T0369283

"My Dream"

By

Rosario Wilson

Order this book online at www.trafford.com
or email orders@trafford.com

Most Trafford titles are also available at major online book retailers.

Printed in the United States of America.

ISBN: 978-1-4269-5902-8 (sc)
ISBN: 978-1-4269-5901-1 (hc)
ISBN: 978-1-4269-5903-5 (e)

Library of Congress Control Number: 2011903781

Trafford rev. 04/05/2011

 www.trafford.com

North America & international
toll-free: 1 888 232 4444 (USA & Canada)
phone: 250 383 6864 ◆ fax: 812 355 4082

I dedicate this book to my Mother_ MRS Juanita Palisoc and
Brother Rogelio Palaganas (Etong)

Chapter 1

The Beginning

I was born June 22, 1950 in Sual, Pangasinan, P.I., on a hot summer day. I was also born two months early; this started me on my journey earlier than normal. I was in my late teen before I gain my normal weight. I have two brothers and three sisters.

As far back as I can remember, I recall seeing a lot of our neighbors in and outside of our house watching a Witch Doctor perform some type of a ritual on my Mother by chant tang and beating her with the Tail of a Sting Ray Fish, to rid her of an evil spirit.

I was so frightened, I became horrified, so I ran and hid under our table; I could hear my mother speaking in another voice. The Witch Doctor said, an evil spirit had taken over her body and he had to beat my mother with the Sting Ray Tail until the evil spirit left her body and promised not to return. All of our neighbors started praying for my mother. The ritual continued for seem like forever; then finally it was over.

My mother had a complete recovery from the ordeal. My father usually spent most of his time away from us; my mother had to feed and clothes all of her kids. In order to do this she had to stay with a well to do family as a live in Maid. She left Barrio Alyaga and went to a neighboring Barrio to work. We were left in the care of my Grandmother and Aunt. I remember playing with my brother Etong and my sister Linda in an empty small room when my Grandmother started shouting at my Aunt, asking why she allowed us to play in that

1

room as if she was mad at us kids; she said this room was occupied by Little Peoples, that was the reason it was not used for a Sari Sari Store. As you can imagine, my family was very superstitious; they believe there exist family of Little Peoples who possess power to inflict harm upon you in various ways if you pose a threat to them.

I was very young and didn't understand what was going on, so I did what I was told and stayed clear of that room. My Grandmother was very religious, every night at around six

O' clock we would pray and go to bed.

After a few weeks passed my sister Linda wanted to return to the little room where the Little Peoples stayed, so we went inside; we saw in the dirt floor mounds of dirt in different sizes. My sister Linda kicked several of the mounds and we ran out of the room.

That night my sister Linda had a high fever and blisters appeared all over her legs.

When my grandmother found out sister Linda was sick, she asked us where have we being playing that day; I told her we had being playing in that room. My Grandmother was very upset. I told her how sorry we were and we would not return to that room again.

The next day my Mother came home; my Grandmother explained to her what had happened to my sister. They begin to prepare different kinds of foods, coconut oil and water. Before dark my Mother and Grandmother took the food and put it inside of the little room, then they walked around the building several times praying and asking the Little Peoples to forgive my sister Linda and take away her sickness. After our six o, clock prayer, my Mother and Grandmother went back to the room and removed the food and coconut oil. They returned to the house and took the coconut oil and rub my sister Linda legs with it. The next day she was feeling good and the blisters had disappeared from her legs.

After seeing the miraculously disappearing of the blister from my sister legs, we were sure the Little People had forgiven her for trying to destroy their home.

My Grandmother gave us a small house that was located about one half mile from her house, so my Mother moved us into this house right away.

My oldest brother Celino was grown and living alone, my oldest sister Melda was married and living with her husband, next to her was my sister Rose and brother Etong, they both lived at home with me and my sister Linda, who was the youngest.

Finally, school started; my mother registered me and my sister Rose for school. Sister Linda was not old enough to go to school and my brother Etong could not talk, so he stayed at home. I could not understand why my brother Etong was not going to school because he was older than me; my Mother explained to me that the school did not teach sign language. She also told us brother Etong suffered a real high fever when he was a baby and the nearest doctor was about fifty miles away, so there wasn't any Medical help for him other than what she could give him. Every day when we left for school, my Mother left for work; I did not know exactly where my Mother worked or what she did, but it was enough to put food on the table and clothes on our backs. Every time we asked our Mother the where about of ours Father, she would always reply...somewhere; she would never tell us where.

One day my Mother, my sisters and I were pounding the rice to remove the brown hush and my brother Etong was in the house boiling the pig food. All of a sudden we heard a loud scream from our house...it seem as though everyone in the neighborhood heard the scream and came running to our house. When we arrived at the house we saw that brother Etong had try to remove the container of hot food from the fire and spilled it on his right leg. Brother Etong has a real bad burn on his leg and there was not a Doctor close by and if, there were, my Mother could not afford to pay for services. So my Mother cleaned and dressed his wound herself. My brother suffered for two or three days with pain, because we didn't have anything for pain. Mother stayed home from work for about three days to clean and dress his wound; finally he was feeling better, so my Mother went back to work.

Before we realized it, the school season was over; during school vacation, Mother stayed home and took us out into the rice fields to gather the rice left behind by the farmers, we went to the river to catch fish and snails. When we get lucky and catch a lot of snails, my Mother would sale them at the Market. We also, shared our catch with our Grandmother and other nearby relatives. We dried a portion of the fish and shrimp we caught, so we can have food during the rainy season, because when it start raining it's almost impossible to go out and catch any type of fresh fish.

When Mother finished gathering the rice and drying the fish and shrimp for the rainy season, it was time for her to go back to her job as a live in Maid. So she would leave us again with my Grandmother; after a month or two she would return with rice, sugar, salt and all other food necessities we used daily.

One day our Grandmother called all of the kids inside her house; she said she had a big surprise for us. When I came inside I saw a man smiling at us. My Grandmother said, give your Father a hug. I thought to myself, so this is my Father; where have he been for all of these years? I was seven years old and seeing him for the first time.

Mother came home the next day. I guess someone told her my Father had returned home. Father and Mother got together and decided that he would stay, so my Mother and Father got a job working in the rice fields. The owner would pay them sacks of rice, chicken and vegetables; sometime they would give them a few pesos.

Once the owner of the rice field paid my parent with two sacks of rice in the husk; this rice had to be dried in the hot sun and pounded so it would come out of the husk. The next morning around eleven o, clock, my Father spread the rice out on mats to dry in the sun. Father told me to watch the rice and keep the birds and chicken away. Around noontime, I had to use the bathroom, so I went into the bushes nearby; all of a sudden, I heard my father yelling for me. When I came out of the bushes, I could see that the chicken had gotten into the rice. Father took off his belt and commenced beating me, he continued until he beat me to the grown. Mother and Grandmother were screaming for him to stop beating me. Afterward, My Father and Mother had a big argument, so he left home again the next day.

My Mother left us in my Grandmother care and went back to her old job as a live in Maid. Finally school was out again, my sister Rose was graduating from the six grades. The school had a play with her playing a mother with four kids. The play was very nice, but the old people who attended the play had superstition ideals that she was too young to be playing someone with four kids; they believe that it will cause her to have a lot of kids when she grows up. When my Mother is away at work, the kids are responsible for feeding the pigs and chicken, we would go into the rice field and pick the different plants that grow in the field. We would carry the plants home and cut them up and boil them in a big pot for the pigs. One day while I was chopping the plants for the pig food, I accidentally chopped my thumb; I was lucky I didn't chop it off, my Grandmother washed and dressed my thumb and stopped the bleeding. During this ordeal I was in such pain; I almost passed out, then finally the pain subsided enough for me to relax somewhat.

After this ordeal, my Grandmother started to look in on us more often and had us to stay in her house at night. My Grandmother was also taking care of our Great Grandmother, who was 110 years old. One night all family members gathered at my Grandmother house to be with her in her last few hours on this earth. We were up all night. The next morning my Great Grandmother passed away. We decided to go home; everyone was there except my sister Linda, we all started looking for her, finally we thought maybe she had went home, so we left my Grandmother house and went home. When we arrived, I saw Sister Linda sitting on the grown crying. Everyone was wondering what had happened to her; she saw us and started to explain what had happened. She said she had came home and tried to get inside the house, but the steps; like always was removed as a security measure to keep other people out when everyone leave the house. She had tried to climb a wood pole to enter the house.

When she looks up, she saw our Great Grandmother reaching down to help her in the house. She was completely startled, because she knew our Great Grandmother was dying back at our Grandmother house, she lost her grip and slipped back down the pole and caught her leg on a rusty nail. Everyone was completely puzzled, because this had happened at approximately the same time our Great Grandmother had passed away.

That night sister Linda started to run a high fever. I didn't know what to do or think… my Great Grandmother had died and my sister Linda now was running a high fever and no one were sure as to whether she would pull through or not. My Grandmother sent for my Mother. When she arrived she and my uncle took her to the town where my mother worked to see the doctor. The only transportation available was a horse drawn carriage, called a Calesa.

When they returned with my sister everyone was surprised and called it a miracle they made it to the doctor in time to save her life. After five days passed, we buried my Great Grandmother. My Mother decided to stay home with us. She decided to gather Fish, Shrimp and whatever she could get from the rice fields and sell it to the Market to make a living for us.

My Mother tried everything she could think of to make money; she even learned to make floor mats...the mats was used by almost everyone to sleep on in their houses.

Mother learned to make real nice design in the mats. The mats were made out of palm leaves; Mother would buy the young palm leaves and dry them in the hot sun. After they dried she would cut them into small strips about one fourth inch wide and use them to make the mats. My Mother would do the outside work during the day and weave the mats at night; sometime she stays up to midnight, weaving mats. I would stay up and help my Mother with her mat weaving...she taught me to make different design around the edge of the mats; I was only seven years and three months old.

My Mother provided for us just as well as we were when our Father was around. She made us happy and we really loved her for it. Alyaga, Pangasinan, P.I. were a very nice place to live and we were very happy living there.

Before school started my Father came back to live with us. He wanted to move to Canan, Pangasinan. My Father Aunt's husband had died and she wanted him to come and bring his family to help her work the rice fields. My parent decided to sale our pigs and chicken to raise money for the trip.

When we arrived in Canan, I met a lot of my Father relatives that lived close by his Aunt place. We finally got settled in my Father's Aunt's house and everything seem to be going all right until the money ran out that my Mother got from selling our pigs and chicken.

My Mother asked my Father when we were going to start working the fields, he said he didn't know, because his Aunt could not decide if she wanted to let someone work the land or sale it. Mother decided that she had to find her a job. She found a job as a live in Maid, so she had to leave us again, but this time we were left with our Father.

My Father was with us for a month after our Mother left for work. He decided to leave us kids in his Aunt care. A few weeks later my Father Aunt got sick, so my Mother had to leave her job and come home to take care of her and us kids. My Father left without telling us where he was going or when he would be back, so we didn't ask anyone about him. My Father Aunt later died. After her death we stayed on in her house.

One day when I came home from school I had a very big surprise; my oldest sister Melda and her husband had come to stay with us a while, because she was pregnant. The earliest I remembered being with sister Melda were when I was three years old. She lived in Aguilar, Pangasinan. My Mother left sister Linda and me in the care of my sister, because the only job she could find was as a live in Maid and my Father only stayed long enough to get my Mother Pregnant. I was almost five years old when I realized my sister Melda was not my Mother. I remembered living with them in a small house by the river. I never will forget when I was living there; I was always feeling sick and my stomach was very big. Sister Melda took me to see a Doctor in Aguilar. The Doctor gave her medicine for me to take. Early the next morning before I ate breakfast; my Sister gave me the medicine to drink and told me not to eat any food. A few hours later my stomach started hurting, I knew I had to use the bathroom, so I told my sister Melda; she took me out back and dug a hole for me to go in. When I was finished she told me to look down into the hole; when I saw all the worms moving around in the hole, I was so scared, I started crying and screaming, because I thought the worms was snakes. My sister hugged me and said thank God the medicine had brought all the worms out. For the next week I ate slice pineapple and kept looking into my bowel movement for worms.

A few weeks later my sister Melda and her Husband took my sister Linda and me to live with my Great Grandmother in Alyaga, Pangasinan.

My sister and her husband settled in with the family. Then came rainy season, it seem as though it would rain every day and night. My sister Melda was working outside one day and she slipped down; she was hurt pretty bad. That night the baby came and died a few hours after birth. I thought this was the prettiest baby I have ever seen. My sister named the baby Erlinda. Every time I would think of the baby I would cry, because I felt that somehow this baby was cheated out of life. Sister Melda and her husband built them a small house near us in Canan and settled into the community. My Brother-in-law decided to visit his relatives in Aguilar for a while, so he left that day.

My Mother came back from her job to spend a few days with us. Right after she arrived home, she became very sick; she could not walk, so Sister Melda called a Doctor to our house. The Doctor arrived and begun examining my Mother. He decided to give her something for the pain until he could figure out what was wrong with her.

After a few minutes my Mother started foaming at the mouth. Everyone started screaming and shouting at the Doctor, because they thought my Mother was going to die. They lost confidence in the Doctor and decided to take my Mother to the Hospital. They went out and called a Jeepney to take her to the Hospital. Sister Melda later found out the Doctor had given my Mother the wrong medicine. When my Mother arrived at the Hospital and was examined; they found that she was suffering from appendicitis. The Hospital staff prepared her for surgery; as soon as the surgery started the power went out and there was no backup generator, so they had to use candles to complete the surgery.

Sister Melda came back home from the Hospital and told us what had happen to our Mother and the difficult surgery that was performed by candles. She also, told us that our Mother would be in the Hospital for a few days. Then she told us some more bad news; she was leaving for Aguilar, to see her husband. This meant that we small kids would be left alone for at least two days.

I had finally dozed off to sleep, when I heard someone knocking at the door. Sister Rose got up and opened the door. I also got up, but I went to the bathroom; I saw Pedro, one of the young men in our neighborhood, he wanted to talk to my sister Rose. When I came back from the bathroom I sat in the living room with my sister and Pedro. Pedro sensed that I wanted to stay with my sister, so he told me to go to bed, because I had to go to school the next day. I asked my sister if she would be o.k. She said yes, go to bed. I didn't argue, because I was very sleepy…I went to bed.

The next morning when I woke up, I saw Sister Rose crying, I asked her why she was crying; she said Pedro had raped her. She told me she wanted me to stay home from school today and accompany her to the Mayor's House. When we arrived at the Mayor's House, my sister Rose explained what had happened; the Mayor asked me had I seen Pedro in our house. I said yes, I had seen Pedro and he told me to go to bed, but I didn't know he was going to hurt my sister. The Mayor told us he would investigate the case.

About two days later, sister Melda and her husband returned home and went to the Hospital to bring my Mother home. My Brother-in-law owned land in Aguilar; he sold part of his land to pay my Mother Hospital bill. A few days after my Mother was discharged from the Hospital, my Father returned home again. When he found out what had happened to Sister Rose he got his sword and went to the house of Pedro. He said when he find Pedro he was going to kill him. Everybody in the neighborhood was scared because they knew my Father was very mad. The Parent of Pedro went to the Mayor and promised him Pedro would marry my sister.

Both families met at the Mayor's House and the Mayor married my sister and Pedro. Now that my sister Rose will be staying with Pedro; I will miss doing the fun things we use to do together, but life must go on.

My Father is leaving again, but this time I know why he is leaving…my Father is in the Philippines Constabulary (PC), he is subject to be going all over the Philippines Island in the Defense of our country. I can understand him being away all the time, but I can't understand why he does not send money to my Mother to help her feed and cloths us.

Turning eight years old was not much of a change in my life style. We did the same things…went to school every day and when school was out for the summer; we would go into the rice fields and pick rice left over by the big farmers. Sometime the owners of the rice farms would see us scrapping rice behind them…they would leave us several big bundles of rice, and we was very happy.

School had just started and I was in the second grade; when my Father's Nephew told my Mother they were selling the house. Mother started looking for a house for us. My Father niece told my Mother we could move in a newly built Nipa hut; I call it the Little House on the Prairie, because it was so far from where everybody else lived. His Niece was pregnant and wanted to live close by her parent house.

We moved into the new house and to our surprise, we had twice the space to use for planting fruit, vegetables and a little rice if we want to. The only bad thing was the amount of miles we were from everybody else and the school. If I took a short cut through the fields and mountain path it about three and a half miles and if I took the road, it was about four miles. My Mother was very happy with our new place, because she could plant a big vegetables garden and sell the vegetables to the Market. Everyone pitched in helping to keep the plants watered and weeded. Once we planted our Garden it really started growing. Our neighbors came by and exchanged fruit and nuts for our vegetables. They would also, exchange baby chick, and whatever they had in abundance for our vegetables. This really helped us to get back on our feet again.

My Mother continued to design and make floor mats for sale to the market; she never stop, she is always doing something to make money for us, because she couldn't count on my Father to help her take care of the kids. My Mother made most of our clothes…she did everything for us. On weekends and after school, my Mother would take us to the nearby mountains and gather wood. We would bring it home, cut it into pieces fourteen inches long, bundle it up and put it aside to be sold at the Market and Sari Sari Stores nearby.

We had plenty of food on the table, clothes on our back and a nice place to stay, we was a very, very happy family; until one day my Brother-in-Law came and told my Mother, sister Melda was planning on leaving him. I had a feeling about their marriage, because the last time they had a big fight, my Brother-in-Law left and went to Aguilar where his relatives live. He returned to Canan, because sister Melda came for him and told him my Mother was sick and needed help with the Hospital bill. They also, decided to stay in Canan close by us to try and save the marriage.

My Mother pleaded with sister Melda, telling her my Brother-in-Law was a good husband and provider and she should really think about her marriage before doing something she will regret. During the same time sister Rose and her Husband were having marriage problems. Pedro's family didn't completely accept Sister Rose into the family, because of the forced marriage. I promised myself I wouldn't get married, when I grew up. A week later sister Melda and sister Rose disappeared. Sister Melda husband came to our house and asked, my Mother if she knew where sister Melda had gone. Mother told him she didn't know sister Melda had left. My Brother-in-Law stayed around for a couple of day and finally he left going to Aguilar.

Sister Linda and I continued to wake up early in the morning and go to school; sometime we would help brother Etong water the vegetable garden before we left, but most of the time we would do it in the afternoon when we get home from school. Brother Etong usually does most of the work around the house, because he didn't go to school.

When my Mother comes home for the weekend, she would take the wood we had bundle up and the Vegetable to the nearby Sari Sari Stores and the Market and sell it. When Mother is away at work, Sister Linda and I would do all of the washing, ironing and cleaning of the house; when we are not helping brother Etong water the plants, feeding the chicken and chopping wood. The only problem I had with the work around the house was putting hot charcoal in the iron to heat it for ironing clothes. I would call brother Etong to help me. My Mother taught us everything she could about how to survive when life don't seem to be treating you fair. Sometime we laugh, sometime we cry and sometime we got angry at one another, but we always loved each other. I guess this is a part of life itself...there are good times and bad times.

Three months has passed and we haven't heard any news about my two sisters; we can only pray that they are doing okay. My Father's niece came to visit my Mother and brought some bad news, she wanted the house we were living in back. The next day my Mother started looking for a place for us to live. One of our neighbors close by told Mother she could build a small house on his land. Mother was real upset about having to move us around so much. She made a deal with our neighbor to buy the land. So we started building the house, everyone helped, even the property owner came by and helped. When the house was finished, we moved in our new home. The property was not as large as the place we had left, so we couldn't plant a very big vegetable garden. My Mother accepted this and started working harder at whatever she could do.

One morning my Mother and brother Etong went to the other side of the mountain to gather some wood. At three o' clock they had not returned, so we begin to worry about them. Finally around four o, clock my brother returned by himself, we asked him, where our Mother was…he could only reply by using sign language. He would put both hands together and point toward the mountain. We could not figure out what he was trying to say.

We decided to tell a grownup about this situation, because we didn't know what to do. So we went to our Cousin and explained what had happened to him, he said we should wait a while longer before doing anything. Just before dark we saw my Mother coming home. We all ran out to meet her; she was carrying a lot of vegetables and rice. I asked her what had happened. She said they had been arrested for picking up wood on the other side of the mountain. The property owner has signs up prohibiting the gather of wood on his land. The Owner had tied her and brother Etong hands and took them to the Mayor's office to be questioned as to why they didn't see the signs on the trees prohibiting the gathering of wood. She explained to them, she couldn't read and brother Etong could not talk and she was gathering wood to sell to the market so she could feed her children. She said the Mayor felt sorry for her and gave her the vegetables, rice and five pesos. They told her when she comes, to gather wood again, she should see the Owner so they can show her the area where gathering wood is not prohibited. She thanked the people that had tied her and brother Etong hands. Now we know what brother Etong was trying to say, when he would put both hands to gather and point toward the mountain.

The new place where we are allowed to gather wood, also, have palm and coconut trees, my Mother would gather some of the leaves to start making mats again for sale. About six month later sister Rose returned home and my Mother was really mad at her for not telling her she was leaving. She told my Mother, sister Melda had pawned her wedding ring and her dog Sampaguita to get enough money for the trip.

I remember playing with Sampaguita, when I lived with my Sister Melda and her husband in Aguilar. My Brother-in-Law would take Sampaguita out hunting and she would catch wild birds and ducks. Sampaguita was a beautiful dog; she had very pretty shiny white hair. I asked Sister Rose, who had Sampaguita, so I could go by and visit her. The next day I went to see Sampaguita. She still remembered me; she jumped around playing with me the same way we always play. When I had to go she started whining and I started crying… the new owner told me, I could come anytime to visit Sampaguita. When I got home I told my Mother about Sampaguita. She said if she can save enough money she would go get Sampaguita. One day My Mother decided to go get Sampaguita, when she arrive the owner told her Sampaguita had ran away and got run over by a bus.

Sister Rose and Pedro got back together. Before long she was pregnant, My Mother told Sister Linda and me to stay with her for a while and help around the house. Mother got her old job back as a live in Maid/Nanny, so my brother Etong was left at our house to take care of the goats and the house while we was away.

One night sister Linda and I were sleeping on our mat, suddenly I felt someone touching me, and I didn't know what to do, so I pretended to be asleep. Sister Rose asked Pedro if I was asleep; he said he didn't know and tried to remove my panties.

Then Sister Linda turned over in her sleep and he got up right away. He told Sister Rose he could not have sex with me while my other sister was lying beside me. Then I knew Sister Rose wanted her husband to have sex with me, because she was pregnant and didn't want to have sex. I was so frightened I could not cry. The next day I told Sister Linda to always stay by my side when we are sleeping. Sister Rose finally had her baby and I couldn't wait to go home and get away from her and Pedro. When she come and asks me to help with the baby, I would go and stay for an hour or two and made sure I was gone before Pedro came home from work. I never told anyone about this disgusting incident. Pedro worked in Malasique as a barber.

Sometime people would come by his house and get a haircut. Pedro would cut brother Etong hair once in a while.

The weekend started off real nice, Mother came home to be with us, but things soon changed when sister Melda's Husband came to our house to talk to my Mother. He told her, his marriage was over and started to rip up his wedding pictures. Mother explained to him how sorry she was that their marriage didn't work. She also, explained how busy she was trying to raise the small kids and couldn't keep up with what's going on with the older married kids. My Brother-in-Law finally left brokenhearted and went home. He sold his house to a neighbor and left Canan; he said he was never coming back.

During the summer months it get real hot and fires seem to break out on their own, one day when sister Rose came with her baby to visit us. Everyone was sleep or half asleep on the floor mats. Sister Rose had put her baby in a make shift swing and he was asleep. All of a sudden we heard our neighbor yelling fire, fire, fire, get water and put out the fire. The bushes and grass was burning real close to our house, so everyone was getting water to wet down the house. Sister Rose ran out of our house clutching a pillow instead of her baby. She had left her baby in the house, in the swing. Mother saw what was happening and ask, sister Rose, where her baby was, she was so nervous and crying she still didn't realize she was caring a pillow instead of her baby. Brother Etong ran into the house and got the baby. The neighbors managed to put the fire out and saved our house. We thanked the neighbors for their help and God that everyone was safe. Everyone thought it was really funny watching Sister Rose clutching a pillow and yelling my baby, my baby.

School had started, Sister Linda and I were coming home from school, when we heard the kids behind us shouting, the sack man is coming, the sack man is coming. So we took off our shoes and ran with the other kids. Our shoes were made of wood...we run faster with them off. We ran until we came in front of several Stores where older people were standing around talking about the sack man. They said, some rich people had built a smoke tower and the smoke tower would work better if they would put a small kid in side to be sacrificed. The man with the sack would grab a kid and put him or her in the sack.

The man would take the kid to the tower and the kid would never be seen again. We ran home and told our Mother, she had a week off work. She said she had heard about this sack man and she wanted us to walk in a group with the other kids when we come home in the afternoon. We had to start caring lunch, because we had always come home for lunch. Sister Linda, our Cousin and me would have a picnic every day. We exchange our food and laugh at what each other had for lunch. We had fried dried fish, boiled eggplant, chopped tomatoes, boiled eggs and the most important item, boiled rice. When we finish lunch we would play a game with uncooked cashew nuts. We would throw the cashew against the wall, if your cashew came within a hand length of another person cashew you would win the nut...I would always win a lunch pail full of cashew nuts. I would take them home and let brother Etong roast them in the fire. We would snack on the cashew and listen to the drama program on the radio. All the kids in the neighborhood were scared of being caught by the man with the sack, so they stayed close to their homes for a long time before they started venturing out again.

One day my father decided to pay the family a visit, but this time he brought my oldest brother Celino with him. We were very surprised, because we had not seen my brother for almost five years. Brother Celino stayed with us for about three months and left going somewhere again. A few months later the police came looking for my brother; claiming he had gotten a girl in our neighborhood pregnant. My father told the police if they are looking to arrest my brother; they should arrest him instead, because he introduced my brother to this girl. So they arrested my father and put him in jail to serve my brother sentence. My Mother was very mad at my father and my brother for what they had done. She didn't worry about my father being in jail, because he didn't help do anything around the house and he never gave her any money to help out. Sister Linda and I visited my father in jail one day. My father asked the Jailer to let Sister Linda and I spend the night with him in the Jail House; the Jailer agreed and said okay. We didn't know what to do, because we were afraid of our father, so we just kept quiet and tried to relax as best as we could in Jail. The next day my Mother came for us and took us with her to her job. I met the family my Mother was working for; I found out that the lady my Mother worked for was the long lost sister she always talked about. She said when they were small; my Grandmother could not take care of all of her sisters and brothers, so she gave my Aunt to a rich couple, that couldn't have kids.

My Mother and Aunt were very happy to be together again even though they were in an employer/employee status. I played hide and go seek with the little boy and girl, my newly found cousins. My Aunt gave my Mother the afternoon off. She gave Sister Linda and me some pretty dresses. I could tell by the way my Aunt treated my Mother and us, that she was a very nice lady.

Chapter 2
Moving

The whole day was like a dream; my Mother always talked about having two sisters and a brother. I have met my Aunt that lives near Canan; I have never met my Uncle, because he was killed when the Japanese invaded the Philippines in 1942. I can't really get over the feeling of happiness about today's encounters.

My Father was finally released from jail; he came back home and pick up where he left off...doing nothing. After a few weeks he left again...destination unknown. Soon after my Father left, my Brother Celino came back; this time he brought a girl friend with him. My Mother was still mad at him for what he did the last time he came home, but she put the pass behind her and greeted him like a loving mother would greet a son.

My Aunt started letting my Mother come home every night from work, so this gave me the opportunity to go with her to work...I would help my Mother with her household duties and the work she had to do outside. My Aunt would always give me something to take home. I would hear people calling My Aunt, "Doctor", so I asked my Mother why; she said your Aunt is a Doctor and that's why she is rich. I also, played with Jo Jo, my Aunt little girl; she liked playing with me so much, she would come with me home and play. She really liked playing with our animals, because they couldn't have animal in the city.

One Saturday Mother and I was going to the market; she decided to go by my Aunt house to see if more stones was needed to complete the stone walkway in my Aunt back yard. Just before we started to leave for the market; I saw a pretty woman at my Aunt front gate asking for my Mother. My Aunt told her she was in the back yard. I didn't realize it was my sister Melda, because she looked like a movie star. Mother introduced sister Melda to my Aunt; they greeted each other and talked for a while…then we left. Mother canceled the trip to the market and we went home instead. When the word got around that sister Melda was back home; all our relatives in the neighborhood came to see her. Everyone was happy to see her; we stayed up all night talking. I finally got a chance to ask her if she was a movie star; she said no, but she live in Olongapo City where Americans live. The next day sister Melda asked to take Sister Linda and me back to Olongapo City with her. Mother agreed to let us go with her. A few days later we were off to Olongapo City. My sister Melda lived in an apartment building in town. We got settled in and Sister Melda started showing us around. We went to the market, the beach and the movies. I fell in love with the place right away because of all the people and Jeepneys moving around in the streets gave me a thrill to watch.

Sister Melda asked us if we would like to live here in the city close by the beaches; we both said yes, as we jump for joy. She said she would start right away looking for a place to rent near the school and beach area of the town.

Sister Melda decided to return to Canan, Pangasinan to try and convince our Mother to come to Olongapo, City, because of better job opportunity here in the city. She asked her neighbor to keep an eye on Sister Linda and me while she was away. A week later, sister Melda returned with Mother and brother Etong. Mother brought our school transfer papers, so we could be enrolled in school.

The next day we went to see a house on the beach my sister had described to us. The owner agreed to rent the house to my sister; I was so happy to know that we would be living next to a beach. Sister Melda rented a jeepney, which was the number one transportation vehicle in Olongapo City, and we moved our household belonging and clothes into our new house. The house had one bedroom, dining room, kitchen and a small veranda. My Mother loved the place; she said it reminded her of the place where I was born in Sual, Pangasinan. I also, remembered living in Sual, Pangasinan in a house close by the beach…I remembered the Nurse from the Barrio coming to give all the kids in the neighborhood vaccine for the polio and all the kids was running to hide. I remembered hiding behind a boat at the beach. I remembered my sister Melda swimming at the beach. Everyone says she swim like a Mermaid.

I asked Mother about our house we left in Canan; she said, all the goats, pigs and chicken had been sold to the market and she had turned our house and land back over to the previous owner to be sold. The owner had promised to send her the money as soon as the property was sold.

Sister Melda paid the rent on our new house while Mother looked for a job. She came by very often to visit us; we would also, visit her on weekends. Sister Linda and I would visit my sister on weekdays when there is no school and sometime we would spend the night. She would tell us if we come to visit her and she's not home, we should find the box; where she kept a lot of American coins and get money to buy food and wait for her.

One day sister Linda and I went to visit sister Melda and she was not home; we decided to wait for her, so we started making ourselves comfortable…I sat in the window and I saw children buying ice cream cones, then I remembered what sister Melda had told us about the money box. I told Sister Linda to hurry and get some American coins from the box to exchange for pesos. I ran out to stop the ice cream man. We exchanged enough coins to get seven pesos…we bought ice cream. I had the man to put my ice cream in a glass it was very delicious; I couldn't wait to have some more. Finally sister Melda came home, she told Sister Linda and me to get cleaned up, because she was taking us out to eat.

We changed clothing, comb our hair and put Johnson baby powder on our faces. I put my pretty wooden shoes on and tried to walk like a movie star. When we arrived at the restaurant, a black guy was waiting for us; sister Melda introduced him as her boy friend. I hid behind sister Melda because I was afraid of the black guy…sister Linda was even more afraid than I was, because this was the first time we had seen a black man in person; we had seen black people in a movie in Canan that eat white people, so we was afraid he would eat us. We went into the restaurant and was seated; He ordered a lot of different kind of food...we ate our fill. When we finished eating he accompanied us home and spent the night; Sister Linda and I was still afraid so we slept with our heads under the cover even though it was very hot.

The next day sister Melda took us back home in Matain and dropped us off and went back to her apartment. She came back the next day and took us to White Rock Beach, a beach resort that was across the street from where we live. She introduced Sister Linda and me to a lady she calls Mama Ligaya, who was the owner of the Swan Club and the White Rock Beach resort. Mama Ligaya was the lady sister Melda met when she ran away from her husband and came to Olongapo City. Sister Melda had started working the Counter at the small Bowling alley at White Rock Beach; later Mama Ligaya convinced sister Melda to take a job at the Swan Club serving drinks to American Sailors and Marines, because she could make more money. Mama Ligaya told sister Melda that sister Linda, brother Etong and me could work in the bowling alley setting up pins for tips. We did real well on weekends; sometime we made five or six American dollars in about four hours. The Americans was very generous tippers, but for some reason our Mother didn't want us to work there, so we quit.

We had not heard from, or seen sister Melda for over a month, then out of the blue she walks in the door. She had wonderful news... she was getting married again and she wanted the family to meet her fiancé at her apartment. We were in for another surprise because she had changed apartments and her new apartment had all new furniture and appliances. After admiring her new apartment and furniture, we sat down and begin to question sister Melda about her fiancé. Then we heard a key turning in the door...all eyes was on the door, a light complexion black man step into the room and said hello and kissed sister Melda. She introduced him to us; he shook our hand and hugged each one of us. My Mother English was not very good, so she told sister Melda to tell him to promise not to hurt her daughter. Then she wanted to say something else, so she tried to say it in English and she said don't be a foolish dog"; everyone started to laugh at what she said because it was so funny. But Mr. Smith, sister Melda fiancée told Mother not to worry; he would love and take good care of sister Melda. Sister Melda explained to Mother in Tagalog, what he had said. Mother said thank you and hugged him. The following week sister Melda got married by the Justice of the Peace in Olongapo City. Mama Ligaya told sister Melda to leave her apartment and move into one of her house close to the market. It was a nice house with two bedrooms. My Mother didn't like the house, because the house was dark inside even during the day. Being married to an American, my sister could afford a Maid, so my Mother asked her not to get a Maid and let her be the one to take care of her house. So my Mother did the washing and ironing and Sister Linda and I did the cleaning.

Sister Melda and her husband bought land close to the White Rock Beach Resort and started building a big house on it. Before it was finished sister Melda and Mother went to Malasique to visit my Mother's sister. Sister Linda and I stayed at sister Melda house while she was gone, so we could do the cleaning. They were to be in Malasique for three days. My Brother-in-Law took Sister Linda and me to the movies the night they were to return. We were very happy to get a chance to go to the movies. When we returned sister Melda were back and very mad at me. The next day sister Linda and I went home to Matain; brother Etong were happy to see us and he had run out of food for the pigs. My Mother left right away for the Market to buy rice and food for the pigs. I don't know why sister Melda were mad at me; she was even mad at my Mother, because she stopped paying her for doing the washing and ironing. Sometime I think sister Melda was upset because her husband was paying attention to us. My Brother-in-Law, brother Smitty was a very nice person and it seem like whenever he would do something for the family she would get mad.

The work continued on sister Melda new house, but just before it was finished she told my Mother to leave the rental house and move into her unfinished house. Today, I still don't understand why she wanted us to move in the house before it was finished. She was paying the rent on the rental house, so we had no other choice but to move into the house with three finished rooms.

My Father finally figured out where we were at, so he shows up with brother Celino and his wife. Brother Celino and his wife stayed for two weeks and left. Sister Melda would come and visit us occasionally and every so often she would spend the night.

One day Brother Smitty came to the house and surprised sister Linda and me with school bags, paper, pencil and everything we needed for school. We were very happy and couldn't think him enough. Sister Melda found out about it and became very angry... she brought all of her dirty clothes and even some clean clothes and made Sister Linda and I wash them. When my Mother came home she saw what was going on and felt sorry for us and helped us finish washing. Sister Melda was mad with brother Smitty, but she didn't tell him the reason why.

My Mother did not like living in this unfinished house, so she and my Father went looking for another place for us to stay. They met a landowner in Calapacuan, three miles away from where we live... that needed someone to stay on his land and watch his Mango trees. The owner promised to let us live there as long as we want to. My Father built a small Nipa Hut on the land.

My brother Celino and his wife came back, he said he wanted to try and find a job in Olongapo City, because he wanted to stay close by the family. My Father told him he could live in the Nipa Hut with us until he could build his own.

Sister Melda started being nice to us again; she went out and bought me a pig. I named the pig princess. Brother Etong helped me to feed and take care of princess. She got very big right away...she acted as if she was a family member; when we took a family picture outside, princess was there posing for the picture too. She was a very smart pig.

Brother Celino started gathering bamboo to build his house...he accidentally spring his leg, so him and his wife came to our house to get my Mother to try and fix it. Mother was our family Doctor, because she treated all of our ailments. It was approximately nine o, clock when my brother arrived. Mother got her coconut oil and massaged brother Celino leg and when she finished the massage she wrapped it in a white bandage. Just as Mother was finishing wrapping brother Celino leg; sister Melda and brother Smitty came through the door. Sister Melda started yelling at brother Celino, asking him why he was in our house; brother Celino got up and started limping toward the door with his wife…brother Smitty asked me what was going on because everyone was speaking Tagalog. I told him my brother Celino had hurt his leg and my Mother was trying to fix it and I didn't know why sister Melda was mad at him. Brother Smitty followed sister Melda into the bedroom and tried to calm her down, but that seem to make things worse.

She came back out of the bedroom and started yelling, "get out of my house", my Mother and Father was so upset; they told us to start packing our things, so we left at ten o, clock at night carrying all we could on our backs. We all went to Calapacuan to live in the Nipa Hut my Father had built. Brother Smitty wanted to do or say something to help us but I knew he did not know what to do, he was deeply in love with sister Melda and he would not do anything to upset her. The next day we came back to the house to get my books, the dog and my pig; sister Melda was not in the house. We had to walk about three miles back and lead the pig.

We live in a little house on the prairie again…our house was built at the base of a mountain by a rice field. This was a nice Nipa Hut, the floor and wall was made of bamboo. The natural cracks between the bamboo poles allowed fresh air to come into the house and keep it cooled down; everyone seem to like our new house even princess, the pig.

A month later as I was wading in the water along the beach and out of nowhere a dog came and bit me on the leg. I was scared and hurt, so I ran and told my Father about the dog. My Father went to the beach to look for the dog, but the dog was nowhere in sight. He came back to the house and took me to the Medical Clinic; they treated me and told my father to bring me back every day for twenty five days to get a rabies shot. The Clinic was pretty close to sister Melda house and I would always look for her or brother Smitty, but I never got a glimpse of either one.

One day I was going to the Clinic for my shot and decided to pass by my Sister Melda house, and to my surprise…the whole house had being removed from the lot it was built on. I rushed home and told my family; Mother went to see mama Ligaya, because sister Melda and she were very close. When she arrived she asked mama Ligaya if she knew what had happen to sister Melda house; mama Ligaya told her sister Melda had given it to her to be moved to the White Rock Beach Resort. She also, asked if she knew where sister Melda was. Mama Ligaya said, "You don't know that Melda went to the United States"? My Mother didn't say anything she just went outside and begin to cry, because it was very hard for her to believe that sister Melda had went to the United States without saying goodbye.

It's two month before school out and I will finish Elementary school and start my first year of high school next year in the seven grades; this was a real big affair for me and my classmates, because the school conducted a Graduation exercise for the six graders. The girls in the graduating class usually wore white outfits. My Mother, God bless her soul; started saving a little money on the side when she was paid for washing and ironing other people clothes. My Mother would wash during the day and ironed at night so she could take her customers their clothes back the next day. My Father left again... where he went no one knew.

About two weeks from my graduation date; Mother took me to see a seamstress to be measured for my white dress. She bought me a pair of white shoes to match my white dress. I was very surprised when she told me she was having my hair done at the beauty shop. Mother has always told me how happy and proud she was of my work in school; now I can tell that she is proud of me, because she is doing everything in her power to make my graduation day a success.

I was the second valedictorian in my class and was awarded a ribbon; my Mother had to come upon the stage and pin the ribbon on my chest. She was so proud she was crying tears of joy. After pinning the ribbon on she gave me a very big hug. Everyone was happy for me.

One day Mother was delivering the clothes back to her customers that work in the Swan club; when she was about to leave she saw mama Ligaya coming toward her. Mama Ligaya told Mother she had heard from sister Melda and sister Melda wanted her to give my Mother money if she need it to help pay for my schooling. Mama Ligaya told Mother Sister Melda was a good daughter; not knowing that my Mother still hadn't heard from Sister Melda since she went to the United Stated. My Mother only smiled and walked away.

When the rainy season came it was real hard for Mother to wash, dry and iron her customer's clothes and return the clothes the next day. So when my Mother ran out of money to buy food she decided to take advantage of Sister Melda offer of money for me to go to school. When she delivered her customers clothes in the Swan Club; she stopped in to see mama Ligaya and get fifty Pesos. Mama Ligaya was eager to give her the money and record it in her ledger.

Mother decided to get her old job back as a live in Maid during the rainy season. She would stay with a family during the week and come home on the weekend. Sister Linda, brother Etong and I were left to take care of all the chores around the house. We would also, go into the rice fields and catch frogs and snails and bring home to be prepared for food. I really liked the way my Mother cook the frog legs in vegetables.

During the rainy season money was scarce, so we had to improvise; we would go out into the rice fields and along the mountainside searching for small Bamboo, Frogs and snails. We would catch as much as we could and bring it home to be cleaned and cooked.

Brother Etong could not talk but he was very smart...he knew where to go to find the most frogs, snails and bamboo. One day he took me to the other side of the mountain to look for food; we had being walking for quiet sometime and I had began to feel tired, then we came to a patch of little small brown stools...I soon realized that the small stools was mushroom. We loaded up all of our containers and headed home; I was so happy thinking about having mushroom when we get home; I almost started to run.

When we arrived home, brother Etong took the mushroom and washed them several times in water and spread them out on banana leaves and rolled the mushroom up in the leaves and put them on the grill. They were allowed to cook until the banana leaves started to burn. Finally the mushroom was cooked; my brother open up the leaves and the aroma filled the house and started my stomach to groan. I begin to eat; I didn't realize how much I was eating until I looked at my brother and he was watching me and smiling. Brother Etong always felt good about himself when he did something to make us happy; he would gladly give up his share of food or clothing so it would be more left for us.

The rainy season finally came to an end; my Mother started taking in washing and ironing to be done at home, so she gave up her live in Maid job. The end of the rainy season brought my Father home. When he arrived he started helping brother Celino finish building his house. This effort also inspired everyone else to pitch in and help brother Celino finish his house. Brother Celino had taken quite a while building his house because he had to build a little at a time due to the lack of money to buy materials.

This time my Father seems to have made up his mind to stay around for a little while longer than usual. He would not go looking for a job; he only wanted to stay around the house and beat up the kids. One occasion he beat brother Etong and tried to put him into a rice sack. Mother was really upset with my Father, because he tried to find a reason to beat us kids and never went out looking for a job. My Mother and Father would fight a lot about him not trying to find a job, but that then change his mind at all. Then Mother got pregnant; I am twelve years old and my baby sister Linda is ten years old...I asked myself, why now?

My Mother didn't stop taking in washing jobs, because she had to feed the family. Then one day she was outside washing and we heard her yelling for help as she made her way toward the house. I knew something was wrong, because she was holding her stomach. We helped her inside the house and called for the Midwife that lived nearby, because Mother didn't want to go into Olongapo City to see a Doctor. The Midwife came and checked her out and told Mother to get some rest. Mother finally fell asleep.

Brother Celino wife, Maria finished my Mother washing. Later that night Mother started bleeding and hurting, my Father called the Midwife back to our house. My Mother lost the baby...it was a boy. That next day Father buried the baby near our house. A week later Mother is back washing and ironing clothes for her customers.

Sister Rose, her husband and baby came for a visit; Sister Rose told Mother that she didn't want to return to Pangasinan with her husband, because his family was always harassing her because her husband was forced to marry her and her husband would never speak up for her. Mother told Sister Rose she could stay with us even though she realized that she was the only person in the house working to feed the family. So now she has two more mouths to feed, because sister Rose husband left and returned to Pangasinan.

Once again, it's time to register for school and I will be starting my first year of high school. This time I have to ride a Jeepney to Jackson High School in Olongapo City. The Jeepney fare is 70 centavos each way and I was given 1 peso for lunch and as always 1 peso didn't buy very much lunch and I would get hungry before the day was over. I would study as hard as I could, but studying is hard on an empty stomach. Sometime I had to go to school without lunch money, if my Mother wasn't pay on time for washing.

After being hungry and dizzy at school one day; I decided to quit school, so I told Mother and she would not hear of it...she decided to try and borrow money from mama Ligaya. When we arrived at her home; she told mother that she didn't need to borrow money from her, because sister Melda ask her to let her have money anytime she need it to send me (Ambing) to school. Sister Melda always called me Ambing...I have several nicknames- Ambing, Rosa, and Vicky. When I was real young I was sickly and the old people believe that my name was causing me to be sickly, so they would change my name. Mother asked for fifty pesos and mama Ligaya gave her the money and wrote it down in her book. Mother and I left for the market; we bought our basis food necessities and kept the rest of the money for my school meals and transportation.

When the Mangoes started to get ripe enough to eat; brother Etong, Sister Linda and I would take bags of mangoes to the fishing boat landing to exchange for fish. The fisherman was always very nice and generous when they traded with us...Sister Linda and I was very happy even though we had to wade out to the boats and end up getting completely wet. Sometimes we didn't have mangoes to trade for fish, but the fisherman would always tell us to wade out to the boat and get fish. One evening sister Linda and I came home soaking wet from wading out to the fishing boats and Mother saw us before we changed into dry clothing; she said hurry and get into dry clothing because we are going shopping at the nearby market for training bra for Sister Linda and me. When we came back home she made us promise to wear the bra's every day. When we brought fish home Mother would clean and prepare the fish to be dried in the sun. When the fish is completely dried; she would either sale it to the market or packet it in a big container to save for the rainy season. Mother would also take some of the fish and make fish sauce. My Mother could not read or write, but she had a great business mind for providing for her family because our Father was never around and when he did show up he would not get a job and help out. My Mother would always share with our neighbors when we would get a lot of fish or any food item and they would do likewise. The majority of the time our neighbors would trade food items with us. I always looked at my Mother as if she was a Saint because I never heard her complain about anything; she just accepted everything for what it was, and kept on pushing.

One day we were let out early from school, so I came home and to my surprise everyone except my father was gone somewhere. I went behind the curtain we had stretched across the house for privacy in the sleeping area and started to change out of my school clothing. Before I could remove my dress my Father came behind the curtain and pushed me to the floor...he was trying to rape me, but I kept fighting him off...he told me if I didn't stop fighting he was going to kill my Brother, Mother and me. I kept fighting, but he was on top of me; then I heard brother Celino call out for my Father; Father jumped right up leaving me on the floor.

I stayed there a few seconds thinking God for letting my Brother come back at the right time. I got up and straightened my clothes just before my Brother came in the door. When he walked in the door and saw me, he said," I didn't know you were home early"...I was so scared I couldn't say a word.

When everyone came home that evening and the family was eating; my Father was laughing and telling jokes like nothing had happened. My Brother Celino asked me again why I was home early; my Father started eying me real bad, so I told my brother the teacher had let us out early.

Now I realize why everyone had found a reason to not be alone at our house with my Father... Sister Rose, my Brother wife and even my brother Etong; they all had a reason to leave the house. After that ordeal I always felt sad and didn't have a reason to smile. I never told anyone because I didn't want my Father to kill my Mother, my Brother or me.

From that day on, I would never come home early unless I was sure someone else was at our house beside my father. Finally my Father left going to Pangasinan to visit his step Brother...I prayed to God to never let him come back.

In my third year of high school, we were told that sister Melda had cut us off, we was not getting any more money for my schooling. I started working with my Mother...washing and ironing her customers clothing on weekends. Helping my Mother on the weekend was working out pretty good until she got sick. Mother was sick for almost a month and there wasn't any money to buy food, so I quit school in the middle of my third year of high school and started washing and ironing for my Mother customers. Sister Rose got a job as a Hostess serving drinks and conversation to American Sailors and Marines at the Top Hat Night Club. Working as a hostess; she learned to dance and speak English.

When I was not washing and ironing clothes, I would accompany brother Etong and Sister Linda to the rice fields to gather the left over rice. Sometimes we would be lucky enough to arrive at the rice fields before the farmers complete their harvest and they would leave more than normal on the ground for us.

When Mother finally recovered from her sickness and started working again; I started to baby sit sister Rose son, Jerry. I gave up the ideal of returning to school and concentrated on helping the family make ends meet. Finally after two years Sister Rose husband came back looking for her...for the life of me, I couldn't understand why it took him two years to decide that he needed his wife. We told him she had a job working in a Night Club.

Sister Rose came home that night after work and to her surprise he was there. They spent the rest of the night talking and finally planning their trip back to Pangasinan. I really thought she was making a mistake going back with her husband because she had saved a little money and was doing very good without him, but love conquer all.

I was finally getting use to the ideal of Sister Rose leaving and returning to Pangasinan with her husband. As if nothing else could go wrong in our household…my Father return from his two years visits with his step Brother. His Brother had given him enough money to come to Olongapo City and get us and take us back for a visit. I prayed to god my Mother would say no, but he kept on begging and she finally gave in. So we packed for the trip and left to visit Father's Brother Family. When we arrived Father introduced us to our new relatives. My Uncle wife was a School Teacher and they had two kids. They lived in a nice big two Story House. After finally being properly introduced it was time for dinner; we were ushered into the dining room to eat first. We were served dried fish and boil rice. When we had finished we went back to the living room so they could have a turn at the table. While we were sitting and listening to the radio Mother got thirsty and went into the kitchen for water; as she passed through the dining room she notice that the menu had changed…they were eating pork adobo, Vegetable and rice. My Mother realized what was happening…they was saving the better food for themselves and this was I first visit. That night Mother told Father that we were being treated like dirt and they decided we would go home the next day. When we arrived home Mother told Father to never take us to a place where we would be treated like dirt again. My Father seem to be a little upset when Mother told him his Brother's Family was not good relatives.

The next day when I woke up Father was gone again and I was happy again. Mother also left early that morning to deliver the clothes she had wash and ironed to her customers at the Swan Club. Just before she left coming back home Mama Ligaya stop her and asked, "Have she seen Sister Melda since she returned from the United States? Mother said no. Mama Ligaya told her sister Melda was back and had gain weight. Mother came home and told us about sister Melda return…I was happy she was back even though she had not seen a need to come by our house and say hello. I often wonder why, but I guess she is the only one that knows for sure.

We decided to carry on as if she had not returned and let her decide when we would see her. After a few weeks she finally showed up at our house with the floor manager of mama Ligaya nightclub. Everyone greeted her as if we did not know she had arrived a few weeks earlier. Mother was the first to tell her she had gained weight; she said, the reason she had gained

Chapter 3

The Job

Weight was because she didn't go anywhere but to the Movies, and to visit her husband relatives because she could not drive a car. Mother started to prepare lunch, but sister Melda said no, because she wanted to take us out for lunch.

Mother told brother Celino wife to keep an eye on our house while we was gone. So we left for Olongapo City. Mother, brother Etong, Sister Linda and I caught a jeepney with sister Melda. When we arrived in Olongapo City, we went to the Shangri La Restaurant. Sister Melda ordered all different kind of foods; I was so full I thought my stomach would burst. When everyone was finish eating, Mother asked the waitress for a container to carry the leftovers... sister Melda said no, she would buy more food if she want it, but Mother insisted on carrying the leftovers home. Everyone thanked sister Melda for taking us out to eat. Sister Melda told Mother that mama Ligaya had built her a house in Olongapo City and she would like to help her support the family. She wanted Sister Linda and Me to live with her; Mother finally agreed, so Sister Linda and I packed and left with sister Melda.

When sister Linda and I finally settled in at her house...I understood why she wanted us there; We cooked and cleaned her house, I became her personal secretary...sister Melda never learned to read and write; Mother said, every time sister Melda went to school, she would fight the boys and the teacher. She would have to leave work and go to the school and bring her home, so she finally decided to stop sending her to school. My family was always on the move when sister Melda was growing up, and that didn't help at all. Brother Smitty, sister Melda husband was stationed in Viet Nam and sister Melda wanted me to write him a letter almost every day. I was very happy to be able to do something for sister Melda, because she was always there for me.

Mama Ligaya found out that I was not going to school, so she offered me a job working in her money exchange booth outside of the Jet Club; working for eighty pesos a month. I was so happy I couldn't wait to get started. The job was changing dollars to pesos for Sailors and Marines that were stationed at the nearby Naval Base and the American Ships that visit the Philippines. When I first got paid; I gave all of the money to my Mother, she told me to keep half of my pay so I could buy clothes for myself. I really liked my job...nearly every time the young sailors and marines changed their money and had small change coming to them; they would leave me the change, because they said it was too heavy to carry in their pockets. The change they left during a month period was more than my regular pay...I was very happy with my job. I met a lot of young American guys; they would stand by my Money exchange booth and try to hold a conversation with me. Sometime they would go across the street to the restaurant and buy food for me. I often think that this job is the best thing that ever happen to me and it's all because I can read and write," I thank God for giving me the strength and my Mother for working day and night to try and keep me in school as long as possible.

One morning I went home to visit my Mother, and to my surprise; Sister Rose was back again with a new baby girl named Gina. She had left her husband again...I asked her what she was planning to do. She said she was going to the Top Hat Club to ask for her old job back.

I left that afternoon and went back to Olongapo City; I had to be at work at five o, clock. When I got off work that night I went back to sister Melda's house; she was still awake, but Sister Linda was asleep. I told her about Sister Rose coming back home with another kid. Sister Melda had received two letters from brother Smitty...I read them to her, she asked me to answer the letters the next day. When

I went to bed I started thinking about the thing brother Smitty was writing about in his letters. He wrote about the snipers shooting into the camp where he was living and him having to wear a helmet and carry a gun everywhere he went even to eat.

The next morning Sister Melda and I was up early; we got started answering brother Smitty's letters...she was dictating and I was writing; finally we finished the letters and had breakfast. Sister Melda wanted to see Sister Rose new baby, so we left for Calapacuan for a visit. When we arrived sister Melda greeted everyone with a big hug and we sat down for a long chat. Sister Melda started discussing her plan to build another house; bigger and stronger than the last one she had built at White Rock Beach Resort. She continued to chat, finally Mother interrupted her and told her Brother Celino lived in the house next door...sister Melda didn't say a word, so Mother went next door to get my Brother Celino, but he had left for the mountain to get bamboo to build a chicken house. Sister Melda decided to go over to my Brother house and introduce herself to his wife. Sister Rose was very quiet; you would hardly notice she was there unless you see her. Sister Melda saw Sister Rose's daughter, Gina and immediately fell in love with her; she didn't miss an opportunity to carry Gina around the house and play with her. Sister Melda and Gina looked somewhat alike; you could mistake them to be Mother and Daughter.

Finally it was time for me to return to Olongapo City to go to work; I reminded sister Rose about seeing mama Ligaya about getting her old job back at the Top Hat Club...I told her sister Linda and brother Etong could baby sit her two kids while she was at work. I bid them goodbye and left. Sister Melda said she was staying for a while because she wanted to talk with brother Celino when he returned home. I thought to myself, why does she wants to see him now; I remember the last time she saw him she was throwing him along with all of us out of her house at White Rock Beach...then again maybe her being away for a while has changed her altitude.

When I got off work that night and came home; sister Melda was still awake, she said   she was going to give brother Celino money to start buying wood to build her new house. I was happy for whatever reason they had for getting past what had happened in the past and treating each other like family.

Sister Rose got her old job back and right away she seem to forget she had kids, because at first she would come home once a week then maybe every two weeks. Mother told me to go to her job and tell her to come home to her kids. After several times going by her job looking for her; I finally caught up with her and relayed Mother messages to her…she promised she would come home, but she never showed up. When I went back to Calapacuan, I told Mother, Sister Rose was living in her friend apartment and I had told her what she had said. Mother said, tomorrow we will find her and see why she want come home and visit her kids. The next day Mother arrived very early at sister Melda house to accompany me to the apartment where Sister Rose was staying. When we arrived Sister Rose was just washing up for breakfast. Mother asked sister Rose, what she plan to do about her kids and why she haven't came back to see them. Sister Rose replied," If you need money…here is money…buy food for them". Mother said your kids need you not your money, because they have plenty to eat. Sister Rose said, she was going to write the kids father and tell him to come and get them. I knew then that Sister Rose wanted to get rid of her kids, so she could run around town and have fun with her boy friend. Mother was so mad at Sister Rose she walked right out of the apartment and started calling for a jeepney. I took the money sister Rose had offered to Mother and followed Mother to the street to catch a jeepney. When we got into the jeepney; I convinced Mother to take the sixty pesos and accompany me to the market and buy something for the kids. We purchased clothing and toys for the kids. I went home with Mother to Calapacuan to watch the kids play with their new toys.

I stayed for about two hours watching the kids play with their toys before I returned to sister Melda's house in Olongapo City. When I arrived I was surprised to see Sister Melda at home, because she has lately being going around town a lot. I told her about the episode with Sister Rose; she said Sister Rose was sick in the head. I went into my room and started getting ready for work; Sister Melda came to the door and asked me to write brother Smitty a letter for her before I went to work. Sister Melda speaks English better than me…it often puzzle me her being able to speak English so well and can't read or write it. When I write my brother in law I often imagine I was writing my husband or boyfriend and telling him the things my sister have me to write brother Smitty. Usually it's the same thing over and over... how much she love and miss him and how she wished he was home. Sometime the wording would change when she would have me to write something about the family. When I read his letters to her; they always seem to say the same things...I miss you, I can't wait to see you and how much she love him.

One time sister Melda asked me to write brother Smitty about the storm we got caught in on our way to visit my Mother in Calapacuan. We left early in the morning for Calapacuan for our weekly visit; it was raining very hard but we were determined to go visit our Mother. So I got my raincoat and Sister Melda wanted to be cute and got her umbrella. We caught a jeepney and were on our way; after we were a few miles outside of Olongapo City at a place that's called the Zigzags, where the road wounds around the mountain. The jeepney came to a stop and we saw the road covered with mud and rocks. The jeepney driver said "this is as far as I go", so we got out of the jeepney and started walking around the mud slide and it was still raining very hard. We walked a couple of miles before we saw a jeepney coming toward us; we flagged it down and told the driver what had happen to the road. The driver decided to turn around and go back to Calapacuan, so we climbed aboard. We arrived at the jeepney stop, which was about a half a mile from my Mother's house across a rice field. It was still raining very hard, but we were still determined to visit our Mother, so we headed across the rice field. We came to brother Celino house first, he and his wife yelling out the window asking us why we was walking in the rain. We didn't reply or stop; we kept going until we came to our Mother's house. As soon as we stepped in the door Mother started balling us out for being out in a rainstorm. We were soaking wet...sister Melda's umbrella had folded the other way and my raincoat was plastered to my body. Mother gave sister Melda and me dry towels so we could dry ourselves. I went and found some of my dry clothing and changed; sister Melda had to use Mother robe because she didn't have any clothes at my Mother house. Mother made coffee and told brother Etong to go outside and catch and kill a chicken, so she can make some chicken soup. Brother Etong brought the chicken in the house and gave it to Mother. She took the chicken into the kitchen and dressed it; then started to prepare her chicken soup receipt. When the soup was finished, Mother told brother Etong to go next door to brother Celino house and invited him and his wife over for lunch. While waiting for brother Celino and his wife to arrive; Mother started again to remind us how important it is to not go around in a rainstorm. Sister Melda had a slight grin on her face as she listened to Mother talk…I knew then that she was not listening to Mother warning because I knew she like doing dangerous things. When Brother Celino and his wife arrived, we all sat down and enjoyed the chicken soup.

When we get together like this we always end up telling stories about something that happen in the past that we thought was funny or very moving, so today was no exception. Sister Melda started first to tell her story about our Mother. "She said when my Mother was pregnant with me; there was a big cat that always would sneak into our kitchen and still our food…we had a small cat that everyone loved that was not a problem, but this big cat come out of nowhere.

Mother tried unsuccessful to get my Father and Brothers to kill the cat. So she decided to go it along. She left some food out one night and found her a hiding place nearby to wait for the cat. Sister Melda laugh pointing at me saying "that was the reason I was born premature and look like a cat." Then she continued with the story. Finally the cat came and Mother struck at him with a big stick and missed him and hit our small cat. The small cat died. My Mother was so upset about the big cat and felt real sorry for the small cat causing her to have premature birth and I was born two months early. She said, "Ambing is the little cat and everyone laugh". We asked Mother what happen to the big cat; she said sadly, he never came back. Sister Melda said, jokingly, you killed his girl friend. Everyone started laughing again.

Now it was Mother term to tell a story;" she said, my story start when the Japanese invaded the Philippines, it was only four of us at that time, Melda, Celino, your Father and me. As soon as everyone heard about the Japanese coming, they started running and hiding… we decided to dig a cave to stay in until they left our village. We spent half the night digging our cave behind our house in the wooded area. We continued to dig every night until finally it was large enough for four people to survive in. Yours Father and I moved what food and some clothing we had into the cave and begin our stay. Our bathroom was an old pot with a lid on it and your Father would carry it out and away from the cave and bury the content. He would also, go fishing and snail hunting at night.

We would never leave the cave until night for any reason. Sometime we could hear the Japanese passing close by our cave and we often had to cover your Sister Melda mouth with our hand so they would not hear her making noise. Every once in a while your Father would venture out doing the day to visit other families in the area and trade food items. He would always take snails because they were easy to keep alive and trade them for such items as sugar, salt and sometime coffee. We were very lucky, because there was a river close by and your Father did not have to go very far to fish. The entrance to the cave was straight down, so we had to put a ladder in it to enter. We had dug two areas out, one on each side of the entrance. Living in the cave was not so bad because it was cool most of the time. Just about everything we did was done at night, so we wouldn't make any noise doing the day when the Japanese are moving around. Being close to the river we would also take our baths, wash our clothes and clean whatever cooking pot and pan we had. Finally we got use to living in the cave. When the American came and ran the Japanese from the Philippines we would still spend the night in the cave on various occasions."

I could only imagine what it would be like living in a cave; I thought to myself...my Mother had a very hard life and I could see where she had gain all the wisdom and knowledge as to how to survive on little of nothing. I broke the silence and said wait a few minutes before starting the next story. I got up and started outside to use the restroom and sister Melda followed me. When we returned I said I want to tell my story; Mother asked, are you guys sleepy yet? Everyone answered no, and asked for more stories.

I begin my story saying Mother, do you remember when Sister Melda lived in her first apartment in Olongapo City and we were staying in the house near White Rock Beach? Yes! She said. That was when typhoon Dading hit no other place in the Philippines but Zambales. The wind was blowing so strong it blew a small black bird from his nest. I took it inside our house to care for it. Brother Etong and I scrambled to find small grasshoppers, worms and bugs for it to eat. I looked across the room at brother Etong; I could see in his eyes and the nodding of his head that he also remembered helping me to take care of the baby bird. Brother Etong found a small cardboard box and put holes in it so the bird could get fresh air and Mother gave me a piece of her old clothing to put in the bottom of the small box. That night the major part of the Typhoon came through with wind sounding like a freight train...it was really scary. No one slept well that night. Sister Linda and I kept close watch on the small bird, because we could not sleep. The next day everyone was up and about checking for typhoon damage to ours neighbor's houses. I came to our Mango trees in our backyard; they looked horrible, it seems as if all of the mangoes had blown off and was lying on the ground. Sister Linda, brother Etong and I started picking up the mangoes; we gathered over three bushels of mangoes. My Mother pickled some of the mangoes and wrapped some in cloth to slow the ripening process and stored them away in boxes. Three days later it was still raining, but that did not stop sister Melda from coming to check on us. When she arrived brother Etong, Sister Linda and I were in the bedroom feeding my bird worms and grasshoppers. Sister Melda came into the room to get a towel to dry her legs off and brother Etong left the room. Sister Melda, Sister Linda and I started playing with the bird. Sister Melda said your bird is almost ready to fly...where did you get the bird? I told her he was blown from the tree in our yard during the high winds. I got up and went into the kitchen to wash my hands; then all of a sudden I heard a loud yell... saying, "Oh my goodness". I ran back into the bedroom; Sister Melda had sat on my bird. I started to cry because I was really mad and upset at Sister Melda. Brother Etong came back into the room and tried to console me; he tried to tell me pointing toward the tree he would get me another bird if I stopped crying.

When I finished my story and looked around the room at everyone; I could see them looking at Sister Melda and finally she said, "It was an accident". My sister-in-law said, jokingly" Melda is a bird killer"... everyone started to laugh.

Someone said it is eleven o, clock we need to make some coffee if we plan to stay up any longer. Brother Celino said, it's my turn to tell my story, so he started...I remembered when the first time I visited Mother's house that was close to the road near White Rock Beach in Matain. Father and I took this little small Bangka boat and made a sail boat out of it. I said Yeah! Sister Melda said, let him tell the story. I said o.k. Then Mother and Linda said, wait we have to go to the bathroom. They lit a candle and they were off to the bathroom. On her way back Mother stop in the kitchen for more coffee. Brother Celino started his story again...I found out from Father that the Americans Marines was using the other side of the beach for a shooting range. He stopped and looked at Sister Melda and asked her if she still remember. She said, yes! Sister Linda and I both said, yes! He started his story again...I know everyone should remember he said. This is one of the times that Sister Melda really got so mad at me she would not talk to me at all. Melda, Father and I decided to start a business together. Father told us about the American Marines using a place called the Quarry on the other side of the beach for a practice shooting range and they was not allowed to leave the area for weeks at a time. So we decided to take beer, soft drinks and sandwiches to the Quarry to sale to them when they are not shooting. Father and I provided the labor and boat; Sister Melda provided the money to buy everything including an icebox. Our business was doing real good; it would do even better when Sister Melda was around, because the Marines was trying to impress her, so they would tell us to keep the change and buy even more beer. This place turned out to be a money maker...we sold everything as fast as we could get it. When sister Melda got sick; we took Sister Linda, Ambing and Mother along that particular day. As you probably remembered when it was time for you to return home the water were so rough you had to spend the night. That night the Marines started shooting up flares and when they came down they came real close to the tent where we were staying. Everybody was real scared...Mother got mad at Father and me; because she thought it was too dangerous for us to be there. The next day the water had finally calmed down so Mother and the kids could go home. Finally sister Melda started feeling better, so she came back to help Father and me with the business and just like always business started to get better.

We continued our business and were making a lot of money until one night I put the money under the blanket as usually and we went to sleep. The next day we woke up late because of the noise from the Marine camp. I looked around and found our camp area was in shambles and our money gone. When Sister Melda found out about it she did not believe what Father and I told her, so we had to shut down the business because there was no money to buy more supplies to sale. Father sold his boat and left Matain and I left also. His story left everyone stunned trying to figure out when this incident took place. It was not a problem for me to figure out when it happen…it was the night sister Melda came and put us out of her house in Matain. Now I know the reason why she did it.

The next day Mother woke up early and started fixing breakfast, she was out of coffee, so she stirred fried some rice until it was brown; she then boiled it and made coffee. Breakfast was real good that morning; I ate so much I decided to go back to sleep. Sister Melda asked brother Celino to go and check the road and see if it was clear, so we could return to Olongapo City. When I woke up it was three o, clock; sister Melda said the road was clear and we could go back to Olongapo City. I had slept right through lunch…Mother told everyone to let me sleep because I had to work that night. Sister Melda said let's go home, so we left for Olongapo City. When we arrive at her house the power was still out. We went inside and I started to get ready for work. As I was leaving sister Melda said she would accompany me; she wanted to see mama Ligaya before I went to work. When we arrived at her place, she said there was no power, so I could go home because she was not going to open up a money exchange booth when there is no power. Sister Melda and mama Ligaya talked for a while and then we went home.

A lot of strange things happened while I was working in the Money Exchange booth in front of the Jet Club. One day I was sitting in the booth waiting for someone to come by and exchange American dollars for Pesos; all of a sudden someone threw a rock and hit the Money Exchange booth, I jumped up out of my seat and looked outside and saw four or five Filipino guys fighting throwing rock and boxing each other. I ran inside of the Jet Club and told the Manager what was happening in front of the club and Money Exchange booth. I was completely terrified because this was the first time I had seen people fight each other that way. I saw one guy get hit in the head with a rock; he fell down in the street with blood coming from his head. No one would go and help the guy in the street; then finally an American guy picked him up and put him in a jeepney and took him to the hospital. The Club Manager explained to me why no one would help the guy…the guy was in a gang fight, he had crossed over into another gang territory and everyone was afraid to get involved because they have been known to kill each other and other people. To my surprise there were two gangs in Olongapo City; the OXO gang and the ZIGI ZIGI gang. I grew up in the country and this is the first time I have ever heard of a gang…I guess you will live and learn when you come to the city.

I had just got to work one day, when one of the girl that work in the Jet club behind the Money Exchange booth came by and asked me to keep her radio until she return. I said, O.K.! I put it behind the booth counter. A few minutes later I had to go to the bathroom inside the Jet Club, so I closed the booth door and left. When I returned and opened back up, my friend returned and asked for her radio. I asked her whether she had taken the radio because it was gone when I returned from the bathroom. We looked again behind the counter, but the radio was nowhere in sight, so I went outside in front of the booth and asked the little girls that sold handkerchief if they had seen anyone around the booth while I was gone.

One of the girls told me the lady that's always high on red devils stopped at the booth and went to Lucy Mar Drug Store. My friend and I went to Lucy Mar Drug Store and asked about the radio; she told us that the lady had pawn it for five pesos about the same as one dollar in American money, so we got the radio back and I promised myself I would not be responsible anymore for other people property. I went back to the Money Exchange booth and thanked the handkerchief girls for helping me get the radio back. They came over to my booth and we talked for a while; I found out that we was all about the same age, so we became friend; when the American would come to my booth to exchange dollars for pesos, the handkerchief girls would stand by my booth and sell them handkerchief. There was never a dull moment when the American Sailors and Marines came by to exchange dollars to pesos...sometime they would ask me if I had a boyfriend and I would ask them what was that, they would laugh. Sometime they would stand in front of my booth and act as if they don't want to leave. They would continue to ask me out or tell me they want to marry me. I was to embarrass to ask them to leave, because I couldn't imagine what they would say. Finally I got use to them asking me out and to marry me, so I would tell them I was too young to get married.

One day, sister Melda came to the Money Exchange booth to visit with me; she pulled up a chair beside me in the booth. Finally one of the young Sailors came by to talk with me again and Sister Melda started asking him questions, so he asked her to work in my place so he could take me out. Sister Melda laughed and told him to go across the street to the Shangri-La Restaurant and bring us an order of chop suey and fried chicken. The guy left and returned a few minutes later with the food. Sister Melda started to laugh and told him she was only kidding around. He quickly told her he did not play around and he was not playing when he told her he liked me very much. From that day, Sister Melda would go with me to work and hang around my booth all the time watching me. I didn't know why she was hanging around so much, and I was somewhat afraid to ask. Then one day this young man came up to my booth and started talking to me. Sister Melda told me the guy was kind of cute and he was about my size. I was completely surprised all I could say was what! I had not considered having a boyfriend yet; I could not understand why she was saying these things to me. I guess she was lonely for her husband and want to do something to pass the time. Every day she kept coming to visit me on the job; then one day she came and brought me a surprise, it was a beautiful ring. I immediately put the ring on and thanked her for being so thoughtful. The young sailor that always tell me how much he like me came by and was startled when he saw my new ring. He asked me right away, who was the lucky guy. I told him no one, but he walked away looking sad and disbelief. Several more of my regular customers came by and asked the same thing, so now I am really puzzled; I closed my booth and went inside of the Jet Club and found the Manager and asked him about my ring. He told me that it was an engagement ring and if I wear it everyone would know that I was engaged to be married.

I thanked the Manager and returned to my booth. Sitting in my booth, I started racking my brain trying to figure out why sister Melda would do something like that to me. I decided to keep the ring and only wear it when she is around. One Thursday sister Melda and I decided to have a family picnic at White Rock Beach on Friday. Sister Melda gave me fifty pesos to buy food and drinks, so when I left work I went straight to Calapacuan to tell my Mom and give her the money to buy everything. Sister Melda said she would meet us at the beach. When we arrived at the beach Sister Melda was already there with an American friend. She introduced everybody and I went swimming; I had been in the water for a couple of hours when I noticed my finger was looking like a prune, so I slipped the ring off and let it drop into the water. When I came out of the water I made sure she could hear me when I said oh no! I have lost my ring. She heard what I had said, she told me that I should have taken it off before entering the water, but not to worry she would get me another one, I immediately told her not to bother, because I can't seem to hold on to valuable things. Everyone had a great time at the picnic; I had to go to work that afternoon. I was a little tired when I arrived at work, but was attentive enough to catch a guy trying to pass counterfeit money; he had two ten, one twenty and four five dollar bills. I yelled for the Manager and the guy took off running and was out of sight when the Manager arrived. The Manager told the Security Guard to keep a close watch on my booth, because the guy may come back. Just as the Manager had figured, the guy came back to my booth and asked for the real ten dollar bill he had gave me, I started yelling for the Security Guard and the Manager; everyone ran to my booth, but the guy was long gone and he never came back. I took the real dollar bills and gave the Manager all of the counterfeit bills. This was a wonderful Christmas gift for me. I use the money to buy my Mother a nice towel set and an embroidery pillow case for her Christmas present. Because every time I went with Mother to the market, she would always stop and admire the pillowcases and towels.

Early December sister Rose husband came from Pangasinan to get his son, Jerry; he said he couldn't afford to take care of two children, so he was only taking Jerry and leaving Gina. He asked my mother if she would keep Gina...she told him if we eat Gina would eat. The next day he left going back to Pangasinan with his son.

Christmas Eve came and Sister Melda and I left Olongapo City and went back home to Calapacuan bearing food and gifts. Sister Rose also came to Calapacuan with gifts and toys for her two kids. When she arrived she found out that her husband had came by and pickup her son and carried him back to Pangasinan. She asked us why someone had not notified her that her husband had come and taken Jerry. I told her I had come by the Top Hat Club where she worked and left messages for her to come home. Everyone I talked to said they had not seen her for at least two days. She said no one had given her the message. Mother told Sister Rose she knew where her kids was living she just didn't want to come home. That was all that was said on that subject. Then everyone pitched-in to help Mother prepare all of the food before midnight, because it is the custom in the Philippines to get up eat and open present at midnight. When we finally got the food prepared; everyone was lounging around and trying to figure out who got what for a Christmas present...Mother told us the present are suppose to be a surprise and everyone laugh. At the stroke of midnight the food was placed in the middle of the floor and everyone gathered around it with his plates. We was so thankful that everyone could be together again for another Christmas dinner. Finally we had finished stuffing ourselves, so now was the time to start opening the presents. Mother was so happy for all the gifts she received...Sister Melda gave her a pair of pajamas with a lot of embroidery on it, I gave her the towel set and the embroidery pillowcases and Sister Rose gave her forty pesos. Mother said thanks very much for your gifts, but you didn't have to bring gifts because all I want is for you to be here. Sister Melda gave me perfume and I gave her an embroidery pillowcase set that said, "Mr. and Mrs." I gave Sister Rose a nightgown and she gave me a pair of earring. I also, gave brother Etong a shirt and handkerchief set. Everyone was very happy, so we said good morning and went to bed. Everyone except my Mother slept late Christmas day. Mother got up and washed her new pajamas, towels and pillowcases.

When we finally did get up Brother Etong went next door to check on Brother Celino house, because they had went to Pangasinan to spend Christmas with his wife family. Sister Melda and I got Brother Celino a carpenter set for Christmas. I know he will like the present because he always considers himself a carpenter; now he will have the tools…he should be very happy. We stayed in Calapacuan for two days just lounging around and doing nothing but enjoying each other company. Mother finally took time out for a little relaxation; which she seldom does. Finally our vacation was over; Sister Melda, Sister Linda and I had to return to Sister Melda house in Olongapo City. The first order of the day was clean up the house. We cleaned the house from top to bottom and change all of the linen. I was already tired and I had to return to work that evening.

The next day after we had finished breakfast; my brother-in-law Smitty arrived home for a vacation. I often wondered why he didn't come earlier and spend Christmas with his wife…I never asked, but it did puzzle me.

The next day Sister Melda woke me up very early and told me to fix brother Smitty breakfast because she was going to the market and wouldn't be back when he awake. I went back to sleep for a while and finally did get up when Sister Linda woke up. We got up and clean up and started our breakfast. After we had eaten Brother Smitty came out of his room and asked for Sister Melda. Sister Linda looked at me…I told him she had went to the Market and asked him what he would like for breakfast. He said, he didn't want anything and he would wait for Sister Melda. He took a seat in the living room. Finally he said, it nine o, clock already and she not home yet. I asked him again what he wanted for breakfast. He said, in a snappy voice, do you have soup in the can? I said, yes, Chicken and vegetables soup. He said o.k. Give me the vegetable soup and crackers.

At ten o, clock Sister Melda came in the door, she was carrying vegetable, pork and large shrimp. She said she had walked all over the market looking for the large shrimp for Brother Smitty lunch. Brother Smitty was happy she was at Home; he even thanked me for fixing his vegetable soup.Sister Melda told Sister Linda and me to clean the shrimp right away because she wanted to prepare it for brother Smitty lunch. The shrimp was very large…I think three or four of the shrimp would be a meal for one person. When we finished cleaning the shrimp, we started preparing the vegetable and rice for our lunch. I decided to watch Sister Melda cook the large shrimp…she mixed flour, salt and pepper in a paper bag and put the shrimp inside and begin to shake the bag. She told me to peel three Irish potatoes and cut them up in pieces the size of my finger and wash and steam some string beans. Brother Smitty had a nice lunch and he really appeared to have enjoyed it. After we had cleaned up from lunch and was sitting around talking; Sister Melda said she told mama Ligaya she wanted me to stay at home until Brother Smitty went back to Viet Nam. Mama Ligaya had agreed and got someone else to work in my place. I said o.k. As if I had a choice.

That night Sister Melda brought some of her clothes into the room I shared with Sister Linda; I thought she wanted us to wash them, but she didn't say anything, so we decided to wait until she told us what to do with the clothes. Early that next morning we found out why she had left the clothes in our room…she came in our room and put the clothes on and left for the market. She told us she didn't want to wake Brother Smitty. I could not understand why she wanted to leave that early going to the market when she usually tells me or Sister Linda to go to the market. She came back from the market late that day and without any food items; she said she couldn't find the big shrimp…I said to myself, she could have bought some pork, chicken or beef instead of coming back empty handed.

Brother Smitty told her not to worry about getting the shrimp; he would take us all out to lunch at the Admiral restaurant. We all got ready and went to the restaurant. When we arrived and were seated; Brother Smitty asked us what we wanted to eat; I said can we have fried chicken, Linda liked fried chicken too. He told Sister Linda and me we could order whatever we wanted to eat. Sister Linda ordered chop suey and white rice…we all laugh thinking that we really have to have rice. We can't seem to get alone without having rice as part of our meal. Brother Smitty ordered beef fried rice and a coke and Sister Melda shared Linda and my order. The food was delicious; when we finished our meal; we went to the Naval Base to watch a movie. First we went to the movie at Cubic Point, but the movie was not starting for some time, so we went to the movie close to the main gate…it was just starting when we walked in. We had our seats and enjoyed the movie.

After the movie we went outside and it was still light. Brother Smitty said let go by the small mini mart and get some snacks to take home. He bought candy, peanut and cashew nuts and we went home. When we arrived home everyone went to his room; I started to get board; I really want to go back to work, but Sister Melda want me to be around so Brother Smitty could have someone to talk to when she is away.

Brother Smitty's month vacation past by so fast it almost slipped by me. He said his goodbye and was off to Subic Bay Naval Base to catch the Navy's ground shuttle to Clark Air Base near Angeles City, Philippines. Sister Melda accompanied him to the Naval Base and said her last goodbye. I really feel sorry for Brother Smitty having to return to Viet Nam…I remember reading one of Sister Melda letter when he would telling her about him having to wear helmet and flight jacket and carry a rifle with him at all times. At night I often pray for Brother Smitty to stay safe. He also, told her about the snipers always shooting at their camp and he would keep his rifle beside his bed every night.

The next day I returned to work and Sister Linda went back to Mother's house in Calapacuan. I was really and truly glad to be back at work. Days came and went…Sister Melda spent a lot of time away from home; sometime she wouldn't come home at all…I would go home to Calapacuan. Sometime Sister Rose and I would get together and go to Calapacuan together. Since Sister Rose husband took her son away she seems to be spending more time in Calapacuan with her daughter. For some reason Sister Rose would come around more often; she even came and spent the night with me at Sister Melda's house.

Sister Melda started spending even more time away from her apartment, so I would go to Calapacuan and help brother Etong with his chores…feeding the pigs, chopping wood and help rake leaves to smoke the mango trees. When the mango trees start to bloom everyone would always smoke the trees to protect the tree's blossom from insects.

Every time I visit Calapacuan and stop by Brother Celino's house, his wife would tell me he was away somewhere. I said to myself, here we go again…first the Father running around away from home, now the son is following in his footsteps. I would try to say something comforting to her… like he may be looking for a job or he will be back very soon. Then I would return to Sister Melda house and get ready for work.

One evening I had just got settled in my booth when Sister Rose came bearing bad news; she said I needed to return to Sister Melda house and get the clothes she had written on a list. I asked what's wrong. She told me sister Melda was in the Hospital. I was so surprised and scared I said, why! What's wrong? Where is she? I got shaky and didn't know what to do. I asked her, which Hospital she was in? She wouldn't answer, so I ran into the Jet Club and asked the Floor Manager to cover for me until I get back. He asked what was wrong, I told him sister Melda was in the Hospital and I had to go and I needed him to take my place for a while. He said he would cover for me…Sister Rose and I went to Sister Melda house and got the items that were on the list. We went out and caught a tricycle; I asked her again…which Hospital Sister Melda was in? She said follow me and I will show you. She had the tricycle to stop in front of a hotel. She got out and told me to follow her. I said this does not look like a Hospital to me. I was really and truly surprised and upset because she would not tell me what was going on. I followed her into the hotel and she knocked on the door. To my surprise, Sister Melda opened the door with a big smile on her face; I could see a man sitting on the bed and she introduced him to us as her friend. As upset as I could possibly be; I said I thought you was in the Hospital…you and Sister Rose tell me a big lie and have me to get off work for something like this. I told her I was going to work. She tried to give me some excuse about me having the key to her house and Sister Rose did not have one, so they had to tell me a lie in order to get her clothes. I left the hotel very mad and feeling sorry for my brother-in-law in Viet Nam. I think that was what she was doing when Brother Smitty was here on vacation… making all the fuss about trying to find big shrimps at the market; she was just making excuses to be with her new friend. On my way back to work I kept racking my brain trying to understand why she or anyone else would do a crazy thing like that. I know I will have to lie when I get back to work…just as I figured the Manager of the club ask me if Sister Melda was alright. I lied and said she was all right and would come back home tomorrow. He asked what was wrong with her; I told him I really didn't find out because I was in a hurry to return to work. He walked away with a puzzled look on his face. I sit down in my booth and started to thinking about Sister Melda and the mess she is getting involved in. I thought, here is a young lady with a very, very nice husband that will do everything in his power to get her what she wanted and she found a need to sleep around with another man while he is away. I thought this was disgusting, and tried to put it out of my mind.

Just when I was about to calm down; Sister Rose popped up at my booth and started to try and explain the role she had played in the lie she and Sister Melda fabricated. She said she didn't have a key to Sister Melda house and they knew I had a key, so they lied to get me to go and get the clothes. I told her to forget the matter; what has happened has passed.

Then she opened her bag and gave me money for Mother and asked me to tell Mother she wouldn't be coming home for a while. I asked her why and what was she going to do? She said nothing! And I see you later. Then left and went across the street and got into a jeepney. When she got into the jeepney she kissed the driver. I said, well! Here we go again.

When I got off work that night, I went straight to Calapacuan even though I was scared because of the rumor about the jeepney drivers seeing a lady in white in his rear view mirror while passing the cemetery and when he look again she had disappeared. Since then most of the jeepney driver refuse to pass by the cemetery past midnight on the road to Calapacuan. I decided to go anyway. When I arrived in Calapacuan; the store beside the road was still open. This made me feel a little better, so I got out of the jeepney and went across the field to my Mother's house. Usually my Mother or brother Etong would wait for me at the store, but not tonight, I am all along. When I arrived I gave Mother the forty pesos Sister Rose had sent her. I told her Sister Rose was not coming home for a while and I thought she have a boyfriend that a jeepney driver. Mother said what! She walked away shaking her head. I was very tired so I went to bed. The next day I woke up at about nine o, clock, I guess I was really tired the night before; my body still felt weak and drained of energy. Mother looked at me and asked if I was all right; I told her I feel as if I don't have any bones. She said maybe you are catching a cold...you need to take care of yourself.

I left early that evening going to Olongapo City because I wanted to see if Sister Melda had came home. When I arrived I knocked on the door, but there was no answer so I let myself in. I took a shower and dressed for work. When I arrived at work I could see through the door of the Jet Club and a lot of girls was huddling around a table and just as I was about to sit down; my friend knocked on the door of my booth...I opened the door and she said come and go with me, so I closed my booth door and went with her. She took me to the table where all of the girls had being huddling around. Now I could see an old woman sitting at the table. My friend told the old lady to read my palm. The old lady said, sit down and reach for my hand. She looked at my palm and told me; I was going on a trip and when I return I was going to meet someone that I would want to marry or stay with. She said, I can't explain it any better because everything is a little cloudy now, but when you return from your trip come and see me. Then my friend said it's going to cost you one peso. I said you didn't tell me it was going to cost me a peso. The old lady said pay me when you return from that trip I was telling you about. Just as I was about to leave the table a group of American sailors walked into the club and all of the girls left the table to meet the sailors. I asked the old lady to look at my palm again...she looked and told me that when I return from this trip I was suppose to go on I would find someone here wanting to marry me.

I asked her, where she will be when I return? She said, look for me around here; just ask anyone here they will know who I am. I thanked her and returned to my booth. The time just breezed by, before I knew it; it was time for me to go home.

When I arrived home I looked into Sister Melda's room and to my surprise she was in bed asleep, so I went to my room and went to bed. The next day I was awaken to the smell of food...garlic fried rice, dried fish, fried eggs and coffee. I jumped out of bed and rushed to get clean up for breakfast. It was a nice big breakfast; I was surprised sister Melda took time to make breakfast normally she would wait and have me do it.

We sat down to the table to eat; then she started to talk about what she wanted to do come Christmas. She said she was going to go shopping early, so she could get nice present for everyone. I said to myself, why not? You have the money. We finished breakfast and I cleaned the kitchen. Right after I had finished cleaning the kitchen, Sister Rose arrived for a surprise visit. I asked her where had she being keeping herself; she said, around. We went into my bedroom to talk, but as soon as we got comfortable and started to talking Sister Melda, called for me. I went into her bedroom. She handed me three letters from brother Smitty to read to her because she can't read. His letters was mostly the same…He was telling her about things in Viet Nam and how the Viet Cong was using small kids in the war. I almost fell asleep reading all three of his letters and thinking it was really bad for the kids getting involved in the war. I really didn't like reading his letters, but I didn't have a choice because Sister Melda could not read.

One day she got sick and asked me to write the President of the United States. I asked her for the address…she told me to address the letter to President Johnson, Washington, D.C.; I did and hoped it would reach him. A few days later Brother Smitty was knocking at the door. I opened the door and there he was standing there smiling and he grabbed me and gave me a big hug. I don't know whether the letter we sent had any influence on him getting leave to come home…I didn't think anymore about the letter; I was just glad to see him. He asked for Sister Melda, I told him she was in San Rogue Hospital; He changed his clothing and left for the hospital. About an hour later, Brother Smitty came back and he seem to be real upset, he told me that the Hospital staff said, there was no one at the hospital by the name of Melda Smith, so he went to mama Ligaya place and asked her about Melda. He said mama Ligaya was totally surprised about Melda being in the Hospital. I agreed to accompany him back to the Hospital; when we arrived I asked for Sister Melda and they showed us to her room. Sister Melda was real surprised when we entered her room. She acted as though she was upset with me for bringing Brother Smitty to the Hospital.

I don't know today what was wrong with her…my guess… she had had an abortion. Brother Smitty asked her why she didn't go to the Hospital on base; she gave him some kind of an excuse about not having time or transportation. He accepted the excuse like everything else she dished out, because he loved her so much. Sister Melda stayed in the Hospital about three more days before she came home. Everyone was helping out at her house…cooking, cleaning and washing clothes; Mother came and brought Gina, Sister Rose daughter. Brother Smitty liked playing with Gina and calling her little Rosie.

All of the family members came by and did whatever he or she could to help out while she was in bed. Brother Smitty vacation was only two weeks and the time passed so fast he even was surprised. When he left Mother lit in on Sister Melda about the things she was doing to hurt her marriage. She didn't say what Sister Melda had done, but I think she knew. She was telling her how great a husband and provider she had. Sister Melda listened, but as always…that was all she did. Mother asked her why she had given the Hospital a different name and explained to her some of the things that can happen to you in a Hospital, such as, she could die and no one would know. She didn't believe something like that could happen to her. That was the first time I saw Mother really get on Sister Melda about the way she was running her life. She tried to make her understand that God had given her a good life and she should take advantage of it. Sister Melda's recovery was very swift; before the family realized her condition she was up and about. She was making her usually rounds I guess; because most of the times I come home from work she would be away and would remain away all night.

I was sitting in my booth one day and to my surprise; Sister Melda appeared out of nowhere with a big smile on her face. She said, the circus is in town…I want you to go to Calapacuan when you get off work and tell everyone to come to my house tomorrow evening, so we can go to the circus. I was excited about the circus too. When I got off work I went straight to Calapacuan. I told everyone…Mother, Sister Rose, Sister Linda and Brother Etong about the circus being in Olongapo City and Sister Melda wanted to take the whole family to the circus. Everyone arrived early at Sister Melda's house; we left for the circus ground and arrived around six o, clock. The sailor I saw her with in the Hotel was waiting at the gate; Sister Melda introduced him as an old friend she met a long time ago and she was surprised to see him at the circus. She gave everyone some spending money and told us to go wherever we wanted to go and meet back at the gate at ten o, clock. Everyone started going in different directions, Sister Rose and I wanted to see the Octopus Kid. Everyone left Sister Melda talking with her friend at the gate. After the Octopus Kid we walked around and watched the rides and games. Finally we decided to take in another show; a little over half way through the show Sister Rose looked at the time. She said, we are suppose to meet at the gate at ten o, clock, I told her we only had a few minutes left before the show finish and I wanted to finish it. The show finished at ten fifteen and we headed for the gate. When we was approaching the gate I saw everyone standing and waiting; Sister Melda turn around and looked in our direction... she looked very mad. As soon as we got to the gate she asked us where had we being; I told her we was in the middle of a show and we stayed to finish it. She said, I told you to meet here at the gate at ten o, clock. I said, yes, but I wanted to finish the show. She slapped me in the face while her boyfriend looked on; Mother didn't see her slap me, but Sister Rose, her boyfriend and several other people at the gate did. I walked away toward the waiting jeepneys; Sister Rose followed and asked me where I was going. I told her anywhere except Sister Melda's house. I told Sister Rose I would see her Christmas, which was two days away. I caught a jeepney and went to Sister Melda's house and pickup some of my clothing and went to the Jet Club to try and catch my friend. She was still there when I arrived, so I asked to spend the night at her place. She said, yes, I have an extra bedroom and you can stay as long as you want to. She asked me what was wrong and I explained to her everything. We went to bed. The aroma of the brewing coffee woke me up. I got up and went to the bathroom and cleaned up. I came out of the bathroom and sit down in the kitchen area to a breakfast of: Hot rolls with margarine and sardine. After breakfast we sat for a while laughing and talking; finally my friend had to go, so she got up and took a shower and was off to meet her friend at the Jet Club. I asked her as she was leaving not to tell anyone, especially the club manager that I was staying at her place. She promised me she would not tell a soul.

I went to work that night and was getting comfortable in my booth when Sister Melda came by. She asked me to come back to her place. I couldn't wait to say, no! I also took the opportunity to tell her...I was seventeen years old and I will not accept being slapped around by anyone. She left my booth in a hurry. I don't know where she went. I stayed a second night with my friend; then I went home to Calapacuan, it was Christmas Eve. When I arrived, Mother said, your Sister Melda were here looking for you, I said, I saw her yesterday. Mother said, where have you being staying? I told her I had being staying with my co-worker. She said, what's going on with you and your sister? I told her that Sister Melda had slapped me when we were at the circus. She said, no one had told her anything about it. She said, Sister Melda had asked everyone to spend the night at her house after they left the circus. She asked had anyone seen you; we figured you were staying with your Sister Rose. The next day Melda asked me had you came home. I said, no! We had breakfast and came home to Calapacuan.

I didn't have to work on Christmas Eve, so I stayed home; Sister Rose was off work also, so she came home to Calapacuan. All of the kids were there except Sister Melda and Brother Celino. Brother Celino's wife spent Christmas Eve with us; she helped Mother prepare our Christmas meal for midnight. When we had finished our midnight Christmas meal and exchanged gifts, we were all sitting around on pillows and wrapped in blankets. This is what we normally do on holidays or whenever the family got together...we would each tell about an incident that involved us all. So tonight was my turn. I started by saying...do everyone remember the big storm that hit this part of Luzon island when we moved into the Nipa hut Father built before this house. Everyone said, yes! I started again...the wind and rain was very strong, you could hear the wind sounding like a freight train...the bamboo on the side of our house was being blown away...the wind gust seem as though it would blow the roof off the house...Sister Linda, Brother Etong, Mother and I would hold on to the roof when the wind would start gusting real hard. We continued to pray and hang on to the roof. Mother said, yes! Yes! I remembered and now to think about it, I think God the roof didn't fly away with us hanging on to it. Sister Rose said, yes! Thank God, because you could have being somewhere on the other side of the mountain with the roof. After my story everyone hurried to get coffee and return for the next story. Mother said it's my turn and began her story saying…I remember when the Japanese invaded the Philippines; I would visit my brother in Sual, Pangasinan as often as I could. My brother was the only kid in our family that had an education. He was married and in the Philippines Navy. I interrupted her saying…I thought you had only one brother. She said I have only one brother alive and continued her story. When the Japanese came they recruited people to be informers. They would cover the informer head with a paper bag and bring him into the barrio and let him point out the people that plotting against the Japanese. As always there were individual that didn't have money and they would sale their soul for a few pesos. The informers would go from town to town with the Japanese pointing out people that against the Laws of the Japanese. Sister Linda can't seem to keep still, Mother stop her story and asked her what was wrong with her? She said, I have to go to the bathroom. Everyone said, hurry up Linda and started to laugh. Sister Linda hurried to get to the bathroom and return. Mother said take your time Linda I will wait until you return before I start again. Sister Linda came rushing back to her seat and Mother started her story again. She said, things was not really bad for the men in our village, but if someone is acting as an informer for the Japanese that made things a little different. The Japanese would arrest and torture you even if they only heard that you said something bad about them. Everyone was quiet as a mouse while Mother was telling her story. It was two o, clock in the morning and I still was not sleepy, because the story was so intriguing.

Mother continued…every time the people hear of the Japanese coming to their town they would run and hide, because they didn't know who the Japanese was looking for. Once my Brother's wife and I was at the market shopping for food; the Japanese came looking for someone they believe was hiding in the market area…we left so fast we forgot to buy the rest of our food". Everyone eyes were glued to Mother lips as they started to quiver; I thought she was about to cry. I asked if she was all right, she said yes! And started to continue her story…"One night my Brother came home to see his wife and family; he was in the Philippine Navy so he had to sneak in. I took my kids,

Celino and Melda to visit my brother at his place he did not want to be seen, because he knew there were informers around. My Brother never left the house; the only people that knew my Brother was at home were his family and his wife family. Three days later we were all sitting around talking when someone said, "the Japanese was coming," My Brother ran and hid in the closet in a basket of clothes. The Japanese searched the house and found him; they brought him out in front of his house and shot him dead in front of his family."

Mother started crying and we cried with her; finally she stopped crying and wiped her tears away. Sister Linda asked, who told the Japanese my uncle was home? She said, she didn't know for sure but she had a good idea it was one of his wife relatives. Mother began her story again...the only reason they killed him was because he were in the Philippine Navy. In my memory it seem like yesterday; I will remember this incident until I die. After we buried my Brother, your Father and I took Melda and Celino and started living in the cave he had prepared. We did all of our traveling and searching for food at night. We stayed in the cave until the Philippine was liberated by Mac Arthur." Mother ended her story saying, "let's go to bed, it's almost morning."

We almost slept through the whole day; we missed breakfast and lunch. We finally got up around three o, clock and ate again. Everyone was still talking about Mother Story and how General Mac Arthur had liberated the Philippine. I had read in my Social Studies book about the Japanese occupation of the Philippines, but I couldn't imagine things being so gruesome until I heard my Mother story. I asked Mother whether my uncle wife received any money from the Philippine Government for the lost of her husband. She said yes, she receives a check every month for the rest of her life, if she does not remarry. I asked her when was the last time she seen my uncle's wife? She said, the last time I saw her was in Pangasinan; she invited me to my niece wedding. I said I never knew that she invited you to her daughter wedding. She said, of course not! You were too young to remember what was going on...do you remember when the Nurse came to give the kids their Vaccination in the Barrio? I said, yes!

Then she said, do you remember the lady that pulled you from your hiding place under the boat? I said, yes! She said that was your uncle wife, she never forgot me, because we are the survivors of the Japanese killing and torturing.

I returned to work the next day…sitting in my booth daydreaming as I normally do when things are slow; today I was thinking about the time when I was much younger and we was living in Sister Melda's house at White Rock Beach. You could see the ocean from the house; I would sit by the window looking out at the ocean waves moving back and forth. I would think to myself…the ocean stretch all the way to the mountains and to the United States and other countries… the ocean goes everywhere. I would wish that I could be like the ocean, so I could travel to the other side of the mountain and maybe to the United States. I also, remembered my Mother snapping me out of my daydream, saying," It's time to go to bed now, you have to go to school tomorrow". Just as always someone or something would snap me out of my daydream…here come Sister Melda, she pull a chair into the doorway of my booth and sit down. She asked me how was Christmas in Calapacuan; I told her everything was fine…she and Brother Celino was the only one who didn't make it home. She looked at me…trying to put on her sad face and said, "will you come home tonight, I am sorry that I slap you; sometime I don't think about what I am doing…my boyfriend got you a big teddy bear and some perfume for Christmas and I got you the seven days embroidery panty set. I said, thank you! You can keep the gifts; I don't want or need them. She got up and left.

A few hours later Sister Melda's boyfriend came by; he said, "A belated Merry Christmas to you" and I said the same to you. He smiled and said, "I bought you a Christmas present and left it with your Sister Melda…how you like it. I said, thank you! But I told my sister to keep the present because she always get mad at us when someone buy us a present, even my brother-in-law…she is a very jealous person. He stared at me for a second and said, "Bye! Tell your sister I said hello". Then he left.

Right after Sister Melda's boyfriend left, Sister Rose came. I said you are not working tonight, she replied, everything is slow tonight… the U.S.S Ranger is the only ship I know that's in port…I know one guy that's on the Ranger, but he has duty tonight. I said it's being real slow for me to only two Sailors have come to get their dollars exchanged. Sister Rose said, "thing should pick up next week the U.S.S Ticonderoga and the U.S.S Forrestal are coming into port. The Club Manager came to my booth and said, "Let's go home early tonight". I counted my money and said to myself; things are really slow I normally would exchange five to eight hundred American dollars when the big ships were in; tonight I only exchanged less than a hundred American dollars. Sister Rose and I left the money exchange booth and took the money to mama Ligaya home behind the Swan Club. Mama Ligaya was still awake when I arrived. She asked me to tell sister Melda to come see her when she got a chance. I said o.k. And goodbye.

Sister Rose and I decided to take some food home, so we bought cooked noodles, hot rolls and cheese spread ... Brother Etong liked the cheese spread in the can. We caught a jeepney for Calapacuan. When we arrived Mother said, "You are early tonight". I said, yes, Things are very, very slow tonight. Mother called our sister-in-law who lived next door over to eat with us. When she arrived I asked where my Brother was. She said, "he' with his Father and some other people looking for buried treasuries. I said to myself, he's looking for treasuries all right...women treasuries. I had often wondered how she and my brother met, so I decided to ask her tonight. I said Sister Maria, We never knew just how you and brother Celino met. She looked at me and took a sip of her coffee and said, "You know that I am older than your brother". I said no, I thought he was older than you. She continued ...every month I had to go and pick up my monthly check at the Government office. I received a monthly check because I was married to a world war two veteran. I interrupt saying we didn't know you was married before. She continued...My cousin son knew your Brother, he and your Brother were accompanying my cousin one day at the Government office and they introduced your Brother to me. We started dating and ended up living together. All my relatives were mad at me; my Sister was so mad she wouldn't speak to me. I interrupt again and said I remembered about the time when you and my Brother got together...you and him came to visit us in Canan, Pangasinan at our little house. She said yes, it was a very small house just like the little house on the prairie. We all laugh. I said that's a very long time ago. She said, yes! And continued...we lived together like husband and wife. My only kid, Celia, was with my in-laws. We were the talk of the town…we didn't get married because I would lose my monthly check I received as a widow. We vowed to each other to stay together for better or worse. We lived together in my house in Villasis, Pangasinan for about five years; then one day I went to pick up my check and I was told that I was cut off because I was married. I said why you didn't take someone there to prove you was not married. She said, "I went to my Uncle and my Sister for support…my uncle said, no, …my sister said I was a fool and your Brother was only using me, because he wouldn't try and get a job; all he wanted was a place to eat, sleep and someone to make love to. She also, said that I was embarrassing the family. I finally told your Brother that I was not getting any more money from the Government and I guess he would be leaving me now. He really surprised me when he said that he was not going to leave me and if I wanted to leave, Pangasinan; he would take me to Subic, Zambales, because he had relatives there. I started the next day trying to sale my pigs, Chicken and my house so we could move to Calapacuan, Subic, Zambales. She said, "Look at me now; Celino want come home to me and my relatives hate me.

Sister Rose interrupted with her big mouth and said, you have got a husband that's never around. I told Sister Rose she had a husband that was not around. She said her situation was different because she left her husband. Sister Maria looked as if she was going to cry, so I went to her and gave her a big hug and told her she would always be my sister-in-law. I looked at my watch; it was almost one in the morning, so I said goodnight and went to bed. As I lie in bed, I started to thinking about Sister Maria losing everything because of the love she had for my Brother. I said to myself, love is blind.

The next day Sister Melda came to Calapacuan, she stopped at Sister Maria house and said hello to her. Then she left and came to Mother house where we was. She said hello to everyone. I told her mama Ligaya wanted her to stop in and see her. She wanted to know why…I told her I didn't know why because mama Ligaya didn't explain to me the reason. She finally said o.k. Then walked into the kitchen where Mother was standing and gave her a bag containing the ingredients for her favorite dish…beef neck bones, Irish potatoes, bananas and cabbage. She asked Mother to cook it her favorite way. Everyone pitched in to help...Brother Etong cut the firewood for the stove and Sister Rose and I washed and cut up the vegetables. Mother cooked the food and put it on the table. We called Sister Maria over to share the meal. Everyone was sitting around talking when we finished eating; I was even talking to Sister Melda. I should have known Sister Melda was up to something when she arrived with the bag of food. She had cornered Mother and asked her to tell me to come back and live with her. Mother finally told me that she didn't want me to have to come home to Calapacuan at night by myself, so she wanted me to stay with Sister Melda. I told her I would go back to Olongapo City with Sister Melda. I notice Sister Maria seem to be in a good spirit as soon as she came into the house, but I didn't say anything to her about it. Finally she pulled out a letter and read it to us ...Brother Celino and my Father would be home in two weeks. I said to myself, that old man is coming home again. The letter stated that my Father and Brother Celino had formed a treasury hunting teamed with a family living in Olongapo City; Mother knew right off the family the letter was addressing. She remembered the wife in this family as being a schoolteacher and the husband as one of her patients she performed her healing massage on. Mother was real good with her hands and her famous coconut oil she used. She has massaged countless people backs, arms and legs and got them up moving again. This also jogged my memory of something that happened to me along about the same time we met this family. I remembered taking a shower and seeing the water running down my leg and turning red. I started to yell at the top of my voice...Mother and this schoolteacher came and explained that I was growing up and this was the sign of becoming a woman. Sister Rose said, "It happened to me too", and everyone started to laugh. Then the focus was on Sister Linda, who was younger than me and had her first period before me. She said very bashful, I was at the White Rock Beach when it happened. Sister Melda said, jokingly, I don't want to swim at the beach now, Linda blood is in the water". After Sister Maria's story, I left with Sister Melda going back to Olongapo to her house. When we arrived at Sister Melda's house I reminded her again to see mama Ligaya. She said o.k. I will leave with you when you go to work. We both went to our room; I lied down and fell fast asleep. I was awakened by the pounding on my door…Sister Melda said, "wake up, it's four o, clock are you going to work"? I said yes and jump out of the bed and started to get ready for work. We were out of the house by five and caught a tricycle to the jeepney stand and caught a jeepney. We stopped in front of the Swan Club…Sister Melda got out and the jeepney proceeded on as I waved goodbye. I arrived about two minutes late; the lady that works the day shift didn't hesitate to let me know I was late. I told her I was sorry and there was a lot of traffic. She said o.k. And she would see me tomorrow. At about five thirty that evening Sister Melda came by. She said, Ambing as if she was mad at me…Mama Ligaya gave me this letter from your boyfriend, he wrote the letter using Vicky Delarosa instead of Vicky Palaganas. I told her I was going to tell mama Ligaya about it, but every time I plan to tell her she would be sleep when I arrive to drop off the money from the exchange. I took the letter and looked at it…it was from Jerome, I thought he was still on the base and was coming by to see me tonight. I was real puzzled; he had told me he would be at the base for a month…maybe he left early…I couldn't wait to read the letter. Sister Melda didn't leave like she normally does; she stayed and made small talk…I guess she was waiting for me to read my letter. We continued our small talk for quite a while, and then mama Ligaya stopped at my booth. I told her how sorry I was for using her last name without asking…I told her I didn't want the other girls here to see my letters and I didn't want my Mother to know that I had an American boyfriend that was the reason I used her last name. She told me it was o.k. And I could be her Daughter just like Sister Melda. I could tell that Sister Melda didn't like mama Ligaya to be nice to me; she wanted her to be mad at me. So the three of us continued to make small talk and they would tease me about having a boyfriend. About twenty minutes later Jerome came up to my booth. When he saw mama Ligaya I could see that he was frightened a little. He thought mama Ligaya was my Mother. He stood by the door of my booth…Sister Melda asked him if he wanted to exchange his American dollars to Philippine pesos. He didn't say anything, he only pointed to me. Then I introduced him to them and they knew why he was there. He asked if mama Ligaya was my Mother…I explained to him we only call her mama and that she was the owner of the money exchange booth, Jet Club behind it and the Swan Club up the street.

I guess he was still nervous because he asked if we could go across the street to the Shangri La Restaurant to eat. I told him I had to work. Mama Ligaya said, go with him have fun and take Melda. Bring me some fried chicken when you return. Jerome asked if fried chicken was all she wanted. She said yes. At the restaurant, Sister Melda and I ordered noodles with vegetables and Jerome ordered shrimp fried rice and fried chicken to go for mama Ligaya. I asked Jerome why he had written me a letter and he was still here. He said the ship was scheduled to leave, but something went wrong with the engine, so they had to stay and fix it. He didn't want me to think he would leave without saying goodbye, so he wrote the letter.

When we returned to the Money exchange booth, mama Ligaya was still smiling at Jerome and me; she took the fried chicken and started to leave, then stop and turned around and asked Sister Melda was she coming with her. Sister Melda looked at me and left with mama Ligaya. Jerome kept me company for a while and finally left going back to his ship. When I arrived home that night after work Sister Melda and Sister Rose was still up talking and eating bread rolls. I sit down and joined them; Sister Rose said her boyfriend was coming to the Subic Naval Base tomorrow. He is stationed on board the U.S.S. Enterprise. She said he was a Navy corpsman in a Marine Detachment. I listened to them talk for a while then I went to bed.

The next day Sister Melda and I went to the market; when we came to a money exchange booth she took from her bag one hundred American dollars and exchanged it for pesos. The first thing she bought was one kilo of pork and lemons. We continued to walk through the market looking around; then all of a sudden a man bumped into Sister Melda as he was going the opposite direction. We kept walking until we came to the section where ladies dresses was displayed; Sister Melda picked out a dress she liked and open her bag to get money to pay for it...her money was gone. She searched her bag two or three times and still couldn't find her money. Then she remembered the guy bumping into her earlier. She was so mad she couldn't talk to me. We started to walk again and finally she settled down a little and asked me if I had any money. I said yes, but it's in my bag back at the house. She said o.k. You can pay for the tricycle when we get there.

When we got home I went in and got money to pay the tricycle driver and Sister Melda went into her room. When I came back I asked her how she wanted me to cook the pork. She said," cut the pork in small pieces add lemon juice, soy sauce, garlic and black pepper and cook it like adobo...please don't put vinegar in it". Sister Rose finally woke up at about eleven when she smelled the food cooking. I also cook rice, because we have rice with all of our meals.

When the food was done; I put it out on the table and told everyone the food was ready. Sister Melda came from her room and took a seat at the table. She looked around at Sister Rose as if she wanted to cry. Sister Rose asked her what was wrong. I told her that Sister Melda was robbed at the market. Sister Rose said how did it happen? I said, as we was walking through the market a man bumped into Sister Melda and took her money. Sister Melda, finally spoke and said, "one month allowance is gone". I said it take me about five months to make that much money. She said yes I know, I really wanted to buy that dress for you, but now I can't; I will have to write your brother-in-law and have him to transfer some more money to my account.

After lunch I got my pen and paper, because I knew she wanted me to write Brother Smitty and explain to him what had happened. When I finished the letter Sister Melda took it to the Naval Base and mailed it. The Naval Base has a more reliable mail system than Olongapo City. When Sister Melda left for the base, she said don't wait up for me tonight; I wander where she will stay tonight.

I asked Sister Rose if she would be coming back to the house tonight; she said, if Mike doesn't come tonight she would come by my money exchange booth before I get off work, but if he does, they would stay in the hotel. We lay around the house until about three that afternoon...Sister Rose decided that she wanted to get her hair fix, a manicure and pedicure. I said yes, I want a manicure and a pedicure too. So we got up, got dress and went to her favorite Beauty salon. I had my nails done in a nice light color; she had hers done in a real red color. They gave her a real nice haircut...she looked like a china doll to me.

We returned to the house and were surprised to see Sister Melda had returned. She asked where we had been. I said we went to the Beauty salon for a manicure and pedicure. She looked at Sister Rose and said," you got a haircut", and Sister Rose said yes, how do you like it? Sister Melda said, "You look like a Japanese and went back into her room". She called me to her room and gave me the Christmas gift she and her boyfriend had bought me. I knew she felt bad about slapping me, so I just took the present and said thank you. I returned to the room I shared with Sister Rose, she had changed into a pretty red dress made Chinese style...she looked so pretty, this is the first time I have ever seen Sister Rose dress up like this. She looked just like a China doll. She said it's time for me to go and walked out the door. She seem to be in a very happy mood, I guess it was because she was meeting her boyfriend. I was very happy for her.

When I started to get ready for work Sister Melda came in the room and said, "do you know that Sister Rose sleep around with jeepney drivers"? I said oh yes, I have known for quite a while Sister Rose had a boyfriend that a jeepney driver. I have to go to work, see you later.

That night I was so busy I didn't have time to sit down, because there was American Sailor everywhere...the U.S.S. Enterprise had come to town. I exchange over five hundred American dollars to Pesos. When I finally got off work and went home that night I realized how tired I was; my legs started to ache. I saw Sister Melda come out of the bathroom, so I asked her for aspirin. She gave me the aspirin bottle and asked if I was very busy tonight. I told her I was so busy I didn't remember sitting down at all. She went back to her room to bed. I guess Sister Rose and her boyfriend got a room at the hotel tonight because I didn't see her at all. I couldn't wait to get in the bed...I went right to sleep.

I woke up about 9 A.M. the next morning, I peeped into sister Melda's room...she had left going somewhere; I guess she went to the market. I washed up and prepared a small breakfast for myself. Just as I was finishing breakfast Sister Linda came by. She said Mother sent her to get some money from me to give to Sister Maria, because she had taken sick and didn't have any money for medicine. I gave her twenty pesos...she left right away going back to Calapacuan. I went back into my room, about five minutes later Sister Melda came in the front door carrying big bags of food. I thought to myself...She got the money from somewhere, but I didn't dare ask her where. To my surprise, she started cleaning and preparing the food for cooking. She normally has me to do it. Once she finished cleaning and chopping up the vegetables, she put the vegetables in the pot...I said to myself, this woman is going to cook. I also, watched her clean and prepared a fish for cooking. When the food was cooked I went to the table and ate so much I could hardly breathe.

I told Sister Melda Sister Linda had come by for money to buy medicine for Sister Maria. She said, "I don't see why Brother Celino want send her some money". I said he probably don't have any to send. He should be home next week. I arrived at work around 5 P.M., the lady that works the day shift was all excited, she said she had exchanged all of the pesos she had and wanted me to wait until she could turn in the American dollars to mama Ligaya and get more pesos. I said o.k. And she left. Twenty minutes later she came back with more pesos. I had Sailors and Marines waiting in line to exchange their dollars. I knew this was going to be another one of those nights where I wouldn't get a chance for a break. I turn around once and peeped into the club that was behind me...there was only standing room inside. I said to myself, everybody except me would be rich tomorrow...The Hostess, Shoe Shine boys, Little girls selling handkerchief, and all Businesses around the area, but I would only get my eighty pesos a month...there is one good thing about my eighty pesos a month, I get it even if there are no ships in port.

Up until midnight the streets were filled with American Military Men, I think I saw a few U.S. Air Force Airmen from Clark Air Base. I wonder why they are here because the base is about fifty miles away. They finally started going back to their ships. I closed up and called it a night. That week came and went very fast, and all of the big ships left and went back to sea. Everyone including the Police, Snatchers, Club Hostess, Hotel Owners, Movie Theaters and above all the Night Club Owners...They all Made money from the American ship visit. I almost forgot the Fireman, they was very busy too...the market and a Movie Theater was set on fire while the ships was in...my guess... someone was paid to set the fire. It seem as though everyone was trying to make money from the ship visit. I only saw Sister Rose a couple of time that week and Sister Melda she was running in and out of the house too. I guess the only person I remembered seeing for a while was the lady that wash our clothes.

Finally the slow days are back I can breathe again. Sister Melda, Sister Rose and I went to Calapacuan to Mother's house. Brother Celino and Father was back, Sister Maria had a surprise for us. Her Daughter had arrived from Pangasinan. We was introduced, I liked her right off, so I decided to stay at Brother Celino's house for a while and talk. I ask her how long she would be staying in Calapacuan; she said forever if she could find a job. I told her mama Ligaya had a job opening at the Money Exchange where I work. She asked me to take her with me to work the next day so she could apply for the job. I said o.k. And went to Mother's house next door. I said hello to Father and hug Mother. I looked around for Brother Etong, then I remembered… Brother Etong always leave the house when my Father is there, so I guess he is camping out in the mountain somewhere. Sometimes I think my Father abused Brother Etong, because he couldn't talk and tell what was going on. He is old enough to take care of himself, so when Father come home he leave home. I always made an effort to spend time with Brother Etong when I come home; Brother Etong, Sister Linda and I were very close, we always spent time together. Mother and my Sisters went in the kitchen and my Father was left in the living room playing with Little Gina, she was sitting on his lap. I didn't like her sitting there so I went over to where they were sitting and started playing with Gina. Finally I got her from his lap and started playing with her on the floor. She had a homemade toy made from a sardine can with bamboo wheels. This brought back memories to me…I remembered playing with a toy like this when I was a little girl. I yell out to Mother, who made the toy Gina is playing with? She said," Your brother Etong made it". I can still remember the toy I played with, it was made from a sardine can with wheels made of coke bottle top.

Sister Rose and I had the day off from work, so we could spend time with the family today. Just before supper Brother Etong came in the door with an arm full of firewood. This was quite a surprise for me because I had figured he wouldn't be coming home because

Father was there. When he put down the wood and turned around, he seem very flush in the face, so I asked if he was all right and what he had for lunch? He told me he had boil bananas for lunch. I said o.k. It's almost dinnertime. He smiled and asked whether the pigs had been fed. I told him Sister Linda and I had fed the pigs. We all found a place on the floor to eat dinner because there was not enough room at the table. Just as we were getting started Brother Celino came into the house and asked what we was having for dinner. Mother told him, chop suey, noodles and fried fish. He brought a bowl as if he knew what we were having. Mother took his bowl and filled it up and gave him some fried fish.

After dinner the family gathered around in the living room to hear someone tell about an experience he or she had. Tonight it was Sister Rose turn. She started her story saying, when I first started to work as a Bar Hostess; I had a problem communicating because I couldn't speak English. So I tried to use sign language like brother Etong, to communicate. Once I was sitting at the table with an American Sailor and I wanted to go to the bathroom…I got the attention of my companion and pointed at myself, the bathroom and my chair; trying to let him know I was going to the bathroom and would come back to my seat. He looked at me a little puzzled and finally said o.k. That worked all right, so I decided to use sign language from then on…If I wanted my companion to buy me a drink, I would pick up a glass…point at it…point at the bar and point to myself. The Sailor would immediately give me some money for the drink. I would go to the bar and get my drink and return with his change. I would hand him his change; he would point at the money in my hand and then to me…when he wanted me to keep the change. I thought to myself this is working out very well. One night I was very hungry, so I got my companion attention and started to rub my stomach and point at the door. I kept rubbing my stomach and pointing at the door, but he didn't understand what I was trying to say. I thought to myself…this is a stupid Sailor. Finally I got up and pull him to the door and led him next door to the Restaurant. When we got inside the Restaurant the Sailor said, oh, I thought your stomach was hurting. We sit down and ordered food; when we finished he even asked for a bag for the left-over food. I asked Sister Rose could she speak English now. She said, I can speak a few words of English, but it's hard for me to open my mouth and say it. Sister Melda said, jokingly, so you are a mute waitress. Everyone start to laugh even Sister Rose.

My Father had being sitting around all evening not even saying a word he was only listening to what everybody else was saying. Finally out of the blue he said, "Ambing, why don't you get a job in the club like your sister Rose and buy me a Rolex watch? Everybody became very quiet and started looking at each other. Mother broke the silence…She said to him, you are not going to tell Ambing or Linda to do anything…you haven't done anything for them since they was born; now that they have grown up you want to tell them where they should work…what kind of Father are you anyway? I have had to swallow my pride and watch two of my Daughter work in the clubs and that's because I married a no good husband like you. Mother was very mad at my Father…this is the first time I had ever seen her real mad. Brother Celino came back to Mother's house…Mother jumped on him; she told him he was just like his Father, a useless husband, you come home when you are ready; you don't seem to care whether we are living or dead. You and your Father are worthless…get out of my face before I do or say something I will regret. Father and Brother Celino left and went to Brother Celino's house. Mother was so mad she started talking to herself.

When we were all settled in to go to sleep that night; I thought to myself, what would happen if I told Mother about the day Father tried to rape me and Brother Celino came home just in time to spoil his attempt…I think she would probably try and kill him and end up in jail…I thought, what would happen to us? That is the reason why I didn't tell anyone what had happened. Before we fell asleep Sister Maria came over and asked for Father suit case and the rest of his clothes; Mother packed his suitcase and told Sister Maria to tell him go and don't come back. We all went to sleep without saying another word.

The next morning I work up smelling fried dried fish and coffee. Mother got up early and cooked breakfast. I got up and got cleaned up and went next door to Brother Celino's house to tell his stepdaughter, Celia we would leave at 10 A.M. for Olongapo City to see about the job at the money exchange. My Father had already left going somewhere.

I said to myself, good I hope he does not come back. Brother Celino asked me what had happened last night to make Mother so mad; I told him what Father had said. Brother Celino didn't say a word he just looked at me puzzled. I left and went back to Mother's house. When I walked in the door Sister Melda was leaving, and Mother, Sister Linda, Sister Rose and brother Etong was going to the Movie. I turned around and left with her and Gina. We stopped on our way at Brother Celino house to get Celia. As we walked away in the distance I could hear Mother tell sister Maria and Brother Celino to keep an eye on her house and if she was late getting back they was to feed the pigs. When we got to Olongapo City we split up, Sister Melda and Gina went to her house and Celia and I went to see mama Ligaya. As we rode down the streets Celia ask what was in all of the buildings that lined the street. I told her they were Nightclubs, the place where all the American Sailors and Marines spend their leisure time. Wait until you see all the lights light up tonight, you will understand. We arrived at the Swan Club and went around back to mama Ligaya home. I knocked at the door, mama Ligaya came to the door and invited us in. I introduced Celia to mama Ligaya and told her Celia was looking for a Cashier job. She told Celia she had a job in the money exchange booth at the Top Hat Club, she could have if she could start work the next day. Celia said she could start the next day and almost jumped for joy. Mama Ligaya told me to show Celia how to get to the money exchange booth she will be working at; she gave me money for the jeepney, so Celia and I left and caught a jeepney to the Top Hat club. I explained to her that the Money Exchange booth was attached to the club the same as the one I work in at the Jet Club. When we arrived at the Top Hat Club, I showed her where she could catch a jeepney to go home. I gave her a fake American dollar bill and explained to her about people trying to pass fake money at the money exchange. I told her how important it was for her to take her time and look at the money before exchanging it. When I was satisfied she could find her way back and forth to work, I took her to a restaurant and bought her lunch. She thanked me for lunch. After showing her around and having lunch, it was time for us to part, so I gave her a few more words of wisdom…when she get to her job tomorrow she should make a list of the dollar exchange rate; one thru twenty dollar that way when she get real busy she can look at her list instead of trying to calculate the number of pesos to the dollar amount. I also, told her to try and arrive a few minutes early so she will have time to settle down from the jeepney ride, and above all, take her time counting the money. She caught a jeepney for Calapacuan and I went to sister Melda's house. When I arrived I looked in on Sister Melda and little Gina, little Gina was asleep. Sister Melda said, "Please don't make noise and wake her". I step back and sit down at the kitchen table. I told Sister Melda about Celia getting a job right away, she said, that good as if she didn't really care. I decided to take a nap before I go to work. Just as I nodded off I heard someone coming in the front door, it was Mother, brother Etong, Sister Linda and Sister Rose coming from the movie. I got up and went in to greet them…everyone was real happy about seeing the movie…Brother Etong tried to explain to me what happen in the movie. They had watched a Chinese Movie with a lot of martial art in it. Mother seem to have enjoyed herself… she was smiling a lot. Sister Melda said, "Spend the night here don't go back to Calapacuan, I will go to the market and buy more food; come with me Brother Etong and they left. Everyone decided to spend the night. I told Mother to take my bed because I was going to work and wouldn't be back before midnight and when I do get back I would sleep on the floor. I went to my room and started to get ready for work; Mother came in and ask if I was going to eat before I went to work. I said that I would get a barbecue hot dog at the stand where I work. When I started for the door Sister Melda and Brother Etong came in with their arms full of food she had purchased at the market. I said see you later I have to go to work…don't forget to leave me some of that food. At work that night everything was very slow, because all of the big ships had gone to sea. Just before closing time I heard screaming and shouting in the club behind me; the door to my booth leads right into the club, so I got up and went into the club after closing the door to my booth. The Club Manager and the Security Guard was trying to separate two girls that was fighting. I knew both girl…one was the counter girl and the other one was a Hostess. I found out later the girls were fighting over the Security Guard. The Hostess accused the Counter girl of trying to take her boyfriend, the Security Guard, but the Counter girl was only asking the Security

Guard to keep an eye on the Bar, because a drunken Sailor was giving her a hard time because she was rejecting him.

The Club Manager told the Security Guard to keep his business and girl friends at home not here in the club. It was very late so the Manager closed the Club and I closed the Money Exchange booth and everyone went home. On my way home, I couldn't keep from thanking about the Hostess in the club having a Sailor boyfriend and when his ship leaves they would be with their Filipino Boyfriend. I said to myself what a life. Sister Rose has two boyfriends just like the other Bar Hostess. I arrive home about one in the morning. Mother had waited up for me and warmed up the food. I carefully walked around everyone sleeping on the floor and made my way to the kitchen table to eat. As soon as I sat down Sister Rose came home, so we ate together.

I didn't eat very much because I was going to bed right away. We talked for a while then we went to bed. I let Mother Have my bed and I found me a spot on the floor. The next day Mother was up early again cooking breakfast; I was awakened again by the aroma of the coffee she had brewed. Finally everyone was getting up to wash up for breakfast. We all gathered around on the floor for breakfast, because the table was too small. We had a little of everything we liked...Fried garlic rice, beefsteak, fried eggs, coffee and oval tine; it was a great breakfast.

Sister Melda broke the silence and asked Mother if she thought Celia would like Calapacuan, Mother said she hope she would like it, because Maria, her mother, need someone to help her...Brother Celino always leave her. After breakfast Mother and Brother Etong left going back to Calapacuan; Sister Melda gave Mother a sack of rice and some money. I called them a tricycle, so they wouldn't have to walk too far to catch a jeepney. Sister Linda and Sister Rose went into the bedroom Sister Rose and I share. Sister Melda took little Gina into her room. The last few months Sister Melda has really gotten attach to Gina. Sister Rose started to read the letter she had received from her American boyfriend, Mike; she said his ship would be back to Subic Bay Naval Base either May or June. The letter contained a money order for thirty dollars; I looked at her and said let's go shopping. She looked at me and smiled and got up from the bed and left the house going somewhere. Sister Melda came into the room and asked where Sister Rose was going. I said, I didn't know, but she has received a letter from Mike with a money order in it. Sister Melda said, "She is going to spend it on her Filipino boyfriend". Sister Linda and I looked at each other without saying a word. Sister Melda looked at little Gina and said, "I should adopt her because she is here all of the time". Again Sister Linda and I looked at each other without saying anything. Later we had lunch; I decided to take a nap right after lunch so I wouldn't get sleepy at work.

I woke up around three and showered and dressed for work. I told Sister Melda I was going in early to check on Celia to see how she was doing on her first day at work. I caught a jeepney and went straight to the Top Hat Money Exchange booth that was located right outside of the main gate of Subic Naval Base. When I got out of the jeepney and started walking toward the booth she saw me and started smiling. I asked how her first day at work was going. She smiled and said, "I love it". I said it good you had a chance to start working here while business is slow. She looked surprised and said, "what do you mean business is slow; I thought it was very busy today. I said wait until the big American Aircraft Carrier come into port, that's when you will really get busy.

We talked for a while; then I left going to my job. When I arrived I saw a man working in the booth, I went into the booth and he said he was working in his wife place because she was sick. So we counted the Money and I took over. He said he worked as a bartender at night...he and his wife had two children; he kept them doing the day and his wife kept them at night after work. I sit down and looked around; I could tell that it was going to be a very slow night. I opened the door and looked back into the club; the Hostess was lying around and trying to keep awake. They played the jukebox and dancing together to pass the time. I closed the door and settled back into my seat...closed my eyes and the next thing I heard was a Sailor saying wake up sleeping beauty; I need pesos. I got to my feet and exchange his twenty. He left my booth and went to the front door of the Club and went inside. Five or six Hostess met him at the door. He looked over and saw the door to my money exchange booth and told the Hostess he wanted to talk to Sleeping Beauty, Me in the booth.

He got a chair and sit down beside my door; he asked me my name and if I would like a drink I said yes, and my name is Vicky. He gave me money to buy the drink. I came out of my booth and went into the Club to the bar and bought a coke. I returned with his change and he told me to keep it and buy another drink later. He talked and listened to the Music from the jukebox and drunk about four beers. He looked at his watch and said, "Its eleven o, clock, what time do you get off work". I said twelve forty five. He said, "I will see you later sleeping beauty, Vicky". He looked at me again and smiled then left. Shortly after he left the girl that works behind the Counter came over and gave me six pesos; I said what is this money for? She said it the money you make when someone buy you a drink and you sit and talk. One of the Hostess said, "You should work in the bar because you make more money, you made more money than I did tonight". The Club Manager said don't talk to her that way, she does not want to be a Hostess. They stopped talking, but I could tell they were jealous of me, because the Sailor wanted to talk to me and instead of them. Now I know how the Hostess make their money…they make a commission on each drink they get, the drink the Sailor buy for himself and when the Hostess leave the Club with a Sailor or Marine.

While sitting in my booth I thought to myself…I made six pesos and the change from the twenty he gave me to buy a coke…I will use it to buy hot bread rolls and sweet rolls to take home. When I went home I stopped by the Bakery and bought the rolls. Sister Melda was still awake when I arrived. I told her I had bought rolls and what had happen at my job. She asked if the bread rolls were still hot, I said yes. She acted as though she didn't hear what I had said about what happened to me at the money exchange. She just sat at the table and ate the rolls. I went to bed.

I was doing practically the same thing every day, going to and from work every day. Before I realize what was going on a month had passed…Celia had changed from the day shift at work to the night shift, she really did like her job. Sister Melda and her boyfriend had came by Celia money exchange booth…Sister Melda introduced her friend to Celia. One night sister Melda came home acting very mad, she said Celia was trying to take her boyfriend. I didn't know she had another boyfriend. So she started taking out her anger on Sister

Rose and me. She said the reason Sister Rose didn't come home every night; she was living in an apartment with her Filipino boyfriend. She accused me of knowing that Sister Rose was living with her Filipino boyfriend. I had an idea Sister Rose was seeing a Filipino guy, but I didn't know she was staying with him. I just assumed that when she didn't come home after work she was going to Calapacuan to Mother's house.

Sister Melda started staying away from her house more frequently. I guess she is staying with her boyfriend when she does not come home at night. I really don't understand Sister Melda, she accuse sister Rose of running around with the jeepney drivers while she is married, but Sister Rose and her husband has separated a long time ago...She is doing the same thing only she and her husband is not separated. Sister Melda spend a lot of time away from home, so I don't get to see her very often...When I get home after work sometime I ask Sister Linda about her...she said Sister Melda ask her to read Brother Smitty's letters to her and then she would leave again.

The end of the month...it's my payday...I went to the market and bought food as always to take to Mother in Calapacuan. I never forget my Mother; she works very hard to support her family. There is one thing good I can say about Sister Melda...she has always given Mother money and bought food for her. When I left the market I went straight to Calapacuan to take the food. Sister Melda, Sister Linda and little Gina were there. I thought what a big surprise. We was sitting around talking about nothing in particular when Sister Maria came over and brought her nephew that was visiting from Pangasinan. She introduced him to everyone. Sister Melda told him she and I would show him Olongapo City. He said he would like that very much, so when we left going back that afternoon to Olongapo City, He packed a bag and we took him with us. Sister Melda told him he could stay in the living room and put his clothes in one of the bedroom. When I went to work Sister Melda and him would go places. This went on for a few days before Sister Rose came home. We introduced him to her; right away she liked him, so she started coming home after work. She would show him around the next day.

One day Sister Melda and I was in her room reading one of Brother Smitty letters...Sister Rose and Maria's Nephew knocked on the bedroom door and told us they was going to the market; it was about nine that morning when they left...they returned at about three that afternoon and said they had went to the Church and the Beach. Sister Melda whispered, "I bet Sister Rose took him to the hotel". I really didn't like hearing her say that about Sister Rose; she think everyone is doing the same thing she doing. I guess she is trying to justify what she is doing. I went and took a shower and got dress for work. He said he was leaving this afternoon and returning to Pangasinan, thanks for showing him around. I said goodbye and have a nice trip back. The month of May came quickly; the U.S.S. Enterprise came back to Subic Bay Naval Base just outside of Olongapo City. Mike, Sister Rose American boyfriend was stationed on the Enterprise. Sister Rose was very happy about Mike being in town; she brought him to Sister Melda's house and introduced him to us. We swapped greetings and they left going back down town. Sister Melda looked at me and said, "He is a real nice guy". She turned around and went into her room and changed clothes. She came out and said, see you tonight. I mumbled o.k. She closed the door and left. I went to my room to lie on the bed for a while...I said to myself; it's going to be real busy tonight. A few minutes later I had drifted off to sleep. I was woken by the loud noise coming from the door.

I got up and opened the door...it was Sister Rose...Sister Melda never gave her a key. I asked was anything wrong, she said, there is nothing wrong, but Mike had asked her to marry him. I said that was good...Mike is a real nice guy. She asked where Sister Melda was. I told her I didn't know. It was time for me to get ready for work, so I got clean up and dressed for work. I picked up my bag and started for the door...Sister Rose mind seem to be everywhere except in this house, I said see you tonight and don't forget to lock the door on your way out. She mumbled, "I guess I will get clean up and meet Mike later tonight". Two days later, it was raining real hard...it was only one in the afternoon but it was dark like it was night. Sister Melda and I were home together for a change, when someone knocked on the door. I opened the door and there stood Mike soaking wet. He was looking for Sister Rose, He said they were supposed to meet today but she never showed up.

We had not seen her in two days. We got him inside…Sister Melda went and found a shirt and a pair of pants that belong to her husband. She gave it to him so he could change out of the wet clothing he had on. The shirt fitted him but the pant was too small, so he made do with only the shirt. We decided to accompany him to some of the places she might be…We checked the Theaters…had the management to put a message on the movie screen, telling her to come home right away. We went to the Top Hat club and the Beaches, but we came up empty handed. We told Mike we was very sorry about what had happened, but he need to return to his ship and we would tell Sister Rose when we see her to contact him. I gave him Mother Address in Calapacuan, so he could write her if he didn't get a chance to see her before his ship sailed. He said take this twenty five dollars and give it to her…please tell her my ship will be leaving in three days and I will write her. Sister Melda gave him her umbrella and we said goodbye to him. I looked at the money in my hand…I said to myself this is almost one month pay for me…what is wrong with Sister Rose? Is she afraid to have someone that really cares about her? Even Sister Melda is upset about the way she is treating Mike.

I went to work that night and the rain kept coming down; the club Manager had to almost board my booth up completely just to keep the rain out. With all the rain business was very slow, so I had a lot of time in my booth to just sit and daydream. I would think of the time I sit by the window when we lived at White Rock Beach; I would look out at the Ocean and wish I could go where the Ocean goes on the other side of the Mountain. Then someone would walk up to my booth to change dollars to pesos and snap me right out of my change of thought. It kept raining real hard through the night and finally stopped about mid morning the next day. Sister Rose came home the next day; she said she saw the messages for her to come home on the movie screen; her and her Filipino boyfriend came outside and when she saw Mike with us she got scared and they went back into the movie. Sister Melda asked her why she didn't meet Mike like she agreed to do. Sister Rose told her she forgot about meeting him. I said to myself, how could a woman being engaged to marry a man forget to meet him for a date? Only sister Rose could do something like that. Sister Melda really surprised me when she told Sister Rose that she should wait until Mike ship leave before seeing her Filipino boyfriend...people get kill doing things like she was doing.

Then I realized that they both was doing the same thing; only Sister Melda was running around with other American Sailors, so I just shut my mouth and listened to them go at each other. Finally Sister Rose said, "I do what I want to with my life", and then Sister Melda took it a step further and said, "If you don't want to listen to what I am saying then you are free to leave my house". Sister Melda went into her bedroom and closed the door and Sister Rose left saying she was going to Mother house in Calapacuan.

All I could think to say was what's going on with my Sisters; I loved them both and there was no side to be taken because both of them was doing the same thing...I could only sit and listen to them fight. Both of my sisters are older than me anyway and if I had said something I am sure they would not have listen to me.

Sister Melda came out of her room all dressed up and said, "I will see you later", and left the house. I guess she was still mad at Sister Rose because she left without telling me where she was going...Every time she left the house she usually tell me where she was going. This episode changed everything; she was away from the house sometime all day and night...then for a day or two I don't see her at all.

One day I went past the Top Hat Money exchange booth and I notice another lady was working there instead of Celia. The next day I went to Calapacuan to visit Mother. I had to pass Brother Celino house before I got to Mother house; when I was close enough to see who was sitting on the porch of Brother Celino's house, I was very surprised to see Celia there. I stopped and asked her was she still working days? She said, "If I worked days I wouldn't be here now I would be at work...I am home because your Sister Melda got me fired. I tried to talk to mama Ligaya, but she wouldn't listen to reason. My next question was why? What happened? She said Melda saw me talking to her boyfriend...I only talked to him because he stopped... she had introduced him to me a few days earlier, so I talked to him when he stop by...Your sister is a very jealous woman...when her boyfriend come off the base he pass right by my booth, so he stop and say hello; I guess she saw him talking to me...she is very dangerous to be around.

I asked what her plans were now; she said she had no plan. I asked Sister Maria where was Brother Celino, she said he was with some people from Olongapo doing some Treasury Hunting. I told Celia, if she still want a job, she should check the Gifts Shops right in the area where she was working in the money exchange booth, because I saw a couple of Help Wanted signs in their windows…try to go today if possible.

Then I went next door to Mother House. I yelled through the window to Mother; she looked around very surprised to see me. She was cooking…I went inside…Sister Rose and her daughter little Gina was there asleep. I didn't see Sister Linda and brother Etong, so I asked Mother where they were hiding. She said, "They were in the back feeding the pigs", so I went in the back where they was and started talking about the pigs. Brother Etong went to get firewood for the kitchen and Sister Linda and I went inside the house. We sat down at the table and had coffee.

Sister Rose finally woke up and went in the next room and cleaned up. She came back out and sat at the table with Sister Linda and me. Mother finished cooking and put the food on the table…we start eating…Sister Rose said, "One night when it was raining real hard she decided not to come home and stayed at the Swan Club in the section where the House boys slept. The next morning Sister Melda came in the Swan Club as she was coming out of the door leading to the House Boys room; Sister Melda became very angry and started yelling at me with everybody looking on. I didn't say anything to her, I left".

I said, Sister Melda, has not said anything to me about you; it might be because she is never home very much. Sister Rose tried to tell me about Sister Melda getting Celia fired. I told her I knew all about it, because Celia had told me. Sister Rose left the table and came back with a small box; it contained a watch she said Mike had sent her. She also, showed me some legal papers, application for Fiancé Visa, she had to fill out and send back to Mike. I told her she should take the papers to the lady working at the Travel Agency in the Swan Club and get her to type them for her. I also, told her to tell the lady I sent her because the lady and I went to school together and she would do it for me. If you are not in a hurry to leave this afternoon I will go with you to the Travel Agency and you can get it done right away. She agreed to wait for me. Mother said, "Rosie don't mess this up; you have an opportunity to make a better life for you and your daughter Gina...Look at your Sister Melda...she never has to work... she never hungry...her husband always send her money to spend". She said, "I am not asking you to be jealous like her...always wanting to be the one on top...don't want to see anyone in her family get ahead...I just want you to have a nice life and be happy". She said," please don't misunderstand me, I love all of my children the same". Mother looked as if she was going to cry, so I changed the subject and asked Brother Etong, how many babies did his pig have? He put up eight fingers. I looked at Mother and said that's a lot of pigs...they will bring a lot of money when they get older.

I looked at my watch and told Mother I had to go because I had a few errands I had to run before I go to work. Sister Rose looked at me and picked up her bag...we said goodbye and left. When we passed Brother Celino house Celia yelled out, wait for me; I am going to Olongapo to check on the job at the gift shop. So we left together for Olongapo. We stopped at the Swan Club Travel Agency, Sister Rose and I got down from the jeepney and waved goodbye to Celia. We entered the Travel Agency and I introduced Sister Rose to the Lady. The lady looked at me with a puzzled look on her face. Finally she asked have we met before. I said we were classmate in our second year of high school. She said, "Oh yes", you was the girl that was very skinny...when you came to P.E. class we would say to you, what are you exercising...your bones and everyone would laugh. I said yes I am the one, I explained to her what I wanted her to do for Sister Rose. She assured me it wouldn't be a problem...she would take care of it right away. I told Sister Rose I had to go, so I turned around and started for the door. I looked up and saw Sister Melda getting out of a jeepney. She asked where I was going. I said I was going home and she gave me some money and said stop by the market and get food to take home. She told me what she wanted me to buy; then I caught a jeepney for the market. Sister Melda was going to see mama Ligaya; I wonder what she up to now. Mama Ligaya owns the Swan Club, the Travel Agency/Money Exchange Booth that in one side of the Club, the Jet Club, the Top Hat Club and the White Rock Beach

Complex. Her Home was behind the Swan Club...She also own two additional Money Exchange Booth...one in the Top Hat Club and one in the Jet Club. The White Rock Beach Complex consists of: A Hotel, Bowling Alley, an Olympic size fresh water Pool and several Beach Cottages. Mama Ligaya was a very rich woman. She has two sons and her adopted daughter Sister Melda. Sister Melda was married to a Filipino in Pangasinan...she ran away and left him and came to Olongapo City and met mama Ligaya. Mama Ligaya liked Sister Melda right away, so she more or less adopted her, but not legally. Mama Ligaya usually let her have her way with anything that involved her business. That's how she was able to get Celia fired from her job. She acted the part of a spoiled child. She was very beautiful and she knew it and wouldn't let you forget it. The Jeepney driver said, "Market" and brought me back to reality. I got out of the Jeepney and went into the market area to do my shopping. When I finished my shopping I caught a jeepney and went home. I went inside the house expecting to see Sister Melda, but she was nowhere in sight, so I put up the food and started cooking lunch. I had lunch and started to clean the house.

After I finished cleaning the house and lounging around for a while, it was once again time to go to work. I thought Sister Melda would be home before I left, but she was nowhere in sight. I caught a jeepney and went to work. I arrived and relieved the lady that works the day shift...I sit down and tried to get comfortable...a few Sailors came by to change their dollars to pesos. Then I looked up and saw Sister Rose coming toward my booth. I saw a large letter in her hand. She said, "The papers have being typed and ready to be mailed". I told her to take it to the post office in Olongapo City and mail it. She said no, she wanted me to get one of the American Sailors to mail it on the base. I explained to her that I do know Sailors that come by my booth, but sometime they get drunk before they return to the base. She insisted that I get someone to mail it on the base. Finally a Sailor came by that I knew and I asked him to mail the letter on the base...I gave him jeepney fare and money for the stamp. He asked about the missing return address for the letter...Sister Rose assured him it was all right to mail it that way. We thanked him as he left with the letter.

Sister Rose left my booth and went into the club. As soon as she left I saw Celia coming toward my booth looking very cheerful. She stood by my booth telling me she had gotten the job at the Gift shop and she was going to start training the next day. She said she wanted to tell me earlier about her good news, but she didn't want to come to Sister Melda's house. She said the gift shop had everything in it and she was very anxious to get started working there...she said, "It's getting late, I have to go home now" and she left. I glanced over my shoulder and I saw Sister Rose talking to one of the Houseboys that work in the Club. The Houseboys clean up the club and help the Hostess when a lot of Customers are in the Club. I said to myself...I wonder what that's all about. Then I turned around and saw Sister Melda approaching my booth with a strange man...I thought to myself; I am very popular today. She introduced me to her boyfriend and Sister Rose came over...she introduced her, saying..."this is another one of my sisters as if she was mad". Her boyfriend asked her how many sisters she has...she said, "There are four of us...the youngest is at home. He said, "Four sister, ha...well you all are very beautiful...he whispered to me, you are very cute. I smiled as they left. Sister Rose went back in the corner of the club where the Houseboy was standing and started talking again. I sat down again on my stool...I said to myself... this is going to be a very long night. Finally it was time to close up and go home...I rushed home and went to bed.

The next day I got up and peeped into Sister Melda's room...she was still asleep; I started back to my room when I heard a knock at the door. It was Sister Rose she had come to pick up some of her clothing. She went straight to the room we shared and started gathering her clothes. She gathered as much as she could carry and left. Sister Melda came out of her room and asked if the person she heard talking to me was Sister Rose. I said she came to get her clothes. Sister Melda asked if she took all of her clothes. I said no, and she will be back to get the rest of her clothes. Then Sister Melda wanted to know what I was cooking for breakfast, I said whatever you want. She said, "Go to the store and buy bread rolls and eggs, and make some coffee". I went across the street to the store and purchased the rolls and eggs. When I returned Sister Melda had finished her shower and was all dressed up. After I prepared our breakfast we sat down at the table and enjoyed it. We finished breakfast and lounged around for a few minutes. Sister Melda got up and left without telling me where she was going. I decided not to stay there by myself, so I cleaned the kitchen and got ready and left for Calapacuan to visit Mother. When I arrived I found out that Sister Rose was not bringing her clothes to Calapacuan, she was taking them somewhere else. I gave Mother half of my paycheck, so she decided to go to the market and buy food for the pig. She and brother Etong left for the market they took two small pigs with them to sale. Mother asked me to stay with Sister Linda and little Gina until she return. Sister Linda was fourteen years old. I asked her if she wanted me to try and get her a job at the Money Exchange booth I was working at. She acted as if she was not interested so I left her alone. We decided to go outside and get some guava from the guava tree; Sister Maria saw us at the tree and came out to help us get the fruit.

Just as we was finishing gathering the guava; I saw Mother and brother Etong coming across the field carrying the food she had bought for the house and the pig. Brother Etong was all smiles caring a sack of pig food on his head...He was a very strong young man. Mother and Sister Linda started cooking lunch. Sister Rose arrived just as we were sitting down to eat lunch. She was looking as if something was wrong...Mother told her to sit down and have some lunch...she sat beside Gina and gave her a little hug. Mother asked her if something was wrong. She said she was pregnant. We all was very surprised...Mother seem a little angry when she asked who was the father of the baby. Sister Rose said the Baby father was Mike.

Mother said she had a letter for Sister Rose from Mike and asked her was she sure the baby father was Mike; because she knew Sister Rose had being running around with other guys. Sister Rose assured her she had used protection when she was with other men. I didn't say a word I just sat and listened to Mother and Sister Rose talk about Sister's Rose affairs. When they finally stopped talking; Sister Rose started writing a letter to Mike...then she changed her mind and decided to finish the letter in Olongapo City, so she left before taking the time to read the letter she received from Mike. I lounged around playing with Gina and went to sleep...Mother woke me sometime later and asked if I was going to work that night. I said, yes and got up and left for Olongapo City. When I arrived at Sister Melda house she was still away, so I changed clothes again and left for work. I arrived at work on time...the lady I relieve was very happy.

I moved the chair around and got comfortable for the night. Then along came Celia with news about her first day of training on her new job. She said she liked working in the Gift shop better than the Money Exchange booth plus she got paid twenty pesos a month more. She also said she would have an opportunity to collect a commission, because the shop had a small bar in the back. When the customers come in they could buy beer or soda from the bar while looking around in the shop. Finally she had to leave going home because it was getting dark, I wished her luck with her new job...I leaned back in my chair trying to relax before all the customers start showing up...a jeepney pulled up and stopped in front of my booth; Sister Melda got out and started for the door of the Jet Club in a hurry; she bumped into my friend as she entered the door and didn't bother to excuse herself. My friend the hostess said something to Sister Melda and they started yelling at each other. The club Manager came over and pulled the Hostess away from where Sister Melda was in an effort to stop the fight. Sister Melda shouted at the girl saying she would not be working in the Jet Club anymore because she was going to get her fired. Sister Melda came over to the door of my booth and told me my friend would not be working at the Jet Club any longer. I calmly asked her what had happened...she said when she came into the club door she and my friend bumped into each other and my friend wouldn't say she was sorry. I guess she saw Celia at my booth, because she asked me what was Celia doing here as she walked away. I said Celia was telling me about her new job. She said, "Good for her" and I almost fell out of my chair because she was the one that got Celia fired in the first place. I told my friend I was sorry about what had happened to her and she said, "don't be sorry, your sister is the one who should be sorry".

I guessed the Club Manager went to see mama Ligaya earlier that night because when I closed up and took the money to mama Ligaya's place she asked me what had happened. I said Sister Melda had rushed into the door of the Club and bumped into my friend as she was coming out the door and they started yelling at each other. Mama Ligaya said the Manager of the Club had been to see her, but Sister Melda hasn't arrived yet. She said she instructed the Club Manager to tell the Hostess if she see Sister Melda come into the club to stay clear of her if she wanted to keep her job…because your sister Melda is going to ask me to fire the Hostess. I said Mama they both was wrong…she looked at me as though she was upset with me and said, "are you saying Melda is wrong"? I could sense that she was upset so I said good night and left. When I arrived home Sister Melda was there fumbling around in all of the drawers and boxes… she asked me if I knew where the towel set I got her for Christmas was; she sounded as if she was mad, so I said no, but I would help her look for the towels. We continued to look until about two in the morning…I told her I was sleepy and was going to bed…she stopped looking and went into her bedroom and closed the door.

The next day when I woke up she was already up and making coffee…I brushed my teeth and got cleaned up. When I came back to the kitchen she told me she had being invited to a beach party. I said so that was why you were looking for the towels last night. She said, "The towels match her swim suit". She reached down and grabbed her beach bag and left. I am alone again here at the house…the first thing I started thinking about was Sister Rose…I hadn't seen her in over a month. Here it is the second week of June nineteen hundred sixty eight and she is out there pregnant somewhere and we don't have the any idea as to where she is living.

The following week I decided to visit Mother in Calapacuan, when I arrived in Calapacuan and started walking across the rice field to Mother's house it started raining very hard. Sister Rose was behind me and just as I opened my umbrella she stepped underneath it with me; it scared me because I didn't know she was behind me, so I jumped bumping her and we both fell down in the mud. We got up and I gave the umbrella to Sister Rose and started wiping the mud off her. Sister Maria saw us coming and started out her door with an umbrella; I yelled and told her not to worry about the umbrella because I was going to try and get cleaned off in the rain. As soon as we walked into Mother's house she said, "I told you not to coming in the rain"; I said it was not raining in Olongapo when we left. She said, "go in and change your clothes…she gave Sister Rose her house coat so she could get warm right away. Mother was still a little upset… she said she hope the baby was all right. She went in the kitchen and started making chicken and rice soup for lunch. We sat around talking and waiting for the soup. I really like Mother's chicken and rice soup…I couldn't wait until it was ready. Finally it was ready… we got our bowl and filled them with the soup…I ate so much until my little stomach seem as it was going to burst. Everyone said they had eaten too much…even little Gina said she ate too much. The rain had finally quit and the sun came out and I put our wet clothes out to dry. I came back and lie down on the floor with little Gina and went to sleep. When I woke up I looked around for Sister Rose, but she was nowhere in sight so I asked Mother where were Sister Rose. She said Sister Rose was next door visiting with Sister Maria. I got ready and left for Olongapo. When I came to Sister Maria's house; I stopped and asked Sister Rose if she was going with me back to Olongapo. She said she was going to spend the night here in Calacapuan, so I left.

When I arrived at Sister Melda's house in Olongapo she was taking a shower. I asked her how she liked the beach party; she said the rain ruin the party. I said it had also rained in Calapacuan. I told her about the accident Sister Rose and I had had in the rain, but she didn't say a word…she only looked at me and went into her room. I went to my room and got dressed and went to work. The next day before Sister Melda left on her daily trip to somewhere…she never tell me where she go everyday…Mother came with bad news…Sister Rose had a miscarriage. I felt real bad about the miscarriage… somehow I felt that I was partially the blame because if I hadn't jumped and bump into her when she scared me; we wouldn't have fell down in the mud. Mother took a seat at the dining table and I came over and joined her. She said she was going to the market to buy food and sanitary napkins for Sister Rose because she was bleeding heavy. I asked if Sister Rose was all right except for the bleeding. Mother said she would be all right, but she would have to take it easy for a few days. Mother got up from the table to leave for the market…I told her I was going with her to the market; Sister Melda went into her bedroom and got some money to give to Mother; she gave Mother one hundred pesos. I told Sister Melda I would see her tonight when

I get off work. Mother and I left for the market...we arrived at the market and started looking around. Mother bought Brother Etong a shirt, a nice ribbon for little Gina hair and Medicine and sanitary napkins for Sister Rose.

When we finished shopping we went home to Calapacuan. Sister Rose was there lying down on the floor on a mat...she was rubbing her stomach as if she was in pain. I felt really sorry for her losing her baby. She looked at Mother and asked what was she going to do... she had told Mike she was pregnant. Mother said that the only thing she can do is tell him the truth and if he really love her loosing the baby wouldn't change a thing.

I went into the kitchen...Brother Etong was washing beef neck bones and Sister Linda was cooking rice. I said; guess Mother is going to cook my second best soup dish because I could see the ingredient on the kitchen table. Mother always cook a nice hot soup when it raining or if someone is sick. When the food was ready, Mother fixed Sister Rose plate and told her to try and drink as much of the beef soup as possible so she could regain her strength. Everyone started to eat the beef rice soup...Sister Linda took some next door to Sister Maria. Sister Maria gave Sister Linda some Guava fruit to bring back. When I saw the Guava I knew I just had to take some with me to Olongapo, so I asked Mother, she said I could take them all because there was plenty of them on the tree in the back...brother Etong wanted to know if I wanted more, because he could go in back and climb the tree and get more. I said thanks! I would go with him after we finish eating. Little Gina said she could climb the Guava tree. Mother said Gina I told you I didn't want you climbing that Guava tree anymore because you might hurt yourself. Sister Linda said yea, she climbed the tree just like a little monkey...everyone laughed. Mother said keep an eye on my baby when you go out in back. When I finished eating and cleaned the kitchen; Brother Etong, Sister Linda, little Gina and me took a basket and went in back to gather Guava. Sister Linda climbed up the Guava tree and commenced throwing down Guava to us... Guava was falling everywhere...I said be careful, take your time. I decided to climb the other Guava tree; when I reached for the big fruit I saw a snake and almost fell out of the tree, but brother Etong caught me. I told Mother about the snake...it was a long skinny green snake...Mother said it was not poisonous and ask if I had killed the snake; I said no, I think we both was scared of each other...I said I had almost fell to the ground, but brother Etong had caught me. She said it was good I didn't get hurt and asked what the time was. I said it was eleven thirty seven the same time as Sister Linda said it. She said as she walked away, the guy should still be there...Vicky I will be back before you leave.

We heard Sister Maria yelling mail, so everyone except Sister Rose ran outside. Sister Maria said you have mail and a package. Brother Etong ran and met her and got the mail...he brought it to me because he couldn't read. I looked at the letter and package; it was for Sister Rose. I went inside the house and called out twice to Sister Rose in a very low voice ...she answered what! I said you have a letter and a package from Mike. She sat up and tried to open the package, I could sense that she was very weak so I opened it for her. She removed the top layer of paper and another layer; I said maybe there is only paper inside...everyone laugh. Finally she removed the last layer of paper...there was a small box inside... Sister Rose opened it; there was a pretty bulova watch with diamond around the face...she put it on her wrist and laid back down on her mat. I heard someone coming in the door; it was Mother. I asked Mother where had she gone; she said she had went to see the guy about a number to play concerning that snake I saw in the Guava tree...do you remember me asking you whether you had killed the snake or not? Well it is good you didn't kill the snake...I tried what the old people use to say about betting on snake...I asked the guy what number to play; he told me to play seven eleven back to back. I asked Mother what does back to back mean; she said it when you box a numbers...you can win either way it come. I asked why she didn't bet five pesos instead of one; she said she only wanted to see if it would happen. I asked her when she would find out if it's a winner. She said maybe tonight or tomorrow morning. Sister Rose sat up again and asked Sister Linda to read Mike letter to her. Everyone got quiet when Sister Linda started to read the letter. He said he love and miss her and he had gotten his leg hurt...Sister Linda paused for a moment and looked at Sister Rose...everyone said don't stop keep reading...Sister Linda said, "don't rush me"...

she started reading again…Mike said by the time you get this letter I will be back in the United States getting well…he said he never received the Visa papers she sent him. Sister Rose said she sent the papers a long time ago…I don't know what is happening to me. She turned and looked at me and said, "Maybe the guy didn't mail the paperwork". I said I didn't know what had happened; I had told her to mail the paper at Olongapo City Post Office, but she insisted on giving it to one of the Sailor to mail on the base. Mother said stop blaming each other; leave your sister so she can get some rest. She said Rosie stop thinking so much so you can get well. Sister Rose lay back down and I looked at my watch it was time for me to go so I said goodbye to everyone, hugged Mother and picked up the basket of Guava and walked out the door. Sister Maria was sitting on her small porch…She said," you have more Guava"; I said yes, thank you and kept walking across the field to the jeepney stop.

I caught a jeepney to Sister Melda's house in Olongapo City where I once shared a room with Sister Rose. When I walked in the door Sister Melda started yelling at me telling me I was ungrateful and was a no good sister. This really upset me so I started yelling asking her what I had done to make her so mad. She yelled…you remember the towel I was looking for a few days ago? Well I saw the towel hanging on a cloth line in back of the Swan Club where the houseboys hang their clothing to dry. I found out that Sister Rose has been sleeping around with one of the Houseboys. I said, wait a minute! I told you the same night you asked about the towel that I didn't know where the towel was; why are you yelling at me? She said," I feed you, dress you and give you a place to stay and you steal from me, that why". I said, do you remember when I first came to live with you, you said that you kept some money in your drawer and if I need money I could get it, but I haven't touched your money…I started crying; I said yes you feed me and give me a place to stay, but I carry my own weight around here…I do the cooking, the cleaning, washing and ironing and act as your secretary…writing your letters…you are our sister; why are you counting what you do for us? I said, you are my oldest sister and of course you should help us, because you have money. I continued crying…you treat us like your Maid not your sisters. I went into my bedroom and lie down and cried myself to sleep.

It was around four that afternoon when I woke up. I got up and got ready for work…I left without checking to see if she was still home…I didn't want to see her and say goodbye. When I arrived at work, I made myself as busy as possible because I didn't want to think about what had happened this afternoon. Finally I saw my friends the girls that sale handkerchief to the Sailors and Marines coming across the street in my direction. When they arrive they notice the puffing around my eyes and asked if I had being crying. I said yes, my sister and I had a fight. My friend said oh yes! We do that to at my house…that why I would like to go away for a while…I have relatives in Angeles City, where the U.S. Air Force Base is located… no one want to go with me; would you like to go with me? I said no! I have to work. Finally they left when they saw a group of Sailors coming down the other side of the street. I was hoping that business would pick up, but it remained slow.

I heard someone knocking on my door from the inside of the club; I opened the door it was Sister Melda's boyfriend. He said hi cutie, Melda's Sister. I said hi, Sister Melda is not here. He said, "I came to see you" and pulled up a chair to the door. He asked when was my off days from work; I said when there are no ships in the harbor, Holidays, Storms and maybe if the building burn down. He laughed so hard he almost fell from the chair. He said, "You are joking"; I said, no I am not, but I did forget we also close on Christmas and New Year. I asked what did he want from me. He said, "I want to see you"…"I want to take you to a movie and take you out night clubbing. I said, you are my sister boyfriend…why you want to do that? I don't want to go out with you. He whispered, we are only friends"…just friends". I said I still don't want to go out with you. I am a nice guy he said…we are not going to do anything you don't want to do…I just want to go out with you on your off day. I said, just like before, my off days are, Holidays, no ships in the harbor, Typhoon come, or the building burn down, o.k. Then he asked if I work every night. I said, yes! And I sleep all day. He laughed and asked if I wanted a drink; I said yes if he was buying I would have a coke, so he got up and went to the bar counter and got our drinks. He returned and pulled a table over to his chair for his drink. He sat there for a while drinking his beer and watching me work; then finally asked me if I was working tomorrow. I said yes I would be working tomorrow because I work every day. He asked me again if I ever get a day off on Saturday or Sunday. I said no because those are our busy days. Then he started to look restless and got up and said he would see me tomorrow; I said I would be here working tomorrow. He said goodnight and gave me twenty pesos and told me to buy myself another drink and he left.

I closed early that night because I wanted to try and catch Celia at the jeepney stop before she left for Calapacuan. As I got closer to the jeepney stop I saw her standing next to a jeepney; I yelled for her to wait for me. She looked up and saw me and started to smile and wave. When I came up to her I told her I was going to Calapacuan too. She asked why I was going to Calapacuan; I told her Sister Melda and I had a fight, so tonight I wouldn't have to hear her big mouth. We climbed aboard the jeepney and it pulled off for Calapacuan. Celia said she really like her job...she make one hundred pesos a month plus commission and tonight she made thirty pesos in tips. She said sometime the customers would tip her in American money as high as a ten dollar bill...your Sister Melda can have the job at the Money Exchange if she want it. I told her I was very happy for her.

We arrived at the jeepney stop in Calapacuan and got out of the jeepney and started across the dark field. We used Celia small flashlight as we crossed the field; she passed it to me when we arrived at her Mother's House and I continued on to my Mother's house. When I arrive at Mother's house everyone was sleep except Sister Rose; I asked her how she was feeling. She said she was feeling o.k. except from being a little sore. Mother heard us talking and came into the room and asked me why I was here. I told her Sister Melda and I had a fight about the towel Sister Rose took from her. Sister Melda said we stole the towel. Sister Rose said she had only borrowed the towel. I asked her why she didn't tell Sister Melda she wanted to borrow the towel instead of taking it? I said we had being looking all over for that towel and she should have let Sister Melda know about the towel. Mother became a little upset with Sister Rose and told her to never take anything from Sister Melda. She said now you have your sister mad at Vicky. Mother looked at me and said "don't go to your Sister Melda's house for a while"...wait until you are sure she is not home then go and get you a few clothes to wear for a while.

Sister Rose said she have to get the rest of her clothes from Sister Melda's house too. Mother told Sister Rose she needed to rest three more days; then she could go and do whatever she wanted to. We sit for a while then Mother said she had forgotten to give me five pesos because she had given everyone else five. I asked her what were the five pesos for? She said the number she played was a winner. I said what number? She said the Snake number. I said oh you won ha! She said yes I won one hundred pesos. I said well I guess the old saying about betting on a snake is true. She said I don't know whether it's true or not maybe I just got lucky…I just wanted to see if the number would win. I said Mother keep the five pesos and buy something for yourself. I went to bed and fell asleep right away.

The next day after I had breakfast I went next door to my Brother's house. Celia was sitting on their small porch; she saw me coming and started to smile. I step up on the porch and had a seat. We talked about her new job; she said she meets a lot of Sailors and Marines; some of good and some of bad, but she had met one sailor that like her and wanted her to live with him when he get an apartment…she told him she would think about it, because she was working to help her Mother. He said he would help my Mother too. I asked if he had proposed marriage to her she said no, he just want to live together for a while and see how things work out.

We continued talking about my job and her job; then we heard a noise…it was a motorcycle coming across the field. Celia said it was her boyfriend and she wonder why he was coming to her house when she had told him she would see him tonight. When he was close enough to yell at, Celia asked him why he had come to her house. He didn't say a word he only looked at us and smiled. Celia and I stepped down from the porch and walked over to where he had ridden up on the bike. By that time everyone from Mother house and Sister Maria had came out to see what was going on…Celia introduced her boyfriend to everyone…I stayed and talked with Celia and her boyfriend for a while, I left and went back to Mother's house. I told Mother I was going to Olongapo to get some of my clothing; she wanted to go with me, but I convinced her to stay and keep an eye on Sister Rose in case she get sick again. As I came by Celia's house she saw me and called for me to wait for her and her boyfriend, because they was going to Olongapo too. I looked at the motorcycle and said we can't all fit on that thing. Her boyfriend assured me that we could, so Celia and I got on behind him and we were off. When we finally arrived at Olongapo; we stopped at the tricycle stop and after thinking them for the ride I caught a tricycle to Sister Melda's house. I walked around the house listening for sounds, but I didn't hear anyone moving around inside, so I opened the door and went in...there were no sign of movement in sister Melda's bedroom, so I hurried and packed some of my clothes and left. I went to the jeepney stop and caught a jeepney to Calapacuan. When I arrived Mother asked if Sister Melda was home; I said no, I didn't see her anywhere. I turned and Sister Rose walked passed me, I said, now you are walking real great ... pretty soon you will be able to go everywhere. Mother said, not yet! Then she went to the stove to check on the bath water she was heating up for Sister Rose. Mother had put leaves from the Guava tree in Sister Rose bath water. This was an old family remedy use for just about everything. Mother separated the leaves from the water and had Sister Rose to strip down and get into the small tub. Mother bathed her whole body in the water. A few minutes later I asked Sister Rose how she felt...she said she felt as though she could move around as much as she wanted. We all was very happy that Sister Rose was finally able to get up and about.

Mother looked at me and said, "we are going to have another grown woman in this house in five days", and so to celebrate we're going to roast a pig and cook all the dishes you like...we will also invited all of your old classmates. I said don't cook too much, because I don't know if all of my friends are coming...they are busy working too.

I said maybe this should be just for the family, but Mother insisted I should invite all of my friends. I heard a motorcycle coming...I guess Celia and her boy friend is on their way back...then the sound went away...a few minutes later I could hear it again, so I looked outside in the direction of the sound and I could see the motorcycle leaving with one person on it...I guess he came to drop Celia off.

Sister Rose was up and about, so I decided to give her the key to Sister Melda's house, but she decided it would be best if she just went there and knocked on the door and tell her, she had come for the rest of her clothes. I reminded her to be careful when she get to Sister Melda's house because Sister Melda is very moody.

I looked at my watch...it was four in the afternoon...times for me to be leaving because I had to go to work. I said my goodbyes and left...as I passed Brother Celino's house Celia came out, she was going to Olongapo too. I asked why she didn't ride with her boyfriend; she said he was in a hurry to get to the motorcycle shop before it close at four.

I asked her if she had decided to live with him when he get his apartment; she said she was still undecided because she was making good money at her job and he had not asked her to marry him. Finally we arrived in Olongapo; we said goodbye and went to where we work. When I arrived at the money exchange booth I could see Sister Melda's boyfriend through the door leading into the club; I quickly closed the door hoping he would not see me, but he saw me and came over...pulled up a chair and table close to the door leading into my booth. He said, "Hello pretty; I have been waiting for you". I said why! I told you I have to work today. I know, he said, you work every day. He sat at the table drinking beer and watching me work. Around six o, clock he said he was hungry; I told him to go and get him something to eat...he wanted to know what I wanted to eat...I said don't worry about me; I will get me a barbecue hot dog at the stand when I get hungry. He got up from his seat and opened his wallet... pulled out a five dollar bill...dropped it on the table saying, "This is for your food and left". I said you don't have to give me money for my food...he kept walking. I closed the door again and pick up my Magazine and started to read it.

A few minutes later someone else was knocking on the door. I got up and opened the door...there stood Sister Melda, mad as always. The first thing she said was what is my boy friend doing here? I saw him sitting in the door talking to you. I said he wasn't doing anything; he just wanted to talk. She said, "you are just like Celia trying to take someone boyfriend. I said Sister Melda, I am not trying to take your boyfriend...first of all he said he was only your friend and I don't like him for a boyfriend anyway. But you are forgetting just one thing...you are married...that really hit a nerve...she started yelling at me and I yelled back. She said she had hired a cleaning lady and

I didn't have to come home...now you can't steal from me anymore. I said you are still accusing me of taking your towel...I didn't take your towel; Sister Rose took your precious towel. She said tell my boy friend we will meet him somewhere and left. I didn't have the slightest idea as to what she was talking about. As she left I saw the club Manager coming toward me. He moved a chair to get closer to me and asked me what was going on. I really didn't want to tell him my business, but I knew I had to tell him something, so I said Sister Melda said I was ungrateful and left. He said he only came over to try and stop something bad from happening...your sister has a little money and she act as though she own the place... you remember the time she and the Hostess got into a fight...well I almost lost my job...I explained to the boss I didn't have anything to do with the fight, but your sister blamed me...there was another girl at the Top Hat Money Exchange that was fired because she said the girl was trying to take her boyfriend. I said yes I know about that girl, she is my sister-in-law daughter. He looked very surprised and said, "Your relative". I said yes, I guess I will get fired now. He assured me that mama Ligaya would not fire me; he said she like the way I work and think I am a very nice girl...she also think you and Melda are so different you don't seem like sisters...that's why I am so sure she will not fire you...I have to get back to work now...take it easy and you will be all right.

I closed the door again and looked out front of my booth and saw my friend across the street selling handkerchiefs; I waved and called her over to my booth. I asked if she still wanted to go and visit her relatives in Angeles City; she said she did, but have not found anyone to accompany her. We talked a while and finally she had to go. I sit back down in my chair and tried to read my magazine again.

Things went very smooth for a while; I had a few customer stopped by for change. Then around ten I heard someone knock on my back door again; I opened the door and it were Sister Melda's boyfriend. I said I thought you had gone back to the base. He said no not yet, but I have brought you some monkey meat (barbecue pork on a stick). I said I have eaten already. He said take it with you and snack on it when you get home. I tried to give him his change from the five back, but he told me to keep it. He went to the bar and got a beer and came back and pulled up another table and chair. He talked while I was working until around eleven and said goodbye and went back to the base.

At closing time; I closed the booth up and started counting the money; I counted it for several time before I realized I had put the change he had gave me into the cash register. I quickly removed it and hurried to turn the money in to mama Ligaya. I turned over the money and hurried out to catch Celia at the jeepney stop so we could ride home to Calapacuan together. I saw her waiting at the jeepney stop; I waved to her and she started to smile. We both decided to order and take home some noodle and bread rolls.

When we arrived in Calapacuan; I saw Brother Etong waiting at the small store by the jeepney stop. We both were glad to see him because we didn't like walking across the dark field alone. I gave him the noodle and barbecue pork and I carried the small flashlight as we walked across the field. We arrived at Celia's house and I said goodbye and continued on to Mother's house. When we arrived it was one thirty in the morning…Mother was still awake…we tiptoed in trying not to make noise, but everyone woke up anyway. Brother Etong put the food on the table in front of Mother…she opened the package saying you brought a lot of food. I said yes someone gave me the barbecue; then I finally saw how much was in the bag…it was at least twenty pieces, so I had Brother Etong to take six pieces next door to Sister Maria and Celia. Everyone was awake now, so Mother warmed the barbecue in the oven and made coffee. We all sit around eating noodles, bread rolls and barbecue pork. Sister Rose said the barbecue was her favorite; she would buy a stick of barbecue and a coke and it would fill her up. Sister Linda said, "Mother we can barbecue some pork like this on Vick's birthday. Mother looked at me and asked if I had invited all of my friends; I said yes, but they can't come because they have to work. Mother said, "More for us then". Sister Rose said, "More for me"… little Gina said more for me too…everyone started to laugh. I said to little Gina, you have a little stomach, you can't finish one barbecue and then she started smiling.

I decided to tell Mother what had happened to me at work; I said Mother early this evening at work one of Sister Melda's boyfriend came by and sit and talked with me for a while; during that time I think Sister Melda saw him at my booth, because as soon as he left she came over and accused me of trying to take her boyfriend. I tried to explain to her that I was working and didn't have any intention of try to take her boyfriend, but she kept yelling telling me that I was trying to take her boyfriend just like Celia. I don't like her boyfriend, but even if I did it shouldn't be a problem with her because she is married. Will you please tell me what's wrong with her? Mother said the only thing she could think of that may have something to do with the way she act is; when she was little going to school she was bitten by a dog. The family didn't have money to take her to see a Doctor, so she got leaves from the Guava tree and crushed them… she applied the leaves to the bite on her leg and wrapped it real tight with a bandage…since then she have being a problem child…when the moon is full that's the time she starts to act up…when she was going to school she would fight the boys and her teacher…she would put thumb tacks in her teacher chair…it became so bad that we had to take her out of the school…that's why she can't read and write. I asked Mother if Sister Melda was crazy and need to be in a Hospital. She said no Melda only act up when there is a full moon just like a werewolf in the movies…when there is a full moon any small thing happen to her…she would blow it out of proportion. I am not sure about Mother Explanation, but I do know that there are certain times when she is very nice and the other time she act like a witch. Mother said try to avoid your sister when there is a full moon, because she can be sweet, loving and kind most of the time. I said that I still think she need to see a head shrink Doctor. Mother said it is almost three in the morning; you better go to bed because you have to work tomorrow. Sister Rose said she would be going to Olongapo tomorrow…Mother said be sure that you avoid your Sister Melda…why do you think I am telling Vicky to stay here for a while. Sister Rose said she just want to go to Olongapo. Mother said o.k. Remember what I said.

The next day I slept until about eleven and was awaken by the smell of food being cook. I got up, washed up and sit down at the kitchen table and tried to find out what I had missed so far. Everyone was outside except Mother who was cooking; she said Sister Rose had already left for Olongapo. I said well I guess she is really feeling good now; maybe she can go back to work. Sister Linda came back inside with a package and a letter for Sister Rose from Mike's Mother. She put the package on the table and I picked it up to try and examine it, but it didn't rattle at all. Mother said let eat, so I put the package down and set the table.

Just before we finished eating Sister Rose came back. I asked her where did she go; she said I went to get my clothes from Sister Melda's house, but a lady was washing clothes there, so I left. I said why didn't you ask for your clothes? She said because I used your key to get in...I thought no one was home. I said why did you go in my bag? She said she didn't want to wake me. It really upset me, so I didn't say anything else. Then Mother said don't you ever go into her bag again; if you need something from her you should ask for it... that's how all this mess got started anyway...you taking something that didn't belong to you...that's why she didn't give you a key to her house...can't you understand you are making a mess of things? Everyone sat quietly eating without a word.

When everyone finished eating Sister Rose opened her package... she pulled from the package a maternity dress...she said well I guess his family know I am pregnant. Mother said you had better write and explain to Mike how you lost the baby, so he will know what's going on.

Around one that afternoon I decided to take a nap; little Gina wanted a nap to, so she lay down beside me and we drifted off to sleep. Sister Linda woke me at three so I could get clean up for work. Sister Rose came and asked to use my key; she promised she would make sure no one is home before she enter Sister Melda's house. I really didn't want to let her have the key, but Mother had made us promise to try and avoid Sister Melda, so I didn't want to cause Sister Rose to have a problem with her. I also knew she needed her clothes so she could return to work, so I let her have my key. I said be careful and bring back the key. She said o.k. And walked out of the door.

Finally it was time for me to go to work, so I got clean up and dressed and left for work. I arrived at work and got settled in for the night; business was a little slow tonight, so I had a chance to read the magazine I had being keeping in the booth. Around six that evening Sister Rose came to my booth. I asked if she had gotten her clothes;

she said when she arrived someone was in the house, so she hid in the shrub to wait for whoever it was to leave, but she finally gave up because the mosquitoes was too bad…she would try again tomorrow. She stayed and talked for a while; then decided to leave and come back when I close the money exchange. At closing time she hadn't returned, so I closed up and went to mama Ligaya place to turn in the money. Mama Ligaya usually would be sleep when I arrived, but tonight she was awake. When I came in she said she wanted me to work the day shift tomorrow, because the lady on day shift was sick and she could only find a school girl to work…she wanted the girl to work the night shift so she could go to school. I said o.k. And left for Calapacuan.

When I got home I asked Mother to wake me up early because I had to work the day shift at work. She said you had better get to bed now so you can get as much sleep as possible. I went to bed. Mother woke up early and started breakfast; the aroma from the coffee brewing woke me up…I looked at my watch…it was a quarter to six…I laid there and went back to sleep. Mother woke me up at seven and I told me that Brother Etong had gotten my bath water ready, so I got up and got my bath and dressed before breakfast. Sister Rose woke up and said she was going with me to Olongapo, so she could try again to get her clothes.

Finally we left for Olongapo; when we arrived we split up; she went to Sister Melda's house and I went to work. It seem really different working here doing the day…everything seem to be moving very slow…most of the Sailors and Marines are at work doing the day. I sat calmly in my booth counting the jeepney and Sailors passing by. At around lunchtime the girl that works the bar counter came over to my booth and asked if I had lunch already. I said no! I would get something later. She said she was going to get noodles for her lunch and would bring me some back; I said wait! I will give you some money to pay for half of the noodles. She said it was o.k. She would pay for the noodles. Later she returned with two plates of noodles… we sat, chat and ate the noodles. When we finished eating I thanked her for lunch and she went back to work at the counter.

Around one that afternoon I was counting the money I had in the cash register when Sister Rose ran up to my booth. I asked what was wrong; she said Sister Melda had tried to kill her. I said when! She said when she arrived at Sister Melda's house no one was there, so she started to pack her clothes in a suitcase...when she filled the suitcase she got a pillowcase and started to fill it...Sister Melda and her maid arrived; when she saw me in your room she got very mad... she asked me what I was doing there and if I came to steal something again? I grab the suitcase and pillowcase and started for the door and Sister Melda got a knife and started toward

Chapter 4

Running Away

Me…the maid said no, no Melda, so I turned around and threw my arm up to try and block the knife from hitting my chest and it caught me in the arm. I said oh my goodness! Did you get your clothes? She said yes she was able to get her clothes, but she left them at a friend house. I asked if she still had my key; she said yes and she had seen Sister Melda and her maid going to mama Ligaya place when she came by on her way here to see me. I became very scared and really did not know what to do.

I took eighty pesos from the cash register and asked Sister Rose to stay and cover the booth until I returned. She said where are you going? Don't take too long. I left looking for Elizabeth my friend that sale handkerchief; after walking around for a while I saw one of the girls and asked where Elizabeth was; she said she was over in front of the Silver Dollar club selling handkerchiefs. I went straight to the Silver Dollar Club and sure enough she was standing out front talking to a Sailor. I walked over to her and asked if she still wanted to visit her relatives in Angeles City. She said yes! With a great big smile. I said do you want to go now? She said yes I only need a few minutes to go home and get some clothes. I said o.k. I will meet you at the bus station. I went straight to Sister Melda's house, because I wanted to get there before she returns. When I arrived there was no one in sight so I went in and packed my clothes; then I remembered her telling me if I ever need some money I could get some from her drawer in her room, so I looked in the drawer and there was only a ten dollar bill and some change. I took the ten and left in a hurry. I was very scared...I thought to myself, if she stab Sister Rose... she probably would kill me if she caught me in her room. I was so nervous and scared I don't know how I got to the bus station... Elizabeth brought me back to reality when she said are you ready. I said yes! How much will it cost to go to Angeles City? She said how about we visit your relatives in Manila first? I said what! I thought you wanted to visit your relatives; that's why I wanted to go with you. When she said that I completely forgot that I was scared. I said please make up your mind as to where you want to go. She said o.k. Can we just visit your relatives first in Manila? We agreed to go to visit my relatives first, so we went to the ticket counter and purchased our ticket to Manila. Finally we boarded the bus; my mind was drifting all over... am I making the right decision...will my Aunt welcome me to her house...will my Mother be worrying about me...is this trip part of my destiny...will I finally be able to go all over like the ocean that I always day dream about? Finally I snapped out of my daydream and realized how fast the time had passed; I looked out of the bus window and could see that we was arriving in Manila. Then I noticed Elizabeth sleeping comfortable beside me; I wondered if she was having mix feeling about our trip. I thought to myself she couldn't be thinking anything about the trip to be sleeping as sound as she is. I woke her up and said we are in Manila. As soon as the bus stopped we grab our luggage and disembarked from the bus.

I called a taxi...Elizabeth asked where were we going...I just looked at her for a few seconds then I said we are going to visit my relatives. Then she asked if there was something wrong. I didn't answer her I just gave the taxi driver the address of my Aunt, which was Mandaluyong Rizal. The driver asked if it was before or after the railroad track; I said after the railroad track next to the market. Elizabeth said you know where you are going as if she thought I was lost. I said yes! I know the place my uncle use to work and the people there know my relatives too. When we arrive I asked the neighbors if they knew the where about of my cousin Dadong. One of the neighbor said he was just right here a few minutes ago...maybe he went next door. We went next door and I saw him sitting and talking with one of his neighbors. I called out to him and he looked around with a surprise smile on his face...where do Auntie live? He said the family is not here now they went back to Pangasinan to help plant rice. I said where do you live? He said I live on the other side of town and I can't take you there, because it is dangerous at night ...how about you and your friend get a hotel room tonight; I will take you there it not very far from here. He called a taxi and we left for the hotel. When we arrived at the hotel Dadong whispered and asked me if Elizabeth worked in a nightclub as a Hostess. I replied very upset...she do not work in a club...why you ask something stupid like that anyway? He said he heard that most of the girls in Olongapo City worked in a club. He could tell that I was upset with him so he decided to leave us right away. As he was leaving he said to us make sure you lock and put the chain on the door when I leave and I will be back tomorrow. The moment he closed the door; I walked over and locked it and put the chain up. I looked at Elizabeth with a sigh of relief although she looked as if nothing at all was concerning her. We sit around and made small talk; finally it was bedtime. I got into bed and started thinking about my situation...should I stay here in Manila even though Auntie is not here or should I go back to Olongapo; then I thought of Elizabeth relatives in Angeles City... maybe we will go there and stay with them for a while...finally I decided to let tomorrow bring whatever it will or may...I will deal with it. I went to sleep.

The next day Elizabeth and I got up and took our showers and had breakfast; my cousin was nowhere in sight, so we waited until check out time and he still had not showed up, so we decided to leave Manila. I told Elizabeth it was time we visited her relatives in Angeles City, so we called a taxi and left for the bus station. Upon arrival we went straight to the ticket counter and purchased our ticket to Angeles City. We spent most of the day waiting for our bus...finally we were off to Angeles City. When we arrived I said to Elizabeth... we are here...where do your relatives live? She said around; let's get a place to stay first its getting dark. I said if your relatives live here why can't we stay at their house? She didn't say anything she just kept walking and looking around. Finally we saw a boarding house with rooms for rent. We knocked at the door and the owner came to the door. We asked what was the price of a room for the night. The owner said come on in its only for tonight you can stay for the night. Then the owner left us in the room. There was no furniture or bed only an empty room. I took my robe from my suitcase and spread it on the floor and folded some of my pants for a pillow. Elizabeth said she would sleep beside me. The owner knocked on the door and gave us two pillows and a sheet; I guess she was watching us from the window and saw we didn't have anything to sleep on. We thanked the owner for the bedding and she left the room. I closed the door and came back and lie down. My mind took off like a jet plane I was thinking about everything…Sister Melda and Sister Rose…My Mother how much she will be worrying about me and oh yes, my birthday tomorrow. My head seem as if it was going to burst from thinking so much. Finally I drifted off to sleep; I woke up about nine that morning, but Elizabeth was up and gone. I got up and got dressed the door opened she came in acting very happy. She said I have found a place where we can stay for free. I said wait a minute; I thought we was going to visit your relatives. She said I went to where they live, but they don't live there anymore. Then I said well let's go home. She said no let's stay for a while like we are on vacation. She picked up the bed sheet and started to fold it so we could return it to the owner. I really didn't know what to do so I decided to stay just like she had wanted to do. We returned the sheet and pillows to the owner. She said if you decide to come back just see me and I will take care of you.

We said thanks and picked up our luggage and started walking down the street. I ask Elizabeth how far we have to go because my luggage was getting heavy. She said just around the corner is the place I am talking about. I said I am getting hungry plus today is my birthday I am eighteen years old today. My friend said yes it is your birthday June 22. I asked again where was the place. She said it's right here let's go inside. We step inside the door; I saw a man coming over to us; he introduced himself as the Manager of the Club. I shook his hand thinking to myself, why am I at a nightclub. He asked us to follow him upstairs where the rooms for employees were located. He said this is the room you will be staying in let me know as soon as you decide what you want to do. He turned around and went back down stairs. I asked Elizabeth what did the Manager mean when he said let him know what we decide to do. She said he want to know if we want to stay and work in the club downstairs. I said I am not going to be a club hostess. She said don't you like the room? We have a bed, chairs and a closet to hang our clothes...I love it.

Then I heard a knock at the door; it was the Manager, he said it's time for lunch...come downstairs and eat. I thought to myself, what kind of trouble I am in now. We followed the Manager back downstairs where he introduced us to the club hostesses. We had lunch and talked with the other girls for a while then we went back upstairs. When we got back upstairs I said, let's go back to Olongapo. She said let's stay for a while if you don't want to work here its o.k. I will work so we can have some money. I didn't tell her about the money I had saved for emergency. I said lets walk around tomorrow and see if I can find me a job. She said you should work in the club where you can get a commission; you don't have to go out with the guys if you don't want to...just sit and talk with them. I said no! I don't want to be a hostess in a club, so please help me find another job tomorrow. She said well if that what you want; I will go with you tomorrow. We decided to lie down and take a nap. Finally we both fell asleep.

Around six that afternoon, Elizabeth woke me up and said it was time for her to go downstairs to work. She asked me to go with her at first I said no, but finally gave in and accompanied her downstairs. We had a seat at one of the table and started to make small talk; then a lot of Air Force guys came in...they was station at the U.S. Air Force Base nearby.

I got up to go to the ladies room and one guy followed me trying to get me to dance with him. I said excuse me; I am going to the ladies room...I went straight back upstairs. When I passed one of the rooms I could hear a baby crying so I peeped in and saw an older lady sitting on her bed with a baby. She said please come in and she introduced herself and her baby girl. She said her baby was one week old. She asked if I was working tonight. I said no! And went to my room. I found a deck of card and started to play solitary. A few minutes later Elizabeth came upstairs. She said the Manager was looking for me and she had told him I was not feeling good. I repeated to her that I didn't want to work as a hostess. She turned around and went back downstairs. I played solitary until I got sleepy then I went to bed. I don't know what time she came back to our room.

The next morning Elizabeth and I went to take a shower down stairs; there was a line so we got in line and finally was able to take our shower and get cleaned up for breakfast. After breakfast we went walking around the neighborhood looking for me a job...we tried the Money Exchanges first...they were not hiring, so we decided to go to the market area...we caught a jeepney for the market. We arrived at the market and started walking to the stores and booths asking if they needed help. Finally when it was getting very hot; we decided to go to the restaurant we saw across the street and order a snow cone. When we came to the door I noticed a help wanted sign in the window...I open the door and started walking very fast to the counter. Elizabeth said wait for me I am coming to. I slowed down for her...when I came to the counter an old woman was sitting there in a chair. I asked her was they still hiring. She said yes! I need three waitresses to start work right away. I said I would sure like working here if you will hire me. She said she would hire both of us if we want to work. My friend said she had a job already, so the lady looked at me and asked when could I start working. I said today! She said how about tomorrow. I said o.k. I will be here. She said wear a white shirt or blouse with pants or skirt and come at nine tomorrow. I thanked her and said I will see you tomorrow and left.

As soon as Elizabeth step out of the restaurant door. I said we have to go back to the market so I can buy me a white blouse or t-shirt. She said I have two t-shirts you can borrow. I said I want to buy at least one white blouse in case I get dirty. When we got to the market, we looked around for a while. Finally I spotted the white blouse I wanted. I decided to get four blouses. I paid the cashier fifteen pesos each for the blouses and went back to our room.

The Manager was waiting for us when we arrived. He asked me if I had decided to stay and work in the club. I said with a big smile on my face;" I have a job". Elizabeth asked if I could continue staying with her. He said she have a job and I guess she have to stay somewhere...as long as she pay for her food and boarding it's o.k. Elizabeth and I were very happy. We went upstairs to our room to sit down and relax and thank about our jobs. My job pays one hundred pesos a month plus tips and my friend worked for a commission in the bar downstairs. We decided to take a nap before Elizabeth left for work. I woke up around six that evening. Elizabeth had left for work, so I decided to try and go back to sleep...I heard a lot of noise outside, so I got up and went to the window, I could see a lot of people in the street yelling. Finally the police came and quieted everyone down. I went back to bed to try again to go to sleep, but all I could do were to think about my job I would be going to tomorrow. I tossed and turned for a while longer and finally went to sleep.

The next morning I woke up and looked for Elizabeth but she hadn't made it back from last night. I got my things together and went down stairs to the shower. I returned to our room and checked the t-shirt I had washed last night to see if it was dry. It was still damp so I pressed it with the iron and finished drying it. I got dressed and went downstairs and had breakfast. When I returned to our room I looked again for Elizabeth, but she still hadn't showed up. I left at a quarter to nine for work. It took about ten minutes to ride from my room to the restaurant. When I arrived the Owner explained a few things about the job; she said I was to work the left side of the dining area and the other girl would work the right. We was given a blue and white apron that fit around your waist...it had two pockets...the owner said jokingly, fill those pocket with tips. She also gave us a hair net to wear at all times while we are working. We started serving lunch at eleven; it started off very slow then all of a sudden the place was full of customers. Around three that afternoon we sit down and ate lunch. The owner said we should come in around ten from now on, so we can have lunch before the customers arrive at eleven. She said we could eat free in the restaurant while we are working and also, take a break when things start to slow down. I thought to myself this is a very nice lady. I counted my tips. I had fifteen pesos in tips just for lunch alone, I was very happy with myself.

We started serving dinner at five and it last until nine. Dinner was the busiest meal; our dining area was full most of the time. Some people were good tipper the other one had a hard time separating themselves from their money. Finally my first day of work was over, I went straight home. While riding in the jeepney on my way back to our room I finally realized what the owner was saying to me as I went out the door. She said that I would only be working five day a week because her niece worked there on Saturday and Sunday. I really didn't have a problem with having two days off to rest it will be nice. When I got to my room I was so tired I went to sleep with my uniform on. From then on I didn't see Elizabeth very much…my schedule was so much different from hers…I would leave around ten in the morning and return about nine thirty at night…I only saw her on my off days. Sometime we would go shopping on my off day. She said she makes three or four times the money she made selling handkerchief in Olongapo. I found out she had told everyone I was her sister even the club Manager. I think that was one of the reasons he agreed to let me stay with her.

One night she got invited to a party at the Airmen Club on the Air Force base. She asked me if I wanted to go with her. I said no! I don't think I should. Then she asked me if I would keep the lady baby next door so she to go with her. I said o.k. I will keep the baby. She hurried next door to tell the lady the news. Now I know they had already plan to ask me to baby sit. About five minutes later the lady brought the baby, diapers, blanket and milk. I took the baby and they left for the party. The baby was real good she didn't cry very much. We fell asleep together. Later that night she started to cry again. I looked at my watch it was two in the morning. I said to myself I wonder where else they went. I change the baby diaper and gave it a fresh bottle of milk and she went back to sleep. At around five that morning I was awaken when Elizabeth unlocked the door and came in. They both said they were really sorry for staying away for so long. Elizabeth said the party was over around one, but they went to someone house after the party. The lady said come on in my room and eat some hot rolls and drink coffee. I followed them into her room and sit down on the bed. The lady gave me some rolls. I said they are still hot. She said yes we stopped the boy riding the bike selling hot rolls…she said your friend tell me you are not her sister…you only ran away together. I was very surprised; I really didn't know what to say; I guess Elizabeth decided to change her story. I decide to clear things up, so I said I didn't run away; I left home to visit my relatives in Manila, but they had Left and went to Pangasinan.

Then we decided to visit Elizabeth relatives here in Angeles City. Maybe she can get her story together and tell you where her relatives live, because I have not seen them. I think Elizabeth ran away...I think she planned this a long time ago...she just waited till she found someone to go with her...I came with her, but I was not running away...Every since we arrived here I have being trying to get her to return to Olongapo, but she is happy here working with you guys down stairs in the club. I left and returned to my room because I was very upset with Elizabeth. I decided to take a shower, so I got my things together and went down stairs and took a shower. I returned to my room and went to bed. My weekend was finally over. I woke up around eight that Monday morning and went for my shower. When I returned I looked for Elizabeth; I hadn't seen her since early Sunday Morning when they returned from the party. I guess she have being staying with the lady next door when she got off work. I left around a quarter to nine that morning. When I got there the owner said go in the kitchen and get your lunch, so the other waitress and I went to the kitchen and fixed our plates. We came back to the dining area and sit down and ate our lunch. At eleven the owner got up and turn the window sign to open...a few minutes later the customers started coming in...I don't know why most of the customers always come and sit on my side of the dining room, so naturally I would end up doing most of the work on the floor.

A man and his pretty wife with long hair almost down to her waist; came in and sat down on my side of the dining room. I immediately took menus to the table and went to the next table...on my way back they were ready to order...I took their order. When it was ready I served the food to them and went to the next table. On my way back the customer with the pretty wife called me to his table. He accused me of putting hair in his food. We went back and forth a couple of times...I called the Owner over to his table and explained to her what the gentleman was accusing me of...there was a hair in his food but it was too long to be mine...looking at the length of his wife hair. I figured it was her hair. The Owner quickly pointed out the length of the hair and the fact that my hair was much shorter than the strand that were retrieved from his food and of course, I was wearing a hair net to prevent loose hair from falling from my head. The gentleman apologized to me and when he finished his meal he left me a ten pesos tip. At closing the owner explained to me that this was a frequently occurrence and I shouldn't get discouraged. She said oh by the way! If you like some of the left over dessert please take some home with you. So I wrapped up some of the dessert and left for my room.

When I arrived at my room Elizabeth was lying on the bed. She said she was not feeling well...I called the elder lady that lived next door over to my room. When she came in I told her Elizabeth was sick and I didn't know what to do. She touched Elizabeth forehead and said she was burning up with fever. I got a container of cold water and wetted a small towel and placed it on her forehead. The lady gave her some of her medicine for fever. I decided to watch her for a while, so I took off my work clothing, put on my robe and lay down on the floor next to the bed; I figured if I lie on the bed I would go to sleep right away because I was very tired. I did fall asleep right away. When I woke up she was sitting on the side of the bed drinking coffee and eating the dessert I brought home from work. I asked how she was feeling; she said she was feeling a lot better than she was last night. I got up, washed my face and brushed my teeth...went down stairs to breakfast.

When I finished breakfast I came back upstairs to my room. I looked at my watch and it was time for me to start getting ready for work, so I got all of the things I need to take a shower and went back down stairs. Whenever I go to the shower I often wonder why the shower was put down stairs and everyone lived upstairs. There was one thing I was glad of and that not having to be at work before ten in the morning, because if I had to come early in the morning I suddenly would be late...everyone seem to take a early shower even though they work late at night.

The time really passed fast...its July the twenty fourth and I am getting my first paycheck...with my paycheck and the tips I had save; I had quite a large bank role compared to what I was getting in Olongapo. Sometime I would go shopping, but I only bought my basic necessity and came back to my room. Every time I had a long talk with Elizabeth I would try and get her to return to Olongapo with me, because I was afraid to travel alone. She would always say stay a little longer I don't want to return to Olongapo I like it here.

One Saturday afternoon I was standing in front of the club trying to decide if I should go up to my room or go shopping. A Sailor came up to me that looked very familiar to me. He said what are you doing here? Your sister is looking for you. Now I knew who he was; he was a Sailor that occasionally come by my Money Exchange booth in Olongapo and talked to me. Before I could answer him; he asked if I was working in the club. Elizabeth came out of the club just as he was asking me about the club and asked him what he was doing in Angeles City. He turned around and asked her the same thing. Then he started asking me more questions again...when I will be going back to Olongapo. He just was not giving me a chance to answer any of his questions.

He said I am going to tell your sister you are here. I said no! Don't tell my sister where I am at, but I really hoped he would tell someone in my family so they would come and take me home. Elizabeth was really worried thinking that the Sailor would tell where we are. We had being away for six weeks and I figured that was long enough to be away from home to prove a point. Two weeks later when I came back from work Elizabeth couldn't wait to tell me that my sister was here looking for me. I said was it my Sister Rose? She said no! It was your oldest sister and she will be back tomorrow. I said she is not coming back tomorrow.

I went upstairs and change my clothes and decided to go back downstairs in the club with her. When I entered the club and looked around I could only see a few people sitting around drinking and listening to the music from a jukebox. I was very thirsty so I went to the bar and ordered a coke. I returned to the table where Elizabeth was sitting. As soon as I sit down at the table a young man came over and asked her to dance...she said o.k. And followed him out on the dance floor. I sit watching her dance and trying to forget about the news I received about my sister. I really wanted to go back to Olongapo and somewhat wanted to stay with Elizabeth here in Angeles City. Elizabeth had said that the lady behind the bar talked with my sister when she was here looking for me, so I decided that I wanted to hear what she said first hand. I went over to the bar and asked if she was the lady that spoke with my sister when she came in the club. She said yes! Your sister had her boyfriend with her...I told her there was two sisters here, but one worked at a restaurant and would be here after work...I don't know which restaurant she is working at. I called your sister that works here over to the bar and told her what was going on, but she said she was not your sister...she was your friend...your sister from Olongapo was almost about to cry, so her boyfriend took her out of the club. I said thanks! I started back to my seat, but decided to go upstairs to my room instead. I opened the door to my room, walked in and went straight to bed. I laid in the bed for a few minutes thinking about everything; then I finally drifted off to sleep.

Early the next morning the Manager of the club woke us banging on the door. I opened the door and the Manager said your sister is downstairs. I said o.k. We will be downstairs in a few minutes. We grab everything we needed for a shower and hurried downstairs to the shower. We finished our shower and returned to our room and got dressed quickly.

I took a deep breath and we started down stairs. We walked inside of the club...Elizabeth hid behind the door...I saw Sister Melda coming toward me with her arms out stretched and crying. She was trying to talk while hugging, crying and squeezing me to death. We moved over to a corner in the club and tried to talk but someone played the jukebox, so I said let's go up to my room. She told her boyfriend she would be right back. When we got in my room I explained to her that I sleep and eat here, but I work in a restaurant. She asked me where were the restaurant. I said it is across the street from the main market.

She said pack your suitcase I am taking you home. I said I have to get my paycheck, because I owe for my food and lodging. She said don't worry I will pay for it, so we went back downstairs to see the lady at the counter. Sister Melda asked how much did I owe and the lady checked her book and said she owe the club one hundred and sixty pesos. The lady asked her if she was paying for Elizabeth to. She said yes! I called Elizabeth over to the counter and told her that my sister would pay for her food and lodging if she wanted to return to Olongapo. She said no! She wanted to stay here in Angeles City. I gave her a big hug and told her to go by the restaurant and get my two weeks pay and pay for her food.

I followed my Sister and her boyfriend out of the club. We caught a jeepney that was almost full of passenger; I had to sit on my sister lay...I think she wanted it that way anyway. My sister started sniffing again as she was trying to talk to me. We arrived at the bus station and purchased our tickets to Olongapo. Finally we boarded the bus... We sit in the same seat...She said mother was so mad at her she gave her a choice...find me and bring me back or she will stop speaking to her. My sister started trying to tell me how sorry she was about the things she did to me...she started crying again...I started crying... her boyfriend started crying too. We finally got it together and calmed down.

The time passed so fast we was arriving in Olongapo City before I realized it. We disembarked from the bus...Sister Melda's boyfriend said goodbye! He would see us tonight and left going to the Naval Base. Sister Melda and I caught a jeepney to Calapacuan. We arrived about one that afternoon everyone was crying...My Mother, Brother Etong and Sister Linda...little Gina was just standing and starring at us.

When things finally settled down my Mother asked me what had happened. I couldn't wait to tell her...I started from the time I left Sister Rose at the Money Exchange booth and finished with the arrival of Sister Melda in my room in Angeles City. She said she was glad I was all right. She also said she told Sister Melda if anything happen to me she would never forgive her. Sister Melda finally put Mother mind at ease when she said that I was working in a restaurant and not a nightclub and was sharing a room with my friend that sold handkerchiefs in front of the Jet Club in Olongapo. Mother said she was glad that I had a friend with me. I could see a sense of calmness in Sister Melda face while she was looking at Mother...She knew she had pleased Mother when she found me and brought me back home. After all of the hugging and kissing was finished and I had told my story at least three times; Sister Melda told Mother we need to go to Olongapo and see mama Ligaya and straighten thing out, so I could get my job back. Mother said o.k. And take care of your sister... I will see you tomorrow.

We left going to Olongapo. When we arrived at mama Ligaya house she accused me of taking eighty dollars from Sister Melda. She said if you had taken eighty dollars from me I would have your face in all of the newspapers. I said mama! I don't know anything about eighty dollars the only money that I took was ten dollars, which I was told that I could get if I needed it...I don't steal. Mama Ligaya looked at Sister Melda and changed the subject...she asked me when could I go back to work. I said tomorrow and she said oh! By the way, I still owe you one hundred and thirty pesos. I was very surprised, but I didn't say a word, because I knew this was Sister Melda's ideal. Sister Melda said take the money Vicky, so we can open you a saving account at the bank. I took the money and we left for the bank. When we finished at the bank we caught a jeepney to Sister Melda's house. Her Maid was still at her house, so she introduced her to me. Sister Melda told the Maid to start dinner early because we was going out tonight. I followed her into her bedroom and sit down beside her on the bed; we talked for a few minutes about the trip back. Finally I asked her about Sister Rose and Celia. She said Sister Rose was working in the Money Exchange booth at the Top Hat Club and Celia has a steady boyfriend now. I asked her if it was the guy with the motorcycle; she said yes...I have a guy I want you to meet; he is the friend of my boyfriend...we're to meet them at the Swan Club tonight.

She looked at her watch and said we had better get cleaned up before dinner, so we took our showers and got ready for dinner. After dinner I got up to go to my old room and I saw the Maid sitting on the bed folding clothes...Sister Melda came up behind me and said that she wanted me to stay in her room for a while. We went into her room and started lounged around; I was sitting on the side of her bed until I got sleepy, so I stretched out on the bed. I guess I drifted off to sleep right away, because Sister Melda shook me and said wake up it almost six o, clock; we have to start getting ready. I got up and washed up a bit and changed my clothes. Sister Melda said that I could use her perfume and lipstick. I said thanks! But I don't like the red lipstick...do you have any with a lighter color? She said look through my collection and you can have whatever color you like... there are some earring over there in my jewelry box...you can have the set you like. I said to myself, is this really my Sister Melda? She seem sincere about me

Chapter 5

Cupid Intervention

Sharing her jewelry. I found a set of diamond studded earring and asked if I could have them. She said that I could have anything in her jewelry box, so put the earring on... she looked and said good! Now we can go and meet them.

We hailed a tricycle and went to the main street and caught a jeepney. I asked sister Melda why we had to ride a tricycle when we come up and down our street. She said the tricycles had to stay on the street off the main drag because the jeepney ran the main streets... they have different territory to operate in. Sister Melda said stop right here to the jeepney driver. We got out of the jeepney and went into the Swan Club. I could see her friend sitting at the bar with another young man. We walked up to the bar and I said hi to Sister Melda boyfriend and he introduced his friend to me. He said this is J. C. Wilson. We call him Wilson. He got up from his stool and shook my hand. When we touched and I eyes met I felt like this maybe the one man I have being looking for. My heart started beating real fast... my mind was gone. Then I snapped out of it when someone said lets go nightclubbing. I followed everyone toward the door. Then I heard something drop behind me...I looked...it was an ice cube...I knew the girl that threw it...Sister Melda turn around and went over to the girl and told her something and came back. She said the girl won't try that again. We continued on outside and hailed a jeepney. We climbed aboard the jeepney; Sister Melda and her boyfriend sit on one side of the jeepney and I unconscious sit down beside them leaving Wilson sitting on the other side by himself. When the jeepney pulled off our eyes met and Wilson asked me to sit by him. I got up to move across the aisle to his seat...he reached over and grab my hand and helped me to the seat.When I sit down he continued to hold my hand; I could feel this strange feeling coming over me...I asked myself, is this love at first sight? I know this man make me feel as if I have lost myself control. Working in the Money Exchange booth have given me the opportunity to meet so many young men that I have lost count of, but neither one of them have made me feel like this when I shake their hand. Then I started to think about what the old lady said to me when she read my palm...she said I would go on a trip and when I return I would meet someone that would take me away from here... my mind was running faster than the jeepney that we was riding in...someone was saying something to me...I looked...I looked at Wilson...it was him. He asked again...what are you thinking about... you are so quiet...Please say something. I couldn't think of anything else to say, so I said, "something" and everyone laugh. I finally got control of myself and asked where are we going. Sister Melda said yes, where are we going...how about the new club...the Place to Play Club? Sister Melda said she knew the owner of the new club and it was the cousin of mama Ligaya.

We arrive at the new club and went inside...the club were packed walls to walls people...we finally found an empty table and sit down. Sister Melda's boyfriend realized that it would take quite a while before someone would come to our table to take our order, so he asked us what we wanted to drink and started for the bar; then suddenly turn and asked Wilson to come with him. Wilson got up and accompanied him to the bar. As I watch him walking toward the bar, I wondered what he was thinking about...was he having the same kind of feeling as I was...did he like me...was he wishing the night would never be over as I was? I guess Sister Melda wasn't saying anything to me, because I wasn't hearing anything. They returned to the table with our drinks...Wilson sit back down beside me...our eyes met...the music was too loud for us to do any talking, but our eyes was saying enough. The band played a slow song and Wilson asked me to dance. While holding me in his arms he asked me if I had a boyfriend; I said no! I know a few Sailors that come by where I worked at before, but no boyfriend. I didn't speak real good English but I am sure he understood what I said. I didn't ask him if he had a girl-friend.

The music stop and we went back to our seats. It was time for another round from the bar, so they returned to the bar again. I asked Sister Melda why did that girl throw an ice cube at me; she said don't worry she will never do that again. I said I have seen her before...is that Wilson girlfriend? If that his girlfriend maybe he better go back to her. I became a little upset; when they return I guess Wilson could tell that I was upset. He asked what was wrong and sister Melda said she told me the girl in the Swan Club that threw the ice cube was his girl friend. Wilson said that he knew the girl in the Swan Club and he also knew other girl that was hostess in a club, but tonight he had met me and this was different and he feel like he always wanted to be with me. That was the exact words I had hope he would say to me. The night was going very fast; I didn't want it to end, but you can't stop Father Time. They were Sailors stationed on the Naval Base and had to return to the base that night.

We went outside of the club and caught a jeepney to the main gate of the Naval Base. We got out and said goodnight. Sister Melda and I started walking back to the jeepney stop; I looked back and saw Wilson coming to catch us...I stopped...he came up to me and said I will see you tomorrow o.k. I said I have to start working tomorrow morning in the Money Exchange booth outside of the Jet Club. He grasped my hands and pulled me close to him and kissed me on the cheek and said with a great big smile...goodnight again. Sister Melda and I caught a jeepney and went home. When we arrived I looked inside my room and the Maid was sleeping in my bed. Sister Melda saw what was happening and said I could sleep in her room tonight and I could get my room back tomorrow. We went into her room and jumped into bed, but neither one of us could go to sleep, so we got up and went into the kitchen to look for something to eat. I found some liver worth spread and we made liver worth sandwiches. As I sit at the table eating my sandwiches, I started to thinking about Wilson and how he made me feel. Sister Melda interrupted my thought asking me if I was thinking about Wilson and if I liked him. I said very much!

She said she was going to find out if Wilson was married. The word married brought my thoughts to a complete stop. I asked her if she thought Wilson was married, because I didn't see a wedding band on his finger. She said that anyone could remove their wedding band from their finger if they want to keep their marriage a secret. I said like you, because you have taken your wedding ring off. She looked at me kinder funny and said lets go to bed; you have to work tomorrow. I guess I hit a sore nerve when I reminded her about her wedding ring. I went to bed more puzzled now than before about Wilson... finally I did fall asleep. The next day while I was getting ready for work, I could hear Sister Melda talking to her Maid. She said she needed her to move back to her house, because her sister had returned and needed her room back. She also said that she would increase her salary to pay for her transportation back and forth to work. The Maid said o.k. And left the room.

Finally it was time for me to go back to work...I was thinking of everything except work...I wondered if this is love...can it be love? I was riding on cloud nine even in the jeepney, if the jeepney had not stopped for another passenger at my stop I would have went right pass it. I really couldn't figure out what was happening to me...it feel as if a new part of my body has woken. I have met a lot of young men but no one has made me feel like this before. I got out of the jeepney and started for the front door of the Swan Club. A girl was standing outside of the door as if she was waiting for me...I looked at her... she said someone is inside waiting for you...I said my Mother... she said a guy. I thought to myself...do I know a guy that come into town this early...I started to walking real fast...I went straight to the bar counter instead of going upstairs to pick up the money for the Money Exchange. My heart started to pounding so hard I believe I could hear it...it must be Wilson...I still couldn't see clearly who he was...I started walking even faster...then I could see that it was Wilson sitting on the bar stool. I had to get myself together, because I didn't want him to know I was this happy to see him. He turned around to face me as I walked up to the counter. He had a big smile on his face...I think he was just as glad to see me, as I was he. Before he could say a word I started asking questions...why are you here so early? Did you go straight to the base when we left you guys last night? Before he could answer, I said I have to go upstairs to count my money for the Money Exchange...are you going to be here when I comeback or are you going back to the base? Finally I let him answer...he said I will be here when you come back. When I was walking away toward the stairs, I said to myself...slow down and take it easy with the questions, because your English is not very good and he might not understand everything you are saying.

When I got upstairs mama Ligaya had just woke up and was lounging around on the bed as if she was dreading to get today started. I asked who was working the night shift. She said the lady that was working the day shift before I left town. She gave me the money and I hurried to count it because Wilson was waiting for me. When I finished counting the money I said good day to mama Ligaya and went downstairs. Wilson was still waiting at the bar. I asked him if he was going back to the base. He said he was going with me to my Money Exchange booth. We went outside and caught a jeepney to Money Exchange booth at the Jet Club. Everyone including the Club Manager welcomed me back. I opened up the booth and put my money in the drawer and got ready for the first customer. Wilson pulled up a chair to the booth door and sit down. I asked him if he had breakfast all ready. He said his cook on the tugboat had prepared him a big breakfast. I asked him why he didn't work today. He said he took the day off to be with me. From that moment on I felt as if I had known him forever, but I realize we only met last night. I wonder does he feel the same way as I do about our relationship...Am I in this alone? A tapping on the booth counter snapped me out of my thoughts; a Sailor had arrived wanting to exchange his dollars. When my customer left I sit back down and couldn't help noticing Wilson watching every move I made. We continued in I effort to learn as much as possible about each other in the shortest time possible. Father Time kept creeping along with our conversation and before long it was lunch time. Wilson said it was lunchtime and he was going across the street to the Shangri La Restaurant to eat lunch; he asked me what I want him to bring back for me to eat. As always, I like noodles, so I asked him to bring me back noodles.

When Wilson left the girl at the counter got noisy and came over asking about my vacation, but I knew she just wanted to find out the status on Wilson. I paused and looked at her for a split second and decided to tell her what she really wanted to know...Wilson was my boyfriend. Then I remembered the old lady that was reading everyone palms in the Jet Club, so I asked my nosey girl friend if she knew what happened to the old lady. She said no one really knew her name or where she came from...everyone only remember her coming in the club...it seem as though she disappeared into thin air.

She asked why Wilson had come out into Town so early; I told her he had taken the day off work. She looked around and saw Wilson coming through the door and she got up and returned to the counter. Wilson came over to me and gave me the food container. I started to put it aside, but Wilson wanted me to go ahead and eat, because he was staying a while longer. I got up to get me a drink from the bar...I asked him if he wanted something to drink. He said yes, I would like a beer and gave me the money to pay for our drinks. I got our drinks and returned to the booth and ate my lunch while he watched. Finally after sitting for so long I could tell that he was getting a little restless. A few minutes later he saw one of his friends passing...he jumped up and said he was going to catch him and he would be back by the end of my shift.

When he left I started to thinking about what the old lady had told me about meeting someone...Could Wilson be the one...if I could only see her again and ask. A jeepney stop in front of my booth and the lady working the night shift got out...I looked at my watch...I thought to myself how time had passed so fast. She came in and we counted the money and just as I was leaving the booth Wilson came back and asked if I was leaving for home now. I said yes I have just been relieved. He asked if we could meet somewhere to night. I said yes, where would you like to meet? He said right here in front of the Jet Club at about seven. I said o.k. Seven will be fine. I caught a jeepney and left for home. When I arrived Sister Melda was getting ready to meet her friend later that night. She asked me what I was doing tonight. I told her I was meeting Wilson at seven in front of the Jet Club. She said I am meeting my friend at the Supreme Club, I will wait for you and we can go together. I said o.k. We sit around making small talk for a while. I decided to go and take a shower and get ready for tonight. Sister Melda said the Maid had cooked dinner, so I needed to eat something before I went out tonight. I ate dinner and brushed my teeth again and it was time to go. We went outside and caught a tricycle to the jeepney stop. We got into a waiting jeepney and we were off to meet our dates for tonight. We arrived a few minute early so we waited in front of the Jet Club for our dates to arrive. A few minutes later I saw Sister Melda boyfriend and Wilson coming down the street toward us.

There seem to be something wrong with Wilson, because he just bump into my sister boyfriend. When they walked up to us, I could see that Wilson was drunk...I was completely disgusted...my night was ruined...I didn't know how to act around a drunken guy...all of a sudden I thought about just turning around and going back home. Then Sister Melda boyfriend said let's go into the Supreme Club and everyone turned and started down the street to the Club. I followed behind everyone. I didn't really know what to do other than follow alone with everyone else. We went inside of the club and were seated. As soon as we was seated Wilson wanted to dance, so he grab my hand and tried to pull me out on the floor. His friend finally got him to sit down, because he was falling all over the place. I were completely disgusted...I felt sorry for him...I wandered if he will be doing this all of the time...I like him very much, but the man I am looking at now is different from the man I met a few days ago. Sister Melda looked at me and said Wilson is drunk...it's still early...where where he drinking at? I told her that I didn't know and that he was with me all day until three this afternoon and he left with another friend. Wilson friend apologized for him, because he could tell that I was either mad or embarrassed. While I were sitting there my mind started running away with thought...is this the man I thought I loved at first sight...it can't be...look at him ...he don't know who I am...I have seen people drank but they didn't act or look like him. I couldn't take this seen any more, so I told Sister Melda I was going home, because I have to work tomorrow and Wilson is completely out of it anyway. I got up from my seat and Wilson tried to pull me to him and kiss me...I pushed him away. Sister Melda told her boyfriend she was going home with me and for him to take Wilson back to the base. We said goodbye and left the club. When we got home Sister Melda said she have never seen Wilson drunk like that before, and maybe someone had put drugs in his drink. Then I started to think about him again. Why would someone do that to him? I felt very sorry for him, so I prayed for him to be strong and safe that night. I got into bed and finally calmed down enough to fall asleep.

The Maid woke me up and said that breakfast was ready, so I got up and went to the bathroom and got cleaned up. I went back into my bedroom and got dressed for breakfast. I came back to the kitchen and got my breakfast. Sister Melda came out of her room brushing her teeth. When she finished brushing her teeth she poured herself a cup of coffee and sit down at the table with me. We made small talk until she finished her coffee. Then she decided to go back to bed. I got my things together and left for work. I stopped at the Swan Club to get the money for my booth. While I was counting the money she gave me a letter. I glance at it to see whom it was from and continued to count the money. I will read the letter when I get to my booth and settle in. Mama Ligaya said she was changing me to the night shift starting the next day, because the lady on the night shift has a sick kid. I said o.k. And left for the Money Exchange booth.

When I arrived at the Jet Club and went into my booth, I immediately started to get everything situated so I could sit down and relax before the customers start arriving. Once I got comfortable I remembered the letter I had in my bag, so I retrieved it and started reading it. This young man was very upset because he hadn't received a letter from me, so this is his final letter to me if I don't write him. I really don't know what to say to this guy...he is very nice, but I don't have any feeling for him. Then I thought about how I felt about Wilson and I didn't want anything to come between him and me, so I said to myself, I guess this will be the last letter you will write, because I am in love with Wilson. Then I heard someone knocking on the booth window...it was one of my friend that sale handkerchiefs in front of my booth. She asked where have I been and I told her I had been around. Before she could say anything else someone called her up the street, so she ran up the street toward the person that was calling her. I tried to see who it was but the person was too far away. I sit back down and started thinking about Wilson...would I see him tonight...I really hope so. Then I realized I was getting very sleepy, so I opened the door to the booth and let fresh air come inside. I had a few more customers to come by…sometime they would stay and chat for a while. Before I knew it; it was five in the afternoon and time for me to go home. My relief was on time. She asked if I had talked to mama Ligaya about coming in on the night shift tomorrow. I told her I had and asked how her kid was getting alone. She said the kid was feeling better. I gathered my thing and went out and caught a jeepney for home.

When I arrived the maid was leaving for the day; she said my dinner was ready and I said o.k. I will see you tomorrow. I peeped into Sister Melda room, but she was gone, so I sit down and ate dinner. After finishing dinner and washing the dishes I went into my room and sit on the side of the bed. Just like always in recent days, I started to think about Wilson. If I could only see the old lady again that tell your fortune; I could ask her where my relationship with Wilson was going. I was thinking about everything…my job… My Mother…should I tell her about my relationship with Wilson… finally I decided to just let thing workout by itself and stretched out on my bed. I fell asleep…I felt someone tugging on my shoulder and saying, wake up! Wake up! Wilson is here…I saw him while I was on the base and he wanted to come with me home and surprise you. Well I was surprised. I got up and washed my face and brush my teeth again. I hurried to the living room to see Wilson. When I walked into the living room Sister Melda got up and went into her room. I casualty walked in and sit down in the chair across from him and ask what was he doing here? He said I wanted to see you, that's why I am here. I said you have other girl friends, why you don't go see them? He said because you are the one I want to see…let me see your address book. I said what address book you are talking about? He said the one your sister told me about. I said to myself, why did Sister Melda tell him about my address book? So I said wait here I will be right back. I went into Sister Melda's room and asked her why she had told Wilson about my address book. She said Wilson had asked her if I had a boyfriend and she said I didn't have a boyfriend she knew of, but I had a sizable collection of addresses in my address book. So I went into my room and got my address book and came back to Sister Melda's room and hurried to copy down some of the addresses in my book. I went back to the living room where Wilson was sitting and sit back down across from him. He asked to see my address book and I gave it to him. After looking through it for a few seconds, he asked me which one of the guys in my book I was serious about. I said neither one. Then he said I am serious about this. Please tell me which one. I said I am serious too... neither one. He gave the book back to me and said, tear it up. I got up and went into Sister Melda's room and started acting as if I was talking to her she started giggling...I said stop he will hear you...I copied some more of the Address from the book.

I returned to the room...he was not smiling...he said if you care for me then tear up the book. I said," What! Then stared at him for a brief second and said these are only addresses, they don't mean a thing. He said if they don't mean a thing then tear up the book. I gave him the book and said you tear it up...he did...he even burned it. When he finished burning the book he said give me the copies you made when you went into your sister room. He had figured out what I was trying to do, so I got up and went into my sister room and got the copies for him. When I came back with the copy he told me to tear it up. I tore the copy up...I didn't feel bad, I probably would have done anything he asked me to, because I have this burning feeling in my heart and it intensify more and more when I am with him. This time I sit down beside him... he tried to kiss me...I let him...I felt like I was in heaven when I was in his arms. I don't know just how he feel about our relationship, but it seem as though he want me all to himself and that fine with me. He wanted to know all about my job...how much was my salary and just how often I had to work. I told him my monthly salary were eighty pesos a month. He said he would give me a hundred pesos a month if I stop working in the Money Exchange. We talked about how I used my pay; I explained to him how important my salary was to me. I told him that I gave half of my salary to my Mother, because she didn't have a steady job. He said not to worry; if I quit the job at the Money Exchange he would give me one hundred pesos and also help my family. He asked me to please seriously think about what he had said and let him knew when he return, because he had to work the next night. That's all I remember hearing him say between kisses, which I didn't want him to ever stop.

Sister Melda walked into the living interrupting us saying she was off to meet her boyfriend…did we want to come along. We both were silent, so she said she would see us later on that night. We were somewhat glad she was leaving, because we wanted so much to be alone. When she was gone he held me in his arms and we talked and kissed and talked some more. We really got to know each other thoughts and deep feelings. About ten that night we were shocked out of our little dream world when Sister Melda came back home. Wilson senses that it was time for him to go so he kissed me goodbye and said he would see me after his duty the next day.

I went outside with Wilson and called a tricycle and reminded Wilson how much he was suppose to pay, because the tricycle driver would sometime try and over charge American. He boarded the tricycle and left for the base and I went back inside the house. I went to Sister Melda's room to talk about Wilson; I told her I think Wilson was very serious about our relationship. She said don't you get to serious about him because I haven't found out whether he's married or not. I was totally convinced that Wilson was telling me the truth about him being single. I just couldn't picture him being married and saying the things he have said to me. I could sense and feel the love he had for me and I loved him back. I told her I was going to bed, so I went into my room and got ready for bed. When I got into bed my mind started to wondering about everything…was he married… did he love me…was I being naive, because I were so young? Finally sleep interrupted my thoughts as I drifted off to sleep.

The next morning I woke up feeling sluggish, I didn't let that stop me. I got cleaned up and had my breakfast. I was about to finish my coffee when Sister Melda came into the room. I told her I was going to Calapacuan to visit Mother. She said if I would wait she would accompany me to Calapacuan. She had breakfast and went to the back porch and told the Maid we was leaving and would return before she left for the day.

When we arrived in Calapacuan everyone was busy cleaning frogs. I quickly joined in to help them with the cleaning. Mother saw the frog p on my hand…she told me to wash it off quickly, because the p will cause warts to grown on my hand. I quickly washed my hands and left the cleaning to Brother Etong. Brother Etong had caught the frogs early that morning and brought them home. He always looks for something to help feed the family. Mother started preparing the vegetables to be cooked. Sister Melda surprising step in and volunteered to help her prepare the vegetables. Sister Linda was in the living room playing with little Gina. I took a seat at the kitchen table near Mother...I broke the news to her...I said Mother I have met an American Sailor that I like very much...he is a very nice guy and he seem to have very serious feeling about me...I held my breath waiting for her reply. She said Sailors have a girl friend in every port and she doesn't think they are the marrying kind. I looked at my Mother with all of the seriousness my little body to produce and said that I like him very much. She understood how I felt because she looked at Sister Melda and said keep an eye on your sister.

Then she turned to me and asked how old Wilson was. I said he is twenty-one years old. She paused for a while and said he is still young maybe he will be all right...I like to meet him one of these days. I said thanks Mother for the vote of confidence. Then changing the subject...I asked how Sister Maria was getting alone. She replied... as well as she can be...your brother Celino left home and have not returned yet...I feel so sorry for her, because of the way your brother is treating her...he is just like his father...always running around and chasing other women...I gave up on your father a long time ago... thank God he have not come back. Brother Etong was listening in on our conversation and I could see in his eyes and smiles that he was glad Father had not returned and hope he will never return. Mother said your Sister Maria's daughter has a steady boyfriend, he is a Mexican American Sailor... her daughter is helping her now.

Finally the food was cooked and on the table, so we all sat down and ate. I always eat a lot when Mother cook, so when everyone finished stuffing their stomach, we cleaned off the table and washed the dishes. Now it was storytelling time. Mother started because she had a new topic and she had hoped it would benefit me. She begin saying...most all of the Sailors have a girl friend in every port... your Father was in the Philippines Constabulary and he was sent all over the Philippines and I know for a fact that he had a girl friends all over...Once he returned home with a young lady he claimed was his Aunt Sally's daughter that lived in Pangasinan...I welcomed the young lady to our house. Your Father had to go outside to the rest room…I kept talking to the young lady and finally asked her how was her Father, Mr. Henry was doing? The young lady assured me that her father was doing just fine…I knew that Mr. Henry had been dead for five years. I was really mad…my husband bringing a woman here right under my nose…taking me for a fool…I didn't know what to do…finally I decided to let it go until tomorrow…That night when we all laid down on our mats to sleep my dear husband was at my side…I tried to pretend that I was asleep, but I fell asleep…the chicken started crowing and woke me up…I reached for your Father…he was gone…I looked around in the dark room and saw him across the room kissing the young lady…I jumped up and went into the kitchen where the bow and arrow was kept hanging on the wall. I grab the bow and found an arrow…I tried to shoot both of them, but the arrow kept slipping from my hand…I was so mad that I could not think straight…they jumped up and grab their bag and ran outside.

I followed them trying to get the bow and arrow to work… neighbors came outside to see what's was going on; then I realized that I was in my pajamas and ran back in the house…your Father and the girl ran out without their shoes they only had enough time to grab their bag…your Father never came back for a very long time. Sister Melda said, "You're a woman Robin Hood". Everyone Laughed, I asked Mother what happen to the bow and arrow; she said she burned it and their shoes for firewood. Sister Linda asked if they came back for their shoes. Mother said no. Mother looked at me very serious with a twinkle in her eye and said, I have told you this story, which is true, and I hope you can understand the point I am trying to make… when men in the Military go from place to place they find girl friends in those places…even your Father does it too…please be careful in this relationship…don't get to involved to quick, because you can get hurt…look at your Father, he never send or bring any money into this house…I have to take care of the family by myself.

Mother told sister Melda again to make sure she keeps an eye on me. Sister Melda asked me the time and I told her it was 2 P.M. and she said we would have to go back to Olongapo, because she was meeting her boyfriend at five. I said o.k. I have to work tonight too. So we left for Olongapo. When we arrived the power was out and the maid was waiting for the power to come back on so she could do the ironing, Sister Melda told her to go and cook and when she finish she could go home early. Sister Melda went and took a shower so she could get ready for her date. I waited patiently for her to finish in the shower so I could take my shower, eat and go to work. Finally she came out and I went in and took my shower. As soon as I came out and dried off the power came on. I was so happy the power came back on because I didn't want to work in the Money Exchange booth by candlelight. All of the bad people…robbers, rapist and gangs come out when the power is out.

When I arrived at the Money Exchange booth I saw a man working the booth, he said he was the husband of the lady that took my place working days. I asked when she would be back to work; he said she would be back the next day. I said good night to him and took my seat; then I noticed it was getting a little chilly so I closed the door of the booth.

Before I could really get comfortable, someone started knocking on the door, so I opened it…it was Sister Rose. She pulled a chair up from one of the tables and sit down. The first thing she said to me was, "You are back", I said yes I am back home again…what are you doing now? She said she was just bumming around. I told her that I knew about her and Sopring staying together. She said yes, they were living in a small place in Barrio, Barretto. I asked her was she still writing Mike; She said not recently, the last time she heard from him, he told her they had to remove one of his leg and she have not heard from him since. She said she had lost interest in Mike because she really liked Sopring, he were a really hard working man and he cared about her and had promised to take care of her if she quit working at the Top Hat Club. Sopring worked in the night Club as a Houseboy, he help clean the place and assist the hostess with their orders from the bar. She said she still works at the Top Hat Club for Commission only…she would not accompany anyone outside of the bar and Sopring wanted her to stop working completely when they get a better place to stay. She said Sopring wanted a better life for her and him and she trusted him to make a better life for her. I said I hope you and him will be happy, because everyone deserves a good life.

I said Sister Melda introduced me to a Sailor by the name of Wilson; she said yes I have seen him because she introduced him to me when I was working in the Money Exchange booth at the Top Hat Club...do you remember going away and leaving me her in the Money Exchange booth; well mama Ligaya asked me to work the booth At the Top Hat Club for a while, but I quit because the Sailors and Marines would come by and grab and pull on me all the time...I got tired of it and quit working in the booth...Wilson is a nice guy. I said that I think so to, and I believe he is serious about his feeling toward me. She said I wish you all the luck in the world with him. I thanked her and asked about her daughter Gina. She said her and Sopring was going to get her as soon as they get a larger place... things are moving a little slow in their life, but they are determined to make a good life for themselves. She also said that Sopring had told her he loved her and would dedicate his life trying to make her happy. I told her that was wonderful, because most of the Filipino men would not have anything to do with a girl that works in the club as a Hostess. Before we could finish our conversation about Sopring, he walked up to the booth door and said hello to Sister Rose and me. Sister Rose quickly asked him if he had met me; he said he had seen me around and spoke to me, but we haven't been formally introduced, so we shook hands and said hello. Sopring asked Sister Rose if she was going to work that night. She told him she was not going to work and that she had came to meet him. She then asked him to go into the club and get her a coke because she was really thirsty. He started to the bar and turned and asked me if I would also like a coke. I said no and thanked him. When he came back he gave Sister Rose her drink and took a seat next to her. They started talking about things they wanted to do when they save enough money. Before long everybody on the streets was going home and all the businesses was closing up for the night...that was my cue to close up my booth and go home. Then I remembered that I would start back to working the day shift tomorrow morning, so I started to speed up my closing process. Finally I had my booth closed ...I thought to myself...I hope Wilson will be off work tomorrow...I can't wait to see him again. I said goodnight and goodbye to Sister Rose and Sopring. I told Sister Rose to take Sopring to Calapacuan the next time she go see her Daughter

Gina and Mother. I started to leave and the Club Manager asked me to wait for him. He came to me and said it was dangerous for me to be along in the streets because the light on one side of the street were out, so he accompany me to the Swan Club to turn in the money from the Money Exchange booth. Upon arrival I saw Sister Melda waiting for me; she was carrying a small flashlight. The Club Manager wife was waiting for him too; she had a hand full of candles and she gave Sister Melda and me four of the candles and told us to be real careful because the street light had being acting weird for quite a while. We thanked her for the candles and said good night. When we got home it was one thirty in the morning. We hurried to get ready for bed. Sister Melda lit one of the candles and placed it in the middle of the floor even though the lights were still on. She said she would leave the candle on the floor just in case the power goes out and we have to get up for some reason and we wouldn't stumble over something and hurt ourselves. I went to bed and fell asleep right away, because it had being a long day for me. I don't know if the lights went off or stayed on all night, because I didn't wake up until the next morning.

I got up that morning even though I didn't feel like going to work, but I was determined to go in and work that morning. I looked around for the Maid, but she was nowhere in sight, so I started breakfast. I made coffee and went across the street to the Sari Sari Store for bread. When I came back Sister Melda was up; she asked me if I were working today or tonight. I told her I was working today. She said Wilson would be off tonight. I said o.k. I can't wait to see him. I told her the coffee were ready. She said she would have a cup of coffee and go back to bed. I finished breakfast and got ready for work.

When I arrived at mama Ligaya place to pick up the money for the Money Exchange; she were still counting the money. She said she was not feeling very good. We made small talk for a few minutes while she was counting the money. When she finished I took the money for my booth and left. When I arrived at the Money Exchange booth the power were out. I thought to myself what was going on with the power. After about an hour it came back on. The time was going pretty fast...at around ten I saw Wilson coming down the street...I were so glad to see him. He came up and gave me a big kiss; I kissed him back. I asked him why he was out in Olongapo so early; he said he didn't have to work so he came out to see me. He pulled up a chair and sit down beside me and held my hand and started to caress it. I had a small wart on my right index finger and I was trying my best to keep him from seeing it. Finally he asked me why I was holding my hand half closed. I was so embarrass, but I managed to tell him that a frog had p.p. on my finger and gave it a wart. He smiled and told me not to worry about my wart and kissed my hand. Then he said, "I have something serious to ask you". I said o.k. Please do. He asked me if I were eighteen years old and if I had ever slept with a man. I were somewhat surprised, but I also knew he were serious, so I answered his question. I told him that I were eighteen years old and had never slept with a man. I also reminded him that I had previous told him that I didn't have a boyfriend. He told me that he had fallen in love with me and he didn't want me to continue working in the Money Exchange booth where all the guys come and talk to me and certainly didn't want them to try and touch me. He asked how much I were getting paid to work in the Money Exchange. I told him I was getting paid eighty pesos a month and I was helping my mother. He said he would give me eighty pesos a month and help my Mother if I would stop working in the Money Exchange. He said I didn't have to give him an answer right away, but he did want me to think about it. I were speechless and surprised for a brief moment, because I didn't know that he was this serious about I relationship. Finally after getting over the initial shock I assured him that I would think about it and let him know my decision as soon as possible. He got up from his chair and said he was going across the street to get a manicure and he would be right back. He gave me a quick kiss and left. I few minutes later a girl by the name of Lucy came over to my booth and asked me what her steady boyfriend was doing in my booth. I asked her whom were she talking about, because Wilson was the only guy that had been at my booth. She asked why I didn't come and work in the Club and be a Hostess, because I was trying to take the girls steady boyfriends away. I said Miss Lucy I work in the Money Exchange booth and I don't try to encourage your boyfriend to come and talk to me; when they come and change their money they stay and talk for a few minutes. If you don't want your boyfriend to come to my booth then tell them to stay away.

When Wilson came back I were still mad. I told him to tell his steady girlfriend that I was not trying to take him away from her. He asked whom were I talking about? I said Lucy your steady girlfriend...you better go to your girlfriend, because I don't want her or anyone else coming here and telling me they are your steady girlfriends...you better go now. He turned around and left; he said he would be right back. I felt kinder bad not giving him a chance to explain before I asked him to leave. I sat back down and tried to get comfortable and stop thinking about what had happened. I heard someone knocking on the door of my booth; I opened the door it was the girl that work behind the counter. She said she were going across the street to the restaurant to get something to eat for lunch and if I wanted something she would bring it. I looked at my watch...it was eleven o, clock. I said yes I wanted something for lunch...bring me some chicken adobo. I gave her ten pesos. She asked me if I were sure that chicken adobo was all that I wanted. I said yes and she was off to the restaurant. When she returned she brought me my chicken adobo, a coke and a piece of cake. She said today is my birthday and I brought you a piece of my cake. I gave her a hug and wished her a happy birthday. When she left I sit down and ate my lunch thinking about how gentle Wilson was when he would hug and kiss me. Then I thought about him even kissing my hands. Then I thought maybe I have yet to meet the right guy for me. My change of thought was broken when one of the girls that selling handkerchief came up to my booth counter and told me she saw the guy that sit in my booth standing outside of the Silver Dollar Club talking to Lucy. I said I knew he was her boyfriend and he come by and talk to me sometime. She said I have to work the other side of the street I will see you later. When she left I closed up and went to the ladies room. On my way back to my booth I saw someone standing beside the door that leads into my booth... my heart started to pound so fast I barely could control myself... could it be Wilson...did he come back...please God let it be him... what if he came back to only say goodbye? I hurried to my booth... it was Wilson...our eyes met...he held out his arms...I ran into his arms...he kissed me like never before and I kissed him back. We were brought back to reality when a Sailor started banging on the counter asking to change his dollars. I quickly changed his dollars and let him go on his way. I turned around to see what Wilson were doing and he had taken a seat by my chair; he said please sit down I have something very important to tell you. I took my seat beside him. This was the second time I had seen Wilson look so serious. He took my hand and said, "Vicky I am really and truly in love with you and I don't want to see you hurt like you was when that girl came by earlier today". My heart started moving so fast I thought it was going to jump out of my chest. He said when he first met me he knew that I was the one for him, but he wanted to be sure before he committed himself, because his experience with the ladies here in the Philippines has proven to be a very short relationship…like they would be with him today and someone else tomorrow. He realize they were Club Hostess and he have not spent any time with girls other than club hostess before he met me, but he had to be sure of my feeling before he would reveal his feelings. He said when you got upset with me when that girl came over; he knew then that I care for him and wanted to be with him. He was so right; I couldn't think of anyone else in the world that I wanted to be with other than him. He said do you still remember me asking you to quit this job and let me take care of you…well I still feel the same way…I don't want these Hostess in your face talking about being my girl friend and definite don't want the drunken Sailors and Marines to be coming by here pulling and tugging on you.

This is the first time anyone other than my relatives had showed any real feeling of love and caring for me…I was overwhelmed…I started to cry. He asked me what was wrong. I couldn't answer, so he said please don't cry I am not going to leave you. He wiped the tears from my face and kissed me again. Then he asked me if I had lunch; I said yes, how about you? He said no, but he would get something later on. Sitting there beside him…my mind started to wondering again…I thought to myself; this is it…I will not hold back my love …I will trust him to do right by me, because now I know he love me as much as I love him. I don't know how long we sit there saying nothing. Then finally he said to me say something and I said, "Something", He laughed and said do you remember the first time we met and I said say something and you said something. We both laughed.

My customers started arriving to get their dollars changed. A few Sailors came by and Wilson said hi to them. He told me that they worked on Tug Boats like him on the base. Wilson sat quietly for a while and watched me work. Finally he broke the silence and asked me if I had thought anymore about quitting my job. I told him yes and I was going to quit as soon as my boss could find someone else. I turned and looked at him; he appeared to be real happy now. Then he became serious again. He said the reason he wanted me to quit my job here is because there are so many bad people hanging out in the street that will do anything including trying to rob my Money Exchange booth, and he didn't want me to get hurt. He took my hands and pull me to him and kissed me...I kissed him back...I had almost forgotten that I was working; then I came back to reality...I told him I had to try and concentrate on my work. As I turned from him to the booth counter I finally realized what I had done. I had completely let my barriers down and allowed myself to be swept off of my feet. Once again I found myself thinking to myself even though he was sitting behind me...if he care enough for me to want to take care of me...I guess I will be safe with him.

From out of nowhere one of my friends that sale handkerchiefs appeared at my booth counter. She saw Wilson sitting behind me, so she asked him if he wanted to buy a handkerchief. Wilson pulled a handkerchief from his pocket and held it up for her inspection. Then she said in our native language...he really likes you and then she was off to explore the other side of the street. When she disappeared from the counter Wilson asked me what my friend say to me to make me smile like I did. I told him she said that she think you really like me. He said she is right I do like you very much.

We continued talking about ourselves until the night shift lady came. She asked me if Wilson were my boyfriend. I said yes and pickup my belonging and walked out the door with Wilson. We decided to have an early dinner, so we went across the street to the Shangri La Restaurant. I purposely went to the side of the restaurant where one of my friends worked. I guess I wanted to show Wilson off. My friend promptly came to our table; she said she hadn't seen me for quite a while, but she did hear that I had gone to Angeles City. I said yes I did go to Angeles City on vacation. She smiled and asked to take our order. I ordered Noodles and a coke and he ordered a shrimp salad and a beer. I looked at him and said, "Shrimp salad and beer"... he smiled and told the waitress to change his drink to water.

Finally the waitress returned with our order. We had our meal and left going to Sister Melda's house where I live. When we arrived she was laying across her bed. She got up and came to the living room where Wilson and I were sitting. She said hello to Wilson. I figured it was time for me to tell her what Wilson and I was planning to do, because I knew mama Ligaya would tell her as soon as I quit my job. I took a deep breath and said, "Sister Melda, I am quitting my job and staying home, because Wilson don't want me to work and he is going to give me enough money to take care of myself". Sister Melda sat down in the chair like she was really upset. She accused Wilson of being married. He looked at her with a puzzled expression on his face and told her she must be thinking of someone else, because he have had a few girlfriend around, but he was not married. Then she accused him of having kids back in the United States. Wilson asked her where she had gotten her off the wall ideals about him being married and having kids. She wouldn't answer him; she angrily got up and started for her room. Then turned and said in our native language...He is married Vicky and he has kids too.

Wilson was really puzzled about what sister Melda had accused him of; he asked me what she had said to me in Tagalog. I told him what she had said and assured him that it didn't matter. He said he knew I was feeling a little doubt as to what was going on, but I could be sure that if he was married he wouldn't have told me that he was in love with me and if he was looking for someone to just fool around with he could have chosen one of the girl that work in the club, because they don't care who they mess around with...I don't want to hurt you, I just want to love you...Your sister introduce me to you...now that I am serious about you she trying to break us up...what's wrong with her? I told him I didn't know why Sister Melda had changed the way she feel about him, but I didn't wanted him to worry and I hadn't changed the way I feel about him. We hug and kissed.

The door of Sister Melda's room opened and she came out and said she would see us lovebirds later and left the house in a big hurry. It was a relief to see her leave, because she had caused me a lot of tension and mix feeling about my relationship with Wilson. I knew for a fact that I love him and wanted to be with him and couldn't help wondering if this feeling was brought on because of the way Sister Melda is acting. As we sat and looked at each other I knew that this was the man for me and I wanted to give myself to him. I have met a lot of young men in my life, but Wilson is the first one that I have had strong feeling for from the first time I laid eyes on him. So this is what love is all about...having a powerful desire to make love to the man you love for the first time. I don't know how it feels to make love, but if it make me feel as good physically as it does mentally; I know I will love it. I could tell by the way Wilson was looking at me that he wanted to make love to me as much as I wanted to make love to him. Finally the words came from his mouth...will you go with me to my hotel room...I love you and want to make love to you. The only thing that surprised me about what he said was that he wanted to go to his hotel room. I wanted to go to my room, but I didn't want to change a thing about this moment, so I said yes and went into my room and grab a few things to take with me.

When we arrived at the hotel; I started thinking about what my Mother would say if she knew what I was about to do, so I asked him to go in first and I would follow. I looked up and down the street for any familiar face...I didn't see one, so I hurried into the hotel. Wilson was waiting at the hotel desk and saying something to the desk clerk and gave him some more money. He knew that I was shy about being in a hotel so he started for his room and I followed him. As I was walking down the hall behind Wilson; my mind started to wandering...I am in hotel 456...I have passed this hotel going to work countless times...I remember the big shining numbers...could Mother be somewhere outside and saw me coming into this hotel? My change of thought was broken when we arrived at the door to his room. He unlocked the door and we walked into the room. He turned around and asked if the room would do for the weekend. I said you don't have to go back to the base tonight; he said no, I have the weekend off. I walked over to the bed and took a seat. He started for the door and said he would be right back. My mind started rambling again...is he nervous like I am...do he really and truly love me...am I making a big mistake...mistake or not...I am here and I love him and will always love him. The door open and he walked in with two beers and a coke. He said that he forgot to ask me if I wanted something to eat or drink, but he brought a coke any way. I told him that I didn't want anything to eat and the coke would be fine. He opened one of the beers and took a drink; I knew that he was a little nervous to; this made me feel a little better. He sat beside me on the bed and took off his shirt. I said oh! I forgot to bring my nightgown; he told me I could use his undershirt, so I took it and went into the bathroom. I sat down on the side of the bathtub. Then I thought, "What have I got myself into now", then I heard him call out if I was all right. I said yes and got up and took my clothes off and put his shirt on and came out. I walked straight to the bed and lay down beside him wondering what would happen next. I was very nervous and started shaking; he asked if I was all right...I said yes! He tried to cover me with the sheet...I guess he thought I was cold...then he reached for his beer. I thought to myself; is he nervous. Then he wrapped his arms around me and started to kissing me passionately...I kissed him back...he took my shirt off and I gave myself to him the best as I knew how.

When it was over we laid in each other arms gasping for air. I was so engrossed in the act I almost forgot the pain I felt when he entered me. He was very gentle with me and when the pain went away and I started to enjoy myself. We lay speechless in each other arms; then my mind started to doubt the serious of our relationship...what if I get pregnant? Will he marry me? What if Mother find out? Then I said to myself, "I am fully committed, I love this man...what happens... happens. He kissed me and broke my chain of thought. Finally we drifted off to sleep.

The next morning we had each other again...got up and took our showers and started to get dress. Wilson noticed a blood stain on his undershirt that I had worn and ask if I was all right. I assured him that I was all right as I was getting dressed. I had to go home and get ready for work. It was about five that morning when we left his hotel room. He said he was going back to the base and change clothes and would come back by the Money Exchange to visit with me. I left first because I was still afraid someone would see me and tell Mother. He followed me out a few minutes later and went back to the Naval Base.

When I got home Sister Melda was not there, so I decided that I wanted to take a bath. We didn't have a bathtub, so I used the container the Maid uses to wash clothes. I filled it about half full with warm water and sit in it until it started to get cold. The bath was very soothing. Just as I finished toweling myself off Sister Melda came home. As soon as she came into the house and saw me, she asked if Wilson were still sleeping. I said Wilson is not here and he didn't stay here last night. She said well I didn't see him on his Tug Boat. I said, oh! You slept on the Tug Boat. She said she just didn't see him on the Boat. I said he didn't sleep here either and I have to go to work now...see you later. When I arrive at mama Ligaya place to pick up the money for the Money Exchange booth; I told her I was leaving my job. She asked me why; I told her my boyfriend didn't like for me to work in the Money Exchange booth. She said oh! You have found yourself a boyfriend...what ship is he on? I said he is not on a ship; he is station on the Naval Base. She said she was glad I had found someone that was stationed on the base, because the Sailors on the ships go away all the time. She asked when I want to quit; I told her as soon as she could find a replacement for me. She said she could probably find me a replacement in about five day. I thanked her and left for the Money Exchange.

When I arrived and got out of the jeepney I saw Wilson standing in front of The Money Exchange booth smiling. He met me and gave me a kiss. We turned and went inside the Jet Club to the Money Exchange both. Wilson pulled up a chair to the door of the Money Exchange and sit down. I got everything ready in the booth so I could serve my customer when they arrive. When I finished I sat by the booth door close to Wilson. He held my hand and looked at me and said, "You still have the wart". He got up from his chair and said he would be right back; I asked where he was going and he said he was going to the Drug store a few doors down the street. When he returned he was caring some sort of a blade in his hand. He sat down and reached for my hand. I pulled my hand back and ask what he was going to do to my hand. He said he was going to remove the wart from my finger. I immediately asked if it would hurt; he assured me that it would not hurt, so I gave him my hand and he took the blade and carefully removed the small wart from my hand. He was right it didn't hurt at all. When he finished he looked at me and smiled; then said now you don't have to hide your finger.

Wilson and I made small talk as we enjoyed each other company; before long it was lunchtime. Wilson asked me what I wanted for lunch; I told him I would like chop suey and rice. He asked if I were sure that was all I wanted to eat; I said I was very sure. He left and went across the street to the Shangri La Restaurant. While he was gone my customers started showing up to get their dollars changed to pesos.

From out of nowhere a guy that I have known for quite a while was standing at my booth smiling...he wanted to talk about old times, but I wanted him to just leave before Wilson come and see him. I tried to act as if I were too busy to talk hoping he would leave, but he just kept talking. I kept looking across the street at the door of Shangri La Restaurant...I knew Wilson would be coming out any minute. Suddenly the door of the restaurant opened and Wilson came out... my friend were still trying to talk to me even though I was acting as if I was completely uninterested in what he was saying. Wilson came in the door of the Jet Club and around to my booth door. He gave me the food and asked me what I wanted to drink. I managed to get the word coke out...Wilson looked and saw the young man standing outside of my booth...then turned around and went to the bar counter for my coke.

The young man were still outside of my booth trying to invite me to his Ship's Squadron party. I told him I couldn't go to his party; he wanted to know why...finally I told him my boyfriend didn't want me to go...he said bring your boyfriend. I said to myself...please leave, but he didn't want to leave. I turned around and looked through the door toward the bar counter...Wilson was paying for the drinks...I knew he would be back any minute now...someone from down the street called the young man...he looked at me and said he had to go and would talk to me later. Wilson came back with the sodas and asked me who was the guy I was talking to and what he want. I said he was a guy that I knew that was station on a ship and he wanted to invite me to his Squadron Party. Wilson asked if I were going to the party; I assured him that I was not. I opened up the container for my food and started to eat. It seem as if everyone wanted to change their dollars as soon as I started to eat. Wilson asked if he could help me with my customers. I told him I could handle them because I was use to eating and working the same time.

Finally business did slow down and I was able to finish my food. The young man from the ship kept his word and came back, so I introduced him to Wilson and added that Wilson was my boyfriend; He said hi to Wilson and left in a hurry. Then as if nothing else could go wrong; one of the Club Hostess came all the way over to the front corner of the building where I enter the Money Exchange to flirt with Wilson. She were close enough for her body to touch him…she asked him if he wanted to dance with her…he said no…she asked why… Wilson said real loud would you mine, I am talking to her, pointing at me. I pretended not to see or hear what was going on by concentrating on my work. She acted as though she didn't believe he was talking to me…she asked if Wilson was my boyfriend and I said yes! She walked away mumbling that she though he was sitting by himself.

When she left, Wilson said this was the reason he wanted me to give up my job in the Money Exchange, because everyone seem to think that if you are out in the public you are fair game. As he held my hand, I could sense that he was about to tell me something, but the music from the blaring jukebox behind us stopped him. The record that was playing was maybe the last time by James Brown. Wilson said he like the song and asked if we could make it our theme song. I said yes! I like it too. When the record finished playing Wilson went over and played it again. Just as the record was ending the lady that works the night shift arrived, so she and I got busy counting the money so she could relieve me. When we finished counting the money; Wilson and I went out front to get a ride home. Wilson asked me if I would like to see the Tug Boat that he work on; I said yes! We caught a jeepney to the jeepney stop close to the base. When we arrived at the gate he signed me in as his guest. We hailed a taxi and were off to see his boat. When we arrive he told his cook to prepare his special recipe for fried chicken. Then he took me on a tour of his boat. When we reached the Pilothouse of the boat, he pulled from a drawer a bottle of liquor; he said that he would drink it all if I didn't tell him that I love him. I said what! What's wrong with you? You know that I love you. Do you really think that I would give myself to you if I didn't love you? He said he still like to hear me say it. I grab for the bottle…he pulled it back and said say you love me and you can have the bottle, so I said I love you twice and we hugged and kissed. We went back down to the level where the Cook was cooking the chicken. The Cook said you are just in time to sample the chicken, so Wilson and I sat down at the table and he served us the chicken. The chicken tasted exceptionally good, so I asked him what was in his batter; he was happy to tell me, so I made a note of his recipe for future reference.

Soon the meal was ready; he placed everything on the table. I ate my fill of the strange food that tasted real good, but the thing that really stood out was the fried chicken, I had never tasted chicken cooked like that before. I don't remember too much more about the food we ate that night because I was thinking more about Wilson kisses and hugs…it seem as if I am on cloud nine when I am with him. Now I understand why people do strange things when they are in love.

Finally it was time for Wilson to take me back to the main gate, so I could go home. We caught a taxi to the main gate and Wilson signed the guest list that I was leaving and told me he would see me in a few days. I went over to the jeepney stop and caught a jeepney home. I got home about ten that night and sister Melda to my surprise was at home. She asked where I had been and I told her I had dinner on Wilson's boat. She said she had told me Wilson had kids back in the United States and if I didn't believe her I could ask her boyfriend. I thought to myself, I wish she would butt out, I wanted to say it to her, but we always respected our elders. I just went to my room and she did the same.

The next day before I left for work Sister Melda asked me to tell Sister Linda about me quitting the job in the Money Exchange, so she could apply for it. I didn't want to go to Calapacuan, because I was not ready to talk to Mother about Wilson, so I told Sister Melda I would contact Sister Rose and let her tell Sister Linda about the job.

When I arrived at mama Ligaya to pick up the money for my booth; I told her about Sister Linda needing a job. She asked me if Sister Linda could count money well enough to work in a Money Exchange; I said Yes! She finished grade six in school. She said oh! She finished the six grade in school...tell her to see me right away. I said o.k. And left for the Money Exchange. When I arrived I didn't go into the booth and set up; I went over to the bar area to see the Club Manager about the whereabouts of Sopring, Sister Rose boyfriend. He said Sopring was at work in the back. I asked him to tell Sopring when he finished what he was doing to come see me. Before I could get in my booth and get setup Sopring came by. He asked if I wanted to see him; I said yes, I need you to tell Sister Rose to go to Calapacuan and tell Sister Linda to come by Sister Melda's house tomorrow. He said Sister Rose was at the Top Hat club and she said she was going to Calapacuan to pick up some of her clothes. I said if you are not busy please go and tell her to come by here before she go to Calapacuan. He said yes and he would leave right away, so he could catch her before she left for Calapacuan. He left and caught a jeepney for the Top Hat club. About fifteen minutes later I saw them getting out of a jeepney and coming to my booth. Sister Rose walked in and asked me what I wanted with her. I asked her if she wanted my job in the Money Exchange booth. She said no right away, so I asked her to go to Calapacuan and tell Sister Linda about the job and if she want it, meet me at Sister Melda house tonight. Please don't tell Mother I am quitting my job; I want to tell her myself when the time is right. She said she would not tell Mother and asked me for jeepney fare to Calapacuan. I gave her twenty pesos and told her she could keep the change after she gave Linda enough for jeepney fare to Olongapo City. Sister Rose and Sopring left and went toward the bar and I closed the door to my booth and tried to relax my mind.

The first thought came into my mind was Wilson; I knew he said he would be back in two days, but I wanted to see him now. The more I thought about Wilson the more the walls of the Money Exchange booth seem to be closing in on me. I wanted to get outside and go wherever he was so that I could be with him. I wondered if he was thinking of me as much as I was thinking of him. Wilson told me he was going to find us a place to stay, so I could move out of Sister Melda's house and we could be together all of the time.

Once we get a place of our own, I plan to tell Mother about Wilson and me. Finally I looked out of the booth window and saw a young man standing in front of the booth tapping on the window trying to get my attention. I snapped back to reality and realized what was going on...wake up he said; you were sleeping with your eyes open. I managed a smile and took his money and exchanged it. He left with a big smile on his face. I sat back down...the walls started to close in on me...I got up again...went outside of my booth...closed the door and walked around outside of the booth. I said to myself...I must be going crazy, because all I could think about was Wilson. I went back inside of my booth. All of the regular customer I knew came by and said that I looked as if something were on my mind. I would just smile and exchange their money as fast as I could, so they could be on their way. I kept looking at my watch, because the time seems to be dragging. Finally the lady that works the night shift came and I was so happy. All I could think of was getting home and hoping Wilson would find a way to get off and be waiting for me.

When I got home Sister Linda was waiting for me, so I said hi and we will talk as soon as I change my clothes. I turned around and asked her if she knew where Sister Melda had gone to. She said Sister Melda had left to meet her boyfriend for dinner. I said oh, by the way...what are we having for dinner? She said Sardine cooked adobo style. When I finished changing my clothes I came back into the living room where she was sitting and took a seat beside her. I explained to her why I was giving up my job at the Money Exchange.

I explained to her that I had a boyfriend and as soon as he finds an apartment I was going to move in with him. I told her his name was John C. Wilson and he was stationed on the Naval Base where Sister Melda's boyfriend worked. I made her promise not to tell Mother about my relationship, because I wanted to be the one to tell her when the time is right. She promised me she wouldn't breathe a word of my love affair to our Mother. I also reminded her...if she want my job, she need to accompany me to mama Ligaya place the next day for her interview. We finally got together as to what we was going to do the next day and fixed our plates and started to eat dinner. Talking to Linda had finally got my mind of Wilson, so I asked her if she would like to go to a movie when we finish eating dinner; she was very happy about going to the movies. When we finished eating dinner I washed dishes and cleaned up the kitchen while she got ready to go to the movies. Finally we were off to the movies. We decided to watch a Tagalog Movie about Vampires. We went in and took our seats and the movie started right away. Sister Linda got into the movie right away, but I couldn't concentrate on the movie; I was thinking about Wilson and wishing that he were with me instead of Sister Linda. I could only imagine what we would be doing...kissing and holding each other very tight. As my mind drifted off into fantasyland all of a sudden the audience started to scream...I asked Linda what had happened; she said that the vampire had bitten the neck of the girl in the movie. Finally the movie was over I could not remember anything about the movie, because I had being daydreaming about being with Wilson. We went straight home and to bed. Sister Linda asked me to leave the lights on because she was afraid of the dark after watching the movie. We left the light on I don't know who turned it off, but it was off when I woke up the next day. We got up early and got cleanup and had breakfast...went out and caught a jeepney to mama Ligaya place for Linda's interview. When we arrived mama Ligaya was ready for us; she asked Linda a few questions and said she will do fine for the job. She had also counted the money out to take to the Money Exchange. We took the money and were on our way.

We arrived at the Money Exchange booth and opened up for the day. We had a few minutes before anyone would normally come by, so I took the opportunity to explain to Linda what to expect. I helped her to make a dollar to peso conversion list, so she could use it when she has a lot of customers. I could see that she was a little nervous, so I told her how nervous I was my first time on the job. I told her not to be afraid because she has the conversion list; if she use it she won't come up short at the end of the day. I told her I would be here every day until she get use to doing the job. She said, o.k. And finally settled down and had a seat. In about fifteen minutes our customers started arriving to get their dollars changed to pesos. I found me a nice spot in the booth and sit back to watch Linda work the booth. While sitting there watching her; I could hear a song played on the jukebox back in the bar behind our booth...Maybe the last time by James Brown...my mind started to wonder again...where is Wilson... what is he doing? I guess I just drifted away from reality for a while, because the next thing I remembered were Linda shaking me and calling out my name. I looked up and saw a young man standing in front of the booth counter smiling at me. He asked me why I was not working the booth; I told him I was quitting my job and were training my sister to take over. He said both of you are very beautiful and picked up his pesos from the counter and left. When he left Linda said she liked working in the Money Exchange booth. I said that I was glad she liked the job, but there is one other thing she would have to watch out for...fake money. The American servicemen did not try to pass fake bills, but the local guys would try very often. I also showed her how to check the bills to see if they were faked.

As I sat and watch Sister Linda work the booth; I could see that she were enjoying herself and I were very happy for her. Finally it was lunchtime, so I told her I was going across the street to the Shangri La Restaurant and order noodles for lunch; she said good, will you please buy a barbecue hot dog too. I left for the restaurant. I went inside and had a seat near the door to wait for a waitress to take my order. A waitress promptly came over and took my order. I told her the order was to go. As I sit waiting for the order a young servicemen that comes by my Money Exchange booth very often, came into the restaurant...looked over and saw me. He came to my table and sit down. He asked what I was doing in the restaurant. I said, "Ordering my lunch".

The waitress came back to the table; he ordered his food and insisted on paying for my food. I quickly told him that my order was to go because I was training my sister to take my job at the Money Exchange Booth. He wanted to know why I was leaving my job. I wanted to tell him that I was getting married, but I didn't know how Wilson would react to that kind of news, so I told him I had another job. The waitress came with my food. I tried to pay for it but she said she had added it to the young man bill. I took my food and said goodbye on my way out of the door. I stopped by the barbecue stand and bought a hot dog for Sister Linda and continued on my way to the Booth. I tapped on the booth door and she opened it with a big smile. We got comfortable and started to eat our lunch. A couple of customer came by to change their dollars...she got up and made the exchange. I told her this was the way it would always be...as soon as you start to eat...customers would arrive...she smiled and kept eating her food.

About ten minutes before our shift end the husband of the lady that works the night shift came in. He said that he was going to relieve us now, because his wife was going to be coming late. I introduced him to my sister…they greeted each other with a big smile. I told him that Linda was going to be working in my place because I was leaving my job. We turned over the money to him and walked out front and caught a jeepney home. As soon as we walked in the door Sister Melda came out of her room and asked me if Wilson was coming out tonight. I said no he has duty tonight, but I will see him tomorrow. For some strange reason I was hoping that Wilson would surprise me and come out tonight even though I knew he had duty. Sister Melda asked Sister Linda if she liked her job at the Money Exchange. Sister Linda with a big smile said, I love it. Sister Linda and I went into our room to change clothes so we could start cooking dinner. I told Sister Linda she could have the next day off so she could go to Calapacuan and see Mother and pick up some additional clothes. I showed her some of my clothes that she could wear if needed…she liked my blouses, but not the skirts, because she preferred to wear pants. I had forgotten that Sister Linda dress like a tomboy. When we started dinner Sister Melda said she was not staying for dinner, so we should only cook enough for us. Sister Linda and I prepared rice, fish and Philippine vegetables for our dinner. When we finished our dinner and cleaned up the kitchen we sat down to rest. As soon as we sat down Sister Linda wanted to know about Wilson. She asked if Wilson was tall and nice; I told her he was about medium height and very nice. Sister Melda came out of her room and said that he is a very married man and she walked out of the door. We looked at each other and didn't say a word. When we were sure she had left; Sister Linda asked me what I was going to do. I assured her that Wilson didn't have a wife. I told her Sister Melda was only saying Wilson were married, because she found out that Wilson is in love with me and she resent the ideal of someone being in love with me. We were tired and start to get sleepy, so we decided to go to bed. As I lay in my bed I said to myself over and over…one more night…one more night; then I fell asleep.

The next morning I got up early and took a shower and started breakfast. I tiptoed around in the house because I didn't want to wake

Sister Melda and Linda. Just as I was getting ready to head out the door Sister Linda woke up and said she would see me tonight. I told her I was bringing Wilson to the house tonight so she could meet him. She said, o.k. As I left the room I told her not to tell Mother about Wilson when she go to Calapacuan today. I didn't want Mother to hear about Wilson from no one but me, because I wanted to make her understand why I have waited so long. I hurried out the door and got a ride to the Swan club so I could pick up the money for the Money Exchange booth. I was also hoping that Wilson would be waiting for me there, but to my surprise he was not there. I picked up the money and left for the Money Exchange booth. I thought to myself...he will be waiting at the booth for me...I strained my eyes for a glimpse of him as the jeepney came to a stop, but he was nowhere in sight. I opened up the booth and went inside and got everything arranged to receive my customers. I was feeling real down, because I wanted to see Wilson, so it was very hard for me to get into my work. One customer came by to exchange forty dollars and I gave him change for twenty. The customer said wake up I am not drunk yet...I gave you two twenty's dollar bills. I quickly apologized to him telling him that I thought he had given me two ten's dollar bills. I gave him the correct change and he was on his way. I sat back down and my mind started to ramble again...where is he...he suppose to be off duty today...has he changed his mind about being with me...he promised he would be here today...if he don't come out today I don't know what I will do. I started to feel real down and disgusted; I thought maybe I put my "out of money" sign in the window so I will not be bothered.

Finally one of the girls came by and said she was going to get something to eat from the restaurant across the street and asked if I wanted something; I said no, I would get something from the hot dog stand later. I really didn't feel like eating anything anyway, because I had only one thing on my mind and that was Wilson. After she left I left the door to the booth open, because I couldn't decide whether I was cold or hot. I was just sitting there feeling very lonely and alone. I thought...why be in love make you feel like this. I got up and went to the bathroom and put water on my face to try and snap out of this low feeling. I returned to my booth and opened the door and step inside then turned to close the door behind me. Wilson was standing in the door looking at me. I said oh! You made it. He said hi! And gave me a big kiss. He got a chair from one of the table in the club and placed it by the door of my booth. He quickly sat down and said he have a surprise for me. What kind of a surprise I asked? He said I have found a place for us to stay. My heart started to pound so hard and fast I couldn't tell whether I was happy or scared. I asked him where the place was located. He said on first's street just passed that furniture store he pointed his finger at. He said that was the place he had being earlier trying to get them to deliver a bed for our place. I said I had being looking outside all morning and I didn't see him. He said maybe he were inside the store when I was looking…I asked them to deliver the bed this afternoon, so I will meet the delivery person at the apartment at about three this afternoon. He looked at his watch and said its one o, clock now, I have two hours to find some linen for the bed. I said that I have some bed lining at Sister Melda house. He said he would give me some money tomorrow to go shopping and get our own stuff. I felt very happy now; it seem as if a hundred pound weight was lifted off my shoulders. He got up and closed the booth door. He grabbed me and held me real tight and kissed me. When he held me I felt like I had died and gone to heaven. It felt so good to be kissed by the man I love. I couldn't think of any place I rather be other than in his arms. Wilson promised me he would be back as soon as the furniture company delivered our bed. When he left I felt very different as if I had accomplished something. Before I knew it, it was time for me to get off work; the lady that works the night shift had arrived. We counted the money and she relieved me. I said goodbye and looked around and saw Wilson coming. He said he was sorry it took him so long to return, but the furniture store had not delivered the bed, but he had asked the girlfriend of his friend Jones to take delivery of the bed when it arrive.

We left and went by the furniture store and they assured us that they would make delivery today. When we left the furniture store Wilson asked me if I were hungry; I guess he heard my stomach making noise…I finally realized I hadn't eaten anything since breakfast. I said yes and we went to our favorite restaurant the Shangri La to eat. We went inside and found us a nice table in the corner and waiter for the

Waitress to take our order. The Waitress arrived and took our order. As we sat holding hands we talked about the furniture we needed for our apartment. We decided to go to the apartment as soon as we finish our dinner. Wilson said we would also go and tell Sister Melda we had a place of our own after I see the apartment. We finished our dinner and left on our way to the apartment. When we arrived Jones and his girlfriend had left, so Wilson explained the living situation to me. He said that he wanted me to remember that we would be staying here only temporary, but for now, we would be living upstairs and Jones and his girlfriend would be living downstairs. We went upstairs to our room and saw our new bed. Wilson looked at me and asked if I like the place. I said I like it, but I thought you and I would only be here. He said remember I said this is only temporary until we can find us another place. We sat on our new bed and started kissing. I said we had better go to sister Melda's house and get the pillows and lining before we go too far. He kissed me again and said let's go. Just as we was about to leave our room Wilson said oh, I almost forgot to show the entrance to the roof where we can go outside and relax. We went outside on the roof; I could see quiet a distance from our apartment. I tried to imagine being on the roof watching him as he make his way to the apartment. Wilson said how you like the roof. Snapping out of my deep thought…I said I like it very much. We left the roof of our apartment and went down stairs and caught a jeepney to sister Melda's house. When we arrived Sister Linda was sitting at the kitchen table. I introduced Wilson to her and they each greeted each other. After the introduction Sister Linda went into the bedroom. Sister Melda were in her bedroom with the door open, so I told her Wilson and I have an apartment now. She came to her bedroom door and said, good for you in English then she started to speak Tagalog. She said I told you he was married and have children in the States…I am your sister and you don't listen to me.

Wilson looked at me…I explained to him what she had said. Wilson said I don't understand why she continues to insist that I am married? That's is one of the reasons I wanted us to have a place of our own, so she would not be around to tell you all of these made up things that's untrue. I assured him she was only upset because she was losing her Secretary. I said that I was sure Sister Linda would become her Secretary now that she has moved in to stay. We sat there in the living room making small talk because we knew our conversation was being monitored. Wilson said that he wanted me to meet him at our apartment the next day at about quarter to six in the afternoon or he could give me the apartment key now so I could move all of my things after I came back from the market. I said no, I wanted him to be at the apartment when I arrive. He said o.k. He would wait for me at the apartment. It was getting kind of late, so he gave me two hundred pesos and said this is what I will give you every time I get paid...one hundred for you and one hundred for food; if you need more money don't hesitate to ask. He leaned over and kissed me...I pushed him away and pointed to the door of Sister Linda room. He said she was not coming out of her room because she has been hiding in there ever since he arrived. He kissed me again and I kissed him back and that started a chain reaction, so I said we had better stop before we end up on the floor. We both laughed. He said it was time he had to return to the base. He gave me an extra hundred pesos to pay for the bed lining so we kissed again and he left for the base. As he walked out the door he turned and said goodnight sleep tight don't let the bedbug bite. I said we don't have bed bugs in our bed because we always change the sheet. He looked at me kind of funny and smiled saying that he was only joking. I said oh. A joke, then I said the same thing to him, goodnight sleep tight don't let the bedbugs bite...we both laughed. This time when he left I felt more at ease...I didn't feel like my heart was being ripped out. I guess it was because I was more confident of our relationship and I knew he would take care of me.

Sister Linda finally came out of her room with a slight smile on her face. I said its ten thirty already and you are not sleepy yet. She said I have been thinking about going to work tomorrow. I said I thought you liked the job. She said I do and that's why I am excited about going to work in the Money Exchange tomorrow. We both got ready and went to bed. I didn't lie there daydreaming like I normally do; I went to sleep right away.

The next day I woke up early before everyone else, so I could go to the market and buy the sheets and pillowcases for our apartment. I rushed to the market to get them so I would have enough time to wash

and hang them out to dry so they would be dry when I meet Wilson at
the apartment in the afternoon. At the market I purchased matching
sheets and pillowcases and a couple of towel set. When I returned
home Sister Linda had left for work and Sister Melda was taking a
shower. I found the container to wash my things in, but I couldn't
find any soap, so I went across the street to the Sari Sari Store for
soap. When I returned and started to wash Sister Melda yelled out
the window...what are you doing out there? I said that I was washing
my bed lining; she said the girl is coming tomorrow to wash. I know,
I said, but I need this bed lining tonight, because I am moving into
my apartment today. She said you are really serious about moving in
with him ha. I said yes, don't you remember him telling you that we
have found an apartment? She said I never thought I would ever see
the day you moving out. I looked up toward the window and she had
disappeared. I got up and went inside to get clothe pins so I could
hang the lining on the line to dry in the sun. When I finished washing
I went inside to take a shower. I got everything together and started
my shower. Sister Melda came by and asked me to come to her room
when I finish. I thought, "What she want now"? When I finished my
shower I wrapped a towel around my head and went into her room.
When I came in she said sit down and read your Brother letter. I
read the letter...Brother Smitty was coming home in three months. I
thought she would be real happy about the news, but all she said was,
"It take that long". I got up and went into my room to dry my hair.
When I finished drying my hair I started to pack some of my clothes.
I left some of my clothes on purpose, because Mother come by every
so often and iron ours clothes even though Sister Melda have a Maid
to do it. I just was not ready to explain my relationship with Wilson
to Mother. My Mother has always insisted on doing something for
us even though she doesn't have to. It seems to make her happy
when she does something to help us. That afternoon before dark I
called a jeepney to load my stuff; Sister Linda had come home from
work, so she helped me to load my clothing in the jeepney. I asked
her how her day went in the Money Exchange; she said she loved the
job and it didn't tire her out. After loading my stuff I climbed in the
jeepney and gave the Driver my new address. When I arrived at the
apartment; Wilson was already there and waiting for me. He helped

the Driver unload the jeepney and turned and asked if this was all of my things. I said, it was all except a few clothes I left so Mother would not find out that I had moved. We carried my clothes along with his into the apartment. When I was hanging the clothes in the closet I noticed that Wilson had a lot of black clothing. I asked him if his favorite color were black; He said why do you ask that? I said almost all of your clothes are black and you have on a black shirt now. He said I guess so...I always feel comfortable in black clothes. He started putting the lining on the bed; I noticed he was doing a good job, which surprised me. I told him that I didn't know he could fix a bed like that; he said I know what I am doing because I do it all the time on my boat. Then he came over to me and pushed me down on the bed and started kissing me very gentle, then it started to intensify; we were all over the bed...someone yelled out...Wilson... Wilson... Are you up there? Wilson answered yea man! We will be right down. We went downstairs and Wilson introduced me to Jones's girl friend. We both said hi. Wilson said do you remember Jones; he is the one that cooked the fried chicken on the boat. I said yes, it was very good. We made small talk for a while then Wilson and I went back upstairs. We started again where we left off. We christen our new bed in rare form and fell asleep. I woke up the next morning and went to the bathroom. When I came back I looked at the time it was five in the morning. I woke Wilson up and told him to hurry because he may be late for work. He said I forgot to tell you that I have a few days off work. He reached for my hand and pulled me back into the bed for a repeat performance.

We made love like it would be our last time for six months. We left our room only to go down stairs to take a quick shower or get something to eat. While we were down stairs getting something to eat; Jones was sitting on the couch drinking a beer. He ask Wilson what we were doing upstairs all of the time, because he never see us down stairs. I was embarrassed, so I ran back upstairs to our room. I don't know what Wilson said to him after I left, but he followed me back to our room. He came in and closed the door and walked over to our bed where I was sitting. He had that look on his face again, so I knew what would follow. We made love again and after that I fell asleep in his arms. Those two days passed by very quickly; we almost forgot the date, because we only ate, sleep and made love. While down stairs eating that afternoon, Jones was home also, so Wilson and him started to make small talk. Wilson asked him what the date of the month was because we had not really notice whether it was day or night while in our room. Jones said man today is Sunday what have you being doing up stairs? Wilson looked at me and said he had to go back to work the next day.

Monday morning around four Wilson and Jones were up taking a shower and dressing for work. The Naval Base main gate open at five and they had to be at their work site by six thirty in the morning. When it was time for Wilson to go he acted for a moment as if he didn't want to leave me. I didn't want him to leave either, but he and I both knew that he had to go to work. He had that look on his face again as he kissed me goodbye. I whispered in his ear that he had to leave now so he wouldn't be late. He turned and forced himself to leave. Later that day I was in our room thinking of my new life; I heard Jones girl friend calling me and asked me to come down stairs, so I went down stairs to see what she wanted. When I reached the bottom of the stairs I saw Sister Melda sitting on the couch. I quickly tried to introduce the two, but Jones girl friend said they had met already. I asked Sister Melda to come up to my room. When we entered my room Sister Melda said she thought I had my own apartment. I explained to her that this was only temporary. She asked me if I knew the girl down stairs belong to a street gang. She said she didn't know which gang it was, either OXO or ZIGGY, ZIGGY gang. I said to myself…here we go again…now she is trying to scare me into returning home.

Every since Wilson told her that he was in love with me, she has been doing everything she can to break us up. Now she is trying the scare tactic. Finally she left. I followed her to the front door and closed it behind her. When I turned to go back upstairs Jones's girl friend came out of her bedroom and said she didn't want a lot of people coming to the apartment. I told her I had not invited a lot of people to the apartment and that were my sister that just left. She said as though she was upset…I just wanted to let you know. She went back into her bedroom and I went upstairs.

Around five that afternoon I started getting ready for Wilson to come home. I remembered Wilson showing me how to get out on the roof, so I went outside on the roof so I could see Wilson as he made his way down the street to our apartment. I stood on the roof peering down the street for any sign of Wilson…then I saw him coming. I ran back into our room and sit on the bed to wait for him to come through the door. Suddenly my wait was over…he was standing in front of me with his arms outstretch. We hugged and kissed. I thought he would never let me go. Then he released me long enough to ask if I had eating dinner. I said yes, how about you? He said he had eaten before he left his Boat. We sat on the bed holding each other. He said he wanted me to get ready so we could go out night clubbing. Our apartment was about a block and a half from the main drag where all of the nightclubs were located. Wilson waited patiently while I got ready to go. Finally we were ready to go, we locked our room and went down stairs. Jones and his girl friend were nowhere in sight. On our way outside we decided to walk to the main drag. We decided to go to the Supreme Club located about three doors down from the Jet Club Money Exchange Booth where I use to work. We entered the club and were seated. Before we could order one of Wilson's friend came over to our table; Wilson introduced him as Billy Joe Sanders the chief Engineer on his Boat. He shook my hand and said hello and I greeted him likewise. Wilson decided not to wait for someone to come over and take our order; He went up to the bar for his drink…I didn't want anything to drink. Sanders took a seat at our table, we made small talk for a while, but I kept anxious awaiting Wilson to return. I saw him standing near the bar talking to one of the club Hostess.

They stood in front of the bar for almost fifteen minutes talking. I begin to get upset about the way Wilson were acting…Wilson friend sensed that I was getting upset, so he excused himself and went to the bar for another beer. Finally one of the guys I knew from my work at the Money Exchange came by our table and asked me what I was doing in the club. I thought…oh no! I don't want Wilson to see me talking to this guy, but he seem to be real busy over by the bar talking to someone else…I guess I can talk to this guy too. He pulled a chair over to my table and sit down. He said, so this is the reason I haven't seen you at the Money Exchange booth…you are working in the club now. I said no! I don't work here…I am here with my boyfriend and just as I said that, Sanders was coming back to my table. The guy thought Sanders was my boyfriend, so he got up and said I will see you around. Wilson finally decided to come back to our table. As soon as he sat down he asked me who the young man that came to our table was. I asked him who was the girl he was talking to…I guess I felt a little jealous for the first time. He said that was Lucy's friend…you remember Lucy…the girl that wanted to be my girlfriend. I asked him what she want from him. He said nothing! We were just talking. I said yes! You were just talking…you almost forgot I were sitting here waiting for you to return. I were very upset and it showed, so he said let's go home. We got up from the table and he said goodbye to Sanders. On our way to our apartment Wilson asked about the guy that came to our table again. I thought he had forgotten about that guy. I guess he was watching me while he was talking to that girl in the club. I told him that I had met that guy while working in the Money Exchange booth and he thought I was working in that club. You are forgetting that I knew some guys before I met you. We went into our apartment and up to our room. Wilson pulled me into his arms and kissed me…for the first time I could smell the beer and cigarettes smoke on his breath. I didn't like the smell but I kissed him back because I love him. I wonder why I hadn't smelled the beer and smoke before…I guess he had brushed his teeth and goggled real good before he see me. I guess I will have to put up with the cigarettes and beer smell, because I love being with him. We made love and fell asleep. The next thing we heard was Jones yelling…wake up man its time to go to work.

We went night clubbing almost every night. Wilson started getting drunk and dancing with the club hostess and leaving me at our table. Sometime he acted as though he had forgotten about me and stayed away from our table. I felt very hurt watching him dance with the girls in the clubs. I even wanted to cry, because I was not use to being in a night club all of the time. One night after he got drunk he started to slow dance with one of the club hostess. I didn't mind so much if he danced a fast dance with the girls, but I would not sit and watch him dance a slow dance with one of the girls. I decided that I had enough; I got up and went to our apartment and left him in the club. When I got back to our apartment I took off my clothes and went to bed. I really don't know why I decided to go to bed because I knew

I wouldn't fall asleep. I laid in the bed thinking about everything... Maybe I should leave him...what can I really do...if he will slow dance with someone else when I am there, what will he do if I am not there? My stomach felt as if someone had stuck a hot poker in it. I knew, after all is said and done, I love him and I wanted to be with him. Finally I heard him come in the door; I acted as if I was asleep, but I am not sure he knew I was there, because he was so drunk he just lay down beside me and went to sleep. As I lay there I started to cry. I guess I cried myself to sleep, because the next thing I heard was Jones yelling...wakeup man it's time to go. Wilson dragged himself from the bed and got ready to leave for work. When he left I acted as though I were still asleep, so he kissed me and said goodbye. As soon as he was downstairs I got up and got ready to leave.

At six o, clock that morning I was in a jeepney on my way to visit my Mother in Calapacuan. Just as I walked in the door of Mother's house she asked me why I had come this early in the morning to visit. I told her that business at the Money Exchange was very slow so I was given a day off. I did my best to keep from looking her in the eye because she can tell if I am stretching the truth. I asked her where was Gina; she said Sister Rose her mother had picked her up the day before. She turned and looked me square in the eyes and asked what was wrong. I quickly turned away, because I wanted to cry real bad and tell her what was wrong. Then I looked out of the window and saw Brother Etong feeding the chicken.

I said I think I will go out and help Brother Etong feed the pigs. I hurried outside hoping to get away from her before she figured out what was going on with me. I ran out and picked up one of the feed buckets to help Brother Etong. He turned and looked at me with a big smile. I wanted to tell her but I was not sure that it was the right time. When Brother Etong and I finished feeding the pigs. I went next door to my sister-in-law house; she was just getting up that morning. I looked at my watch it was nine o, clock, so I took a seat on the porch next to her window so we could talk. When she finally came out on the porch she asked me if something was wrong with me. I thought to myself...everyone is reading my mind. I said there is nothing wrong I was just thinking about work. Then she asked if I was still working at the Money Exchange...I said yes! I didn't want to tell her about my boyfriend. She made coffee and we drank coffee and ate bread rolls. She talked about her daughter Celia and Celia boyfriend. She said that Celia boyfriend was really helping them out a lot. I said that's good because my no good brother is out running around not sending money here to take care of you. She said don't worry about it because when he get tired he will come back home. I thought to myself…she must really be in love with him. I really know the feeling because I am really in love with Wilson, but he like to party and get drunk all of the time. He forgets I am with him sometimes. When he is not drinking he is a very gentle, loving and caring person. Since we moved into our apartment all he want to do every night is go out partying. I don't know what I am going to do. Sister Maria interrupted my thought and asked again if I was all right, because I seem to have a lot on my mind. I wanted to tell her about my boyfriend, but I didn't want her to know that he was a drunk. Mother called from next door, so I got up and went to see what she wanted. She said she was going to the market and asked if I was staying for lunch. I said yes and I was spending the night too. She said she was taking Brother Etong, because she was buying feed for the pig and she wanted me to go next door and visit with Sister Maria until they return.

When Mother and Brother Etong left for the market I didn't go next door I took a seat by the window and my mind started to wonder… Does he know how much he is hurting me…does he care? He likes to take me out night clubbing and show me around, but as soon as he starts drinking he forgets I am with him. I remember the first time I saw him; I fell in love with him, the smell of his cologne, and his gentle touch. I wonder if he loves me as much as I love him…he always tell me he love me…that's what I can't understand…if he love me so much why does he get drunk and dance with club hostess and forget I am around…maybe I am not pretty enough for him…I really don't know what to do…our love affair seem like a game to him…I felt sorry for myself and I couldn't hold the tears back any longer and started to cry. I lay down on the floor and cried myself to sleep.

I don't know how long I was sleeping before I heard Mother voice talking to Brother Etong as she came in the door. She said she had bought a pineapple at the market and Brother Etong was cutting the hull from it. I said o.k. I would have some later I just wanted to lay down for a while. Mother started to cook and I started thinking about Wilson again. I remember the first time we made love in Hotel 456. It was like him and I was the only people in the world. I felt really and truly in love and I think he loved me too. To love and be loved is a wonderful feeling. I reached for one of the pillows nearby and hug it thinking of Wilson. I wonder if he's thinking of me. My mind started wondering…maybe he is just using me…he have had his fun with a young eighteen year old girl…maybe he want to leave me now… maybe I should just leave him and make it convenient for him…I have to be realistic with myself; he is an American Sailor use to partying with a lot of girl…I am just a young girl that haven't experienced a lot of partying and running around…he like partying with his friends every night…I am not sure whether I am being used or not…he have plenty of money to spend and like to party all of the time…maybe he just don't want to deal with a party pooper like me and want me to leave on my own…if he don't want me anymore I wish he would tell me. My head started to hurt because I was thinking too much. I asked Mother for an aspirin. She went to the kitchen and got an Aspirin and a glass of water. I took the Aspirin and sat down by the window.

Brother Etong had finished preparing the pineapple and brought me some in a small dish. I looked at him and forced a smile and told him I had a headache and would eat the pineapple later. He smiled and went to put the pineapple away. Then Mother came and sat beside me and said she knew something was wrong with me because she couldn't remember a time when I turned down my favorite fruit. She asked if Sister Melda and I had a fight. I said no! Then she asked if I was having problems at work. I said no! I am not having a problem at work; I just don't feel good now. Mother said o.k. She would leave me alone so I could get some rest. When Mother left my mind started drifting again…Wilson is a nice caring guy, but he hurt me…I wonder if he know what he is doing or maybe he only pretends to be nice and caring…I can't forget how he looked the first time he said he loved me. Mother said let's eat and snapping me out of my daydream. I got up and took a seat at the table. Mother had prepared my favorite vegetable dish with barbecue fish. I ate a little bit because I was not really hungry. I felt so down and out and I could tell that Mother was worrying about me and wanted to help me solve my problem. I was not ready to tell her what was on my mind...I wanted to cry, but I didn't want them to see me crying, so I excused myself from the table. Mother looked at me and said she knew there was really something wrong and she hope I would talk to her later about my problem. I repeated to her that I just didn't feel good and I wanted to sit down and think. She said o.k. Maybe we will talk later. Mother and Brother Etong finished eating and cleaned up the kitchen; then they went out back to feed the chicken and pigs. When they left I sat back down beside the window on the wooden box where I once kept my clothing. I started to thinking about what I wanted to do...go back to work and make some money...it would have to be the Money Exchange because I would not take a job as a Club Hostess and sale myself to the highest bidder...I will not ask Wilson for money even though he promised to take care of me and give me one hundred pesos when he get paid, but lately he would only come home and tell me to get ready to go nightclubbing...He would get drunk and start dancing with the hostess in the club and forget about me...this cannot be love...He is using and abusing my love. I tried to clear my head and stop thinking, so I got a mat and a blanket from the corner of the room and spread the mat out so I could lie down and tried to go to sleep. I covered my head with a pillow and drifted off to sleep.

The next thing I heard were Mother calling me and telling me it was four o, clock and asked if I were going to work today. I said no I was spending the night. She said o.k. Go back to sleep. I lay around for a while and tried to go back to sleep; then finally decided to get up. I folded the mat and blanket and stored it in the corner and brushed my teeth and washed up. When I was putting the mat and blanket away I heard the sound of a motorcycle, so I decided to go outside and see who was riding it. I figured it was Celia boyfriend, because he has a motorcycle. Outside I couldn't see anyone, so I went next door to Sister Maria house. She was sitting on her porch. I asked who was riding the motorcycle. She said she didn't know because it just passed by and didn't stop. I climber up onto the porch and took a seat beside her. She said I guess you thought the motorcycle belong to Celia boyfriend. I said yes! We made small talk for a while and then I started to get depress again. So I excused myself and climbed down from the porch and walked back toward Mother's house. I decided to walk around outside for a while. I saw the pigs playing in the mud in their pen and they seem to be very happy. The chicken running around having fun with each other and there was a nice gentle breeze blowing against my face. I thought to myself... everybody and everything seem to be happy but me. I have always wanted to be love and in love, but I guess I will have to give him some space so he will realize what he's missing. I turned and saw Brother Etong doing something in the corner of the yard. I asked him if he would like to play the Songka game. He smiled and indicated by sign language that he would like to play. So we went into the house to find the game; we found the game, but we couldn't find the small seashells use to play the game. We decided to use small stones instead, so we went back outside to find enough small stones to play the game. Mother and Sister Maria noticed Brother Etong and me picking up stones, so they came over to inquire about what we were doing. I explained that we needed small stones to substitute for the small seashells we normally use to play the Songka game. Everyone joined in to help find enough small stones to start the game. Suddenly I remembered where there were a lot of small stones. I explained to everyone that we should find a lot of small stones at the spring where we get our water. Everyone quickly agreed, so we all walked over to the spring and sure enough; there were more than enough stones to use to play the game.

After gathering up the stones we went back to the house to play the game. Brother Etong and I started playing first while Sister Maria and Mother watched. After watching for a few minutes Mother got up and went in the kitchen to start cooking. A few minutes later she asked Brother Etong to get some firewood for the stove, so Sister Maria took his place. She and I were having a lot of fun playing the game when Brother Etong returned. He motioned for us to keep playing and he would play later. I really got into the game and before we realized how long we had played Mother said it time to eat. We put the game to the side and went straight to the table. I had developed a real big appetite, so I filled my plate and asked Brother Etong for the Pineapple he had saved for me. I commenced to stuff my stomach; everyone seems to be in a real eating mode. When I finally finished I was really stuffed. When everyone had finished eating; Brother Etong and I volunteered to clean the kitchen and put away the food. Mother and Sister Maria pulled out the Songka game and started to play. I could hear them talking, laughing and having a lot of fun with the game. I was glad to see Sister Maria laughing and having fun, because my brother were always gone running around the countryside chasing other women. I really could relate to her feeling because my boyfriend was causing me to hurt inside the same way. When we finished doing the dinner dishes and cleaning up; Brother Etong went outside to feed the dog. I got my mat, blanket and pillow and spread the mat out on the floor. I sat down in the middle of the mat hugging my pillow and watching Mother and Sister Maria play the game. I am glad I thought about the Songka game because it snapped me out of a real unhappy mood. Finally everyone started yawning and getting sleepy, so Sister Maria said she was going home and go to bed. When she left Brother Etong got his mat and spread it out near the door. Mother shared the mat with me. She asked me how Sister Linda like her job. I told her Sister Linda love her job, because it not a very hard job working in a Money Exchange both. The biggest part of the job is counting money and Linda can count very well. I made sure she understood everything about the job before I left her alone. Mother said I am glad you helped her to find a good job so she can help herself...how are you doing? I knew Mother had figured out what going on with me, so I decided this was the time to tell her about Wilson. I said Mother I met a very nice young guy and before I finished my sentence she asked very calmly is he's Sailor?

I said, yes! And she asked if he was the same guy Sister Melda introduced me. I said, yes again. She said do you remember me telling you about Sailors having a girl friend in every port; well it's true. I know you said he is a young guy, so I guess he has started to play around with other girls...is that what worrying you now? I said that's part of it. Well she said, you and him are very young and have a lot to learn about yourself and other people. When you start to learn about other girls and boys you may see someone else you like and you move on to them and before long you realize you have made a circle...let me give you an example: You see two dress in a store window one nice and one fancy; you like both dress...

you try on both dress...you see that the fancy dress look the best but the nice dress is more your style, so you end up buying the nice dress...you work in a Money Exchange booth you're not around people that like to party and have fun with different guys...the girl in the club are fancy and like to party with different guys...you are nice and simple...if he really like you he will come back to you...do you understand what I am trying to say? I said yes I think so. Then she said, don't worry yourself...you are still young...you will find another Sailor or guy that will love and care for you for who you are. I could tell that Mother was getting sleep as she explained part of the birds and bees to me. Then her voice was silent; I knew she had fallen asleep, so I hug and kissed my pillow pretending that it was Wilson. As I lay there clutching my pillow I made sure I didn't bump Mother and wake her. I lay there for quite a while clutching my pillow thinking of Wilson; Finally I fell asleep.

The next day I heard Mother telling everyone to be quiet, because she didn't want to wake me, but I was already awake. I took my pillow and cover my head to block out the sun that was streaming in through the window. I guess it had rain last night, because the sun was shining real bright just like it does after the rain. I thought for a few minutes about what Mother had told me before she went to sleep; I know she was right and I am glad we had that talk, because I feel real good about myself now, so I decided to get up and join the living again. I thought to myself...I am young like my Mother said and I can find me someone else that will love me for who I am. I got up and brushed my teeth, then I heard Mother and Brother Etong coming in the house each caring a bucket of water. Mother said, good you are awake because we have brought you water so you can take a bath. I said thanks! Mother went in the kitchen and started cooking breakfast. I took my bath and felt really refresh and alive. I felt as if I had awakened in a new world. I also managed to sing a little as I took my bath. I heard Mother in the kitchen saying someone is feeling better today. I just smiled to myself as I dried my hair. Suddenly I smelled the aroma of garlic fried rice and dried fish Mother was cooking. I could even smell the coffee, so I hurried to dry my hair so I could get to the table and eat. Finally it was dry and I rushed to the table and sit down. I told Mother that she cook real great all the time. She smiled and said go ahead and start eating, I am going to help your brother to bring more water to do the dishes.

I started to eat breakfast before Mother and Brother Etong could come to the table. I ate too much as always when I am at Mother's house. When I finished I took a seat beside the window on my favorite wooden box. Mother and Brother Etong was in the kitchen at the table now. I was alone at the window. I tried not to think of Wilson; I fixed my mind on what Mother had said about the nice dress...if he loved you he will come back and buy the nice dress. When Brother Etong finished breakfast he excused himself to go outside and feed the pig. Mother said wait for the plant food she was cooking for the pig. I said I wanted to help, so when the plant food was cooked we mixed it with the table left over and gave it to the pigs. I enjoyed watching the pigs eat and making their funny sound. They even would try and bite each other. I told the pigs that they have a lot of food there is no need to fight. Brother Etong laughed at me. Then I thought I heard Sister Melda calling me, so I turned around and I could also hear Mother calling me. I went back inside the house but no one was there. I heard Sister Melda calling me again, so I went outside in front of the house. I saw Sister Melda, Wilson and Mother coming toward the house. Sister Melda said, your boyfriend is crazy he drag me out of the house early this morning to try and find you. When I saw Wilson I thought my heart skipped a beat I don't know whether I was happy or sad to see him here at Mother's house. Sister Melda said again, your boyfriend is crazy. Everybody went into the house... Mother asked what was going on...Sister Melda told Mother Wilson had came to her house and begged her to bring him to Calapacuan to see me. Mother asked why he was trying to find your Sister Vicky. Sister Melda looked at Wilson and Me and tried to explain what Mother had asked in English. Wilson couldn't take it any longer, he hug and kissed me. Mother was really surprised and she said, will someone please tell me what's going on? Wilson and I were sitting on my wooden box by the window holding hands. I tried to speak, but Wilson cut me off and saying looking straight at Mother, I love your daughter Vicky and I want to marry her. I looked at Sister Melda she was so surprised she almost lost her footing. Wilson turned to Sister Melda and said please tell your Mother what I said. After gaining her composure, she said in Tagalog...Wilson want to marry your daughter. Mother said, now I know why Vicky came here the other day acting so funny. Mother turned and looked Wilson straight in the eyes and asked him was he serious about wanting to marry me. Wilson looked at Sister Melda for the interpretation of what Mother said. Sister Melda explained to Wilson what Mother had said. Wilson said yes! I want to marry her...all she have to do is say yes to my proposal, because I have found out everything we need to do to get married here. If she agrees to marry me, then all we need is her birth certificate to start the paperwork. I sat there looking at my Mother, I could tell she was very happy about the prospect of me getting married. I started to think...Wilson seem to be serious about what he is saying or maybe not...maybe he is trying to impress my Mother...I have to take this one step at a time...I had this same mix feeling the first time we made love in 456 Hotel...I don't know what to believe. When Sister Melda finished interpreting to Mother what Wilson had said, Mother looked at me and said, he's is serious about you, are you going to marry him? She seems to be real happy for me, even though I didn't believe it would happen I said yes. It made Wilson very happy too, because he started to explain to Sister Melda and Mother about getting my birth certificate so he could submit the marriage request. I turned and looked at everyone in the room as they were smiling and telling me how happy they were for me; then I saw the look on Brother Etong face, he was the only one that could tell that I had my doubts about marrying Wilson. I got up from my wooden box and pulled Wilson up alongside me and introduced him to Brother Etong. They shook hands and greeted each other.

Brother Etong spoke using sign language telling me that Wilson really loves me and I should be happy. Then he turned around and pick up two buckets as he left for the spring to get some water. Wilson and I followed him to the spring. The spring was at the side of the mountain where my family had driven a bamboo stick in a tiny hole that was leaking water from inside of the mountain. The bamboo stick was perfect because a steady stream of water ran out through the bamboo stick. When we arrived at the spring Wilson saw my Brother placing the bucket under the end of the bamboo stick filling the bucket; he was astonished at what was happening.

He asked if we drink the water and I said yes! So he stuck his hand under the stream and tasted the water. He said the water was cold and had a sweet taste. I said yes! The water is very good. Wilson asked me if anyone had caught malaria from drinking the water. I said look at that long bamboo stick...the water is coming out of the mountain not from the top of it. Wilson said he thought it was rainwater coming from the top of the mountain. I smiled and said that we don't drink water from the hill. He smiled and gave me a big hug and kiss. Finally both of Brother Etong bucket was full, so he pick up them up and started back toward the house; Wilson took one of the bucket to carry. When we came near the pigpen; he motion for us to go to the pin. When brother Etong poured water on the backs of the pigs they would lie down in the dirt and wallow. Wilson said there was no use trying to give them a shower they would get dirty again. I said that were the idea...getting wet and get dirty. I guess Brother Etong understood what Wilson had said because he started to laugh. We went back inside the house when Brother Etong finished wetting down the pigs. Sister Melda was helping Mother clean and dress the chicken my Mother had killed. She said Mother was going to cook chicken adobo for Wilson. Wilson and I took a seat back on my wooden box. We couldn't resist the urge to hug and kiss. Wilson finally got serious, he said that he loved me and was very sorry for what had happen that night; the last thing he wanted to do was to hurt me. He said please don't get mad at him anymore because he couldn't take being away from me. I said that I were the one having problem taking what was going on between us... everything is happening so fast maybe we should just take things easy for a while and let it cool down.

I am only eighteen years old, still young and don't know too much about what's going on in my surrounding. I really think we should give ourselves more time and see where this relationship is going. He held me real tight and said he wanted to marry me so we could be together all the time. When he said that my heart skipped two beats just like it did the first time we met. I said to myself...I have to control my feeling and keep him from sensing how much I want to be married to him. I kept telling myself...don't believe everything he's saying...you are young...wait and see what happen.

We started kissing again and Sister Melda said we're going to eat in a few minute lovebirds. I got up and went over to the kitchen table and fixed Wilson plate. I put rice and chicken adobo in his plate. He started eating then he stopped and said this is the best chicken adobo I have ever eaten. I told Mother what he said and she was so happy she gave him some more adobo on his plate. Brother Etong had finally returned from the store with coke and ice, so Mother gave Wilson some coke in a glass with ice. I really enjoyed eating Mother chicken adobo, but I didn't say anything because Mother seem so happy that Wilson liked her cooking.

While everyone was sitting around relaxing after dinner Sister Melda said she had a date with Wilson friend, so she had to return to Olongapo City. Wilson and I said our goodbye and left to accompany Sister Melda to Olongapo City. Wilson told Mother before we left that when he got paid again he would give me enough money to pay for mines and her fare to our old hometown to get my birth certificate. In the Philippines the groom pays all of the wedding expenses. I still hadn't told Mother that Wilson and I were living together. I continued to let her believe I was staying with Sister Melda. When we arrived in Olongapo, Sister Melda went to her house and we went to our place. We opened the door and looked around for Jones and his girlfriend, but they were gone, so we went upstairs to our room. We opened the door and went straight to the bed and made passionate love like we hadn't seen each other for over a year. I felt so good to be back in Wilson's arms. We fell asleep. I guess after about a half hour, we heard the door slam downstairs. Wilson got up and went down stairs to see who was downstairs. I followed him to the door. When Wilson got to the bottom of the stairs I heard Jones say man I didn't know you was up there...is everything all right...is your girlfriend back?

Wilson said everything is o.k. I could hear everything they said. Jones said let take our girlfriend out to the club tonight. Wilson said he would have to ask me. I ran back and jump in the bed. Wilson came into the room and said Jones want us to go out to the club with them tonight. I asked him what time did he want to leave. He said oh! Whenever you are ready. I got up and got my things together to take a quick shower, so I went downstairs and Jones was sitting on the couch smiling. He said hi and kept smiling. I said hi and continued on my way to the shower. When I finished and went back upstairs Wilson went down to take his shower. While he was gone I got dressed and waited for him to return. Wilson returned to our room and got dress and we went downstairs. Jones girlfriend was still getting dress so we sat down and made small talk until she came out of her room. It was about six thirty when we left so we decided to walk to the main drag. We crossed the street right in front of the Money Exchange booth where I use to work. I heard someone speaking to me saying hi and I turned around to see whom it was when Jones girlfriend said, do not talk to her. I didn't pay any attention to what she said, I said hi back to the girl, because I knew her. The girl said that's why I haven't seen you in the Money Exchange booth you have a boyfriend. Jones girlfriend looked at me very angry and said I told you not to talk to her...she belongs to the ZIGGY ZIGGY Gang and I belong to the OXO Gang. Then they started to fight...Jones tried to pull his girlfriend away and Wilson grab me by the arm and we kept walking. Wilson asked me what was going on because the whole conversation between the girls was in Tagalog. I told him that those two was in different gangs that why they were fighting. I don't know what happened to them because Wilson took me completely away from the fight. We decided to give up going to a nightclub and go to the movies instead. We arrive at the movie just in time for the first feature. I don't remember the name of the movie, but I do remember that it was a Chinese Movie.

When the movie was over we went to our apartment. Jones and his girlfriend were sitting on the couch down stair waiting for us. Jones was very upset because his girlfriend was telling him everything except the truth. He asked me what started the argument. Before I could answer him his girlfriend started talking in Tagalog telling me it was my fault that the fight started because she had warned me to not speak to the girl and I did anyway.

I told her I knew the girl and if she speaks to me I was going to speak to her. Jones looked at his girlfriend and told her to shut up. Then Wilson said man my girlfriend don't know anything about girls being in gangs, she just speaking to the girl because she know her, but your girlfriend don't want Vicky to speak to her...so I figure that's her problem...she want to fight anyway...so let her fight without us. Jones looked at me so I told him the same thing Wilson had told him. His girlfriend tried to talk over me so he could not understand what I was saying, so he told her to shut the f—k up in a real loud voice. When we left going upstairs they were arguing back and forth. Wilson was very upset about what happened. He said he was going to find another place and get me away from Jones girlfriend, because he doesn't want me to have to deal with her again. So we went to bed, made love and forgot about everything that happened that night.

The next morning our alarm clock went off...Jones from downstairs saying wake man it's time to go to work. Wilson got up, dressed and kissed me goodbye. He left me some money so I could go to the market and buy me something pretty. I went back to bed and slept till around nine that morning and got up and started getting ready to go to the market. I heard someone knocking on the door and I opened the door and a strange little girl was standing there. She said that her Auntie wanted to see me downstairs. I followed her downstairs. Jones girlfriend was sitting on the couch looking very mad. Before I could inquire as to what she wanted she said that her and Jones was doing us a favor by letting us stay upstairs...I really don't want anyone to stay here because I don't know if you are one of the ZIGGY ZIGGY Gang member...how am I suppose to know whether you are in a gang or not...you talk to the gang members. I thought to myself...this girl really do believe I am in a gang. Then she said we will beat anyone until they can't stand anymore...so you think I am scared of them...I will kill anyone that get in my way. When she said that I got scared and started to cry. When she saw me crying she calmed down a little; then she asked me how I become to know that girl that she was fighting. I said Sister! Because she was older than me so I tried to respect her even though I knew she was out of her mind. I said I use to work in the Money Exchange in front of the Jet Club before I met my boyfriend...everyone around the Money Exchange knew me and she is one of the girl that I see everyday...if she speak to me I speak back to her.

That's why I don't understand why you are fighting her just because I spoke to her. I don't know anything about Gangs I just work in the Money Exchange trying to make a living and I don't runaround in the street. I have to work and help my Mother. She said I just want to make sure you are not one of the Gang member…don't tell this to your boyfriend or Jones, because I don't want to have to hurt someone…I have tried to change my way of life, but if someone cross me, I will try and bury them with me. I thought to myself…what have I got myself into now. She said did you understand what I said? Just don't cross me and nothing will happen o.k. I said o.k. She said don't tell your Sister Melda; because I have seen her before, but I don't know if she is in a Gang…like I said don't cross me. I went back upstairs to my room. I was so scared I didn't know what to do. I didn't want to tell anyone because I didn't want someone to get hurt especially Wilson. I thought to myself…I didn't know that Gangs was around here…I am living in an apartment with one…my God have I being living in a closet and couldn't detect what was happening around me…I remembered she said that if I didn't tell anyone nothing would happen. I promised myself that I wouldn't tell. I heard a door close downstairs, so I went out to the top of the stairs and listen for any sound. Finally I decided she had left and I quickly ran downstairs and out the front door. I caught a jeepney to Sister Melda's house. When I knocked on the door she opened it as if she was expecting me. She said she thought I was Sister Linda knocking because she had forgotten her key. She asked why I had come to her house. I told her I wanted to pick up some more of my clothes. She said I should have told Mother Wilson and I was staying together. I said I wanted to wait until Mother and I go to Pangasinan to pick up my birth certificate next month. She said I have told you about Wilson having kids back in the United States, he have a girlfriend in the jungle, (The main drag where all of the Night Clubs are located) and you know the girl that work in the Swan Club. I thought to myself…Sister Melda is not helping my situation at all, she is making it worse…tell me stories about Wilson and I am scared to death…what am I going to do? I went into my old room and lay across the bed, because I felt very weak and mixed up. I went right to sleep. Several hours later Sister Melda knocked on the bedroom door and asked me if I was going to eat lunch.

She said she had prepared beefsteak for lunch. I said yes! She said well come on then because the food is getting cold. I washed up and went to the table. We ate our food and talked about Brother Smitty coming home soon and that he was trying to get stationed at Sangley

Point, Philippines. I asked her where was Sangley Point. She said it was in Cavity City, near Manila...he might end up somewhere in the United States, but she hope he will get Sangley Point...Linda and I wrote and told Smitty that you have a boyfriend and he wrote back and said tell my favorite sister-in-law I said congratulation. I said oh no! You told him I have a boyfriend. She said yes! If I hadn't told him when he comes he would have been very upset...I can hear his mouth now...why didn't you write me about my favorite sister-in-law...she is too young, too sweet and bashful to have a boyfriend...so I had Linda to write and tell him. Then she asked what was I planning to do when Mother come here to pick up the Money Wilson promised for me and her to go to Pangasinan to get my birth certificate. I told her I had plan to come and stay at her house so Mother would not find out about me staying with Wilson until we get the paperwork taken care of. She said don't say I haven't warned you about Wilson and went into her room. I cleaned the kitchen and put up the food. When I finished I sat in the living room for a while trying to think about what I was going to do next. A few minutes later Sister Melda called me and asked if I would come in her room. When I walked in she was sitting on her bed with a deck of cards in her hand. She said sit down. I am going to teach you to play Solitary. This will keep you from being so board while sitting and waiting for Wilson to come home. I thought to myself...so that's what she be doing in her room all of the time. I sit down on the side of her bed. She shuffled the cards and laid them out one at a time. She said you see...this is a very easy game to play...I do it to kill time...you will be surprised to see how fast the time pass. After a while she said now you try it. I tried it a few times and finally got the hang of it. I looked at the time and it was almost three that afternoon, so I told her I had to get back to my apartment in case Wilson comes home early. I went outside and caught a jeepney and left. When I arrived at the apartment Jones's girlfriend was waiting for me. She said where have you been, I knock on your door and no one answered.

I told her that I went to pick up a few things from my sister house. She said did you cross me? I thought she asked me if I had bought her a cross. I said you didn't tell me to buy you a cross. She laughed and said no! I told you earlier not to cross me that mean you are not to tell anyone what we talked about this morning. I got scared again and said no! I haven't told anyone. Then she pointed at the lady sitting on the couch and said, this lady will be working here cleaning the house and washing clothes…you and I will each pay half of her salary…she will not live here, but will come twice a week…one day she will do my clothes and will do yours the next day…each day she will clean the bathroom where you and your boy friend make a mess…propane is used to cook our meals…you will pay half for it. I said just how much all of this is going to cost me? She said forty pesos a month or twenty pesos every two weeks when my boy friend is paid… remember this is between you and me…don't tell your boy friend or Jones. The lady sitting on the couch looked at me and said she's not going to tell. I turned and ran upstairs to my room and lay down on the bed. I thought to myself…when is this going to end…my Father tried to rape me, then told me if I tell he would kill everyone…this devil woman is telling me not to tell and if I do she will kill or hurt the one I tell. Now I will have to give the money I have being giving my Mother… what am I going to do? I started to cry…I felt like I was having a bad dream…I wanted to wake up and realize it was only a dream, but my God! This is real. I looked at my watch…I thought to myself…Wilson will be here soon and I can't let him see that I have being crying, so I got up and put some powder on my face to try and hide the tear traces. Finally I heard Wilson coming through the door. He asked me what I am doing upstairs and why I don't go downstairs sometime. Before I could answer he gave me a big hug and kiss. I felt better after he kissed, because I thought he was trying to get upset with me too. I told him I had been downstairs and had just come back to our room, why? He said Jones asked him why I always stay upstairs and don't come downstairs even though we share the living room…he think you are afraid of him.

I almost said that I was afraid of his devil girlfriend, but I said instead, you know I was working around a lot of people when I worked in the money exchange, so I am not afraid of talking and dealing with Sailors. He said don't worry about that…let's go out? I said are you tired, you have being working all day. He said no! And sit down on the side of the bed. I got up and walked over to the closet and started changing my clothes. He stood up and grabbed me and pushed me over on the bed and started kissing me and I responded. Then we stopped when we heard the rain on the tin roof...we started kissing again and again, we made love and it was just wonderful as always.

We decided to stay home because it was raining real hard. Wilson went downstairs and came back caring a beer in each hand. He sat down on the side of the bed and started to caress my back while sipping his beer. Finally he said that he think we should start going to the movie more often instead of the nightclubs. I thought to myself... this is the best ideal he has had in a long time. He asked me what type movie did I like and I told him I like the one where the guy always ride a horse. He said oh yes! You mean western movies...I like Chinese movies. I said I like to watch them too, but my favorite is the one where the guys ride the horse. He smiled and said he have to use the bathroom, so he got up and started to go downstairs, I followed him because I had to use it too. We moved quietly downstairs to the bathroom so we would not wake or disturb Jones and his devil girlfriend. We finished using the bathroom and ran back upstairs. Wilson said we had better go to sleep because he had to go to work a little early the next day. We undressed again and before I could put my nightgown on he was pulling me down on the bed. We made passionate love again. When we finished I laid in his arms thinking...I don't want this to end...I want it to last forever...I fell asleep.

The next morning Wilson and Jones left early going to work. I got my things together and quickly ran downstairs and took a shower. I wanted to leave before Jones girlfriend was up and about. I came back upstairs and dressed; then I quietly started downstairs, I made it to the front door before I heard her bedroom door open. She asked me where were I going this early in the morning and I told her I was going to visit my Sister Linda.

She said you have another sister. I said yes I have three sisters. She said o.k. Remember what we talked about. I opened the front door and left. I wanted to go to Sister Melda's house, but I decided to go to Calapacuan, because she always talks about Wilson. When I arrived in Calapacuan, I had to walk across a field to Mother's house. I had to pass Brother Celino's house before I got to Mother's house. To my surprise Brother Celino was sitting out on his porch. I said Brother

Celino you are back home. He said yes! I decided to stop by for a while, so I climbed the stairs to his porch and gave him a big hug. I took a seat beside him and turned to speak to my sister-in-law; when I noticed her appearance; her eyes looked as if they would pop out. I asked her what was the matter and she just started crying. My Brother said that's enough crying. I asked if someone in the family had died. She said yes, I am the one who is dead or might as well be dead. Your brother said he was leaving me for another woman because I can't have kids...what am I going to do...I have lost the only income I had by staying with him...now he's going to leave me for someone else. She started crying again and got up and went inside the house. I asked my brother why he would tell her something so cruel...he's never around anyway? He said I have to have children, I am getting old...I found another woman she is young and beautiful. I thought to myself...another no good man...I left before I disrespected my elder. I went to Mother's house and called out to her as I walked in the door. She turned and asked me why I was there so early. I said no special reasons I just wanted to see her and Brother Etong. She was busy cooking breakfast, but she wanted to know how Sister Linda was doing on her job. I told her Sister Linda was doing real well on her job. She said that she had come by Sister Melda's house around nine a few days ago and we were gone. I told her if she wanted to see us, she need to arrive before seven in the morning because we normally leave for work at seven. She said oh, it wasn't anything important I was going to the market and since I pass close by Melda's house I decided to stop for a while. I heard someone coming in the door and it was Brother Etong caring firewood. Mother said to him don't go anywhere now, we are going to eat breakfast in a few minutes. Brother Etong took a seat beside me and I asked him had he being catching frogs lately. He said yes! Not as many as before.

I turned to Mother and asked her why Brother Celino was acting so cruel. She said he is acting just like your Father...they don't care who they hurt. Your Brother and Maria had a fight yesterday about him having another woman. I said why does he have to come back home, he should stay away and never come back. Mother said I shouldn't talk that way about my Brother. I said yes he is my Brother, but I feel very sorry for Sister Maria, I am a woman too. My Brother is doing the same thing my Father does, running around and having different women. Mother said she couldn't do anything to change his mind, because he is a grown man and have a mind of his own. When we finished eating, Mother and I went into the living room and took a seat on my box. Brother Etong started cleaning the kitchen. Mother asked me what my boyfriend name was. I smiled and said Wilson…you forgot it already…He is doing fine…I see him almost every night. She said we have one more week left before we go to Pangasinan. That's right I said, make sure you come to Sister Melda's house on the sixteen and spend the night, so we can get an early start to Pangasinan. I really want to make the round trip in one day. She said your Brother Etong want to go and visit your Grandmother in Alyaga, Pangasinan. I said, that will be fine, we will drop him off in Alyaga and proceed on to Sual and get my birth certificate. I felt sleepy and I told Mother I was going to take a nap. She said go ahead, because she wanted to go next door to Brother Celino's house and talk with him for a while. When I lay down my mind was very clear, I was not thinking about a lot of things, so I drifted off to sleep right away. Suddenly I heard noise at first I thought I was dreaming, but I knew that voice…it was Sister Rose. I looked at my watch. It was ten thirty and I thought to myself…everybody is come home to Calapacuan. Sister Rose said hi Vicky what are you doing here…is Wilson with you? I said no! I am visiting Mother. I looked around and saw Mother sitting at the kitchen table talking to Brother Etong, I grab Sister Rose and pulled her to the side. I spoke to her in English so Mother couldn't understand what I was saying. I said Mother don't know that Wilson and I are living together, she think I am still working In the Money Exchange…please don't tell her what's going on. She promised me that she would not tell Mother my secret. Brother Etong and little Gina came in the living room. I told Gina she looked very pretty in her yellow dress. She smiled and sat beside Sister Rose. Mother asked me what time I was returning to Olongapo City to go to work. I told her I would be leaving around three in the afternoon. Sister Rose said I thought you were. Then I looked at her and frowned. Then she said oh! You work at night again. I said yes! I change shifts every now and then. Mother told Sister Rose to fix Gina plate, because we were going to start eating lunch now. We had boil rice, adobo squid and boil eggplant. We put lemon and soy sauce on the boil eggplant. I almost ate too much. When I left the table I thought the zipper on my pants was going to break. When I said that I had ate too much, little Gina held her stomach and said she had eaten too much. Everyone laughed and pointed at her stomach. Sister Rose and I started talking about Brother Celino. Sister Rose said, Mother told her that Brother Celino have another girlfriend. I said yes! They had a big fight last night. Why don't you go over there and see what they are doing. She said I don't think so, our sister-in-law may get a big knife and chop Brother Celino head off...I better leave them alone.

I looked outside and notice that it was getting dark as if it was going to rain. I decided to leave for Olongapo City now before the rain come. Sister Rose thought it was a good idea to leave now too. We said our goodbyes to Mother and started for the jeepney stop. Brother Etong accompanied us to the jeepney stop with his umbrella. We made it to the stop before it started to rain. I told Brother Etong to hurry back to Mother's house before it started raining hard. He closed up his umbrella and started running back to the house. On our way to Olongapo City Sister Rose told me she and her boyfriend had rented a room in Barrio, Barretto. And they were making a good life for themselves. When we came to Barrio, Barretto she stop the jeepney and got out. I told her I would take care of her jeepney fare. We waved goodbye. When I arrived in Olongapo City I decided to go by the Money Exchange booth and see Sister Linda before I went to my apartment. I tried to scare her; when I reached for the door she jerked it open scarring me. We laughed in surprise. She said what are you doing lovebird? I said lovebird! She that's the word Sister Melda always uses. I told her I just wanted to stop by and see how she was doing...do you still have a lot of customers? She said when it rain business get a little slow, but the big ships are here I guess no one want to come out in the rain.

She said when I get home tonight I hope Sister Melda is not there because I want to relax tonight. I said what's wrong? She said when you left I became her Secretary; had to read and write letters to brother Smitty for her...she don't seem to care what time it is when she want it done...when I get home sometime it is very late, but she still call me in her room and have me to either read or write a letter for her. I looked at the time it was getting pretty late in the afternoon, so I told Sister Linda I had to go to my apartment because Wilson would be coming home very soon. We said our goodbye and I left. When I arrived at the apartment I didn't see Jones's girlfriend, I went straight upstairs to my room. I decided to change clothes and get ready to go to a movie, because he said we were going to start going to the movie instead of the clubs. After I finished changing clothes I went out on the rooftop so I can see him when he comes down the street. I waited and waited for him, but he didn't come home; I felt tired so I went back to my room and lay across the bed. I thought to myself…maybe he had to work because sometimes a big ship come in and he have to work. I fell asleep. I heard the bedroom door open and hit the wall. It was Wilson he looked as if he was going to fall on top of me on the bed…I got up before he fell on me. I checked the time it was eleven thirty. I yelled at him, where have you been…I have been waiting for you. He didn't say a word he just tried to pull his pants off and only got them half way down when he fell on the bed. I don't think he know who I am. I pulled off his pants and let him sleep. I took off my clothes and put my pajamas on and went back to bed. I was very mad at him, but I did finally go to sleep. Then he started waking me calling me different names. I pushed him to the other side of the bed. I guess around two in the morning he fell out of the bed. I put his pillow under his head and cover him with a sheet and left him on the floor because he was too heavy for me to pickup.

The next morning Wilson fumbled around and finally got dressed for work. He asked Jones for an Aspirin, Jones said he didn't have an Aspirin in his room but there were some on the boat at work. I watched him silently as he got ready to leave for work. He tried to kiss me goodbye, but I turned away. I didn't know that stale alcohol could smell so foul on a person breathe until he tried to kiss me.

The smell lingered for almost ten minutes after he had left the room. I waited till I heard the front door close then I went downstairs to use the bathroom. When I finished using the bathroom I hurried back upstairs, because I didn't want to see Jones's devil girlfriend. I went back to bed; I was so mad at Wilson I cried myself to sleep. I woke up around ten that morning and went downstairs and took a shower. I returned to my room and got dressed. I decided to go visit

Sister Linda at the Money Exchange. When I arrived she was really busy changing Sailors dollars, so I took a seat and waited until she had a break. I decided to treat her to lunch and asked her what she likes to have for lunch. She said Philippine vegetables, so I went across the street to the restaurant and got our food. I went to the bar in back of the Money Exchange and got two paper plates. My friend at the bar asked me had I came back to work, I said no I was only visiting my sister. We took the food from the bag and put it into our plates. We start eating our lunch. Sister Linda said that the restaurant didn't know how to cook Philippines vegetables right...Mother could cook it much better. I agreed and told her I would go to the Shangri La Restaurant next time, because I think they cook their food a lot better. After we ate lunch I sat around making small talk and watching Sister Linda do her work. I felt sleepy so I went back to my apartment. When I arrived I looked around for Jones's girlfriend, but she was nowhere in sight so I rushed upstairs to my room. I lay across the bed for a quick nap, but I didn't wake up until I heard my room door open. I opened my eyes and Wilson was standing over me; I turned my back to him. He sat on the side of the bed and said he was sorry about last night...he had being invited to a party on base last night and had had too much to drink. I asked him why he had come home early...maybe he should go get drunk again...that seem to be the only thing he want to do anyway. He laid down beside me on the bed and I turned to keep my back to him. He managed to get his arms around me...I didn't fight him...he kept saying he was sorry about last night. He said it's three thirty let's go to the movie. I said go and get the girl you were talking to in your sleep last night and take her. He started kissing my neck and the side of my face.

He said you are the girl for me...I love you and I am very sorry for hurting your feeling and I will try my best not do it again. He was really getting to me...the smell of his cologne and his kisses... before I knew it I was kissing him back. He said let get something to eat and go to a movie. I said o.k. And got up and change my clothing. On our way downstairs I asked Wilson had he seen Jones and his girlfriend. He said Jones was still on the boat and his girlfriend was off somewhere visiting her relatives. I said that's why I haven't seen her lately.

We went to the Shangri La restaurant, I ordered a fried chicken dinner and he ordered a shrimp salad. After dinner we went looking for a movie showing Chinese film. After several stops we found one. The movie was very exciting Wilson is crazy about Chinese movies, so he really enjoyed the movie. When it were over we went straight back to our apartment. Wilson said tomorrow I get paid so your Mother can get your birth certificate. I told him I would have to spend the night before going to Pangasinan at Sister Melda's house… don't come to the apartment go to Sister Melda's house…Mother and Brother Etong will be going with me. He said wait a minute! I though your Mother was going to Pangasinan alone. I said I have to go in case they need me to sign for the birth certificate. He said I don't want you to go. I said I thought you wanted me to get my birth certificate… Mother said we be gone only one day. I changed into my nightgown. He looked at me and said you are going to come back right? I said yes! We jumped in the bed and started kissing and hugging. We were the only one in the apartment that night, so we played around and made love as loud as we wanted too. We finally got exhausted and we went to sleep.

Then ringing of the alarm clock woke us up. Wilson got up and got ready to go to work. On his way out I told him to be careful because he was by himself this morning. He kissed me goodbye and said there were another Sailor living on the other side of the building that will be walking with him to the jeepney stop. I said I see you tonight…oh! What time will you be home tonight? He said I might be a little early. I went back upstairs and climbed back in bed. Around seven that morning I was awaken by someone knocking on the front door. I got up and went downstairs to see whom it was; it was the cleaning lady, I let her in so she could get started washing clothes and cleaning the house.

I went back upstairs and took the lining off the bed and got all of my dirty clothes and took them downstairs to her. I went back upstairs and cleaned my room and let the cleaning lady do the rest of the house before she started washing the clothes. With the cleaning of my room and supervising the cleaning of the rest of the house, the day surprisingly went by very fast. By four o, clock all the bed lining were dry, so I put all fresh lining on the bed. Around five the cleaning lady left for the day. I told her to come back the next day, because Jones's girlfriend will be back. I thought to myself...Wilson is not home yet, he told me he was coming early. I made sure everything in our room was in order then I went out on the roof to wait for him. I waited and waited until around eight thirty; I was really upset, crying, cold and mad, so I went back to my room and put my sweater on. I lay on the bed and started to shiver, I didn't realize how cool it was out on the roof after dark. I couldn't figure out what had happened to Wilson, I change into my pajamas and went to bed so I could warm up. I laid there in my bed thinking to myself...is this the life that I am going to have with him...I don't know if my love can survive with his lies... what's happening to me? I cried myself to sleep.

I woke up around three the next morning, but Wilson and Jones hadn't showed up yet, so I went and used the bathroom and came back upstairs and packed my clothes. I laid back down on the bed to wait until daybreak, but I fell asleep and slept until around eight that morning. I got up to get ready to leave the apartment and heard someone say go upstairs and tell the girl to come down here. I knew it was the big mouth of Jones's girlfriend. Her niece came upstairs to my door and knocked. I answered the door and asked what do you want? She said her Aunt want to see me downstairs. I said o.k. I will be down as soon as I changed clothes. I could still hear Jones's girlfriend talking to someone down stairs. After changing my clothes I went down stairs to see what she wanted. She was sitting on the couch. I asked her how she enjoyed her vacation with her relatives. She said I don't want to talk about my vacation, I want to talk to you and your boyfriend...you have stayed her for a month already...you suppose to pay half of the rent...your boyfriend got paid yesterday, but you haven't given me the rent money yet. I said you are not here yesterday plus Jones and Wilson didn't come home. Why are you saying I didn't give you the rent money? We are not the one who made the deal to split the rent...Jones and Wilson made the deal to split the rent...I didn't make a rent deal with you.

She said if you want to stay here tell your boyfriend we are doing him a favor by letting him stay here and split the rent. I said why don't you tell him yourself when he come here tonight; he is the one with the money not me. She said the cleaning girl came here yesterday to wash your clothes; why haven't you paid her yet? I said now wait a minute! You said that we will pay the cleaning girl once a month... she will do my clothing one week and yours the next...it only being two weeks...plus I am upset about what you said about my boyfriend not paying his part of the rent and you said I haven't paid the cleaning girl and it only been two weeks...what are you thinking? I thought to myself...maybe she needs money for drugs. Then she said don't go anywhere today before your boyfriend get home...I need to pay the rent; I were suppose to pay it yesterday. I said you were not here yesterday. She said just don't go anywhere...I don't like people who cross me...I don't want to hurt anyone. I went up to my room I was really scared. I went outside on the roof to look for a place so I can cross over to the next roof and leave, but the space between the buildings was too wide for me to jump. I went back inside and sit on the side of my bed. I thought to myself...I hope Wilson comes here instead of going to Sister Melda's house tonight and Mother and Brother Etong don't arrive early at Sister Melda's house...what am I going to do...Jones's girlfriend had locked the front door and was sitting on the couch in the living room. I got hungry and went downstairs. I pretended to use the bathroom. When I came out I saw a loaf of bread on the table so I walked over to the table and got a piece of bread and drunk a lot of water. She was watching me as if she wanted to grab me and really hurt me. She even told her niece to stay in the living room. I thought to myself...if this is the end...let me die quickly...I don't want to suffer. I slowly made my way to the stairs trying to act as though I wasn't afraid. I went up the stairs and to my room. I locked the door behind me and tried to push the bed in front of the door, but it was too heavy. I decided that I wouldn't go back downstairs if I had to use the bathroom I would go out on the roof. Around three that afternoon I heard voices down stairs, so I went to the door and cracked it so that I may hear better what was going on downstairs. It was Jones and Wilson I sit on the bed and waited for Wilson to come to the room.

When he came in the door I ran to him and hugged him real tight. He asked me what was wrong. I told him Jones's girlfriend want the rent money and I told her that I didn't have any money to pay rent and that you are the one with the money...she is very mad because you didn't pay her yet…we need our own place. He said I am still trying to find a place for us…I will be right back. Wilson went downstairs to talk with Jones. He said Hey man! Didn't I give you my share of the rent money yesterday? Your girlfriend is mad at mines because she said I didn't pay my half of the rent. I was standing at the top of the stairs and could hear the whole conversation. Jones said I got you man! Don't worry about it I don't involve my girlfriend in our deal. Wilson said I didn't make a deal with your girlfriend I made it with you. Then Wilson came back upstairs and said let's get out of here. I hurriedly got ready and we went downstairs together. Jones's girlfriend was sitting on the couch and she smiled and said I was just playing with you and you got serious. Jones said shut up woman! Sorry man. We went straight to the front door and left. Wilson asked if I had eaten. I said no, and we went to the Magnolia Restaurant. Wilson ordered his favorite, shrimp potato salad and I ordered pepper steak and rice. I was so hungry that I started to order two servings. We finished eating and went out front and caught a jeepney to Sister Melda's house. Mother and Brother Etong hadn't arrived yet. Wilson and I took a seat in the living room and started making small talk. Sister Linda was in her room relaxing, sometime I think she be hiding from visitors. Sister Melda like being the center of attention; so she was going in and out of her room. Finally Wilson and I conversation lead up to me asking him what happened to him last night…I been waiting for you all day…you said that you was coming early to the apartment. He said that he had to work. We started hugging and kissing and Sister Melda came out of her room again. She said hey, love birds what are you going to do tonight? Wilson said I don't know what Vicky has planned, but I thought we were supposed to stay here. Vicky, her Mother and Etong are leaving for Pangasinan early tomorrow. I said we like to go nightclubbing with you guys tonight. She said I am suppose to meet him at seven tonight…what time is it Wilson? Wilson said it is six o, clock.

She went back into her room. About ten after six Mother and brother Etong arrived. Wilson said hello Mrs. Palaganas. Mother had a very happy smile on her face…she said hello and forgot Wilson name, so she asked me in Tagalog…what was Wilson name. I said Wilson Mother. Mother then turn and said hello Wilson and everyone started to laugh. Brother Etong smiled at Wilson with a hello nod of his head. Sister Linda came out of her room when she heard Mother and Brother Etong come in. Mother and Brother Etong sat at the kitchen table. Sister Linda busied herself checking the food to see if it had cook. I got up from the couch and went in the kitchen to find out why Mother was late coming here tonight. I said Mother you said you was coming early, what happened? She said I waited to ask your brother and his wife to feed the pigs while I am gone. O.k. I said. As I went back to sit down beside Wilson I was thinking...I am glad she didn't arrive here early and find out that I haven't being working, but living with Wilson. When I sit down I notice Wilson looking a little worried, so I asked him what was wrong. He said are you sure you will come back? Sister Melda heard Wilson when he asked me about coming back. She said Wilson it take only one day to go and come back...she said in Tagalog, Mother tell Wilson it only take one day to go and come from Pangasinan. Mother held up one finger and said one day Wilson. Wilson said o.k. Half smiling. Sister Melda said are you guys ready to go now? Both Wilson and I said yes and started for the door. Sister Melda gave Mother enough money to take Sister Linda and Brother Etong to the movie. Sister Linda turned to Brother Etong and said we're going to the movie and he started smiling and shaking his head in agreement. Mother said after we eat then we will go. We caught a tricycle and left. I asked Sister Melda where was we going to meet her boyfriend and she said in the jungle. I asked her why people call that section of Olongapo City the jungle. She said in the beginning the white and black military guys went to separate clubs to have fun in Olongapo City and for some reason they started calling it the jungle where the blacks hung out at and the whites hung out on the main drag called Magsaysay drive. Now black and white go all over and party, but they still call this part of the city the jungle.

Wilson was holding my hand so tight it felt like the blood had stop circulating, so I pull my hand from his grip and shake it so the blood would start to circulate again. Sister Melda's boyfriend was meeting her in the Harlem Club, so we went in and were seated. Sister Melda went to look for her boyfriend in the club. Wilson and I sat and kissed and watched the crowd while she was gone. A few minutes later she returned with her boyfriend and they joined us at the table. Her boyfriend looked at me and said hello little bit. I guess he thought I was a little girl because I am skinny. I said hello to him. Wilson asked me what I wanted to drink and I told him nothing. Then he asked Sister Melda and her boyfriend what would they like to drink. Sister Melda said she wanted Rum and coke and her boyfriend said he wanted a beer. Wilson asked me again what would I like to drink and I said nothing...I am not thirsty. Sister Melda's boyfriend said man you are going to save some money tonight. She is not expensive to take out and turn to look at Sister Melda. Sister Melda said oh! So you think I am expensive to take out...well I have my own money to buy my drinks. I don't need you to buy me a drink. He said I didn't mean to say you are expensive. I was only making small talk with Wilson. Sister Melda kept going on and on about the drinks until the waitress came with the drinks. Then Wilson paid for the drinks and told the waitress to bring me a coke. I ended up getting a drink anyway. I think Wilson did that to quiet Sister Melda down about the drinks. We sat and had a few more drinks and made small talk. Finally it started to get late so Wilson said he was going back to his boat tonight because I was leaving early the next morning for Pangasinan. He asked me if I was still coming back. I said yes I am coming back. Then he asked if I love him and I said of course I love you...don't worry I will only be away for one day. He smiled and said I guess I can make it for one day. Sister Melda's boyfriend had to go back to his boat also. We all got up and went outside and caught a jeepney to the base main gate. We kissed and said goodbye and started walking in our separate ways. Wilson turned around came and grab my hand. He wanted me to promise again that I was coming back. I said I promise I will come back. He said I love you and don't forget it; then he kissed me again and again. Sister Melda said lovebirds! Let's go home Vicky.

Wilson turned around and started walking toward the gate feeling down. I didn't want to leave him feeling that way, because I really did love him and I knew that he love me too. When we arrive at Sister Melda's house everyone was back from the movies and asleep. I got undress and ready for bed. I told Sister Melda we were leaving at five in the morning. She said o.k. I will set my alarm clock for four.

I went to bed, but I couldn't go to sleep because I started to thinking again...what if Wilson don't really want to marry a Filipino...what if I get pregnant...what would happen to me and my baby...maybe he just wanted me around to show the other guys he can have a girl that's not a club hostess. I kept turning from one side to the other. I guess Mother heard me moving around, because she said you better go to sleep Vicky. I tried not to move but I couldn't get Wilson off my mind. I just couldn't sleep, so finally the alarm clock went off at four. We all got up to get ready for our trip. I took a quick shower to revive my body it felt sleepy but I couldn't go to sleep. In the shower I started thinking again...why is it so important to him that I get my birth certificate...what if it just for show to make me think he want to marry me...I can't do anything if I get pregnant and he leave me and return to the States. Mother said hurry up in there we have to catch the bus at five thirty. I snapped out of my daydream and said o.k.

Finally we were ready to go and we went to the Victory Liner bus station. We got our tickets and were off to San Fernando, Pangpanga our first stop. We caught a train from Pangpanga to Malasique, Pangasinan. We had to take a Calesa (a horse buggy) to my uncle house. On our way to my uncle house, mother was talking to the driver and found out that he was our cousin. When we arrive at my uncle house in Alyaga, Pangasinan, Mother Aunt had come over to meet us. I have always called her Grandmother, but she is my Auntie. My Auntie said she was glad we had brought Brother Etong to help her son take care of his animals because he was having a very hard time by himself. She gave me a big hug and told me I had really grown into a beautiful young lady. Some of the kids I knew when I was in the first grade had gotten the word that we would be coming to Alyaga, so they came over to see me.

One of the girl said we are all grown up now and the other one said yes! And I have one kid...how about you. I said I am still single but I have a boyfriend. Mother called me and said we had to leave now to catch a Calesa back to Malasique, so we can catch a bus to Sual, Pangasinan. We said goodbye and we was off. When we got on the bus I went to sleep and slept all the way to Sual. When we arrive Mother woke me up and we caught a jeepney to the Municipal Building. I could tell that we were close to the Ocean because I could smell it. I remembered this smell when I was growing up here in Sual, Pangasinan, I felt like I was home again...this is the place where I got my first childhood shot...I played hide and go seek beside the ocean behind the boats...I said oh! I am home again. Mother said we're here now. Let's get your birth certificate. We went up to the big counter and a man came over to help us. I told him I wanted to get my birth certificate. I gave him my date of birth and he went over to a cabinet and got a big book and looked and looked in it. Finally he asked mother had she registered me in Dagupan City. Mother said why I would register her over there. The man asked again what year I was born. She said June 22, 1950 and her Father registered her birth not me. He wrote the information down on a piece of paper and started to look in the big book again. Finally Mother looked in the big book with the man. Then I took a turn looking in the big book. The man said I will check in another book. I started to get upset, so I asked to see the first book again. I checked the pages all the way to July 22, 1950 and I saw what had happen. They had registered my date of birth as July 22, 1950 instead of June 22, 1950. I showed the mistake to the man and asked him if he could change it to June 22, 1950. He said if he made a change in the record book he would get in trouble. I said well I guess I will have to be reborn again. He said you're lucky to have two birthday to celebrate. He typed out the birth certificate and gave it to us. We quickly ran out to catch a jeepney to the bus station in Dagupan City. When we arrive the last bus had left for San Fernando, Pangpanga. Mother said we have to stay here tonight, so we caught a jeepney back to Sual to spend the night at my Uncle Wife house. I said o.k. I know Wilson is going to be upset when we don't show up. Mother's sister-in-law was very happy seeing us again.

   She and Mother talk about their kids and how things had change since they have seen each other. Mother said do you remember Ambing...this is Ambing. She said yes I remember Ambing; she is the one that was hiding under the Bangka Boat. If she hadn't sneezed I would have missed her and she would have missed taking her vaccination because we had found everyone else. I said to myself... now I know where I have seen this lady; she is the one that pull me from under the Bangka Boat when I was hiding from the Nurse. Ambing were a nickname that was given to me, the old people believe that if you are sickly giving you a new name will keep you from getting sick again.

We sit around talking about old times and how things have change since we live here in Sual. Then it started to get late so everyone decided to turn in for the night because we had to leave early the next day to catch a bus to San Fernando to make our other connections to Olongapo City. I went to sleep right away because I was really tired. The next morning we were up and around early. My Aunt said the bus to San Fernando doesn't leave until ten today...why don't you go by the Market and look for souvenir to take back to Olongapo City...I am going to Dagupan City to the market. Mother asked me if I wanted to go with them and look around in the market until it was time to go and catch the bus. I agreed to go, so we were off to the market. When we arrived I started looking around at the different things they had for sale. I found a nice pair of slippers for Wilson. As soon as I paid for the slippers Mother asked me why had I bought slippers for Wilson? I told her that I liked the slippers and wanted him to have them. My Mother was very superstitious; she believed that if you buy your boyfriend slippers or shoes he would run around all the time. She said well if you love him and he loves you it may make a different. It was time to leave for the bus station so we hugged my Aunt and said our goodbyes and left for the station. When we arrived the bus was filled almost full. We hurried onboard and took our seat. As soon as the bus pulled out heading for San Fernando Mother and I fell asleep we didn't wake up until the driver said Olongapo City connection. I woke Mother up and we hurried off the bus. We bought boiled banana, peanut and coke before boarded our bus to Olongapo City. Mother seems as if she was enjoying our trip.

Mother said I am really glad we had the chance to spend some time with my sister-in-law...she really loved my brother...he was killed by the Japanese and she has never remarried...her love for men died with him. Mother said tell me about Wilson and before I could respond she said you both are young...the trouble is he is an American...he goes all over the world and meet a lot of people... you are a Filipino you has just started to blooming like a flower... you don't know very much about your surrounding yet...he does because he travel around meeting a lot of girls...they party, drink and smoke...you are a house girl not a party girl...I really worry about you because you are my Daughter and I love you...I pray to God that he really love you. I said Mother I really love him and loving and being loved is a part of life; I guess I will have to take my chances with him and hope that he love me back. Mother turned and looked at me and said you really have grown up...you sound like an older woman...I just really want a good life for you because I never had one...we will be home before dark. My heart started to pound in anticipation of seeing Wilson; I really missed him. I want to see my Wilson... I said to myself...come on bus and move fast...I want him to hug, kiss and caress me like he always does...if I only could fly I would be there already.

Finally we arrived in Olongapo City; I hurried to call a tricycle so Mother and I could ride home. The tricycle drove up to Sister Melda's house and I quickly got out and knocked on the door. Wilson opened the door in surprise, he looked as if he was going to faint. He took my hand and pulled me to him. He hugged and kissed me. I could feel his heart pounding...he was so over whelmed by my return he forgot to help Mother in the door with the packages she was carrying. Finally he came back to reality and grab the packages from Mother and carried them to the table...he told Mother he was sorry that it took so long for him to help her with her packages. Mother just smiled and said o.k. Sister Melda said, with her big mouth, take your boyfriend home, he is driving me crazy; I told him not to worry you would be back, but he couldn't keep still. Wilson said I wanted to come to Pangasinan to look for you but I didn't know the first place to start looking. Mother turned to Wilson and said Melda! Tell Wilson what I am saying...now you have Vicky birth certificate do what you suppose to do so you can be together...I know you said you love my Daughter...you have my blessing...do the right thing.

Sister Melda repeated to Wilson what she had said. Wilson told Mother he would do the right thing. Mother and Sister Linda left going to Calapacuan. Sister Melda said I am meeting my boyfriend at seven what are you love bird going to do? Wilson said we are staying home tonight. I went over to the kitchen table and got the slippers I bought him. He tried them on and said they fit perfectly. We went into the bedroom I use to share with Sister Linda and start kissing and hugging. When everyone had left, Wilson said let go to the apartment. I didn't really want to go because I knew Jones's devil girlfriend, will be on my back again. I said o.k. I didn't want Wilson to know what was going on between us and I remembered what she had said about crossing her. I have to go back to the apartment because I don't want her to think that I am crossing her. I thought to myself...what am I going to do now...I guess I will have to play it the same way I played it before...act like she is not around...if she is around, act like I am not afraid. Wilson and I got the bags that I brought and we left for the apartment. When we arrived Jones and his devil girlfriend was nowhere in sight, so we hurried up to our room. We just wanted to be alone together. I really missed him and I know that he missed me too, because he can't keep his hands off me. We ran straight to our bed and made love like we had been apart for a month. As I lay in his arms I felt save and content; then I felt asleep.

The next thing I heard was Jones voice saying get up man it's time to go to work. Wilson got up and dress for work. He asked me what I had plan for the day. I told him I plan to visit Sister Melda. He said well! I will see you around five thirty this afternoon. He sit down on the side of the bed and started kissing me again, then he realized he had to go so he jumped up and readjusted his pants on the way out of the door. I covered myself and went back to sleep. During the next few weeks we would go out to the club or a movie, but we spent most of the time in our room. Everything was going pretty smooth except my encounters with Jones's devil girlfriend. She always tried to scare me. I made it a point to avoid her, but sometime she would catch me when I am down stairs using the bathroom. I would pretend that her threats didn't matter at all. I would just go on about my business and ignore her piercing eyes. Sometime she would come up stairs and peep in my room, but if she doesn't say anything I just keep cleaning or doing whatever I am doing at the time.

One day as I was relaxing in my room I heard the front door down stairs slam real hard. I got up and went down stairs to see what was going on. When I got to the bottom of the stairs I could see Jones's girlfriend standing and clinching her fist. I asked her what was wrong. She said why do you want to know...you going beat her up for me. I said no! I just wanted to know what happened because I heard the door slam down here. She said if you don't want to get hurt you better go back upstairs. I turned around and went back upstairs to my room. Around lunchtime I got hungry, so I went downstairs to get me something to eat. She was sitting on the couch with a knife in her hand. I went straight to the kitchen and got bread, liver spread, a big glass of water and a knife. I said to myself...now I have me a knife if she comes close to me. I will stab her too. I tried to pretend that she was not sitting on the couch, so I would not be so scared. I started for the stairs, when I reached the bottom of the stairs. I said to myself...if she just sit there and don't move. When I reached the top of the stairs, I quickly ran into my room and locked the door. I sit quietly on the bed for a few minutes listing for footsteps coming upstairs. I said to myself maybe she is not going to follow me. I spread a towel on the side of my bed for a make shift tablecloth and put my food on it. I had a small picnic by myself. As I was eating my food I couldn't help thinking...what was wrong with her...she need help... what make her act like this...she want to threatened and fight little old me...I can't understand it...I haven't did anything to her, but she want to control what I do...now she is sitting down stairs with a knife in her hand and starring down at the floor...if she come upstairs I am not going to open that door...if she start trying to kick it in maybe someone from next door will hear the noise and come over. I really hope Wilson come home early and tell me he have found a new place for us. I finished eating and put everything away. I lay down on the bed thinking about my situation and before I knew it I was asleep. Around two o, clock the door down stairs was slammed again wakening me up. I got up and slowly opened the door and listened for any sound from downstairs. I went downstairs and looked around to see if she had gone. I didn't see or hear anyone so I ran back upstairs and to get my things so I can take a shower before Wilson arrive.

I hurried taking my shower, when I finished; I opened the door slowly and looked out to see if she had returned. When I was satisfied she had not returned I quickly ran out of the shower and up the stairs to my room and locked the door. I toweled my hair dry and got dressed. When I finished dressing, I sit there on the side of my bed waiting for Wilson to come and hold me tight, so I can forget what's happening here with this devil woman. When Wilson is around I always feel safe. But sometime I get scared for both of us, when she, the devil woman start acting up. I know she belong to a gang and is a troublemaker, but I don't know how far she will go when she get mad. That why I want say anything to Wilson about her, he may say something to her and she get mad and try hurting him or have someone in her gang do it. I rather get hurt than let something happen to him. So I take the insults and the threatening from her and keep it from him, because I love him very much. Suddenly I felt the need to use the bathroom again; I opened the door very slowly listening for any sound; I couldn't hear anything, so I went downstairs to the bathroom. When I finished I opened the bathroom door and Wilson and Jones was coming in the front door. Jones and Wilson said hi almost the same time and I said hi to them. Wilson gave me a big kiss and asked me if I had eating, I said no! We went upstairs and he said get ready we're going out. He sat down on the bed and I started to rub his shoulder. He grabbed me and pulled me down beside him and started kissing me and we were on our way. My stomach started to growl and he heard it, so he stopped and asked if that was my stomach. I said yes! He said you are hungry I thought you went to visit your sister today. I said I didn't feel good so I stayed home and only had a sandwich. Then we started hearing noise from downstairs, it was Jones and his devil girlfriend fighting. Wilson said let's wait for a while before going downstairs, so we waited and listen to what was going on downstairs. Finally we heard them go into their bedroom and close the door, so we hurried downstairs and out the door. We walked to the Magnolia Restaurant in the Jungle and went inside an ordered our usually, shrimp potato salad for Wilson and chop suey and rice for me. We savior our food for more than an hour; while discussing our next move to finding another apartment. Wilson said there was a list of approved furnished and unfurnished apartments in the housing office on base.

Wilson said he was going to check the list as soon as he can and see if we can afford to rent one of the furnished apartments. When we finished our meal we decided to take a walk over to Magsaysay drive and see what's showing on the movies. Most of the movie theaters were on Magsaysay drive. We walked up Rizal Avenue to where Rizal Avenue and Magsaysay drive intersect and turn up Magsaysay drive in the direction of the Naval Base. After checking all of the theaters we realized that we had seen all of the movies that were showing, so we decided to go home. I was tired anyway, so we caught a jeepney and went home. When we arrived at the apartment we found Jones sitting on the couch drinking a beer. We said hi to him and he looked up and said hi. Wilson asked him if he had more beer and he said yes! Look in the refrigerator. Wilson went to the refrigerator and took out two beers and we went upstairs. We went inside our room and closed the door. Wilson took a seat on the side of the bed and started to drink his beer. I thought to myself...I guess he will get drunk on those beers. I started to get ready for bed. I tried to unzip the back of my dress when the zipper got stuck, so I asked Wilson to help me with it. I turned my back to him and he unzipped my dress. I went to the closet to hang it up and he said come here Sweetheart. I was startled when he said Sweetheart. I said why are you calling me Sweetheart, my name is not Sweetheart...is that your girlfriend name... you can't remember my name? I was very upset with him. I put my nightgown on in a hurry and sit on the side of the bed. He kissed me and told me that Sweetheart, Dear, Honey and Baby are pet names that you call someone when you love them; He said that I could call him one of those names if I wanted to. He kissed and hugged me again. I said o.k. I lay back in the bed thinking...now he call me his Sweetheart...it felt good knowing that I belong to him and I am his Sweetheart...I like it better than Vicky...it has a sweet sound to it. He started caressing me while he was drinking his beer. He finished his beer and got up and put on his pants. He said he would be right back.

I thought he was going for more beer, but he went to the bathroom instead. He came back and took off his pants and jumped in the bed and started kissing and caressing me all over again. We made love; when we finished I lay in his arms thinking...why is love like this... it feel so good to be with the man you love...I know now what love is all about...love is caring for each other...love is sacrificing to protect each other...love is hurting and being hurt sometimes...love is life...love is the one that conquer all. These are the things that I have realized while being with the man I love. Loving him is just like I am living in a fantasy world; it feels so good that I don't want it to end. I fell asleep.

The next morning I was woken by voices coming from downstairs, Jones and his girlfriend was up early, because we had the alarm clock in our room and it had not rung. A couple of minutes later the alarm went off. Wilson got up and got dress for work, he said he was going to check the listing of apartments in the Housing office before he comes home today. He wanted me to be ready to go and see the apartment that available as soon as he gets home. I promised him that I would be ready to go when he return. He kissed me goodbye and left for work. I went back to bed thinking…what will the devil woman do today, now that we are all alone…I hope she have somewhere to go so she want be watching every move I make…sometime I think Wilson ask her to watch me, but I quickly discard that ideal…I know he love and trust me. I finally drifted off to sleep.

I was woken again this time I heard screaming and yelling; then I heard a knock on my door. I asked who is it? The voice said my Auntie want to talk to you downstairs. I look at the clock it was eight o, clock in the morning; I said tell her I will be right there. I got up and put my robe on and went downstairs. When I reached the bottom of the stairs I took a deep breath and calmly ask her what did she want. She started yelling you or your boyfriend has thrown up all over the bathroom…why don't you clean the bathroom when you or him get sick…do you think I am your Maid? I said I didn't get sick and I don't think my boyfriend got sick, because he only drunk two beers last night and I don't think he will get sick from two beers. She yelled you don't think! Looking up from her seat on the couch as if she wanted to hit me.

She said the bathroom has always been clean until you guys moved in here now it's never cleaned. I said have you asked your boyfriend about it, maybe he did it…he drinks a lot of beer. Then she realized that that her boyfriend does drink a lot of beer, so she calmed down. She said I have something to tell you about Jones and your boyfriend…when I went to visit my relatives a few days ago; Jones and your boyfriend spent the night with another woman…I am telling you this so you can prepare yourself for the worse…you remember telling me that both of them didn't come home that night…both of them spent the night with girl from the club...promise me you want tell them what I said...don't cross me now. I said I promised. She said I know the girl they was with, one work in the Silver Dollar Club and the other one works in the Birdland Club...I have girlfriends all over the jungle they are in my OXO Gang; they tell me everything they see...we use to hurt people that cross us...they didn't tell me the name of the girl your boyfriend was with, but they said she is very pretty and is older than you. Her words were tearing my heart out, my stomach was in a knot and I couldn't breathe comfortable. I remembered Wilson telling me he had duty that night after he got paid. I started crying and she stopped talking for a minute; then she said that why Jones and I always fight...I know you hear us fighting...I want to kill or hurt him real bad, but I don't want any witnesses...you and your boyfriend staying here, so I have to play it cool...you think you have a man...you are a fool to believe we are the only one in his life...they have girls all over the Jungle...Jones promised me that I would be his steady girlfriend, but as soon as my back is turned he run to the Hotel with the first girl he find...you think I am happy about that...what if he give me a sickness...that's why I am telling you this so you can get ready for the worse...your boyfriend has a lot of girlfriends too...he is more handsome than my Jones. All I could do was cry, because I didn't know whom to believe anymore. When I met him he had girlfriends and I knew two of them. I thought to myself...maybe it was Lucy or the girl that works in the Swan Club that he had in the Hotel. I finally pulled myself together and stopped crying. We sat quietly on the couch.

Her niece broke the silence when she said the shower is clean Auntie, do you want me to cook breakfast now. She said yes! Fry me two eggs and some spam; she turned and asked me how many eggs did I want. I said two. She told her Niece to go to the store before she starts cooking and get some bread rolls. Her Niece picked up her bag and left for the store. Jones girlfriend calmly said she was going to find out if Jones got sick last night. She said if you decide to move out and go back to work in the Money Exchange and have some trouble in the Jungle; all you have to do is come knock on my door and tell me what's wrong and I will take care of it. I almost told her she was my problem, but I didn't want her to get mad again, so I said thank you! As I sat there in the couch beside her, my mind started wandering again...what's going to happen to me if Wilson decide he like the girl in the club better than me...what if I get pregnant and he decide to marry an American instead of me...what will happen to my baby and me...maybe he just want to play around with the girl in the Philippines...what if I am just one of his toys, he keep me until he get tired of me, then cast me away? Jones girlfriend Niece broke my chain of thought when she said I have finished cooking and the food is on the table. She said let eat now, we will finish our business when they get home. We got up and went to the table and started to eat breakfast. I was not very hungry, but I ate one egg and a roll, because she is trying to be nice to me. She said if you ready to take a shower when you finish eating; go ahead the shower is clean now. She said she would take her shower when I finished. I thought to myself...what did her Niece put in the food...I haven't never seen her act this nice before...if there is something in the food I want her to continue eat it, maybe she will continue to be nice. Then she calmly said please don't tell anyone what I told you about my OXO gang in the Jungle...I have tried to change my way of life...I try not to hurt anyone, but people sometime cross you...that the time when I can't promise to control my other way of life...killing and being killed...I want you to promise me you want tell anyone o.k. I said o.k. Then I excused myself and went upstairs to my room. I fixed the unmade bed and sit down on the side of it. I thought...what have I got myself into now...Wilson is cheating on me...Jones girlfriend is going to kill me if I say something to him about what she said he did...I thought he really loved me...what kind of love is this?

I was getting a headache so I lay down on the bed and hugged my pillow close to my chest; my stomach was in a knot it was just like a burning sensation reaching all the way to my heart. I thought...my love... my life... my youth... everything. I have given it to him; what else can I give? Well I guess I asked for this, I let it happen, because I love him. I lay there thinking over and over what did I do wrong; finally fatigue set in and I fell asleep. I was woken by Jones girlfriend big mouth downstairs, she was calling. I went downstairs to see what she wanted. She said my Niece is going to the market do you want her to get something for you? I said yes! Buy me two milkfish, that's what we will have for lunch. So I ran back upstairs and got the money for the fish. I gave her five pesos for the fish. Then they left going to the market; I went back upstairs to get my things for my shower. I felt very relax and not scared for a change. I went in the shower and started to sing a little. I spent twice the amount of time that I usually stay in the shower. When I finished my shower I ran upstairs and sit on the side of my bed and towel dry my hair.

Later I went downstairs and started the rice cooking; I wanted it to be ready when they return, because it didn't take too long to fry the fish. After I finished in the kitchen with the rice, I went into the living room and sit down on the couch. I started thinking about what Wilson had said to my Mother. He said I love your Daughter and want to marry her. I wonder if he was telling her a lie…that really worried me because I didn't want her to get her hope up and find out it was just a lie. Mother has did all kind of work just to make sure we had something to eat; if she finds out that Wilson lied, it will break her heart. How am I going to explain this to her? I remembered the look on her face when she gave him my birth certificate and told him to do the right thing. Oh! My mind is wandering again; I have to stop this. A few minutes later Jones girlfriend and her Niece came back from the market with all of the food and put it on the kitchen table. She told her Niece to cook some rice and I said I had cook rice already. Then she told her Niece to clean the fish. I sit at the table and helped her cut up the vegetables. We had string beans, eggplant, bitter melon and okra; I got the big frying pan and started cooking the vegetables. I put a little cooking oil in the pan…added chopped garlic and brown it…added chop pork and let it brown…added chopped tomatoes and salted shrimp and let it simmer for a while then added the rest of the vegetable and stir fried everything until the vegetable was tender. She said the food smell real good; I didn't know you know how to cook this kind of food. She told her Niece to hurry and cook the fish. Jones girlfriend was the first one to get to the table and start eating. She said the vegetables are real good I should have watched how you cooked the vegetables. I said that's the way I learned; I watched my Mother cook. She didn't wait for us to get to the table, before she started eating. After I finished helping her Niece clean the table and wash the dishes, I sit on the couch with her. We talked for a while like we were civilized. She said you are young and pretty…you think you have a nice young man…he's the one the girl in the club want… someone that don't know about them yet…I know because I wanted it too…I been through that kind of life with different young guys. My stomach started to tighten up again while listening to her. She said I was happy when Jones said that he wanted to go steady with me, because I could be out of the club for a while…I could be with one man until he get tired of me and then back to the club. She looked as if she was going to cry. Then she said I am getting old I don't know what I am going to do…working in the club marks you as a bad girl, because you have been with a lot of men. I thought…why is she telling me all of this now? She said when I started in the club; I was young and very beautiful and every Sailor I met said that he love me and later I see him with another girl…now when someone say that to me I just say you want my body…I become wiser around Sailors…I tell them if you don't have money you don't get my honey…before I go with them I ask for the money first, because sometime they take you to the Hotel and don't have money; they get your honey and don't give you any money. I said what did you do with your money? She said I didn't save any money I just buy me pretty tight dresses and party…Sailors love my tight dresses…they even say that they want to marry me. I said did you ever marry one? She said no! How am I going to marry someone that just wants my body and the other girl body too? She seem as though she was getting upset so I just sat, listen and kept quiet.

She said it's too late for me to meet someone and get married… I started my life working in the club…you said that you worked in the Money Exchange and you are young and haven't worked in the club; you can find a man that will fall in love with you and leave the other girl alone…what I am saying is you need to forget your boyfriend, because he like older pretty women, not to old but older than him…I know, because my OXO gang friend is one of them he like…her name is Lucy…I didn't want to tell you where she works. What she told me was real upsetting. I said to myself…I know Lucy, but I didn't know she was in a gang. She said there is a lot of us in the Jungle…we hurt other girl that take our boyfriend, but we don't fight each other, because we know it only a job and we don't cross each other…we use to beat up other girl; we brake their arm, leg and sometime they end up in the hospital for a long time…If Sailors cross my gang we would drop drugs in their drinks and when they pass out we would get their money from their wallet and put the wallet back…We took watches and jewelry too…that how we made extra money…you have to be fast and clever; I started when I was young. I started yawning. She said are you trying to go to sleep on my story? Before I could answer. She looked at the time and said it's three thirty I guess I better take a shower…don't tell anyone what I told you…I like you because you are quiet…I wanted to tell you about me. She got up and went into her room. I went upstairs to get ready before Wilson came home. I started thinking…what am I going to do, I think Wilson has a girlfriend in the OXO gang. I hope it's someone else not Lucy. Oh! What am I thinking? I started to feel sorry for the Sailors that cross the girl in the OXO gang; I can't tell anyone about this. I guess I have to try and pretend this is not happening to me. I wish I could wake up and find out that this whole mess involving living here in this apartment was a bad dream. The longer I live here the more bad stuff I learn about what's going on. Maybe the next time I talk to Jones girlfriend she will tell me that she and her gang have killed someone. Oh boy! Maybe I will go back to Calapacuan and live with my Mother and get my job back in the Money Exchange. Just like everyone says…I am young and pretty and can start over again. I feel like I have been used and abused sometime…I don't know what or who to believe anymore.

I want to believe Wilson when he tell me he love me and want to marry me, but Jones devil girlfriend has been telling me all of this stuff about him liking older girls. I looked at the time it was five thirty; Wilson is suppose to be home already. So I put some baby powder on my face and went out on the roof to wait for him. This time I took my sweater because the last time I came out on the roof I got chilly. I thought to myself…he will be coming in a little while and I will be able to see him…my sweetheart is coming home from work. I even made a song…my sweetheart is coming home from work… my sweetheart is coming home from work. I kept singing it to myself until about seven o, clock; and then I got tired of waiting and went downstairs to the bathroom. When I finished I decided to go ahead and eat, so I went into the kitchen and ate fried fish and rice. I went back up to my room and sit on the side of my bed; I started counting the panel in the window; I counted them over and over. Finally I hear footsteps coming up the stairs and the door to our bedroom opened and it was Wilson. I could smell the liquor on his breath as soon as he walked in the door. I looked at my watch and it was eight thirty. I thought…it's only eight thirty and he is drunk already. He said get ready we're going out. I said you're drunk already, why are we going out? He said it again…get ready we're going out and meet your sister and her boyfriend in the Supreme club. When he said we're meeting your sister; I agreed to go because I didn't want Sister Melda to know that I was having a problem with Wilson drinking. I got ready and we left and went to the Supreme club. Sister Melda and her boyfriend were there so we joined them at their table. We said hi to them and Sister Melda said hi, but her boyfriend said hi little bit to me; he always call me little bit. We sit down and ordered our drinks; I started watching the girls dance with the Sailors in the middle of the floor. When they played a slow record Wilson wanted to dance, so we went out on the dance floor and started to dance, we almost lost our balance because he was to drunk. I said let's sit down now. He insisted on dancing; I thought to myself…I wish this song hurry and finish, when it finished Wilson didn't want to sit down, he wanted to wait for the next record to play. I walked away and left him in the middle of the floor. When I came back to the table by myself Sister Melda asked where was Wilson. I turned to look but back where I left him, but he had disappeared. The music started and I saw him dancing with one of the club hostess.

Sister Melda saw him about the same time as I did; she got real upset and told her boyfriend to go and get Wilson. He returned with Wilson and Wilson sat down and tried to kiss Sister Melda. Her boyfriend said man that's not Vicky, that's my girlfriend. Sister Melda said Wilson what's wrong with you…don't you know who I am? I am Vicky's Sister. Sister Melda said you better take your boyfriend home before he get into trouble. Her boyfriend told Wilson he better take me home. Wilson didn't want to leave. Sister Melda was very upset, she told her boyfriend to get a jeepney so they to take us home. He went outside and got a jeepney and came back to help Wilson out to the jeepney. They went with us to the apartment. Her boyfriend helped Wilson upstairs to our room. I went back downstairs to talk to Sister Melda. She was still upset. I told her he would be all right. She said my boyfriend drinks, but he controls it when he's with me...did you and him have a fight. I said no! He just likes to drink. She said you come home and leave him if he continue like this...I never seen him drunk like this before. Her boyfriend said we have to go now... see you later little bit. I said thank you and goodnight. I went back upstairs and remove Wilson shoes and clothes. I put on my nightgown and lay down to try to go to sleep. I started to thinking...I am not use to this kind of life...I have to really give this some serious thought... is this the life I want...all he wants is to drink and party...is this the way it will always be...I better get out of here...Jones girlfriend was right, I am young and pretty and can still make it out there...I will leave him if he get drunk like this tomorrow night and let him find someone else to use and abuse.

I got up and finished packing the clothes I had started packing the time before when I started to leave him. He had been in the closet several times and had not notice the box of clothes in the corner. I went back to bed. The more I thought about my situation the more I was convinced that I need to leave him. I thought...I really and truly love him...that's why it's so hard for me to leave him...if he love me like I love him, he would protect and care for me and make me feel save like I always feel when I am in his arms. I cried and cried as I hugged his back until I fell asleep.

The next morning he didn't want to get up and go to work because he was still somewhat drunk. I kept at him until he got up and put his clothes on. Jones was calling from downstairs telling him to hurry so they wouldn't be late. Finally he was dressed and he kissed me and left without saying anything. My heart ached when he left, I wanted to tell him that I love him, but he left in a hurry. He didn't say he would see me tonight.

After I finished my shower that morning I went to see Sister Melda. She asked me what I was doing there so early. I said oh! I just wanted to get out of the apartment for a while; I can't take it anymore. She said what happened? Did you and Wilson have a fight after we left last night? I said no! I just can't take his drinking anymore and

I started to cry. She said I have never seen Wilson drunk like that before; he didn't know who I was last night. She said this is what we will do; I will come visit you this evening and if Wilson is drinking you will come home with me...you need to leave him for a while. If he is single like he said he is then he is going to want you back...don't cry I know it hurts sometimes.

She said I told you he is married...we will see if I am right or wrong. I thought to myself...even if she is wrong she will still insist she is right...she is the winner of all augments right or wrong...she is my sister and crazy too...like Jones's girlfriend she is a very sick woman. Well I guess I will see what happens tonight; I pray that he has not been drinking.

When I went back to my apartment I didn't see Jones girlfriend, so I went upstairs to my room. I felt very down knowing what I might have to do tonight. The time went surprisingly fast that day; before I realized it Wilson was coming upstairs from work. When he came in the door I could smell the alcohol on his breath. He sat on the side of the bed and started talking about seeing another apartment. I heard Sister Melda call me from downstairs. I went downstairs. She said you need to come with me now. I went back upstairs and told Wilson I was leaving with Sister Melda. He didn't say anything, so I went to the closet and got my clothes. Then he said I don't want you to go. When he said that my heart almost jumped out of my chest; I had to be strong so I kept walking to the door. I wanted to go back and hug him, but I kept walking toward the stairs. I didn't know if he was following me to try and stop me from leaving.

I tried to look over my shoulder to see if he was behind me, but I didn't see him. I thought maybe he just don't care anymore. Sister Melda and I left and went to her house. I went to the bedroom that I use to share with Sister Linda. I sit on the bed; then I lay down and started to cry and cry. Finally Sister Melda felt sorry and came into the room and tried to comfort me. She said I told you he have a wife, if he didn't he would have tried to stop you from leaving... he didn't even follow you outside. She was not helping me at all with what she was saying; it only made me feel worse. She said let's go to Pangasinan and see Brother Etong, if you like you can stay there for a while. She didn't say anything to make me feel better; I ended up crying myself to sleep.

Early the next morning she woke me up and said let's get ready to go. I got up and got ready to travel. We caught a jeepney to the bus station. When we arrived the bus for Pangasinan was loading up, so we bought our tickets and quickly boarded it. During the bus ride to Pangasinan I tried to sleep, but I felt so down and out all I did was daydream. When we arrived at my Grandmother house we asked the where about of Brother Etong. She told us that my Uncle and Brother Etong was on the other side of the river and would be back in about a week. We sat and made small talk for a while. Finally I couldn't take it anymore, so I told Sister Melda I wanted to go back to Olongapo City. She said we just got here. I said we were just coming to see Brother Etong, but he is not here. We said goodbye to my Grandmother and left for the bus station. Sister Melda said if I knew you didn't want to stay I wouldn't have came here. I kept quiet; I didn't want to auger I wanted to return to Olongapo City, so I can be close to Wilson. I just want to be close to him I don't care if he has a girlfriend now. On our way back to Olongapo City, we made small talk until I fell asleep. We got back to Olongapo City in time for Sister Melda to keep a date with her boyfriend. Before she left the house she told me to stay home and if I just had to go somewhere I could visit Sister Rose in Barretto. She said she was going to look around for Wilson and see if he has another girlfriend and if he asked her where I am she was going to tell him I was in Pangasinan.

She said don't plan on going to the Money Exchange yet; I will tell you when to go there. When she left I stayed in my bedroom thinking of no one but Wilson. I thought to myself...I don't care anymore about him drinking and maybe having another girlfriend... if that's what he want; I just want to be with him. That night when sister Melda came home, she said she saw Wilson dancing with one of the girl in the club; she couldn't tell whether they were sitting together in the club. I said its o.k. They were only dancing. I am going to work Sister Linda shift tomorrow morning. She said that's o.k. You will be working during the day while he is at work and he want see you.

The next morning I got up and went to work. Being at work was just plain torture all I thought about was Wilson. When some of the customers that I knew before come around and try to talk to me; I couldn't really concentrate enough to make them feel that I care about what they were saying. It was a long drawn out lazy day that went very, very slow. I wish I could push the time up so I could get off and go home. I checked the time again it was five o, clock and the lady that works the night shift is not here. Sanders, one of Wilson friend came by and saw me in the Money Exchange. I thought Wilson would be coming behind Sanders so I ran in the bathroom. When I came back Sanders was gone and the lady was there to start her shift. I hurried to turn over everything to her so I could go home. As soon as I got home Sister Melda said get ready we're going out with my boyfriend. I jumped in the shower and when I came out I put my pink and green dress on. I even let my hair down to my shoulders. We met her boyfriend at the Supreme club; we stayed there for a while, but we didn't see Wilson. Sister Melda told her boyfriend she wanted to go to the new club, The Place to play, so we left and walked down the street to the new club. The club was filled almost to capacity, but we managed to get seated. Sister Melda ordered rum and coke and a coke for me. One of Wilson friend saw us and came to say hi. Sister Melda asked him had he seen Wilson and he said I saw him a few minutes ago in here. I started looking around and finally saw him talking to one of the girl on the other side of the club. My stomach started burning like it was on fire all the way to my heart. Sister Melda saw what was happening, so she told me to dance with her boyfriend. He got up and said come on little bit. We went out on the dance floor and danced a fast dance, when we got back Wilson was sitting at our table looking at me. He held my hand and I felt just like I did the first time we met. We sat there holding hands. Sister Melda said lovebirds go dance, but he didn't move he just sat there looking like he wanted to grab me and hug me. This time he wanted to act nice with me. Then someone played our theme song, maybe the last time by James Brown. He asked me if I wanted to dance; I didn't say anything I just nodded. When we got on the dance floor he held me real tight and kissed me. I felt like we was the only one in the place; it felt so good to be in his arms again. I knew that I didn't want to be without him anymore. When our song was over we sat back down at our table. He held on to my hand. He said he love me and was never

going to let me go again. Sister Melda said we have to go now. I said
I want to stay with Wilson. Sister Melda and her boyfriend got up
said goodbye and left. Wilson said let's go find a place to stay tonight.
We went to the Magnolia Hotel and went to the restaurant first and he
ordered his favorite dish, shrimp potato salad, I didn't want anything
to eat because I had eaten before I left home. I sat and watched him
finish eating his food. After he finished, he went to the front desk and
got a room. We went to our room and he locked the door. He removed
his shirt and hanged it in the closet; I sat on the bed watching him;
then he removed his t-shirt and gave it to me. I turned my back to him
so he could unzip my dress. He fumbled with the zipper and finally
made it work...he kissed me on my shoulders as I pulled my dress
off. I went to the closet and hanged my dress and put his shirt on.
He had stopped looking and started staring at me. I asked him what
was wrong. He said nothing! I just love you and missed being with
you...I never want to be without you. Then he held me and kissed me
over and over; I had to push him away to catch my breath. I started
to cry, because I was so happy; he said don't cry, it sounded like he
was crying too. We made our way to the bed and made love like there
was no tomorrow. As I lay there in his arms I thought to myself...
if I die I want to die this way, with the man I love. We lay quietly
for a while; then we talked about an apartment of our own. He said
we are getting a place close to Sister Melda's house. The people will
be moving out the end of September 1968. I asked him what he was
going to do about the apartment.

He said we will pick up the clothes you left tomorrow...wait at
your sister House and we will go there together and get your clothes.
He kissed me again. I said what happened to our bed? He said I told
them to come and pick it up, because I didn't want it anymore. When
you left I told them I have to give up the apartment, because you had
left and I wouldn't need the bed anymore. He said now that you are
back I am going to get the apartment that I looked at before. Then he
started kissing and caressing me over and over again. I said we better
go to sleep. He said are you sleepy? I said no! But you have to go to
work tomorrow. So he hugged and held me real tight. I think he was
watching me, because every time I moved he would pull me even
closer to him, so I stopped moving and went to sleep. The next thing I

heard was someone knocked on the door and said sir it's time to wake up. Wilson said o.k. Thank you! Wilson and I got up and got dressed; I gave him his t-shirt back. We went out of the hotel together and caught a jeepney to the base main gate. Wilson said he was getting off work early today and would meet me at Sister Melda's house. He kissed me and was on his way to through the gate. I said see you later sweetheart. I went back to the jeepney stop and caught a jeepney to Sister Melda's house. When the jeepney pulled off I could see Wilson watching me from the main gate; I watched until we were buried in the morning traffic and I couldn't see him anymore. I thought to myself...whatever happen from this day on, I promised myself to stick with him no matter what...for better or worse...I will be with the man I love...I want let anyone tell me I can't be with him.

When I arrive at Sister Melda's house I stopped at the Sari Sari store across the street and bought bread rolls. I opened the door of her house and went straight to the kitchen to start breakfast. I boiled some water to make oval tine drink and fried eggs and spam. I wanted breakfast to be ready when sister Melda wakes up. Just before I finished she came out of her room; she asked me what happened to me last night. I told her Wilson and I had spent the night in the hotel. She said what happened to the apartment. I said Wilson didn't want to stay there without me so he gave it up. I said we are getting a new apartment the end of September. She looked at the calendar on the wall and said that's only five more days. I said yes, it want be long before we move in it.

He wanted me to stay here and he will stay on his boat until the people move out the end of this month. She said you are going to need a lot of thing to get started in your new place. I told her our apartment is furnished...all we need is cooking utensils and propane stove to cook our food. She said that's good you are getting a furnished apartment. We sat down at the table to eat breakfast. I had bread rolls and oval tine and she ate eggs, spam, and rolls and drank coffee. She said your brother-in-law is coming home; he will be stationed at the Naval Base in Cavite City...I am glad we want be going back to the States. We finished breakfast and I started cleaning the kitchen. She took a shower and got dressed; she said she was going to the base and check to see if there is more mail from Brother Smitty. I said I would stay until Wilson comes. She said I want you to go to the market later on and buy some fresh vegetable and a milkfish for lunch and don't forget to clean the fish. I said o.k. And went into my room; I laid across the bed and my mind started to wondering again...oh boy...we're going to have our own place...my very own place with Wilson...I don't want anything else but his love and care. Then Sister Melda called me. She said Vicky come here. I went to her room and asked what was wrong. She said would you zip me up? I can't reach it. I smiled as I zip up her dress, because I remembered that I had to get Wilson to zip my dress up. She said I am going now. I went back in my room and started getting my thing together so I could take a shower. All of a sudden, I heard someone banging on the door. I quickly ran to the front to see who were there; it was Sister Linda. I said what's wrong? She said I have to go to work but my clothes are here and I need to change; I also need to take some of my clothes to Mother House, so I can leave from there when I go to work...what's for breakfast? I said eggs, spam and rolls. I turned on the stove and boiled her some water for the oval tine. When she started eating breakfast I told her I was going to jump in the shower later. I said take your time eating, it's only seven thirty; you have an hour and a half before you have to be there. I said Wilson and I are going to have our own place in one week.

She said that's good you are back together again...I am very happy for you. I said yes! I am very happy too. She said yes I could tell by looking in your face that you are happy. I said I am going to take my shower while you finish eating. She said o.k. I went in the shower and before I knew it I was singing. This was a quick shower normally it take me a lot longer to finish. I use to be dragging when I take a shower and Sister Melda always tell me that I take too long in the shower. She said that I was trying to drown myself. Sister Linda said that I looked very happy, but my singing is running the bugs out of the house. We both laughed; I said oh! My singing is that bad huh. She said no! I just wanted you to laugh. I said so I can use my singing to run the bugs away huh. And we both laughed again. Finally I was ready to go to the market, so I told her we could walk to the market and she could catch a jeepney from there to work. We left the house walking. She said do you still think you can walk faster than me?

I said yes! And started walking as fast as I could; I step on a rock and almost lost my balance. She said you're the winner; you always beat me in our walkathon and running contest in school. I said that's because you always let me win...you don't want me to lose. She said Oh well; I just didn't want to beat my sister...I couldn't understand why our teachers in school always put us opposite each other, they knew we were sisters...that's why I didn't really compete against you...I didn't want you to lose. I said I was trying very hard to beat you; now I know you let me beat you on purpose. She said well we're grown now and it wasn't really a big deal so let's forget about it. We arrived at the market and she caught a jeepney to work. She said I will see you sometime after I get off work; I am staying in Calapacuan at Mother's house now. I said o.k. Tell Mother I said hello. Then I got busy looking for fresh vegetable. I finally found the vegetables I was looking for and even found a fresh milkfish. I called a tricycle to ride back home. When I got home I looked for Sister Melda, but she hadn't returned, so I got busy cleaning the fish and cutting up enough vegetable for our lunch. I started cooking the rice, so all we have to do when Sister Melda get home is cook the vegetable and fish. I sit down for a while in the living room and my imagination kicked in. I said to myself...if we get the apartment I would buy flowers for the table, nice simple curtains for the windows and a nice ashtray for my sweetheart. Oh! I like the sound of sweetheart. Then I felt hungry so I looked at the time it was eleven o, clock so I went in the kitchen and started cooking; I cooked the fish and vegetables just like Mother had taught me. When I finished I looked at the time again and it was twelve o, clock so I decided to go ahead and eat because Sister Melda was late. When I tasted the food I wanted to pat myself on the back because it really tasted good almost as good as Mother. When I finished eating I got up and cleaned the kitchen. I had to stay busy, because if I don't I would start thinking about Wilson and never get anything done. I thought to myself...he will be with me all the time very soon...so Vicky get busy. Then I heard Sister Melda coming in the front door. She said I am really hungry... have you cooked the vegetables yet? I said don't you smell it? She said I am catching a cold that's why it took me so long to get back...a lot of people was in the Doctor's office...I wanted to leave but I got stuck in the room waiting for the Doctor...that's why I am in a hurry I am very hungry. She got her food and sat down at the table and started eating. She said this is very good, now you have to learn to cook American food, because Wilson is not going to eat what we eat. I said I could learn to cook American food; I will just watch and ask people how they fix or cook it. It will be easy to cook American food; if I can learn to read and write I can learn to cook too. She said o.k. Smarty! After she finished eating she went to her room. I had to wash her dirty dishes and clean the kitchen again. When I finished I went into my room and sat on the bed. I looked around for something to do. Finally I decided to lie down on the bed; I got my pillow and hugged it pretending it was Wilson and fell asleep. I were sleeping real good, when I heard Sister Melda saying, Vicky Wilson is here open the door. I got up and opened the door and said I will be out in a minute. I ran to the bathroom and brushed my teeth and washed my face so I would look and smell fresh when Wilson kissed me. When I finished I went to the living room and Wilson said hi sweetheart and I said hi sweetheart back to him. He smiled and said come sit beside me, so I can kiss and hug you.

Sister Melda came in the room and said oh! Love birds! That's enough smooching; she went into the kitchen and got her playing cards and returned to her room. Wilson and I started kissing and hugging again; finally I said let's go into my room, so we went into my room and continued our smooching. We kissed so much my lips started to burn. Wilson look at the time it was four in the afternoon, so we decided to go to the apartment around five thirty and get the things we had left in our room. He said when he got paid the end of the month he was going to give me some money to buy kitchen utensils. I said o.k. Then he started kissing me again. We played around in my room until about five fifteen. Then he said we better go now so we can catch Jones before they go out. On our way out the door I told Sister Melda we was leaving for the apartment. I called a tricycle and we left. On our way pass twenty fifth street we tried to get a glimpse of the apartment we was going to get the end of the month, but the tricycle was moving too fast. In a few minutes we was at the end of the line for the tricycle; we got out and caught a jeepney to the apartment. When we got there Jones and his girlfriend was sitting on the couch. We said hi to them. Jones and Wilson started talking about something on the base, so I went upstairs and his girlfriend followed me to my old room. She looked to make sure Wilson was not coming upstairs. Then she said while you were gone Wilson and his friend had two girl up here; I don't know what they were doing because they closed the door...one of the girl was very young I don't know either one of them...When they left I look at the bed sheet and there were blood on it...maybe one of the girl had her period and slept in the bed. They had girl here almost every night. I said that I knew Wilson had a girlfriend. Then Wilson came in the room and she left and went downstairs. Wilson asked me what Jones girlfriend was telling me. I said don't worry about it...why our bed sheet have blood all over it. He said I don't know how the blood got on the sheet...what was she telling you...you shouldn't believe what she say because she is just jealous of us. I got upset because he insisted on finding out what she had told me. So I told him what she had said...she said you and your friend brought two girl up here when I was gone...I don't want to know if you did, just don't do it again...I left for a little while and you get someone else right away...I thought you said that you love me...I was gone not even a week and you exchange me already.

He pulled me close to him and kissed me and said let's get out of here. We picked up the clothes and sheets and went downstairs. We said goodbye to Jones and his devil girlfriend. On our way out the door she said in Tagalog, he has a girlfriend. Jones said shut up woman! Jones understood a few words of Tagalog that why he told her to shut up. Wilson asked me what did she say. I told him she said that he had another woman. I was so glad to be leaving this place I could just scream...I have been threatened, made a prisoner in my own room and just plain scared to death by this devil woman. I hope I will never see her again; she is crazier than sister Melda and that's crazy. Wilson said let drop these clothes at your Sister's house and go out. I said o.k. We dropped our things at Sister Melda's house and went to the Shangri La Restaurant to get something to eat. We ate our favorite food and went nightclubbing. I told Wilson to go to the bar and get his own drinks and not let the club hostess bring them to him. We danced and had fun; the time went to fast, before we knew it, it was time for Wilson to leave going back to the base. Wilson was in complete control of his drinking; I was very proud of him and the way he conducted himself. We went outside of the club to catch a jeepney. We kissed and said goodbye. Wilson said I will see you tomorrow Sweetheart and got into his jeepney. I said goodbye and climbed into my jeepney and went home. On my way home I remembered the last thing Wilson said to me...I will see you tomorrow Sweetheart...that made me feel strong, because I like the sound of it. When I got home I think everyone was sleep, because I didn't hear a sound. I went to my room and tried to separate the dirty clothes we had pickup at the apartment. When I finished I changed into my nightgown and went to bed. As I lay there in my bed I started to thinking about Wilson... what he is doing now. I thought to myself...does he really love me... does he miss me as much as I miss him...are we really getting a place of our own soon...are we going to stay together forever this time? Oh! I don't know what to say or think; I guess I will have to wait until the end of the month. I grab my pillow and pretended it was Wilson... closed my eyes and finally went to sleep.

The next morning I woke up early, I thought maybe I will go back to sleep until around nine, but I remembered Sister Melda's Maid was coming in around seven to wash clothes. I got up brushed my teeth and took a quick shower. When I finished my shower Sister Melda was getting up. She said if you go to the market today bring me a lemon back for my cough. I said I thought the Doctor gave you some medicine for your cough. She said yes, but I want to drink lemon tea...don't you remember Mother always making lemon tea for us when we get sick? I said yes! And she would also make chicken soup. She said you better buy two pounds of chicken...use half of it for the soup and the other half for adobo, so you and the Maid will have something to eat for lunch. I am getting ready to go to the market; do you want me to fix your breakfast first? She said yes I could fix her some coffee and hot rolls. I said I think I will have the same thing; I fixed the coffee and rolls and brought it to the table. We sat down to have our breakfast. Sister Melda said just think, in a few days you will be moving into your new apartment, I really think that better than living in the same place with that girl; I am still trying to remember where I seen that girl before...I know, oh! Forget it...you are out of that apartment now. She said I don't know why you stayed there as long as you did and not know anything about that girl; I think she is a druggie or a Gang member…oh! I don't know where I have seen her before, but you better go to the market. I went into my room and got the dirty clothes and took them out back to the Maid. Then I caught a tricycle to the market. After I found out that there was Gangs in Olongapo City, I will not walk alone; I always catch a tricycle or jeepney. The tricycle have their territory that they can work in the same as the jeepney and the drivers all have identification badges, so I feel pretty comfortable riding. If one of the drivers say or do something to you, you can get their badge number and report them. The drivers are not allowed to go out of their territory to give you a ride. I got out of the tricycle and started to look around for lemons and the rest of the thing I had planned to buy. I stopped to look at some pot and pans; I made a mental note to come back here when Wilson give me the money and buy some for our apartment. I saw a nice dress that I like very much. I thought to myself…if I just had the money to buy that dress; I know Wilson will think I look very pretty in it. I walked on by the stand and caught a tricycle. The driver said well you got me again; the last time I gave you a ride you was with another Lady…I live on the other end of your street…the other lady always ride my tricycle. I said I think you are talking about my Sister. He said that's your Sister? I said yes! He drove me straight to Sister Melda's house. I didn't have to give him any directions. I took all of my packages out of the tricycle and went into the house. I put everything on the table. Sister Melda came out of her room and asked for the lemons. She said she wanted to make lemon tea right away. I gave the lemons to her. She said wow! These lemons are very big. I said yes, I took my time and picked them out for you. She started to make her lemon tea. I took out the chicken and washed it; I separated part of it for adobo and I gave the rest to Sister Melda for her chicken soup. She said I want to marinade the adobo chicken and put it aside. She started preparing the chicken soup. Then the Maid came around from the back and knocked on the front door; she said that we were out of soap. Sister Melda gave her some money to buy some at the store across the street. I watched Sister Melda make chicken soup; she tried to make it like Mother and she did a very good job, because

I ate some for lunch, it was delicious. The Maid thought it was very good too; she ate two bowls full of the soup. I told Sister Melda I wanted to cook the adobo for dinner. She said yeah! Maybe Wilson will eat some. I remembered Wilson eating adobo at Mother's house in Calapacuan and he loved it. I hope he like it tonight. Sister Melda went back into her room and I cleaned the kitchen and washed the dishes. When I finished the Maid had started hanging out the clothes on the line outside, so I went out and helped her. When we finished, I came inside and went to my room and gathered up my thing so I could take a shower. I went into the shower and the Maid went into my room and started to iron the clothes that were left over from the day before. When I finished my shower I came back into my room and sit on the side of the bed and started drying my hair with my towel. Then I heard something drop right down beside my foot, it was the iron. I jumped up and screamed, because it gave me a good scare. Sister Melda yelled, what's going on in there? I said we had an accident with the iron everything is all right. The Maid picked up the iron and continued to iron the clothes.

When I finished drying my hair I laid down on the bed. Then my mind started wondering...do I have to wash and iron my Sweetheart uniform, or do they do it on the boat? I can cook him some food in our own kitchen...we can sit on our couch and no one can tell us what we can or can't do. The Maid interrupted my thoughts saying ...I will check the clothes and see if they are dry. I sit up on the side of the bed to wait for her to bring my clothes inside so I could fold and put them in a box under my bed. Suddenly she burst through the door with an arm full of sheets. I said that's good! I can fold them now. She said the towels are still damp. I said o.k. I will get them later on. She started back ironing the rest of the clothing. About two hour later the Maid said I have finished ironing. I look at the time it was four o, clock. I thought to myself...four already! I told the Maid to go home and don't worry about the rest of the clothes that was on the line; I would take care of them. She said o.k. I will see you next week and left. I went outside and got the towels and brought them inside fold them and put them in my box under my bed. I went in the kitchen and started cooking the adobo and rice. Sister Melda came out of her room, she said I smell adobo; what time is it? I said I guess your nose has cleared up a bit. She said yes I can smell the food... let's brown the chicken and add some more water and chopped white potatoes. I said that's not the way to cook adobo. She said yes, it's still adobo chicken you just add some potatoes, American style, in case Wilson want to go out and eat; you and him can eat here instead. Oh yes! He can save money so we can go to the movies. She turned and went back in her room.

Around a quarter to six Wilson came; just before he knocked on the door I opened it. He said how did you know it was me? I said I was looked out the window when I heard a tricycle pull up. He hugged and gave me a big kiss. Sister Melda said is that Wilson out there? I said yes! It's Wilson. He sat down in the living room; I asked him if he wanted a coke and he said no. Then he asked if I had eaten. I said not yet. He said let's go out and eats Tacos at the Palladium Club and Restaurant. I said how about we eat chicken adobo right here; Sister Melda has cooked already? He said o.k. We will get Tacos next time. I told Sister Melda we were ready to eat. She said go ahead and eat I am trying to get ready to go out. I Fixed Wilson plate, rice and adobo and put it on the table. He sat and waited for me to fix my plate and come to the table. We ate our adobo and rice and drunk a coke.

I had smelled beer on his breath, so my mind started thinking... why does he smell like beer if he just came from work...maybe he stopped at a club or maybe they have beer on the boat. Sister Melda broke my chain of thought when she came out of her room and said I will see you later love birds I have to go. I said I thought you were going to eat; she said just put the food up and I will eat when I come home tonight. As soon as she walked out the front door my mind started wondering again...maybe he stopped to see his girlfriend before he come here...does he like her better than me...does he compare us...does he like her better because he stop their first? Then Wilson said are you all right Sweetheart...what are you thinking about? I said nothing! And I started back eating. He said this food taste like the food I ate at your Mother's house and it has potatoes in it. I said Sister Melda said it American style. He smiled and said yes we eat a lot of potatoes in America and you eat a lot of rice here in the Philippines. When he finished eating he went into the living room and sit down. I started cleaning the kitchen; Wilson came back to the table and asked if I need help with the dishes. I said no! There are only two plates and the pot and pans; I can do it by myself. He gave me a quick hug and a kiss and went back to his seat. He asked if we had some beer; I said no, but I can get some across the street as soon as I finish with the kitchen. After I finished cleaning the kitchen I told him I was going for the beer; he wanted to go with me, but I told him if they see me with an American the price of the beer will double. I told him to give me the money and I would go alone and get the beer. He gave me five pesos and I ask him how many beers he wanted. He said two would be fine, so I left and went across the street and got the beer and brought him his change back. He was really surprised to find out that the beer only cost sixty centavos, because he normally pays two pesos for a beer in the club. I went in the kitchen to find a bottle opener; I opened one of the beers and gave it to him. He told me to sit on his lap. I said I am too heavy to sit on your lap. He said you're too small to be heavy and pulled me down on his lap. We started smooching and more smooching; finally I said you better drink your beer before it get to hot. So he stopped and said it want be long before we move into our apartment. I said yes! I can't wait. Then he started kissing me again and again; I felt like I was getting drunk too. He drink, kiss me and smoke...kiss drink, and smoke. I felt dizzy already, so I said let me sit in the chair before I fall down. He said I am not going to let you fall. I said to myself...right! I feel like I am drunk now from the beer and smoke taste kisses.

I didn't drink or smoke and I was having a hard time getting use to the smell or beer and smoke...I will have to work on this because he drinks and smoke. He looked at his watch and said I have a couple more hours before I have to go back to my boat...I am not sure whether I have the duty tomorrow or not, but if I do I will see you the next day, my pay day. I will come early and we will move into our apartment...I can't wait to be alone with you in our own place. I said come into my room and reached for his hand. He followed me into the room. We sat on the bed and started kissing again, the kissing started to intensify and Wilson said we better wait until we get our place. I said why can't we do it right here in my bed? I think he was surprised at what I said. He said I really want to do it very badly, but we have to consider where we're at, in your Sister's house...I would feel real bad if she walk-in on us. I sat quietly thinking...he has got me all hot and bothered with all the kissing and now I can't relieve all this energy I have built up. I got up and went in the kitchen to get a glass of water and he followed me in the kitchen and got the other beer. I asked him if he wanted me to get more beer before the store close at ten; he said no the two was enough for tonight. I thought to myself... thank you! Because when he went back to the base I didn't want him to be drunk...especially when he had to change from a tricycle to a jeepney to get back to the base. I forgot being hot and bothered and calmed down. I sat in a chair across from him so we wouldn't be doing a lot of kissing. We started to plan some of the things we would do once we moved into the apartment. He said he was going to stop drinking so much and we will stop going out nightclubbing a lot. I thought to myself...please don't say that, because I don't want you to bite your tongue.

Finally it was time for him to go back to the base. He said I have to go now Sweetheart. I said already! Then I went outside and called him a tricycle. He hugged and kissed me goodbye. I told him if the tricycle or jeepney Driver gives him a problem get their license number and I would report them. I also, explained to him how much he was to pay for each ride, because the Drivers try and charge American more than Filipino.

As soon as Wilson tricycle pulled away Sister Melda rode up in a tricycle and asked if that was Wilson she saw in the tricycle. I said yes. We went inside of the house. When we got inside Sister Melda said I am hungry...do you have some more of that adobo? I said yes, do you want me to warm it for you? She said yes, but I have to go to the bathroom first. I went in the kitchen and warmed the adobo. It started smelling so good that I decided to have some more. I fixed her and me a plate. When she came out of the bathroom we sit at the table and ate. She said this adobo taste better when it is left over. When we finished eating; she said I feel real sorry for my boyfriend, because I told him your Brother-in Law will be coming home maybe the end of next month, in October...he may come around the middle of October and try and surprise me, because he like to surprise me. I said to myself...I think he knows you're cheating on him, but he love you so much that he pretend that it's not happening. Sister Melda said wake up Vicky it will be all right, just two more night away from him. I got up and put the food away again and clean the kitchen and washed the dishes. I went to my room to relax for a while. As soon as I sit down Sister Melda knocked on my door. She asked me if I knew where her beach towel was at; I told her I had put the towels in her bottom drawer with her bathing suit. I said why, are you going swimming? Yes, she said I am going to White Rock Beach...mama Ligaya want me to come to her party tomorrow. She asked me if I wanted to go with her; I said yes! I haven't been swimming in a long time. She said do you have a bathing suit? I said no, but I have a pair of short pants that I used in High School that I can wear. What you are going to use for a top, she asked. I said I would use a t-shirt. She said I guess that will be all right and went back into her room.

The next day she got up and cooked our breakfast. I asked if she still have a cold. She said it's almost gone. After breakfast we got dressed and I called a tricycle. The tricycle took us to the end of our street by the market and we caught a jeepney to White Rock Beach. We arrive around ten that morning and went in the lady room and changed into our swimwear. When I came out all of the guys was looking at me. Sister Melda was really and truly surprised that the guys were admiring me from a distance.

Sister Melda called mama Ligaya son and asked him to get us an inner tube, because we were going to swim in the beach. We got the tube and went over to the edge of the beach. We went in and swim for a while and she said she was going for another inner tube and would be right back. When she came back she said that mama Ligaya don't want me to swim in the swimming pool because the clothes I had on was inappropriate. I said its o.k. I want to swim in the beach anyway. A few minutes later Larry, mama Ligaya's son came and said the party is over by the swimming pool...why are you swimming in the beach. I said I just wanted to swim in the Ocean. He said when you get tired of swimming in the Ocean come up to the swimming pool...there is plenty of food. I said thank you Larry. He said your sister is having a lot of fun on the diving board. I said yes, I know I can hear them. He left and returned to the swimming pool party. I was paddling around on my inner tube when I heard Sister Melda calling me she was carrying something; I started paddling toward the shore to see what she wanted. When I paddled to shore and pulled my inner tube out of the water she was standing waiting with a plate of food. I found a place to sit down and said this is a lot of food. She said I got you a hamburger, pork on a stick, and a hot dog; I didn't think you wanted something you are not use to eating. I said thank you! When I finish eating I am going home. She said o.k. I am going to stay for a while longer. I said don't stay in the water to long because your voice sounds a little hoarse. She turned and left me sitting there on the beach eating my food. When I finished eating I carried the inner tube to the deck of the swimming pool. Larry saw me coming and came got the tube and put it away. Then some of the Sailors started whistling at me. One of the Sailors called Larry and whispered something in his ear. I went to the ladies bathroom and changed clothing. When I came out a couple of Sailors came up to me and asked me why I have changed clothes and where Iam going? Sister Melda rushed over from the swimming pool. One Sailor asked her why she hadn't told them she had a sister here at the party. Sister Melda said she is shy, she don't like being around people. I almost told her that she told me mama Ligaya didn't want me in the swimming pool, but I said I have to go enjoy your party. As I left going to the road to catch a jeepney, I heard one of the guys ask Sister Melda why she didn't introduce her sister to them. I kept walking toward the road to catch a jeepney back to Olongapo City.

My Mother live about ten minutes away from White Rock Beach, but I don't want to go there because she will be asking a lot of questions about my birth certificate and what Wilson is doing. The jeepney ride carry me around the mountainside close to the Ocean; I tried to see if there were a Tug Boat out there maybe it was Wilson's boat, but I didn't see a Tug Boat. I thought to myself...what is he doing now...is he working or thinking about me...does he miss me as much as I miss him? Then someone in the jeepney yelled a child! The Driver jammed his brakes and almost threw me across the jeepney. One lady was real mad at the Driver and said watch where you are going, you almost hit that kid. The Driver said stupid kid! Where is the parent...why they don't watch their kid? One of the passengers said it is good you didn't hit that kid, because a bus Driver hit a kid last year and the kid was hospitalized and didn't die. He said the

Driver of the bus said he should have back the bus back over the kid and made sure it was dead that would have been an accident. Now the bus Driver is still paying for the Hospital bills and supporting the kid family because they have to take care of the kid because it can't feed itself. Someone asked could the kid parent work? He said no! The kid Mother is in shock and is crazy and the Father have to take care of both of them. One person said I think I rather go to jail than work for them and one other guy said I think the guy should have run over the kid again and call it an accident. Everyone in the jeepney had something to say about the bus accident. When I arrived in Olongapo City I asked my tricycle Driver had he heard about a bus running over a kid. He said yes, it was in a small barrio between here and Zambales. He said he hear of bus Driver running over people all of the time, he guess the Driver are sleepy or just bad Drivers. When I got home I went straight to my bed and went to sleep. I woke up around six that afternoon and looked around the house to see if Sister Melda has come home, but she had not come home yet. I felt a little hungry, so I went into the kitchen and made a sardine sandwich. I sat down at the dining room table and ate my sandwich and drunk a coke. I begin to think to myself...tomorrow Wilson and I will move into our apartment...our place...our own living room...our own kitchen and bathroom...oh! I can't wait until tomorrow. Then I heard someone opening the front door; it was Sister Melda and she look as if her cold had gotten worse.

She went straight to the bathroom to take a shower. When she came out she asked me if I had eaten. I said yes, I ate a sardine sandwich, would you like me to fix you one? She said no, I ate a lot of food at the party. I asked if the party was over; she said no, the party would go on until ten tonight...the guys probably will sleep on the beach after the party is over...I had to come home and get ready to meet my boyfriend tonight. I told her Wilson had duty tonight but will be off tomorrow and we will move into our apartment. She said that right, you're not going to be here tomorrow night...I better go to Calapacuan and ask Mother if Linda can stay with me for a while or maybe I will go by the Money Exchange tomorrow and ask Sister Linda to come by my house when she get off work. She left going to meet her boyfriend. I found myself alone again and I started thinking…is this going to happen tomorrow or Will Wilson just hide from me or maybe he's not getting the apartment and is on his way to the United States…he said he have duty today. Oh boy! My stomach is turning into a knot. I am scared, maybe he is thinking of me. Then I said to myself…wake up Vicky! It's going to happen…you will be with your Sweetheart tomorrow. I got up and walked around in the house looking at the walls. I went to my room and lay down and hugged my pillow and pretended it was Wilson. I even kissed the pillow. I said to myself…I am crazy or losing my mind. I got up and went into the kitchen and got a glass of water and sat down in the living room. I was getting real jittery, thinking Wilson maybe, Wilson had returned to the States. I wish I could push up the time; I wanted tonight to be tomorrow night, so I can see what is going to happen. I looked out of the window for him; I knew he was not out there, but I looked anyway. What will I do tomorrow if he doesn't show up? What's happening to me, all of this thinking is going to give me a nervous breakdown. I went back to my room and got one of his shirts from the box under my bed. I put the shirt on my pillow and hugged it until I fell asleep. I woke up at five thirty the next morning and took a shower. I wanted to be ready if Wilson came early. I went back in my room and started towel drying my hair; I was so nervous and tense that I didn't sit while I was drying my hair.

I heard Sister Melda say is that you Ambing? I said yes! She said why you wake up so early; I know you are moving today, but it's not even six o, clock and people are still sleeping. I said I can't sleep anymore and I want to be ready when Wilson comes so I took a shower. She said well you are up already, will you make some coffee and buy some spam and rolls if the store is open. Cook some eggs too. I said to myself…I just wanted to get up early; I don't want to do everything. I continued toweling my hair. I started thinking…I will have to get up early and fix Wilson breakfast and coffee or does he drink oval tine? I will fix whatever he wanted to eat or drink. Oh! It will be a good life just being with him. Sister Melda came out of her room and said I thought you had gone to the store. I said the store is not open yet. She said the light is on in the store; you better go now so you will be first in line to get hot rolls. I left to go get her precious rolls. When I got to the store they were just opening up. The storekeeper said oh, you're early today, are you going to work this morning? I said no! Somebody got hungry early this morning. I got the rolls and they were still warm. My sister was right the rolls are warm, if you get them early. On my way back to the house I said to myself…I woke up early to wait for Wilson, not to do all of the things she want me to do…she is hungry…well get up and cook. When I came in the house she said when you cook the spam can you make it crisper. I said spam, oh! I forgot it, so I went back to the store. The lady said did you forget something? I said yes! Spam. She said you're still sleepy. I didn't answer I just took the spam and left. I said to myself…how can I remember everything if I have my mind on something else, Wilson…did he wake up this morning or maybe he forgot me. I said today is the day I don't have to wait any longer. When I got inside of the house I went straight to the kitchen to cook the Queen's breakfast. Just as I was getting started the Queen came out of her room and said don't scramble my eggs; I want them sunny side up. I said do you want me to cook your eggs when the sun comes up, or do you want me to cook them later on…what is sunny side up? She laughed at me and came in the kitchen and said no! To cook eggs sunny side up, you only cook them on one side and leave the yellow showing on the other side…that's called sunny side up. I said I have never eaten any eggs cooked like that. I thought…Wilson don't like sunny side up, he like scrambled like me.

I cooked the Queens Eggs sunny side up and fried the spam crisp just like she wanted it. Now she asked if the coffee is ready. I said not yet…She must have gotten up on the wrong side of her bed. All I wanted to do this morning was wait for Wilson; now here I am in the kitchen cooking for the Queen…do this…do that. When I finished cooking breakfast I called the Queen. I said your food is cooked come get it before it gets cold. She came in the kitchen and started eating. I went into the living room and sat down. She asked if I was going to eat. I said not yet! I will eat later when I am hungry. Then she said I forgot that I put my wet bathing suit and towel in a bucket in the back; if you are not doing anything right now; will you wash it before it starts to stink the Maid is not coming until Thursday. I said to myself…I just want to sit down here in peace and not be bothered. Then she said buy some soap from the store, because we're out. I stood up really mad and said give me the money. She got up and went in her room and got the money for the soap. When she passed by me I wanted to smack her. I am losing my wit early this morning. All I really want to do is sit down and try to get my thought together, but the Queen has me running errands and during all of the choirs here in the house. I took the money for the soap and went to the store and got the soap. When I returned the Queen had finished eating and returned to her room leaving a dirty kitchen and dishes behind. I said to myself...take me away from this house Wilson. As I put the food away I noticed that she left two slices of spam from a total of six and four rolls from a total of twelve...she must have been real hungry. I cleaned the kitchen and dishes and went to the bathroom to wash the Queen's bathing suit and towel. Just as I was getting started, she came in the bathroom and told me she wanted to take a shower before I wash the bathing suit and towel. I got up and went back in the living room and sit down to wait for her to finish her shower. My mind begun wandering again...maybe Wilson and I could take a shower together...we could do anything we wanted no one could say no. I heard her voice ring out... I am finished. I said to myself...I better get started doing this before she think of something else for me to do. I washed the bathing suit and towel and hung them out to dry; then I sat down outside in back of the house away from the Queen to get a breath of fresh air. The early morning wind was gently blowing across my face. I could smell the burning of leaves and food cooking from a distance.

The way the wind was gently blowing against my face reminded me of the way Wilson gently kissed my face, lips and neck. Oh! I thought...I better go into the house before I get excited thinking about Wilson. I went inside and checked the time; it was almost nine o. clock in the morning and Wilson wasn't anywhere in sight. I decided to eat breakfast before the Queen comes out of her shell again. I ate the two slices of spam and two rolls and had a glass of water. When I finished my breakfast I went into my room. A few minutes later I heard the Queen say Vicky, I will see you later if you're still here when I return. I came to the door of my room so I could better hear what she was saying. She said don't get your hopes up...if he comes that good for you, but if he don't come that's good for you too, because I told you he was married and have kids in the States…if he comes I know you will be very happy…good luck. Why did she have to say that? Now she have me thinking again…what am I going to do…he told me that he love me and wanted to marry me…where is he now…did he stop to see his girlfriend in the club or has he left and went back to the States? Well I am still young I can find another man to love me and not play games. I went back to my room and lay down hugging my pillow and pretending it was Wilson and I was in his arms. I got up to go to the bathroom and heard a tricycle drive up to the house. My heart started beating very rapidly as I peered through the window and saw Wilson in the tricycle. I quickly ran to the mirror to make sure I was presentable for my Sweetheart. Then I waited by the door; I heard him knock on the door, but I waited for a few moments so he couldn't tell I was just waiting by the door. I opened the door he was standing there with a big smile on his face; he hugged and kissed me right in the doorway. I knew the neighbors were watching but I didn't care. After he finally released me from his tight grip he stepped inside and closed the door. I felt like I was holding my breath waiting to hear what he had to say, good or bad. Then he said sit down I have something to tell you. We will go to the apartment to take a look first and see if we like it and if it is clean. I don't want to take our things in a dirty place…are you ready to take a look? I tried to stand up but I was too nervous. He asked if I was all right. I said yes! O.k. He said let's go then. I said wait I will call a tricycle. He said no, it just up the street we can walk…you don't mind walking do you? I said no, I don't mind walking, so we left walking going to our apartment. When we got there Wilson said that's the apartment, the one in front…let me see if the Owner is in. He went in the back and returned with the Owner of the apartment. He introduced me as his Fiancé. We both said hi and she opened the door of the apartment. There were a living room, dining room, kitchen, bedroom and bathroom. I really like the closets. The lady said there is a stove for cooking but we have to supply our own propane…you have a complete set of living room, dining room and bedroom furniture. If you have a problem with the bathroom let me know and we will take care of it right away. Wilson said how's the neighbors? She said the neighbors are real quiet. Wilson asked me how I like the place. I looked around and said I like everything except the darkness inside, but that can't be help because there are apartment on each side of the apartment. Wilson said I guess we will take it. She said when would you like to move in? Wilson said how about today? She gave Wilson the key and left. We went into the bedroom and sit on the bed and started kissing; we almost baptized the bed without lining. Wilson said we needs to think about some of the thing we will need when we move in here...pot and pans, a four piece china set and silverware...I will get propane today and we can get our stuff in your Sister's house. Let's get something to eat. We could have Tacos at the Palladium Club and Restaurant. I said o.k. And we left to get Tacos. We arrived at the Palladium club and Restaurant and he ordered four Tacos for himself and two for me. He ordered a beer and a coke for me. I thought... we are supposed to move in today and now he is drinking beer. When the waitress returned with our order. I said so this is the Taco you have always talked about; I opened the shell of my Taco and saw that it contain lettuce, tomato, and some kind of meat. I took a bit of my Taco and it tasted good until it started to burn my mouth. I said my God, what are they trying to do...kill someone? Wilson said what's wrong? I said the Tacos are too hot, I don't want it.

He asked me if I wanted to order something else. I said no, I wasn't really hungry. He took my two Tacos and ate them. When he finished eating we went back to the apartment to get the propane bottle so we could have it filled. We took the empty bottle to the Propane dealer and traded it for a full bottle. When we got back to our apartment Wilson hooked up the propane bottle to the stove and tested it out. It worked right away and I was very happy. We left and went to Sister Melda's house to get our things. We got our thing and started walking carrying them to our place. The people were watching us carrying our boxes to our place. After we put away our stuff Wilson asked me to go across the street and get him some beer. I told him to get coke, but he insisted on having a beer. I left and went across the street and asked the lady if she had cold beer. She said yes! I told her I wanted two. She asked if we were the new tenants. I said yes, we just moved in today. I turned around and looked at our apartment window and saw Wilson standing and looking out of it. The lady gave me the beer and I gave her the money. She said if we run out of money before Wilson get paid we could charge what we need until he get paid. I said thank you! She asked me my name. I told her it was Vicky. She said the name on the store's front is mines. I looked at the sign; it says Cindy's Sari Sari Store. I said bye to the lady and went back across the street. When I got inside Wilson asked me what the lady and I talking about that took so long. I said next time you can go and buy your own beer if you think I take too long. I got a little upset...I don't drink beer, so I don't like to buy it...I do it for him because I love him. I said she asked if we were the new tenants moving in and that we could buy stuff on credit until your payday if we wanted to...her name is on the sign on the front of the store. He said oh, she is the Owner of the store. I didn't answer his question I went to the bedroom and started hanging up clothes in the closet. He followed me and said let's do the bed now and you go to the market and get some glasses and plates; we can finish the rest tomorrow. He gave me money for the glasses and plates and fifty pesos for me. He said he would give me the rest of the money when he got paid again because he had to buy the propane. I didn't say anything I took the money and went to the market. I walked around in the market looking for a bargain on kitchenware.

First I bought a big handmade bag to carry everything I buy. I bought glasses, plate, pots, pans and two towels to wrap the glasses. I put everything in my big bag. Just as I started to prepare to leave the market and go home; I saw the tricycle Driver, he knew that I live close to Sister Melda's house, he was buying cigarettes. I called him and he came over and asked if I was going home. I said yes and he took my big bag; just as we were heading to his tricycle I remembered the pillows we needed; I asked him if he would wait until I got the pillows. He said he would and he took my bag to the tricycle. I bought two pillows and quickly walked over to the tricycle. I got into the tricycle and we were off. I told him where I wanted to go; he asked me if my sister and I had moved. I said yes I have, but my sister is still living there. We were talking so much we almost passed the apartment. I stopped him in time and he got off his tricycle and got my bag out of the back and followed me to the door; I knocked on the door and Wilson opened the door and let us in. Wilson took the bag from the Driver and I said thanks and paid him and he left. We sat down in the living room and I showed Wilson all of the things I had bought. He said you have got a lot of stuff; I guess you will have to go back for food tomorrow. I said yes, I would go early in the morning I am much to tire to go back today. He said he would have a copy of the key made tomorrow so both of us will have a key...you're going to the market tomorrow, you can have a copy made there. I said o.k. And went in the bedroom and to my surprise he had made the bed real nice and tight. Then I remembered the pots and pans still in the living room, so I went back to the living room and asked Wilson to help me take the pots and pans into the kitchen so I could wash them. I said I want to buy the thing where the dishes dry. He said oh yes, a dish rack. I said yes a dish rack. I thought...I have learned another English phrase. He grabbed me and started pulling me toward the bedroom. I said wait my hands are still wet. He wouldn't stop...he started kissing and telling me how much he love me. Suddenly he had swept me off my feet and was caring me to the bedroom...laid me on the bed...pulled the bedroom curtains and started undressing me. He quickly undressed and jumped in the bed. We did an outstanding job in christening our new bed. Completely spent, we held each other in a tight embrace and fell asleep. When I woke up it was eight thirty that night. I got up and headed for the kitchen. He asked me where I were going. I told him I were hungry and was going to find me something to eat...are you hungry? He said yes! I looked around in the kitchen and couldn't find anything I wanted to eat, so I decided to go to the store across the street.

I asked Wilson if he wanted anything from the store. He said yes, I want beer. I said to myself...here we go again. I asked him how many beers he want. He said one would be enough. I left and went across the street and bought sardine, bread and beer. As soon as I walked back in the apartment I realized I didn't have a bottle opener for the beer. Wilson said he wanted to try and open the beer with his small knife. I gave the beer to him and he managed to open it with his small knife. I told him I would get a bottle opener the next day at the market. I went in the kitchen and made two sandwiches and came back in the living room and set with him. I had a glass of water with my sandwich and he had a beer with his. Our living room furniture was made of solid wood without cushions; it get very hard after awhile sitting on it, but we didn't mind too much because we were in our own apartment. We finished our sandwiches and Wilson peered out the window to see if the store was opened. He asked me if I knew what time the store closes. I said I think around eleven o, clock and it was ten thirty already. He said the lights are off in the store. I said I guess they are closed. We sat and talked until Wilson finished his beer; then we went to our bedroom.

This were our first night in our new apartment; it felt so good to know that we could do anything we liked and no one would be watching us or trying to tell us what to do. We sat on the side of our bed talking about some of the things we plan to do. Wilson asked me if I had enough money to buy our food the next day when I go to the market. I told him I had thirty- five pesos left from the money he gave me. He gave me twenty more pesos so I could buy a can opener and a knife. I got up and put the money in my bag and got my nightgown from my drawer. I put my nightgown on hoping it would appeal to Wilson, because I bought it just for him. He didn't disappoint me by not noticing it; he called me right away to come to him on the bed, but I told him I had to go to the bathroom. When I came back he asked me where I got my sexy nightgown. I told him I bought it from the market and was saving it for our first night in our apartment; I want our first night to be a memorial one. He said you look very sexy in it and pulled me down on the bed and started kissing me. A few minutes later my sexy nightgown was cast aside to make way for a wonderful love making session. We lay in each other arms very silent as our bodies calmed down...we fell asleep.

Around four the next morning we woke up; he didn't have to be up until about four thirty. I went back to sleep, but I think Wilson remained awake because when I woke up about thirty minutes later he was watching me sleep. I asked him if there were anything wrong. He said It's hard for me to believe that I have you here in my arms and we're in our own apartment; would you please pinch me, because I want to make sure I am not dreaming. I pinched him on his arm; he said now I know I am not dreaming and he hugged me very tight and kissed me. He said I have to go to work now and got up and got dressed. I told him to be careful as he walked through the market area to catch a jeepney. I went back to bed, but I couldn't go back to sleep, so I just laid around waiting for daylight to come. I wanted to go to the market and finish my shopping. Finally I got up and took a shower and when I finished I made up the bed and cleaned the room. I went into the living room and took the towel from my head and started towel drying my hair.

Around seven that morning I started getting hungry, so I got dressed and went across the street to the store. I bought two eggs and oval tine and returned to the apartment and went straight to the kitchen. I prepared my breakfast boil eggs, bread and hot oval tine. I were very happy with everything especially the apartment even though we only had a few pieces of furniture. I said to myself...the main thing is I have Wilson with me now and no matter what life brings; we would be all right, because our love is stronger now that we're together. I decided to make a list of the things I need to do and buy at the market. Having a key made was on the top of my list. When I finished the list; I said to myself...I hope I have enough money to pay for all of these things.

I checked the time and it was eight o, clock already, so I got my big bag to carry my things in and left for the market. I spotted the guy making keys right away; I gave him my key and he made the copy and said sixty centavos please. I paid him and said to myself... that was very cheap. Then I begin looking for the rest of the things on my shopping list. I had everything except the rice and I noticed that the bag was getting heavy so I decided to get ten cups of rice instead of twenty.

After buying the rice I hailed a tricycle and put my big bag on it and we were off to my apartment. I tried the new key in the door lock; it worked perfectly. I took my bag straight to the kitchen and set it down and went to the living room to catch my breath. When I sat down I realized just how tired I had gotten carrying my big bag, but I still felt very happy with my present situation...this is the life I always wanted...to be loved and needed. I got my purse and counted the money that I had left from shopping; it was twelve pesos, I said to myself...I could buy some more rice, fish and vegetables the next time I go shopping.

After resting for a while I went back to the kitchen and put up all the grocery. I decided to start cooking my lunch so I cleaned and washed two cups of rice and an eggplant. I fried the eggplant and put vinegar and soy sauce on it and put it aside to wait for the rice to cook. I went to my bedroom and laid down; I said to myself... this bedroom belong to Wilson and me...before my mind take me too far; I better check and see if the rice is cooked. I got up and went into the kitchen and sure enough it was cooked and ready to eat. I fixed my plate and went into the living room to eat. I made a mental note to myself to buy fish and chicken the next time I went to the market. When I finished eating I went into the kitchen and put everything up and washed the dishes. I thought maybe I would go to Sister Melda's house and return the key to her house. After I finished cleaning the kitchen; I got my bag and left for Sister Melda's house. I decided to knock instead of using the key so I wouldn't scare her if she were sleeping. She came to the door and opened it and asked me why I didn't use my key. I didn't explain I just followed her into her bedroom and gave her the key. She said someone had told her they saw me a street up from her house. I said yes, my apartment is just a street up from here; you can come visit if you like. She kept playing solitary on her bed. I watched her for a while. Finally she asked if I had bought playing cards so I could play solitary while I was alone. I said not yet. She said I am going to buy you a deck of cards; I will give it to you the next time I see you...did Wilson go to work? I said yes, is Sister Linda going to stay with you now? She said yes, after work she would be coming straight here starting today...I think your Brother-in-Law is going to surprise me when he come home. I said that's what you said the last time we talked...I have to go now...you can visit me when you are not busy. She said o.k. I will see you later and followed me out of her bedroom into the living room. She said goodbye as I left the house. I walked back to my apartment; when I opened the door I felt very happy knowing that no other person other than Wilson lived here with me...just my Sweetheart Wilson, the man I love. I went straight to my bedroom and sit down on the side of the bed. I thought...this is a lot softer than the hard chairs in the living room. After sitting there for a while, I remembered the extra pillows we had in the closet. I got right up and went to the closet and got one of the pillows and placed it on the couch made of wood and sit down on it. This was great, all I need is another pillow for my back, and so I quickly returned to the closet and got the second pillow. I sit down on one of the pillow and put the other one behind me for my back. Now this is very comfortable I thought. I opened the curtains and sit back down thinking...now I can sit in the living room and see what's going on out front. I looked at the time, it was four o, clock, only thirty more minutes before Wilson come home. I got up and went to the bathroom and just as I came out I heard someone knocking on the front door. I went to the window and looked out; it was Wilson, he's coming home early today. I quickly opened the door and let him in. He came through the door and hugged and kissed me. He said he feel as if he was dreaming...coming home to be with me. I pinched him again. He said o.k. I am not dreaming and kissed me again. We sat down in our living room on the hard couch. I asked Wilson if he wanted one of the pillows. He said no I don't need one...do you want to go see a movie in the Grand Theatre? I said yes; just give me a few minutes to get ready. Then he asked if I had gone to the market. I said yes, and I have twelve pesos left. He said keep that and he would give me ten more pesos to buy more food if I need it. He said I would be eating on my boat, so don't worry about cooking dinner for me when I come home...the only time I would eat here would be when I am off on the weekend or come home early... on the weekends I will eat can food because we don't have a refrigerator to keep our meat... just prepare your food like you normally do and don't worry about me eating. I said o.k.

He gave me a big kiss as if it was time to go to the movie. Then he looked at his watch and saw that it was only four- thirty. He said let go in the bedroom and relaxes for a while. I said o.k. And followed him in the bedroom. He sat on the side of the bed and stared at me. He quickly jumped up and closed the curtains to the bedroom windows and came back took off his shirt and lay down beside me on the bed. I pinched him again. He said that's hurt and I said I don't want you dreaming that I am not here...we're together now. He pulled me over to him and squeezed me so tight I could hardly breathe...and started kissing me. We raced to the top of mount ecstasy and calmly floated back down. We fell asleep. When we woke up it was eight o, clock.

He said well I guess we will go to the movie tomorrow. I said o.k. I am going to fix me something to eat. He got up and put his clothes on and started for the door. I asked him where he going. He said he was going across the street to the store for some beer. I will be here when you come back. He returned with two beers and a coke for me. We sat in our living room and drink our drinks. I said to myself...being with the one you love is a very good feeling...talking together... laughing together...just being there for each other...doing whatever else you want in life, because you have each other and you can take care of all the bad things and enjoy the good things the world has to offer. I am so happy to be just sitting and watching him look at me. I am proud to be his woman. I guess he feel the same way about me, I hope he does. We finished our drinks and Wilson said let's go to bed it's getting late. We got up and went into the bedroom and went to bed. I told Wilson to make sure he set his alarm clock. I felt real safe and comfortable lying in his arms, before long I drifted off to sleep. Early the next morning around three- thirty; I was woken by Wilson kisses and caresses; I couldn't resist because I wanted it just as much as he did. As we lay there relaxing our spent bodies the alarm went off. Wilson got up and got dressed he said he would take a shower on his boat. He hugged and kissed me goodbye and said I will see you tonight Sweetheart. I followed him to the door and told him to be careful on his way to work. I closed the door and returned to bed. I fell asleep right after getting comfortable in bed.

I slept to around seven thirty and got up and went into the bathroom and brushed my teeth and combed my hair. Finally I was ready for breakfast; I made garlic fried rice to eat with my eggs, sunny side up. I took my plate and a glass of water into the living room where I had my breakfast. Sitting there eating and thinking to myself. I wondered what Wilson was having for breakfast. I promised myself that one day I would be preparing three meals a day for Wilson. Right now I can only prepare Philippine dishes, but I will learn to prepare American dishes. I know he likes Philippine Adobo dishes, because he had it at my Mother's house and he said he liked it. After finishing breakfast I decided to take a shower and go to the market. In the middle of my shower the power went off, so I hurried and dried myself off wrapped my towel around my body and went into the living room where there was light. I sat in the living room window and towel dried my hair. I looked around outside to see if everyone had lost power. I made a mental note to myself to buy candles when I get to the market. When I finished drying my hair I looked around in the apartment to see if I was missing a necessity that I need for the house. The only thing I figured we needed was a flower tray for the living room coffee table. I went in the bedroom and got my bag and left for the market. I decided to walk to the market because it was only about a block and a half away. When I arrived at the market I could hear a group of people talking about extending the area further down the street toward my apartment. I said to myself...that will be good, right outside my apartment less than a block away...I want need to ride a tricycle neither going or coming from the market.

First I walked through the market looking for the things I need and once I see them I will price them and compare the price at other location in the market. Finally I bought candles, matches, plastic tub, fish and a dustpan. I carried everything over to the parking area for the tricycles; the Driver helped me load my things in the tricycle for my trip back to the apartment. As soon as I opened the apartment door I went straight to the kitchen and put everything on the table. I said to myself...something is missing...my Sweetheart ashtray. I will have to get him one, but I have to clean the fish first because we don't have a refrigerator. I cleaned and fried the fish. While cleaning the fish I remembered that I was supposed to buy a dish rack.

I decided to go back to the market when I finished frying my fish and get the dish rack and ashtray. I count my money to make sure I had enough to buy the thing I wanted to get. I didn't have enough left from the money Wilson had given me to spend for the house, so I decided to use twenty pesos of the money I was saving to give to my Mother. I closed my bag and left for the market walking. When I arrived I found a nice white shinny glass ashtray and a dish rack. I walked back to my apartment; it was very hot around ten o, clock. I went inside and started to feel dizzy, so I went back outside across the street to the store and got me a cold drink and a small block of ice. When I returned to the apartment, I washed and chopped some of the ice for my drink. I poured my drink in the glass over the ice and had a seat in the living room. I drink it right away because I was very dizzy and hot. I sit there for a while, then I looked at the time; it was twelve o, clock. I said to myself...maybe that's why I am dizzy... I need to eat. I decided to warm the fried rice I had left over from breakfast and eat it with the fish I fried before I left for the market. After eating lunch I felt a lot better, so I washed the dishes and cleaned the kitchen. I use my dish rack for the first time; I was very happy with it. Every time I turn around I would feel dizzy so I went and sit down in the living room and started looking out of the window at the people passing by. I thought to myself...this is not helping me, so I went into the bedroom and lay down and hugged my pillow until I fell asleep. Later I woke up and wanted to go to the bathroom. When I started to get up I noticed that I was still very dizzy, so I lay back down. I had a very powerful urge to go to the bathroom, so I forced myself to get up and use the bathroom. When I finished I hurried back to the bedroom and lay down again. I fell asleep. A few hours later I was awaken by a lot of people in the street talking. I looked at the time it was three o, clock, so I decided I should fix my hair because Wilson may come home early. I sat down in the living room combing my hair. I could see through the window the people still standing around discussing something. I decided to go outside and see what they were talking about. They were talking about the market extending into our neighborhood.

I had heard the rumor about the market when I was there shopping earlier that morning. I could hear opposing views about the market extension, but there would be a vote by city official that will determine whether the market will be extended. After listing to the discussing for a while I decided to go back inside, because I still wasn't feeling very good although I was not dizzy. I got me a glass of water and sit down in the living room and drunk it. Then the front door opened and Wilson came in. I said Sweetheart you're home early today. Then I smelled the beer on his breath. He kissed me and told me to get ready, because we were invited to his friend house for dinner. I said I thought we were going to the movies tonight. He said we would go some other time. He followed me into the bedroom when I went to change my clothes. He noticed me when I felt dizzy and quickly sat down on the bed. He asked me what was wrong; I said I didn't know, I just feel dizzy sometimes. When I was changing my clothes he said you bought a pretty flower tray and ashtray. I said so you like it ha! He said I love it...this place is starting to look like home. I asked him where his friend lived; he said his friend live on Gordon Street near the Naval Base. When I finished changing I said I am ready to go. He said would you be all right? I said yes, I just don't know why I feel dizzy sometimes. We left and caught a jeepney to his friend apartment. Their apartment was on the second floor; we had to use the outside stairs to enter their apartment. We climbed the stairs and Wilson knocked on the door. Their Maid opened the door and let us in. Wilson friend immediately introduced himself as C.B. and his wife as Jean Powdrell. I could tell right off that C.B. was very arrogant and didn't have any manners at all. His wife Jean was a very nice lady; she made me feel right at home. We took our seats and I could smell the food cooking in the kitchen and it almost made me sick. C.B. wanted to introduce me to his Maid; I think because we both were Filipino, so he asked me to accompany him to the kitchen where he introduced the Maid. We said hello in Tagalog. C.B. opened the pot that was cooking on the stove to show me what he was cooking. He was boiling ox tail and seasoning it with vinegar and soy sauce. I told the Maid that it smelled vinegary; she said yes, it's suppose to be adobo American style.

She said C.B told her to put tomato sauce, onion and potatoes in it also...she smiled looking at me. C.B. said what are you two talking about...are you calling me a stupid American? I said no, we were talking about the food you are cooking. He said oh! I thought you were talking about me. I left the kitchen going back to the living room and C.B. followed me. When I sat back down Jean asked me if I wanted anything to drink. I told her I would like a glass of water. When I spoke in English I spoke real slow spacing my words, because my English was not very good. Jean noticed how I was speaking and asked if I was all right. Wilson said she is a little dizzy...I think it is the hot weather. Then C.B. said I am a Doctor and I think you are an anemic. Jean laughed and said leave Vicky alone...she is blushing and embarrassed already. Then C.B. told Wilson to help himself to all of the drinks in his small bar refrigerator. Wilson didn't disappoint him, he got up and went to the refrigerator and got a beer. Wilson came back to the couch and sit down beside me and started drinking his beer. I sat and watched him and C.B. drink beer and talk loud. Jean asked me if I drank beer; I said no, I don't drink any liquor. She said that's good. The Maid called C.B. into the kitchen; he got up and asked me to come too. I followed him into the kitchen; he wanted me to taste the meat and see if it was done. The Maid gave me a small piece of the meat and I tasted it. The meat was very tender and I suppose done. I said the meat is very tender. C.B asked the Maid if the rice was cooked already. She said the rice was almost done. Then Wilson and Jean came into the kitchen and asked C.B. what was going on. C.B. said we are trying to see if the meat is cooked already. Jean said I guess the food will be done in a little while, so we sit back down in the living room. We sat and talked and I tried to use my broken English slow enough so everyone could understand me. I can understand English real well, but I have a problem speaking it real fast. The Maid came into the living room and announced that the food was ready to be served. Jean got up and ushered Wilson and me into the dining room. Their kids finally came out of their room; Jean quickly introduced the two girls, the oldest one was named Lois and the youngest was named Penny. We were served Adobo ox tail and rice, which was very tasty.

I kept thinking about the name Lois that sounds like Lucy...this name follow me everywhere I go...it remind me of Wilson old girl friend Lucy. Jean asked me how I liked C.B. cooking and started to laugh. I said it is very good. Wilson and C.B. finished eating and went straight to the cabinet where the liquor was kept and started to fix mix drinks. They continued to drank until around ten o, clock. Jean had put the kids to bed earlier. I guess she was ready to go to bed because she started to turn out lights in the house. I told Wilson it was time to go home, but he didn't seem to want to leave; I told him that I didn't feel good, but he and C.B. kept drinking. I stood up and Wilson pulled me back down on the couch; I said we have to go now because you have to go to work tomorrow. He got up from the couch moving as if he was going to fall down. I said goodbye to the Powdrell and thanked them for inviting us into their home. Jean said you are welcome, but C.B. mind were someplace else. We left their house and walked to the main street (Magsaysay drive and caught a jeepney to go home. Wilson almost went to sleep on our way to our apartment. I helped him to get to the apartment. When we got inside he went straight to the bedroom and lay across the bed. I removed his shoes and clothing and covered him with a sheet. I undress and put my nightgown on and lay beside him thinking...why he have to get drunk when we go out...who will protect me if I am attacked... why he can't control his drinking? I hugged my pillow and went to sleep.

At four thirty the next morning the alarm clock went off and Wilson got up and sat on the side of the bed. I asked him if he was going to work; he said yes, and asked if I had something for his headache. I said you need to buy you some medicine for your drinking headache, I don't know what medicine to buy for drinking too much...you was so drunk last night...why do you have to get drunk when you take me out? He said please I have a headache. He got dressed and kissed me goodbye and left for work. I really felt sorry for Wilson having a bad headache; I guess it was because he drank that liquor C.B. Had last night. I went back to bed, but I couldn't go to sleep because I was worried about Wilson having a bad headache. I got up to go to the bathroom and the room seems to be moving around, so I held on to the door. I couldn't imagine what was happening to me; I got a glass of water and drank it all and slowly walked back to the bedroom and lay down. I tried to go back to sleep, but I just kept thinking about Wilson. I covered my head with my pillow and tried to force myself to fall asleep. Finally I did fall asleep.

Around nine that morning I woke up feeling hungry; I decided to get up and fix me something to eat. I fixed the bed before I went into the kitchen to cook me something to eat. When I got to the kitchen I felt dizzy and felt as if I want to throw up. When the dizzy feeling passed I felt like I wanted to eat some fruit, so I cleaned up a bit and left for the market to get fresh fruit. When I got out of the tricycle at the market the dizziness had returned so I walked around in the market very slow until I had picked the fresh fruit I wanted. I caught another tricycle and went back to the apartment. I went straight to the kitchen and washed the fruit and set down at the table and had my fill. I couldn't understand why I had a craving for just fruit this morning because I didn't usually eat that much fruit at anytime. The fruit was so delicious; I felt better so I went and sit down in the living room. Around eleven I decided to take a shower; when I finished I came back to the living room and towel dried my hair. When I finished drying my hair I decided to have some more fruit for lunch. I really can't understand it; I usually can't go for no more than one meal without eating rice and today I only have a craving for fresh fruit. I thought to myself…tomorrow I would go to the market early and get some more fresh fruit. After finishing my lunch I sat down in the living room and suddenly I felt very sleepy, so I lie down on the couch and fell asleep. The next thing I heard was the front door opening. I got up to see who it was; it was Wilson coming home early. He said hi sweetheart and came over and kissed me. I said hi and asked why he was home so early. He said they had finished up early so he came home. He asked if we could go to the bedroom and I said yes, because I knew he was still feeling bad from last night drinking. He undressed and lay down on the bed and I lay down beside him and we went to sleep.

We slept to around four thirty that afternoon before Wilson woke up. I asked him if he was all right and he said he was o.k. And he was not going to drink liquor again; he would only drink a beer. Then he asked me if I wanted to go to C.B.' house; I said that I really didn't want to go anywhere, but I will go with him if he wanted to go. He said we will only stay for a little while, so I got ready and we left on our way to visit the Powdrell. When we arrived and knocked on the door, C.B. answered the door. He looked as if he was drunk. He said come on in. we had a seat on the couch in their living room; I could hear Jean and the kids in one of the bedroom.

She promptly came out and greeted us. She offered us a drink, I said no thank you, but Wilson couldn't wait to get a beer. He decided that he didn't like the liquor C.B. was drinking. Wilson told C.B. that the liquor had given him a bad headache. Jean said yes and a hangover too. Wilson said C.B. I don't know how you continue drinking that liquor…it almost killed me. Jean said C.B. had gotten use to drinking liquor and it does not bother him. We sat around making small talk for a while. Finally C.B. asked me if I would accompany him to the market the next day because I could bargain with the vendors better than him. Jean asked him why he doesn't send the Maid to do their shopping. He completely ignored what Jean had said and asked Wilson if he would mind if I went with him to the market. I was hoping Wilson would tell him no; I couldn't go with him, but he said no man I don't mind if she go. I said I will get whatever you want just give me the money. He said no I would pick you up and drive you to the market. He asked Wilson to give him our address. I asked Jean if she would be coming too; she said no, because she had to stay and take care of the kids...tomorrow was the Maid off day. We made small talk till around ten o, clock and I told Wilson it was almost ten and time to go home. Surprisingly he said o.k. And we said our goodbye and C.B. said I would see you tomorrow when I pick you up for our market date. I said to myself...I hope you forget about tomorrow market date. When we got home I asked Wilson why did he agree to let me go to the market with C.B. when all C.B. had to do is give me the money and I would get whatever he wanted...he also could stay at home and let Jean and I go to the market. Wilson said just do it this time and it will be the last. I didn't really feel good about the ideal of going with another man some place without Wilson or a chaperon. He kissed and hugged me, but I was still upset. I thought to myself...this is Wilson friend and he trusts him, so I guess I have to trust him too. Wilson asked if there was something to eat in the kitchen; I said there is can food and bread in the kitchen cabinet, go and look. He went into the kitchen and fixed and ate corn beef and rice. I went to the bedroom and got ready and went to bed. When he finishing in the kitchen he came to the bedroom to get ready for bed. He got into the bed and tried to hug and kiss me but I turned my back to him because I was still mad about him agreeing to let C.B. pick me up and take me to the market without him. I thought to myself... what if C.B. wanted to do something to break us up...this would be his chance...he always act as if he don't like me being with Wilson. Wilson started again trying to kiss me and make me face him in the bed. Finally I gave in and we made love and I went to sleep in his arms because as always I felt safe in his arms.

The alarm clock went off at four that morning, but instead of getting up and getting ready for work, Wilson started hugging and kissing me and I knew what was next. Finally when it was all over I lay spent in the bed with hardly enough strength to say goodbye to him as he left for work. I grab his pillow and hugged it as I drifted off to sleep. I woke up around seven that morning; when I got up I felt dizzy again, so I walked slowly to the bathroom. I washed my face and brushed my teeth and slowly walked into the kitchen and got my kettle to boil water for oval tine. I figured that the oval tine would help me get pass my dizzy spell. I went into the living room to wait for the water to get hot. I went back into the kitchen and checked the water; it was hot enough to make oval tine, so I mixed a cup for me and set it on the kitchen table to cool down and went into the bedroom and made up the bed. I thought to myself...the oval tine should be about right now, so I went into the kitchen and retrieve my cup and returned to the living room to relax and have my oval tine. I sat silently having my oval tine; when I finished I decided to take a shower because C.B. was suppose to pick me up around nine that morning. During my shower I started to thinking about my condition...why I am having dizzy spells and have a sick stomach. I decided to explain to Wilson exactly what's happening to me when he comes home. I finished my shower and went into the living room and started towel drying my hair. I had a craving for fruit and hot boiled eggs, so when I finished drying my hair I went into the kitchen and started boiling two eggs. As soon as the eggs were done I took one out and took the shells off it while it was still hot. I ate it and the left over fruit for my breakfast. When I finished I thought to myself... that was not a bad breakfast. I lounged around in the living room and kept an eye on the window for C.B. Finally I heard someone blowing a car horn outside; I looked out the window and saw C.B. standing beside his car. I thought to myself...I had better hurry before he starts blowing his car horn again. I grab my bag and went outside to meet him. I asked him why he didn't knock on the door. He said he didn't know my neighborhood, so he didn't want to leave his car. I got into the car and we were off to the market. I told him to park his car in front of the market. I decided to try and explain to him about how the Vendors price their goods.

I told him if they see an America their prices go twice as high, so I need him to tell me what he wanted and how much he wanted to spend. Then I could bargain with the vendors, but he would have to stay away from me so they wouldn't think we are together. He agreed, and said he wanted jumbo shrimp and pig blood. He gave me the money and I made the purchase. When we started back to his car I asked him was he going to buy some pork; he said no, he would buy the pork from the Naval Base Commissary. Before we got to the car I started to feel dizzy again, so I had to stop and hold on to something to keep from falling down. C.B. asked me if I was all right; I said yes, it's just the heat here in the market. We walked slowly to his car; then I thought about my fruit, so I told him to go home and I would catch a tricycle home. He wanted to wait for me but I finally convinced him to go. I went back to the fruit stand and picked a mixture of all the fruit at the stand. I went across the street and caught a tricycle to my apartment. When I arrived at my apartment and started for the door; I almost felled down the tricycle Driver asked me if I was all right. I said yes as I walked slowly to the door. I opened the door and went straight to the bedroom; I laid my bag on the floor and lay down on the bed. As I lay there on the bed trying to figure out what was wrong with me; I decided to tell Wilson I would go to Calapacuan tomorrow to see my Mother. I lay there for a few minutes then I started to feel a lot better, so I closed my eyes and went to sleep.

Hunger woke me up, I glanced at the time it was one o, clock already. I thought to myself...that's why I am hungry. I got up and picked up my shopping bag and slowly carried it into the kitchen. I put all of the fruit into the sink and washed the fruit until it were squeaky clean. I put four pieces of mixed fruit into a bowl and put the rest away for later. I sat at the table and ate the fruit in the bowl it tasted wonderful. When I finished eating my stomach felt as if it was going to get upset; I thought to myself...now my food want to come back...what's going on with my body? I really have to tell Wilson about my sickness because I need to see a Doctor. I got up and went into the bedroom and lay down again; finally I went to sleep again. I don't know how long I had slept before Wilson came home and woke me up. He shook me and asked if I was all right; I told him that I was sick and had being vomiting. He said that I should go and see a Doctor the next day without fail.

He said maybe you ate some spoiled food because we don't have a refrigerator. I said no, because I always buy fresh fruit, meat and vegetables everyday...I don't eat leftover. The only food I have eaten today is fresh fruit that I bought when I went to the market with C.B.

He said how did your trip to the market go? I said everything went fine once I explained to him how things work at the Market. He leaned over and kissed me and said you need to go and see a Doctor tomorrow. I said I am going to see my Mother then maybe I will go see a Doctor. He said there is no maybe about it; go see a Doctor so you can find out what's wrong with you. Wilson lay down beside me on the bed and said let's go to the movies tonight and if we have time maybe we will stop and have a drink at one of the clubs. I said o.k. I thought to myself... what is wrong with him...I am laying here dizzy and about to throw up and he want me to go nightclubbing tonight...well I guess I will if I feel all right after the movie. Wilson went across the street for beer at the Sari Sari store. I stayed in bed because I was very sleepy. He came back and started drinking his beer and looked as if he was restless. Around three he said he had to go out for a while and he would be right back. I sat up in the bed and said I thought we were going to the movie tonight. He said the movie doesn't start until around seven we have plenty of time, plus I will be right back. He kissed me and left. I thought...what is wrong with him...he knows I am sick, yet he leaves me alone here to wait for him.

I got up and slowly walked into the kitchen and got a drink of water; I decided to fix me something to eat, so I decided to have something different. I cooked some rice and fried some eggplant. The smell of the eggplant cooking started to turn my stomach, so I hurried to finish frying the eggplant. I went into the living room to wait for the rice to cook. Finally the rice was cooked, so I cut up a ripe tomato and ate it with my rice and eggplant. I felt a lot better when I finished eating so I went into the bedroom and made up the bed. I decided to change my clothing and get ready to go to the movies because Wilson said that he would return very soon. After getting ready for the movie I went into the living room and sat down to wait for Wilson. I sat watching the people walking by. After a few minutes I decided to get me a pillow from the bedroom and lay down on the couch in the living room and try to relax until Wilson came home. After what seems like an hour or two, I looked at the time and I could see that we wouldn't be going to the movie tonight. I looked out the window at all of the lights coming on because it was getting dark; I could see all the bugs flying around the lights looking so happy.

I wish I could fly and maybe I could be with someone instead of being here all alone and lonely. Then my mind started to wonder… maybe Wilson want to get away from me because I am sick…he said we were going to the movie, but he's nowhere in sight…maybe he went to see his other girlfriend because I am sick…I pray that I am wrong…maybe he going to leave me because he doesn't like having a sick girlfriend. Finally I couldn't hold the tears back; I started to cry, so I got up and went into the bedroom and lay down on my bed. I hugged my pillow as I cried myself to sleep. I woke up around ten that night and looked around for Wilson. I lay there until around ten thirty and I heard him come in the front door. He was so drunk he was having problem standing up, so I helped him to the bed and to undress. I said where have you been? You said we were going to the movie, but you went out and got drunk…look at your shirt! It has lipstick all over it. He said that's your lipstick. I said that not my lipstick color. He said maybe someone put it on me. He stopped talking and started to snore. I thought to myself…I love him to much…I know he had a Hostess girlfriend before I met him…I pray to God he doesn't give me a sickness. Then he started to mumble someone name in his sleep. I put my pillow over my head and went to sleep. Around two in the morning I heard the closet door open; he was up trying to use the closet for the bathroom. I jumped up and showed him to the bathroom. I stayed until he finished using the bathroom and took him back to the bedroom. We went back to bed and to sleep.

The alarm clock went off and I got up and went to the bathroom. When I came back he was still sitting on the side of the bed. I asked him if he was going to work. He mumbled out a yes. I said I don't know what time I will be back from visiting my Mother and seeing the Doctor today. He took out his wallet and gave me twenty pesos. I didn't know how much the Doctor visit would cost so I took the money. He got ready for work and kissed me goodbye as he left. I decided to get up and get ready to go to Calapacuan; I wanted to be ready to leave as soon as the sun comes up. At day break around six that morning I left on my way to Calapacuan. I took a tricycle to the jeepney circle and caught a jeepney that was pulling out for Calapacuan. I sat quietly riding because my stomach was feeling upset. I took an orange from my bag and removed the peeling from it and held it up to my nose. The smell from the orange peeling helped somewhat to settle my stomach. When the jeepney arrived at Calapacuan I got out and started walking slowly across the rice field to my Mother's house.

When I arrived everyone was up and about Sister Linda, Sister Rose, Gina, Brother Etong and Mother. As soon as I walked in the door Mother asked me what was wrong I looked as if I was going to fall down? I said I am sick. She said do you have the flu? I said no, I am dizzy and can't seem to hold anything on my stomach... every time I smell food cooking my stomach get upset. She said sit down and went and got me a glass of water; she looked me over and said you're pregnant. I said pregnant! She said yes! I thought you promised me that you were going to wait until you get married before you and Wilson started sleeping around. I said we are going to get married because Wilson has submitted the paperwork to the Navy requesting permission to get married. I know it is taking a long time but we are going to get married. She said so you and Wilson decided to have a baby now...what if he decide not to marry you...what you and the baby going to do...remember you're still a baby too...you are acting just like the Hostess in the club, sneaking around and getting a hotel room. I said we're not sneaking into the hotel; we have an apartment and just waiting for the paperwork to be approved. She said why you haven't told me about your apartment? I said we were going to tell you as soon as the paperwork came back...are you sure I am pregnant? She said yes I am sure you are pregnant...how could you let this happen...I told you to wait until you get married before you jump in bed with him...I pray to God that Wilson take the responsibility and do what's right...you kids never listen to what I say to you...you all live dangerously...you just act before you think. Everyone sat quietly listening to Mother sermon. Finally she told Sister Linda to find some dried fish so she could start breakfast and she told me she was going to take me to see the Doctor after breakfast to make sure I am all right. I said Linda please don't cook the fish inside the smell make me sick, so Brother Etong took the fish outside and cooked it on the grill. Sister Linda fried the eggs and cooked the rest of the food inside.

Mother started on me again; she said you are pregnant now, I hope Wilson will do the right thing and marry you. Sister Rose looked at me with a smile on her face and said you are pregnant, ha. As I sat on my favorite wooden box, I admitted that I didn't think about being pregnant at anytime; I thought I had a stomach virus or something...what will I tell Wilson. Sister Rose said you are going to have a little Wilson.

I got a sleeping mat, a blanket and a pillow and lay down to rest until breakfast was ready. Finally breakfast was ready; we all had our breakfast; when we finished breakfast Mother got ready to take me to see the Doctor. When she had finished changing we left for the Doctor's office. When we arrived the Doctor took urine, blood and listened to my heartbeat. We returned to waiting room to wait for the result. Mother said from now until you have your baby you can't lift heavy things you will have to take it easy because this is your first baby. Finally we were called back into the Doctor office. The Doctor said you're pregnant Mrs. Palaganas and anemic too... here are some prescriptions that will help you and the baby and take care of your morning sickness...this medication is to be taken for nine months. I said how many months am I pregnant? He said unless I am mistaken, you are two months pregnant...if you have a problem you can come in and see me; my Clinic is open six days a week. We thanked the Doctor and left. We caught a jeepney back to Calapacuan. Mother told me she would let Sister Linda stay with me until the baby came, because the first pregnancy is usually a little sensitive and I don't want you to lose the baby...ask Wilson right away if it will be all right for Linda to stay with you until the baby come.

When Mother and I got back to Calapacuan everyone wanted to know what the Doctor said. Mother said I told her before we left she was pregnant; we just needed the Doctor conformation and a treatment plan for her pregnancy...the Doctor said she is two months pregnant. I spread a mat on the floor and lay down and went to sleep. I woke up in about an hour later thinking...what will Wilson do or say when I tell him I am pregnant...what if he doesn't want a baby... maybe he will leave me...what if he think the baby is not his and he leave the baby and me...oh! What am I going to do? Mother broke my chain of thought when she said what are you thinking about...

stop thinking too much because it's bad for you during your first pregnancy. I said I just don't know how I am going to tell Wilson I am pregnant. She said that why I have always told you not to jump into bed with the first guy you think you are in love with...now you're pregnant and both you and Wilson is very young...I don't know if Wilson is ready to be a Father...most American that get their girlfriend pregnant either leaves the baby here in the Philippines or let the girl get an abortion...remember if he don't want you to have the baby, come home and we will take care of my Grandbaby...you are not to abort the baby...we maybe poor but we will find a way to take care of the baby...love is blind...you made a big mistake, but there is no turning around this is a one way bridge...go home and tell him you're pregnant and if he don't accept the baby don't push it, just come home and we will take care of the baby.

When I got up to leave Sister Rose said she was leaving too. I said goodbye to Mother, Brother Etong and Sister Linda; I told Linda I would let her know about staying with me as soon as I talk to Wilson. Sister Rose and her daughter Gina, Live in Barrio Barrietto; where the jeepney stops before Olongapo City. We caught a jeepney and were on our way. The gas fumes started to bother me so I reached into my bag and got my orange peel and held it to my nose. Little Gina said she wanted some orange too. I showed the orange peel to her and let her smell it. I whispered to her...I always smell the orange peel to keep from smelling the underarm odor of the men in the front seat. Then she looked and saw most of the women holding their nose when the guy lifted his arm. She started to laugh, she laugh until we arrive in Barrietto. The jeepney stop in Barrietto and Sister Rose and Gina got out of the jeepney; I told her I would take care of their fare and said goodbye.

When I arrived in Olongapo City I caught a tricycle to my apartment. Wilson had not arrived so I went straight to the bathroom; when I came out I got a glass of water and sit down in the living room to wait for him. Around three thirty I saw a tricycle pull up and Wilson got out in a hurry. He hurried into the apartment and started asking me questions so fast I didn't have time to answer him... what did the Doctor say? What's wrong with you? He even forgot to kiss me. I said sit down and I will tell you, so he sat down.

I said I am pregnant. He said what! You're pregnant. Oh boy! I didn't expect you to get pregnant right away. I said what are we going to do? He said I don't know let me think…I don't make enough money to take care of a baby. I felt real bad then about being pregnant. I said this is our baby…I know we're young to have a baby, but I am still pregnant and don't know what to do. I started to cry; he hugged and kissed me and said he will think of something o.k. I said o.k. Wilson started pacing back and forth and finally said let's go to C.B. house. I said I don't want to go. He kept at me until I agreed to go. I went into our bedroom and got ready to go. When we arrive at their place; Jean greeted us warmly as she let us in. C.B. said hi boy! Come on in and have a seat. We sat and made small talk for a while. Finally Wilson said boy I need to talk to you. C.B. said Jean take Vicky in the kitchen, we need to have a little man-to-man talk.

Jean and I went into the kitchen and sit down; I could barely hear Wilson telling C.B. that I was pregnant. Then C.B. said in his loud voice…do you think it's your baby? Jean looked at me and kept listening to what C.B. were saying. Finally Jean got up and went into the living room and told C.B. that we could hear everything he was saying. He said I am just trying to help this boy straighten out things because he may not be the Father of the baby. Jean said C.B. do you know what you are saying? I walked into the living room and everybody turned and looked at me as if I had done something wrong. Jean asked me if I was pregnant. I really didn't want to say anything at all, but I seem to be the center of the conversation, so I said yes! I found out today. I really didn't know why Wilson was discussing my pregnancy with C.B. anyway, because every time I see him he usually drunk or on his way. Then C.B. said do you think he's the Father of the baby you are carrying? I was so startled that I couldn't speak. Jean said C.B. that's none of your business. C.B. said you don't know the women in Olongapo. Wilson didn't say a word he seem to be o.k. With what C.B. was saying to me, he kept drinking his beer. I wanted to leave at that time, but I sat patiently waiting on C.B. to shut his mouth, but he was really getting drunk then. I asked Wilson if we could go now, but he just looked at me as if he agreed with what C.B. had said. I don't know why, but I was waiting for Wilson to tell me that he didn't think the baby was his…

if he does, I will leave and he will never see me or the baby again… it look like he have C.B. doing his dirty work asking me all of these questions. I sat calmly waiting for whatever may happen, because they both were getting drunk. Finally C.B. started acting as if he was going to pass out, so I stood up and tried to show all the anger that I could without screaming and said these people need to go to bed, we better go home. Then Wilson finally stood up and started for the door. I looked at Jean and said thanks for your hospitality. She said don't mind C.B. he just talk too much. We left and went home. When we got inside I went to the bedroom to change and get ready for bed, but Wilson went back out and across the street to the store. He came back with a can of corn beef. He went into the kitchen and cut up and onion and stirred fried it with his corn beef. I kept watch on him while he was cooking the corn beef because he had been drinking and seem to be a little tipsy. I didn't say a word to Wilson about what had happened at C.B. house even though my blood was boiling.

I kept wondering what Wilson had said to C.B. for him to ask me if I had gotten pregnant by my Filipino boyfriend…was it Wilson ideal or did C.B. ask on his own accord. Wilson of all people should know better; I haven't given him any reason to believe that I have been unfaithful to him from the first day I met him until now. I had never seriously thought about having a boyfriend until I met him…I think Wilson is trying to hide from his responsibility, because if he wasn't he wouldn't have allow C.B. to talk to me like that. He knows that I have been faithful to him; I even quit my job to please him, because he didn't want other guys talking to me. I guess I am all along again with no one to protect me from wrongful accusations. I have been tried and found guilty by Wilson and C.B. and neither one has really given me the benefit of the doubt. They act like I got pregnant all by myself. Wilson seem to have forgotten that we made love three or four times a day; if you make love that often there is a good possibility that you will get pregnant. We went to bed; we lay there with our back to each other. He didn't kiss me goodnight…I am glad he didn't try because I would have turned away. I was really mad at him for letting me down in my time of need. Somehow I was waiting for him to tell me to my face that he didn't believe he was the

Father of my baby, but he never mumbled a word. I had made up my mind to pack my things and go home and never see him again.

That night it was very hard for me to fall asleep; I know I had to be strong, but I kept thinking over and over...C.B. was poisoning Wilson's mind with the lies about the girls in Olongapo City...yes, he said that he love me countless times, but they was only words. My love for him is unwavering and living proof is in my stomach, but he will have to figure it out himself. After all I have said and done for him he still have doubts about my love. I guess he think I am like my Sister Melda or his girlfriend he had in the club. His drinking doesn't help the situation at all; when he's drinking he forget about me, some of his friend say bad things about me, he either don't care or too drunk to know what's going on. I realize I don't speak good English, but I speak enough to know what they are saying. I maybe young but I am not stupid...now Wilson is treating me like I am stupid with no feeling at all. Oh! What have I gotten myself into now? I thought I had a mutual love affair, but now everything seem to be going wrong; I am being blamed for getting pregnant although I know it is my fault because I let it happen, but I also know it takes two to make a baby...my poor baby...what am I going to do...your Father don't want to accept you. Don't worry I will take care of you even if I have to scrub floors on my knees.

I felt a slight headache coming on from all of the worrying trying to figure out Wilson next move. I looked at the time it was two in the morning, so I hugged my pillow and tried to go to sleep. I kept trying thinking...I better go to sleep so my baby could sleep; I put my pillow over my head and finally drifted off to sleep. I didn't hear the alarm clock go off at four that morning. The only thing I remembered was Wilson kissing me on the cheek and saying goodbye. I went back to sleep and slept almost half of the day. I woke up feeling hungry, so I decided to get up and cook me something to eat, because I didn't want my baby to get hungry. I went across the street to the store and bought carnation milk. When I returned I mixed it with sugar and water and drunk it along with my meal. I had a half can of milk left so I put it in a bowl of water to keep the ants from it. The little ants are always popping up unexpectedly. The water in a bowl works sometime; I even tried putting salt and pepper in the water, but they swim across to the can of milk. I figured if I drink milk and eat real good I would be all right until Wilson gave me some money for my medicine. He had seemed very upset when he found out I was pregnant, so I didn't tell him about the prescriptions that had to be filled. It's only a few more days before he got paid; I can get my prescriptions fill when he gives me some money. I know my baby will be all right until then. I rubbed my stomach to tell my baby that his or her Father and I love it very much.

The time seems to fly; it seems like it was only a few minutes ago I had finished drying my hair after my shower. Then I heard Wilson coming in the door. He said hi and kissed me. I didn't say anything about what had happened last night while he and C.B. was drinking. I just waited for him to say whatever to me. He asked me how I was feeling. I said that I felt dizzy, but the Doctor said I would be all right if I take my medicine. He said what medicine? I showed him the prescriptions the Doctor gave me. I said I would wait and have the prescriptions fill when you get paid. He said give me the prescriptions and I will get them filled now. He took the prescriptions and was off to the drug store. I had just finished combing my hair when my stomach started churning. I hurried to the bathroom. I decided to stay in the bathroom for a while. Just as I came out of the bathroom Wilson came in with my medicine. He said C.B. was right you do have a slightly anemic. I said yes the Doctor said yesterday that I needed iron for my blood. He said the other pills are for the baby and me. Wilson said three of the pills have to be taken until you have the baby, but the other one is for morning sickness and you can stop taking it when you no longer have morning sickness. I said thank you for the medicine and hugged and kissed him. He kissed me back. I asked him where he got the medicine; he said that he bought it at the Pharmacy across from the market and that I could buy it at any Pharmacy in Olongapo City. He also added; don't forget to take your medicine every day. I said o.k. I promise. We went into our favorite room, the bedroom and decided to take a nap. We lay on the bed making small talk until Wilson asked what the Doctor said about making love. I said the Doctor said it was all right to make love, just relax and don't force it. That was all Wilson wanted to hear, he started kissing and touching me all over and before I knew it; I were wanting it as much as he did. We made passionate love. Finally when our body was completely drained, we lay motionless in each other arms until we fell asleep.

We woke up around four thirty that afternoon and decided to go out for dinner. I got up and went into the shower and he followed me. He came in and grabbed me from behind and started kissing me. We started all over again in the shower; realizing it was not enough room in the shower, Wilson carried me to the bedroom and we made love again. We lay around in the bed for an hour or two too tired to get up. Finally Wilson gained enough strength to get up and go across the street for beer, bread and corn beef. I asked him what he were going to do with the bread. He said make a corn beef sandwich. I said I thought we were going to the movie. He said we would go another time when I stop feeling dizzy. I thought to myself…being pregnant making love two and three times in the afternoon was taking all of my energy. I said o.k. We will stay home tonight and I will prepare our dinner. I made corn beef hash and rice. While I prepared our dinner Wilson sat in the living room drinking beer. Finally he said that smells good. I also noticed that I didn't get sick when I smelled the food cooking after taking my medicine…maybe the medicine had started to work right away.

While waiting for the rice to cook, I went into the living room and sat down with Wilson. Finally the rice was done and I fixed our plates and we ate our food in the living room. Wilson said the corn beef is very good with rice. I said yes, it's even better with a potato chopped up in it. We finished our meal and I washed the dishes and came back into the living room. I noticed Wilson had his mind on something else. I asked him if he was all right. He said yes, and stood up then he bend down and kissed me. He said he was going out for a while and would be right back. I said are you going to your boat? He said no, I have to catch the guy that owe me some money. I said why not catch him tomorrow…I thought we were going to stay home tonight? He said I would be right back. I said don't stay to long, its eight o, clock already. He left without saying another word. I thought…here I am all along again…I wish I knew what else he wanted in life…he have me, the woman he said he love…a place to stay and he can buy beer or whatever he want to drink right across the street. I guess he want one of the hostess in the nightclub sitting on his lap kissing him with her hand in his pocket. Maybe he likes to compete with the other guys for club hostess. He have to have some reason for wanting to leave me here and go into the street...I am here in his bed and belong to no one but him and carrying his baby...he walk out leaving me here by myself...why didn't he want me to go with him? He tell me he love me every time he comes home, why can't he see or tell that he's hurting me when he leaves me like this and go out. I started crying again, I felt so lonely without him. I went into the bedroom and lay down and hugged my pillow. Then I remembered I was pregnant, so I rubbed my stomach, maybe my baby is crying too. I said to myself... stop crying Vicky you have a baby to think about. I rolled over in the bed and looked at the clock, it was almost ten o, clock. I got up and put my nightgown on and went back to bed. I hugged my pillow as I closed my eyes and finally drifted off to sleep.

Suddenly, I was awakened by Wilson falling into the bed it almost scared me to death. I got up and helped him undress for bed. I often wonder how Wilson can be so drunk and still find his way to our apartment. I think he play drunk so I will leave him along, because he know he has done something wrong. I will play along with his little games, one of the days he will change and I will be here waiting to pick up the pieces and move forward. I lay down beside him watching him sleep, I like to touch his nose and eye lids while he sleep, sometime he would try to hit my hand as if it was a fly, but he never wake up. I don't know why I like to do it, but I do it every time he goes to sleep before I do. I looked over at the clock on the table it was eleven o, clock; I thought to myself...I better go to sleep, so I held my pillow instead of him and went to sleep. Wilson woke me up again talking in his sleep, he was calling some girl name, so I put my pillow over my head and went back to sleep. I really don't know what I would do without my pillow, because I pretend that it is Wilson when I am alone or he's drunk and sleeping on his side of the bed. Sometimes I put his cologne on my pillow and hug it pretending that it him. Believe it or not it helps. I don't know, I guess I am so madly in love with him that why I always find myself pretending so much. All of the hurt and loneliness is tearing me apart, but I know I have to be strong not only for me but also my baby. I have already decided to let him run around until he realize that everything he has being looking for is right here in his apartment.

He woke me up again as he jump out of bed hurrying to get dress, because he forgot to set the alarm clock. He mumbled that the alarm clock didn't ring and he was running late for work. I don't remembered if he kissed me goodbye, because of all the commotions. I went back to sleep and slept until hunger woke me up. I got up and went to the bathroom and washed up. When I finished in the bathroom I cooked my breakfast and sat in the living room and ate it. I also took my medicine because I didn't want to experience morning sickness again. When I finished breakfast I cleaned the kitchen and the bedroom; I decided to take it easy and not do too much house work at one time, so I went back into the living room and sat down. While sitting there in the living room I decided to clean just one room a day so I wouldn't exert myself and hurt my baby. After sitting for a while I decided I had better take a shower now because sometime the power and water is shutoff. I remembered that I have not saved any water lately, so when I finish taking my shower this time I will fill the usual containers with water to be use when the city shut off the water and electric power.

I hurried and finished my shower and towel dried my hair. I thought to myself…it is good that I have finished cleaning up because Wilson may come home early and we can go see a movie. I put my towel away and went into the kitchen to see how much fruit I had left. To my surprise, I had enough to last me until I went back to the market. I usually eat lunch around eleven, but after looking at the fresh fruit I had left, I decided not to wait until eleven and started eating at around ten that morning.

After eating my lunch I decided to go outside in the front on the narrow stoop and get some fresh air. Just as I was really enjoying the fresh air a jeepney came speeding by; normally the apartment manager would wet down the street in front of the apartments to keep the dust down. I don't know why he decided not to do it today. I ran inside and closed the apartment windows to keep the flying dust from coming in. after thinking about the dust and our water situation; I now know why the street was not wet down…the market was extended into our neighborhood and all of the booths use quiet a lot of water, so the city shut it off from time to time to conserve. I also see why some of the residents didn't want the city to extend the market area into our neighborhood; it has been causing problem every since the addition was opened up. I got my dusting equipment and dusted the living room furniture because the dust from the road came in through the open window. When I finished dusting I sat down to take a rest. My mind started to wonder again...Wilson said he will be home early today, he normally come around three thirty...I wonder why he hasn't arrive yet. I sat waiting for what seem like hours and started to feel sleepy, so I went into the bedroom and lay across the bed. I woke up around five thirty that evening feeling hungry I got up and went into the kitchen to fix me something to eat. I opened a can of squid and warmed it up. I really didn't feel like cooking rice so I ate the squid with bread. When I finished eating dinner I sat in the living room staring out the window as the streetlight started to come on. Finally around seven thirty Wilson came home, I could smell the liquor on his breath as soon as he came in the door. I was already upset about him coming late, now here he comes smelling like a bar. He came in and sat down across from me. He didn't kiss me like he normally does, so I knew something was up. He said in his most serious voice, I need to talk to you about your pregnancy...you know a lot of people think that if you are pregnant and your boyfriend is an American...the baby is not his. I said what are you talking about? Do you mean that people will think that the baby is not yours? Is that what you are saying? I was beginning to get real mad at him. Then he said that he knew of a Hospital that would perform an Abortion. I said what you mean when you say Abortion. He said when the baby is still small in your stomach the Hospital will remove it. I said what do you mean remove my baby? I almost got sick in my stomach, but I tried to be calm and understand what he was saying. I couldn't hold back any longer, I started screaming...you are not going to kill my baby...if you don't want my baby then you don't want me...why are you listening to what other people are saying...I maybe poor but I am not going to kill my baby...you must be out of your mind...tell your friend C.B. to stop trying to poison your mind to kill my baby or maybe you need to move in with him so he can tell you what to do with your life. Wilson said I just want to help you because we're still young and can have another baby later when we can afford it. I said I don't think we will have a baby later; this will be our last one...you do whatever you want to do...I am going to keep my baby. I left the room and went into the bedroom crying and closed the door behind me. I was so mad I could hardly breathe. I lost a lot of respect for him because he worries about what other people think about him. He act as if he can't think for himself...just because someone else has doubts about whether this baby is his or not shouldn't have an effect on what he think...now because of what his friend say he want to get rid of our baby. This is so upsetting to me; I hope it doesn't cause me to lose my baby. Finally he came into the room and sit down beside me on the side of the bed. He started caressing my back trying to comfort me, but I told him to leave me alone and stop touching me. I think he was waiting for me to tell him to leave me alone, because he got up and left the apartment. I sat there crying and thinking...I can't believe what's happening to me...is this the man I fell in love with...what's wrong with him...why can't he stand on his own feet and make his own decisions? I got up and got a glass of water. Just then, I didn't care whether he came back or stayed away. I decided to go to Calapacuan tomorrow to see my Mother so I went to bed because I was very tired.

A few minutes after I drifted off to sleep I felt the bed move as he took off his shoes. He got undress and got into the bed beside me and went to sleep. Finally I went back to sleep. It seem as though I had just went back to sleep when the alarm clock went off the next morning. Wilson got up and got dressed for work. He said he would be home early today. I said I don't care whether you come back or not. He bended over and kissed me on the cheek and left for work. I stayed in the bed a few minutes before deciding to get up and get cleaned up for my trip to Calapacuan. I left around six thirty that morning on my way to my Mother house. When I arrived I saw Mother standing in front of the window brushing her teeth. When I was close enough she asked me why I was out so early in the morning. I said I wanted to eat fried dried fish and garlic fried rice. I decided not to tell her what was going on with me because I was upset and didn't want her to get upset too. She told brother Etong to get wood and start a fire in the stove so she could cook the food I like. She asked me if I was still feeling all right. I assured her that I was. I told her the medicine I was taking was helping me a lot. She said that's good...how is Wilson doing? I said he is doing all right and going to work every day.

Mother cooked breakfast and we ate breakfast making small talk. When we finished Brother Etong told Mother he was going to burn some dead leaves under the Mango trees. I looked at Mother and said I didn't know that the Mango trees had started blooming. She said yes, they have started already. I told Brother Etong I would help him later on; He looked at me and smiled pointing his finger at my stomach. Then he pointed his finger at his eyes indicating that he wanted me to watch him instead. The food was very good; when I stood up I realized I had almost ate too much, but Mother assured me that it was all right she said I was eating for two.

I asked Mother how was Sister Maria, my sister-in-law getting alone; she said Maria was doing just fine...her Daughter would come visit her twice a week. I said that's good. I wonder why I didn't see her this morning when I came pass her house. Mother said she was probably still asleep. I told Mother I was going to go next door and visit her for a while. Brother Etong left to get water to wash the dishes.

I left and went to Sister Maria's house; when I arrived she was sitting on her porch drinking Coffee. As I climbed the steps I asked her how she were doing; she said I am doing o.k. I heard that you are pregnant. I said yes, and I have a boyfriend. I don't know if you seen him, but he has being here before. She said I think I was away the last time he was here. I said when he comes back again I will introduce him to you. We sat and talked for a few more minutes until Brother Etong came by with the water to wash the dishes. I told her I had promised Brother Etong I would help him rake the leaves under the Mango trees, so I left following him back to Mother's house. She said o.k. I will talk to you later. Brother Etong took the water into the house and came out and got a rake for the leaves. Mother and I followed him in back where the Mango trees were located. Mother and Brother Etong started raking leaves; I picked up a long stick pretending to rake the leaves. When they had raked enough leaves under the trees Brother Etong set them afire. The smoke from the dry leaves would run the insects from the Mango trees so they wouldn't destroy the blossom on the tree. Mother left going back to the house and I stayed with Brother Etong to watch the fire and keep it smoking. Suddenly I heard Sister Maria yelling my name; Mother heard her yelling too so she came out of the house to see what was wrong. Sister Maria were trying to tell me that a young man was coming and she though he maybe my boyfriend. I said o.k. And started looking in the direction she was pointing and saw Wilson coming. Wilson was walking toward Mother's house when Mother pointed in my direction and he saw me standing under the Mango tree. I pretended that I was raking leaves as he walked toward me. He exchanged greeting with Brother Etong and asked me what I was doing. I told him we were smoking the Mango trees to get rid of the flies and bugs that harm the blossoms. Brother Etong started raking more leaves, so Wilson looked around and saw the rake Mother was using; he picked it up and started helping Brother Etong rake the leaves. Mother was really surprised to see Wilson helping Brother Etong rake the leaves. When they finished raking and burning the leaves I left and went to Mother's house for a drink of water. I didn't act as if I was mad at Wilson, because I didn't want Mother to know what was going on. Wilson followed me into the house. I sat down in my favorite place on a wooden box by the window.

Wilson came over and tried to kiss me. I said what do you want from me…I don't have anything…we're a poor happy family…now I have your baby inside me and you want to get rid of it…just go back to your friend C.B. or to the people that telling you it's not your baby…if you think it's not your baby you can leave now…I am going to keep it. Mother and Brother Etong came in the house. He asked me if I had told my Mother what had happened. I said no, I don't want to worry my Mother with my problems. He said I need to talk with you, but I don't want you to get mad at me here. I said I am already mad at you, but I am not going to let my Mother know it…you hurt me, you really, really hurt me…I though you loved me, but I see you just want to use me…what kind of love do you have for me? Then he said could we go home now? I said why do you want me to go home with you if you don't want my baby? I don't want to go home with you. Mother walked over in front of Wilson with a glass of coke with ice in it trying to ask him if he wanted it. He said yes, thank you! I asked where they got the ice for the coke. Mother said she had sent Brother Etong to the store for ice and coke for Wilson. Wilson didn't understand what Mother was saying in Tagalog, so he thought she knew about us and was mad at him. He asked me if she was mad at him. I said no she was just telling me she had sent out for the coke. He said thanks again to my Mother for the coke. I repeated what he said to Mother in Tagalog. Wilson started again trying to persuade me to come with him to our apartment. He said when I told your Mother and family that I love and wanted to marry you; I was very serious and meant every word I said... I still love you and want to marry you...I told you that we have to wait to be interviewed by the base Chaplain before our marriage request would be approved and I am still waiting for our appointment...I am very serious about our relationship...I am very sorry about the things I said to you last night...I had being drinking and was not thinking straight. I was really upset about last night and really didn't want to listen to his excuse for his action. Mother interrupted our conversation and asked whether we were going to stay for lunch. I explained to Wilson what she had said. He said he didn't want to stay for lunch he just wanted to go home and talk to me. I decided to give in and go home to hear what he had to say. I told Mother we were not staying for lunch.

Wilson guessed what I had said to Mother and kissed me; Mother was standing in the room looking at us so I kissed him back. We said goodbye to Mother and Brother Etong. Mother said take care my children. We left going pass Sister Maria house, we saw her sitting out on her porch as we came up to her house. She asked me if Wilson was the guy I had being talking about; I said yes, he is the one and the Father of my baby. We stopped and I introduced Wilson to her; I told him this was my Brother Celino wife. We stopped for a few minutes making small talk. Finally we left and went home to Olongapo City he held my hand all the way as if he thought I would run away. We arrived at our humble apartment, a very lonely place sometimes for me and my baby. I had being thinking to myself all the way home...please let him be the man I fell in love with and not the man that worried about what other people are saying. As soon as we entered the apartment I went straight to the kitchen for a glass of water. We decided to sit in the bedroom because our living room furniture was made of solid wood and we didn't have cushions. Sitting on the side of our bed Wilson held my hands as he attempted to explain his pass action. He said last night I being drinking and was not thinking rationally, I was and still scared to have a baby, because I don't know if I make enough money to take care of it...plus we both are too young to have a baby...we are going to be stuck in the house all of the time. I jumped in right there and said so that all you are thinking about...going out and partying with your friend... worrying about what they are saying...what do you want me here for...is it just to show them that you have a girl friend that doesn't work in the club? You tell your friend C.B. everything; you discussed my pregnancy with him before you discussed it with me. Sometimes I wonder whether you want me to be more like the hostess in the clubs, because you hang around the club with them all the time. Yes, I am in love with you and I thought you loved me too. That's the reason I quit my job at the Money Exchange, so I could spend all of my time with you. I guess having my baby is going to break us up, because I am not going to give up my baby. He started saying he was sorry over and over; then he started kissing me. I said stop, do you think kissing me will stop me from being mad at you? He said please don't be mad at me; we're not going to get rid of our baby we are going to keep it...please don't get mad at me I can't stand for you to be mad at me that's why I left last night...we are going to take care of our baby and when our marriage is approved we will be married.

I started crying; I had to cry and let go of my hurt feeling. He started crying too, and then I knew he felt bad about what happened and realized he loved the baby too. We started trying to comfort each other and before we knew it we was making passionate love. I really do believe that making love is good for whatever ail you. I felt safe once again as we lay totally relaxed in each other arms and fell asleep. The last thing I remembered thinking about before I fell asleep is; I really love him very much...I can't stay mad at him...I know I would follow him to the end of the earth, because I want to spend the rest of my life with him. I woke up feeling very hungry, so I decided to get up and cook something to eat. Wilson asked me where I was going; I said I was going in the kitchen to cook something to eat. He said that's right we haven't had lunch yet; we can get dressed and go out and get something to eat. I said no! I would fry some spam and cook some rice to eat with it and make you a spam sandwich. He said if that what you want to do o.k. I left him in bed and went into the kitchen and started cooking. I would check on him every now and then and give him a big kiss. He kept asking me if I would forgive him; finally I said yes, he tried to pull me back into the bed. I said let me go finish cooking. He let me go, so I went back in the kitchen and finished preparing our food. When the food was ready he decided to go across the street for a beer. When he returned we sat down and ate our food. He said looking at me, pretty soon you would need maternity clothes, but not now. He smiled and gave me a big kiss; I kissed him back even though the foul beer and cigarette smell on his breath almost make me sick sometimes. I put up with the smell of cigarettes and beer because I love him. He looked at his watch and said, let's go and catch the movie matinee. I said o.k. Just give me enough time to clean up the kitchen and get dressed. Finally I was ready to go so we left for the movie. For almost two weeks things went real well; we would either stay home or go see a movie. Finally his payday came and he stopped off at the club before coming home, guess he stopped in to see his girl friend that work in the club.

He arrived home around ten that night drunk as always. I helped him to get undress and into the bed. All the time I was thinking to myself...why does he always do this to me...he tell me he doesn't make very much money, but it seem to me he always has enough to go to the club and party with the hostess...I started to feel upset again thinking about the way he act...when he is almost broke he stay at home with me and occasionally go to a movie, but as soon as he get paid he stop at the club before coming home and party with his friends. I guess he want to spend his money before he get home so I won't ask for it, but I never ask for any money other than what he promised me and the money to buy food. He swear that he love me, but I don't think he know what love is, because if he did he wouldn't treat me this way. I know I love him that the reason I stay with him. It is really upsetting to me to think how he is treating me. Sometime I think he think I am stupid, because he doesn't seem to think I can smell the cheap perfume the hostess wear all over him. I guess I am stupid somewhat because I let him get away with the thing he is doing, but I can't help it because I love him too much to let him go. The hurt and pain is still in my heart and I keep wondering why he continues to do this to me. I know the hostess in the club only want his money; I am sure he knows that too, but he still like to party with them. I guess I am really jealous of the hostess in the club because he seems to want to spend his time and money with them. I guess I will have to decide whether I want to stay with him or go it alone. I started to think…maybe I would leave him…the loves I give him don't seem to be enough. I got undress and went to bed; as I lay there beside him I started to think again…I don't think he is ready for married life…I don't know if he really turned in our application for marriage to the U.S. Navy…the only thing I know for sure is he like to hang out with the hostess in the club. I started crying again; I got my pillow and put it over my head so he couldn't hear me. Finally I cried myself to sleep. The next morning the alarm clock woke us up; he got up and started to get dress for work. I laid there with my back turned to him because I didn't want to see him I just wanted him to leave I had had enough of the way he's treating me. He said I would see you after work; I said if I am home, I am going to visit Sister Melda or some place.

He tried to kiss me; I said go back to your girl friend in the club… catch a sickness…that what you want…I don't want to be involved. He tried to kiss me again; I said please leave me alone. He left going to work. I laid there thinking…I will go back to my job at the Money Exchange; I can work till I am seven month pregnant that will give me enough time to save some money for the baby. My head started hurting; I was too afraid to take something for it because it may harm the baby. I tried to stop thinking so I could calm down and maybe my headache would go away. I got up and went to the bathroom; on my way back to bed I stopped by the kitchen for a glass of water. I returned to bed, but sleep would not come, so I lay there looking at the empty ceiling. Finally I decided to get up and fill up my water containers because the city turns off the water without notice. When I finished filling the water containers and putting them aside; I decided to take my shower too before the water was cut off. When I finished my shower I went into the bedroom and sit on the side of the bed and towel dried my hair.

When my hair was dry I made up the bed and got dress to go and visit Sister Melda. I put my medicine in my bag and walked to Sister Melda's house. Just before I got to the door I decided to go across the street to the Store and get some hot rolls. I got the rolls and went back to Sister Melda's house. I knocked and she came to the door and opened it; she asked me why I was out so early and I told her I was trying to catch her before she left home. She said well, I am not going anywhere today...oh! You brought fresh rolls...we will fry eggs and spam. I said you clean up and I will start cooking, so she went into the bathroom to get cleaned up. I cooked the eggs and spam and brewed some coffee. I looked for cream or milk for the coffee, but I couldn't

find any, so I decided to go across the street again and get a can of carnation milk. I yelled to her I was going to the store and would be right back. When I returned she had finished her shower and was sitting at the table eating bred rolls. I told her I had got milk for her coffee, so she could drink coffee now. We ate our breakfast and made small talk. I didn't tell her I was pregnant, because I knew she would say the same old things about Wilson. After we finished eating she got up and went into her room. She said I would do the dishes later. She stayed in her room for quite awhile before I decided to wash the dishes and clean the kitchen. When I finished in the kitchen I went into my old bedroom and lay across the bed. A few minutes later Sister Melda asked me to come into her room. She had a letter from Brother Smitty that she wanted me to read to her. I sat down and read the letter to her; Brother Smitty said he love and can't wait to see her in about one month. I said to myself...it won't be long now. I gave the letter back to her and she took it as if she was in deep thought. Then she started playing solitary card game. I left her and went back to my old room.

Around nine that morning I was laying there about half asleep when I heard someone knocking on the door. I got up and went to the front door; I looked out the window before I opened it and saw that it was Wilson. I thought about knot opening the door, but I opened it. He came in the door and said I forgot to tell you we have an appointment with the Naval Base Chaplain today. I said that's because you didn't come straight home last night...you stopped and partied with your girl friend…go to your girl friend and leave me alone. He said please listen this is important…we have an appointment today at ten thirty to see the Chaplain…let's go home so you can get ready for the appointment. I said I don't want to go. He said we have to go because we have to have the Chaplain approval on our marriage application. I thought to myself…is he for real…well two can play this game, so I decided to call his bluff and go. I said I have a dress here that my sister gave me; I will try it on so you can see if it's nice enough to wear to the appointment. He said o.k. Sister Melda, I guess she heard us talking and came out of her room. She said hello! Wilson you didn't go to work today. He said I went to work but I had forgotten about our appointment to see the Base Chaplain today about our marriage application. She said what! Oh good! Good luck and went back into her room. I went back to my old room and put on the dress Sister Rose gave me and came back and showed it to Wilson.

He said he like the dress, so I went back inside to find an underskirt to wear with it. The underskirt I left in my old room was gone so I asked Sister Melda if she had one that I could borrow. She said she didn't have one. I told Wilson that I didn't have an underskirt to wear with the dress. He said it was all right because the dress was thick enough where you couldn't see threw it…don't worry you look very pretty. I said in a low voice, what about my stomach? He said what stomach! It's not showing at all. Finally we were off to the Naval Base for our appointment. I didn't really believe Wilson about the appointment, but I did love him and I wanted it to be true, so I went with him to see if he was telling the truth. I was fed up with the way he had being treating me and had decided to go back to my old job. I thought to myself…if he gave me any indication that he lying about this appointment just to get me to come back to the apartment; I will leave him forever. We went to the Chaplain Office on the Naval Base just like he said. When we arrived the Chaplain Secretary said come in and have a seat the Chaplain will be with you in a few minutes. We had a seat and waited a few minutes and the Chaplain asked us to come in his office. The Chaplain said a few words to set us at ease; then he looked at me and said if you marry an American and go to the United States you will not see your family for a long time. Wilson tried to say something, but the Chaplain cut him off and said let her speak. I said as strong as I could with my broken English...I love him...I will go with him anywhere he goes...I will come and visit my family whenever I can. He said that what I wanted to hear and he signed out marriage request. He said he would forward our papers to the Commander in the Philippines for his signature. He was looking at me as he shook Wilson hand and said you treat her right. As we stood up to leave the Chaplain said you two look good together...God bless you. We thanked him. Wilson asked him how long will it take for our papers to come back. He said at least two to three months. We thanked him again and left.

When we got outside Wilson said now all we have to do is wait...I was very happy the way you answered the Chaplain...I thought you was a little nervous. I didn't say anything we just kept walking toward the main gate of the Naval Base. Wilson said let get something to eat when we get outside the gate. I looked at my watch and said oh yes! Its eleven thirty already. We stopped at the first restaurant and ordered lunch. When we finished we decided to go to the movies. We liked Chinese movies, so we checked a few movie houses and finally found one we wanted to watch. After the movie we went to our apartment. As soon as we arrived Wilson went to the store across the street for beer. I went straight in the apartment and sat down and waited for him. He came back with two beers; he put them on the table and went to the bathroom. When he came back he sat down beside me and pulled out his wallet and gave me one hundred and sixty pesos for food; he had promised to give me two hundred and sixty pesos whenever he got paid. I didn't ask him about the hundred pesos he had promised me. We sat and made small talked for a while before he started talking about what he wanted to do when the baby comes. He said he would get me a Maid to do the cleaning and provide company for me here in the house while he is at work. I said how about my Sister Linda; she will need a place to stay here in Olongapo City when Sister Melda move to Cavity City. He said Linda can stay here, but I still want to get you a Maid to do the housework. I thought to myself...how is he going to pay the salary of a Maid when he can't give me the hundred pesos he promised me if I leave my job...I have used the money to help my Mother...now he wants to hire a Maid...he always claim that he doesn't get paid very much, but he always have enough to go partying with his friends in the club…I guess he will completely stop giving me the hundred pesos when he hire a Maid…I guess I will have to keep admiring the dress in the market I have planned to get…I don't want to complain about the money, but for the last couple of paydays he haven't given me the extra money he promised…of course, he always have enough to go partying in the club.

He started drinking his last beer and said let's go sit on the bed in the bedroom this chair is too hard. I followed him in the bedroom and sit down beside him on the side of the bed. He got both pillows and propped himself up in the bed and I moved over close to him and laid my head on his chest.

I lay there a few minutes while he was still drinking his beer; I felt sleepy and closed my eyes, the next thing I felt was Wilson raising my head from his chest and sliding the pillows under it. He looked at me and said he would be right back. I was still half asleep; I asked him where he going…wait I will get ready and go with you? He said no, I will be right back, I have to see someone…go back to sleep. It was around seven when he kissed me and left. I got up cooked and ate my dinner. I sit down in the living room staring out the window at the night flies and bugs flying around the night light post. They seem to be happy just flying around in the light. I thought to myself…I should be happy too, but here I am sitting and waiting for the man I love to return. I really wanted to be with him out nightclubbing, but I guess he don't want me with him because I am pregnant or maybe he think I am ugly now that I am pregnant, but I am not showing. For whatever the reason he has left me here alone and this is breaking my heart. I thought I had found a man to share my love and life with, but he always finds a reason to leave me here at home alone. He always say he will be right back, but I know he is not coming right back; he will stay until he get drunk and then come home falling over everything. When he get in the club he forget about me; sometimes I think that the only reason he want me around is to have some to make love to at will and to brag about to his friends, because I am not a club hostess. He wanted to keep me at home away from the other guys; that's why he wanted me to quit my job at the Money Exchange. I think he worry too much about what other people do and think. He wanted to keep me away from the other guys, but he want to party with the girls in the club. He swear to me that he love me; I guess he doesn't understand how much it hurt me when he leave me alone and go out partying with his friends. I take all the abusive treatment and stay by his side, because of my unconditional love for him. Lately I have being worried about my baby and how my heartbreak and crying is affecting it. I pray to God he or she is not feeling the hurt and pain I am feeling. I decided to go to bed. When I got into bed I started to cry, so I got my pillow and put it over my head and cried myself to sleep.

Around eleven that night I was woken by the noise in the kitchen and the smell of food being cook. Got up and went into the kitchen and saw Wilson trying to cook and stand up; he was very drunk so I told him to sit down and I would finish cooking the food. I finished cooking the food and gave it to him and he ate all of it. I asked him why does he get so drunk and he mumbled something back and got up and started for the bedroom. He lay across the bed fully dressed; I managed to get him undressed and covered up. I could smell the cheap perfume, cigarette smoke and liquor on him; I lay back down in the bed beside him and started to cry again. I took my pillow and put it over my head again and cried myself to sleep. The next morning the alarm clock ringed and I pretended I didn't hear it; I didn't move in the bed because I didn't want to see his face. I was very upset with him. He tried to kiss me and I turned my back to him. I wouldn't say goodbye to him but he did manage to kiss me before he left. As soon as he left I got up and got ready to visit my Mother in Calapacuan. It was five thirty and still kinder dark when I left that morning on my way to Mother's house. When I arrived they had just started getting up and getting ready for breakfast.

I was surprised seeing Sister Linda there. Mother said it is too early for you to be traveling by yourself and you are pregnant…there is a lot of crazy people out there. I lay down on the mat beside Sister Linda, because she didn't want to get up, she wanted to lie around a while longer. Brother Etong was already up and feeding the chicken. When he finished he brought firewood inside so Mother could start cooking breakfast. Sister Linda and I continued to lie around on the mat. I told Sister Linda to wake up, because she had to go to work. She said I don't have a job anymore Sister Melda got me fired because I don't want to write her letter at twelve thirty that night. I had being working the day and night shift because the other lady was sick. When I got home around twelve thirty that night Sister Melda asked me to write Brother Smitty a letter; I told her I couldn't write it then but I would do it the next day...she got upset...when I woke up the next morning she was gone, so I got ready and went to work. When I got to Mama Ligaya place to pick up the money for the Money Exchange booth. Mama Ligaya said she had replaced me with someone else, so I could have time to write letters and do whatever Sister Melda wanted me to do.

I looked around to see if Sister Melda was still there, but I didn't see her so I came home to Calapacuan. I said you mean Sister Melda got you fired. Mother said yes! Your Sister Melda; I asked Sister Linda what was she going to do. She said she didn't know yet. I got up and went over and sit at the kitchen table and Sister Linda got up and put the mat away and got cleaned up. She came back and sat down at the table with me. I said Wilson and I have been talking about asking you to stay with us when Sister Melda move to Cavity City. Mother said that would have been nice if she hadn't been fired from her job I said well she still can stay with us until she find another job so she can have a place to stay when she get off work. Mother started cooking breakfast; she cooked fried dried fish and eggplant with egg. The food was smelling real good and I started eating the dried fish and Sister Linda start to laugh because I had almost ate it all. Mother started frying more dried fish. Before she finished frying the fish Sister Rose and Gina came in the house. Mother asked her why she was out so early too. Sister Rose said her boyfriend Sopring had left early to work as an Apprentice Carpenter. Mother told Sister Linda to help Brother Etong to get water so we could start eating breakfast. I got up and put the food and plates on the floor because there were only four chairs at the table and we all couldn't sit at the table. Finally we took our seats on the floor and started eating breakfast. I put more fried fish on my plate and dug in. Sister Linda said Vicky has almost eaten all of the dried fish. Mother said leave her alone she's eating for two now. Sister Linda said she eats a lot of food but she is still skinny. When we finished eating Sister Linda picked up all of the dishes from the floor and took them into the kitchen to be washed. Mother sat on my favorite wooden box, so I took a seat beside her. I asked Sister Rose how things went with her doing her first pregnancy. She said everyone called her crazy Rosie, because she didn't realize she was pregnant until she started craving for weird food...she wanted to eat barbecued string beans in the hull and eat it with butter. Sister Linda and Gina said Yuk! Sister Rose said she even tried to climb the neighbors fruit trees...she would choose the real ripe fruit...a neighbor came out and told her to get down before she brake her neck...she was so upset she threw fruit at the neighbor...the neighbor called her husband and told him to come get his crazy wife.

I said I don't remember you climbing fruit trees. She said you and Linda was gone to school...one day I went to another neighbor house and they thought I was trying to steal their fighting rooster and asked me what I was doing in the chicken pin...I told them I was trying to smell the dark dried chicken poop. Everyone started laughing and shaking their head. I said wait don't say another word I have to go to the bathroom. When I finished everyone else took terms going to the bathroom. Finally everyone was finished and ready for the story to continue. Mother said wait until I get me a cup of coffee. She got her coffee and came back. Sister Rose continued her story...she said one day her Mother-in-Law was sweeping the dead grass and chicken poop in the yard...she swept it up in a pile and burned it...I took a stick and separated the burnt poop from the burnt grass and put some of it in a handkerchief so I could smell it at will...my Mother-in-Law called my husband and told him to take me to see a Doctor. Everyone laugh at her and said she really did go crazy when she was pregnant. Mother said I have known people to hurt themselves and their baby while being pregnant...you need to be careful of the things you do...your Sister Vicky only problem has been the smell of food, but this is early in her pregnancy...sometimes in your last month of pregnancy you can start craving different things or want to do weird things...your Sister Rose is the only person I have seen do crazy things. Mother got up and said she had to go and feed the pigs, Brother Etong followed her. That finished the story telling session. I asked Sister Rose if she plan to stay with Sopring. She said yes! That's why he's studying to be a Carpenter during the day and working at night as a Waiter. Please don't tell Mother I am pregnant; I don't want her to know yet. I said you had better tell her, because she can tell by looking at you and the way you act, especially when you do crazy things. She said I don't feel those strong urges to do crazy things sometime I feel a little dizzy and crave Mother cooking; that's why I am here now. I said to myself...I like Mother cooking too and I also like being here with family when I am hurt and mad at Wilson... it makes me feel good and I don't feel lonely anymore. She said how is Wilson doing and I said he doing all right. We decided to go next door to our sister-in-law house and see how she was doing.

When we got there she was outside sweeping up the dead grass to be burned. I asked what she was doing, she said she was cleaning up because Brother Celino was coming home and bringing his pregnant girl friend. I said in surprise, he bringing his pregnant girlfriend to your house? She said yes, don't worry about it I have gotten use to always being alone...I have forgiven him for what he put me through, so now we're friends. I said to myself...that's what happening to me...Wilson running around with the girls in the club...what if one of them get pregnant and say the baby is his...what will he do...what will I do? Oh! I better stop thinking because I may start crying here. I said to myself...three pregnant women, Sister Rose, my brother girl friend and me...I wonder who will have their baby first. Mother came by and said she was going to the market and would be right back. I asked her to buy the small bananas that could be boiled because I wanted to eat some for lunch. She said o.k. And continued on her way to the market. Sister Rose and I left Sister Maria and went back to Mother House. I looked back and saw Brother Etong helping Sister Maria sweep the dead grass. When we got inside we got a cool drink of water and started the rice cooking so it would be ready when Mother return with the fresh fish and vegetables. Then the conversation came up about Sister Maria. Sister Rose said I can't understand what's wrong with her; she is going to let our Brother bring another woman in her house...she is crazy. I said yes, she is crazy in love with our Brother...you know what they say about love...love is blind. Sister Linda jumped in the conversation and said Sister Maria is the one blind; she can't see what our Brother is doing to her...he going to bring his pregnant girlfriend into her house...how blind can she be? I said to myself...I am one of the blind one too, because I let Wilson run around with Hostess in the club and still forgive him when he come home...it hurt but if you love someone the hurt go away when they come back to you. Sister Rose said Vicky what are you thinking about? I said nothing...I think I better lay down for a while and Sister Rose said let's lay down together. Little Gina came over and said let me comb your hair Auntie Vicky. I said o.k. Thank you! Sister Linda gave her a comb and she started combing my hair. Her combing my hair felt so good, I drifted off to sleep. When I woke up Mother had returned and boiled the bananas.

When she saw that I was awake she told Sister Linda to bring the boiled bananas to me. I said umm! Bananas, I sat up and started eating the bananas. Sister Rose said give me half of your banana and Mother said don't eat what your sister is eating, because you will be sleepy like her...get one and eat it by yourself...you know she is pregnant, if you eat what she is eating you are going to feel the same way she's feel. Sister Rose said oh yes! I forgot about that. Everyone ate a whole banana even Brother Etong. Mother started cooking the fish and I went into the kitchen to help her cut up the vegetables. I snapped the long string beans so they could be mixed with the other vegetables. Mother mixed the string beans, eggplant, squash, tomato and garlic. Once everything was cut up and ready, Mother began stirring the salted shrimp, garlic and tomato in the frying pan. The aroma was overwhelming I began to get hungry. Later she added the rest of the vegetable to the frying pan and cooked them until they were nice and tender. She finished cooking everything around twelve and said let's eat. We all got up to help get the food situated so we could eat. Brother Etong got the plates and placed them on the floor so everyone could eat together, because the dining table was too small for everyone to get around. Sister Linda got the rice, I got the bowl of mix vegetables and Mother got the fish. We put it all in the middle of the floor so everyone could get around it. I said oh Mother! This is really good. She said smiling at me; it is good you are enjoying it. I ate too much, my stomach seem like it was going to burst. I guess it were because I ate three boiled banana earlier. After lunch Brother Etong and Sister Linda cleaned the kitchen and washed the dishes.

Sister Rose said when you get ready to go let me know so we can leave together. I said o.k. But I am not in a hurry to leave.

We sat around making small talk for seem like an hour or two when I heard my sister Maria yelling...Vicky! Vicky! Your boy friend is coming. I looked out of the window and sure enough he was coming in a hurry. I was happy to see him, but I didn't want him to know it. I met him at the door and said what are you doing here? Before he said a word he kissed me and I kissed him back because I didn't want Mother to know I was mad at him. Then he said hello to everybody and told me he need to talk to me. I said about what? He said we need your Mother permission to get married because they thank you are too young to get married. I said I thought they said everything were o.k. After we saw the Base Chaplain? He said everything is o.k. But we still need your Mother permission to get married...this is what we have to do...get a Lawyer to draw up a statement saying that your Mother is giving you permission to get married and have your Mother to sign it...we need to do this right away because they are holding up the paperwork until they get this statement...we need your Mother to come to Olongapo City tomorrow early so we can see a Lawyer and get this statement done. I explained everything to Mother and told her she need to come to my apartment in Olongapo City the next day...bring Sister Linda so she could show her the way...Wilson and I are going home. Sister Rose said I am leaving too. Mother said Rose leave Gina here she is really enjoying herself...I will leave her with Maria tomorrow, because it shouldn't take very long to sign the papers Vicky need me to sign.

Wilson, Sister Rose and I left going to the jeepney stop to catch a ride to Olongapo City. You have to board the jeepney from the rear, so when the jeepney came we got onboard and sat close to the rear of the jeepney. The jeepney doesn't have a/c or windows in the back. Sister Rose and I held our nose when the jeepney took off, because one of the passengers in the front of the jeepney had very strong underarm odor. Wilson said someone need to take a shower. The guy sitting in front held his arms close to his body. Sister Rose and I started to laugh. Finally we came to Barretto, Sister Rose stop...she got out of the jeepney and started to pay her fare, but Wilson told her he would take care of it. Sister Rose smiled and waved goodbye. When we got to Olongapo we caught a tricycle to our apartment because jeepney are not allowed to carry passenger in our area. Wilson and I didn't say very much on our way home we just sat and held hands. Wilson is a very loving and caring person when he's not drinking, but when he start drinking he forget what respect is or who you are...there is one thing I can't understand about him...when he drunk and almost can't stand up...he still remember his way back home...sometime I thank he is playing a game with me ...he play drunk so I don't get mad or to avoid me giving him a sermon about the way he act.

I really do believe that if he would control his drinking he would be a wonderful guy to be with...he is loving, caring and very respectful, but when he show his other side while drinking...if you are hurting and bleeding and need help...forget it...you will bleed to death...because he will pass out and go to sleep. That's why I worry about him so much when he leave and go out by himself, maybe something will happen to him and I want see him anymore. I just pray that he will be safe. When we got to our apartment I kept silent I didn't say anything about the way he had being acting. I was tired anyway and really didn't want to hear him try and lie his way out of the fix he's in. When he not drinking he wanted me to act like nothing has happened. At first I thought drinking was his only problem, but I know now that he like to party with the Hostess in the club. So I try and give him the silent treatment and pretend he is not here...I always pretend one way or the other when he's not home. When he try and kiss or hug me I will walk away...I will let him see how it feel to be hurt by someone you love. Sometime he makes me want to try and stop loving him, but I can't because I will always love him no matter what. I will always be around until he doesn't need me anymore... maybe he will get tired of partying and devote his time to me and our baby...I hope it want be too late for us.

Wilson said would you like to go to the movie tonight? I just looked at him. He came over and started hugging and kissing me saying how sorry he was and please forgive him. He sounded like a broken record over and over saying sorry please forgive me; sometimes I wish I could take what he is saying and smash it like a record...I am tired of listening to it...why cause himself to have to say sorry all of the time? Just don't do what he is doing again. I kept turning and trying to avoid his kisses, but he kept trying until he finally got me square on my lips; I couldn't fight it anymore I gave in and kissed him back. I thought to myself…what a fool I am…what I will do for a good kiss… his kisses always make me melt light a candle; that's why I can't stay mad at him and he know it…I guess I am a fool madly in love with him. Before I realize what was going on, we were in the bedroom in bed making passionate love; today I still can't remember whether he carried me to the bed or I walked.

After our lovemaking we was so exhausted we fell asleep. I woke up around five o, clock looking for something to eat. He said let's get cleaned up and go on the Naval Base and get something to eat. We got up and got ready and left for the Naval Base. We arrived at the main gate of the Naval Base and Wilson got me a visitor pass. We continued on to the Spanish Gate Restaurant and ordered sandwiches and fries. We finished our meal and started walking back to the main gate. Wilson turned in my visitor pass and we left walking across the bridge that separated the base from the city. There were three movie houses on the main street, Magsaysay drive. We decided to walk down the street and check the movie house and see what's new playing. We finally found one we had not previously seen, the title of the movie were the Blind Swordsman. We bought fruit from the fruit stand outside of the movie; we got the Seriggulas a fruit about the size of a plum and very sweet and juicy. We enjoyed the movie while snacking on our fruit. When it was over we decided to walk for a while before catching a jeepney. We held hands as we walked down the street talking about the movie. We really like the scene where the blind Swordsman killed a fly flying around in the air just by listening to the sound. There were a lot of killing but all in all we still like the movie. We were still talking about the movie when we arrived at our apartment. Wilson went across the street and bought two beers and came back and joined me in the living room. He told me he was going in to work the next day, but he was coming right back so we could meet with the Lawyer and get the papers drawn up. I said o.k. And got up to get ready for bed. He was still sitting in the living room drinking his beer. As I put my nightgown on I could see him through the bedroom door watching me. I thought to myself… not again. He said come here. When I got close to him he pulled me down so I could sit on his lap. He started kissing me and finally said let's go to the bedroom. Before I could say anything he had me up and was carrying me into the bedroom. We made love again and fell asleep in each other arms. The next morning the alarm clock went off and Wilson got up and got dressed for work. He kissed me goodbye and told me not to forget our appointment with the Lawyer. I said o.k. And decided to sleep for a few more hours; I don't know why, but the nights seem to be getting very short and I wasn't getting enough sleep. I went back to sleep and was later woken by someone knocking on the door. I really wasn't ready to get up, but I could hear the knocking and I recognized the voice of the person calling my name; it was Sister Linda. I got up and opened the door and let them in. Mother said we have come early so we would have time to eat breakfast... I brought bread rolls. I said sit down I will get cleaned up and try and wake up. Mother asked if the furniture belong to me. I said no, we are going to buy our furniture very soon. She said I would start cooking breakfast just show me to the kitchen. Sister Linda said there is a bedroom, a living room. Dining room and a bathroom in this apartment. I said yes, and if you decide to stay with us you can use the dining room for your bedroom...then you want have to far to travel to work. I went into the bedroom and fixed the bed and lay my clothes out that I plan to wear today and returned to the living room. I could smell the aroma of the spam and egg being cooked. Mother prepared a breakfast of spam, eggs with onion, bread rolls and coffee. We ate our breakfast. Mother looked around in the apartment and said this is a nice place; now all you have to do is buy your own furniture a little at a time until you get it all. I really enjoyed my breakfast; I always eat more when someone else cook especially when Mother cook. I got up and excuse myself because I had to take a shower and get dressed before Wilson got home. I went in and took my shower and came out and towel dried my hair. I got dressed and came back and in the living room and joined Mother and Sister Linda. We started talking about Wilson; Mother said she didn't know American acted the same as we did...she remembered Wilson helping Brother Etong rake leaves under the Mango trees and carry water. She said she think he is a very nice young man. Suddenly the front door opened and Wilson came in with a big smile on his face. He said Mrs. Palaganas is here and ready to go. He said hello to everyone and gave me a big kiss. He told Sister Linda to wait until we return before she left the apartment because he wanted to talk to her. She said o.k. And we left for our appointment.

The Lawyer office was very close to the market area so we just walked to his office. We went in and was seated; the Lawyer asked where were my Father and Mother told him my Father were dead, so he gave her the papers he had drawn up and she signed them and we were on our way. Wilson was very happy and I was happy too. When we got back to the apartment Wilson told Sister Linda she could stay with us and go to school at night and get her High School Diploma…that way I would have company and she could finish high school…would she like doing that? She said yes, but I made sure she understood what he was saying, because her English was not too good. I told her again in Tagalog what he had said. My English wasn't much better, but I understood it better than I could speak it and Wilson helped me a lot with my English. Wilson told Sister Linda to check with the school and find out when they start registering for night school so she could start on time. She said thanked you and said she would continue to check with the school. Mother said we have to go back to Calapacuan now, but Sister Linda would return when the school starts. Wilson thanked Mother and gave her a big hug. When Mother left I could tell that she was very happy because Wilson had convinced her that he really wanted to marry me. When they left Wilson said he was going to the base and turn in the paperwork before it get lost. I said o.k. Do you want me to go with you? He said no, I would just go and get it over with, so he kissed me and said goodbye and left. After he left I started to feel a little hungry so I went in the kitchen to fix me something to eat. I saw that we still had food left over from breakfast, so I went across the street and bought me a coke to drink with my lunch. After fixing my lunch I sat in the living room and ate it so I could look out the side window for Wilson. Sitting there I thought to myself…please come back home soon…I started to get lonely…he promised he would be right back as soon as he turned in our paperwork. I got tired of waiting in the living room so I went in the bedroom and lay down and went to sleep. I don't know how long I was asleep, but I was woken by the smell of beer when Wilson trying to kiss me. I looked at him making a quick survey to see if he was drunk, but he seem to be all right. He said get up and get ready we're going out.

I said where are we going? He said we're going to C.B. house. I said I don't want to go to his house he thinks I am like the Hostess that work in the clubs. He said he knows now that you are not one of the girls from the club and he also know that we're engaged to be married...please get ready o.k. I got up, cleaned up and dressed and we left. When we arrived C.B. started acting real nice to me, he couldn't wait to offer me something to drink. Jean came into the living room and asked me to join her in the kitchen. As soon as I entered the kitchen she said congratulation, I didn't know Wilson were serious about you. I said yes, I think he is serious...we are waiting for our marriage application to be approved, but it seem to be taking a very long time. She said I been through that military red tape before...I thought marrying a Sailor would be easy, but you are still required to request to marry even in the United States...my Maid is off today so I am cooking today... do you like fried chicken? I said yes. She said well, I am cooking fried chicken, sweet peas and mashed potatoes. I begin to get hungry as I sat there watching her cook the food and smelling the aroma of fried chicken. I guess she sensed that I was hungry, so she gave me a small piece of chicken to taste...I told her it was very good chicken. She said thank you... Wilson came by here around twelve thirty and got C.B. to drive him on the base, they returned around three fifteen. He told me that you and Wilson would be coming by for dinner tonight. I thought to myself...that's why he didn't come home early...he was running around with C.B. on the base. I became mad again, so I told Jean I was going to sit in the living room for a while. I had to get away from her, because I didn't want her to know I was mad at Wilson. Jean was a very nice person, but her husband drink a lot like Wilson. I sat there in the living room and acted as if I was enjoying myself. Finally jean said dinner is ready, you can eat at the dining table or in the living room. C.B. and Wilson got their food and went into the living room to watch television while eating. Jean fixed the kids plates and sat them at the table. Jean and I joined C.B. and Wilson in the living room. I like all of the food except the sweet peas.

Jean asked Wilson when we are getting married. He said as soon as our application is approved. We continued to make small talk and watch television until everyone was finished eating. I offered to help Jean with the dishes, but she said don't worry about them she would do them later. We sat back down in the living room and watched C.B. and Wilson drink. Finally Jean started yawning, so I told Wilson we had better go home…he surprised me and got right up and said man we have to go now. C.B. said it's still early, it's only ten o, clock. Jean said yes, but you have to go to work tomorrow. So we said thanks for inviting us into your home. Jean said anytime, you are always welcome to come to our house. We left and caught a jeepney to the market and a tricycle to our apartment.

When we arrived at our apartment I went straight to our bedroom and changed into my nightgown and went to bed. Wilson said I didn't get drunk tonight sweetheart. I didn't say a word I just laid there with my back to him. When he came to bed he tried to kiss and caress me, but I didn't respond to his advances I just turned away from him and tried to go to sleep. Finally I did fall asleep I guess he did too, because I slept until around three in the morning that when I heard him get up and go to the bathroom. When he came back to bed I got up and went to the bathroom too. When I returned I tried to go back to sleep, but Wilson had another ideal, he started kissing and caressing me and I lost my will to resist him…we made passionate love. I guess when you love someone it easy to forgive and forget. He always knows what to do when I am mad; he coaches me into making love. We fell asleep again only to be woken by the alarm clock. He got up and got dressed; we kissed goodbye on his way out the door. I went back to bed and fell asleep. Suddenly I heard noise coming from my bedroom window; it was someone calling out my name. Between the loud noise of a tricycle and the yelling, I couldn't make out who was calling, so I got up and opened the front door to see who was calling. It was Sister Melda. I asked her if there were something wrong and asked her to come in. She said your Brother-in-law is back and I am in a hurry to go to the Naval Base…tonight we will be by to go nightclubbing with you and Wilson.

Tell Wilson to tell my boyfriend to come here tonight, because I want Wilson to introduce him to us. I also want Wilson to invite my boyfriend to go with us nightclubbing. Oh! By the way, we will spend the night with you and Wilson. I closed the door as she turned to leave. I thought to myself…what is wrong with this woman…she want her husband to meet her boyfriend…I wonder why she hadn't told me that Brother Smitty had came home, so I could come and visit with him…she only live a couple of streets down from me. Now she wants to go out nightclubbing and want Wilson and me to bring her boyfriend alone. She didn't let her family know that Brother Smitty was back; now they will be leaving for the Sangley Point Naval Base in Cavite City. This means that none of us will get a chance to spend any amount of time with him before they leave. Well I can't waste time trying to figure out her motive for doing all the stupid things she does; I had better start cleaning my apartment so it will look nice when Brother Smitty come. I usually keep the apartment clean my only real problem is dust that comes in from the street the apartment manager usually wet down the street in front of the apartment building, but since we have a water shortage it hard for him to do it regularly. When I finished cleaning the kitchen I made me some breakfast and ate it. After sitting for a while in the living room I decided to get up and finish cleaning the apartment. It took me about two hours to clean the rest of the apartment including taking a couple of breaks.

Now it was time for me to take a shower and get cleaned up because Wilson may come home early. I was finishing up my shower when the water pressure started to dwindle down to just a small stream. I finished showering thinking…I was glad I had saved some water the day before in my containers because there is no telling how long it will be off. I went into the bedroom and started towel drying my hair, finally it was dry and I looked at the clock beside the bed and it was lunchtime. I thought to myself…wow! The times really go fast. I decided to fix and have myself some lunch. After lunch I walked around in the apartment to make sure I hadn't missed anything while I was cleaning; then I decided to take a nap. I lay across the bed and drifted off to sleep, I was woken when I heard the front door open. I got up and went into the front room and it was Wilson coming through the door. I said you are early today.

He said yes, I saw your sister's boyfriend and he said he was coming by our apartment tonight. He gave me a big hug and a kiss. I said Sister Melda wants us to go nightclubbing with her and my Brother-in-law tonight and they also, want to spend the night with us. Now you will get a chance to meet Sister Melda's husband. Wilson said but her boyfriend is coming here. I said she plan it this way so they can see each other again before she left for Sangley Point…she wants you to introduce her boyfriend to her and my Brother-in-law and ask him to go nightclubbing with us. He said your sister is playing a dangerous game…let go in the bedroom I want to lay down and relax for a while. I followed him into the bedroom and he lay down on the bed; I lay down with him and within a few minutes he was sound asleep, I guess he was very tired. It took me a while longer, but I finally drifted off to sleep. I slept for around two hours and had to use the bathroom, so after using the bathroom I decided to stay up, I started doing a few things in the apartment to keep busy until Wilson woke up.

Around five that afternoon Wilson's friend arrived, so I invited him in and asked him to have a seat in the living room. I went into the bedroom and woke up Wilson and told him his friend had arrived. He got up and went into the bathroom and I went back to the living room to entertain his friend until he came out. His friend asked me how I was doing and I told him I was doing fine. Wilson finally came out of the bathroom and both of them said hi to each other. We sat in the living room making small talk for a while; Wilson decided to go across the street to get some beer for him and his friend. As soon as he returned with the beer and sat down with his friend, Sister Melda and her Husband arrived. Wilson introduced his friend to her and Brother Smitty. Brother Smitty hugged me and asked how his favorite Sister-in-law was doing. I told him I was doing fine. We sit around making small talk until Brother Smitty asked Wilson had he turned our marriage request in. Wilson said I have turned the paperwork in we're just waiting for the Commander of Naval Forces in the Philippines approval. Brother Smitty said I would be working on the Admiral staff, so if I see your request I will make sure the Admiral see it right away.

Wilson said that would be nice man if you do that for us. Then Brother Smitty turned to me and asked me if I really wanted to get married. I said yes, then he said smiling...you are still acting bashful with me...you are still the same Ambing, quiet and bashful, that's why you are still my favorite Sister-in-law. Then he asked to use the bathroom, he wanted to shave, because he didn't get time to shave earlier because they was packing everything for the move to Sangley Point. Wilson said sure man! Make yourself at home. Sister Melda said we're taking you guys out for dinner, before we go nightclubbing, so you had better get ready. When Brother Smitty came back into the living room Wilson asked his friend if he wanted to go nightclubbing with us. Naturally he said yes, because it had been prearranged. He said he would meet us in the Harlem Club after he had his dinner. He got up to leave and told Sister Melda and Brother Smitty it was nice meeting them and he left. I just sat there thinking to myself...how could she treat Brother Smitty like this...he is one of the best guys I know...she knew Brother Smitty wanted to see me and meet Wilson, so she took advantage of the situation and planted her boyfriend here so she could see him again. Finally it was time to go, we decided to walk to the market area and catch a jeepney. We caught a jeepney and went straight to the Magnolia Restaurant, which was located about three or four doors down from the Harlem club. We had dinner and brother Smitty volunteered to take care of the check. Wilson and I thanked him for the dinner as we left for the Harlem club. When we arrived we saw Wilson's friend sitting at a table waiting for us. Everyone said hi again as we took our seats. Everyone ordered drinks except me, because I felt full from our dinner. We sat making small talk and drinking. Wilson and his friend started getting drunk; I could understand why his friend was getting drunk, Sister Melda was leaving town, but I just couldn't understand why Wilson was getting drunk or had someone put something in his beer. Wilson started acting as if he didn't recognize us. He laid his head on Sister Melda's shoulder and Brother Smitty tried to explain to him that I was his girlfriend not Sister Melda. Finally Brother Smitty said let's take him home...he is acting as though someone slipped some drugs in his drink...he can't take care of himself, so we had better go and take him and Vicky home. Sister Melda said goodbye to her boyfriend, he looked as if he wanted to hug her, but shook hands instead.

Brother Smitty helped Wilson up and we started for the door Sister Melda followed us. When we got halfway down the stairs she said she had forgotten something and turned around and went back up and into the club. Brother Smitty continued to help Wilson to the bottom of the stairs and to the street. Brother Smitty called a jeepney and Sister Melda arrive just as the jeepney was pulling up. She looked as though she had been crying, so I asked her if she was all right, she said she think she was catching a cold. I said to myself...I think that long goodbye had brought tears that why she was sniffing. I am pretty sure her boyfriend is sniffing too.

When we arrive at the apartment we started preparing our sleeping arrangement. We had only one bed, so we took the top mattress and put it on the floor in the dining room. We had extra pillows and lining that we fixed the bed with. Wilson wasn't any help so we put him to bed so he could start sleeping it off. Sister Melda got ready to go to bed, but Brother Smitty wanted to talk to me. He said you know I want you to have a good life, because you are my favorite Sister-in-law, but I don't like what I see happening to you... your boyfriend drinks a lot...you're very young and naive and look at you, I can tell that you're in love with him...I want something better for you. Sister Melda said Smitty are you coming to bed? He said I will be right there... I am talking to your sister. He said don't worry! When your marriage application come across my desk I will make sure the Admiral see it right away...if he really want to marry you the paperwork want be an excuse...I still thank you deserve better...I hope he change and be a good husband to you. He said good night and went to bed. I got up and went into the bedroom where Wilson was sound asleep. I got undress and put my nightgown on and went to bed. Laying there beside him I started to thinking...He never get that drunk just drinking beer...maybe someone did put drugs in his drink...I was told by Jones girlfriend that Hostess does it a lot of times...even Brother Smitty thought someone may have tampered with his drink. I closed my eyes and tried to go to sleep, all of a sudden Wilson fell out of the bed, I didn't try and lift him back in the bed; I just put a pillow under his head and covered him. When he has been drinking I don't try and wake him because he accidentally pushed me one time; now that I am pregnant, I don't want to take a chance. I got back in bed and tried to go to sleep. I turned over and looked down beside the bed as he lay there snoring...I lean over and kissed him goodnight. Finally I fell asleep.

The next morning when the alarm clock ringed, Wilson got up from the floor and crawled into bed beside me. He asked me why he was on the floor and I told him he had fell out of the bed and I had covered him up. I asked him if he was going to work, he said no he had the day off. We went back to sleep and I slept until I heard Sister Melda talking to Brother Smitty in the next room. I got up and went to the door and asked if they were ready for me to fix them breakfast. Brother Smitty said don't worry about him because he wasn't hungry. Sister Melda said as she laughed, what was you guys doing last night, I heard a loud noise like someone falling on the floor...was you doing something on the floor? I said no, Wilson fell out of the bed. She said I think you two were doing something on the floor. Brother Smitty said leave her alone can't you she is bashful and is blushing. Sister Melda would not let it go; she asked me again in Tagalog if Wilson and I were making love on the floor. I guess Wilson heard us talking, so he got up and came into the room. Everyone said good morning. Brother Smitty said he was going to the base to rent a car from Special Services for their trip to Sangley Point in Cavite City. Wilson said I would go with you...I think Special Services open up around eight. Sister Melda told Brother Smitty she would stay with me until He and Wilson returned. I went into my bedroom and took off my nightgown and put an old dress on to wear until everyone finish using the shower. Around eight Brother Smitty and Wilson left for the base. As soon as they left Sister Melda said she had somewhere she had to go and if Brother Smitty return before she does tell him she went to mama Ligaya house. She rushed out in a hurry. I was left alone, so I decided to cook me some breakfast. After breakfast I cleaned my bedroom and the living room and dusted the furniture. I decided to go ahead and take my shower now, because everyone would be returning very soon. I wanted to be ready to do whatever when they return. After my shower I took a seat in the living room to towel my hair dry. I sat close to the window because the wind was blowing a little bit so it would help my hair dry a little faster. Finally it was dry so I went back into my bedroom and put a little make up on and got dressed. Just as I was finishing dressing I heard a noise out front, I went into the living room and looked out the window; I saw Wilson, Brother Smitty and Sister Melda coming toward the apartment. I went back into the bedroom and took a final look in the mirror and came back to greet them in the living room.

As I walked into the living room they were coming through the front door. I said hi and walked over to Wilson side. Sister Melda said we can't stay very long because we have to meet our driver on the base and leave from there for Cavite City. Brother Smitty looked at me and said don't worry about your marriage request, as soon as it arrive at Sangley Point I would make sure it is forwarded right away to the Admiral for his approval...don't forget, we want you to come to Sangley Point for Thanksgiving dinner. We assured him that we would come. Then we hugged and said our goodbyes. I felt real sad that Brother Smitty and Sister Melda was leaving going to Sangley Point Naval Base; I wish they could be stationed here at this Naval Base. I think Wilson sensed that I were feeling down, so he hugged and kissed me and promised we would visit them at Sangley Point. We sat there in the living room making small talk. Wilson wanted to talk about us; he said he wanted Sister Linda to come stay with us, because he wanted someone to be with me when he is at work... he wanted me to go to Calapacuan the next day to see if she would come and stay. We talked about getting married as soon as we get our approval back...he even told me that he was going to stop drinking a lot and save some money for us and the baby...he said we would stop going nightclubbing so much and go to the movies instead. We stayed in bed most of the time that day talking about the things we wanted to do and making love. I was very happy and relaxed because I was with the man that I love and always wanted to be with. I guess that why I always forgive him when he does stupid things. That night after we made love I slept so sound that I didn't hear the alarm clock ring the next morning. Wilson shook me and kissed me goodbye...as he left he said don't forget to go to Calapacuan and ask Linda to live with us. I stayed in bed a while longer until the sun was up. When the sun started shining through my bedroom window I got out of bed, took a shower and got dress for my trip to Calapacuan. When I arrived Mother was cooking breakfast, she asked me why I was up and about so early. I told her I had come to ask Sister Linda to come live with Wilson and me.

Sister Linda was lying awake on her sleeping mat in the corner; she was listening in on our conversation, so she immediately got up and said she wanted to come and live with me because she had started going to night school in Olongapo City. She said if she came to live with me Brother Etong wouldn't have to wait for her at the jeepney stop here in Calapacuan every night she went to school. I said I told you when you start school you could come live with me. She said I didn't want to impose on you and your boyfriend. I said Wilson told me to come ask you to stay. Mother said that's good Wilson want Linda to stay with you...did you see your Brother new wife that staying in your Sister-in-law house? I said what! You are telling me that Brother Celino is back with another wife and staying in the same house with his first wife...why does she let them stay in her house? Mother said because love is blind...she is happy to share your Brother with another woman. I didn't say anything because I knew Wilson had done the same thing to me. Mother said Linda get your Brother Etong from outside so we can eat breakfast. When Sister Linda came back with Brother Etong, Sister Rose and her daughter Gina and Brother Celino and his new wife followed them in the house. I thought to myself...where did everyone come from? Brother Celino ushered his new wife in the house and introduced her to Sister Rose and me. His new wife name was Rosie and she was pregnant too...now there are three of us pregnant at the same time... Sister Rose hadn't told anyone beside Sister Linda and me about her being pregnant. We all sat in a circle around the food placed on the floor because there wasn't enough room at the table for all of us. We enjoyed a breakfast of rice, fried eggplant with egg, fried dried fish, bread rolls and coffee and oval tine. I asked Brother Celino why he didn't bring his first wife with him to breakfast. He said she had eaten breakfast at her house. Finally Brother Celino new wife broke the silence and told brother Celino to ask Mother could they stay with her for a while. Mother said I told Celino when you and he first arrived that it wasn't appropriate for him to bring a second wife to live with his first. She looked at Celino and said I don't know what's wrong with you...you never got a job when you was with your first wife, now you have another wife and she is pregnant…what are you going to feed them?

I hope you are not counting on me feeding you and your wife… you need to find a job so when Rosie have the baby you can buy the baby some clothes…it's easy to make a baby, but you have to have money to feed and clothe it…one other thing…you bring your second wife back here to live in the same house with your first…you never know what's running through your first wife mind…what if she decide to poison you and Rosie…I am not saying she would do something like that, but you never know what a person will do if they are really in love with someone and see someone else taking that person away…oh! Didn't I tell you what almost happened to Vicky when she was almost six years old? Everyone said no! What happened? I said Mother please don't start until Linda and brother Etong pickup all of the dishes and plates and put them in the kitchen. She said o.k. But don't start washing the dishes until you hear my story. Finally everyone had gathered around sitting on the floor; I sat between Mother and Brother Etong. Mother began telling the story of the doll maker. She said the doll maker was young and very beautiful. She was also considered a very religious woman. She makes all kinds of beautiful dolls…wooden dolls, ceramic dolls, cloth dolls and porcelain dolls. She could paint perfect faces on the dolls. She had a dark secret. She didn't have a boyfriend, so finally she met a young Indian man, he even wore a head turbine and she fell in love with him right away. No one knew exactly where he came from, but he was rich and lived in a big house. He had also met a young lady in a nearby Barrio that he visited very often. The girl from the nearby Barrio had been seen several times at this young man house. The doll maker became very jealous of the other girl. Finally the Barrio had a Fiesta and the doll maker dressed up real sexy and seduced the young man. After that the young man started taking her to his house. Before long she got pregnant. Sister Rose interrupted Mother and asked if the young man married her. Mother said let me finish the story o.k. She continued saying…everyone in the Barrio started talking about her being pregnant without a husband. The doll maker went to the young man and begged him to marry her so the baby would have his name. The young man was in love with the girl from the other Barrio, so he refused to marry the doll maker.

The doll maker told him that she was going to make her baby hate any person that fall in love with it. She said you would pay for what you are doing to my baby and me... you will never see this baby. Brother Celino interrupted and said that he had heard the story about the doll maker before in Alyaga. He heard the old people saying that the doll maker had sold herself to the Devil. Mother said that part of the story. Brother Celino wife said let your Mother finish the story. Mother said the doll maker stop going out doing the day and only went out at night. She made a doll just like the young man she carried it when she went out at night to see him. She really loved him and wanted to be with him. Finally the news came out in the Barrio that he was getting married to the other girl. After the news came out bad things started happening. First, the young man new wife started to have stomach cramps that wouldn't stop, so he took her to see the Doctor. The Doctor couldn't find anything wrong with her. The young man took his wife home. Sister Linda said if her stomach was cramping all the time...did she eat? Mother said yes; please let me finish the story. She continued...his wife started getting skinny because she was in pain most of the time and didn't feel like eating very much. The young man didn't know what to do, so he decided to take her to see a witch doctor, but the witch doctor couldn't help her...he started taking her to every Doctor or witch doctor he heard of, but no one could help her. His wife finally died after he had spent all of his money trying to help her recover. Her sickness was a mystery. Sister Linda said what happened to the guy? Mother said he became sick himself; every time he would leave his house his legs would start hurting so bad he would have to turn around and go back home. He was house bound, a prisoner in his own house. Brother Celino wife said did the doll maker have her baby? Mother said I will be right back; I have to use the bathroom. Everyone said oh no! Brother Etong left to feed the pigs, so everyone got up and stretched while they was gone. When Mother came back she said well, it's almost ten o, clock now, so I will finish telling the story after lunch. Sister Rose said we want to know about the doll maker baby. Mother said again, I will tell the rest of the story after lunch. Everybody had to wait and wonder what happened until after lunch to find out what really happened.

I thought to myself…everyone wasn't listening when Mother said the doll maker was very young and beautiful…I don't think she will have a problem finding someone else. Mother told Brother Celino to start a fire in the stove and Sister Linda started helping Mother cut up the vegetables. Sister Rose and I got the mat, pillows and blankets and lay down on the floor to rest while lunch was being cooked. Gina went outside to see the pigs and help Brother Etong feed them. When Sister Linda finished with the vegetables I told her to go and pack her clothes so we could leave as soon as we had lunch and Mother finish her story. Sister Rose said Linda is going to stay with you? I said yes, she would be staying with me while she attended school at night. We lay silent for a while and I closed my eyes and drifted off to sleep. Suddenly I was awakened when I heard Brother Celino first wife next door calling Brother Celino and asking whether he and the second wife was going to have lunch with her. He told her no he and his second wife was having lunch at Mother's house. Mother told Brother Celino to ask his first wife to come and have lunch with us. She said she had fixed her something already.

When Mother finished cooking lunch, everyone hurried to finish so she could finish the doll maker story. As soon as the dishes and cooking utensils was cleaned and put away; Mother said it look like everyone can't wait to hear the rest of the story. She said the doll maker went to see the sick Indian guy again. She asked him to marry her again, but the guy said no again. He said that when my wife died my love died with her; I can't love or marry another woman. The doll maker left and promised she would not come back again.

Finally it was time to have her baby, so the Midwife came and delivered a baby and a snake. The Midwife told everyone in the Barrio what had happened doing the delivery. She said that night right after the baby came a snake or worm, she wasn't quite sure which one it was, crawled out and went into a hole in the floor of the house. She never did see it again. Sister Rose said maybe she just had worms. Mother said that's what everybody said… everyone referred to the baby as the Mystery Baby…a week later the Indian guy died from a mysterious bite on the neck.

The people thought maybe a snake bite him while he was sleeping, but his house was two stories high and well built, so a snake shouldn't have been able to get inside. The news about the Indian guy death was all over the Barrio. Someone even told the doll maker that her baby father was dead. The doll maker said that the Indian guy was not her baby father. Brother Celino wife said I thought the Indian guy was the father of her baby. Brother Celino said I told you the doll maker sold her soul to the devil...that's what all of the old people in the Barrio says. Mother said yes, that the story...when the baby became five years old her Mother started teaching her how to make dolls and the things to say and do as she stick the dolls with pins. The doll maker really loved her daughter, so she taught her how to protect herself even though it was the bad way.

When the little girl started school, the doll maker problems begin...every time the little girl got mad at one of her class mate they would have pain in their arm, leg or just anywhere on their body. Everyone said she was a little devil girl. Sister Rose said she is a witch, I saw a girl like that in the movie...the voodoo woman... it's not only happening here it happening all over the world even in America. Mother said I guess that what it called in English, voodoo. I said let Mother finish the story. Mother said the girl was growing up to be a very beautiful young girl...one day in school the doll maker daughter saw a boy she liked, but he had a girl friend...the little girl tried to use her powers to hurt the boys girlfriend, but it didn't work...the little girl was very upset that her powers didn't work, so she finally told her Mother what had happened...her mother told her to get some of the girl hair. My brother wife said they could hurt you if they get some of your hair...I heard about witches in other Barrio doing things like that...they are very powerful. Mother said may I continue the story? Everyone said yes! Mother said when the little girl finally got a piece of the girl hair; she took it home to her Mother. When the doll make performed her ritual trying to hurt the girl it came back and hurt her. Her daughter asked her what had happened and the doll maker said the girl has power too and it was stronger than her power.

The Daughter became very, very angry her Mother had never seen her angry like this before. The girl told her Mother to use all of her power to hurt the girl; she didn't care if it killed her. Brother Celino said I guess she is more of a bad witch than her Mother…she want her Mother to kill the girl. Mother said it's her Mother fault because she taught her to do all of those bad things…now the Daughter like to use her powers to do bad things. The doll maker decided to try and find out who was the girl parent and relatives. She found out that the girl was a relative of hers and that the girl Grandfather was a very powerful witch doctor known throughout the Barrios too. The doll maker told her Daughter that she couldn't hurt or destroy a relative, but her Daughter insisted on her eliminating her competition. The doll maker didn't know what to do or say to her Daughter, because she loved her Daughter very much and didn't want to disappoint her. She also realized that she had taught her Daughter to use bad things against people to get her way, so she had to decide whether to use her power to hurt a relative just to satisfy her Daughter. Sister Rose said what did she decide to do? Mother said she did what her Daughter asked her to do. She decided to hurt the girl legs instead of killing her. She figured if the girl couldn't walk to school and other places she wouldn't be a threat. The doll maker made a doll the image of the girl and broke the leg of the doll. When she broke the doll leg she felt her leg snap and she passed out. Sister Linda asked why the doll maker suffered a broken leg. Mother said maybe the girl has power too and reversed the spell on the doll maker…some of her close relatives had power. I asked Mother what else happened. She said the doll maker Daughter came home after the dance she went to in a nearby Barrio and found her mother crying in pain. The Daughter asked her Mother what had happened to her. The doll maker said I can't try and hurt that girl anymore, she has some kind of protection or maybe she is a witch like us. The Daughter said if you can't take care of her I would do it myself even if it kill me. The doll maker begged her Daughter to just leave the girl alone, but the Daughter left leaving her Mother on the floor crying in pain…She went out into the night. Everyone asked where did she go? I said let Mother finish the story, I have to go home because Wilson is probably at home already.

Mother said people think she went out in the woods to meet her twin, the snake. Sister Rose asked if she really had a twin that was a snake. Mother said that's the story that everyone has been telling…

the Midwife said the baby was born with a twin worm or snake…it disappeared to fast to tell whether it was a worm or snake…no one other than the Midwife knew what had happened at the childbirth. Mother said the girl leg was hurt a little, but she was able to get around, but the doll maker leg was broken. The girl continued to go to school and date her boyfriend. Finally the doll maker Daughter convinced the girl and her boyfriend to walk with her in the woods; she told them she had something very important to show them… everyday she had asked them to accompany her to a special place in the woods…they went with her even though the girl was still limping on her bad leg. When they got to the wooded area the doll maker Daughter said meet my twin, the snake. The girl and her boyfriend were very scared and surprised because they had heard about a girl being born with a snake twin. The doll maker Daughter told the snake you are my twin and you must do as I say…kill the girl for me…kill her now. Brother Celino said I heard the story about people killing a big snake in the woods. Mother said please let me finish the story. She said when the doll maker Daughter told the snake to kill the girl; the girl took from her bag a small pouch and told her boyfriend to run and get help, she would take care of the snake. When the snake started to attack her she threw the content of the pouch in face of the snake. The powder substance in the pouch blinded the snake and the doll maker Daughter…both of them felt the pain from the powder substance as it blinded them. The boyfriend returned with the people from their Barrio. They attacked the snake with big knives and killed it. The doll maker Daughter died alone with the snake, which surprised everyone, because no one placed a hand or knife on her. The people figured that the reason they died together, there was only one heart between the two. Everyone wanted to know how something like that could happen. Mother said in this world there are a lot of mysteries that go unexplained. That's why I wanted to move out of that Barrio…the doll maker tried to teach your sister Vicky to be a witch, but I didn't let it happen…I told her if she try it again she would not be sitting down anymore, she would be laying down on her back.

After the death of her Daughter she promised herself she wouldn't use her powers again to hurt anyone…she continued to make dolls for sale, because she couldn't walk and she had to have something to do to make a living. Mother said the doll maker was a distance cousin. Someone asked Mother if she was a witch. She said yes! All of you are under my power fly, fly away. Everyone laughed. Brother Celino wife said oh boy! Vicky you was almost a witch. Mother said Celino you need to move your wife out of the house with your first wife because you can never tell what a person may do. I said Mother if you had not found out that the doll maker was trying to teach me to be a witch; what kind of witch you think I would have been? She said I don't really know, because I was always away at work...maybe you would have been a good witch...you never know...I personally think you would have been a good witch, because you are a very loving and caring person and you always respect your elders. She kissed me and told me to always be that way. I got up and looked around for Sister Linda and said it is time to go maybe Wilson is home already. We said our goodbye and left for Olongapo City.

When we arrive at the apartment I was surprised to see that Wilson had not came home. I got busy showing Sister Linda around in the apartment and told her she will be sleeping in the dining room because we had only one bedroom. I also told her about saving water every night because the city would turn it off without notice. After showing her around and explaining to her some of our routine, we sat down in the living room and started discussing the market extension. Sister Linda said that's good the market is in walking distance. I told her she would be going to the market to buy our food and I wanted her to make sure she bought the very shinny fruit. She said o.k. I will. Then we heard Wilson coming through the front door. Wilson said hi to Sister Linda and gave me a big hug and kiss. I followed him into the bedroom and as soon as I walked through the door he grab me and started kissing me again. I told Wilson I would be right back so I went into the living room and told Sister Linda to cook her some rice and corn beef so she would have something to eat before she went to school. She said o.k. I will start now so I can leave before three o, clock because I have to be there at three thirty...I will be back home around nine thirty tonight. I gave her my key to the apartment just in case Wilson and I went out nightclubbing.

Wilson came into the room and told Sister Linda he was going to give her twenty pesos a week for school. She said thank you

Brother Wilson! I turned and started back to the bedroom and Wilson followed. As soon as he closed the bedroom door he grab me and started kissing me again. Wilson is a very loving and caring person when he not drinking, you can talk to him and he will listen and give you the attention you deserve. He asked me what time Sister Linda was leaving for school. I said around three and he gave me five pesos for Sister Linda to use for snacks and jeepney fares. I took the pesos to Sister Linda. She said thanks! I am going to get dressed before I eat and leave for school. I said be careful and get a tricycle tonight if you are afraid to walk back to the apartment tonight. She said o.k. I turned and went back into the bedroom to check on Wilson and found him fast asleep. I went back to the living room where Linda was still getting ready for school. I asked her if she had enough uniforms for school. She said she had three set and that was enough for now. I said o.k. Let me know if you need anything else for school because Wilson said he would get whatever you need. Finally Sister Linda was ready for school so she sat down and ate her dinner and left for school. I decided to let Wilson sleep because he seems to be a little tired when he came home. He woke up around four, but didn't get up he just lounged around on the bed, so I lay down beside him and played with his nose. He said what are you doing? I said I want our baby to have your nose and face. He said my big nose…I want the baby to look pretty like you. Then he kissed me. All of a sudden he got quiet and started looking around in the room. I asked him what was wrong. He said pretty soon we would have to buy baby clothing and a baby crib…when I get paid we will start buying clothes for the baby to start out with…I don't want you to breast feed the baby if that's alright with you. I said that's fine with me…whatever you want. He said we would also start saving some money for a living room set that's not hard to set on like the one that came with this apartment. He hugged me real tight and got up and went into the bathroom. When he came back he asked me what I was having for dinner. I told him I was having corn beef and rice that Linda had cooked. He asked if there were enough for him too. I said yes! I will fix you a plate.

I went into the kitchen and cut up some onion to add to the corn beef. I stir fried the onion and added some garlic. I added the stir fried onion and garlic to the corn beef. The rice was ready so I put some on his plate and topped it with the corn beef and onions. I gave him his plate and went back and fixed mine. When I came back to sit down at the table with him; he said this would be real nice if I had a beer. I said o.k. I would go across the street and get beer…how many beers do you want? He said just one. I left and went across the street for beer. When I arrived the owner reminded me that Wilson owed eighty pesos. I asked what have he being getting here to owe you that much. The owner had a list showing that he had been getting beer, corn beef and bread. I said I will tell him and left the store. When I got back to the apartment I told Wilson that the store owner want him to pay his eighty pesos bill tomorrow when he get paid. He said you mean to tell me that I owe that much? I said every time you get drunk you stop by the store and get beer and corn beef…I was surprised that you owed that much in two weeks…that's was a month pay for me when I worked in the Money Exchange. He said don't worry I will try not to get credit from them anymore…I think they added more to my bill because I was drunk…but I will pay it off tomorrow, so I want owe them anything anymore. We ate our dinner in the living room. Wilson asked me what time Linda would be back from school. I told him she would be back before ten. He continued to drink his beer and I got up and put the dirty dishes in the kitchen sink. He said don't worry about washing the dishes I will wash them when I finish my beer so I came back into the living room and sat beside him. I thought to myself…I really wish he would be loving and caring all of the time. If he would act like this all of the time our life would be perfect. He finished his beer, kissed me and got up and went to the kitchen to wash the dishes. Looking at him washing the dishes I thought to myself…I wish I could see this side of him forever… we would be very happy, but his drinking always spoil things…I will enjoy this moment even if it's only for a little while. If he's not drinking he is one of the most wonderful guys in the world. I am in love with his good side I guess I will have to forgive him for his bad side until he realizes the damage it is doing. I am hooked on him and want to spend the rest of my life with him no matter what. Thinking of how loving and caring he was being today I didn't notice that he had finished the dishes until he kissed me. Then he asked me would I mind if he went over to C.B.'s house. I said to myself…here we go again. I said go ahead and visit your friend…I waited for him to ask me if I wanted to go with him, but he never did he just kissed me and left. I thought to myself…the moment of loving and caring was great while it lasted…I will take whatever I can get and carry it in my heart forever. Once again I was left alone; then I thought…I am not alone, I have my baby, so I rubbed my stomach and promised my baby I would never leave it alone.

I looked around the apartment to see what else we need to do to make it more like a home; then I thought about an iron and ironing board. Yes, I thought…we need it so we can take care of Sister Linda school uniforms…it good Wilson get paid tomorrow, now I can buy some more of the things we need for the apartment. I sat down again in the living room close to the window, so I would have a nice view out of the window; I watch all of the people small and large walk by. Some held hands and the other walked by their selves …some was dressed raggedy and some was dressed to kill, but they all seem to have some place to go. I didn't have a radio or a television I spent my idle time sitting and watching the people pass by. I thought to myself…how much I missed the stories my family tell after each meal…their happy laughter…sometime sad and crying…we were very happy together even though we were very poor…we loved each other and it kept us going through the real bad times and the good times…no matter what life brought upon us we stuck together for better or worse…this can't be my destiny, because I think God have something better for me, so I will wait for Wilson to change, because he can't continue to be this way forever…he will change his bad ways one of these day and I will be here waiting. I got tired of sitting on the hard wood furniture in the living room so I went into the bedroom and sat on the nice soft bed. Our living room chairs seem very hard I guess maybe it is because I am pregnant, because I always sit on a wooden box at my Mother's house and it didn't bother me. I looked at the clock by the bed it was almost nine I thought…Linda would be home before ten.

I got up and put my nightgown on getting ready for bed. Then I heard Wilson coming through the front door. He has come home early, I was so surprised I looked at the clock again to be sure of the time, and he wasn't drunk, but he had being drinking. He kissed me and asked if I was getting ready for bed. I said yes, and he closed the bedroom door and started to get undressed for bed. He asked if Linda had a key to the apartment. I said yes, I gave her my key. He hung his clothes in the closet and got into bed and pulled me down next to him. I started playing with his face and nose. He said stop doing that I want to play with you for a while. He started hugging and kissing me so gently. I asked him what was wrong. He said I don't want to hurt the baby. I told him that the doctor said we could make love anytime as long as he doesn't push me very hard or hit my stomach…we can make love the same as always. I could tell that he understood about the baby now, because the kissing and caressing started to intensify. We made love just like it was our last time and lay exhausted in each other arms. He told me how much he loved me and kissed me goodnight. I kissed him back and went to sleep. Around one o, clock the next morning I woke up and went to the bathroom; on my way back I decided to check on Sister Linda, because I didn't hear her come in after school. She was sleeping very soundly, so I tiptoed back into my bedroom. When I got back into the bed Wilson pulled me close and hugged me. I felt real safe and secure as I drifted off to sleep. At four thirty the alarm clock went off, Wilson got up talking about how short the nights are getting as he dressed for work. He said I will be getting paid today and will be home early. I said o.k. I will be here waiting for you. He kissed me and left for work and I went back to sleep. That morning around five thirty I heard a lot of noise coming from outside. I got up to see what was going on, Linda was already up. I asked her if she knew what was going on. She said no! We got dressed and went outside to see what was going on…everyone outside was setting up their fruit and vegetable stand, because the market was opening up for the first stand in the new acquired area.

Outside we could see all of the fresh fruit and vegetables in the stands, so Linda and I decided to buy the fruit and vegetables we need for the apartment. I told Linda to ask one of the vendors if they would be here every day. The vendor told her the stands would be open twice a week and today was a tryout day; they haven't decided which days of the week to use, because they don't want to use the same days as the other part of the market. I said this is nice having the market this close to the apartment. Sister Linda said yes! The only problem is the noise early in the morning waking you up. We walked a while longer as we bought fresh fruit, vegetables and fish. I told Linda my hands were getting tired of carrying the food, so we went back to the apartment. At the apartment we washed the fruit and vegetables and put it away. We started eating some of the fruit. Sister Linda started cooking breakfast; we had fresh fruit, fried eggs and rolls and drank hot oval tine.

We sat in the living room and ate breakfast as we watch the crowd of people outside going from booth to booth buying fruit and vegetable. I asked Linda what she did at school last night. She said just the same old thing we studied Reading, Math, Social Studies and Physical Ed...oh yes! We will start doing Crochet as our school project. I said when you start your project I want to work with you so I can learn how to do it...I need something to do while I am alone here in the apartment...I will pay what whatever we need to do the project. When are you going to start? She said right away, when I get the needle and thread. I said I would give her the money so she could buy it on her way to school. She said o.k. I will leave a few minutes early and stop by the market and get what I need. I said tomorrow I want you to go to the market and buy an iron and ironing board so you can take care of your uniforms. She said that right! We don't have an iron and ironing board. I said make sure you buy an electric iron not the one that uses charcoal...having electric here makes ironing a lot easy. She said o.k. But I never learn to use the charcoal iron anyway, Mother use to iron my uniforms...the last time I tried to use the charcoal iron Brother Etong laughed at me because I burned the skirt of my uniform...Mother tried to tell me how to use the iron, but I haven't tried it anymore, I don't want to go to school with a patch uniform...the kids will call me patch Linda. I asked her what she did with her burned skirt. She said Mother made herself a blouse out of it...you know Mother never want to throw anything away...it was a nice blouse...I almost asked for it back because it looked so good. I remembered when I was ten years old Brother Etong would put the charcoal in the iron and I would iron trying to help Mother iron all of the clothes she had taken in. Mother borrowed an iron and ironing board from our neighbor, so I could help her iron. I had ironed about four sheets when I dropped the iron to the floor and burned the corner of the sheet. I dropped the iron because I was very tired and sleepy; I guess I dozed off momentary. Mother yelled are you all right, as she came to me...she thought I had burned myself. I assured her that I was all right. The only thing was damaged was the corner of the sheet that I was ironing. Sister Linda said I remember when that happened Brother Etong and I were asleep and the big thud on the floor woke us up. I felt real bad about the accident because Mother was working so hard trying to take care of the family. Sister Linda said I thought Mother was able to fix the sheet where it wouldn't be noticeable? I said yes, she was able to fix it, but that was more work she had to do...she always took care of us without any help from our Father, the only help she got was from God, whom seem to be with us all of the time.

Mother has done a fine job taking care of her family...look at me I have grown up and fell in love with Wilson, Brother Celino and Sister Rose either married or engaged...Brother Etong is grown and you are a teenager and have a nice job...Brother Etong will always be with Mother, but he can take care of himself and Sister Melda is married to an American...we all are in a good position in life because of her. I looked at the time and told Sister Linda it was about time to start cooking lunch, she said yes, I will clean the fish and I said I would prepare the vegetables. Finally we had our lunch on the stove cooking I could smell the aroma from the food and it made me hungry. I told Sister Linda I was going to take a shower, because Wilson was coming home early today. When I finished my shower Sister Linda went in and took her shower. While she was showering I sat down by the window in the living room and started towel drying my hair. She finally came out and sat down beside me and started drying her hair too. I told her that I would always come and sit by the window while toweling my hair and most of the time I would get a nice breeze through the window.

We sat there for a while trying to dry our hair. I told Sister Linda we had better let our hair go for now and eat our lunch before it get cold, because our hair was almost dry anyway. We got up and fixed our plates. I asked Sister Linda if she would like a coke to drink with her dinner. She said yes, but we don't have any cokes. I said go to the store across the street and get a big bottle of coke, so she left and went to the store and came back with the coke and a block of ice. I said that's good you thought of the ice, now we can have ice-cold coke. She took the ice in the kitchen and chopped up some of the ice for our glasses and poured the coke over the ice. She brought our glasses to the table. I said o.k. Now we're in business let's eat. I ate so much of the food I could hardly breathe. Sister Linda said we cooked the vegetables almost perfect like Mother. After lunch we put away the food and Sister Linda started washing the dishes. I went into my bedroom and checked the time it was only eleven o, clock. I told Sister Linda there was no reason to rush with the dishes because she had plenty of time before she had to leave for school. She said I plan to leave around two this afternoon so that I can stop at the market and buy the things I need for my project. I said well you still have enough time to take a nap before you go so you want get sleepy in class. She said I really don't want to take a nap, I think I will do a little reading until it time for me to go. I said o.k. But I think I will take a nap until Wilson comes home. I went into my bedroom and lay down across the bed and before long I was fast asleep.

Sister Linda woke me up saying Vicky, Vicky Brother Wilson is coming. I said where is he? She said he is across the street at the store. I got up and went into the bathroom and freshened up and came back into the living room to wait for him. He came in the door and said hello to Sister Linda and gave me a big kiss. He told me he had stopped and paid his bill at the store across the street. I said that's good, now they will stop bothering me about it. He held up two beers and said I also paid for these too. When we sat down in the living room I told him we needed an iron and ironing board. He said how much does it cost? I told him I didn't know for sure but I would have Sister Linda to find out when she go to the market to buy her school supplies. He said give me your best guess. I said around twenty- five pesos. He took out his wallet and gave me one hundred pesos, one hundred for food and twenty- five for the iron and ironing board. Then he turned to Sister Linda and gave her twenty pesos for transportation to and from school.

Sister Linda said thank you Brother and left the room. She returned with her school uniform on. Wilson said it's only two P.M. is Linda going to school already? I said no she leaving early so she can stop at the market and buy the things she need for her school project. He asked Sister Linda if she had enough money to pay for all of her project. She said yes Sister Vicky gave me enough…goodbye I will see you guys tonight. When she left Wilson said if Linda ever need money for her school projects let him know and he would take care of it. I said o.k. Then he said I feel a little sleepy let's go in the bedroom. I followed him into the bedroom as he carried his beer. He sat on the side of the bed until he finished his beer. Then he took off his shoes and top clothing and stretched out on the bed. He pulled me down beside him and asked me what kind of perfume I was wearing. I said why you don't like it? He said yes I like the smell it is very pleasant and it make me want to make love. I said I better not use this perfume again because I don't want someone attacking me. He said I don't know why I always feel this way when I smell your perfume… it make me want you more and more. I said I bought this perfume at the market and its name is Intimate Perfume…I am not going to use it anymore if it make you want me…I want you to want me because you love me not because of the perfume. He said you are always on my mind I can't wait to hold you in my arms and make love to you and the smell of your perfume really get me going. Then he started to kissing and caressing me and before I knew it I was at my boiling point. We made passionate love. The last thing I heard Wilson say was if we wake up in time we will go to the movies. I remembered saying o.k.

Around four-thirty I woke up and started to the bathroom I tried not to wake him but he woke up and asked me where I was going. I told him to the bathroom. He said hurry up and come back to bed. I said I thought we were going to the movies. He said later I want to sleep a little more. When I finished in the bathroom I went into the kitchen and got some fruit to eat. I decided to sit in the living room and wait for him to wake up. I sat there for about an hour waiting for him; the wooden chair seem to be getting harder by the minute, so I decided to wake him up. I thought…he had being sleeping for over an hour…he didn't sleep like this before…I would ask Mother what causing him to want to sleep so much when I go to Calapacuan tomorrow. I shook him a couple of times and he reached up and pulled me down and kissed me. He asked what time was it. I said almost six.

He said did I sleep that long? I said yes are you sick? He said no! I am just sleepy all of the time. I said I going to see my Mother tomorrow and find out if I am making you sick. Wilson said how could you make me sick? I said I don't know yet. He said I am not sick so you haven't made me sick...I will be all right don't worry o.k. He got up and sat on the side of the bed and asked me if I had dinner already. I said not yet I have only eaten some fruit. He said get ready and I will take you out to dinner and a movie. I hurried to get ready before he falls asleep again.

We went to the restaurant beside the Grand Theater. I ordered noodles and he ordered beef fried rice. When I finished eating my noodles Wilson had already finished and he asked me if I wanted anything more. I said no I couldn't eat another bite. Wilson paid the check and we went next door to the Grand Theater and decided to watch a Western movie. The movie lasted about two and a half hour and Wilson was sleep most of the time. During the movie I would nudge him trying to keep him awake to watch the movie. He even started snoring because he was sound asleep. I know he didn't watch enough of the movie to understand what was going on. Finally the movie was over and he said let's go home as if he was in a hurry to get there. When we got back to the apartment Linda was fast asleep so we quietly went into our bedroom and closed the door. I started changing my clothes getting ready for bed and Wilson decided to go across the street for a beer. He came back with two beers I wondered if he was going to finish both beers before going to bed. He put one of the beers aside and continued to drink the other one as he sit on the side of the bed looking at me. He kept staring at me so I asked him if anything was wrong. He said you look like a china doll in your nightgown. I said are you sure? Can't you see that I am pregnant with a big stomach? He said what stomach? Your stomach is so flat there is no way a person can tell that you are pregnant...it's still early you probably want start showing until you are around six months pregnant...don't worry about being pregnant you will always be a beautiful woman and when you start showing you will be a beautiful pregnant woman. He started caressing and kissing me. I said hurry up and finish your beer so we can go to sleep and I stretched out on the bed. He hurried and finished his beer and lay down beside me and started caressing and kissing me again. I don't know what's wrong with him he always wanted to make love two or three times a day. Again we made love like it was the last time. When we finished just like always he would tell me that he love me and give me a nice gentle kiss. I would lay in his arms feeling safe and secure; then fall asleep. When the clock started to ring I turned it off. Wilson continued to sleep so I started shaking him telling him it was time to go to work. He got up and went into the bathroom and got cleaned up and came back into the bedroom and tried to lie down again. I said you are going to be late. He held me real tight and kissed me and said take Linda with you when you go to Calapacuan today. I said o.k. be careful and he left.

I saw Sister Linda going into the bathroom and when she came out I told her we were going to Calapacuan today. She said well I will get ready then. I said I am getting ready too so we can eat breakfast at Mother's house. I fixed my bed and went into the bathroom and took a shower. Sister Linda said I would take my shower when I get back. I said that's fine with me, go outside and call us a tricycle it's too dark outside to be walking around. She said Vicky a lot of people are walking outside going to work. We went outside together and caught a tricycle to the Victory Line bus station. I told Sister Linda I was going to buy hot bread rolls to take to Mother's house. She said you had better buy a lot of rolls because everybody will probably be there…you know Brother Celino and his wife is staying with Mother now. I said yes you are right and I am going to buy some canned liver worth too. We caught a jeepney to Calapacuan. We arrived around six that morning and everyone were still asleep. I put the food on the table and Mother startled me saying what are you doing here so early? I said I am hungry and Sister Linda said to Mother your baby is hungry too and we laughed. Brother Etong got up shaking his head and smiling. Brother Etong went outside to get wood for the stove. Mother started folding the blanket and rolling up the sleeping mats. I asked Mother where were Brother Celino and his new wife? She said didn't you see the small Nipa hut outside? They live there now.

I looked out the window and saw the new house built next to Mother's. I said I guess they are still sleep because I can't see any movement in the house. Mother said not to worry when they smell the food I am cooking your Brother will come running. I looked into my bag and pulled out forty pesos and gave it to Mother. Mother said you should keep this money so you can buy clothing for the baby and food. I said don't worry about it Wilson would take care of all the baby needs…later when the baby come maybe I want be able to give you anything, but now it's o.k. She said don't worry about your Brother Etong and me we would be all right. Mother started frying onion and eggs to eat with the bread rolls. Sister Linda said I like the smell of fried onion and eggs it makes me feel very hungry. I told Sister Linda she should watch Mother cooking the food so she can cook it at our apartment. Brother Celino showed up just as Mother predicted. He said Mother what are you cooking? Mother said I am cooking onion and eggs to go with the bread rolls Vicky brought… tell your wife to come over and eat breakfast with us. He said do you have coffee too. Mother said I am making it now.

Brother Etong came back into the house carrying water from the spring. Mother told him to stay inside because we were getting ready to eat breakfast. He smiled and took a seat on his wooden box. Brother Celino came back with his new wife. Brother Etong pointed at Brother Celino wife stomach and my stomach. I said yes and you are going to be an uncle very soon. He smiled and looked as if he was proud to be called uncle. Everyone sit down on the floor in a circle and the food was placed in front of us. We started our breakfast. Brother Etong liked the liver worth so I passed it to him first even though there were plenty for everyone. I broke the silence when I told Mother about Wilson being sleepy all of the time. Mother said does Wilson eat the same food with you? I said yes. She said do you crawl over him when he lay in the bed? I said yes again. She said Wilson is feeling the effect of your pregnancy. Brother Celino said the same thing is happening to him and he feel sleepy and sick a lot. Mother said when you go home crawl back over Wilson from the other side of the bed…if you don't do this he will always be sleepy even at work…this pregnancy is going to be hard on him, so you do as I tell you and he will be all right.

I said what about me? I am the one that pregnant. Mother said you stay home Wilson has to go to work; if you feel sick or sleep you can rest at home, but Wilson can't because he at work. I said I am happy now that I know what's going on I can go home and tell Wilson why he feel sleepy all of the time. I have being really worry about him; I told him I was going to ask you what was causing him to be sleepy all of the time when I visited you today. I said he is an American I don't know if he will believe something like this can happen to him. Mother said you do it anyway, so you can reverse the feeling he having. I said o.k. I will try. Brother Celino wife told Celino we had better go home so I can do what your Mother said to you, so you want be sleepy and feeling sick. Mother said you do it later before you go to sleep. I said Mother why does something like this happens to a man anyway? She said the woman carry the baby for nine months and the Father should feel some of the things we feel carrying the baby because he help make the baby…no one can really explain why a man feel the effects of his wife pregnancy…just being born in this world is somewhat a mystery…life itself is a mystery whether it a good life or a bad life…you are born into it either rich or poor, healthy or sickly and if you live long enough maybe you will have a job or maybe not. We don't have a choice in the matter, but if you look around yourself you will see that things always balance out…do you understand what I am saying? There are something you can explain and some you can't…God is the only one that can explain everything he knows everyone destiny…God brought us into this world and he can take us out of it…try to enjoy the things you have and be thankful that we have each other…I thank God that all of my kids are grown and healthy and I will continue to pray that they will be happy always.

Brother Celino started yawning. Mother said wake up Celino don't go to sleep now you just woke up. Everyone started to laugh. Mother said Vicky, Wilson will be all right too just do what I told you to do and it will help him. Sister Linda got up and started to help Brother Etong do the dishes and Brother Celino wife swept the floor. I asked Mother how was Brother Celino first wife doing. She said she's taking in washing three times a week so she can have something to do. I said I thought her Daughter was helping her?

Mother said she is helping, but she still want to do something… she spends most of her time sitting on her porch looking out into space. I said I guess she is lonely being alone all of the time. Mother said she will be all right...I think she is happy when she is around other people that's why she takes in washing. I asked Mother had she seen Sister Rose and Gina lately. She said they came here the other day; she is pregnant with Sopring baby. I thought to myself...I am glad she finally told her. Mother said there are three of you pregnant now...I don't know who will have their baby first...we will see in a few months. Brother Etong looked around and started counting his fingers and smiling. Mother looked at Brother Etong and said let's go feed the pigs, we need to fatten them up, so we can get a good price for them. I said why do you want to sale your pigs? Mother said because their food is getting too expensive and I can't afford to continue to feed them...I will continue to take care of my chickens and maybe I will keep one of the piglets. I can go back to work washing people clothes; I can't count on your Sister Melda or you giving me money, because you need it too. Don't worry about your Brother Etong and me we will make it all right. I thought to myself...I know Mother is a very strong and smart woman, but I wish I could do more to help her and Brother Etong... Wilson is not rich he makes only enough for us and we have the baby coming too. I asked Mother why she doesn't start buying fish by the bushel and selling it at the market, because that was better than washing people clothes. She said that's just what I was thinking to do after I sale the pigs. I said selling fish or vegetable is better than washing clothes because you are your own boss and if you have some left over at the end of the day you can take it home for use. Mother said yes you're right. Sister Linda said Vicky we had better go now because I have to go to school. Mother said you are not staying for lunch? I said no, we had better go because Wilson comes home early sometime. Sister Linda and I said our goodbye and left for Olongapo City. We made our way to the jeepney stop and caught the first jeepney that came alone. The jeepney was almost full of passengers so Sister Linda and I had to ride in the very back of the jeepney. The jeepney doesn't have windows on its side just plastic flaps, so when the jeepney took off the wind passed through the jeepney from the front to the back.

Sister Linda said someone forgot to take a shower and put her hand over her nose. I sat quietly with my lemon peel over my nose. Linda was very upset and she said very loud...someone didn't wash under his arm...what else did they forget to wash? It smells like a dead rat or a dead fish in here. I opened my bag and gave her a piece of lemon peel and told her to cover her nose with it. Sister Linda was too upset to quiet down. She said these stupid people need to wash under their arms before riding in public...no one want to smell your foul sent. The passengers started looking at each other and putting their arm down to their sides. Someone sprayed some perfume in the air up front. I couldn't keep from laughing at Sister Linda because she was looking like a mad woman...her hair was blowing in the wind and she was so mad...I thought...I have got a mad sister that looks like Frankenstein wife. Finally we made it to Olongapo in one piece... the passengers didn't decide to beat us up. We hailed a tricycle to ride to the apartment. When we arrived at the apartment I had a big surprise, Wilson was on the bed asleep I immediately crawled over him to the other side of the bed. He woke up and asked what I was doing. I told him I was doing what Mother had told me to do to make him stop sleeping so much. I settled down beside him and continued telling him what Mother said. I told him she also said I shouldn't let him eat the same food I am eating so he wouldn't feel the effect of my pregnancy. He said whatever! I want to go back to sleep for a while. I said o.k. He put his arms around me and kissed me. I felt safe and content as I fell asleep in his arms. I was awaken by the smell of food being cooked, so I carefully removed Wilson arms from around me and got up and glanced back at the clock it was almost twelve o, clock. I move slowly through the bedroom door and closed it behind me. I went into the kitchen and asked Sister Linda what we were having for lunch. She said fried eggplant, tomatoes and fried fish. I said that sound good. She said what are you cooking for Brother Wilson? I said nothing now maybe later on, he usually eat before he leave the base. He will let me know if he's hungry. She said I have finished cooking let's eat. She fixed her plate and I fixed mines. I took my plate in the living room to eat. She said I am going across the street and get some ice for the coke that we have left over.

I said that's good I will get our glasses and the coke. Sister Linda came back with the ice and chopped it up for the glasses. We sat in the living room and had our lunch. I asked her had she started her school project. She said yes, but I am still trying to get a handle on it, I will teach you as soon as I figure it out. I said that will be great, I really would like to learn to crochet. She said I got your needle and thread so you can get started when I learn it. When we finished lunch Sister Linda took the plates into the kitchen and washed the dishes. After cleaning the kitchen she showed me the needles and thread I would be using when she start teaching me. I was very excited about the ideal of crocheting my own designs. She said give me a few days to learn how to start; then I will show you how...we will start with white thread first then we will switch to color thread when we learn how to make designs. I said o.k. I can't wait to get started.

Then the bedroom door opened and Wilson came out and went into the bathroom. When he came out of the bathroom he asked us what we were doing. I said I am trying to learn to crochet are you hungry. He said no I just want to lie down for a little while longer... do we have any cokes? I said no I would go to the store and get some. Sister Linda said give me the money and I will go to the store. I said o.k. Bring some ice too. When she came back she chopped up some of the ice and put it in a glass and gave it to me. I took it into the bedroom to Wilson. He sat up and put the pillows behind him and started drinking the coke. He drunk the whole glass of coke and asked for some more. I went back into the kitchen for more coke. Sister Linda said Brother Wilson is real thirsty. I said yes and I hope he will be all right very soon...it really worry me seeing him sleep so much. Sister Linda said Mother said it will take a few day before you will see him starting to get better...we just cross our fingers and toes and hope that your pregnancy want be a bad one. I said Mother said sometime you feel the effect for the whole nine months. She said poor Brother Wilson we will just keep our fingers cross and hope that it would only be a short time. I said yes I am crossing my fingers and toes. We both laughed. Sister Linda said you had better hold onto that coke before you drop it. I went to the bedroom to take Wilson his coke. He asked me what Sister Linda and I was laughing at. I said Sister Linda and I are crossing our fingers and toes hoping you will be all right very soon. He smiled and said don't worry I will be all right. He drank all of the coke again.

I asked him if he wanted more. He said oh no! I don't want to drown myself in coke. I laughed at him. He said you think what I said is funny...come here. I came over to the bed and sit down beside him. He started tickling me and I remembered he was very ticklish under him arms, so I started tickling him. He started shouting uncle, so I quit tickling him and we started hugging and kissing. He stopped kissing and said we had better wait until Sister Linda left for school. I said yea! You just want me to stop tickling you. I started playing with his nose and he said I want to keep my nose. I said I don't want to remove your nose I just want to play with it and look at your handsome face...I want our baby to look just like his or her Father. He said o.k. Go ahead and play with my face. We heard a knock on the bedroom door and Sister Linda said she was going to leave early so she could meet with her classmates and start working on their project. I got up and went into the living room and said goodbye to her. I went back to the bedroom and closed the door. Wilson couldn't wait to get me back into his arms. He looked at me as if he was falling in love with me all over again. Then he started gently kissing and caressing me and my whole body seem as if it was going to melt...his kisses radiated from my head to my toes...I guess this is what heaven feel like...I don't want this feeling to ever end...suddenly I remembered what my Mother said one time...if there is happiness there will also be some loneliness and you have to find a way to balance it...I will take whatever come my way just as long as I can be with Wilson the man I love. Wilson said what's wrong. I said nothing at all and he kept caressing and kissing me. We made such wonderful love it seems as though it was better than the time before. Wilson managed to say I love you before he closed his eyes and went to sleep. I stayed in the bed and watched him sleep for a while; then I got up and got a glass of water. When I finished the water I decided to take a quick shower. When I finished my shower I sat next to the window in the living room to towel dry my hair. Around four o, clock Wilson woke up calling me. I went into the bedroom and found him sitting on the side of the bed. He said where were you? I dreamed that you left me. I said I will never leave you, I was just drying my hair in the living room. I sat down beside him and he hugged and kissed me again. He said I want to make sure I am not dreaming. Then he said I want to take a shower so I can wake up.

I said I had just finished my shower and it was his turn. He said while I am taking a shower would you please go to the store and get me some beer? I said yes how many do you want? He said two would be fine. I decided to get some ice just in case he needed some. When I got inside of the apartment I put the ice and one of the beers in a big pitcher. When he finished his shower he drank one of his beers. I asked him if he wanted something to eat. He said no I just want to have a cold beer. We sat in the living room on our hard wooden chairs. Our living room furniture was made of wood without cushions. I asked him does he feel better after his shower. He said I feel a lot better than I felt this morning…I could hardly open my eyes this morning so I took a shower on my boat trying to wakeup. I said it good you can take a shower on your Tug Boat. He said my Tug Boat is just like a small house it have a kitchen, a shower and bunk beds and our living room is in the kitchen. We have a long table with a bench that we use to eat on and for recreation. I said I remember when you took me to your Tug Boat just two weeks after we met. You didn't believe that I love you so you got a bottle of rum and said if I don't tell you that I love you, you would drink the whole bottle. I shouted over and over that I love you and you gave me the rum bottle. You hugged me and started kissing me over and over. Somehow I felt that if Jones were not cooking Chicken there we would have ended up baptizing your boat. Wilson said I wanted to make love to you that night so bad that after I took you back to the main gate I came back and took a cold shower. I said why a cold shower? Did you put ice in the water? He said smiling no I just didn't use the hot water. Wilson said now that I have you here with me I feel much better. Then he started kissing and caressing me. I said not on this hard wood chair my whole body ache just sitting down here and you think I can make love here…if you want to make love let's go into the bedroom. He said I am about to get use to sitting on this hard furniture. I said that's good I will buy a hard wood chair for you and carve your name on it. He said no thank you! I will buy you a soft chair to sit on and maybe you can lie down on it once in a while. I said as soft as our bed?

Wilson said if it not as soft it would be real close. Sitting there laughing and talking with him it seem as if my life is almost complete… only one thing left to do…get married…why is the paperwork taking

so long. I thought about what Mother had always told her girls...
wait until you get married before going to bed with a man...I loved
Wilson too much to wait...if I had not gotten pregnant she would
not have known I was sleeping with him, but when I got morning
sickness I got scared and had to tell her. Wilson brought me back
to reality when he said I am hungry let go get something to eat. We
got up and hurried to get ready. Finally we were ready to go and on
our way to the Admiral Restaurant. We arrived at the restaurant and
went in and were seated. When I got the menu I looked at the prices
and said wow! Wilson said what's wrong? I said the prices are too
high in here. Wilson said don't worry just order whatever you want
to eat. I said we could order half the chicken and fried potatoes, but
I want rice instead of the potatoes. He said I will order whatever you
want. Finally the waitress came and took our order and came right
back with Wilson's beer. He said this is a nice restaurant. I said yes
the management own the hotel upstairs and the Movie theater next
door...I just don't like their food prices. Wilson said we don't go out
to real nice restaurant very often you deserve to go once in awhile.
I said o.k. But next time take me to a less expensive one. I do thank
you for taking me to this expensive restaurant. Wilson smiled and
kissed me on my cheek. Finally the waitress came with our food. I
started eating my fried chicken with rice and Wilson said you eat
rice all of the time. I said yes Filipino people eat rice three times a
day and Americans eat potatoes all of the time. Wilson smiled and
said yes you are right, you eat a lot of rice and I eat a lot of potatoes.
I said you see! We're almost alike we eat some food more than the
other. When we finished our meal we went next door to see what
movie was showing. Wilson said oh look! They are showing a good
Western movie...let's watch it. Wilson got our tickets and look at the
time...he said we're right on time the movie starts in ten minutes...
do you want any snacks? I said no I am too full to do any snacking
now. We went in and found our seat in the balcony...I don't like to
sit close to the screen it hurts my eyes. We sat down and Wilson put
his arm around me and kissed me and he started kissing me again
and again. I said let's watch this movie.

He quit kissing me for a while, but not for long...he had my lips
pinned down under his and I was getting so hot I almost forgot that

we were in the movie. I said if you want to make love let's go home. He said in a very calm voice o.k. We would finish the movie. When the movie was over he stood up and readjusts his pants. I said are you all right? He said yes! I am all right. He took my hand and we walked hand in hand out of the theater. We caught a jeepney and went home. When we arrive at the apartment Sister Linda was not home. Wilson said let's go to bed and go to sleep. I changed and put my nightgown on then I looked at him and he had that look on his face like he wanted to attack me. Wilson went and checked the lock on the front door and came back to the bedroom. I could tell that he had something on his mind. My lips would say cool down mad man if they could talk. He knows what get me in the mood and didn't waste any time pushing my buttons. As soon as we got into the bed, we got started and he was finished almost as soon as we started. I asked him what happened to him. He said when I left the movie I was very excited. I am sorry I didn't wait for you. I was about to rip him apart when I heard Linda coming through the front door. I decided to quiet down and not say anything else. Wilson just closed his eyes trying to go to sleep. I looked at the clock it was almost ten. I got up and went into the living room where Sister Linda was unpacking her bag. I said have you eaten yet? She said yes I had some snacks at school. I said have you learned how to crochet? She said yes and I will teach you what I know tomorrow. Then she went into the kitchen to eat leftovers. I told her I was going to bed. We said our goodnights and I went into my bedroom and closed the door. I climbed into bed beside Wilson and he put his arms around me and pulled me close to him. I fell asleep in his arms. Around three in the morning I woke up and was feeling very much in the mood, so I started caressing Wilson and it seem as if he was waiting for the opportunity. We didn't waste any time although we tried to hold the noise down to a minimum so we wouldn't wake Sister Linda in the next room. We lied completely exhausted in each other arms. It didn't take us long to drift off to sleep.

Around four-thirty the clock alarm went off as usually Wilson jumped out of bed with a burst of energy. He went into the bathroom and got cleaned up for work. When he came out I asked him if he was still feeling sleepy. He said you know what, I feel real awake and ready to get my day started. I said to myself...I guess doing the things Mother told me to do is working to reverse his sleepy feeling. He came back to the bed and kissed me goodbye. I went back to sleep. A weird smell woke me up and I was feeling very irritable, I got up and went into the kitchen to see what was going on. I discovered Sister Linda cooking something that smelled like fried garlic and onions. The smell was so bad it made me mad. I grab the frying pan and threw the food in the sink and swung the pan at Sister Linda. I don't know what happened to me to trigger that type of behavior. Sister Linda ran into the other room and changed her clothes and left the apartment crying. For the life of me I couldn't figure out why I had acted so weird. I looked around the kitchen and saw food all over the floor, the table and the sink. I thought to myself...well I had better clean up this mess. I cleaned up everything and took a shower and got dressed. I decided to go to Calapacuan because I figured that was where Sister Linda had went.

When I arrived at Mother's house she asked me what had happened. I told her I didn't really know what caused me to act like that. When I smelled the food Sister Linda was cooking something triggered my mind and I started to act like I have never acted before. Sister Linda said she is crazy; she tried to hit me with the frying pan. Mother said is Wilson feeling better? I said yes why? She said that's why you are feeling the effect from your pregnancy...you reversed the effect on Wilson...now you will continue to feel this way for awhile or maybe until you have the baby. I said are you telling me that I will be feeling irritable and sleepy until I have my baby? Mother said you won't be feeling like that all of the time just off and on. Sister Linda said I don't want to go back and live with her if she will be acting crazy like that. Mother said your Sister Vicky is not a crazy woman, she is pregnant and don't like the smell of onion and garlic cooking... try to avoid cooking the food she doesn't like and remember she is pregnant...Linda go and call your Brother Etong he went to get water a long time ago and haven't returned yet.

Sister Linda went outside to call brother Etong and I sat down at the table and started eating breakfast. I asked Mother if it was all right if I drank coffee while I am pregnant. She said you can have some this time, but you shouldn't drink it while you are pregnant. I said I would just drink milk. Mother said that's good you are thinking about you baby...you don't want to hurt your baby...coffee has a lot of caffeine and it's not good for the baby. I said thanks Mother for telling me the things I need to know to take care of my baby. When Sister Linda and Brother Etong came into the house I was almost finish eating. Brother Celino came by and asked if we had brought something from Olongapo City. I said no we only came to visit. He poured himself a cup of coffee and took some of the food from the table and left. I asked Mother if Brother Celino had found himself a job. She said no, he doesn't have a real job, but him and brother Etong go out every day and cut long grass and sell it to people for their house roof. It's not a lot of money but it is enough to buy food. I said I am glad Brother Celino built him a house before his wife has their baby. Now they won't have to worry about somewhere to stay; they can concentrate on food and clothing. I said Mother you need to tell Brother Celino to get a job, so he can stop coming here every time he need something...tell him there is only enough for you and Brother Etong. Mother didn't respond, so I didn't say anymore about it because I know she like having her family around her even if she has to feed them all. Sister Linda said we could go back to Olongapo as soon as I finish washing the dishes, so I can start teaching you how to crochet. Mother said don't worry about the dishes if you have to go I will wash them...just go and remember your Sister Vicky is pregnant. Sister Linda said in a very low voice tone...yea! Mother I will take care of your crazy pregnant Daughter. I grab her arm and pretended to bite it. Sister Linda said you see Mother I told you she is crazy. We all laugh together as we prepared to leave. Mother was in a very happy mood as we left. Brother Etong was smiling and pointing toward his head indicating that Sister Linda and I were crazy. We left and went to the jeepney stop and were lucky enough to catch a jeepney that had seats up front, so we could get fresh air in our faces. The air blew our hair all out of shape, but we didn't care as long as it was fresh.

When we arrive in Olongapo City we brushed our hair down as best we could and caught a tricycle to our apartment. When we entered our apartment I was very surprised to see a monkey moving around in the apartment bumping into everything. I told Sister Linda to go and ask the apartment Manager if they turned the monkey loose in our apartment. Just as she was about to leave Wilson came in the door. He said how do you like my surprise...I went to the store to buy bananas for him. I said I like him, but he seems to be blind. He said he would be all right. I said where did you get the monkey? He said from a guy on the base...his name is Chico. Wilson gave me a banana to feed to the monkey. I said Chico come get your banana as I removed the peeling...I said I think he smell the banana. Sister Linda said laughing...I think he know the smell of the bananas. Wilson looked at me and said now you have some more company. I said to myself...not a monkey. I turned to Sister Linda and said give him some water in one of the bowl...make sure you write his name on it. She came back with a bowl of water for Chico. She gave the bowl of water to him, he grab the bowl and spilled water all over the room. I said the next time you give him water make sure you put it on the floor. I said to myself...what a surprise...someone else to clean up behind. Sister Linda took the monkey into the kitchen and I followed Wilson into the bedroom. I thanked him for the surprise. He said I am glad you like Chico...I am going across the street to get a beer, do you want something. I said no, but maybe Sister Linda want something to drink. He went into the kitchen and asked her if she wanted something to drink. She said yes Brother I would like a coke. He left and went to the store. Sister Linda put the monkey away and started showing me how to crochet. When he returned he asked us what was we doing and went into the kitchen and put the beer and coke on ice in the sink. He opened one of the beers and went into the bedroom. A couple of minutes later he called me. I told Sister Linda we would continue our session when Wilson went to work the next day. I went into the bedroom and closed the door behind me and sat on the side of the bed. He told me he wanted us to meet his friend and boss at a club on Magsaysay drive later on. He said do you remember your Sister Melda's boyfriend?

Well he has another girlfriend we will be meeting them tonight. I said o.k. Just tell me what time so I can get ready. He said we are to meet them around seven, so you can start getting ready around six. I stayed in the room for a while waiting for him to fall asleep, but he was not sleepy, so I went out into the kitchen and told Sister Linda to go ahead and eat I was not hungry. When I returned to the bedroom I snuggled into Wilson arms and went to sleep. The next thing that I heard was Sister Linda when she said I am leaving for school now. I didn't say anything or get up I just eased one of the pillows from under Wilson head and moved to the far side of the bed to try and go back to sleep. I guess Wilson was very tired because he didn't move when I eased one of the pillows from under his head.

Around four that afternoon I woke up very hungry, so I got up and started for the kitchen to fix me something to eat. Wilson woke up and asked where I was going. I told him I was going to the kitchen to cook me some food. He said are you making lunch? What time is it? I said it four o, clock already. He said it late I thought it was around one o, clock...when you came in and got into the bed I watched you sleep until I couldn't take it anymore and I fell asleep too...I guess I was tired and didn't know it. Wilson said come eat in here and keep me company. I brought my plate into the bedroom and sat on the side of the bed and started eating. I was eating with my hand when he asked if we still have fork and spoons. I said yes but it is easy for me to use my hand...when I was growing up I use my hands all of the time. He said I guess it's all right. I said I never use my hand when we go out to dine in public only when I am here behind closed doors...in the Philippines we use our hands to eat. Wilson said I guess it's all right if you want to eat with your hand at home. I said don't worry I am not going to embarrass you when you take me out. He said I am not worry about that I have seen you use fork and spoons when we are out eating...this is the first time I have notice you eating with your hand that's why I asked...now that I know it's the way things are done in the Philippines forget I asked. He leaned over and kissed me.

When I finished eating I washed the dishes and cleaned up the kitchen. Wilson was following me around in the kitchen until he decided to go to the store and buy beer. He said it only five o, clock we would meet my friend at seven. I said o.k. I will start getting ready around six and went into the bathroom and brushed my teeth. When I finished in the bathroom I came out and gave Chico a banana and some water. We had put a leash around his waist so he wouldn't run all over the apartment. Wilson came back just as I was finishing with Chico he had two beers in his hand. I said to myself...I hope he doesn't get drunk when we go out. He sat down in the living room and drank his beer. He called me over to sit beside him. We sat there talking and he was drinking his beer and kissing me. Sometime the smell of the beer made me sick and he smoke too. I just take the smell and never complained. Sometimes I wish he could experience some of the things I go through living with him, but I don't want him to be bothered with this pregnancy thing always being sleepy. Even though he didn't drink as much while he was feeling sleepy I still don't want him to feel that way again. I said to myself…I can take what he is doing to me…I am use to it now. I looked at him and he was drinking his second beer. Before I could say something to him, he said you better get ready now so we can go. I said are you going to be all right drinking that beer? He said I have only drunk two beers I am not drunk yet. I got up and went into the bedroom and started getting ready. When I finished and came out of the bedroom I told him I was ready to go. I was waiting for him to tell me how good I looked but he didn't say a word. We left to meet his friend. When we got there they was nowhere in sight so we got a table and sit for a while. Finally Wilson got up and started looking around in the club for his friend. He found his friend and they came over to our table. His friend introduced me to his girlfriend. We said hi in our native language. The waitress came over and we ordered our drinks. Wilson friend sat next to me. He said little bit you look so cute and innocent tonight…don't get mad at me because I have another girlfriend…I loved your sister, but she wanted to be with her husband. I said I am not mad at you…you do whatever you want.

I looked at Wilson he was concerned about his Boss, so he got up to look again in the other side of the club. His friend said man where are you going? Don't go anywhere now…we will be leaving in a little while. Wilson left anyway. His friend said I don't know what's wrong with Wilson…he can't hold his liquor…he always acts up when he is drinking…don't worry little bit I am not going to leave until he come back. We sat for a while longer and Wilson still had not returned, so his friend decided to look for him. His girlfriend and I started making small talk she told me that she knew I was the sister of her boyfriend formal girlfriend. I said you are right and I am glad he found someone else…he is a very nice guy. She quickly agreed with me. We sat a few more minutes waiting for Wilson and his friend to return. Finally they came back to the table. I asked Wilson's friend where did he find Wilson and he said Wilson was at his boss table when he found him. I couldn't believe that he left us at the table waiting for him while he sat at his boss table. Looking at him as he sat down I knew why he did what he did…he was drunk. I couldn't understand how he got drunk so quick; I know he wasn't drinking that much before we left our apartment. As soon as he sat down he asked me to go with him over to his boss table so he could introduced me to him. When I got up from the table his friend asked me if we were coming right back, because they were leaving as soon as they finish their drinks. I said I don't know but I will be all right, so I said goodbye as I left the table. Wilson's friend told him to take care of me and to take me home before he got too drunk. Wilson said o.k. Man I will catch you later. They left and Wilson and I went over to his boss table. The guy sitting at the table was kinder old and fat. Wilson introduced him as his chief. We took a seat and I sat there watching them drink. Finally his friend asked Wilson if I could dance with him. Wilson looked at me and I said I don't want to dance, but he whispered to me…just dance with him this one time for me he is my boss. I said o.k. He stood up and came around the table and took my hand. We walked out to the middle of the dance floor and we danced around and around it almost made me dizzy.

He asked me where I worked before I met Wilson. I told him that I worked in a Money Exchange booth on Rizal Avenue. He said I figured you didn't work in the club, because you move and act very nice indeed. He said I have my Daughter here in the Philippines. She is with her boyfriend somewhere. I said that's nice. The music stop and he thanked me for dancing with him and I said you are welcome. He walked me back to our table and he even thanked Wilson for letting me dance with him. He told Wilson that he has a very nice girlfriend. I don't know what came over Wilson, because he kept starring at his boss and me as we sat down at the table. Wilson said we have to go home now. His boss said why are you leaving now? It's still early. Just as we were leaving his boss's Daughter and her friend came over to our table. He introduced them to us. Wilson said hi to them and told his boss he would see him the next day. Wilson almost fell as he got up from the table. His boss said are you going to be all right Boatswain Mate. Wilson said yes as we left going home. As soon as we entered the apartment I went straight to our bedroom. I didn't say a word to Wilson because he was drunk and I didn't want to get into an argument with him because Sister Linda was sleeping in the next room...plus he wouldn't remember anything we said the next day. I glance at the clock in the bedroom it was ten o, clock, I quickly undressed and put my nightgown on and got into the bed. Wilson sat on the side of the bed for a few minutes and finally lay down with his clothes on. I got up and removed his shoes and push him to the center of the bed to keep him from falling again. I also tried to remove his clothes but he was too heavy for me to move around so I just let him sleep with his clothes on.

When I got back into the bed I started thinking to myself... well we was happy for a while...he really has a problem with his drinking...a few drinks have him falling all over himself...what will he do if one of his friend ask to share me with him...he forget that I am with him when he start drinking...he know I am pregnant and he should be trying to take care of me, but he got drunk and forgot about me. The only thing I could do was cry and I cried until I fell asleep. At four thirty the next morning the alarm clock went off and I quickly turned my back to him because I didn't want to say anything to him. I was still very mad and he knew I was mad. He got up and found his shoes and struggled to put them on. Finally he got his shoes on. I could tell that he was also struggling with a bad headache...I don't know why he drinks like that because it always give him a bad headache and a hangover. Wilson said he will be home early today and tried to kiss me. I didn't say a word and pretended to be asleep. When he left I got up and went to the bathroom. On my way back I saw Chico he was asleep and I guess Sister Linda was still sleep too because I couldn't hear any movement coming from the next room. I got back into the bed and tried not to think about Wilson. I closed my eyes and finally drifted off to sleep. I woke up hearing voices and I smelled food cooking. I looked at the clock, it was eight o, clock in the morning. I quickly jumped out of bed and opened my bedroom door; I saw Mother in the kitchen cooking breakfast. I thought that's why the food aroma smell so good...fried dried fish and garlic fried rice. I said Mom the food smells real good and what are you doing here in Olongapo City this early? She turned around from the stove and smiled saying I just wanted to see if you and your Sister Linda is doing all right. I said we're fine. She said you're not alright...where did you get that monkey...take it back to the jungle...I know you don't want to lose your baby...the monkey don't belong in the house especially when you are pregnant...he take away all of your strength and patience and maybe cause you to lose the baby. What if he jump on you and you lose your balance and fall? What about all of the noise and the mess he makes in the house you have to clean up? You are suppose to relax and take it easy because this is your first pregnancy and you never know what can happen...Linda take that monkey outside and put him in the Guava tree. Linda took Chico outside and tired him to the Guava tree. Mother said Vicky what have you been crying about...your eyes never lies...I can tell that you have been crying about something? Did you and Wilson have a fight? I said ask Sister Linda. Sister Linda said I never hear them fight they seem to be very happy. Mother said what have you been crying about? I knew I had to tell her something so I told her my stomach had been hurting last night and I didn't want to wake anyone.

Mother said maybe you should see a Doctor. I said you know I always cry when something is bothering me even when I have my period. Mother said I know you are very sensitive to pain even a small mosquito bite. Sister Linda said you mean to say my Sister Vicky cry when bitten by a small mosquito? Mother said yes, that was when she was very small she complained even when the bite is well. Sister Linda said as she was laughing that mean that my sister is a crybaby. Mother said no she is just very sensitive to certain things. I said I am hungry let's eat. We fixed our plates and sit down to eat breakfast. Sister Linda said how about me when I was very small? Mother said you were very different you would always cause even a small mosquito bite to get infected because you liked to play with your sores. I said Yuk what's wrong with her? Didn't it feel hurt when she did that? Mother said she seem to enjoy doing it maybe she thought it would get well sooner. I said Sister Linda you was a very sick child. We all laugh and said we were very sick children. Mother said your Sister Melda has a very strong stomach she always tried to lick her sores like a dog...I really don't know why she does that...it started when she saw a man in the Barrio back in Pangasinan suck the girl leg that got snake bitten she try and lick her sores...she was three years old when she saw it. Sister Linda said oh boy! She is sicker than we are. I said laughing let finish eating my stomach can't take much more of this. We hurried to finish eating. Mother checked the time and said it's almost nine o, clock...your Brother Celino and Sister Rose acted almost alike when they had mosquito bites, they cry all of the time...I would boil leaves from the Guava tree and bathe their arms and legs in it...they wanted you to baby them around all of the time especially at night and I would end up trying to comfort them most of the night...your brother was a crying mama's boy... Rose and Celino was very sensitive to all of the common aliment that went around they gave me more problems than all the rest of my kids. They seem to run a high fever every time they got sick...you have to be very careful with small kids when they have high fever. Your Brother Etong had a very high fever when he was four years old and we didn't have money for a Doctor so we had to use a Midwife; He got well but never talked again.

I said are you saying that he got a high fever from sores from a mosquito bite? She said no, I don't remember exactly how he got the fever I just remember that he had a high fever and almost died...I think God that he got well...even though it took away his ability to speak I am still thankful that he is still with us. I said Brother Etong has been blessed he is a very lucky guy. Mother said we all have been blessed to still be in this world. I guess I had better go back to Calapacuan, I only wanted to check and see if you two was alright... now that I know you are alright I can rest easy on my way back home. Tell Wilson I took his monkey to Calapacuan to make sure you won't lose your baby. Mother got Chico and left. I was glad she took him because I was tired of cleaning up behind him anyway. Cleaning and listening to the noise Chico made was just like a job. I had rather work in the Money Exchange than take care of Chico, but I wouldn't tell Wilson that because I didn't want to hurt his feeling. I know now that worrying with Chico can cause me to lose my baby I am glad Mother came and took him away. I believe my Mother has some kind of Mother instinct, because she came here and knew or felt that I had been crying last night…that's why she came early this morning. Sister Linda said when I finish washing the dishes I will show you how to crochet. I said o.k. I will hurry and take a shower so we can crochet. I quickly made up my bed and hurry into the shower. When I finished I dried off and got dressed and went into the living room to wait for her. Sister Linda came into the living room with her crochet basket. She started me with straight in and out needlework. She said I would show you how to make designs when you get use to doing this part…keep practicing what I showed you and maybe tomorrow I will show you how to do some designs. Sister Linda started doing her homework and I busied myself practicing the needlework she had taught me. I thought to myself…this is very nice it will keep my mind on something besides what going on with Wilson and me. Sister Linda said I heard you crying last night…you can wake me up if you are sick and I will go with you to the Doctor. I said o.k.

Then I remembered I had my towel wrapped around my head, so I went into my bedroom and took the towel off and started combing my hair. I remembered Mother said my eyes were puffed up so I looked into the mirror to see if they were all right. I said to myself…I don't look bad, but my eyes are a little puffy. I guess that how she could tell that I had been crying…as the old saying goes…the eyes doesn't lie. Sister Linda came to my bedroom door and asked what I want to have for lunch. I said go to the market and get a kilo of beef. I want to marinade it in garlic, lemon and soy sauce and cook it. She said are you going to cook it like Sister Melda cook it? I said yes but Filipino style not American style when you mixed potatoes and onions with it. Linda said let's cook it American style with potatoes and onions. I said o.k. If that's what you want, but you had better go now to the market before it is too late to buy beef. She said o.k. I heard her leave through the front door. I decided to lie down for a while because I was feeling very drowsy. I closed my eyes and drifted off to sleep. I guess I had slept for at least two hours because the meat had to be marinade for at least one hour and the smell of the food woke me up. I looked at the clock on the table it was almost twelve so I got up and went into the kitchen and told Sister Linda the food smells good. She said laughing I thought you was going to hit me with the frying pan again. I asked her if she had learned how to cook and marinade the beef from Sister Melda. She said I learned a few things from her, but I can cook most Philippines dishes. I said me too, one of these days I will learn to cook American dishes, so when Wilson eats at home he will be proud of me. The only food that I cook he like to eat is corn beef and rice mixed with onion. He eats it when he is very hungry. Sister Linda said I will eat anything when I am very hungry, I will climb a fruit tree when I am hungry…do you remember me climbing the fruit tree? Do you remember the time when we came home from school and someone had stolen our rice and we didn't have any to cook that night or the next day? We were so hungry we climbed the neighbor's cashew tree and got some fruit. The neighbor got very mad at us and told us when Mother came back she would have to pay for the fruit. We ate the fruit and roasted the cashew in the fire. We took twenty pieces and we ate all of it and drunk plenty of water. We didn't go to school the next day.

I said I bet the neighbors got our rice because there were two families living nearby. We made it until Mother came home and brought more rice. When she found out what had happened she hid a box underneath our floor for the rice. We never had it stolen again. Mother went to the neighbors and told them something they looked as if they were scared. After that the neighbors told us we could get fruit from their tree whenever we need it. I said Sister Linda did you hear what Mother said to our neighbors. She said no! I was busy playing with their kids. I tried to listen to the conversation but the only thing I could understand about the conversation is when they said thanks to Mother. Sister Linda said you could only hear them say thank you to Mother? I said yes! And we had better eat this cooked food before I eat up all of the fruit. Sister Linda said you always eat a lot of fruit even when you are not hungry. I said my baby like to eat fruit. She laughed at me. We ate the food Sister Linda cooked; it almost tasted as good as my cooking… the marinade beef was very good and tender. Sister Linda said I asked the lady at the market to cut off the tender side of the beef for me. I said remember the cut you got so when you return you can get it again. When we finished eating Sister Linda said she would leave the leftovers in the pot. I said o.k. I am so full right now I can't think about food for a while. When Sister Linda finished cleaning the kitchen and putting up the food she started doing her homework. I started practicing my crochet. Sister Linda came over and examined my work and told me I was doing very well and could start making some designs. She opened her book and showed me some of the designs in it. She said which design would you like to do first? I said I like the flowery design so I can use it on the coffee table; she said first I will show you how to make a flower design. I watched as she made the design. Then she said now I want you to try it. I started the design and surprisingly it was very easy to do. She looked at my design and said you know how to crochet you don't need me anymore...you are very easy to teach. I said to myself...now I have something to keep me busy while sitting here waiting for Wilson to come home...I don't have to sit here thanking about him all of the time. Sister Linda said when you make a lot of flowers I will show you how to put them together. I said I can't wait to finish the crochet for my table.

The apartment door open and in walked Wilson, he said hello to Sister Linda and me and we said hello to him. He asked me what I was doing and I told him I was crocheting. Linda got up and put her book away. Wilson bended over and kissed me and asked me to go into the bedroom with him. I followed him into the bedroom and sit beside him on the bed. I sat there waiting for him to say his old familiar word...I am sorry. Just like I expected the first thing he said was I am sorry about last night. I thought to myself...why he always say he is sorry and continue to do the same thing over and over...I am tired of him saying sorry, sorry all of the time. He started trying to kiss me and I turned away because I felt like I was being used. He asked what's wrong. I said nothing! I really didn't feel like arguing with him because Sister Linda was still at home. I lay back on the bed and gave him the silent treatment. He finally realized I didn't want to talk about last night, so he asked me if we had a coke in the apartment. I said no! If you want something to drink I will send Sister Linda to the store for it...do you want a beer? He said no he only wanted a coke. I called Sister Linda and asked her to go to the store and get a big liter bottle of coke and some ice. When she returned she put some of the ice in a glass and poured some coke over it. She knocked on the bedroom door and said here is your coke Brother. Wilson got up and went to the door and got the coke and thanked Linda for getting it.

He came back and sat on the side of the bed and drank the coke like he was very, very thirsty. He lay down beside me and tried to rub my stomach. I turned my back to him and he kissed my neck. I sat up on the side of the bed and he started tickling me. He knew I can't take it when he start tickling me. I lay back down on the bed and started tickling him too. I tickled him in his arms pit and he quickly gave up. I stop tickling him and he asked for more coke. I got up and went into the kitchen and got him more coke. Sister Linda said I am leaving for school now. I asked her if she had eaten. She said she would eat when she return home from school. She left and I went back into the bedroom and gave Wilson his coke. When he took the coke I went back to the living room and sat down. He followed me into the living room and sat down beside me. He said I know you are still mad at me. I said do you think I am happy about the way you treat me? You ask me out to the nightclub and forget that I am with you…you force me to dance with your friend as if I am a hostess in the club…I told you I didn't want to dance with your chief, but you insisted saying just this one time because he's my boss…maybe I should work in the club and then I could pick who I wanted to dance with…you act as if you want to share me with your friend…I thought you loved me… or maybe you are just saying you love me to pacify me. Your friend couldn't understand why you left our table and forgot about me… you had better stop drinking so much or one day you will wake up and find your friend sleeping with me because you tell me to let him do it…you have to try and control your drinking. I thought if you drink here in the house you would be satisfied, but I see that you are not, you like drinking in the clubs and playing around with the club hostess…you even forget that I am with you when you start drinking a lot…I don't know what to do…what do you want me to do? I couldn't hold the tears back any longer I let it all out. He said take it easy you wouldn't want something to happen to the baby. When he said that I remembered the Doctor told me to try and not get upset, so I took a deep breath and tried to calm down. Mother also had told me about getting upset while I am pregnant. I got up and went to the kitchen to get a glass of water. Wilson followed right behind and asked if I was all right. I got my water and started for the living room, but Wilson guided me back into the bedroom. I wouldn't say one word to him because I was really mad at him and I was afraid if I said something I would start crying again. We sat on the side of the bed. He put his arm around me and held me real tight and told me he was very sorry for asking me to dance with his boss even though I had say I didn't want to. He said I will never ask you to do something that stupid again...I don't know what I was thinking about...I am so sorry I hurt your feeling. Finally I said your drinking is the cause of everything... when we are at home you only drink one or two beers, but when we go out your drinking is completely out of control...you want to drink and be with the club hostess. I started crying again. He said please don't cry; remember you are pregnant. I grab my pillow and tried to hug it, but Wilson put his arms around me and hugged me real tight. He took off his shoes and shirt and continued to hug and kiss me. He wanted to make love, but I didn't want to make love...I thought...why should I make love to him if he doesn't really love me?

He treats me like I am a club hostess. I am tired of trying to be everything he wants me to be...he can go and get him a Hostess from one of the club to do all of his bidding. I have had enough of him pretending that he love me, so he can have me here to make love to. He turned my hand loose and said he would be right back. I didn't say a word. I thought to myself...go ahead and leave I could care less... my baby and I will make it all right. I heard the front door open and close. I didn't get up; I grab my pillow and hugged it. A few minutes later I heard the front door open and close again. A few seconds later I could feel him sit down on the bed. Then I smelled beer. I thought to myself...he went to the store for beer...he can't go for one day without drinking beer...everything I have being telling him about his drinking was useless...he didn't hear a word I said...I was just talking to the wall...he has forgotten everything I said to him. I got up and went into the bathroom. After leaving the bathroom I went into the kitchen to fix me something to eat. I took my food into the living room and sat down to eat. Wilson came in and asked me what I was eating; I told him I was eating beef stew and rice. I asked him if he wanted to eat some. He said he ate on his boat before he came home. He sat down beside me and kissed me on the forehead and asked me if I still love him. I stopped eating and swallowed. Then I said what do you think? He said I just wanted to know if you still love me. I said if I didn't love you do you think I would be doing all these things to please you and make you happy? You know what! I won't try and please you like that anymore...if you want someone to dance with your friend...you dance with them...I don't want their hands all over me I am saving myself for the man I thought love and wanted to protect me. I stopped and looked him squarely in the eye and said don't worry I love you and will stay with you...I will learn your American custom of sharing your girlfriend with your friend... it want take long I am easy to learn. Wilson said please! Can't we try and forget what happened...I know I made a real mess of things and I feel very bad about it...I love you very much. I just looked at him and got up and took my plate into the kitchen and washed the dishes. When I finished with the dishes I went into the bathroom and brushed my teeth. After brushing my teeth I went back into the living room and sat down.

Oh! He said I almost forgot to tell you that I called Smitty your Brother-in-law to check on our marriage request. He said it hadn't crossed his desk yet. He also invited you and I to Sangley Point to spend Thanksgiving with him and Melda. I said when is Thanksgiving Day? He said in two week from today. I said o.k. If that's what you want. He said I would put in for a day leave so we can get there the day before. He was silent for a minute. Then he said if we go to Sangley Point would you promised to return with me? I just looked at him. Then he said please tell me you would return with me. I said if I wanted to leave you I would have being gone and no one would know where I went, so don't give me an ideal...I am tired of what you are doing to yourself and keeping me in the middle of it because I fell in love with you. I don't have a choice as to whether I should or should not come back to Olongapo with you. Do you think I want her to know what's going on between us...you drinking too much and destroying my love and respect for you? I don't want my family to know our business...I am young but I am not stupid enough to involve my family in our business...I will always respect you even if you don't respect my love for you...when I am mad at you I don't act that way around my family because I don't want them to know that we have a problem...you don't have to worry about me not coming back with you...I will always be with you and only you until you sale me to the highest bidder. He said what are you talking about? I just wanted to know if you were coming back with me when we visit Smitty and Melda. I said you are not listening to what I have being saying to you. Is my English so bad you can't understand me? I stop talking and looked at him and thought to myself...Is my English that bad where he can't understand me? Then he asked me if I wanted to go to the movies. I said do I look like I want to go to the movies with you? If you want to go somewhere just leave...forget that I have being talking to you for almost two hours...I know you want to see your girl friend in the club so please leave. I got up and went into the bedroom and closed the door. I thought to myself...if I could speak real good English maybe he would

understand what I am trying to tell him...it's really hard to speak good English...I understand it, but it's hard to speak.

I lay down across the bed again trying to calm down. This is too much excitement for my baby. I started taking deep breath and counting to ten and tried to think about something else. The bedroom door open and he came in and told me we would go to the movies tomorrow. He sat beside me and started hugging and kissing me. He said I love you very much and can't thank of the thought of you leaving me...do you love me too? I said I love you very much too. He almost started crying when I told him I loved him too. We started hugging and kissing and one thing lead to another and before we knew it we were laying in each other arms exhausted and out of breathe. I asked him to get me a glass of water and he jumped right out of bed and got it for me. The water was nice and cold and it helped me to calm down. He got back into bed and held me real tight and told me he loved me again and again. I told him how much I loved him as he continued to kiss me. He kept kissing me all over. His kisses always arouse me and I end up giving in to his wishes. He knew the exact thing to do when I am mad at him to change my mood...he would use his kissing power. Finally his kisses stop and he said sweetheart go to sleep now and don't think too much...I promise you I will control my drinking when we are out...I don't want to lose you or make you mad at me...I also promise to not make you cry again...I love you too much. He repositioned my head on his arm as he tried to relax his body. I closed my eyes and thought to myself...

why is life sometimes cruel…Wilson is a very good man, but he is cruel when he drinks too much? I guess Mother was right when she said you have to balance the good with the bad. I guess I am selfish because I want everything to be good all of the time. Well I guess I can't have everything because I am stuck on Wilson right or wrong good or bad. I will always love him. It is said that love conquers all, so maybe I can conquer his love and attention. I closed my eyes again and this time I went to sleep. Suddenly I was awakened by the sound of fire sirens and a lot of noise the people was making outside. I got up started for the front door to look outside and saw Sister Linda coming in the front door.

I asked her what was going on outside. She said the old market is on fire. I said we had better get ready to move in case the fire reach here. Wilson came into the living room and said don't worry about the fire the Fireman can take care of the fire. I looked at Linda and said just get ready in case the fire reach here. Wilson picked me up and started for the bedroom. He said don't worry I will save you from the fire. He laid me gentle down on the bed and lay down beside me and started kissing and caressing me all over again. I thought to myself…I could not believe this man want to make love again. Suddenly I heard someone banging on our front door it was the owner of the apartment. He said get ready to move in case the fire reach here. Sister Linda came to our bedroom door and knocks and repeated what the apartment owner had said. We got up and got fully dressed and started making plans to move our belonging if the fire reached our apartment. Wilson told me to make sure I put my medicine in my bag. We sat in the living room until about one o, clock the next morning waiting to see what the fire was going to do. Finally we heard from the people outside that the fire was out. They said that the fire department from the Naval Base and volunteers Servicemen helped put the fire out. They also said that the fire had destroyed about half of the market area. We silently thanked God that the fire was out and that it didn't reach our apartment.

Wilson broke the silent and asked if the day was Friday and Sister Linda said yes Brother. He said great! I don't have to go to work. Sister Linda said I am going to Calacapuan today to wash my clothing do you have any dirty clothes you would like for me to wash? I said yes! I will put them in your bag. She said I will probably be gone by the time you wake up tomorrow because it take a while to get enough water to wash at Mother House. Wilson said what are you still doing? You can unpack tomorrow let's go to bed. I went into the bedroom to join him. He was already in bed so I lay down beside him and he wrapped his arms around me. He said you know that I love you? I said I know and I love you too. He said all of the people and the noise outside is gone, now we can relax and go to sleep. I was very happy and content lying in Wilson arms. He said go to sleep. I closed my eyes and fell asleep.

I woke up that Saturday morning around nine o, clock, I felt hungry. Wilson was still asleep. I got up and went into the bathroom and got cleaned up. When I finished and came out Wilson was up and on his way to the bathroom. I told him I was going to start breakfast. How many eggs would he like to eat? He said I would like two eggs scrambled. I scrambled four eggs and fried some spam and went across the street to the store and bought some bread rolls, we call the rolls pandisal. We usually eat either rice or pandisal for breakfast. When I returned Wilson had finished in the bathroom, so I told him we would eat our breakfast in the living room. We were pretty hungry so we ate all of the food except two rolls. Wilson said he prefer eating the bread rolls instead or the sandwich bread. After we finished eating breakfast I went into the kitchen to wash the dishes and clean the kitchen. Wilson sat watching me from the living room clean the kitchen. I turned and asked if he was all right. He said I am all right I just enjoy watching you move around. I said come here and help me wash the dishes even though I had finished. He jumped up and came to the kitchen and looked into the sink and said you have finished already. I said so! And smiled at him. He grabbed me up and carried me to the bedroom. We started kissing and caressing each other; then I remembered the tattoo he had on his arm and I had promised myself I would ask him about it. The tattoo was two hearts with two words in it. I rolled on top of his stomach and asked him about the tattoo. At first he didn't want to answer me. I said I guess this person was very important to you for you to put her name on your arm. He said you want to know…please don't get upset. Before I came to the Philippines and met and fell in love with you I had a girlfriend back home in the United States. I was in love with her. When I joined the Navy I thought she would wait for me, but when I came back home on vacation I wanted to surprise her with the tattoo I had gotten in Hong Kong while I was drinking, but I was the one who got surprised… she had decided not to wait for me…I left mad at the world…I started drinking out of control…everywhere I went I got as many girlfriends as I could even here in the Philippines…when I met you I learned to love and trust a woman again. I said I know about the girlfriends you had here in the Philippines before you met me…I knew one of the girl because she use to come and borrow ten or twelve pesos from me when the Navy ships left and went to sea.

I trusted her because she would bring her boyfriend and his friends to my Money Exchange booth when their ship came in. I knew most of the girl that worked in the Jet and Swan club, because my Mother uses to wash and iron their clothes when they had money. I remembered back when I was in the fourth grade I would accompany my Mother to the Swan club to pick up the clothes from the girls to be washed. My Mother had stopped being a live-in Maid, so she could be home with Sister Linda and me. She said she didn't want Linda or me to end up pregnant like Sister Rose did, so she started taking in washing from the girls that works in the clubs. One of your girlfriends that work in the Swan club was a customer of my Mother. I have known her for quite awhile that why she couldn't believe you would prefer me instead her. When I started worked in the Money Exchange I had to go by the Swan Club to pick up the money for the booth. One day when I came into the club on my way to the back to pick up the money for my booth one of your girlfriend called me over to a corner in the club and told me that she had a chance to be your steady girlfriend…if she had known I was going to meet you she would had agreed to be your steady girlfriend and I would not have met you. She said if she want you to come back to her you would come, because she have more to give you than I have. I told her she was welcome to try and get you back. She really upset me and I felt really bad as I left to go to work that day. That day sitting in the Money Exchange booth I thought to myself…if Wilson like her better than he like me he will miss out on my never ending love for him. Wilson said you never told me about that. I said there are a lot of things I haven't told you about your girlfriends because they were you girlfriends before you met me. Do you remember the time when you, Sister Melda and I were leaving the Swan Club and a girl threw some ice at us? I knew she was one of your girlfriends because you acted as if you didn't know what was going on, but Sister Melda went back and told the girl to stop acting like a fool...your girlfriend that works in the Silver Dollar Club came by my Money Exchange booth one day very upset, she told me she was your steady girlfriend and she wanted me to leave you alone.

Wilson said you know that is not true and he started kissing me trying to shut me up. He knew I was about to get upset and start crying and he didn't want me to be upset. Wilson said I was never serious about any of those girl that worked as club Hostess, I was just having fun, but I am very serious about you and our relationship that why I want to marry you...we are here together kissing and hugging each other and we're not dreaming...pinch me I want to make sure. I said pinch me too and we laugh. He said about the tattoo...I can't do anything about it now...I already have it on my arm, but one day I may be able to get it removed, but for now let's try and forget that it on my arm...it is a part of my pass that should be forgotten...please try and forget it even exist, I know I will try because you are the one that I love. He turned and looked at the clock and said eleven o, clock and I repeated what he said, eleven o, clock...I have to get up and cook some rice, but Wilson held on to me and started kissing me again and I kissed him back. His caressing and hot kisses set me on fire...I was hot enough to cook a pot of rice...finally my body reached fulfillment and let go like a raging wild fire that burned everything in its path. We lay silent in each other arms...Wilson closed his eyes trying to go to sleep...I wanted to lay there and relax, but I had to get up and cook something to eat. I got up and started for the bathroom and Wilson asked where I was going. I told him I was going to cook lunch. He said o.k. I am going to sleep a little while...will you be all right? I said of course! In the kitchen I decided to cook some rice and corn beef. I decided to cook the corn beef American style like Sister Melda taught me. I chopped up some onion and Irish potatoes and cooked it with the corn beef. I hope Wilson will like it because it has potatoes in it. Wilson doesn't like fried dried fish or Philippine vegetables, so corn beef and rice was the only thing left I could prepare for him. When I finished cooking his corn beef and rice and my vegetables and dried fish he was still asleep. I decided to eat and let him sleep, because he seems to be really enjoying his sleep. When I finished eating I decided to go into the living room and crochet for a while. While crocheting I thought to myself…I can't believe that I am making all of these nice designs, I can't wait to start putting them together.

I bet Wilson would like my crochet for the coffee table and I am sure Sister Linda will be proud of my work because she taught me how to do it. All of a sudden I heard noise coming from our bedroom, it was Wilson talking in his sleep, so I went to the bedroom and tried to wake him. He woke up sweating all over. I lay down beside him and asked him what he was dreaming about. He asked me for a glass of water. I went to the kitchen and got him a glass of water and he drunk it all up. I asked him if he wanted some more. He said no! And put the glass on the floor beside the bed. He wanted me to lay beside him on the bed, so I sat on the side of the bed and asked him again about his dream. He said I dreamed you were leaving me. I said where was I going? I am not going anywhere. He said I dreamed you were leaving me for another guy. I said I don't think so, because I love you…maybe you were leaving me instead of me leaving you. He said you are not going to leave me right? I said I am not going to leave you unless you tell me you don't want me anymore. He hugged and kissed me again…I guess he finally realized he was having a bad dream.

I said are you ready to eat now? I will warm your food. He said yes, so I got up and went into the kitchen to prepare his food. I heard Wilson in the living room say hey! That's smell good. I asked him if he wanted to eat his corn beef with bread or rice. He said I would eat it with rice this time. I put some rice in a plate and covered it with stirred fried corn beef. I took the plate into the living room and placed it on the coffee table in front of him. I gave him a coke and asked him if he preferred a beer. He said no! I will drink whatever you give me. He started eating his food and said you made the corn beef hash just like they do it in the can…it is called corn beef hash…this is really a good lunch. I decided to try the corn beef hash and see if it was as good as he said, so I went into the kitchen and made me a corn beef hash sandwich...surprisingly it was very good. I told him I wished I knew how to prepare more American dishes. He said I am satisfied with the food you prepare. I thought to myself...one of these days I will learn to prepare more American dishes for my Wilson.

Wilson said I don't care if you cook me corn beef all of the time just don't leave me...I can't take more hurt and disappointment from the girl that I love...come here and give me a big hug. I came over to him and he pulled me down into his lap and kissed me. We went into the bedroom and sat on the bed because it was softer than the living room furniture. We talked about buying a nicer bedroom set and a living room set when we save enough money. He asked me if there were places in Olongapo City where we could buy furniture on installment. I said yes! There are places all over Olongapo. He said that what we would do as soon as we get married. I thought to myself...when will that be...when my stomach get real big or when I have the baby. Wilson said you haven't changed your mind about marrying me...you still love me and want to marry me? He said I don't know what I will do if the paperwork came back from Sangley Point approved and you decided you don't want to marry me. I said maybe you would change your mind about marrying a Filipino. He said no! I am the one scared and nervous because you are pregnant with our baby and you may decide to leave me. I said let's not talk of leaving each other anymore...my stomach couldn't stand it. He said o.k. Sweetheart, remember you are my life I would always love you... just stay with me. I thought to myself...we want the same thing...to be together forever. He started kissing me over and over again until a cool breeze came through our bedroom window. He said did you feel that? I said yes! We have an electric window that gives us cool air without a fan...that's why we stay so cool in our bedroom. He said the two building on each side of our apartment is directing the cool breeze into our apartment. I said that's good because it's very hot out there, but we always get a cool breeze most of the time and that's nice. Wilson said it keep us cool while we are making love. As I snuggled in his arms I said I want to take a nap. He said go ahead I will watch over you while you sleep. When I woke up around two that afternoon Wilson had fallen asleep. I got up and went into the bathroom to see if the water was on so I could save some for my bath.

The water was on but the pressure was real low, so I put my bucket under the faucet to catch what little water that was dripping out. I went into the living room to wait for the water pressure to build up. Around five o, clock I heard my bucket overflowing in the bathroom so I hurried to turn off the faucet. I decided I would take a shower while the water was on. I quickly undressed and got into the shower. I heard Wilson opening the door to the bathroom. He said I am coming in to join you. We started splashing around in the shower and before long we were kissing and caressing. Wilson decided that the shower was too small for what he had in mind, so he carried me into the bedroom and the next thing I knew was I was sweating all over again. We spent that Saturday in and out of bed and we promised each other that we would love and stay together for better or worse.

Sunday morning I got up and cooked our breakfast. Wilson got up and made our bed. I tried to get him to leave it for me, but he said that he has to fix his bed on his boat, so he can fix our bed too. We ate our breakfast of egg, spam and rolls. Wilson promised to take me out for lunch and a movie. He helped me put the dishes in the sink and I washed them. After finishing the dishes I joined him in the living room. I pick up my crochet basket and started crocheting. Wilson looked at the flower design I was making and said they were very nice and he was glad I had found something to do while he was away. He said you learn very quickly that will look very nice when you finish it, but you need to put it away now that I am home...I need all of your attention. I said are you jealous of my crocheting? I just learned how to do this so I can decorate our apartment and have something to do when you leave me home alone...I get real lonely when you are not here, but you are right, I will put up my crochet until you leave. I put my crochet away and started tickling him, but he said uncle right away so I would stop. He picked me up and carried me into the bedroom and laid me gently on the bed. He started kissing and caressing me. I said let's take a shower and get ready to go out for lunch. He said I want to play. I said if we play we would not go out because we will be too tired. He said that's o.k. I still want to play. I thought to myself...what's wrong with this man...he want to make love more and more all of the time...I am not complaining, but

I can't help thinking what he will do when my stomach get real big…
will he turn to his girlfriends in the club?

He suddenly stopped kissing me and said what's wrong? I said
nothing…I was just thinking about something. He sat up on the side
of the bed and said go take your shower so we can go out. I said
are you sure? He said yes! Go ahead and I will follow you. When I
finished I called out to Wilson and told him he had better hurry and
take his shower before they turn off the water. When he came out of
the shower I was still towel drying my hair. He came over to me and
kissed me on my shoulder and said sweetheart you smell real good
and he pushed me down on the bed and started kissing and caressing
me. I said hold on tiger you are always attacking your prey…take it
easy…shouldn't you go back and take a cold shower? He said I don't
need a cold shower you can take care of me. Once again I gave in
and happily accommodated him. We laid completely exhausted in
each other arms. I said forget about going out I don't have enough
strength to move around. He said let's go to sleep. I knew then that he
was as exhausted as I was. We went to sleep I don't know how long
we slept, but I woke up when I heard the front door open and close.
I got up and covered Wilson and went into the living room. When I
walked into the living room Sister Linda said it's me…what did you
cook? I told her I had not cooked anything Wilson and I had been
sleeping all day. She said do you have any clothes hangers? I want to
hang my uniforms up so they want be wrinkle. I said I have plenty of
hangers in my closet…I will get you some. I went to my closet and got
clothes hangers and gave them to her. I said when you finish hanging
up your uniform would you like to go to the market and get some
cooked noodles for our lunch? She said yes, it's pass lunchtime and I
am getting hungry. I said what time is it? She said it is almost one o,
clock. I said buy enough for three because Wilson will be eating too.
When she left for the market I went back into the bedroom. Wilson
asked whom was I talking to. I told him Sister Linda had returned
from Calapacuan and I had sent her to get food for our lunch. He
said that's good! I am feeling hungry anyway. I told him I was going
across the street to the store for coke and ice. He said I guess I should
get up too I have being sleeping almost all day. Before I got back to
the apartment I saw Linda getting out of a tricycle at the apartment.

She saw me coming and told me she had bought the big noodles, the one Wilson likes. We went into the apartment and took the food into the kitchen and fixed our plates. Wilson was in the dining room, so we decided to eat lunch in the dining room.

Sister Linda and I started eating using our folk. Wilson said you could eat with your hand if you like don't worry about me I know it a Philippine custom to eat with your hand. Sister Linda was embarrassed to use her hand so she kept using her folk. As we sat silently eating lunch Wilson broke the silence and said why don't the three of us go to the movies tonight? I said yes and looked at Linda. She said yes I would like to go to the movies with you. Wilson said the movies start around five so we had better leave the apartment by four thirty. Sister Linda and I agreed that we would be ready to go at four thirty. Wilson finished eating his noodle and said he liked the noodles very much. I said I like the way they cook the noodles in the Shangri La restaurant best, but these run a close second. Sister Linda and I washed the dishes and cleaned the kitchen. I decided to take my shower now so I wouldn't be rushing later. When I finished my shower and came into the bedroom Wilson said let leave right away they may have a Chinese movie we can watch until the next one come on. I went out and told Sister Linda to get ready and I came back into the bedroom and finished dressing. Finally we were dressed and ready to go, so we went out and caught a jeepney to Magsaysay drive where all of the movies are located. We had the jeepney to drive slowly down the street so we could check the movie billboards for new movies. We saw a nice Tagalog movie showing at one of the movie house, but Wilson couldn't understand enough Tagalog to watch it. We finally stopped the jeepney in front of the Grand Theatre and got out. We were early so we decided to go shopping in a nearby gift shop. We looked around and priced some of the items in the store. Wilson said Christmas is next month this is a good time to shop around. I looked at some of the embroidery handkerchief that I wanted to get Wilson for Christmas. I found a set that I liked very much...I promised myself I would get it as soon as I got the money. Wilson looked at the time and said we had better go now it's almost time for the movie to start. We arrived at the movie and purchased our ticket and the power went out. We stood in the movie lobby waiting for the power to come back on. Sister Linda said this is my first time coming with you guys I guess I am bad luck.

I said we're still lucky because we're here in the lobby we could be stuck inside the theater and it is very hot in there with the power off. One of the movie's employee said that they are working to start the emergency generator it should be working momentary. About fifteen minutes later we heard the generator come on. We decided to wait in the lobby until the generator started running smoothly. We went to the balcony to find our seats. We decided to set close to the stairs in case the generator stop running. Wilson said don't be scared I am here...do you want snacks and something to drink? Sister Linda said no she was still full from lunch. When we were about half way through the movie the generator started acting as if it was going to stop running. Finally the generator did stop and everyone was very upset. We sat quietly watching the people lighting up their cigarette lighter and matches. Someone finally said the power is back on and we will have the movie going again in a few minutes. After what seem like ten or fifteen minutes the movie came on again. We watched the whole movie and left in a hurry because we wanted to get home before the power went off again. On our way back to the apartment Wilson asked me if we had candles at home. I said yes. Wilson had the jeepney to take us all of the way to our front door. We got out and went inside. Sister Linda hurriedly got our candles and matches and put them out so they would be ready if the power went out again. I put candles and matches in my bedroom, so I would be ready when the blackout come. We always call it the black out when the power goes off. Sister Linda busied herself fixing her mat on the floor so that it will be in place if the power goes off. Wilson decided to go to the store for beer and he asked us if we wanted something from the store. I told him to bring a loaf of bread so we could make sandwiches. I told Sister Linda when Wilson returned with the bread I wanted her to make us a liver worth sandwich. She asked if she could make her a peanut butter sandwich too. I said fix whatever you want just make me a liver worth sandwich. Wilson returned with beer, bread and ice. Linda were happy when she saw that Wilson brought ice too. She said now we can finish the rest of the coke. I asked Wilson if he wanted a sandwich, he said yes, but only one.

I fixed Wilson sandwich and Linda fixed ours. We sat down to eat our sandwiches. I asked Sister Linda how did she like her sandwich. She said peanut butter and liver worth does not mix; it is the worst tasting sandwich I ever had. I laugh saying that's what you get when you try to be different...drink your coke it will kill the bad taste. Wilson said what are you two laughing about? I told him Sister Linda had made her a liver worth sandwich with peanut butter on it and she said it taste very bad. We finished eating our sandwiches and started preparing for bed. Wilson and I went into the bedroom and I started undressing to put my nightgown on, but Wilson said don't put it on yet. I instantly knew what was coming next. We made love just like it was our first time. The only thing I remembered saying before I went to sleep was make sure you set the alarm clock.

The next morning Wilson woke up around four thirty tossing and turning and woke me up. I asked him what was wrong, but he couldn't figure out why he woke up so early. He kissed me and told me to go back to sleep. He sat on the side of the bed for a while and finally decided to get up and get dressed for work. Just as he got up the alarm went off and he grab it and turned it off. He said he was sorry he forgot to turn the alarm off when he decided to get up. He kissed me goodbye and started for the bedroom door. I told him to be careful out in the street. He said don't worry everyone is up and about now and on their way to work. I said be careful anyway. I followed him to the front door and looked outside; I could see a lot of people gathering around the booths in the market area waiting for them to open up. I thought to myself...they will be using this area everyday now for the market booths now that the fire had destroyed the main section...this area was only suppose to be used on Wednesday and Sundays now it look like it will be every day. I closed the door and went back to my room. I got back into bed and went back to sleep. Around seven o, clock Sister Linda woke me up and asked if I was going to the market with her. I said you can go ahead without me this morning, but make sure the fruit and vegetables are fresh and get fish too. I said Linda before you go please go across the street to the store and get some bread rolls for breakfast. She said o.k. And left.

I heard her a few minutes later coming back with the rolls. I decided to just laid around in the bed for a while. Sister Linda was gone about an hour before she returned with fresh fruit and vegetables. She started telling me about all of the changes they were making to the market as they rebuild it. She said they have everything; shoes, clothing, house ware and all kinds of fruit and vegetables. She said they even have several small restaurants where you can order freshly cook food on display...you need to go and see it. I asked her if they had fresh cooked chicken soup. She said yes they have that too. I said would you like to go back and eat breakfast in the market. She said yes smiling and shaking her head. I went into the bathroom and got cleaned up and came out and dressed. We left for the market. When we arrived it was just as Sister Linda had explained, everything was laid out so neat. We went to the small restaurant and ordered our breakfast, I ordered the chicken soup that I was craving for and Sister Linda ordered what she wanted. When we finished our breakfast we walked through the market and admired all of the nice things they had for sale. Finally we were on our way back to the apartment. When we arrived Sister Linda went into the kitchen to clean the fish and vegetables. I went into my bedroom to finish straightening it up before helping her prepare the food she had brought home from the market earlier. After we finished getting the food ready to be cooked for lunch I went to the living room and started to crochet. When Sister Linda started cooking the vegetables and frying the fish she decided to check on me and see how far alone I was with my crocheting. She brought her crochet basket alone to show me what she was doing. She took out the crochet she was working on and showed it to me. I told her how nice it looked and that I wanted to crochet that pattern next. She said when the design are finished you have to soak them in hot starch or sugar water so they can be shaped. They are to be shape before they dry and after drying you will see and like the result. Sister Linda said it takes time to finish each piece, but you will like it when it's finished. Well I said, you not going to be happy when your fish get burned. She said the fish and ran into the kitchen.

I could hear her laughing, so I asked what she was laughing about. She said I have burned the fish on one side. I said don't worry we are going to put it in the pot on top of the vegetables. I continued to crochet until around ten o, clock then I put away my crochet and went into the kitchen to help Sister Linda finish cooking. Finally the food was cooked. Sister Linda said the food really smells good. I said yes it does, you can eat now if you want to. She said no not now, but the smell of the food really does make you hungry. I said I know, because when I am at Mother's house and she start cooking the smell of the food always makes me hungry. Sister Linda came back into the living room and we sat crocheting and making small talk. Sister Linda said my project is due before the Christmas vacation I really hope that I'll have it finished by then. I said don't worry you will have it finished by then...oh! Don't forget that we will be going to Sangley Point to spend Thanksgiving with Sister Melda and Brother Smitty. She said that's next week! I said yes, November 23, American Thanksgiving Day.

Sister Linda and I continued crocheting and discussing the designs. I told her I liked the design she was working on and I was going to copy it when I finish the design I was working on. She said don't worry when I finish it and my teacher grade it I will bring it home and you can copy it...I will give it to you if you want it because it only a project to me...I don't need it. I said that's good I want have to read the instruction from the book. I think I will stop for a while my eyes are tired. Sister Linda said your arms and fingers get tired too...that's the problem you will have with it until you get used to doing it. I looked at the time it was eleven thirty. I said it's lunchtime anyway, so we got up and fixed our plates and came back into the living room to eat. We only cooked one fish so I took the head half of the fish and left the tail part for Linda. We both like the head part of the fish, but I was pregnant and had first choice. We decided next time to cut the fish down the middle and cook it in two parts so we both would have part of the head and tail of the fish. The idea of cutting the fish down the middle and cooking it really had an appeal to us, so we finished eating our lunch and cleaned the kitchen.

As I left to go back into the living room I told Sister Linda to check the water and see if it's still has pressure and if so, we need to go ahead and take our showers and save some water for later when the city turn it off. We took our showers and came out to towel dry our hair. Sister Linda said I want to get my hair cut before we go to Sangley Point. I said your hair is very short now. She said I like my hair short why don't you get yours cut? I said I might get the ends clipped Wilson like for me to wear my hair very long. Sister Linda finished drying her hair and said she was going to take a nap until around two thirty. I said o.k. It's twelve o, clock now. I got up and went into my room and continued towel drying my hair. I sat on the side of the bed drying my hair then I started thinking to myself... my hair reaches all of the way to my waist maybe I should get it cut to shoulder length...I will ask Wilson when he come to let me get it cut tomorrow...that Suave shampoo makes my hair smell fresh and manageable...Wilson always like the smell of my hair. I closed my eyes and drifted off to sleep. I was awakened by the sound of the front door opening. I jumped out of bed and hurried into the living room to see what was going on. I was hoping it was Wilson coming home, but it was only Sister Linda putting out the garbage. She said she was leaving early to meet with her classmates to discuss their projects. Wilson said he would be home around one o, clock but it was almost three; I wonder what has happened to him. Sister Linda said I am leaving now I will see you tonight. I said o.k. Remember to take your small flashlight just in case the power goes off tonight. I decided to wait for Wilson in the living room, so I got a couple of pillows and stretched out on the hardwood couch. After a few minutes I decided to go back into my bedroom because the couch was feeling harder by the minute. I stretched out across my bed and started thinking to myself about Wilson...where is he...is he all right...maybe he had to work late...what happened to him? It's really hard for me when he doesn't come home when he promise. I wish we were married so I could at least go on the base and check to see if he is all right. I thought...if something happen to him what would I do...what would happen to me and my baby...the paperwork for our marriage is driving me crazy, it is taking a very long time to come back...sometimes I think Wilson has changed his mind about getting married...oh, forget it, I can't do anything about it anyway.

I got up and got my crochet basket and started crocheting. I am glad I have learned to crochet, because it takes my mind off Wilson for a while. I had just finished eating my dinner around five o, clock when Wilson came in the door with two Filipino a man and a woman. He introduced them to me as husband and wife or boyfriend and girlfriend; I really wasn't paying attention to what he was saying, because he was drunk again. The guy said this is my boss I work on his boat and if anyone attempts to hurt him I will shoot him. He pulled up his shirt to show his gun in his belt. I became very nervous because I don't like guns. I told the guy he had better hide his gun because there are Gangs in our neighborhood. The girl said I told him to leave the gun at home. The guy said my boss is a good man and I want to help him anyway that I can. I brought him home so he wouldn't be in danger...if you have a problem just tell my boss and I will take care of it. Wilson was sitting in the chair and wanting to lie down, because he was very drunk. The guy said we are going to go now; I will see you tomorrow boss. Wilson got up to accompany them to the door and almost lost his balance, so I got up and closed the door and took Wilson to the bedroom. He lay down on the bed fully dressed, so I took off his shoes. I started feeling upset and thinking to myself...we have been doing real good for a few weeks... he had promised not to get drunk...today he is not only came home drunk, but he brought Gang members from another Barrio home with him...I have told him he have to be careful about whom he associate with...I don't know what's wrong with him...he never thinks about me or what I tell him...I think he only think about drinking...he can't understand that the only people carry a gun in Olongapo City is; Policeman, Security Guard and Gangsters...I tell him over and over to watch whom he associate with, because he could in up in trouble or the Morgue. In the Philippines people feel sorry for a person and his wife or girlfriend if he or she drinks too much. I think that's one of the reason no one has try to rob Wilson on his way home...they figure he doesn't have any money, because he has spend it getting drunk. I felt sorry for myself because the extra money he is suppose to spend on me and the apartment goes to drinking and girl in the bars. It's very upsetting to me, but it is his money because he worked for it and should be able to do whatever he wants to with it. I waited in the living room for Sister Linda because I wanted to tell her that I wanted her to go with me to Calapacuan the next day. Finally she arrived and agreed that we would leave early the next day. I went into the bedroom and put my nightgown on, set the alarm clock and lay down beside Wilson. Then I started thinking...why Wilson never think about me and the promises he makes about him stopping drinking…didn't he know that bringing a man here with a gun would upset me after all I have told him about Gangsters in Olongapo City? My stomach started hurting, so I got my pillow and hugged it tight to my stomach I hope my baby will be all right. I guess my stomach is acting up because things have being so upsetting to me today. I tried to calm down and relax so I could fall asleep. Finally I did fall asleep.

Early the next morning the alarm clock went off right on time and Wilson got up and started dressing for work. I got up and used the bathroom and I noticed that I had blood in my panties. I decided not to tell Wilson; because he can't take care of himself I know he wouldn't know what to do about what's going on with me. I also decided I wouldn't tell Linda either. I went back to bed without mumbling a word to Wilson. When he finished dressing he tried to kiss me goodbye; I didn't respond I only looked at him. I could tell that he was suffering from a hangover as he made his way out the door. As soon as he left I woke up Sister Linda and told her I wanted to go to Calapacuan to see Mother and eat breakfast at her house. Sister Linda said Vicky it's five o, clock in the morning and I am still sleepy. I said get up now you can go back to sleep when we get to Calapacuan. Sister Linda finally got up and I went into the bathroom and got cleaned up. I packed extra under clothes in a bag in case I start bleeding again. I asked Sister Linda for an additional sanitary napkin just to be safe. She asked what I was going to do with a sanitary napkin; I told her I just wanted one. She just shook her head and went and got me one. Finally we were on our way to Calapacuan.

When we arrive at Mother's house everyone were sleep except Mother and she wanted to know why we had come so early. She said your Brother Etong and Gina is still sleep. Sister Linda said I told you it was too early to be coming here. She found her a pillow and lay down beside Mother on the Mat. I decided that was a good ideal so I found me a pillow and lay down on the other side of Mother. Mother said what's going on with you two? Sister Linda said I don't know what's going on with Vicky; she asked me for a sanitary napkin early this morning. Mother almost jumped up to a sitting position and asked me if I was bleeding. I said only a little bit. Mother told

Linda to get up and get the coconut oil from the cabinet and bring two more pillows. Mother put the extra pillows under my feet and started massaging my stomach with the coconut oil. She asked why I didn't see a Doctor in Olongapo City; I said I didn't find out until I got up to use the bathroom this morning. Mother said I hope this doesn't cause a problem with the baby…did you do any heavy lifting yesterday? I said yes, Sister Linda made me work caring my crochet basket. Sister Linda said your crochet basket is not heavy. Mother said stop joking this is a serious matter…has you gotten mad or real upset lately? I almost told her about Wilson bringing the guy home that was carrying a gun, but I said no. She said I am taking you to the Doctor when they open up around nine today…until then I want you to stay right here and relax on this mat. Linda said I am going to relax here too.

All of the talking woke Brother Etong, so he got up and put his mat away. I said see their Linda you have woke up Brother Etong. Brother Etong just smiled as he put his mat and pillow away. Mother told Brother Etong to bring firewood after he get washed up. I started to get up so I could go to the bathroom. Mother said where are you going? I said to the bathroom. She said wait I will get you a pan to go in because I want to see if you are still bleeding. I used the pan and there was only a trace of blood in it. Mother said I want you to lay with your feet elevated until it's time to go and see the Doctor. She rubbed my stomach again and told me to continue to relax and don't think too much. Mother went into the kitchen and started cooking breakfast. I asked her why Gina was here. She said I told you to try and relax and not worry about what going on here…your Sister Rose left Gina her for a while. I didn't say another word I just closed my eyes, held my stomach and started praying that my baby will be all right. I really didn't want to lose my baby because the Father makes me worry all of the time…I think I will stay with my Mother for a while. I closed my eyes and fell asleep. A few minutes later I felt Mother shaking my shoulder. She said I want you to set up and drank this ginger root tea it will warm up your stomach. I sat up and started to sip the tea. I heard someone say what you are drinking. I turned around and saw Gina; I said I thought you was asleep…I am drinking hot ginger root tea. She said that's yucky; I don't like ginger.

I said o.k. Gina I will get you some milk when we go to the market. She said yes I like milk as she went into the kitchen to talk to Mother. She said Grandma what are you cooking. Mother said I am cooking rice so you can eat...I have carnation milk in the can would you like for me to fix some for you? When Mother gave her the milk she said Grandma this is oval tine my Mom fix this for me at home. As I listened to the conversation between the two, I thought to myself...Gina has learned to talk real good. Lying there on the mat I started to think about a lot of things...Chico...where is Chico? I asked Mother where were Chico. She said someone cut his leash and let him go and she didn't have any ideal as to who let him go. I turned and saw Brother Etong coming in the door carrying a bucket of water. Sister Linda must have heard him come in because she got up and put away her mat and pillow. I said Sister Linda give me your pillow I want to hug it for a while. Mother said it's time to eat, so all of the food was put on the floor near my mat so I could reach it. Mother cooked rice, dried fish and eggs for our breakfast. Brother Etong sat beside Gina and helped her remove the bones from the fish. Gina said I don't like onions. Mother said I didn't put onion in the eggs only in the fried rice. We finished our breakfast and Mother said we would leave for the Doctor office around eight thirty, so we would be the first one there. After eating I wanted to brush my teeth before seeing the Doctor, but I left my toothbrush at the apartment. I asked Sister Linda to go outside and get me a branch from the Guava tree, so I could fashion me a toothbrush. Brother Etong signaled to me that he would go and get it. I smiled and thanked him. He returned a few minutes later with a piece of a branch cut about four inches long. He had fashioned one end of the branch so it would easy flare out when you scrub your teeth. I took the branch and wet it and put salt on it and commenced brushing my teeth. Gina said that's not a toothbrush my Mom uses that to spank me on my legs. I said Mother did you hear what Gina said. She said yes and I am going to talk to your Sister Rosie when she come to pick up Gina...now I know why Gina is so happy when she is here...she never ask for her Mother.

Finally it was time for us to leave for the Doctor's office. When the Doctor saw me and asked what happened I told him I got scared and upset last night and when I woke up this morning I notice blood on my panty. The Doctor examined me and gave me a shot in my bottom and told me to take it easy and try not to get upset...if your husband is running around let him do it...you need to take care of your baby and yourself.

I was surprised that he knew what was going on with me. He continued saying I know what's going on out in the street around here...clubs and plenty of girls...you can't let this bother you if you want to have a good pregnancy...just take a deep breath and try and stay calm and remember this is your first pregnancy and you have to be careful...come back if you start bleeding again or if anything else happens. Mother met me at the Doctor door and asked the Doctor what was wrong with me. He told her I just need to take it easy...I gave her a shot she will be all right. We left the Doctor office for the jeepney stand to get a ride home, but I started to get real dizzy and perspiring a lot. Mother took me back to the Doctor office. She told him that I had become real dizzy and started perspiring a lot. The Doctor said I am sorry I forgot to tell her to sit for a while before she left because of the shot...she will be all right there no need to worry...let her sit there in the waiting room for fifteen or twenty minutes before you leave. We took a seat in the waiting room. Mother said sit here for a while I am going to the market and will come back and get you as soon as I finish shopping. I said I would be all right Mother I am here in the Doctor Office. She left and went to the nearby market and returned just about the time I started to feeling myself again. We left and caught a jeepney home. On our way home she gave me a boil banana to eat. Mother bought beef neck bone, cabbage, potatoes, onion, dried fish and carnation milk from the market. She took the food in the house and started preparing it for our lunch. I sat at the kitchen table and watched Mother prepare the food. Sister Linda and Gina were next door at my Brother Celino's house. Mother told me I should lie down and relax for a while. I thought about it and decided it was a good idea, so I got a mat and pillow and before I could spread my mat out Brother Celino, his wife, Sister Rose, Sister Linda and Gina came in. I guess they smelled the food cooking. I just sit down on my mat. Sister Linda asked what the Doctor say was wrong with me. I told her the Doctor said everything was all right and I should take it easy because this is my first pregnancy and sometimes the first one is bad.

Brother Celino wife said that why I don't do very much at our house I let Celino do the washing. I said Brother Celino washing clothes really surprise me. Brother Celino said yes I wash our clothes; I just find a big rock in the water stream and put the clothes on it and hit them until they are clean. Everyone laughed at Brother Celino. Brother Etong came in the door carrying firewood and looking a little puzzle as to what was going on. Mother said don't anyone leave because we are going to eat in a few minutes. Brother Etong looked at me very sad and pointed at my stomach. I said the Doctor said the baby is all right. He put a big smile on his face in approval. I knew Brother Etong was very concern about my baby and me and I made sure he understood that everything was all right. Mother said the food is ready. Brother Celino and Sister Linda went into the kitchen to help her bring the food to our circle so everyone could eat. Everyone started eating. Mother brought me a cup of beef broth she said the broth was good for my baby and me. I drink the beef broth it was very good. Brother Celino said he was taking his wife to visit her relatives in Antipolo, Rizal before she gets to far alone in her pregnancy, but he wasn't sure when they would return. His wife said she wanted to have her baby here maybe they want stay too long. I got another cup of Mother Broth and drink it as I rested on my mat it was very good; I always eat a lot when Mother is doing the cooking. Sister Linda started washing the dishes, Brother Etong took the leftover food outside to the dog; and brother Celino and his wife left and went home next door. I decided to stay for a while longer, so I told Sister Linda to go ahead without me because she had to go to school. She said she wanted to stay a little while longer too. I decided to relax for a while on the mat, but Gina came over and asked for the pillow. Brother Etong signaled to her that he was going to get her a pillow. Sister Linda came over to me after washing the dishes and said that if we left by two o, clock that afternoon she would still have time to go to school. I said o.k. If I feel better we will leave then. I noticed Brother Etong watching out of the window as if he waiting to see someone coming.

I remember doing that when I sat at the window waiting for Wilson…I remember feeling very lonely…here I go again…I better stop or I will be sick again thinking so much. All of a sudden Brother

Etong jumped up and started trying to get my attention as he pointed out the window. Sister Linda went over to the window and looked out; she turned around and said Wilson is coming Vicky. I didn't get up from my mat I just sat there and thought to myself...why does he always follow me...He always manage to make me upset enough to leave and come here...sometimes I think he want me to lose the baby...one day he is as nice as can be and the next day he is bad...I don't know what to think. Brother Etong went outside and met Wilson and said hello and went next door to Brother Celino's house. Wilson came and said hello to Mother and took a seat at the kitchen table. Then he turned and saw me sitting on the mat in the corner, so he got up and came over and kissed me. Sister Linda said hi to Wilson and took Gina outside. Mother told Wilson in Tagalog that I had been bleeding and she took me to see the Doctor. Wilson only understood the word Doctor and he immediately asked me what Mother was trying to tell him about a Doctor. I said she is telling you that I was bleeding this morning and she took me to see the Doctor. He said what is wrong with you? I said I am pregnant and because this is my first pregnancy it is very sensitive...the Doctor told me not to get upset with my husband even though he is running around with the girls in the clubs...I didn't tell him about us, he act as though he could read my mind...if you don't want to have this baby just keep doing what you're doing...bringing people into our house with guns. He said I am so sorry I have put you through all of this...making you angry and everything...I promise I will be more thoughtful. Where did you find that Filipino you brought home with you last night? He said that guy works on my Tugboat as a houseboy...he keep the boat clean. When he flashed his gun I got real scared and upset...I really don't know what to think about you...every two or three days it's always something to upset me. Maybe you should return to Olongapo City and leave me here with my Mother...I want to have my baby...I don't want to get upset with you and lose my baby.

He said when I am drinking I don't think very clearly like the time I told you to have an abortion that was crazy...I love you and our unborn baby and I want our baby to be born healthy I don't know whether you believe me or not, but I think about you and the baby all of the time...I promise you I will control my drinking. I said you are not trying hard enough, so just leave me her and when the baby is born you can come by and visit it when you are not running around in the clubs. Mother came out of the kitchen and said remember what the Doctor told you about trying to relax and not getting upset. Wilson asked me what did my Mother said to me. I said my Mother told me to remember the Doctor told me to relax and don't get upset. Wilson said please don't get upset so your Mother want be upset with me. I said my Mother don't know that I am mad at you…I don't' tell my family my problems they have their own problem to worry about… why should I involve them in our problems? I didn't tell anyone about me bleeding Linda figured out what was happening with me when I asked her for a sanitary napkin. She couldn't wait to tell Mother what had happened. Mother thinks I have being lifting something heavy or doing too much cleaning in the apartment. I haven't told them the real reason I was bleeding…you being drunk and bringing a man to our apartment with a gun. He didn't know what to say he just sit down on the wooden box beside me and buried his face in his hands. Sister Linda and Gina walked in the door after returning from the store; they brought coke, ice and candy. Gina asked me if I wanted some candy. I said no and she asked Wilson if he wanted a piece of candy. Wilson said yes thank you very much. Sister Linda said in Tagalog, it is two o, clock Vicky are we going home now? I said go back to the apartment and go to school. She said I am waiting for you. Wilson said what did Linda say to you? I said she asked if I was going home now so she can go to school. Wilson said please let's go home I will take care of you…I will feed you in the bed…you will not have to get up. I said I could do all of that myself…the Doctor told me not to get mad and upset. I am mad at you, so you and Linda go back to Olongapo City… so she could go to school and you can do your running around. Mother came in the room and said Vicky when you get home make sure you buy beef neck bone and vegetable and make you some beef broth and drink plenty of it.

Wilson thinking my Mother was mad said now she finally figured out what going on and is mad at me. I smiled as I looked at him and said my Mother is not mad at you or anyone else she is trying to get me to go home too…she want me to drink plenty of beef broth. Wilson turned to Mother smiling and said o.k. Give Vicky plenty of broth. She said yes, plenty of broth. He said please let's go home before your Mother get mad for real. I told Sister Linda we were leaving now so she would have time to get ready for school when we arrive in Olongapo City. Don't forget the plastic bag with my clothes in it; I want to take it back with us. Mother came over and kissed me on the forehead and said now don't get upset with Wilson. I was surprised when she said that and I wanted to tell her that I was not upset with Wilson, but I knew she had figured out what was going on so I let it go. I just said goodbye to her and everybody else as I walked to the door. Brother Etong touched my shoulder and pointed to me and down at my stomach and gestured for me to take care of my baby and myself. I said o.k. I will. As we left for the jeepney stop Wilson held on to my hand as if he would never let it go. Mother and everyone else was smiling and waving goodbye to us. We caught a jeepney and had to take a seat in the back; I was very surprised when I didn't smell strong body odor from the passenger in front. When you have the smell of gasoline and body odor mixed it almost is unbearable. Wilson continued to hold my hand in the jeepney; I tried to slip it away but he held on tight and kissed me on the cheek. When we arrived in Olongapo City we hailed a tricycle to ride to our apartment. Wilson and Sister Linda couldn't decide who would ride on the back of the tricycle behind the driver. I said I don't have time for this... let Sister Linda ride on the back so we can hurry and get to the apartment. As soon as we arrive at the apartment I went straight to the bedroom and got into the bed. I knew Sister Linda was going to school so I asked her if she had money to buy what she need at school. She assured me that she had enough. I said o.k.

I will see you when you return tonight. Wilson came into the bedroom and asked if I need anything. I stared at him for a moment then I said I don't need anything at all...if you want to leave go ahead I know you can't wait to leave...do whatever you want to do...I just want to be alone...I don't want to think about anything. He said please don't get mad at me. I turned away and didn't say a word. He lies down beside me and put his arm around me like he really cared about what's going on with me. I said to myself...now that he knows that I have to take it easy for a few day and can't make love...I know he can't wait to have a beer or go to the club...he wants to make love all of the time…let's see what he is going to do next…maybe tomorrow he will sneak out and see his girlfriend…I hope she doesn't give him a sickness and he bring it home to me…he think I believe all of his lies…I had better stop thinking and remember what the Doctor said. Wilson broke his silence and said sweetheart, and before he could finish I said yes you can go and get you some beer I don't want to get up I want to lay here and relax. He said no I don't want a beer right now; I want to know if you would like for me to get you something to eat from the restaurant. I said you want to get something to eat…no! You want to leave and go somewhere and get drunk…will you please go and leave me alone before I get mad and upset. I told you before we left my Mother's house to just leave me there and you could go and do your running around. Now you have me here at home…what do you want me to do? Please just go and leave me alone. I hug my pillow and turned my back. He turned me around and pulled the pillow out of my arms and threw it to the floor. He held me very tight and started kissing me…he told me how much he loved me and asked me to forgive him and give him another chance to prove his love to me…he can't take it when I am mad at him. I said please shut up I don't want to hear anymore of your lies; I don't want to get upset again…I am trying very hard to understand what's happening to our relationship one day I am happy and the next I am sad and it's all because of the things you are doing…you're destroying our relationship, so please be quiet or just leave and do whatever you like.

I got up to use the bathroom and he got up too. He asked me over and over what was wrong; I told him I just wanted to use the bathroom. When I got into the bathroom I decided to change my sanitary napkin and I was very happy that I had not been bleeding anymore. When I returned to the bedroom he was sitting on the side of the bed; I went to the other side of the bed and sit down. He turned to me and started pleading his case again. He said that I was the most important thing in his life and he was sorry for causing me to get sick. I said to myself…do I need this…he always say he is sorry, but as soon as he start drinking he does it all over again. As I lay back down on the bed I turned my back to him and closed my eyes trying to go to sleep. He scooted over to my side of the bed and put his arms around me and kissed my cheek. He said I know I have done some stupid things…I am sorry and I will try even harder to control my drinking. I didn't say a word I just tuned him out and fell asleep.

When I woke up I realize I had my leg on top of his and hugging him as I normally do when I sleep. I also realized I was supposed to be mad at him, so I removed my leg from on top of his. Then I noticed he was awake and watching me. He pulled me back into his embrace and kissed me. I said I have to cook it five o, clock now. He said no you're not going to cook I will go and get us something to eat…what do you want to eat? I said I want to eat Pancit with the big noodles. Go to the Shangri La restaurant for the food. He got up and got dressed and left. I got up and went to the bathroom and checked my sanitary napkin; I was not bleeding, so I went back to the bedroom and stacked all of the pillows together and reclined on them as I lay in bed. As soon as I got comfortable my stomach started to hurt. I thought to myself…what's wrong with me now? I removed the extra pillow and tried to lie still hoping the pain would go away. I lay quietly on the bed rubbing my stomach. Finally Wilson returned with the food; he sensed that something was wrong and he started quizzing me. When I finally got a word in I told him I was all right except my stomach was hurting a little and the Doctor told me it would happen every so often. After he calmed down he put the food on the coffee table in the living room. He asked if I wanted to go to see the Doctor.

I said no and explained to him again what the Doctor had said. He asked if I wanted to eat in the bedroom I told him I would get up and eat in the living room with him. As soon as I came in and sit down he asked if I would like a coke to drink with my meal because he was going across the street to get him a beer. I said I would drink water with my meal. He said are you sure you don't want a coke? I didn't answered I just said to myself…I knew he couldn't go very long without a beer…I am tired of hearing beer, beer…what's with that beer? He came back with two beers and we started eating our dinner. The Pancit noodles was really good; he brought enough for three people so I put some aside for Sister Linda to eat when she come home from school. We finished our dinner and Wilson said you know we're suppose to go to Sangley Point this coming Thursday to celebrate Thanksgiving with Melda…do you think you will be all right to travel that far? I said yes we would be riding a bus not walking. He said I have put in a request for vacation time just for that long weekend. He said just to make sure you would be all right I am taking you back to the bed so you can be comfortable. I got back into bed and he sat on the side of the bed drinking his beer. When he finished his first beer he got up and took his shirt and pants off and closed the bedroom door. He came back and sat down on the side of the bed with the second beer. After finishing the second beer he got into bed and put his arms around me and started kissing me. I didn't respond to his kisses. He said I know I have been acting like a fool; I really don't like seeing you like this. I interrupted him saying to him; I don't want to hear pleas and promises about what you are going to do in the future, because they are only words. What I need right now is to feel safe and loved when I am in your arms...please don't make any more promises. He quiet down and continued hugging and kissing me. Finally, I told him that the Doctor said that I have to wait a few days before making love again and if he can't wait he have to go find his girlfriend in the club to satisfy his needs...if you do go please remember to use some protection. He just held me real tight and tried to kiss me again. I said stop torturing yourself you know I can't make love. He said I just wanted to kiss you and make sure you still love me. I said you know I still love you, but you are getting yourself all work up for a big letdown. He said if I get too hot I would go and take a cold shower. We started laughing and he said I want you to always feel full of laughter like this. We heard the front door open and we said together, "Linda is home". I said is that you Linda? She said yes I am home. I said we left you some Pancit in the kitchen if you are hungry. She said thank you! Are you feeling better now? I said better than I felt this morning, good night. Wilson said don't forget we would be leaving early Thursday for Sangley Point. I said I will remind her tomorrow let's go to sleep. Wilson turned off the light and pulled me tightly into his arms and kissed me goodnight. I closed my eyes as I lay in his arms...I felt safe again.

The next morning when Wilson got up he was in a real good spirit; I told him to turn the bedroom light on. I pulled the sheet back and checked my sanitary napkin for signs of blood and thank God there wasn't any blood. Wilson asked what I was doing and I told him I was checking to see if I was still bleeding, but thank God I was not.

He came over to the bed and kissed me goodbye and said stay in the bed and relax I will see you tonight. I got his pillow and hugged it very tight, closed my eyes and drifted off to sleep.

I was awakened around eight that morning by the smell of food cooking, so I got up and opened my bedroom door; I could see Sister Linda in the kitchen cooking. I said hey! What are you cooking? She said rice, eggs and sausage. That sound good I was hungry and ready to eat. I hurried into the bathroom and washed up and came back to my room and made the bed. Sister Linda said I have finished cooking; I will fix your plate and bring it to you in the living room...do you want milk or oval tine? I said I prefer the warm milk. She mixed oval tine for herself. She said she stop drinking coffee because it made her very nervous. I asked her if she remembered when we were back home and ran out of coffee and Mother would make rice coffee

by stir frying rice until it almost burned; then she would add the amount of water she needed for everyone to have a cup of coffee... she would boil and strain it and pour everyone a cup of it. I like to put milk and sugar in my coffee, but even if we didn't have milk it still was good. I ate everything on my plate. Sister Linda said there are two more sausage in the kitchen do you want them? I said no I am full now. I said Linda please don't forget tomorrow we leave early for Sangley Point; you remembered we are suppose to have Thanksgiving dinner with Sister Melda and Brother Smitty. She said that's tomorrow already time sure do pass fast...I will see part of Cavity City. I said you will see more than that...you will see all of the different Barrio that we pass through...do you know where the Frantranco Bus station is located? She said no! I thought we would be riding the Victory Bus Liner. No Frantranco your Brother Wilson has checked it out already. I can't wait Linda said; I know I am going to like being away from Olongapo City even if it only for one day... are you alright to travel that far? Yes I will be all right for the trip... sometimes my stomach hurt a little and I had a little blood yesterday, but the Doctor said I would be all right. She said that's good because Brother Wilson seems to be very worried about you. I said everyone is worry about me, but I would be all right. Sister Linda said well I guess I will wash the dishes and clean the kitchen; then I will take a nice shower. I said I would follow her in the shower. When she finished I went into the shower and the water pressure was still very strong. When I finished my shower I told Sister Linda to go to the market later on and buy food for our lunch and dinner. She said I will go now before it gets too hot and while the meat is still fresh. I gave her enough money to buy the food and she got her big shopping bag and left. When she left I thought about trimming my hair as I sat on the side of my bed towel drying it. Then I decided against it because I hadn't talked it over with Wilson, because he is crazy about my long hair. The front door opened and Sister Linda came in carrying the food she bought at the market. I thought to myself... wow! She has returned already and I haven't finished drying my hair. She said Vicky I had some money left so I bought you a tangerine for you to use while traveling to Sangley Point. I said thank you for remembering how I dislike the smell of gasoline. I certainly will need it for the trip tomorrow. I got up to help her start cooking the food for our lunch. Sister Linda said go back and sit down...you can explain to me what I need to do from over there...I remembered Mother washing the neck bone real good.

I said yes and put a lot of water in the pot and boil it until it become very tender; then add onion, potatoes, cabbage and string beans... don't forget to put salt and pepper. She said I know I am forgetting something...you remembered all of those ingredients from yesterday. I said yes I always watch Mother and Sister Melda cook, so I can cook for myself later...you can also add other types of vegetables too...I know I want take long to learn how to cook American food. Add a little extra water because Mother wants me to drink plenty of broth. Sister Linda said I remember Mother saying yesterday she wants you to drink plenty of broth. I said you should have bought the can soup. She said the food in the can is not fresh; you need your broth made from fresh vegetables. I said yes everything fresh and we laugh together. I said make sure you keep a watch on the food because I don't want to overcook the vegetables I like for them to still have a little crunch left in them. After a few minutes Sister Linda brought me a cup of the broth; I tasted it and told her it was very good almost as good as Mother Make it. Finally Linda finished cooking. I said I would eat later because I was full after drinking the broth. She said she would eat later because the smell of the food had made her full.

She got her crochet and started crocheting. I decided to go and take a nap. I told her if she get hungry go ahead and eat don't wait for me and please don't wake me if I fall asleep. I lie across the bed and fell asleep momentary. I don't know how long I was asleep before I woke up and reach for the other pillow and saw Wilson sitting on the side of the bed watching me. I started to get up but Wilson said sweetheart just lay down I would get you whatever you want…what do you need? I said I am all right…you come home early. He said I was worry about you so I took off work early. He leaned over and started kissing me. I said take it easy let me get up so I can eat lunch. He said you haven't eaten lunch yet? I said no I fell asleep. I said have you eaten lunch already? He said yes I ate before I left my Tug Boat. I got up and said Linda let's eat I am hungry now. Wilson said I am going to the store and get ice and coke for your lunch. Linda and I fixed our plates and sat down in the living room.

Wilson came back with coke, ice and beer. He said don't get up I will fix your drink, so he chopped the ice for our glasses and added coke. He served our drinks and sit down next to me to drink his beer. He said are you ready for the trip tomorrow? Sister Linda and I said yes we were ready. He said if I am not mistakenly the bus leave at seven in the morning, so we need to leave here about six fifteen so we want be late. We finished our lunch and Linda cleaned the kitchen and washed the dishes. Wilson insisted that I go back to bed and rest, I went to our bedroom and he followed. I told him that I have been feeling all right ever since yesterday, but he still insisted that I lay down. He kicked his shoes off and got into bed beside me. He said put your head on my shoulder I want to hold you. I said I thought you wanted me to relax. He said I do, but I still want to hold you. I put my head on his shoulder. He kept kissing me and drinking his beer. He was kissing me so much that I felt as if I was drinking beer too. He asked me if I still love him; I said yes I will always love you that's the reason I can't stay mad at you when you treat me bad. He didn't say a word he just kept kissing me. Finally I just turned my back to him because I knew what we were working ourselves up to. He said what wrong now? I said both of us are getting hot as a firecracker and you don't know what's wrong. You know that the Doctor said for me to take it easy and not have sex for a few days…I guess you have forgotten already, so please take it easy and give me a little time…if you can't wait leave me here and go to your girlfriend in the club like you always do. He said do you think making love is the only thing on my mind? I just love to kiss you, because I love you so much. We stop kissing and we were silent and finally fell asleep.

I woke up around four that afternoon Sister Linda had already left for school; I used the bathroom and went into the living room and sat down. Wilson was still asleep when I left the room. Finally he woke up and said sweetheart where are you? I said I am in the living room I can't stay in the bed any longer…after laying around all day I am tired of laying down. He said I guess I would get up too. He got up and went into the bathroom and washed up. When he came out he said I want to go to the Palladium Restaurant for Tacos. I said to myself…well here we go again…I know it wouldn't be too long before he would want to leave me and go to his girlfriend. He said would you be all right if I leave you for a little while?

I said do whatever you want to do; don't pretend that you are worried about me. He kissed me and left. I took a deep breath and counted to ten; I didn't want to get upset again. I sat for a while there in the living room and finally got up and warmed the leftover food. I fixed my plate and sat by the window looking out as if I knew Wilson would be coming right back. I sat there thinking to myself…he is very cruel to me…he know that the Doctor told me to avoid sex for a few days…from the day I told him I was bleeding things seem to have changed with him…now he is pretending to go for tacos, but I know that he is going to see his girlfriend…he said that he love me, but I have a hard time trying to understand what kind of love is he talking about.

I finished eating and took my plate into the kitchen. I washed the dishes and cleaned the kitchen. I kept taking deep breath and telling myself that he is only going for taco like he said. I tried counting to ten again, but it was too hard for me to keep from worrying because the same things always happen to me over and over. I thought about my baby and promised the baby I wouldn't get upset and lose it. Maybe Wilson wants me to get upset and lose the baby, but I would show him; I am not going to worry and lose my baby. I thought to myself…Mother made it with six kids without our Father help…I can take care of my baby without a Father too. I went into the bedroom and looked at the clock; it was eight o, clock. I thought to myself... eight o, clock, he must be eating a lot of tacos, because he left here at five o, clock. I decided to try and crochet maybe I could get my mind on something else. While crocheting I thought to myself...I am crocheting very good now; if Wilson decided to leave me for someone else I can always crochet different thing and sell them and maybe I would get my old job back in the Money Exchange booth. I know there are plenty of jobs that I can do to take care of my baby and me. I rub my stomach it was still very small; I wonder what it would be like when it is very large like Sister Rose when she was pregnant with her child; she looked as if she was carrying a big watermelon under her clothes...I guess I will be like that when the baby get larger. The front door open and closed I thought it was Wilson...I felt happy again, but it was Sister Linda coming home early. I said you came home early.

She said yes I finished my test early and the Teacher let me go early. I said that's nice of the Teacher to let you out a half hour early... don't forget to wake up early tomorrow morning. She went into the kitchen and warmed up the food and ate. I went back to my bedroom and closed the door so Linda wouldn't hear me crying. When the man you love hurt your feeling all of the time it hard to keep from crying...I put the pillow over my head let it out...I figured it's best to cry and get it over with than to hold it in and really get upset. I ask myself why do I do this to myself...why do I let him get away with doing me like this? I guess the first girl he fell in love really hurt him that why he never think twice about hurting me. I kept watching the time and wondering what he was doing. I decided that if he doesn't come home Sister Linda and I was still going to Sangley Point and visit Sister Melda. I thought to myself...it's eleven o, clock now and I am going to try and go to sleep. I got the other pillow and hugged it and continued to count to ten. Finally I fell asleep. I don't know how long I had slept before the bed started moving and woke me up. It was Wilson, he was undressing for bed. I could smell the stale liquor on his breath and the cheap perfume the girl wear in the clubs. He tried to kiss me but I pushed him away. I wouldn't dare let him kiss me knowing that he was possible kissing on someone else in the club...he seem to think I am very stupid when he is drinking…he think I don't know what he has been doing. I decided right then to stay a week or two in Sangley Point when I visit Sister Melda. I really don't know how long I can take this kind of life for my baby and me. I started counting one to ten again until I drifted off to sleep. The alarm clock went off at five and I got out of bed and started heating up some water for my bath, because the water would be real cold in the morning. When I finished my bath Sister Linda was up and about; she asked me the time and I told her it was six o, clock. She hurried into the bathroom and got cleaned up and started cooking breakfast. Wilson finally got up with a big hangover; I asked him for Sister Melda address he had gotten over the phone from Brother Smitty. He said I am going to Sangley Point too. I said look at yourself you can hardly stand up and you smell like your girlfriend you left in the club.

He said I am going to take a shower and I will be all right. I said just give me the address and you can stay and go back where you were last night. He said no I am going with you and I will be all right as soon as I take a shower. I thought to myself…I am going to have to do this all of the time with him…forgive him every time he go out drinking and hanging out with other women? Sister Linda said do you want me to buy some bread rolls for breakfast. I said yes and hurry. Wilson finished cleaning up and finished dressing as Linda came back from the store. I asked him if he wanted to eat breakfast. He looked at the time and said it's six fifteen already…do we have aspirin? I told Linda we would take the Spam and rolls with us just in case we got hungry on the way. I gave Wilson two aspirin for his headache. He said it's time to go so we left for the bus station. When we arrive at the bus station our bus was loading up. We got our tickets and boarded the bus; we were lucky enough to get the third seat from the front of the bus. Sister Linda got the seat in front of Wilson and me. Finally the bus loaded up and we started on our way. Wilson still had stale alcohol on his breath and of course he smokes, so I got out my tangerine from my bag and sniffed on it every so often so I wouldn't get dizzy. I could live with Wilson breath and cigarette smoke, but between it and the smell of gasoline; I knew it would give me a headache. When we reached the end of the city limits; we came to the area called the Zig Zag. It got its name from the way the road zigzag around the mountainside. I started to feel a little dizzy, so I reached for my tangerine again. Wilson asked if I was all right. I assured him I was fine. I lay my head on the bus window frame. Wilson said don't lay your head there you will hurt yourself when the bus hit a bump in the road...you can lay it on my shoulder. I said this is fine I would be all right...I guess he think I have forgotten what he did last night...if I had Sister Melda's address this morning I would have left him behind...next time I will get the address and write it down, so I can leave at will. All of a sudden the bus hit a great big pothole and I almost bumped my head on the seat in front of us. Wilson grabbed me and pulled me into his arms so I could lay my head on his shoulder. I tried to go to sleep, but the rough ride and the noise was too great.

Finally we came to our first rest stop; the Vendors were all over the bus selling boil bananas, boil eggs, apples, boil and roasted peanuts and a lot more stuff. I bought a boil banana, Wilson bought roasted peanuts and a coke and Sister Linda bought a coke to drink with the food she brought from home. She shared the Spam and rolls with Wilson. We amused ourselves eating the food we bought from the Vendors as we continued on our way to Sangley Point. We travel close to four hours before we reached Cavity City. We caught a jeepney to the Sangley Point Naval Base main gate. We got out of the jeepney and walked about two blocks before we came to Sister Melda's house. We knocked on the door and Mother opened it; we were so surprised to see her there. Sister Melda greeted us in the living room and introduced us to her private Teacher; she said my Teacher is teaching me to read and write...she have to go now, but she will be back next week. I asked how Mother get here before we did? Sister Melda said I called mama Ligaya and she sent someone to get Mother so I could talk to her...she arrive yesterday. I asked Sister Melda why she didn't tell Mother we was coming so we could have came together. She said she wanted everyone to be surprised to see Mother here. Wilson asked where brother Smitty was. She said brother Smitty had to attend some kind of a conference and wouldn't be home to have Thanksgiving dinner with us. Sister Melda said come in the kitchen I want you to see the turkey. We went into the kitchen and she opened the oven and we saw a turkey so big it barely fitted in the oven. Wilson said how many people you invited for dinner today. Sister Melda said no one but us. Mother said that is the biggest turkey I have ever seen. Wilson said I still have a bad headache; Melda do you have any aspirin? Sister Melda said yes and went and got two aspirin for him. When she gave him the aspirin she said what's wrong with you Wilson? Do you have a hangover? Wilson didn't answer her he just took the aspirin and got a glass of water to wash them down. I didn't say a word, because I knew everyone smelled the stale alcohol on Wilson. He came and sat down beside me and we held hands as always. Sister Melda said it is lunchtime so we can start eating I don't know what time Smitty will be home. Everyone washed up and went to the table. Sister Melda asked Wilson to carve the turkey.

We had corn on the cob, mashed potatoes and Ham and Turkey gravy and of course rice. Wilson carved the turkey and placed the turkey platter in the center of the table. He told Sister Melda she was going to have turkey sandwiches for a month. She said no I want you'll to take what left home to Calapacuan: Mother is leaving with you guys. Everyone ate his fill of the turkey, but I liked the ham better. Wilson said if I didn't have this bad headache I would eat more. When everyone finished eating Sister Melda took some of the food and put it in the refrigerator for Brother Smitty. Mother took the rest of the food and put it in a plastic bag. Wilson said if you don't put that food on ice in a cooler it's going to spoil. Sister Melda said just take all of the food no one here will eat the leftovers; Mother has plenty of dogs and pigs she can feed it to them. Mother and Linda helped Melda put all of the food away and clean the kitchen. Then everyone sat around making small talk. Finally Sister Melda broke the ice and asked about Wilson friend. I was wondering how long it would take before she asked about him. She asked how was he doing and had he being seen out nightclubbing. I told her we saw him one time at a nightclub and since then I haven't seen him.

Wilson said I wish we could stay longer, but I have to go to work tomorrow…thank you for inviting us. We packed up everything and said our goodbye and left for the bus station. Wilson carried the big shopping bag with the food. I looked back and wave to her; she looked very sad standing in her doorway waving at us. We caught a jeepney to the Victory Liner bus station. We arrive just in time because everyone was loading up, so we climbed aboard. Wilson said we almost missed our bus I knew it was suppose to leave at three o, clock. We got seats almost to the back of the bus. Mother and Linda sat together and Wilson and I sat in the seat behind them. He tried to kiss me and I let him, because I didn't want Mother to know I was mad at him. I didn't want my family to get involve or worry about what's going on between Wilson and me...if Mother hadn't showed up at Sister Melda's house I would have let Wilson return to Olongapo by himself. I would have stayed for a few days. I know Wilson would have to leave because he has to be at work tomorrow. Sister Melda surprised me and had Mother to meet us there at her house spoiled my chance of staying for a while.

I looked at Wilson already sleeping before the bus start moving; everything seems to be working out in his favor. The Driver came back for the bus fares, so I woke Wilson up so he could pay our fare. He stayed awake long enough to pay our fares then he went back to sleep. Finally the bus headed out for Olongapo City. When we arrived at the midway point rest stop all of the Vendors came onboard the bus selling fruit, sandwiches, drinks and snacks. I asked Mother and Linda if they wanted anything to eat; Linda said she was still full from the Thanksgiving dinner and Mother said she didn't want anything, but she wanted to get a boil Banana for Brother Etong. I gave her some money to buy the boil banana. Finally the bus was getting ready to move again and all of the Vendors hurried to get off. Wilson slept through the whole thing and didn't wake up until we arrived in Olongapo City. We arrived in Olongapo City around seven o, clock; it was dark already. We got off of the bus and started walking over to the jeepney stop. Sister Linda said she would accompany Mother to Calapacuan so she wouldn't have to travel alone. Mother asked if I wanted some of the leftover food. Wilson said I don't think you should eat that food because it smells spoil already. I said no you take it home for the dogs because you don't want to get sick. We said goodbye and Mother and Sister Linda caught a jeepney and Wilson and I caught a tricycle to our apartment. As soon as I entered the apartment I went straight to the bathroom. Wilson took a seat in the living room waiting for me to finish in the bathroom. When I came out of the bathroom he said I am sorry we had to have such a short stay at Melda's house...we will stay longer the next time we visit. I didn't say a word I just went straight into the bedroom and changed into my nightgown for bed. I had a very long day and all I wanted to do was to relax and go to sleep...I had plan to take a nap on the bus, but Wilson went to sleep before I did so I had to stay awake and watch what was going on...some passengers and vendors will snatch your wallet or watch while you are sleeping. I am sure Wilson remembered me telling him about sleeping on public transportation, but he knew that between my Mother, Linda and me someone would be watching over him while he slept. Wilson got up and followed me into the bedroom. He asked if I was going to bed; I said yes and I am going to sleep too.

I said how is your headache? He said it's better than it was this morning. I said that good, why do you do that to yourself? He didn't answer he just got undressed and sit on the side of the bed. Then he said could we talk? I said what about? Oh! Do you want to explain to me why it took you until one o, clock in the morning to get tacos? I said I don't think my love for you is going to take all the abuse you are dishing out...I was sick for one day and you headed for the streets and the clubs to find your old girl friend...you even have the guts to come back home smelling like their cheap perfume and drunk...you continue to tell me you love me, but you continue to hurt me...I can feel the hurt deep down in my stomach and don't mention my heart, but I take what you are doing because I love you. I started to cry because I was feeling the hurt, but I was determined to tell him how I felt. I said I think you are trying to do the same thing to me as your stateside girl friend did to you...well I am not going to take it...I am not going to put up with you chasing the girl in the clubs and coming home to me...I don't want you to bring home a bad sickness to my baby and me. Maybe you should go back to running the streets and maybe I would go back and get my old job and work and take care of my baby when it born...you don't care about the baby anyway your friend C.B. told you it maybe someone else baby and you seem to believe him. Do you think I am not hurt when you believe what someone else says about me? It is just like being slap in the face. I think I really had enough of your pretending to love me. I think it would be better for us to go our separate ways before we really hurt each other. He said I don't want to hurt you I love and need you. I got up and went to the closet and started packing my clothes. As fast as I took my clothes from the closet to pack Wilson hung them back into the closet. Finally I gave up and went into the bathroom and sat down to try and calm down enough to think. I thought to myself…I can't go to Mother's house because I don't want to bother her with my problems…maybe I will go stay with Sister Rose and her boy friend in Barrio, Barretto, but I don't have her address…maybe I will go and stay with Maria daughter on kissing street.

Wilson couldn't wait for me to come out so he started trying to break down the door. I got up and let him in the bathroom. He picked me up and carried me to the bedroom begging me to stop crying. He put me down on the bed and continued pleading for me to stop crying and not leave him. I didn't say anything I just kept trying to calm down because of my baby. I lay there on the bed with him hugging and kissing me and trying to get me to say something. Finally he started crying when he couldn't get me to talk to him that was the first time I saw him cry. I though a guy was not supposed to cry they are suppose to be strong. I thought he was faking at first, but the tears convinced me. Now both of us were crying. He kept saying you have to forgive me and give me another chance… I know you love me…please don't destroy what we have right now. When he said that I couldn't hold back any longer, I said you think I am destroying our relationship…you need to take a long look at yourself. I am not chasing after another guy…you are the one chasing all of the girls in the club and coming home drunk every chance you get. I started feeling a little dizzy, so I held my head. He asked me if I was all right. I told him I was feeling dizzy and I need some water. He jumped up from the bed and ran into the kitchen and got me a glass of water. He said the water is not cold. I said never mind just give me the water. I took the glass and drunk the water. While drinking the water I noticed that all the clothes I had taken from the closet and put on the bed was hung neatly back in the closet. I didn't say a word because I was trying very hard to calm down. I remembered what happened last time I got real upset. I started taking deep breath and counting from one to ten. Finally I said thanks for the water and calmly lay back down on the bed. Wilson covered me with a sheet and lay down beside me. I tried to move away from him, but he just moved closer and hugged me. We both lay silent in the bed. I closed my eyes and tried to fall asleep. Finally I did fall asleep. The night passed real fast, it seem as if I had just fallen asleep when the alarm clock went off. Wilson hurried out of the bed and got ready for work. He came back to the bed and started begging and pleading for me to wait until he came back before I decided to leave.

Finally I said o.k. I will wait here for you. I would have said anything just to shut him up, because he just kept pleading asking me to stay and don't leave him. I let him kiss me and he left going to work. I went back to sleep. Around seven thirty or eight that morning I woke up feeling hungry. I got up and went into the bathroom and clean up; then I went into the kitchen and prepared my breakfast. I made an egg sandwich and oval tine and took my plate in the living room. I thought to myself...I am ready for whatever happens to this relationship...I can get me a job and start over...I can even find me another man to love and be love by...it appears that my love is not enough for him...things are different than the way I thought it would be between us...I am still young I can find someone else to love me, but I will still wait here for him and see what he have to say. Well I had better take a shower so I can relax and see what Wilson have to say when he come home this afternoon. Life can be very cruel sometimes you never know what life is going to bring you until it is upon you. I thought Wilson would be the man I would spend the rest of my life with, but now there is a question hanging over our relationship. If I had to bet one way or the other I would bet that our relationship won't make it.

Oh! I had better hurry and finish showering before the water is turned off. After I finished my shower and towel dried my hair; I put my make up on and a nice dress that fit above my knee. I looked in the mirror and thought to myself...this dress still fits perfectly and I know I am not a bad looking woman...I can't imagine what else Wilson want that I don't have...I know he like making love to me...so what could it be? I went into the living room and prayed to God that I will be able to deal with whatever he decides to do. If he decide that it's best that we go our separate ways I can do that too, because I am ready to go back to work and do what it takes to support my baby. I went into the bedroom to check the time; it was only eight thirty that means I have to wait at least four hours if he comes home at one like he promised. I decided to do a little crocheting to pass the time and I really wanted to finish the piece I was working on anyway. I got busy crocheting and finally decided to rest my eyes for a while, so I looked out the window to see what was going on outside.

To my surprise, I saw Wilson coming from the market walking; I guess he walked from the jeepney stop at the market. I put my crochet away and sit down to wait for him. When he came in the door he seems very happy to see that I was still at the apartment. He rushed in and hugged and kissed me and begins thanking me for not leaving until he had a chance to talk. He said could we talk in a very serious way. I thought to myself...here we go again. I said yes; just say what you want to say...I am leaving anyway. He said please just listen to what I have to say before you make a decision. I said o.k. Say what you have to say. He said I know that I have hurt you and I am the cause of what happened to you, but you do know I love you...I may not show my love the way you want me to. I interrupted him and said do you mean to say that there are other ways to show your love to me? He said please let me finish...before I met you I was in love with another girl back in the States, but she left me for someone else and I was hurt very bad. When I came to the Philippines I met lots of girls in the clubs and had a lot of fun, but when I met you everything changed because I knew I loved you from the first moment I met you...My thinking have being selfish because I have being thinking only about myself...my friends telling me the baby you're carrying could be fathered by someone else, so my thinking have being very mixed up. Today my mind is clear I know that I love you and wants to marry you and take care of you and the baby when it come...please give me another chance to prove to you that my running around and seeing other girls is behind me now...you are the only girl for me and the one I wants to spend the rest of my life with...please give me another chance to prove what I am saying to you...I will get down on my knees and beg if that's what you want. I said no! I am not God, you don't have to get on your knees to ask me for forgiveness...you only get on your knees to ask God for forgiveness...I don't know if I believe you or not. He said just give me a chance to show you. I said o.k. I will see. He kissed me and acted as if he was relieved. I said why did you come home early today…I thought you said you will be here at one today? He said I just couldn't wait to come and try to straighten out the mess I got myself into plus I love you and wanted to be with you…have you eaten yet? I said yes I ate breakfast, but it's only ten o, clock…I would cook some rice for lunch. He said could we set in the bedroom this wooden chair is very hard. I said yes my bottom is hurting too…it is especially hard when you are skinny, because your bones hurt too. He started laughing as we went into the bedroom. We were supposed to sit on the bed, but we ended up stretched out on the bed propped up with our pillows. The next thing I knew I was in his arms. He looked puzzled at my dress and asked why I was dressed up. I said I was prepared to leave and go away. I figured that I couldn't compete with your other girlfriends so I was going back and try to get my old job back at the Money Exchange. He hugged me real tight and said don't say anything about leaving me. He held me so tight I could hardly breathe. I said let me go I need air. Then he gently kissed me and said don't say anything else about leaving me…I want you to stay with me until you get tired of me. I said I am tired of you already…now what are you going to do? He said you are supposed to give me one more chance to show you that I love you and only you. I said o.k. Show me that you love me. We looked at each other and smiled. He said you're very cute when you talk like that. I didn't respond. He pulled me even closer to him and started kissing me as if there wasn't a tomorrow. He stopped and said I have to take a cold shower. I said don't worry about the shower show me how much you love me. We let ourselves go and let it happen; we made love like we had being waiting a month and it was wonderful as always when you are with the one you love. After we made love and things settled down I went to the bathroom to check if I had started to bleed again. I was all right and I thought to myself…thank you God. Wilson came into the bathroom and asked if something was wrong. I said no I just wanted to use the bathroom. He picked me up and carried me back to the bedroom. He said you're going to get tired of me, because I am off for the whole weekend…we will see who get tired first. I said o.k. I sure would like to have a coke now…would you get me a large coke and some ice from the store? He said let me get dressed, so he started dressing then stopped and looked around at me; he said why are you dressing?

I said oh yea, I don't need to put my street clothes back on...I guess he thought I was going to leave when he went to the store. He seems relieved as he headed for the door. I said don't forget to get you a beer and reclined back on the bed. When he returned he was carrying coke, beer, ice and a can of corn beef. I said you tried to buy out the store. I said I had better cook the rice now if we plan to eat lunch around one, so I got up and started the rice cooking. Wilson said he would watch the rice. I said when the rice start boiling lower the flame under it and let it simmer for about fifteen minutes, but I am here and I can watch it myself. Wilson said no! I would watch it I want you to go back to bed. I said both of us would watch it. Now let's sit down in the living room so I can drink my cold coke. He said o.k. Sweetheart! When the rice boils I would go back into the kitchen and lower the flame on the gas burner so the rice can simmer. I said what do you want me to do with the corn beef? He said stir- fry an onion with the corn beef. I waited until the rice was done before I started stir- frying the corn beef and onions. Wilson took a seat in the living room and lit a cigarette and started drinking his beer. He said come sit beside me. I said I have to cook the corn beef. Finally the food was ready; I said the food is ready do you want to eat now? He said yes I am ready to eat, so I fixed our plates and took them into the living room and we ate. When we finished eating I got up to wash the dishes Wilson tried to help, but I told him this kitchen sink was not built for two. Wilson went back to his seat. As soon as I finished the dishes and started back to the living room Wilson met me and steered me to the bedroom. He said the bed is softer than the wooden living room furniture...I don't want you to think anymore about going back to work, because I am the only one that would be working to take care of us. I said what are you talking about now...I thought we finished talking about what happened...now you are starting all over again... the only reason I would go back to work would be to take care of my baby and me if you leave. You asked me to give you another chance... well I thought that what I was doing...please I want to put everything that happened yesterday or before behind me. You asked for another chance, well it start today...I don't want you to think about any of your girlfriends in the pass, just me.

He said that's what I want to. We hugged and kissed to show each other how much in agreement we were. We stayed in the bed most of the afternoon only getting up to use the bathroom. Around two that afternoon Wilson said let's go to sleep. I said o.k. That's a good idea, so I closed my eyes and tried to go to sleep. I smelled the smoke from his cigarette and opened my eyes and ask what was wrong. He said I just want to watch you while you sleep. I said I thought you were going to sleep too. I will as soon as I finish my cigarette. I turned my back to him and tried again to fall asleep. Finally he finished his cigarette and put his arms around me and we fell asleep.

Around five o, clock I woke up and he was not beside me, so I called out to him and there was no answer. I got up to see what was going on; the bathroom door was closed so I went back into the bedroom and fixed the bed. When I finished I went into the living room and sat down to wait for him. Finally he came out and said I thought you were still sleep...I couldn't stay in the bed any longer... would you like to go and catch a movie? I said couldn't we just stay home sometime...I thought you wanted to spend time with me. He said I just want to make you happy. I said I would be happy if we're together; we don't have to go out and spend money all of the time... we are supposed to be saving money to buy furniture for the living room...are you hungry? He said no I am still full, but I would eat sausage in the can later. I said I am going to cook me something to eat now. He said o.k. I am going across the street and get me a beer do you want a coke? I said no I would just have water with my dinner. He left and went to the store and bought beer and sandwiches bread. After I finished eating my dinner of fried eggplant, chopped tomatoes and rice I washed the dishes. Then I hurried into the bathroom and brushed my teeth, so Wilson wouldn't smell the fish sauce on my breath. We sat in the living room and he started drinking his beer. I said shouldn't you eat before you start drinking? He said I told you I am still full. I said o.k. Go ahead if you are not hungry. He started looking as if he were bored, so I asked him if he were all right. He said I am all right don't worry about me...let's sit on the bed I am tired of this uncomfortable chair. We moved to the bedroom and sat on the bed. He started drinking his beer and kissing me. I said finish drinking your beer and then kiss me. He said what's wrong?

I said I am getting dizzy and I don't know if it the beer you are drinking or the cigarette you are smoking causing it. He said o.k. I would finish my beer and cigarette first so you want get dizzy. Just as I was getting comfortable on the bed Wilson asked me to make him a sausage sandwich. I got up and made the sandwich for him. He ate the sandwich and went to the bathroom and brushed his teeth. When he came back he started kissing me on the back of my neck. Then he stopped and started talking about different ways to make love. He said some people do a position called a sixty-nine, would you like to try it? I said I like the way we make love and I think you do too...have you tried the sixty-nine before? He said no, but we can try it and see if you like it. I said I enjoy the way we make love now. We started hugging and kissing and before long we were very excited and let ourselves go into orbit. We finished and remained in a tight embrace until we fell asleep.

The next day Saturday morning, Wilson was up first and went to the bathroom and came back and sat on the side of the bed. I was not so eager to get up so I stayed in bed for about ten or fifteen minutes longer. He sat on the side of the bed looking puzzled then he asked me where all the beer bottles came from. I looked at him and said whom do you think brought the beer bottles here? He said I am serious. I said I am serious too...tell me who keep going back and forth to the store buying beer? If you don't remember just forget it I would return the bottles to the store later. I decided to get up and take a shower before the water is turned off. When I finished my shower he was still setting on the side of the bed looking puzzled...I guess he was trying to figure out if he emptied all of those bottles last night. I said it's your turn to take a shower you had better hurry before the water is turned off. He said sweetheart come in the bedroom for a minute. I wrapped the towel around my head and went to the bedroom to see what he wanted. When I sat down beside him he asked me if I still love him; I said of course, I would always love him. He said even though I drink too much? I said that our big problem, but you promised to try to cut back on your drinking...I guess it take time for you to get it in your mind to slow down. Don't worry about that now just go and take your shower before the water is cut off, I am going to start cooking breakfast. I finished cooking breakfast just as he came out of the shower, so we sat down to breakfast of scrambled eggs and Spam.

Wilson got two slices of bread and made him an egg and Spam sandwich. After breakfast I washed the dishes and cleaned the kitchen. I came back to the living room and took the towel from around my head and started towel drying my hair. I turned and saw Wilson looking at my hair. He said don't cut your hair I like it long. I said I was planning to ask you if you like it long because I wanted to cut off the split ends. He said let me see what split ends you are talking about. He took my hair in his hand and examined it and said the split ends are not bad...just don't cut it. I said to myself...I guess he think he own my hair too...he don't want me to trim the split ends...I guess I'll let it grow until it reach my bottom maybe he will let me trim it then. He really surprised me when he asked to comb my hair; I didn't hesitate at all, I gave him the comb. He started combing and fondling my hair. He said now you look like a little doll with your hair hanging loose like this. He always knows what to say to me to make me feel good about myself. Then he stopped combing my hair and kissed me on the back of my neck and from there to my lips. He always makes me feel good; he just need to control his drinking. When I get mad at him I try to think of his other side, the loving and caring side. He gave me the comb back and said would you like to go visit C.B. and Jean? If that's what you want to do. We got dressed and went to their apartment. Their maid said they had left and went on the Naval Base. We decided to go to the Base too. We caught a jeepney to the jeepney stop at the Main Gate. We went to the pass office and got a visitor pass for me. We walked around on the base until lunchtime then we stopped at a small cafeteria with seating outside. Wilson ordered a tuna sandwich and coke and I ordered a hot dog and a coke. Eating our lunch we talked about the things we would do when we got married. Wilson told me that when we are married I would get a Military Dependent ID card and I could buy anything that I wanted on the base, but cigarette and liquor because they are control items. He said don't worry about it you don't smoke or drink anyway. We sat and talked until around twelve thirty and decided to go and catch a movie matinee in town. Wilson turned in my visitors pass at the gate and we went to the Grand Theater just outside of the gate. The movie we saw last week was still showing, so we hurried to Del Rosario Theater. We arrived before the movie started; they were showing a Chinese karate movie.

We watched and really enjoyed the movie. The movie was over around four thirty. Wilson said it's only four thirty let go and see if C.B. and Jean have returned home. I said o.k. And we went back to their apartment. When we arrived there their car was in the driveway; I could tell that Wilson was happy they was back home, he had a smile on his face. He knocked on the door and Jean opened the door with a big smile on her face. She said C.B. Wilson and Vicky are here. We sat down in the living room and C.B. came out of the bedroom and joined us. Jean said our Maid told us you guys came by earlier. Wilson said yes we thought we would come by for a while. C.B. said we're moving on the base in December; that's where we went earlier today...we drove around looking at the houses in the neighborhood. I asked Jean if she thought she would like living on base. She said I think I am going to like it...everything is pretty close together, the school, the Mini Mart, Swimming pool and the Commissary and Exchange is five miles away...I can't wait to move. I said Jean I am very happy for you. She said don't forget to visit us on the base. I said I would if Wilson got me a gate pass. She said you call me and I'll get you a pass. I said thank you very much. C.B. said how is little Wilson doing as he pointed to my stomach? I said just fine. CB and Wilson started drinking, I watched Wilson to see if he would remember what he said about controlling his drinking. Jean excused herself and went to the kitchen to talk to her Maid. When she came back she told us they were having fried chicken for dinner and wanted us to stay for dinner. C.B. said of course they could stay for dinner it's not even six o, clock yet...they don't eat dinner at four o, clock woman...tell the Maid to cook up some more chicken. Jean looked as if she was embarrassed by the way C.B. were talking to her. Jean is a very nice and quiet person she just smile and ignore what C.B. say. Wilson caught my eye to see how I was handling the situation, because he knew C.B. was getting drunk. Jean looked at me and said don't pay any attention to C.B. he has been drinking since this morning...we

367

visited some friends on base and he started drinking over there and when I got back home he started again...he is drunk and is going to sleep pretty soon...I am use to C.B. getting drunk...I don't pay him any attention anymore, so don't worry. I said to myself...look like we have the same problem. Jean smiled and pointed to C.B. saying you see he is trying to go to sleep now.

C.B. was falling over on Wilson as they sat on the couch. Wilson pushed him and woke him up. Wilson looked at me and said we had better go and let C.B. sleep. Jean said the food is ready why don't you eat first before you go. Jean told C.B. it was time to eat. He told her to bring his food into the living room. I went and ate at the kitchen table with the kids and Wilson stayed in the living room with C.B. and Jean. Jean stayed in the living room so she could help C.B. with his food, because he was spilling it all over the chair. I enjoyed the fried chicken and French fries. Wilson finished eating and took his plate into the kitchen. When he returned he said Jean we hate to eat and run, but as you can see C.B. need to go to sleep...do you want me to help put him to bed? Jean said don't worry about C.B. I am going to let him sleep right there on the couch...he is drinking almost every day he's use to sleeping on the couch...he will be all right. I said thanks very much for the dinner. Jean said don't forget to visit us when we move to base housing...C.B think we would be moving by this December, but you never can tell...we're on the list, maybe they will call us very soon I certainly would be happy. Wilson said we have to go Jean thanks for dinner. We left and went back to our apartment. I opened the door and look back for Wilson he had turned and went to the store for a beer. I went straight to the bedroom and change into my nightgown, because I was very tired. When I heard Wilson come in the door I met him in the living room he put his beer on the end table and went to the bathroom. I sat down wondering what he was going to do next; he drunk two drinks at C.B.'s house and now he is going to drink beer. He came back into the living room and looked at me and asked why I had my nightgown on it only eight o, clock. I said I am tired and want to go to bed...you can sit here and finish your beer I am going to lay down. He said I am not going to set here by myself; I'll drink my beer in the bedroom. I followed him into the bedroom and he sat down on the bed and said come let me hold you. I lay my head in his lap and closed my eyes. I guess I drifted right off to sleep, because I didn't wake up until Wilson tried to ease my head out of his lap on a pillow. I opened my eyes and asked where he was going he said to the bathroom. I looked at the clock it was ten o, clock. He came back to the bedroom and got undressed for bed.

I asked him why he didn't wake me. He said you were sleeping so good I just couldn't bear to wake you...I knew you were really tired because you had a long day. I said are you going to sleep now? He said I am not sleepy yet, but if you are still tired I guess I would try and sleep. I got up and went into the bathroom and put water on my face to try and wake up; I also used my mouthwash. When I finished goggling I went back to the bedroom. He was waiting for me; he said come here as he held out his hand for me. I climbed back into bed beside him into his arms. He started kissing me gently on the neck. I said you are supposed to be sleep by now. What happened...the beer is keeping you awake? He said I don't know what's wrong with me. I said I know what's wrong...you ate before you started drinking at C.B. and Jean apartment...having food in your stomach before you start drinking would help you keep from getting drunk quickly... remember next time you drink eat first. He said I eat most of the time before I drink; said maybe it is because you took a long time drinking the two drinks at their house. He said maybe you're right. I said yes, you drank the two drinks at their house very slow and when you came home you drank your three beers very slow, so now you know to take your time and drink your drinks real slowly. He said what are we going to do now? I said we can turn off the light and maybe you would fall asleep. He said but I want to look at you o.k. I said do whatever you want and turned my back to him to try and go to sleep. He said maybe if I drank more beer I would go to sleep. I said do whatever you want to do I am going to try and go back to sleep. He got up and looked out of the window and said the store is still open. I said the store don't close until eleven Saturday and Sunday and ten Monday thru Friday, so you have thirty minutes before it close...you still want some beer? He said yes! I said go get some I am staying in the bed. He got dressed and went to the store and bought two beers. He said this is all I am drinking tonight. I said o.k. Enjoy it. He got undress again and lay down on the bed and propped his head up with pillows. He said is tomorrow Sunday? I said yes you have one more day before you have to go back to work. He said yes and five more days before I get paid. I said it is almost December the month is going so fast. He said yes, I was hoping our paperwork would be back by now, so we could start planning our wedding…even if we have to go to the Justice of the Peace.

I said I want to get married in the church. He said what church do you want to get married in? I said I want to get married in the Catholic Church. He said we would see if there are no problems we could do it. He started hugging and kissing me all over again. He always makes me feel good when he kisses. He makes me very hot when he gently kisses me all over. I thought to myself…do I make him feel the same way when I return his kisses? I guess I do because he is all over me. He asked me if I love him I said yes. He said I want you to say I love you. Between kisses I said I love you, I love you, and I love you. When I started saying I love you Wilson started kissing me like a wild man. He almost ripped my clothing off. We made love like there was no tomorrow and lay gasping for air in each other arms. Wilson was so relaxed he didn't have enough energy to get up and turn off the light. I got up and put my nightgown back on and turned off the light. I went back to bed he pulled me close to him and said I love you sweetheart, goodnight. I said goodnight to him and closed my eyes. Sunday morning at four thirty the alarm clock went off; both of us reached for the alarm clock to silence it. Then I remembered that today is Sunday. I said I thought you told me you were off this Sunday. He said I set the alarm by mistake as he turned it off. I got up and used the bathroom and got back into the bed. Wilson pull me close and wrapped his arms around me and we went back to sleep. I slept to around nine and woke up feeling very hungry. I got up and started for the bathroom. Wilson asked me where I were going. I told him I was going to the bathroom to get cleaned up so I can cook us some breakfast. When I finished in the bathroom I went into the kitchen and fixed our breakfast of Spam, eggs and garlic fried rice. I said the food is ready are you ready to eat? Wilson said yes I am ready…you didn't take very long to cook. I said I didn't have to prepare very much food. He said I would eat the Spam and egg…May I have two slices of bread and some butter. I said we have bread but no butter; I could run to the store and get some butter. He said don't worry about the butter, because we don't have a refrigerator to put it in anyway. I said the store has a refrigerator and they would sell you enough butter to use for two slices of bread because people can't afford to buy a refrigerator. He said I didn't know that the Sari Sari store sold it like that.

I said yes they do that here in the Philippines…they will slice it, chop it, or dice it, it depend upon what you want…they would roast half of a pig for you if that what you want. He said I saw a group of people having a beach party and they had half of a roast pig served in banana leaves…there were an apple in the pig mouth. I said so you have seen some of the food we have in the Philippines. He said yes I like most of your food…the only food I don't like is pig blood they cook. I said your friend C.B. like to eat pig blood cooked by his Maid…don't you remembered the time I went to the market with him to buy pig blood? He said yes I remembered you going to the market with him, but I didn't know he bought pig blood. I said I didn't see him eat it, but his Maid says he always eat all of the Philippines dishes she cook for herself. Wilson said could we talk about something else before I get sick…I don't know about C.B. when he drinking he would try and eat anything. I said to myself…you and him act just alike when you are drinking…you can't tell when you have had enough…C.B. act like he is more than anyone else when he drinking…you can't tell him anything…he don't respect anyone even Jean…he curses using abusive language…he think he have all of the answers and is never wrong about anything. Wilson said what are you thinking about? I said I was thinking about some of your friends they are crazy. Some of your friends are very nice too. Wilson said how about me? I said right now you are a loving and caring person, but when you get drunk you turn into another person…very cruel… you even forget that I am with you; the only thing you think about is getting more to drink, but you can control you drinking just like you did last night…you have to slow down and sip your drinks not chug them down…take time to enjoy the taste. He said I told you I would try and slow down o.k. And he kissed me. I got up and took the dishes into the kitchen and started washing them; I said when I

371

finish cleaning the kitchen I am going to take a shower before the water is turned off. He said I am going to get a haircut, so I want have to worry about trying to get one after work tomorrow. I said today is Sunday are the Barbershop open on Sunday? He said yes, people get haircut on Sunday too. When I finished with the dishes I told him I was going to take my shower. He kissed me and left for the Barbershop. I hurried into the shower because I wanted to finish before the water was cut off.

As I took my shower I tried to sing a song by Nat King Cole, but I didn't know the words, so I ended up just humming the song. When I finished my shower; I dried my body off and wrapped the towel around my head and put my under clothing and housecoat on. I went to the bedroom and sat on the side of the bed next to the mirror. I thought to myself...let me see if I am still pretty like Wilson said I am...I put some baby powder on my face so I would look real sexy to Wilson. I took the towel off my head and started toweling my hair. When I finished drying my hair I looked in the mirror and said to myself...now I look like a pretty doll...why do Sister Melda always tell me I am ugly and look like a little kitten...I don't look ugly, why does she say that to me I am her sister...Wilson love and like my looks very much...he had a lot of pretty girlfriends, but he choose me...he is a real handsome guy...I don't think he would fall in love with me if I was ugly like Sister Melda says...she try and make me feel like I am ugly, for a while I really believed her. I know now that she was wrong people always say that I am cute and look like a little doll; I never hear anyone call or say that I am ugly even in anger. Now I know that I am pretty, pretty, pretty and not ugly. I sat for a little while admiring my looks in the mirror. I said to myself...you are young, sexy and pretty...you don't look bad at all. I heard the front door open, so I went into the living room to see who it was; it was Wilson surprisingly returning home early after getting his haircut. He said hi sweetheart did you miss me? I said yes I missed you. In my effort to learn to speak English, I listen to what the person is saying and I repeat what they say. Sometimes it comes out all right. If Wilson say I love you then I would say I love you too and if he ask if I am hungry I will answer either yes or no. It is real difficult to speak English and listen to someone speak it too. If

I don't understand I would not answer at all. Usually Wilson and his friends understand that I don't speak the language very well. Wilson hugged and kissed me and almost carried me to the bedroom. We sat on the side of the bed and he said you smell real good. He really acted like he missed me too. I asked him if he thought I was ugly. He looked at me in surprise; then said if you were ugly I would not have fallen in love with you. He said who told you that you're ugly? I said my Sister Melda. Well he said your Sister Melda is wrong... she jealous because you're pretty, sexy and younger than she is. Then he pushed me over on the bed and started kissing me all over. He always knows what to say or do to make me feel good about myself when I am feeling down and unhappy...he knows what to say to me even when I am mad to make me forget that I am mad. Right now I know what he trying to do; he is trying to raise my temperature and is being very, very successful. I love Wilson very much and I think he love me too, if he kisses me one time he set me off and I can tell that my kisses does the same for him. We have to be very careful when we're out, because if we start kissing our temperature start to rise and we have to head home to put out the fire. Wilson said what's wrong? I said there is nothing wrong. He said you look like your mind is far away from here...what are you thinking about? I said I was just thinking about something. He said what were you think about? I said remember the time we were out nightclubbing with your friend from the base and we were sitting at the table and talking to them when you started kissing me...well about two minutes later you told them we had to go home. Your friend said you just got her man. Wilson said we were kissing like this. I couldn't answer him because he had my lips pended down and my temperature started to rise. He started removing his clothing between kisses and then started at my clothing as if he was going to rip them off. I said take it easy tiger and he shifted into high gear. Finally we let ours self go and made love like there were no tomorrow. We finished drenched in perspiration and gasping for breath. We lay motionless on the bed with our bodies completely spent. Finally we were engulfed in sleep. It was around two that afternoon when we woke up and I decided to get up. We were hungry, but were still feeling spent and didn't want to move. I said I had better get up and cook something to eat. I told Wilson that all I had to cook for him were a can of vegetable soup. He said that would be fine if I had crackers. I got dressed and combed my hair and went to the store and got crackers for his lunch. I went back to the kitchen put the crackers down and washed my hands and started preparing my food. Finally Wilson got up got dressed and came into the kitchen. I told him to go and have a seat in the living room until his soup is finished. After heating the soup I gave him a bowel of it with his crackers. He asked if we had coke. I said no I forgot to get some when I was at the store, so I started for the door then turned around and asked him if he wanted something else. He said oh yes; don't forget to get some ice. I went to the store and got coke and ice and chopped up some of the ice and put it in a glass and poured coke over it. Then took it into the living room and gave it to him. I told him I would be in the kitchen fixing me something to eat. I thought to myself...what I can cook real fast...oh yes; I will warm up the left over from breakfast. Wilson asked for more coke so I took the whole liter bottle into the living room to him. When my food was warm I fixed my plate and took it into the living room and sat beside Wilson on the wooden couch. I started eating my food with my hand. I was very hungry. I became real embarrassed when I saw Wilson starring at me as I ate my food. I asked him what was wrong. He said smiling; you must be real hungry I thought you were trying to eat your hand. I quickly turn my back to him and continued eating my food. He upset me with his small sense of humor. I thought to myself...he know I am very hungry, because I had to fix his food, go to the store for coke and ice and fix my food too...next time he can just fix his own food...I was the first one to mention eating in the first place then he said he was hungry...plus he didn't bother to try and help me prepare our food, or go to the store for his coke, he just sat there and waited for me to do it. I got up and took the dirty dishes to the kitchen and had started washing them when Wilson came up behind me. He said sweetheart I didn't realize you was that hungry please forgive me...I don't want you to be mad at me...I know I should have being paying more attention to you...I should have went to the store instead of waiting for you to go...I wasn't thinking please don't get mad. He kissed the back of my neck and gently turned me around and kissed my lips. I said o.k. Now let me finish washing the dishes. He said o.k. Sweetheart I will go sit down and finish drinking my coke. When I finished in the kitchen I went to the bedroom and started to make the bed.

Wilson said just close the door...don't fix the bed yet...you're wasting your time...you know we will back in there again very soon. I didn't say a word; I continued to fix the bed. After fixing the bed I went to the bathroom to brush my teeth again. Wilson said what are you going to do now? I said I am going to brush my teeth so you want smell fish sauce on my breath. He said you always smell good to me. When I finished brushing my teeth I joined him in the living room and sat in a chair across from him. He said are you still mad at me? I said no. He said why don't you sit beside me? I got up and sat beside him on the wooden couch. As soon as I sat down he started kissing me. I like being kissed by him because it makes me feel loved by him. I never get tired of kissing him back. The problem we have when we kiss a lot is getting excited real easy, so we try very, very hard to control our kissing when we are out in public. Wilson said sweetheart is Linda coming back today? I said yes, she is supposed to come this afternoon. He said have you learned to crochet yet? I said yes I could crochet. He said you never let me see your crochet. I said I will show it to you, but remember you told me not to crochet while you are home because you wanted all of my attention. He said yes I remember saying that to you, so you can show me what you have finished now and do the rest of your crocheting tomorrow when I am at work. He looked at me and smiled and gave me a kiss. I got up and got my crochet and showed it to him. He was really surprised when I showed him the crochet; he said this is very beautiful are you sure you made this? I said yes I made it. He still stared at it in disbelief, so I started a small design that I would later add to it...I continued until I completed it. He said it was really hard for me to believe you could make something like this, but I see it with my own eyes how wonderful and talented you are. I got up and put my crochet basket away, because I didn't want him to think I was not paying attention to him...we have a good and loving relationship and I don't want to spoil it. I want to give one hundred percent of my attention to him. Wilson looked at the time and said the time goes by so quickly...it's four already and I have to go back to work tomorrow. He said let's go into the bedroom and he picked up his ashtray and started for the bedroom. I followed close behind him and closed the bedroom door just in case Sister Linda comes home. He turned around smiling and said I told you not to make up the bed now we're going to mess it up again. He grabbed me and pulled me to the bed as he reached over and pulled the bedspread back. The next thing I knew I was on the bed and he was kissing my legs, stomach, and all over with the exception of my lips. I asked him was he all right? He said keep still I am trying to find the spot where you are tickle. I started tickling him too...when I got to his armpit he said I give up...you win...I don't want to move suddenly and hurt your stomach. We stopped tickling each other and lay there smiling. Suddenly he grabbed me and kissed me on the lips so long and hard I thought I was losing my breath. The next thing I realized was the journey we were on...the wonderful journey two can take where there is enjoyment all of the way...at the end of our journey we lay in each other arms gasping for breath. As we lay on the bed relaxing and enjoying the closeness of our embrace, we heard the front door open and close, Linda had returned. We kept still and didn't mumble a word. After about five minutes we decided she was not going to call out, so I turned my back to Wilson and went to sleep.

That afternoon around six we woke up smelling the aroma of food being cooked. I got up and put my clothes on and tipped out of the room. Wilson was still sound asleep. I closed the bedroom door and went into the kitchen. Sister Linda was busy at the stove. I asked her what she was cooking. She said I am cooking dried marinated milkfish. Mother dried this fish and she wanted us to have some. I said that's good! How is everyone doing in Calapacuan? Sister Linda said Brother Celino and his wife left going to Antipolo, Rizal to visit his wife parent. I said I hope Brother Celino find himself a job they really need some type of income, because his wife is going to have a baby. I hate to say this about Brother Celino but he is very lazy... he continue laying up at Mother house eating up what little food she have for her and Brother Etong...I don't know what's going to happen when their baby comes. I went into the bathroom and brushed my teeth; when I came back Wilson came out of the bedroom. I asked him if he wanted to eat some of the fish Linda was cooking. He came over to the table and looked at the fish and said I don't eat that kind of fish...I like only fried fish with corn meal batter...I am going to the store and get corn beef and you can fix it the same way as you did before and I will eat it with rice.

I said o.k. If that's what you want to eat. When I left I chopped up some onion to cook with his corn beef. When he returned he had beer, ice, coke and corn beef, I took the food in the kitchen and He sat down in the living room and started drinking a beer. I thought to myself...he's supposed to eat before he started drinking beer. I didn't say anything to him I just rushed in the kitchen and hurried to prepare his food before he drink too much. As soon as his food was ready I took it into the living room to him. Sister Linda and I fixed our plates and joined him. Linda and I ate with our hand, she was ashamed to eat with her hands in front of Wilson at first, but now she doesn't have a problem, because Wilson is use to seeing use do it. The marinated fish Mother sent was delicious. When Wilson finished eating he said that was really good as he continued to sip his beer. I took his plate and mine into the kitchen and Sister Linda washed the dishes. I came back to the living room and sit down beside Wilson; we talked for a while. Linda went to the closet and got her mat and spread it out in the corner of the room. We always go to sleep around eight or nine o, clock at night at Mother's house. Wilson said Linda is going to sleep early. I said yes she does that on her off nights from school...I guess she is trying to make up that loss sleep. Wilson said I am going to the store and get more beer and we can finish our conversation in the bedroom...my body is aching sitting on this hardwood chair. He left going to the store. I thought to myself...if we had a refrigerator we could save some money and time instead of running to the store to get one or two beer at a time...he knew that the store closes early on Sunday nights, so that's why he went there right away. I waited there in the living room until he returned and followed him into the bedroom. He put his beer on the floor and sat on the side of the bed drinking one of the beers. Then looked around for an ashtray and suddenly remembered that he left it in the living room. He got up set his beer down on the floor and went to the living room and got his ashtray. I don't mind him kissing me while drinking, but he smokes too and that really makes me dizzy. I do my best not to complain because I love him very much and I don't want him to think that I am trying to stop him from drinking and smoking; he is a grown man and should be able to make that decision himself.

The majority of the time when he is smoking I try to turn away from the smoke without him noticing me. It was getting late; Wilson was still drinking his beer. I got up and put on my nightgown and came back to bed. I put my pillow over my head and tried to go to sleep. Wilson pulled the pillow away and started kissing me. The taste of the beer and cigarette was terrible and I was unmoved. I pretended to enjoy his kiss...I didn't want to hurt him...I love him enough to accept all of his bad habits. Sometimes I wonder why he doesn't think about how I feel about drinking and smoking; I guess he just assume that it doesn't bother me. I have learned to deal with his bad habits; I guess that what love is all about. I just started to drift off to sleep when he finished his beer and asked me if I was asleep. I said I am trying my best to...can we go to sleep now? He got up and undressed and got into the bed. He wrapped his arms around me and said now we can go to sleep sweetheart. He wanted to make love so he started kissing me. I really wasn't in the mood, but I kissed him back and finally he realized that I just wanted to go to sleep, so he said goodnight sweetheart I love you. I said I love you too. As he held me in his arms I felt safe and content and finally drifted off to sleep. The next morning Wilson woke up before the clock ringed. He woke me up with his kissing and caressing. I thought to myself... here we go again. I responded to his advances and before long we were on cloud nine. Just as we were coming off of cloud nine the alarm clock went off we just let it ring and enjoyed the last moment. Finally Wilson reached over and turned the alarm clock off. We thought the timing of the clock was real funny. Wilson got up and got dressed. I said are you going to take a shower? He said I would take a shower on my Tugboat at work. He said I love you sweetheart and kissed me goodbye and left for work. I quickly turned the light out and went back to sleep. Later that morning I woke up and went into the bathroom and took my shower and brushed my teeth. When I came out Sister Linda was up and about; she asked me if I wanted her to start cooking breakfast. I said no we would go to the market and have breakfast there. She said o.k. Just give me a few minutes in the bathroom and I will be ready to go. I continued to towel dry my hair while I waited for her. When she came out of the bathroom my hair was almost dry. She said o.k. I am ready to go.

We left and walked to the market. We went to a small restaurant booth and looked at the prepared food in the glass cage. I told Linda I liked the noodles that were topped with a yellow sauce, egg slices, fried garlic, fried dice fish and chopped onion. She said that's what I want to eat too. We sat down and enjoyed our breakfast. Before we left I ordered two orders to go. Linda said I guess we will eat noodles for lunch. I said yes and we are going to get some fresh vegetable, sardine and corn beef for Wilson to take home. Sister Linda said he really like corn beef. I said he doesn't have a choice I don't know how to cook American food yet, I will learn so he will be happy to have a wife that know how to cook. Sister Linda said yes I am sure he will be happy to eat something other than corn beef. We finished our shopping and started walking back to the apartment. Sister Linda said I enjoy going to the market early in the morning, because it not very hot and you get a nice cool and comfortable breeze. When we arrive at the apartment I put the noodles in a pot to keep from spoiling, because we would eat it for our lunch. Sister Linda said I am going to take a shower before the water is turned off. I said yes you had better hurry…fill up those containers in the bathroom so if the water remains off for a long time we still will have water. I have learned to always save some water because the city turns it off without notice and it usually catch you in the shower with soap all over your face, or trying to brush your teeth. I remembered the first time the water was shut off when I was taking a shower; I had soap all over my face and had to go to into the kitchen to use the pitcher of water we keep for drinking. Now I always think ahead and fill up all of the containers before I start my shower, because the faucet seem to have eyes and can see you when you need the water the most then it shut off…that's why I always tell you to save water. Linda said that happen to me too…one day when you and brother Wilson was out I was taking a shower and forgot to save some water; I had soap all over my face and body when the water went off. I remembered that we always fill the coffee pot with water so I had to go into the kitchen with my eyes closed and find the coffee pot…I was lucky you and Brother Wilson

379

was out because I didn't have any clothes on. I said I told you the faucet have eyes don't forget to save water first. We laughed about our experience with soapy eyes and no water. She said when you have soap in your eyes and it is burning it make you act like a blind person. I wonder how blind people make it without seeing.

I said they have relatives that help them and they become use to getting around by memory. She said yes but how do they live. I said I guess they get use to being blind and learn how to function without seeing...like what we do when we have soap in our eyes we remember where to go in the house to get water...there are school for the blind...they learn to function without seeing...I am happy they have school for them. Sister Linda went into the bathroom and filled up all of the containers and started her shower. I got my crochet and started putting the designs together. Wilson said he like the design I am making. I am happy that I have learned to crochet; I guess if you like what you are doing you can do it very easy. Finally Sister Linda came out of the shower and came over to look at my crochet. She said I have almost finished my project; I have to wash it and soak it in sugar so it will stand up. I said I can't wait to see your project completely finished. I want to make one like it. She took her project out and spread it out on the coffee table. I said Linda you did it, you put on the border color that I like. She said I told you all I have left to do is soak it in sugar, shape it and let it dry...I am not going to soak it yet I have to wait till just before Christmas vacation. I said I will help you so I will know how to soak mines when I finish...I really like the white and purple border on you design. She said I wanted to surprise you, but I just couldn't wait to show you what it look like...it will look even better once I soak it in sugar water, shape it and let it dry... you will really like it when you see it standing up. I said have you started another design? She said yes, and this time I will have a piece of material sawn around the border of the crochet. I said that sound like it will be a nice project. She said yes, I like to crochet it straight and not have material in it. I said I think your teacher is teaching you a variety of crochet designs...that good! Maybe you will learn a lot more in school than I did...oh I am not sorry for myself, because I can read, write and can communicate in English very well...if Sister Melda hadn't stop helping me in school I would have graduated in the top of my class, but that's life I guess it was meant to be…that's why I met Wilson, he is my destiny…everyone has their own road to travel to reach their destiny. If Wilson marries me and takes me to the United States maybe I will get my High School Diploma over there…I am still young and want to learn more. I saw Linda looking out of the window then she asked what time is it? I said its ten o, clock, what's wrong?

She said I see Brother Wilson coming. I said today is Monday why is he coming home early? Wilson walked in the door and Linda and I said hi the same time. Wilson looked very happy as he said hi Linda and hi sweetheart to me. He kissed me and said let's go to the bedroom I want to talk to you. I followed him into the bedroom and sat beside him on the bed. He said I have got good news and bad news. I started getting scared when he said bad news. I thought to myself… is he changing his mind about marrying me, or what? Wilson said while looking so happy, we got our marriage papers back, now we can plan our wedding. My heart started pounding I didn't know if I was happy or what. Wilson kissed me again and again and then he said the bad news is, my heart stopped for a few seconds, then he said the bad news again, it felt like my blood had went to my head and I was going to faint…I couldn't take the suspense any longer, so I said what bad news? Are you leaving me? He said no way as he kissed me, the only thing left for us to do now is get married…the bad news is we have to find another apartment to stay in that's approved by Navy Housing…this is one of the requirements we have to fulfill before we can get married. I said that means that this apartment is not approved. He said I don't think so. The Base Housing office has a list of off base apartments and housing that's approved. I will get some of the addresses and we can check them out; and Friday when I get paid we can put a deposit down on the one we like…maybe we can move Saturday December the first or the second. Wilson held me and kissed me and said sweetheart are you happy now? I said yes I am very happy. He said if you are happy why are you looking sad? He said what's wrong? I said I guess I can't believe this is happening it being a long time coming…it means we can get married before the baby comes. He said all we have to do now is get a place to stay and then we can start planning our wedding…you will have to really take charge when we start buying our furniture, because the local furniture stores will inflate their price if I am alone doing this…first we need to get a bed maybe we can get it on installments then I can make payments every payday…after we get the bedroom set paid for we can start on the next room until we have a house full of furniture. I said let me lay down for a few minutes the news have gotten to me. He said lay down for a while I will go across the street and get me a beer.

I didn't mumble a word the good news was so overwhelming I couldn't talk. When he left for the store I raised up long enough to tell Linda we would be moving maybe sometime this week. Linda said what! She was completely caught by surprise. I said yes we are moving. Before we could discuss it any further Wilson came in with two beers, a liter bottle of coke and ice. He asked Linda to chop up some of the ice for my coke. Sister Linda fixed my coke and gave it to Wilson and he brought it into the bedroom to me. We sat reclined on the bed celebrating the good news about our marriage papers. He sipped his beer and I sipped my coke and we kissed between sips. When we finished drinking our drinks we were still in shock about the good news, so we just silently held each other. Finally Wilson said why don't we get ready and go look around in the furniture stores and check the prices of their bedroom sets…do you think they would let us pay in installment? I said yes, they will be happy to sale you some furniture because they know you can pay for it. I got ready to go and on our way out I told Sister Linda not to wait for us go ahead and eat dinner if we are not back; Wilson and I are going to look at some furniture. The first furniture store we stop at was close to Jackson High School where Linda attends at night. Wilson didn't like the way the bedroom set was made so we went to several more store looking. Finally I thought about the furniture store over by the Market that I visited before. When we arrived the lady that owned the store came over quickly to greet us. I said what happened to all of your sewing machine? She said people have stopped buying sewing machines, so she started selling just furniture. She asked me if I still have my sewing machine. I said yes I still have it. She said are you looking to buy some furniture? I said yes if we find a bedroom set my boyfriend like. Her eyes lit up in excitement when I said yes. Wilson started looking at the Rattan bedroom set and fell in love with it right away. She asked me if Wilson like the bedroom set. Wilson said I like it but it is too small. She said that set is Filipino size we have a warehouse in Angeles city where we can make the set any size you want; we can start making your right away if you want. Wilson said would you sell it to me on installments and I pay every two weeks? She said yes we let people pay by the month so every two weeks will be just fine. Wilson said we're still looking for an apartment and my payday is this Friday.

She said I know your girlfriend she bought a sewing machine on credit and she came and paid on time. She said if you sign an order request now we can start making your bedroom set right away. She said we can deliver your furniture on Saturdays or Sundays just give me two days notice. Wilson signed for the furniture; he said I would let you know what day to deliver when I make my first pay installment this Friday. She said that would be just fine. We said goodbye and left feeling very happy. I looked at the sale order and said four hundred and sixty pesos that too much...we have to pay it off within six months. Wilson said don't worry I can pay forty pesos every payday that is ten American dollars...I think it is very cheap, because in America the price is three times as much...four hundred and sixty pesos is the equivalent of one hundred and twenty American dollars; now I can afford to get us a dining room set too...I will get us a living room set next. When we got back to our apartment Sister Linda was taking her afternoon nap. Wilson went to the store across the street for beer and I went into the kitchen to check the noodles and see if they were still good. I decided not to eat the noodles because they have been out too long without refrigeration. Wilson came back from the store and asked me to fix him a Spam sandwich. I went into the kitchen and fried the Spam for his sandwich and decided to make me a sandwich too. I asked Wilson if he brought ice back from the store. He said no I forgot, but I will go and get some. He left and went back to the store and got ice. Sister Linda woke up and asked what time it was; I told her it was two o, clock and she have one more hour before she have to go to school, go back to sleep. She said I have to go early today and meet with my classmates and discuss our projects. I said o.k. Wake up then. I said I am eating a Spam sandwich; I had to throw away my noodles because they started to smell. Linda said I ate my noodles. I said why didn't you eat mines? She said after I finished mines I was full. Wilson and I sat in the living room eating our Spam sandwiches. He asked me if I were happy about our furniture selection. I said yes, the furniture is made of narra and rattan. This is the best wood in the Philippines for making furniture. That's why I like it. I know you like it too, because I could tell you wanted to take it home today. Right now money and a place to put the furniture is the problem now.

Don't worry we will have it soon maybe tomorrow if we find an apartment. Sister Linda said goodbye as she left for school. We said goodbye and take care. Wilson noticed me watching Linda as she left for school. He said what are you starring at? I said Linda uniform; I use to use that blue and white uniform when I attended Jackson High School. He said what happened? I said I had to quit because there was no money. Sister Melda promised to help me finish high school, but she stopped mama Ligaya from giving us money when she found out that we owed a thousand pesos. She told mama Ligaya that I knew how to read and write and it was time I got a job and went to work. When she returned to the Philippines she got me a job in the Money Exchange booth working for mama Ligaya. I had turned sixteen so I went to work in the Money Exchange where I was working when I met you. Wilson kissed me and said don't worry about working I will take care of you. He said tell Linda when she comes back I said give her uniform to you. I said what am I suppose to do with it? He said I was just joking…tomorrow after work I will check the Housing List of approve apartment in Olongapo City. I said o.k. I can't wait. Wilson said let's go in the bedroom and lay down; I need to relax I am still charged up. We got on the bed and he got right back up and took off his shoes and closed the bedroom door. I said take it easy everything would be all right. He came back to bed and kissed me as if this was our last kiss. I couldn't figure out just what was making him nervous…maybe he were very, very happy or had something on his mind. I asked him if he wanted me to get more beer. He said yes would you please. I got up and went to the store and got more beer. When I returned he were still acting different. I asked him why he looked worried like something is wrong. He said I guess I am very happy because we are almost husband and wife. I said maybe you are thinking to change your mind about marrying me? Maybe you don't want to be tied down with a wife and child...that's what you are thinking about, right. He kept drinking his beer and starring at the ceiling as if he doesn't hear me. I kissed him and said if you plan to change your mind you had better do it right away before it's too late. Wilson turned toward me and said I don't mean to give you the ideal that I want to change my mind about getting married...I will never change my mind...I love you and want to spend the rest of my life with you...I was only thinking about all of the things we have to do before we can get married.

He said I have a lot on my mind. I said I am here you can tell me everything I may not be able to fix the problem, but I can give you my love and support...you will be surprised as to how much just talking about a situation helps. He said you are right sweetheart; I know you can help me and you do; I am just frustrated with the Navy's silly regulation that require us to do all of these thing before we can get married legally. I said well, don't think too much about everything we can take care of them one at a time and before we realize it we will be finish. He said even though you don't speak very good English I understand what you are saying and the point you are making...now you need to help me with my other problem...this. He started kissing and caressing me. I said you are crazy. He said yes I am crazy about you. I said tiger you can take it easy I belong to you no one is going to take your catch away. We hurried removed our clothes; I got out of bed and ran around the bed to see if he would try and catch me. He said you had better stay away from the windows somebody may see my catch. I laughed at him and came back to bed. He took me in his arms and the next thing I realized I was laying in his arms gasping for air. As we lay there starring at the ceiling Wilson started talking about our move from Twenty fifty Street to a new place. Then finally he said let's get cleaned up and go somewhere. I said o.k. Let's go somewhere. After repeating what he just said I got up and went into the bathroom to get cleaned up. As I was coming out of the bathroom he had finally decided to come in and get cleaned up himself. I went back into the bedroom and got dressed, combed my hair and put my makeup on; I was ready to go somewhere, anywhere Wilson wanted to go. Wilson came into the bedroom and said are you ready to go. I turned and looked at him and said yes and don't forget to put your pants and shoes on. He said that right! After he finished dressing we went outside and he finally decided where we were going first. He said let get something to eat and then go visit C.B. and Jean. I said o.k. I am really hungry. We went to the Magnolia Restaurant in the Jungle and he ordered his favorite, a large shrimp salad and I ordered noodles with vegetables. I was surprised when the Waitress asked Wilson what did he want to drink and he said just water.

After we finished our meal we caught a jeepney to C.B. and Jean apartment. We knocked and the kids let us in and went into the bedroom and woke up their parent. C.B. came out first and said they were just taking a nap. After a few minutes Jean came out. As they came out they greeted us and had a seat. C.B. asked Wilson if he wanted a drink of Liquor and Wilson asked him if he had a beer. C.B. said this is some good liquor man it's not the cheap kind that give you a bad hangover. Jean said I had to buy some good liquor for C.B. because he has a problem getting up in the morning every time he drinks that cheap stuff. Wilson said o.k. I will try one drink. C.B. said I want twist your arm if you don't want to drink some. Wilson said you could twist my arm man. I said why does C.B. want to twist Wilson arm? Jean laughed and said Vicky they are only joking. I said you mean they are joking? I started to laugh and they started laughing at me. After everyone stop laughing Wilson told C.B. and Jean that I request to get married has been approved now we can get married. Jean looked at me and said congratulation! You are a fiancé now. I didn't know what a fiancé was, so I said to her, I guess I am. She said I am happy for you. Then I realized that being a fiancé must not be bad, so I said thank you. Then Mr. no respect C.B. said man why hurry, the baby isn't born yet and you don't know if it will look like you. Jean said C.B. leave Wilson alone don't you know you are talking about his fiancé. C.B. said to Jean F--- you woman. Jean looked at me and said Vicky you have to excuse C.B. he just like to curse; every time he opens his mouth the F word comes out...I am use to it...please excuse him. Then Wilson really surprised me when he said man stop talking about Vicky and my baby like that...you know Vicky is not like those girl that works in the clubs; when I met her she was working in the Money Exchange Booth…she is not the girl you think she is o.k. C.B. could tell that Wilson was really serious. He said man I am sorry for talking like that about your woman. Wilson said I don't want you are anyone else to think that all women you meet in Olongapo City are Club Hostess…you are my friend and I respect you and you have to respect my woman and me. Jean said I told you C.B. Vicky is not like the girls that work in the clubs, she is a very nice person. C.B. said yea! Yea! Vicky I apologize for talking about you like that. I said o.k. Then Wilson and C.B. shook hands. I knew then that Wilson was going to protect me no matter what the case and I was very happy to see the change in him.

Everyone settled down and started making small talk until Wilson said we're looking for an apartment that approve by Base Housing. C.B. said you can have this one when we move, but it doesn't look like we will be moving no time soon…we had hope to move by Christmas, but it look like it will be Christmas next year. Wilson said how far up on the Housing list are you? C.B. said the last time I checked it was at least fifteen or twenty names ahead of ours. Jean said the people are moving out very, very slow because they like living here in the Philippines and I can't blame them because you can really save some money living here; it is very hard for us to save any money while living in the States, but here we are saving and still can afford to have a Maid…I am getting spoiled here. Wilson picked up his drink and finished it; I was watching very closely to see what he was going to do next. He said man we have to go now we only came by to share our good news with you and Jean. C.B. said eh! Boy I am truly sorry for what I said about your woman. Wilson said man! Forget about it and they shook hands again. I said goodbye and thank you to Jean. On our way home I thought to myself…it looks like Wilson is trying to control his drinking I really hope that he continue to do it. When we got home I looked for Linda but she had not made it home yet. I thought to myself…I can't believe that it's only nine o, clock; we're home early and Wilson is not drunk. I went into the bedroom and started getting ready for bed. Wilson said are you going to bed now? I said you are not sleepy yet? He said it still early let's sit and talk for a while; I will run to the store and get me a beer. I said o.k. And I got comfortable on the bed to wait for him to return. He came back and said the store had only one cold beer left. I said do you want me to go to the store that beside Sister Melda's old place. He said no it is getting late. He came into the room and closed the bedroom door. He took his street clothes off and reclined on the bed beside me. He kissed me and said we're almost husband and wife. I said we're already husband and wife...you love me...you take care of me and protect me from big mouth C.B. He said C.B. is all right he just curse and talk a lot. I said someone needs to wash his mouth out with soap...maybe he would be all right when he taste the soap...the next person he talk to like that may not be as nice about it as I was tonight...he should never use that word around women or at anytime.

Wilson said we had better stop talking about C.B. I don't want you to get upset...just concentrate on us. I said o.k. What do you want me to concentrate on? He said this! And he started kissing and caressing me. I knew what was coming next; I wanted it to happen just as much as he did. Lying limp there on the bed my mind started to wonder...when my stomach get larger will I still be sexually attractive to him. He noticed that I was thinking deeply about something and asked if I was all right. I quickly said I am all right. Then I got up and went into the bathroom. When I came out I saw Linda coming in the front door from school. I told her not to worry about fixing enough food for me, because I was going to bed. I went back to bed and into the comfort of his arms and went to sleep. The next morning when the alarm went off Wilson hopped right out of bed and got ready for work. He almost forgot to kiss me goodbye. I said have you forgot something? He said sorry sweetheart I was thinking of everything I have to do today. He kissed me and went to work. I tried unsuccessful to go back to sleep, but I couldn't. I just stayed there in bed to wait for Sister Linda to wake up so we could go to Calapacuan and tell Mother the good news. Finally I couldn't wait any longer so I got up and woke her up and told her we were going to Calapacuan. She said it is very early why you are waking me this early. I said come on and wake up we have to go to the market and get fresh vegetables and fish to take with us. She said we're going to Mother's house. I said yes! Now get up so we can go. She got up and went into the bathroom to get cleaned up and dressed. Before we left

I wrote a note to Wilson just in case he came home early telling him we had went to Calapacuan to spread the good news. We left and went to the market and bought fresh vegetables, fish and bread rolls. We caught a jeepney that was waiting to load up passengers, so we were lucky enough to get the front seat. I always tried to get the front seat, because if you set in the back you would smell everyone that didn't take a shower and that smell always gave me a headache. When we arrived in Calapacuan we got out of the jeepney across from the Sari Sari store. I saw Brother Etong in the store buying sugar. When he saw us he came and met us and took our bags. When we came into Mother's house with Brother Etong Mother was surprised because she wasn't expecting someone to be with Brother Etong. We put our bags on the table and Mother looked inside and said that good! You brought bread rolls I was just starting to cook breakfast.

Mother put the fish in the sink to be clean later for lunch. Brother Etong kept signaling how happy he was that we had come to visit. He was real excited about the bread rolls because he likes to dunk them into his coffee. Mother looked at me and asked if I were all right. I said I am all right and I have some good news...the paperwork for our marriage request came back approved...we can get married very soon, but we still have a few things to do before we can; we have to find an apartment that approved by the Navy. Mother said what do you mean by approved? I said they have to approve of the place we stay before we can get married legally...if they don't I want be able to get a Military Dependent ID card so I can use my base privileges like Sister Melda...it's going to take a while to do all of these things. We have to because Wilson is in the Navy and the Navy wants him to live in a nice place so nothing will happen to him and his family. Mother looked very happy. She said that's good you are inside the door now...all you have to do is wait and do the right thing. When we finished eating breakfast Sister Linda got right up and cleaned the kitchen and washed the dishes. She asked what time we were going back to Olongapo City; I told her we would go after lunch. We sat around making small talk until around nine o, clock. Then Mother decided it was time to start preparing lunch; she went to the kitchen sink to clean the fish I brought and to her surprise there were four fish in the bag. She said I thought you only brought one fish there are four here in the bag. I said yes that's right! You can cook one and marinade the others. She said I am glad you brought this food here it will save me the trouble of going to the market. I started to feel a little dizzy, so I told Mother I would lay down for a while. Brother Etong heard what I said and he got up and got a mat, pillow and a blanket for me to lie on. Sister Linda said I will lie down beside you I am sleepy; you got me up this morning too early. After Brother Etong finished putting down the mat for Linda and me he looked at us smiling and pointed to the mat; then he got his bucket and went outside. Sister Linda and I stretched out on the mat and tried to go to sleep; I put one of the pillows over my head and finally drifted off to sleep. I slept for about an hour and half then I got up and sat at the kitchen table to watch Mother fix lunch. Mother said I have started cooking lunch so you can eat before you leave…how is Wilson doing?

I said he is doing all right except he is worry about getting a new apartment and furniture. Mother said everything takes time. I said I thought that once the paper were approved we could get married right away, but we have a lot more to do before the wedding…I didn't think marrying an American would be this much of a problem…we had to wait two months before the request was approved, now we have to find another apartment that approved by the Base Housing office…I wonder what else we will have to do before getting married…I hope Wilson can do all of these things and not get to upset and decided to quit. Mother said I don't think Wilson would do that; I have seen how he looks at you, he really and truly loves you…he is young and can take the pressure…don't worry you're in the door…all you need to do now is find a chair and sit down and wait…you are almost there pretty soon your problem will be over. Sister Linda got up from the mat and said I hope the new apartment is not too far away. Mother said if it's in Olongapo City it is not to far because there is plenty of public transportation to take you wherever you want to go… lunch is ready come on and eat. Everyone hurried and washed up for lunch. The four of us sit down at the table and started eating lunch. I said give me the fish with the head on. Brother Etong gave me the half with the head. Sister Linda said here we go again; I like the fish head too. Mother said I have another fish with the head on; I will get it for you Linda. Brother Etong just smiled and shook his head. Mother said you and Linda never change; you have always like to eat the head of the fish so you can suck the eye ball from the fish head. Everyone was quiet and eating when Mother said I remember when we first moved to Matain close to the beach where all of the big fishing boats came with their catch; you Linda and Etong would trade Mangoes for fish... you would bring so many fish home it would take me a half day to clean them; I cooked some with chopped Mango, barbecued some and dried what was left; we had fish for almost two months. This was the first time I tried cooking fish with green Mango; the receipt came out all right. This was also the time when I noticed that you and Linda was eating only the fish head and sucking out the eyeball. I didn't say anything because the fish was being eaten.

Mother said I started watching you and Linda when you came to the table; I noticed you always put your rice on your plate and took the head part of the fish...I guess I will start cooking you and Linda fish heads only until you start eating the rest of the fish like everybody else...you have to remember we all like to have the head on the fish when we get it; we like to suck the eye balls out too. Sucking the eyeball from the fish head is like sucking the snail out of his shell... do you remember all of the snails we ate when we lived in Alyaga, Pangasinan? We ate snails there and we eat fish here. Linda and I started Laughing. I told Linda it was her fault that we wanted to eat fish like we do snails. She said no it's your fault for asking for the fish head. Mother said it's no one fault, it's just the way you like your fish...remember Linda, your sister is pregnant if she want to eat the head let her have it. I said I have taken care of that Mother; we always cook two fish. Brother Etong smiled and signaled to us that he and Mother do the same. I told Linda to help with the dishes, because we had to go back to Olongapo City. Mother said don't worry about the dishes I will wash them. Brother Etong signaled that he would wash the dishes. When Sister Linda and I was putting up the mat, pillow and blankets in the next room I noticed that Sister Melda had left her living room furniture with Mother. I asked Mother why Sister Melda had left her furniture. Mother said it cost too much to take it to Sangley Point plus Melda has bought a new living room set. I said when I find my new apartment could I borrow it? Mother said yes, Melda is not going to use it again. I said that great! It will give us time to save money to buy our own living room set. Mother said you're thinking like a grown up; I am proud of you...I would never have thought you would marry an American like your Sister Melda...I am happy that I will get to see my Grand children before my time is up. I hugged and said goodbye to Mother and on my way out I said goodbye to Brother Etong in the kitchen washing the dishes. He signaled goodbye and pointed to my stomach indicating that he wanted me to take care of the baby. I smiled and promised him that I would. We caught a jeepney with student passenger from Matain Elementary school where Linda and I use to attend. When they got down at their stop Linda and I got up front in the jeepney.

I asked Linda where she thinks the students are going. She said they was going back to school after lunch...it's twelve thirty and they have to be back at school by one. I said I forgot that they always go home for lunch. She said it being a long time ha! Vicky. I said yes I forgot that I use to do the same thing. She said if I went to school during the day I would be doing the same thing they are doing. I said how do you like going to school at night? She said I am getting use to it; I like going at night because it's not too hot. I said I think I would like going doing the day better, because I would be able to see everything. She said Vicky they have lights all over the school and you can see everywhere. I said I am talking about the darkness on the other side of the fence. She said what are you going to be doing on the other side of the fence when you are supposed to be in the classroom? I said just forget it Linda. We sat silent watching the coastline because there was a big Navy ship going toward Cubi Point on the Naval Base. I tried to make out the ship number, but it was too far away. Finally we arrive at the jeepney stop in Olongapo City and caught a tricycle to our apartment. When I entered the apartment I looked for the letter that I left for Wilson, but it was not on the table where I left it. I went into the bedroom and saw the letter on the bed. I called out for Linda and she came into the bedroom. I asked her if she saw me put the letter on the table in the living room. She said yes Vicky you put it on the table in the living room; maybe brother Wilson came home and read the letter and put it here in the bedroom so you would know he had been here. I said I didn't know he was coming home early today... check the bathroom and see if the water is still on. Linda went into the bathroom and turned on the faucet and said the water is still on. I said o.k. I think I will take a shower now before Wilson return. I went into the shower singing one of Nat King Cole's songs. When I came out of the bathroom Linda said the winner of the singing competition is Rosario Palaganas. She really scared me. She kept laughing and finally said your singing scared the bugs away; they ran into hiding, so you're the winner. I said you're crazy; you had better take your shower before the water is turned off...remember the Monster eyes on the faucet Linda...the faucet have eyes. Linda said you're the one that's crazy; now you are trying to scare me.

When Sister Linda went into the bathroom she stopped laughing and got quiet. Then she called me to come into the bathroom and check the faucet for eyes. Then I realized that I had really scared her telling her the faucet had eyes. I went into the bathroom and assured her that I was only joking about the faucet having eyes. When she finished her shower and came out of the bathroom I started laughing at her. I thought to myself...I would give her the name scary cat. While sitting on the bed looking in the mirror I almost scared myself when I looked and saw myself with one eye. I didn't realize that one of my eyes were cover with the towel I had wrapped around my head. I thought to myself...I had better stop trying to scare Linda because I would only end up scaring myself. Sister Linda came in and asked if I had some baby powder. I said yes and gave her the container. She put some in the palm of her hand and rubbed her hands together and smeared it on her face. I said you use baby powder on your face just like me. She said can't you see that I have a baby face. We laughed and she said you have a baby face too. I looked back into the mirror and she said I got you. We laughed again and she went into the living room and sat down to towel dry her hair. She always wore her hair real short so it didn't take very long for her to dry it. I kept my hair very long and it always took me a long time to dry it. When she finished drying her hair she put on her school uniform. I said it's only two thirty why are you getting dress for school now? She said I am going to my friend's house and sew my material for my next project. I said o.k. Go ahead then, but before she walked out of the front door Wilson walked in. As he came through the door he said hi to Linda and came over and gave me a big kiss. He seems to be very happy, so I guess he have some good news for us. Wilson said I have found an apartment and I think you are going to like it. The apartment is still occupied, but they will be moving tomorrow. The owner of the apartment says we can move in Thursday, but I told him we would move in Friday. I also went to the furniture store and told them to deliver the bedroom set Friday afternoon. I said slow down and take it easy you know I don't understand English real good so slow down so I can understand what you are saying. He spoke real slow and said I am happy because I have found us an apartment. I said where is it located? He said over near the Money Exchange Booth where you use to work on Second Street. I said how many bedrooms?

He said two bedroom, but I didn't get a chance to go in the apartment; I looked at the owners apartment, which he said looks just the same as the one we're moving in...this afternoon we will go by the apartment so you can see the location. I said o.k. He said what did your mother say about our good news? I said my Mom is very happy for us...she said she is happy that we're in the door. He asked what your Mother meant about being in the door. I told him she means we can relax now the hard part is over. He still looked a little puzzled, but I could only repeat what Mother had told me. He hesitated for a few second then he said I am going to tell the Landlord that we will be moving out Friday...we're paid up for the next two weeks here, so they should be able to find a new Tenant within two weeks. He left and went to the Landlord apartment in back. I kept combing my hair trying to get it to dry in a hurry. When he returned he said the Landlord told him all he need to do is drop off the key on Friday and everything will be all right. He said let go in the bedroom, so I followed him into the bedroom he looked so happy I wondered if he had something else to tell me. He turned around and said we're going to celebrate; I am going to the store and get coke and beer. When he came back he went straight to the bedroom again, so I followed him. He gave me a coke and he opened up his beer. He touched his beer to my coke. I asked him why he bumped my coke with his beer. He said we're celebrating because I have found a new apartment and when we touch our drinks together we're making a toast to our new apartment. I said to another apartment. He smiled and said to us and I said to us. He stopped smiling and said I love you; being with you makes me very happy. I just smiled and finished drinking my coke. He asked me if I wanted another coke. I said no I have had enough. He opened another beer and started drinking it. He always gets two beers when he goes to the store, because we don't have a refrigerator to keep things cold. We made ourselves comfortable on the bed propped up with pillows. He said we would buy the rest of the furniture one room at a time...the bedroom and dining room furniture is being delivered Friday...the next room we would take care of is the living room. I told him my Mother said we could use Sister Melda's living room set that she left when she moved to Sangley Point.

He said that is wonderful; we can use it until our new furniture arrives...Linda and I will rent a jeepney and go to Calapacuan and pickup the living room set and you can stay at the new apartment and wait for the furniture to be delivered...have the delivery people to arrange it just like you want it. I said I can't wait I am so excited. He said yes and you excite me. Then he started kissing and caressing me and before long it happened. After catching our breath we drifted off to sleep. Around five that afternoon I felt the bed moving as Wilson were getting up to go to the bathroom. I said where are you going. He said to the bathroom. I closed my eyes and tried to go back to sleep. He came back to the bedroom and said wake up sleeping beauty. I pretended that I didn't hear him. He sat on the side of the bed and kissed me and said it's five o, clock get up so I can show you where the new apartment is located. I got up and went in the bathroom and cleaned up and came out and put on my make up (baby powder). Finally I was ready to go, so we caught a jeepney and went to Rizal Avenue the strip of Night Clubs called the Jungle. We got out on Second Street and walked about fifty yards from Rizal Avenue and about one hundred yards from the Money Exchange Booth where I use to work. Wilson pointed out the apartment through the metal fence and gate. I said that's nice; it has a metal gate. He said yes they close the gate at night to keep the intruders out. I said that's good we're protected from robbers. He said do you think you will like living here? I said it's a nice apartment, but it's too close to the Clubs. I said do you think you will like living here close to the Clubs and everything you like? He didn't really get the meaning of what I was trying to say...he found a place real close to the Clubs and his girlfriends. I guess I have to accept this apartment because it's where he wanted to stay...if I disagree with him about the apartment it will only delay our plans in trying to get everything done so we can get married; if there will be a wedding...we will be living just around the corner from all of the night clubs he likes to hangout in. I started to feel that uneasy feeling again...trying to figure out what would come next. He said let's stop by the Birdland Club tonight. I said I didn't know you hung out in the Birdland.

He said I have a friend that will be there tonight. I said o.k. And followed him down the crowded street. When we entered the club it seem as though every girl in the club knew him and tried to get his attention. He spotted his friend sitting at a table with his girlfriend. We made our way over to their table. He introduced me to his friend and his girlfriend. We took a set and he ordered our drinks. I said would you please go up to the bar and get my coke. He gave me a puzzle look and said I have ordered you a coke already; why do you want me to go to the bar and get it for you? I knew then that it wasn't any use trying to explain to him what the girls may do to my drink or his if they are jealous of me being with him. I didn't say anything else because he was where he likes to be...in a nightclub with girls hanging all over him. I sat there watching him drink his mix drink. I thought to myself...one drink and he is drunk already. I asked him if we could go home now. He said later I am talking with my friend... are you going to drink your coke? Then he poured my coke from the bottle into the glass. I said I am not thirsty yet. He kept looking at me so I picked up my glass and pretended to drink the coke, but I didn't dare drink it, because if they put something in his drink they would put something in mines too. Wilson wasn't concern about what someone would put in his drink all he wanted to do was drink and hangout in the club. One of the girls came over to our table and pulled him out on the dance floor; he started dancing and enjoying himself as if I wasn't there. When he returned to our table I told him to stay and enjoy himself I was going home. I went outside and hailed a taxi; he followed me out and got into the taxi too. He started getting mad at me in the taxi; he said I was only danced with the girl it doesn't mean anything. I didn't say a word I decided to wait until we got home. When we got home in the apartment I told him I would talk to him the next day because he was drunk. I went straight to the bedroom and changed into my nightgown and got into the bed. He came and sat on the side of the bed looking at me as if he was spaced out; I guess whatever they put in his drink make him act like that. If Jones girlfriend had not told me about what the girl in the club do; I wouldn't know what was happening to him when he acts like that.

I keep telling him over and over again to go to the bar and get his drink and not let the girls bring it to him; some of the girls are bad they put drugs in your drink and get you drunk and then they take your wallet and take your money out and put the wallet back in your pocket. Tonight he got mad at me because I asked him to go to the bar and get my drink. I thought to myself...now look at him; he is drunk and had only one drink. I turned my back to him...I really don't think I can live like this forever with him...maybe now he will start listening to me sometimes and he will be all right...he can't seem to understand that all the girls in the club want from him is his money...he said he wanted to try and save money to buy furniture for our apartment; we will see how he does that living around the corner from the Jungle...everyday he will pass by the clubs coming home...it will be hard for him to walk right by them and come home. He tried to turn me around and kiss me. I told him he had better brush his teeth so he wouldn't make me dizzy like him from that drink he had in the club. He kept sitting there looking at me as if he didn't know me; then he started taking off my clothing I decided not to resist him because I didn't want him to fall on my stomach. Finally it was over I looked at the clock it was only nine o, clock and still early. I turned from him and went to sleep. The next morning when the alarm went off he grab the clock and turned it off. He asked me where were his clothes. I said they are on the floor somewhere. He got up and picked up his clothes from the floor and put them on. He came back over to the bed and tried to kiss me goodbye and I turned my back and didn't say a word to him. He knew I was mad, so he quietly left the bedroom on his way to work. I decided I wouldn't think about what was happening; I tried to go back to sleep and was very successful. Around eight that morning Sister Linda knocked on the bedroom door. I got up and opened it; she said he had cooked rice and dried fish. I was still sleepy, but I was hungry too, so I went into the bathroom and got cleaned up for breakfast. I told Sister Linda the water pressure was very weak she had better take her shower and save some water in the container we kept in the bathroom. She said o.k. And hurried into the shower.

When she came out I could tell she was glad that the water kept running long enough to finish her shower. I said there must be a lot of people in Olongapo taking a shower at the same time. She said the City should build a bigger water tank...next time we go to the market we need to buy a big plastic container to save water in at night to use to wash clothes...we didn't have this problem in Calapacuan because we had spring water that came from the mountains...I think we should do what we do at daytime at night; take showers and wash clothes. I said I still need to take a shower at least twice a day, but I didn't tell her why. I said when you're pregnant you sweat a lot. When we finished drying our hair we started eating breakfast. I told her we were moving Friday. She said where is the apartment? I said Second Street facing the Money Exchange where we use to work. She said over there! That's good! We don't have to ride tricycles anymore; we just catch passenger jeepney to go to the market and to school. I said we are quite a distance from the market. She said that's o.k. We ride tricycles to the market now, so when we get there we will just ride a jeepney; it's all the same we have to ride anyway...have you seen the place? I said yes, but I didn't go inside your Brother Wilson say it is up and down and the two bedrooms are upstairs. She said that's good! Now I can have my own bedroom. I said yes it is really good you will have your own bedroom.

This Friday Wilson is going to Calapacuan to get Sister Melda's old living room set; would you go with him before you go to school? She said yes I will go, but I don't have to go to school at all I will tell my teacher I had to move. I said that's good, because I have to wait at the Second Street apartment for delivery of our new furniture. She said I am very excited about moving into our new apartment. We finished eating our breakfast and Linda cleaned the kitchen and washed the dishes. When she came out of the kitchen she said the water is off again. I went into the bedroom and put some baby powder on my face and continued towel drying my hair. I took a seat near the window where a nice cool breeze came in and before long my hair was dry. I thought to myself...next time I get a chance I am going to get the split ends trim from my hair...I will tell Wilson after I have it cut.

When I finished drying my hair; I didn't feel like doing anything else. I started thinking about what had happened in the club last night. Wilson really upset me when he danced with that girl in the club. I can take his drinking and getting drunk, but I just can't take it when he get up and leave me and dance with other girls. I am really tired of trying to deal with two personalities; I don't know how long I can take it. I wander if he realizes how much he hurt me when he does that; what if I decide to dance with other guys? I wonder what he would do or say. I think he would want to beat up the guy. I can't understand why he forget who I am; I guess the drug they put in his drink make him forget everything. He knows about what some of the girls will do to your drinks, because he told me that the Navy lectures them about some of the things to watch out for when they go into town. He doesn't seem to care about anything except getting drunk. I wonder if he knows that the way he treats me causes me to lose respect for him. Maybe he wants me to act like those girls in the club that take drugs and do anything for money. Sometimes I get that feeling; I really don't know what to do sometimes. I am sure he knows that girl he danced with last night. We're supposed to be trying to get married, but it looks like he trying to get closer to the nightclubs and the girls. He knows the Doctor told me not to get upset; maybe he is trying to get me upset so I will lose the baby. I told him before if he didn't want the baby just leave me, because I would keep my baby. He told me that I am the only girl that he loves and he would cut back on his drinking, I am still trying to figure out when he plan to start cutting back...I guess he think I am real naive and stupid. I started to get dizzy thinking about everything, so I decide to try and go to sleep. I put my pillow over my head and closed my eyes. Finally I did drift off to sleep. The next thing I realized was when Linda started shaking me and woke me up. She asked me what did I want her to cook for lunch. I said lunch! Then I looked at the clock it was eleven thirty. She said I have fried the eggplant; what do you want me to cook with it? I said open a can of sardines and stir-fry some garlic and onions with it. She said yes, that's a good idea. I got up and went into the bathroom and got cleaned up again.

When I came out I smelled the stir-fry and all of a sudden I was hungry. When the food was ready I fixed my plate and went into the living room and sat down to eat. I told Linda to go to the store to get ice for the water. When she came back she asked me if I wanted some coke I told her I only wanted cold water. She chopped up some of the ice and put it into a glass and poured water over it and gave it to me. We sat eating silently. I still felt sleepy; Linda asked me if there was something wrong. I said yes I am all right I just feel a little sleepy and I don't know why. Linda said you were acting all right this morning what happened? I said I really don't know this feeling came on all of a sudden and it make me feel as though all of my energy has been drained. She said I hope you are not catching a cold, because that would be bad while you are pregnant. I couldn't bring myself to tell Linda the truth of the matter; I was trying desperately to figure out what my next step would be after what had happen in that nightclub. I don't know if I still want to marry Wilson. I really have some soul searching to do. Then I really started to thinking to myself...I still love him, but everything he does seem to make me doubt whether I can trust him to be the husband he need to be or the husband I want him to be...now we're moving close enough for him to walk to the Clubs...will he stop there before he comes home? I really don't know what to think. Linda broke the silence and said why don't you go back and lay down for a while; maybe you will feel better. I got up and went back into my bedroom. As soon as I entered the bedroom my mind started to wonder again...Wilson is a very loving guy...he is young and likes to party...I love him very much and he know that... he knows that I will always forgive him when he starts to kissing me...I really can't help myself when he kisses me...I guess I will have to stop thinking about myself and start thinking about my baby. I really can't understand Wilson when he gets in the club he seems to forget everything including me. I have told him countless times about the girls putting drugs in his drinks, but he continues to trust them to do the right thing. He should have guessed by now that if he gets drunk on one drink in the club and it doesn't happens at home there is something wrong.

I can't make an issue of it in the clubs because the girls are in Gangs and they would make trouble for him and me...when we are at home I always tell him to go up to the bar and get your own drink...don't let the girls bring your drink, but he quickly forget what I have told him as soon as he get into the club. I guess the only thing I can do when I sense that someone is putting something in his drink is do the same thing I did last night...walk out of the club and hope that he follows me. When I worked in the Money Exchange Booth in front of the Jet Club I heard all kinds of stories the girls told each other about how they would drug a Sailor and take him to the Hotel and let him pass out; then they would get his wallet and take all of his big bills and leave him the small bills and leave the room; then they would return to the Club. That's why I worry about Wilson so much when he goes to the Clubs alone. I always go with him when he ask, but he always treats me so bad when I am there I really don't like going with him. I guess that's why I don't really know what to do about ours situation. Sometimes I think I should just tell him to forget about getting married, because our relationship is not working; we're two different people from different cultures and have a different way of life...his way of life is looking for the next party...should I say this to his face? What will I do? I really love him too much to say that and hurt his feeling. Why life is like this? Sometime you are up and sometimes you are down, love is good and love is bad. Am I going crazy or do I have too much on my mind? Starring up at the ceiling is driving me nuts, what's happening to me? Linda came into the bedroom and said are you sure you are all right? Would you like to see what I am making for my new school project? Linda didn't get any type of a respond from me so she came closer to see what was going on. She noticed that I was starring at the ceiling. She came over to the bed and shook me. I turned to her and asked her what was wrong. She said there is nothing wrong with me, but it sure looks like something is wrong with you. I said oh it does...please bring me a glass of water. She went into the kitchen and returned with a glass of ice water. I sat up in the bed and drunked some of the water. I looked at her and said thank you and then decided to go into the living room and sat with her. I was starring at the window when Linda said Vicky look what I am doing. I turned and looked at the crochet she had in her hand.

I said that is nice Linda I like that purple color. She said when I finish this project and get my grade I will give it to you for your apartment. I said thank you! She said are you going to crochet with me today? I said no not now maybe later; I have a lot on my mind. She said what's on your mind...remember what Mother told you about thinking too much...you need to stop it so you want get sick. She said let's go outside and gets some fresh air for a while. We went outside and looked at the Guava trees that had some fruit and blooms. I said let's get some of the fruit. Linda said no don't touch the Guava tree...do you want it to get sick? When you are pregnant you are to stay away from the tree...I will buy you some fresh Guava when I go to the market tomorrow. We stayed outside making small talk for a few more minutes. Then Wilson came home and asked us what we were doing outside. I said I want to eat that Guava fruit on that tree. He said which one do you want? I said that one hanging right there on the big limb. Wilson reached up and plucked the Guava from the branch and gave it to me. He said let's go inside before the Owner call the Police. Linda was smiling when she said are you happy now? What if the Owner saw Wilson picking the fruit...maybe you and him will get in trouble. I said you're a scary cat...I wanted the Guava, but you wouldn't get it for me, but Wilson got it for me...eat your heart out. Linda just kept laughing at me. Wilson said make sure you wash that fruit before you eat it. I went into the kitchen and washed the Guava and came into the living room where she and Wilson were sitting. I bit into the Guava and said um, um good as I looked at Linda. She kept laughing and finally said spoiled brat. Wilson got up and said let's go into the bedroom. I followed him into the bedroom and closed the door behind me. I continued to eat the fruit in the bedroom. Wilson said you really like that fruit; what is the name of it? I said Guava like Guava jelly or Guava fruit. He said I have heard about Guava, but this is the first time I have seen the fruit. I stopped eating it and held it out in my hand for him to see. He said it have a lot of seeds in it. I said yes that what make it taste so good when you bite into the small seeds and you hear the crunch. He kissed me and said sweetheart, what was you mad about when I left for work this morning? I said let me finish eating my fruit.

I had almost forgotten what I was mad at him about. When I finished my Guava I said don't take me out to the nightclub again...do you remembered me asking you to go up to the bar and get my drink and you insisting on me drinking the one the waitress brought? I have tried to make you understand that the girls working in the club will put drugs in your drink and I am afraid they will put drugs in my drink, because I am with you. Do you remember getting drunk with one drink? He said yes I remember, but what happened last night? When we came into that club I could see the expression on those girl faces; they was jealous of me being with you, so when you refused to get my drink from the bar I decided to leave instead of drinking the drink the girl brought to our table. I figured if I leave you would follow me. I don't want to be in the club with you when you get drunk, because you forget that I am with you. I have seen what happens when we go to the club and you only have one drink and you become so drunk you almost pass out. He said just one drink. I said yes, but when you are at home or at C.B.'s house you drink two or three beers and you don't get drunk. He said I guess they have being putting something in my drink. I said thank you! That's what I have being trying to tell you...I know that those club Hostess will put drugs in your drink and you know it too, but you want listen to me or use common sense and watch what you 're drinking...do someone have to pound it in your head that those girl will put drugs in your drink? That's the real reason I don't want to go out to the clubs with you, because they will put drugs in your drink and you start acting like you are from another world and forget that I am with you. I don't know if we will remain together, because we will be moving closer to your favorite party places...I probably want see you very much when we move to second street. He said you know I have promised to cut back on my drinking...it not my fault that someone put something in my drink and I get drunk on one drink. I said it would never happen if you go up to the bar and get our drinks, but you insist on letting the Hostess bring our drinks. The girl you were dancing with is the one that brought our drinks. He said I was not paying attention to the person that brought our drinks. I said well I were watching what was going on that's why I got up and left hoping you would at least follow me out of the club. He said I don't remember anything you said that happened. I said just forget it; I don't want to talk about it anymore.

Then I got up and went into the living room and sat down. I thought to myself...if he doesn't remember anything that happened why talk to him about it. He said come back to the bedroom I need to talk to you. I said let me sit out here for a while. Then there was silence until Sister Linda said I am going to school now to meet my classmates. I said I would see here tonight. She stopped at the door and asked if I still wanted her to go with Wilson to Calapacuan the next day and pick up the furniture. I said yes Wilson still need her help. Wilson heard Linda and me talking and asked what we were talking about. I told him Linda wanted to know if we still plan to pick up the furniture in Calapacuan tomorrow. Wilson said yes Linda if you still could make it. She said o.k. Brother we will go tomorrow and left for school. Wilson said would you please come into the bedroom so we can talk. I said we can talk out here...what do you want to talk about? He said about us. I said what about us? He said Sweetheart we're almost husband and wife and I don't want you to be mad at me...I am trying to please you...I have cut back on my drinking...I couldn't help what happened last night when someone put something in my drink...I guess the only thing that I can do or say to you is that I promise to be more careful when I take you out to the clubs...please forgive me. He came into the living room and kissed me and I kissed him back. I knew it wasn't his entire fault about what happened last night, but he could have avoided it if he would listen to me sometimes. He took my hand and pulled me up from the chair and led me to the bedroom. We put our pillows together and reclined on the bed like we always do. He said this is our last day and night to use this bed. I said yes! So what! He said please don't get mad again let's kiss and make up. I just looked at him and thought to myself...I guess it's true we are leaving this apartment...we have a lot of memories good and bad in this apartment...it's really bad we have to move; I hope the new apartment will be as nice to us as this one. I hope God will bless us again. Wilson said what are you thinking about? I said I really feel bad about having to move away from this apartment. He said I do too, but we have to...living in this apartment is part of our life, twenty fifth street and the little Sari Sari store across the street... everything will be all right.

He pulled me closer to him and kissed me and told me everything will be all right. We lay silently there enjoying the cool breeze coming from the window. Wilson said it would be nice if the Navy would approve this apartment...I guess we should also be happy that I have found an apartment right away, so we can get on with the other things we have to do before we get married. We can start planning our wedding. He turned to his side and looked me square in the eyes and said I love you and nothing can stop us now...except you...I sometime wonder if you love me...you know that I love you and want to spend the rest of my life with you and our baby. I said I love you too, but the only thing I worry about is your drinking...maybe you get drunk in the club and forget to come home because of the drugs they slip in your drink. He said don't worry I am not going to get drunk in the club. He always makes promises to me; I just listen to him and silently hope he will do what he promises. I decided to try and go to sleep, so I turned my back to him. He said why you turned your back to me...are you still mad at me? I said no I am not mad at you I just want to go to sleep. He said o.k. I am going to the store and get me a beer. He got up and went to the store. When he came back he brought his beer and an ashtray into the bedroom. I knew it wouldn't be very long before he wanted to start drinking beer, so now here he is with his beer and cigarettes. I don't like the smell of cigarette smoke. I got up and opened the bedroom door and came back to bed. He said why did you open the bedroom door? I said because your cigarette smoke makes me dizzy...you know I am pregnant and a lot of things I smell make me sick. He said I am almost finished now. I said that's o.k. Just leave the door open and I will be all right and you can enjoy your cigarette. He said I want to enjoy something else and he kissed me and started tugging at my blouse. I said are you all right? He said between his kisses, I would be in a few minutes. We made love like there were no tomorrow and when we finished I closed my eyes and went to sleep. I was awakening by the smell of food cooking. I thought to myself...Linda has returned home. I looked around and Wilson was not in the bed, so I got up and went into the kitchen. Wilson was cooking something in the frying pan. I said what are you doing?

He said I am cooking you some corn beef so you can eat when you wake up. I said you know how to cook too. He said I try to...I wanted to do something for you. I went into the bathroom and washed up and brushed my teeth. He said I am going to the store for ice and coke then we will eat. I didn't say anything I took a seat in the living room; I just tried to observe what he was doing. He came back with ice, coke and beer and went into the kitchen. He chopped up some ice for my coke and served it to me. I said I would get the food. He said how much rice do you want? I said oh! Are you going to serve the food too? He said just sit down and I will bring your food. He fixed our plates and gave me mines and asked if it was enough food. I said yes it is enough. He took a seat beside me and we ate our food. I started thinking to myself...is this a dream or what. Then I said to Wilson would you pinch me I think I am dreaming. He reached over and pinched my arm; I said I guess I am not dreaming you are really cooking corn beef for me. He said it was getting late and you were sleeping so good so I decided to see if I could find something to make a sandwich; I saw the corn beef and remembered how you had stirred fried it with onions, so I decided to try it...how does it taste? I said it taste good and you have cooked like this before when you were hungry and drunk...don't you remember? He said I don't remember, maybe it was a sandwich instead of stir-fry. I said the food was really good what's for dessert? He said oh! I forgot how about giving me a rain check on the desert? I didn't understand the phrase "rain check", so I asked him if I had to wait until it rain to get desert. He looked surprised then he said no! It means that I would get you some desert at a later date or time like tonight or tomorrow. I said o.k. Just give me my desert whenever. Now I will wash the dishes. I leaned over and kissed him and told him he cooked a great meal. I got up and went into the kitchen and started washing the dishes. After washing the dishes I got a big pan and put all of the dishes, pot and pans inside. Wilson saw me putting the stuff in the big pan and asked why. I told him I was packing for our move the next day. He said that's a good idea; I will help you with the can food in the cabinets...don't worry about trying to pack the clothes; we can hang them up in the jeepney. We packed all of our food, clothing and shoes in big shopping bags.

Wilson said now we're ready to move tomorrow...I will be her around nine o, clock tomorrow morning. I said o.k. I will be ready...I think I will take a shower tonight so that I will be ready tomorrow morning. He said there would be plenty of time to take a shower tomorrow morning…come over and sit by me on this hardwood chair this will be the last night we will sit on it. I said o.k. And took a seat beside him. I said I really like this hardwood furniture, but when you sit to long your whole body start to ache. Wilson said I am getting use to sitting on this furniture…I just gage how long I sit and get up before my rear end start to hurt. Do you think this is Narra wood? I said I guess so, it have all of the nice carving on it…Narra is the best wood in the Philippines for carving and making nice furniture. I could tell that Wilson really likes the furniture, but we had to move to another place. We sat there on the chair quiet for a while. Finally I said I have sat here on this chair more than anyone especially when you leave me alone here at night…I set here watching the light on that pole; sometimes I cry because I feel sorry for myself. Wilson put his arm around me and hugged me real tight. He said Sweetheart you shouldn't think so much; I know that I have being drinking and running around too much, but I promise not to do that again… it was stupid of me to leave you alone and go out running around. We hugged and kissed. I said to myself…if this hard wood chair could talk it would say I am happy for you go and have a good life sitting on new furniture. Wilson said Sweetheart you know that if you marry me we will be moving around a lot; we will see and meet new people and live in new places until I retire from the Navy, so you need to get use to the ideal of moving around a lot. I like living here in this apartment, but just like Wilson said I have to get use to living in different place, because we will move around a lot. I thought I had put all of the moving behind me when I came to Olongapo City; when I was growing up every time I thought we had settled in to a place my family start planning to move again. Now here I go again moving from place to place with my would be husband. This is just like a broken record never ending.

Wilson said let's go to bed we're going to have a long day tomorrow. He got up from the hardwood chair and started for the bedroom and I followed him and closed the door behind me. I got undress and put my nightgown on and all of the time Wilson was standing beside the bed looking at me. As soon as I put my gown on I jumped into the bed and covered myself; I knew he was watching me undress and put my nightgown on. He asked me what was wrong; I told him there was nothing wrong I was just feeling a little chilly. He said don't worry I am coming to warm you up. I said I thought you were tired and sleepy? He said after I warming you up I would go to sleep. He warmed me up just like he said he would. If our bed could only talk it would have a story to tell.

The next morning our moving day Wilson got up before the alarm clock went off. After he got dress he came back to the bed and gave me a big hug and told me he would be back around nine or nine thirty. He kissed me and said I love you sweetheart and left for work. I assured him that I loved him too. When he left he seem a little excited about the move, but I could tell that he was a little sad also, about leaving our first apartment. I didn't try to go back to sleep; I got up and stripped the lining from the bed and folded it up. Linda heard me moving around in my room and came in to see what I was doing this early in the morning. She said what are you doing this early in the morning...we have plenty of time before we leave. I said Linda go back to bed I am going to take my last shower in this apartment. I put the lining aside and went into the bathroom. When I turned on the water the pressure was real strong I couldn't believe it. My first thought was to save some in case the water was turned off, but remembered that I was moving out today to another apartment. When I finished my shower I said thank you to the shower for making my last shower really enjoyable. When I came out of the shower I told Sister Linda that the water pressure in the shower was really strong and it would make her shower a real treat. She said I guess I have to get up now. I said you don't have to get up now I was only letting you know that the shower pressure is very strong...the water pressure is being nice to us on our last day in this apartment...when you take a shower you will see. She got up and went into the bathroom to take her shower. When she came out she said the shower is like a ghost, now that we're leaving it running stronger than ever...you was right Vicky when you said that the faucet have eyes or maybe ears...it know we're leaving, so it is giving us all of the water we want... every day we have a problem with the water pressure, look at it now... there is so much water coming out I don't know how to act. I said we should just be thankful that we had a chance to really enjoy our last shower in this apartment. She said I kind of like this place, but I know we have to move…you have to start moving all over again…moving with your boyfriend and when you get married with your husband and you never know how many times after that. What's going on? We're always moving like when we were growing up…now we have grown up and still moving. I said I guess Linda, we were born to be a traveling family from Barrio to Barrio, from city to city and maybe country to country…maybe that's my Destiny or God's will. Maybe that's the way God want my life to be. I thank God that I have Wilson to share my life with and if it's still his will; I want to have a long life to show my love to him and have his kids…I believe it God's will that I spend my life with Wilson. Sister Linda said Vicky you are so dramatic I know God is watching over you. I said Linda one of these days you will feel and understand what I am talking about…loving someone and spending the rest of your life with without complaint. Linda said we had better get moving or Wilson is going to complain that we haven't finished packing the rest of the things. I said we had better get something to eat first before I get hungry and can't do anything else…go to the store and get some bread and liver worth to make sandwiches and we will cook at the new apartment. I gave her money for the food and she left for the store. When she returned she said the store didn't have any liver worth so she got sardines. I said that o.k. Let's eat. When we finished eating Sister Linda said she was going to clean the bathroom and kitchen so it would be clean when we left. I said yes that's good I am going to dusty all of the furniture and push everything into one corner and scrub the floor.

Sister Linda said we don't need to worry about the floor it is shinning so bright you can see yourself as you walk over it…it shines like a mirror…that's why Wilson like this place so well it has floors and furniture made of hardwood…all you have to do is run a dust mop over the floor and they shine like a mirror. We clean the apartment and sat down to wait for Wilson. Sister Linda said it almost nine o, clock, but don't worry we have all day to move…I told my Teacher I was moving and wouldn't be coming in today. I said that is good now you can stay and help us all day to get settled in the apartment and don't forget you are to go with Wilson to Calapacuan to get the living room furniture. Around ten o, clock Wilson arrived with a jeepney; Linda helped him load up the jeepney. After loading the jeepney Wilson went in the back to see the owner of the apartment. They took a quick tour of the apartment to look for cleanness and damage; the owner said the apartment looked great, she asked if we were moving to another apartment. He said yes, we had to move to an apartment approve by the Navy Housing Office. She told Wilson her apartments were approved by the Navy Housing Office. Wilson told her he wished he had known before he put a deposit down on the new apartment. He returned the keys and we left. When we got into the jeepney I asked Wilson if he knew that the apartment was approved before we moved in. He said no the owner never mentioned anything about the apartment being approved when we moved in; if she had told me we wouldn't be moving now...we will just see how our new apartment works out o.k. Sweetheart. I said o.k. I guess we will have to take the new apartment. When we arrived Mr. and Mrs. Blanco, the apartment complex owner were waiting outside to greet us. Wilson introduced me to them and started unloading the jeepney and carrying everything into the apartment. I told Wilson and Linda to put everything in Linda room until the rest of the furniture is delivered. Finally everything was unloaded and place in a temporary location until the Furniture Company makes it delivery.

Wilson asked me how did I like the apartment. I told him it was all right except it was very hot upstairs, so he and Sister Linda opened all of the bedroom windows upstairs. Standing in the master bedroom Wilson said Sweetheart this is our bedroom you can watch me from this window coming home. He started kissing and hugging me; I said not yet! We don't have our bed yet...let's go down stairs so you can hook up the propane stove and I can cook some rice. When you finish with the stove you and Linda can go to Calapacuan and get the Living room furniture. Downstairs Sister Linda asked me if I wanted her to cook some rice; I told her I would cook the rice so she and Wilson could leave for Calapacuan and get the furniture. When Wilson finished hooking up the stove they left for Calapacuan. I took a quiet tour of the apartment and looked around out back in the patio. Finally my tour was over so I looked for the pot so I could cook the rice. I found the pot under the sink, so I took it out and washed it again and started the rice. I started thinking to myself...a two-story apartment, how in the world am I going to get Wilson upstairs when he is drunk. Someone started knocking on the front door and almost startled me; I answered the door it was Mr. Blanco the apartment owner. He said if we need anything else just knock on his door, which was next door to us. I said thank you! I would make sure I tell Wilson when he comes home. I went back to the kitchen and lowered the flame under the rice pot so that it would simmer. Then I went over to the stair step and sat down. I looked around and started thinking to myself...this place is bare we don't have anything in it not even a chair to sat on or a table to put my food on when I eat...I wish the Furniture Company had delivered the dining table and bedroom set earlier...maybe it would look more like home...looking at this empty place is depressing. I looked at the time and it was almost twelve o, clock that why I am getting hungry. I got up and opened a can of Spam and cut a few slices and fried them. When my food was ready I put some in a plate and sat on the stairs to eat. I really wish I had a cold coke, but I can't leave the apartment and go to the store because I don't want to miss the furniture delivery people.

While sitting on the stair step eating my lunch I notice a cool breeze coming from upstairs from the windows I left opened. I thought to myself...I think I am going to like this apartment it look something like the apartment we shared with Jones and his crazy girlfriend...we're not sharing this apartment with any other couple...I will not be threatened again...this place will be our new beginning... we will get married here...I will have my baby here and watch it grow until we have to move again. When I finished eating I took my dirty dishes to the kitchen sink and washed them. The water pressure was real strong in the sink, so I decided to check the bathroom commode. The water pressure was real strong in the bathroom too, but I think I will save some water tonight just in case the water is off tomorrow morning. When I came out of the bathroom I heard noise coming from outside the front door; I went to the door and saw Wilson and Sister Linda in a jeepney loaded with the living room furniture from Mother's house in Calapacuan. Wilson, Linda and the jeepney driver got out and carried the furniture into the apartment. Wilson paid the driver and gave him a tip; I could tell he tipped the driver because the driver was very happy as he went back to his jeepney. Wilson and

Linda looked very tired; I asked them what had happened. Linda said it was very hard carrying the furniture across the field to the road to load the jeepney. I said I am going to the store to get you and Wilson something cold to drink; at the store I bought beer, coke and a block of ice. When I returned I told Sister Linda that I left her some food in the kitchen; as soon as I told her about the food I remember that I needed some bread to make Wilson a sandwich, so I started back to the store. Wilson said where are you going now? I told him I was going back to the store to get bread to make him a sandwich. I thought to myself…it's good that we have a store close by. When I returned to the apartment I fixed Wilson a Spam sandwich and gave it to him. While sitting on the couch eating his sandwich and drinking his beer Wilson called me to come sit beside him.

When I sat down beside him he asked if I had heard from the furniture delivery peoples. I said no, but don't worry they are still coming. He gave me one hundred pesos for food and gave Linda five pesos for her rides to and from school. He said he couldn't give me the hundred pesos he promised to give me when I stopped work. He said he had to pay a rent deposit on the apartment and a down payment on the bedroom and dining furniture. When he gives me the hundred pesos on his payday I would give Mother half of it so she wouldn't have to take in other people washing. Now I guess she will have to start scraping and washing other people clothes again so she can eat. I started thinking to myself…moving into this apartment and trying to buy furniture is causing us to spend more money…I don't really know what I am going to do about giving Mother some money, I guess I will try and give her at least twenty pesos so she and brother Etong can eat…I know we have to make sacrifice, but I hate that it have to affect my Mother…I will go to Calapacuan tomorrow and see her. Wilson asked me what I was thinking about. I told him I was thinking about going to see my Mother tomorrow and tell her I can't give her money for a while. He said I am sorry Sweetheart but we need the extra money I had for the rent deposit on this apartment…right now we have to do whatever it takes to finish making preparation for our wedding…maybe next payday I will have enough to give you more. I said don't worry about it, we will make out somehow. He said I wonder what's keeping the people that deliver the furniture? I said if they promised to deliver it they will deliver even if it's tonight. Sister Linda said Vicky; I am going upstairs to hang up all the clothes. I said there are extra hangers in my closet if you need some for your uniform. Wilson asked me where did I buy the beer; I told him there were two Sari Sari store close by one in front of our apartment and one in back...you want more beer? How many beers do you want? Wilson said two. I took the money from him and started back to the store. On my way to the store I started thinking to myself...if he had to use the money he promised to give me then he should use the money he is spending on beer; then maybe he could at least give me half of the money...he works very hard, so I guess he deserve to have money to buy his beer...I guess Mother will just have to make do for a while.

When I returned I gave one beer to him and put the other one in the kitchen. He turned and asked me if I liked the apartment. I said I have told you already that I like the place; I have to like it because it is approved and we have to live in an approved apartment before we can get married. Why do they have to give you a hard time doing all of these things before you get married? Wilson said they want us to live in a good environment...as soon as we get these things taken care of we can get married and you can get your dependent ID card and use the Naval Hospital, The Navy Exchange and Commissary; I really want you to be able to get all of your pregnancy checkup at the Naval Hospital. It's not really bad that they do these things I said, but I just want to get them done and over with. I want to get married and move on with our lives. He took my hand and pulled me close to him and kissed me; he led me to the back door and opened it; he said this is where you can do your barbecuing and washing. I said yes, I have being back here already looking and it is nice. He said this is really a nice place we just need to save some money to buy furniture for it. I said what do you think about me going back to work in the Money Exchange? He said if you become my wife I am the only one that going to work; I don't want you working anywhere I can take care of you and our baby, so don't tell or ask me anything about you going to work anymore. I said o.k. Sweetheart I just wanted to help make some extra money. He held me real tight and said everything would be all right...once we get moved in here we will have some extra money. We went back into the living room and checked the time; it was almost five o, clock and the furniture still haven't arrived. Wilson said I guess they will deliver tomorrow. I said I am going upstairs I will be right back. I went up stairs and told Linda I wanted her to go to the Shangri La Restaurant and get our dinner. She said o.k. While following me downstairs. I told Wilson Linda was going to the restaurant to get noodles for dinner; what did he want to eat? He said I would eat whatever you get me. I said would fried dried fish be all right? He said anything except that…tell her to bring me a shrimp salad. He gave me ten pesos to pay for the food. I gave the money to Sister Linda and she left for the restaurant to get our food. Wilson and I went upstairs to look at our bedroom again.

Wilson said there is not very much air stirring in this room it's hot in here…we will have to buy an electric fan. I said I guess we will get one your next payday. He said let's go back downstairs maybe later tonight it will get cooler upstairs. When we got down stairs Linda came in with the food. We put our food in plates and ate our dinner. When we finished eating and Linda was gathering up the dishes to be washed we heard a noise coming from outside. Wilson went to the door to see where it was coming from. It was the people delivering our furniture. They said their truck broke down around three this afternoon and caused them to be late delivering. They started unloading the truck everything went smoothly until they tried to carry the bed frame upstairs. We had to get permission from Mr. Blanco to remove part of the handrails on the stairs to get the frame upstairs. Once we got the bed upstairs and assembled; the delivery peoples helped put the stairs handrail back. When the delivery peoples left Wilson said if he had known that the bed headboard was going to give us that much trouble; he wouldn't have bought it. I told him that the bed looked real good with the headboard and without it the bedroom set wouldn't look as good. He agreed and we went down stairs to admire our first dining room set; it was wonderful. I said we are almost finished with our apartment. Wilson said when we finish paying for the bedroom and dining room set we would get a living room set and return Sister Melda's furniture to Mother's house in Calapacuan. I said don't worry about returning it right away; Sister Melda bought her a new living room set and gave this one to Mother. He said I am still going to get you a new living room set. The apartment owner checked the stair rails again to make sure it was strong. He said it looks and feel o.k. I am going now if you need anything else just knock on my door. We thanked the owner for allowing us to remove a section of the handrail and for helping to replace it. The owner left and went next door to his apartment. It good that he live next door in case something happens and we need him right away. Wilson said we had better go upstairs and put the lining on the bed. When we got upstairs; I went to Sister Linda bedroom to get lining.

She was sitting on the floor crocheting. I said pretty soon you would be putting starch in your crochet so your teacher can grade it before you go on Christmas vacation. She said yes that's right. I got the lining for the bed and took it into the master bedroom. Wilson closed the bedroom door and we put the lining on the bed. We lay down on the bed to test it out. Wilson said this bed is nice and soft and I just felt a breeze coming in that window. I said I think you felt the wind coming from my pillow as I swung it around. He said I thought it was coming from the window. I said it is nine o, clock now maybe the breeze will start stirring later on just leave the window open…I am going downstairs to the bathroom. When I returned I told Wilson I like everything about the apartment except having the bathroom downstairs…I don't think I will like going downstairs at night to use the bathroom…maybe I could use a chamber pot until after I have the baby. He said next time you go to the market check the price on the chamber pot and if they are not too expensive we will get one. I got my nightgown from the closet and started undressing for bed. Wilson said you don't need that now it's a little warm here in the room just lay down beside me. I said don't talk too loud Sister Linda's room is next door. Wilson took my nightgown from my hand and put it beside his pillow. I got into bed beside him. He kissed me and said, "You really have a nice body…golden tan all over". I quickly pulled the sheet over me. He said can't I admire my sweetheart body? Then he pulled the sheet from my body and started kissing me. I said will you kill the light? He stopped caressing me and reached under the bed and got his shoe; he started swinging it all around in the air. I said what are you doing? He said I am trying to kill the light. I said no! And pointed to the light switch on the wall. He said come here I want to show you something; I got up and went over to the light switch where he was standing. He pointed at the light switch and said when it is up it is on and when it is down it is off. I said in my Language "patayin" kill and off is the same...turn off the light please. I thought to myself...I have learn something else about the English language...I guess I still have a long way to go before I can speak good English. Wilson went back to the bed and said come here! I will kill the light later. I said now you're making fun of my English.

He said I would never make fun of the way you speak English I only wanted to correct you...I love you and I love the way you talk... don't think for one second I am making fun of you...I love the way you talk, smile, laugh and above all I love your golden brown body; don't ever forget it...you belong to me and I belong to you. He held me tight and started kissing and caressing me. Finally we christened our new bed and we also found that our bedroom wasn't as cool as the one on 25th street. I was completely drenched with perspiration, so I asked Wilson to go down stairs and get me some water. He came back with ice water to my surprise. He said Linda had bought ice and put it in our water container. After drinking the cold water all I could do was to say thank you for the water, because I was completely drain and the water quickly filled the void. Wilson went to our closet and got a piece of cardboard and used it to fan me and try and cool me down. Finally I did cool down. Wilson told me to put on my nightgown so I wouldn't catch cold. I sat up in the bed and put my nightgown on. Wilson said Sweetheart I am killing the light now. I said o.k. Kill the light and we started laughing. Wilson turned off the light and we kissed and said goodnight. I woke up Saturday morning and decided to let Wilson sleep in, so I went down stairs to the bathroom. I heard Sister Linda following me down stairs; I stopped at the bottom of the stairs to see what she wanted. She said I am leaving for Calapacuan; I will stay today and return Sunday afternoon. I said wait I have twenty pesos I want you to give to Mother; tell her I am coming to Calapacuan Monday to talk to her. I went back upstairs to get the money to give to her. Wilson heard me come back in the bedroom and asked what I was doing. I told him I came back to get money to give to Linda to take to Mother. He said Linda is going to

Calapacuan. I said yes, she would be back Sunday afternoon…she normally go to Calapacuan every Saturday and Sunday and return Sunday afternoon. He said come back to bed it's still early. I said I would be back to bed after I take Linda the money for Mother. I went back down stairs and gave the twenty pesos to Sister Linda and closed the front door behind her. I quickly turned and ran back upstairs. I got back into bed. Wilson said it got kind of chilly in here last night, so I closed the windows.

I said I felt the cold air coming in the windows, but I was too sleepy to get up and closed the windows. He said what are we going to do today? I said what do you want to do? He said I guess we can just lie around here in the bed until we get hungry…then maybe get up and fix something for breakfast…I really just want to lay here and hold you in my arms. I said before you get to comfortable I need to go downstairs to the bathroom. I got up and started for the bathroom again. Wilson followed me into the bathroom and brushed his teeth. When we finished using the bathroom we went back upstairs. I told Wilson I was going to buy curtains for the windows when he get paid again, so we could open the windows wide opened. As soon as we got back in bed Wilson lit a cigarette. I thought to myself…he just got through brushing his teeth and his breath smells o.k. Now he wants to spoil everything by smoking…I wouldn't say anything, but cigarette smoke early in the morning make me sick and dizzy. I got up and told Wilson since he were smoking and was not going back to sleep I was going to cook something for breakfast. He said wait I am almost finish smoking. I came back to bed and he said we have to get your wedding gown and a ring…as you know the ring can't be very expensive… maybe you could look around and price some of the rings her in the city and let me know how much they will cost…if I go they will see that I am an American and jack the price sky high. I told him I would start looking around after New Year and that would give us more time to finish paying for the furniture…everything is real expensive now because of the Christmas holidays. He said that's right! Today is the first of December. I said yes! Christmas is just around the corner. He said o.k. We will start planning our wedding after the holidays…don't worry Sweetheart; we're going to get married even if I have to borrow the money to do so. No, I said we need to stay with our plan…pay for the furniture one at time until we get all we need then we can think about buying something else. He said you are right…we need to get one thing at a time until we finish, because right now we're living payday to payday and we don't have the money to do everything at the same time. He hugged and kissed me. I said let's get dressed and go downstairs so I can cook breakfast. We got dressed and I made up the bed and we went downstairs. I went into the kitchen and started breakfast. Wilson started looking at the walls in the living room and dining room. I asked him what he was looking for.

He said I was only checking to see how many electrical outlets we have. I said how many eggs do you want? He said two scrambled would be fine. I fixed breakfast and called him to the table. We had eggs, Spam and bread for breakfast. I got up and took the dirty dishes to the sink to be washed. Wilson followed me over to the sink and kissed the back of my neck and went into the living room. When I finished doing the dishes I went into the living room and had a seat. He said you know, I really like this apartment it even has a nice patio in back where you can barbecue or just wash clothes…there is also a nice brick privacy fence…I guess that one of the reason this apartment complex is approved by Navy Housing office. I said yes, I saw some other American living in this complex two of them have a car…most of the tenant are white American. He said why are you sitting over there, come over here and sit beside me. As soon as I sat down he started kissing and caressing me. I said not here people could see us through the windows. Wilson got up and went outside and tried to look inside through the windows. When he came back inside he said the windows are one way you can't see inside if you are outside. I said o.k. I just don't want people to see us trying to make love here. He said let's go upstairs where you would be comfortable. I said I am going to take a shower and clean up. He said why can't we just lounger around today is Saturday and I don't have to go to work and don't have any plan to go anywhere…let's go upstairs and relax on our nice firm bed. I reluctantly said o.k. We got up and started up stairs and I noticed Wilson was trying to shake the balancers on the stairs. I said what are you doing? He said I am trying to see if the balancers are strong…it look like Mr. Blanco fixed it real good. I said o.k. Leave that handle alone…he is a Carpenter and knows what he is doing. We entered the bedroom and sat on the side of the bed. Wilson got up and started looking around in the bedroom. Finally something caught his eye it was the fire escape, so he called me over and pointed it out to me. He said this is the fire escape make sure you remember where it at just in case of a fire. I said o.k. Then he walked over to the closet and opened it.

He said we would have to split the closet when he brings some more of his clothes from his boat. He said everything is all right except one thing; during the day it would get real hot in the bedroom because of the metal roof; he said he would get an electric fan as soon as possible…but for now we would have to make do. He pulled me into his arms and guided me toward the bed. I thought to myself… my tiger never lose his appetite he is hungry for more. I sat down on the side of our bed and Wilson quickly opened the bedroom windows. We weren't lucky enough to have the one-way windows in the bedroom, but we didn't worry about anyone looking into our bedroom because all of the nearby houses were one level and our bedroom was on the second level. I could feel somewhat of a breeze coming through the opened windows. When he came back to the bed I could see in his eyes exactly what he wanted to do and I was as anxious as him for it to happen. After making love we fell asleep in each other arms. I woke up a couple of hours later and got up to go down stairs to the bathroom; just as I was leaving Wilson woke up and ask where I was going. I told him I was going down stairs to use the bathroom and when I finish I was going to try and find something to cook for our lunch. He said don't worry about trying to cook something; we will go and eat lunch at the café just inside the Naval Base. I said that's good, because I want to eat a hamburger…I am going to take my shower. He said wait I will take one with you. We got into the shower and one thing lead to another and we found ourselves try to make love in the shower. Finally we decided that I was to short or the shower size wasn't right, so Wilson tried to carry me back upstairs. I told him to put me down so we could move faster. We made it to the bed and it happened again. When I finally got my strength back; I went back down stairs to finish my shower. When I returned Wilson said I guess I will take my shower now; I didn't dare come back down stairs while you where there. I sat on the side of the bed and started towel drying my hair. When it was almost dry I put my clothes on and my makeup, baby powder. When Wilson came back to the bedroom I asked him if my stomach was showing. He kissed me and said your stomach is not showing and you look real good in that dress. I said then I am ready to go.

When he finished dressing we left for the Naval Base Cafeteria. We stopped at the pass office and got me a visitor pass so I could come on the base. Wilson said pretty soon we want have to wait in line to get a visitor pass when we are married; you will only have to show your Military dependent ID card and enter the Base whenever you want to. We walked to the Cafeteria and ordered hamburgers, fries and coke. We sat in the open- air part of the Cafeteria. I said when you brought me here before they had regular table and chairs now they have replaced them with permanent picnic tables made of cement. Wilson said I guess they had a problem with the wind blowing the regular table and chairs away. I said this is very nice they will never move. When we finished our lunch we caught a bus to the Navy Exchange and the Commissary. We didn't go inside we just looked in the windows as we walked around. I asked Wilson if he could buy something from inside. He said yes! What do you want me to buy for you? I said I would like to eat M & M candy like the one Brother Smitty use to buy for me. He said he couldn't take me inside because of the strict Merchandise Control rules on the base. I sat down at the bus stop to wait for him to come out of the Navy Exchange. I thought to myself…if Wilson marries me I will be shopping here one day…if he doesn't change his mind…we still have to wait until we get the furniture paid for…that's o.k. It is better to lay in bed than on the hard floor…we even have a dining room set…it's nice to have this type of comfort…to have this we have to sacrifice something, so we have to wait to get married. Finally Wilson came out of the store and gave me the M & M candy I gave him a kiss and started eating it. He said you have to finish eating it before you walk out of the Main gate because of Merchandise Control. I said I know that; I remember Brother Smitty had to have his receipt when he came through the gate because they check all of his bags to make sure he was not taking something that was not on his receipt. Are they going to do that to me when we get married and I come on base to do my shopping? He said Yes, and don't worry about it he would accompany me when I came to the base to do my shopping. I told him that I could continue to buy the things I need out in town instead of coming on the base to shop and have someone looking through my bags as if I had stole something. He said that is their job to check for control items…the gate guards are trained to look for control items just like I am trained to drive A Tug Boat. I said I know they are trained to look for certain items, but I don't like someone looking through my bags as if I am trying to steal something. We walked around a little while longer and decided to leave the Base. We caught the bus to the Main gate; on our way out the Gate we decide to check the Grand Theater and see what was showing, because we had to pass right by it. I still feel upset when they checked my small purse that was a little larger than the palm of my hand…what did they expect to find…a machine gun or maybe a time bomb? I remembered Wilson saying that they were only doing their job, so I guess I will have to except it. When we arrive at the Movie Wilson said they are still showing the same movie we watch her last week; we decided to walk down the street to the Del Rosario Theater. It was showing the same movie also. I told Wilson I think they run the movies for a whole week and change them on Monday. He said let's go home, so we caught a jeepney going to Rizal Avenue and we got out at second and Rizal. We walked the short distance to our apartment. On our way to the apartment we stopped at the Sari Sari store and bought cokes, ice and beer. When we arrived at the apartment Wilson put the ice in the sink and chopped some for my coke and put the rest in a pitcher and ran some water in it. We sat in the living room and drink our drinks. We notice a cool breeze coming from upstairs because we had the windows open. The breeze felt real good coming from upstairs, but when you get upstairs it not very cool because of the tin roof. Wilson said it not that hot upstairs; if we had a small electric fan it would be nice. I said let's go and see just how hot it is upstairs. We took our drinks and headed upstairs. Wilson said it not bad up here after all; I can feel the breeze coming through the windows. I said it is nice up here. We sat on the bed; Wilson took out his cigarettes and started smoking. I said to myself…I have to get use to smelling cigarette smoke one way or the other. I took another sip of my coke trying to keep from getting sick from the smell of smoke. I really wanted Wilson to feel comfortable as he enjoy his beer and cigarette with me beside him. I often wonder how does he do it…smoke and drink at the same time…does it taste good to him…does it make him real happy? I try very hard to put in my mind that cigarette smoke smells good; I wonder if it ever cross his mind that smoking and drinking beer may taste bad to me when he kiss me.

I can take the beer taste but cigarette and beer together make me feel dizzy. Wilson said are you all right…do you want some more coke? I said I have had enough I want to close my eyes for a while. He said wait let me put my cigarette out; I want to hold you. That made me real happy, so I lay my head on his shoulder and went to sleep. Around three o, clock Wilson woke me up and said let go down stairs it's getting very hot up here. I said what time is it? Wilson said its three o, clock and it's real hot up here the wind stop blowing through the window. I said o.k. We better go before we become like a dried fish. Wilson laughed and said we're swimming in our sweat. We laughed as we went down stairs; I went straight to the kitchen and got me a drink of cold water. Wilson said he was going to the store and gets some more beer. I told him to take the empty bottles so they wouldn't charge him a deposit on the bottles. When he returned from the store; he said Sweetheart the first thing I am going to buy after we get married is a Refrigerator. I said that will be nice, so I can have a cold coke and you a cold beer. He kissed me and said Sweetheart I will try and get all of the things you need, but as you know we have to get one thing at a time. I said all those things don't really matter; what really matters is we are together and I love you and you love me. He said I love you very much and you're right. He stretched out on the couch and put his head in my lap. I said wait a minute; I got up and went upstairs and got a pillow. I put the pillow in my lap and told him to lay his head on the pillow. He put his head on the pillow and asked if he were hurting my leg. I said no! Are you comfortable? He said yes I am real comfortable. I started stroking his hair and tracing the outline of his face with my finger; he went silent and I took a closer look at him and saw that he were asleep. I sat there holding his head in my lap for almost an hour; then my legs start to feel tired so I eased from under the pillow and gently eased it down on the couch. I went to the bathroom and came back he were still asleep, so I got my crochet and started crocheting. While crocheting I kept an eye on him because I didn't want him to roll out of the couch on the hard cement floor. The floor was made of cement and stained a nice reddish brown and very east to keep nice and shinning. Around five o, clock Wilson woke up and went to the bathroom. When he returned he asked me what I did to his head to make him go to sleep so fast.

I said I were only massaging your head and combing your hair... you were asleep before I knew it...you seem to be resting real good so I didn't wake you. He sat down beside me on the couch. I said would you like to lie down again. He said yes, so I put my crochet aside and put the pillow back on my lap. He laid his head on the pillow and I started massaging his head again. This time he laid there looking at me and said you have a nice shaped face, nice eyes and a nice little nose...he held his nose and said I have a big nose. I said so you have a big nose; everybody have a different size nose...I am small so I have a nice little cute nose and you are big and have a big nose... some people have nose shaped like a pig...some shaped like the beak of a bird...everybody nose is different. He said you're still lucky to have a nice small nose. I said we're lucky to have noses to smell... now smell me...do I smell good or what? Wilson said you smell me and I smell you and what do we have? I said forget it, we're not going anywhere with this smell stuff. He said you still smell good to me...even when I am on my Boat I can smell you. I said now you're telling a story. He said it is true every time I think about you I can smell your perfume. I said maybe someone is using my perfume on your Boat. He said no! Just thinking about you I can smell your perfume. I said o.k. You smell me, that's good just think about me only. He said I would because I love only you. He rose up his head and kissed me. I tried to bend down and kiss him back and he pulled me down. I said hold on you need to set up or let me lay down beside you. He sat up and started to passionately kiss me. I said it is too hot upstairs. He said what's wrong with this couch. I said can't we wait until tonight? He said I don't think so. He kept kissing and caressing me. The couch was fine we didn't miss being in bed at all. We laid on the small couch until our body's functions came back to normal. We stayed there until I got hungry; I asked Wilson what did he want to eat. He said what do we have? I got up and went into the kitchen to see what we had in the cabinet. There were some sausage in the can, sardines and corn beef. I said we have sausage in the can, sardines and corn beef. He said I want the sausage; I will eat it with crackers or bread. I put the food on the table and told him I have to use the bathroom. While in the bathroom I decided to take a shower before I cooked me something to eat.

When I finished my shower I went into the kitchen to start cooking. I asked Wilson were he all right; He said yes I am all right I have being waiting for you to come out and cook your food…what are you going to cook? I said I am going to cook dried fish to eat with my rice. He said please open the windows, because the dried fish really smells bad when you fry it. I said this fish were marinade and dried by my Mother and it doesn't smell like the other dried fish. I measured my rice and put it in the pot and turned the fire up. Wilson said what are you doing now? I said I am cooking my rice; it takes a little while for it to cook because it has to simmer for a while after it boils…go ahead and eat. He said I would wait for you…maybe I will go to the store and get me some beer. I said I am dressed already; I will get your beer. I turned the fire down under the rice pot so it would simmer; then went to the store for beer. On my way back I met one of our neighbors that live at the far end of the complex; we introduced our self and she invited me to come visit her when I get bored. I promised her that I would and told her I would see her later. When I came inside the apartment Wilson was setting on the couch fully dressed; He asked me whom I was talking to in front of our apartment. He took one of the beers and started drinking it. I told him he had better eat his food first; I was going to start frying my fish. He said he would wait and eat with me. When I finished frying my fish I told Wilson to come to the table it was time to eat. I watched him eat his sausage and crackers and asked him if that was going to be enough food for him. He said yes, I am not very hungry…that dried fish doesn't smell bad at all, but the other one does. I said even though the other one smells bad it really taste good…don't worry I want cook it when you are home. He said I want you to cook whatever you want to eat; I don't want to stop you from cooking your food even though it smells bad. He got up from the table with his beer and came over to my side of the table and kissed me. He said I am going to set in the living room. I said o.k. I thought to myself…he really love drinking beer…he drinks it like water…I guess a man like drinking beer better than anything else. I finished eating and cleaned the table and kitchen; then joined him in the living room.

I asked him was he happy. He said yes I am happy that you are here with me, I am happy we have our own apartment, I am happy we're sitting here in our living room and will be even more happier when we get married. He said I hope you don't get tired of me and leave before I get a chance to marry you…do you still love me? I said I would always love you no matter what. He said what do you mean when you say no matter what? I said I love you even though you get drunk a lot and hang out with the girl in the club…you get drunk and dance with the girls in the club when we go out…you hurt my feeling a lot. He said Sweetheart; you should know I don't want to hurt you…when I have too much to drink that when I do those crazy things. I said I know that but you're still suppose to know when to stop drinking so you want get drunk, but as soon as you get in the clubs you quickly forget and sometimes forget that I am with you. He said o.k. Let's not talk about that tonight, because I don't want you to get upset and mad at me…I have waited a long time to have you all to myself. I said what do you mean about having me all to yourself? I have been yours ever since the night Sister Melda introduced me to you. From the first time I saw you I knew that I loved you. He said I felt the same way about you when I first met you; I don't know what I would do if you left me…I want and love you more and more each day. I said don't worry I am not going anywhere unless you throw me and your baby out…right now we're together here in our Navy approved apartment and getting married very soon, so don't worry I am yours Tiger. He kissed and held me so tight I had to push away to breathe. I said you have to let me go I can't breathe. He said could we go upstairs now…its nine o, clock now so the bedroom should be cool down now. I said o.k. Let me get a glass of water first. To my surprised it had cooled down in the bedroom and a nice breeze was coming through the opened windows. I undressed and put my nightgown on and joined Wilson in the bed. As soon as I got in the bed he lit a cigarette and started puffing on it. I really don't want to stop him from enjoying himself smoking and drinking beer, but the smell is over bearing. I said to myself…I wish a man could feel what a woman feel when she is pregnant…the smell of smoke and beer how it makes you feel sick and dizzy. I really try hard to take it because I don't want to hurt his feeling…I wish he would put out his cigarette and go to sleep. Then I noticed him looking at me. He said why you look like your mind is far away…what are you thinking about? I said I thought you finished smoking downstairs. He said o.k. O.k. I am almost finish let me go in the bathroom and brush my teeth. I didn't say anything when he said he would brush his teeth, but I was happy. I closed my eyes as I lay there waiting his return. When he returned to bed he asked me if I was asleep. I said no I just closed my eyes. He drew near me and pulled me into his embrace and started kissing and caressing me. I responded and one thing led to another one and before long we were laying in each other arms gasping for air. Our bodies completely spent we finally got enough energy to kiss each other goodnight.

The next day, Sunday morning I got up Wilson was still sleeping so I didn't wake him. I went down stairs to take a shower. I was real happy about the way the water flows from the showerhead. I remembered when we live in our other apartment we would have problems with the water pressure. The Owner of the apartment warned us that sometimes the city would cut the water off without notice, but so far we haven't had a problem. When I finished my shower I wrapped my towel around me and went back upstairs to see if Wilson was awake. He was still asleep so I dressed and went back down stairs and dried my hair. I decided to go to the store and get hot bread rolls for breakfast. When I arrived at the store I decided to buy ice and a liter bottle of coke too. When I returned I chopped up some ice and put it in the pitcher so we would have some cold drinking water. I put everything up and decided to cook some breakfast, so I looked into the kitchen cabinets to see what I had to cook for Wilson…there were Spam and corn beef in the can to choose from. I decided to cook my breakfast first because it takes longer; I decided to cook garlic-fried rice for myself. Just as I got started I heard Wilson coming down stairs. He said Sweetheart what are you cooking? I said garlic-fried rice are you hungry now? He said don't worry about fixing me something to eat I am going back on the Base to my Boat to get clean underwear...I will eat breakfast there. I said today is Sunday can't that wait till tomorrow? He said I will be stinking by tomorrow plus I need to take some more clothes here so I can change when I want to.

I said while you are gone I will go to the market. He went into the bathroom to get cleaned up. I ate my breakfast, cleaned the kitchen and went upstairs to make the bed. To my surprise Wilson had made up the bed before he left. I sat down and fixed my face; then I went back down stairs. Wilson said why don't you wait until Linda comes home tomorrow to go to the market? I said today is market day I can get better bargains today than tomorrow. He said o.k. I will see you later, so he kissed me goodbye and left. I got my big shopping bag and left for the market. The first thing I looked for when I arrived at the market was a covered container that I could use for a Chamber Pot. Finally I saw the container I wanted, so I bought it and the rest of the food except rice, because my bag was getting very heavy. I decided to let Linda get the rice the next day. I caught a jeepney that goes to Rizal Avenue. I stopped the jeepney at Second Street and Rizal Avenue. I had to walk about half of a block to my apartment. By the time I got to the apartment the bag was feeling real heavy. I opened the door and went straight to the kitchen and got me a drink of water. I sat down for a while as I drunk my cold water. I said to myself...I am not going to the market again by myself while I am pregnant. I lie down on the couch and put my legs up to relax for a while. Then I thought about what my Mother said" don't try to carry heavy things while you're pregnant". I got scared for myself and decided to stay on the couch until I was totally relaxed. Lying there on the couch with my eyes closed; before I knew it I was asleep. I slept until Wilson came back. I asked him the time and he said it was almost ten o, clock. He said are you all right? I didn't answer I just got up and went into the kitchen and started cooking lunch. Wilson started upstairs and turned and asked me what drawers did I want him to put his clothes in. I told him to use the top two drawers. When he came back down stairs he said I don't want you to worry about washing my clothes; I will take them back to my boat for washing until we get a Maid. I told him I could wash them but he insisted on taking them back to his boat, so I gave in to his wish. I said I am cooking lunch what do you want to eat? He said I ate a big breakfast on my boat don't worry about fixing me something to eat. Wilson sat in the living room smoking his cigarette. When I finished cooking I went in and sat down in the chair across from him. He said why are you sitting over their...come and sit beside me. I got up and sat beside him on the couch. He kissed me and I almost threw up because of the cigarette smell and taste. I didn't say anything about it I just did my best to bare it. He always likes to kiss me but he never think that the cigarette smell and taste makes me sick and dizzy. Finally the smell was too great so I ran into the bathroom and threw up. When I came back he ask me what was wrong. I told him that I get sick once in a while. He said that's because you are pregnant. I didn't want to hurt his feeling, so I sat back down beside him and didn't say anything about the cigarette smoke. He kissed me and I kissed him back; then I said I am hungry. He looked at his watch and said it is eleven o, clock you should eat your lunch now. I got up and started to the kitchen to fix my plate and he got up and said he was going to get him a beer from the store. I thought to myself...if he didn't smoke or drink we could buy curtains, electric fan and a whole lot of more stuff we need for the apartment...smoking and drinking must be an important feature in his life. Just as I finished eating he came in the door. He said I bought some ice and coke for you in case you want something cold to drink later on. I took the ice and put it in our water pitcher. He opened up one of his beer and sit down to drink it. He always buys two beers because he likes his beer to be cold when he drinks it. We are lucky to have a Sari- Sari store real close to our apartment; it only takes a few minutes to go and come back. After cleaning the kitchen and putting the left over away I went into the bathroom and brushed my teeth. When I came out of the bathroom he asked if I had finished what I was doing. I said yes I am finished. He said come and sit beside me. I sat down beside him and he started kissing me it was like he never kissed me before. He love kissing me and I like kissing him too, but since I got pregnant I have a problem with the smell and taste of his cigarettes and beer, but because I love him and he is a real good kisser I take the smell and taste even though it makes me dizzy. He was making me feel good and forget about the smell and taste of cigarette and beer. He said let's go upstairs. We got up and hurried upstairs and did what we do best.

The next week we did about the same thing; everyday when he came home he would stop at the store and get a couple of beers and bring them home. Sister Linda went to school at night, so we made love downstairs, upstairs and wherever we are in the house. We made love sometimes three times a day. Finally Wilson got paid and was supposed to come home at ten that morning, but didn't show up until four that afternoon. He was drunk and wanted me to go with him out nightclubbing. I told him I didn't want to go because he was drunk already. He sat on the couch and still insisted that I go out with him. When he came home he didn't kiss or give me a hug like he normally do. He continues sitting on the couch acting as if he was trying to figure out who I was. He always finds his way home even though he is falling down drunk. That is one thing I can't quite understand about him. Sometimes when we are out clubbing he forgets that I am with him...he starts dancing with the club Hostess and leave me sitting at the table by myself. I thought things was going pretty good until today...I have no idea where he were at earlier today to get so drunk...he loves to party, but I thought he was giving it up at least for awhile so we could buy some of the things we needed for the apartment. I really don't know what to think or do, because I believe he is running around with some of those girls that work in the club... it scares me to think about him catching some type of disease and bringing it home to me and my baby. Finally he went to sleep sitting on the couch trying to get me to go out with him. I looked at the time it was six o, clock, so I got up and fixed me something to eat. When I finished eating I cleaned the kitchen and went back into the living room to check on him. I decided not to try and wake him up and take him upstairs. I will wait until Sister Linda come home from school and let her help me get him upstairs, because he being drunk maybe he will make me fall down the stairs with him. I sat down across from him trying to think what I was going to do next I said to myself...if Linda go to Calapacuan tomorrow I am going with her...tomorrow is Saturday and Wilson don't have to go to work...I will leave him a note...this will give him a chance to spend some time with his girl friend in the club if he rather be with them than me...I really don't want to catch the sickness those girl often have...I have to think of something to do...Wilson don't know what love is; He have got it wrong...he think love is hurting the one you love...well he is not going to hurt this girl anymore. I fell in love with a kind, loving and caring guy, but he has a cruel side that I hate... the cruel side thinks only of it...partying and have fun.

The front door opened and Sister Linda walked in breaking my change of thought. I said you came home early tonight. She said they are having a meeting so they let us out early...Brother Wilson sleep. I said yes he went to a party today and came back and went to sleep sitting here. Will you help me get him upstairs to bed? I told her we were going to Mother's house tomorrow morning before Wilson woke up. He started moving around on the couch, so I told Linda to take his other arm and help me get him upstairs. When we started pulling him up he got up and we helped him upstairs to the bed. I thanked Linda for helping me get him upstairs. She said Brother Wilson really got drunk at that party. I said yes I guess he really enjoyed himself. I wouldn't tell her that he had been running around in the clubs; I didn't want to get my family involved in my problems. When she left the room I took off his shoes and covered him up with his clothes on. I left his clothes on because he was too heavy for me to try and roll around and I were pregnant too. I got ready for bed and lay down beside him and tried to calm down because I didn't want to think a lot about what was going on. I tried to think about the good times we had together and finally I went to sleep.

Saturday morning came quick when I got up Wilson was still sleep, so I wrote him a note telling him that he had all the time he wanted to spend with the girls in the clubs. I closed the note saying goodbye and I love you. I got dressed and went downstairs to the bathroom and washed up. When I came out Sister Linda was up and ready to use the bathroom. When she finished I said let's go. She went out the door first and I went back to the coffee table in the living room and put the note on the table so he would find it. We left and caught a jeepney to Calapacuan. This time we were lucky enough to get in the jeepney first so we got up front. I really like the cool morning air blowing in my face. Sister Linda said I have all of our dirty clothes, but I forgot to get Brother Wilson's. I told her not to worry because

Wilson took his dirty clothes to his Boat to be washed. I thought to myself...if he doesn't get them washed on his Boat maybe his girlfriend in the club would wash them...he had better make up his mind who he want to be with, me the one who love and care for him or the girls in the clubs...I don't think I can continue to share him with someone else.

Sister Linda said Vicky! Be careful, hold on to that bar so you want fall out of this jeepney and kill yourself. My mind started wondering again...yes, maybe I will kill myself by falling out of this jeepney and maybe he will understand how much he has hurt me... maybe he will blame himself for my death...what about my unborn baby...I can't do that to my baby...the baby is innocent. What am I thinking about? Thinking of Wilson has got my mind all mixed up. Oh God! Forgive me for thinking that way. Sister Linda said Vicky let's go we are here now. I said o.k. She said wake up we need to get out of the jeepney. I said o.k. I am sorry. We got down from the jeepney and started walking across the field to Mother's house. We came to Sister Maria's house first she was sitting out on her front balcony. She said you are visiting early this morning. I said yes, we are trying to catch Mother before she starts breakfast. What are you having for breakfast? She said fried dried fish, rice and coffee. I said o.k. I will talk to you later. Sister Linda and I walked past her house to Mother's house. When we came up to the front door Mother said I thought that was your voice I heard when you came by Maria's house. Brother Etong came out to help Linda with the bag of dirty clothes. I came in the house and took a seat at the kitchen table to talk to Mother. She asked me where was Wilson. I told her that he went back to his Boat and Linda and I decided to come here. I asked her what did she cook for breakfast. She said nothing yet what do you want to eat? I said I want fried dried fish, fried garlic rice and coffee. She said I could cook that now you go and lie down and relax I will call you when it's ready. Linda said I am going to separate the white and dark clothes I am going to wash after breakfast. Mother said take a look at the shed your Brother built to keep the sun off me while I am washing clothes out by the spring. I said you have started back taking in washings. She said yes, what else can I do, your Sister Melda give me money once in a while and you give me money whenever you can, but it's not enough...I know you need your money because you are trying to fix up your apartment...don't worry your Brother and I will make it; we have always been able to survive...take care of yourself and your husband...I am glad to see that someone is taking care of you.

I thought to myself...if you only knew what was going on in my life you would be telling me to come back home so you could help take care of my baby and me...what would she say if I told her that Wilson had split personality a bad side and a good side...if she knew that she would be mad at me for staying with him. Brother Etong brought me a Mango and showed me his slingshot that he used to shoot the Mangoes from the tree. I said Mother do you still have Mangoes on the tree? She said yes there are still plenty of small Mangoes on the tree...your brother use his slingshot to shoot the big ones from the tree...that why that Mango look like something is wrong with it. I looked at the Mango and said it is o.k. I will eat it now. Brother Etong took it and washed it real good he peel and sliced it into thin slices for me. I got up and got some of the dried fish and rice and started eating it with the Mango. Mother said I have finished cooking come let's eat. Sister Linda and brother Etong came to the table and everyone started eating. Mother looked at me and said you eat that Mango like it isn't sour...that young green Mango is very sour...I guess when you are pregnant you will eat anything even if it bother you. I said it taste very good...maybe I will go with Brother Etong and climb the tree. Mother said I will buy you some Mangoes from the market just don't try and climb the tree while you are pregnant...you don't want the tree to get sick like Wilson did, do you? I said I forgot that I am pregnant. I looked at Brother Etong and said we can use your slingshot. He smiled in agreement. I finished eating the Mango. Sister Linda said it is too early for me to be eating green Mangoes. I said then there would be more for me. When everyone finished eating breakfast Sister Linda started washing the dishes. Brother Etong and I went outside to the Mango tree. I took a small basket to carry the Mangoes in. When we got under the tree I saw eight or ten large Mangoes in the tree. I pointed them out to Brother Etong and he commenced shooting at them. The first Mango he hit came down with a thud. I picked it up and told Brother Etong that I really liked it...keep shooting so we can get some more. He kept shooting them down until we had the big one that I had pointed out to him.

He said we would get more when they get bigger. I told Brother Etong thanks for the Mangoes. He looked at me with a big smile signaling that I was welcome. I went back into the house and told Mother and Linda I had Mangoes if they like to eat some. Mother said save me some to cook with the fish later...I am going to the market now...do you want anything special to eat? I said I would like to eat beef neck bones cooked with cabbage and potatoes. She said oh! I was already planning to cook that for you. I said o.k. That's all I need. I said Mother I have something for you...I opened my bag and took out the twenty pesos I was keeping for her. I said here is some money I wish I could give you more, but you know my situation. Wilson had stop giving me the hundred pesos he promised because we were trying to get furniture for our apartment. I will continue to give Mother some money even if I have to cut back the amount of food Sister Linda and I eat at the apartment... eating two meals a day won't be bad I will just get up late in the morning and eat lunch instead of breakfast and if I get hungry before dinnertime I will drink a lot of water. I better see if Sister Linda need help washing the clothes. I said Linda do you need me to help you wash the clothes. She said do you want Mother to get mad at me...she don't want you to do anything while you're pregnant...I can do it by myself because we don't have very much to wash. I said o.k. But if you need help I will be over at Sister Maria's house. I left and went next door. When I got there Sister Maria said I am glad you came by because I have some Guava fruit left for you I picked from the tree...the tree leaves hide most of them but I found a few for you. I said yes I know, every time I look for them in the tree I always sit down under the tree on that big rock and focus for a while then finally I start spotting them behind the leaves...even though you focus for a while there are some right in front of you but you can't see them. She said that because there are magical small people living under that tree. I said you know about them living there too...when we first moved here that Guava tree was very pretty with that big rock underneath it. I use to sit and sometime lay down on the big rock under the tree. If I had to move around I would say sorry if I step on someone that I can't see...I set for a while longer then suddenly the Guavas start appearing right over my head...I would eat all I can and lay down on the rock and say thank you tree.

When my Mother called me I would try to get some to take with me but they suddenly disappeared behind the leaves. I tried real hard to spot more Guavas on the tree, but I couldn't so I left to see what Mother wanted. Sister Maria said they are there but hard to find. I said I think that tree is getting very old and lonely looking...it use to look real pretty especially when it was in blossoms, but now like me it has grown up and got older and no one talks to it like I use to. I guess the big rock has grown old too it is turning black and the Guava tree is falling apart. She said you and the rest of the kids use to play around that tree even though the magical people live there too, but they didn't mind you playing and sitting on the big rock they enjoyed having you around...you have grown up now and have your own family; I guess everything is falling apart without the other to lean on. She started crying. I asked her what was wrong. She said oh! I just remembered when your brother left me...don't worry I am all right...it takes time to get use to being alone. I said I am so sorry about the way my brother has treated you. I sat there for a brief moment then I started thinking about Wilson...I had said goodbye to him in the note that I left on the table. I was really depressed about the Guava tree, the big rock that I use to lay on and Sister Maria... now Wilson comes into the picture. I didn't really know what to do...I want to cry, but I didn't want to tell her my problem. Then she asked me if I wanted something to drink. I said no thank you...how is your Daughter getting alone? She said she is doing all right...she come to see me every two weeks or sometimes once a month...I am not worry I wash clothes for the people that live right across the field. She pointed at the house near the road close to the jeepney stop. I said that's good that it's close by. She said yes that why I am not worry if my Daughter don't visit me very often and give me money...she have her problems too, but she still give me money once in a while when she can spare it. I said to myself...that once in a while phrase is very common in our family, but a little help is better than none at all. I saw Brother Etong run pass Sister Maria house as he was going across the field. He must have seen Mother coming and decide to go and meet her and help her with the packages. Sister Maria and I watch Mother and Brother Etong draw near her house.

When Mother came pass the house she told Sister Maria to come over and have lunch with us. Sister Maria said o.k. I am coming. I saw Linda come by going to the cloth line where we hang our clothes to dry. Well I said to Sister Maria, I am going to help Linda hang the clothes out to dry don't forget to come for lunch. When I got to the cloth line where Sister Linda was hanging out the clothes to dry; I asked her if she had put starch in her uniforms. She said yes, they would be ready to be ironed tomorrow. After we finished hanging out the clothes to dry we went into the house to see what Mother had brought back from the market. I took a seat at the kitchen table and look in the bag to see what she had bought. To my surprise she bought some Mangoes. I took one from the bag to eat and Linda saw what I was doing, so she said I want a piece of that Mango. Mother said if you don't want to be sleepy all of the time you had better get a Mango of your own and don't eat the same one Vicky is eating. Sister Linda said I forgot that Vicky makes everyone sick. Mother said do not eat part of the one she is eating. Linda took a Mango from the bag and shared it with Brother Etong. I looked at Linda and said there will be more for me…does it make your mouth watery watching me eat this Mango? Everyone started laughing. Then Mother said all of you make my mouth watery eating it as though it is so crunchy. Mother took a Mango from the bag and started eating and said oh! It is to sour. I said yes, but it is good. Then Sister Maria came through the door and said look who here with me. Everybody said Wilson it's Brother Wilson. He came in and said hello to everyone. I went to him pretending like I was glad to see him. We kissed and I pulled him into the living room and said what are you doing here…I left a note telling you to go out and have fun with your girl friends…I don't want to be with you anymore because you like running around with the girls in the club. He said I was not in the clubs in Olongapo I was at a Squadron beach party on the base…I was invited by a friend…I got drunk, but I still came home. I said yes you did come home, but you smelled like cheap perfume. He said I don't know about the smell maybe it was the liquor that spilled on my clothes…please don't get mad at me…don't let your Mother know that we're fighting.

He said why did you leave me a note telling me goodbye, and you said that you love me. I said I do love you, but I can't take you running around partying in the clubs with your girlfriends...when you come home smelling like perfume it always hurt my feeling. Sweetheart, he said when I woke up and found your note downstairs it almost scared me to death...I ran back upstairs to check your closet to see if you had moved out. When I saw your clothes in the closet I realized that you was mad at me and probably came here to your Mother's house. Just to be sure I checked Linda room and saw that she was gone too, so I quickly got dressed and came here. I heard Mother said let eat, so I asked him had he eaten already he said no, so I fixed his plate and mines. We took a seat on my favorite wooden box in the corner and ate our food. I asked him how did he like the food and he said I like it very much...I've eaten boiled cabbage and neck bone before, but I ate it with corn bread instead of rice. Mother brought Wilson a glass of coke with ice I guess she had sent Brother Etong to the store for the coke. Wilson told her the food tasted real good and thanks for the coke. I explained to her what Wilson said in Tagalog. She said o.k. I am glad he like it. Then I explained to Wilson in English what she said to him. Mother asked Wilson if he wanted more food. I explained to him again what Mother had asked him and he told me to tell her he had enough. Finally we were left alone, so I was quiet while I was thinking about my situation. Wilson asked me if I were all right I told him I was all right I was just thinking about him... every time he get paid he come home late and drunk...never think to tell me he would be late. Now you tell me that you went to a Squadron party on the base; I think you went out clubbing just like always. I really don't know if our relationship is going to work out. He started looking around in the house and asked me if we could go home and talk. We can talk here because they don't understand what you are saying, so don't worry. He said I still would like to go back to our own place. I said you don't want to be with me at that apartment, because if you did you would stay there and stop running around drinking and chasing the girls in the clubs. He said you know I really want to be with you and I am trying hard to control my drinking. I said I thought you like being with me, but it seem that you like running around more than staying home with me. When you run around like that it really tear my heart out…would you like it if I ran around with other guys? I really don't think so. He said all I can say right now is that I promise to stop running around and getting drunk especially when I am with you so I can take care of you…please let's go home before your Mother figure out that something is wrong. I said if you are worried about that why do you keep doing what you are doing? My sister-in-law came over and said goodbye to us. Wilson asked me what did she say and I told him she only said goodbye. He quickly said goodbye to her as she was leaving the room. He turned to me and kissed me; I kissed him back because Mother was watching us. Wilson started pleading again asking me to leave and go back to our apartment with him. Mother came over to where we were standing and asked Wilson if he wanted some more coke; I told him what she said and he said maybe a little in a glass, I took his glass and filled it with coke and ice. Sister Linda told me she was staying until Sunday afternoon before returning to the apartment. I had planned to stay, but everyone was expecting me to leave with Wilson so I finally gave in and agreed to go home. I told him next time I got mad at him I was going somewhere else so he couldn't find me. He said I love you and I know that you always come to your Mother's house to calm down…you don't want your Mother to worry about you…that's why I am worried that she will find out that we're fighting. I will never tell Mother about our problems; I don't want my family involved in my problems…the only thing I have told her about is our money problem and I explained why I couldn't give her more money. He said that remind me, you left me before I could give you the money to buy food and I also forgot to make a payment on the furniture; please take care of it for me. I said o.k. I will do it Monday. He gave me one hundred and forty pesos, eighty for grocery, forty to pay on furniture and twenty for Sister Linda school. Here again He didn't give me the hundred pesos he promised to give me if I stopped work.

I guess he spent it partying, but that's o.k. Because the only thing that matters is we are together and we have food to eat and a place to stay. Wilson asked me what I was thinking about; I said oh, I was only thinking about us. I told Mother we have to go back to Olongapo. Then Brother Etong came over and reminded me to take the Mangoes and Guava fruit. I told him I would take only one Mango and the

Guava, because Mother needed the rest of the Mangoes to cook with her fish. He put the fruit in a bag and gave it to me, he always seem very happy when he give me something. I took the bag and we said our goodbye and left. We had to walk pass Sister Maria's house she was sitting on her porch. I said thanks for the Guava and goodbye as we walked pass her porch. When we pass the Guava tree I touched one of the branches of the tree and closed my eyes and said thank you. Wilson asked me if I was all right. I said yes, I was only paying my respect to the tree...when I was a little kid I use to lay on that big rock under those guava trees...I played under that tree almost all of the time when we first move here. He said I often wonder why the big rock was in the middle of the trees. That rock was very pretty when I use to play on it. Wilson said it looks very old now. I said that because no one plays on it anymore...what do you expect? We use to play on that rock everyday and it looked gray and very shining. He said well it look very black now. I said it got old like me...all grown up. Wilson stopped and hugged and kissed me in the middle of the rice field. It was good there were no rice in the field, because the way he kissed me I almost forgot I was in the rice field. That's why we try not to kiss too much...when our lips touch every nerve in my body move as if we had an electric shock. I said we had better stick to holding hands and He agreed. At the jeepney stop we held hands and looked at each other. Finally the jeepney came and we were off to Olongapo City. We held hand during the jeepney ride and finally we were at Second Street we got down and walked the short distance to our apartment. When we got inside we closed the door and windows downstairs and went upstairs and opened all of the windows for fresh air. He led me to the bed and we made love like we hadn't seen each other for a month. When we finished he said I love you Sweetheart and I said I love you too Tiger. We fell asleep in each other arms.

Around three that afternoon we woke up with our bodies drenched in sweat; Wilson got up and sat on the side of the bed. He said we really need to buy an electric fan for our bedroom it is really hot up here this time of the day...let's go downstairs before our brains start frying up here. I said I need a real cold drink. He said o.k. Sweetheart I will go to the store and get coke and ice...you can get dress while I am gone and meet me downstairs. I thought to myself...if we only had an electric fan I could stay up here all day if I wanted to…I guess we would have to suffer until we saved enough money to buy an electric fan. I got dressed and went down stairs and took a seat on the bottom step of the stairs. I thought to myself…why is it cooler down here than upstairs…where is the cool air coming from? I heard the front door open and Wilson came in. He said you want believe what happened to me at the store…a small boy tried to sale me some red devil. He tried to sale you some red devils? Yes! But I told him I didn't want any and he kept insisting that I buy some…the guy at the shoe shine stand told him to leave me alone and that I live in The Blanco Apartment. The young guy went inside the building across the street. I said I am going to ask Mr. Blanco if he know the people living across the street…I think they are drug dealers, because they are harassing the people that live over here. Wilson said don't worry about it the shoeshine guy told him that I live here and he left me alone. He bends over and kissed me and went into the kitchen and chopped up the ice for my coke. He came back into the living room with the glass of coke. He asked why I was sitting on the stairs. I told him it seems to be cool there. He sat down beside me and said well I guess it is cool here, but it is real hard on your behind…it reminds me of the hardwood furniture in our apartment on twenty fifth street… let's set on the couch close to the window it should be cool there. He opened the window and there was a little breeze coming in. The cold drinks help to cool me down and Wilson was drinking his favorite beer. We sat there real close together; Wilson started kissing me every now and then and I felt as if I was getting dizzy tasting the beer on his lips. I didn't complain at all because he was happy and with me. I like being with him too; I didn't worry about the small things he did. I got up and told him I was going to take a shower.

He said he would take his shower when he finished drinking his beer, so I went upstairs and got my towel and clean clothing. I came back down stairs and went into the shower. I thought to myself as the water flowed strongly from the showerhead…this is not like the shower in our old apartment on twenty fifth street where you had to save water and worry about the water being shut off while you was soaped down…I really like this shower. I finished showering and got dressed and called out to Wilson …you are next. He said o.k. And got up to get ready for his shower. I sat on the couch in the living room and started towel drying my hair. I thought to myself...the longer your hair the longer it take to dry...maybe I will ask Wilson when he finishes showering if I can cut my hair. When he came out of the shower I asked him if I could cut my hair to shoulder length. He said no!!! I don't want you to cut your hair...your hair belongs to me. He sat down beside me and took the comb and started combing my hair. He said your hair is black and shining and very pretty. I said yes, but it is long and hard to manage and take forever to dry. He said you have plenty of time to dry your hair...you are not going anywhere... please don't cut your hair I like the way it flows down your back when you walk. I said maybe I want cut it for a while. He said great! Let's go to the movies they have new movies showing now...we can get something to eat first. I said o.k. And went back upstairs to change my clothing. I didn't waste any time changing because it was getting hot upstairs. Finally we were ready to go so we left and walked down to Rizal Avenue to the Magnolia Restaurant. I ordered beef fried rice and Wilson ordered his favorite shrimp salad. When we finished we caught a jeepney to the jeepney stop across from the Navy Base main gate and walked to the Grand Theater. There was a Western movie showing starring John Wayne. We watched it and I really enjoyed it. I told Wilson the next time we go to the movies I want to watch another movie with John Wayne, because I like Western movies. He said you really like Western movies. I said yes they are just like real life there are good times and bad time, plus they have girl working in the Saloon just like they have girl working in the clubs in the Philippines...I didn't know they have girl working like that in the States.

He said there are girls working in Saloon and clubs all over the world...they are entertainers...do you feel like walking with your date? I said yes why not; let's walk back to our apartment. We started back to our apartment walking and holding hand. I asked him if he had been to other countries while he was onboard ship and met other girls. He said yes, but there wasn't really enough time to really get to know them. I asked him where some of the places he had been were. He said Hong Kong, Japan, Korean and just about all over the Far East...let's take a short cut home. He guided me to a small dark street where Vendors was selling barbecue hot dogs and chicken on a stick. I told him I didn't want him to use this dark street at night because the police do not patrol them and people get beat up and robbed up and down these dark streets...do you remember seeing the guys standing up against the building back there...I have seen them all over town even in the market looking for a chance to snatch a purse or grab a watch from someone...they even train their kids to do the same thing, so please don't take a short cut through an alley stay on the main streets. He said o.k. He would never take a short cut again. We continued down the side street to Rizal Avenue. I said see there are the Navy's Shore Patrol patrolling Rizal Avenue and not the side streets...you didn't see them patrolling that dark street because they will get robbed too. Finally we came to Second Street and Wilson stopped to get two beers to take to the apartment. He asked if I wanted to get coke and I told him I didn't want to drink coke at night. When we arrived at our apartment we saw our next-door neighbors standing outside their apartment. They said hi and introduced themselves to us. Their names were Larry and Pat. We stopped and talk for a while and finally went into our apartment. They were the only American couple living in the Blanco apartment complex. I said Larry and Pat seem very nice and he said yes they are here in the Philippines, but they are different back in the States. I didn't really understand the meaning of what Wilson was saying until now. As soon as we entered our apartment Wilson started kissing me. I said hold on tiger you haven't drink your beer yet, it's going to get hot. He sat down on the couch and started drinking his beer.

I went upstairs to see if the room had cooled down enough for us to go to sleep. There was a nice cool breeze coming in the window...I thought to myself that's wonderful. When I came back downstairs he pulled me down beside him and started kissing me again. One thing led to another and we were up and on our way upstairs. I guess he was ready to see my golden body and I was more than ready to show it to him. We jumped in bed and made love like it was our last time. When we finished we laid completely drained in each other arms. I remembered hearing him say good night and I said good night to him and closed my eyes and fell asleep. The next day was a Sunday morning; I woke up but didn't want to get up. Wilson woke up too and asked me if I wanted to get up. I told him no I just wanted to lie around for a while, so I snuggled up to him and laid my head on his shoulder. It wasn't very long before my stomach started telling me it was time to eat something. Wilson heard my stomach and said I guess we need to get up and get some breakfast. I got up and went downstairs to the bathroom and washed up so I could start cooking breakfast. I cook scrambled eggs and Spam for Wilson and opened a can of pork and beans for myself. I called Wilson, he was in the bathroom and told him breakfast was ready. He came out and came to the table. We sat down to eat he looked at me and asked if the can of pork and beans was all I was going to eat. I said yes that all I feel like eating this morning. When we finished eating breakfast I washed the dishes and cleaned the kitchen. Wilson decided to take a shower while I was cleaning the kitchen. When I finished in the kitchen Wilson had finished his shower and was sitting in the living room. I decided I would take a shower too, so I went upstairs and got my robe and under clothing and came back downstairs to take my shower. When I got downstairs I saw Sister Linda coming in the front door with a bundle of clothing. She said hi to Wilson with a big smile. I asked her why she had come back early. She said I have to get my school project ready for tomorrow as she went upstairs. I went into the bathroom and took my shower. When I finished I came out to towel dry my hair.

Wilson was still sitting on the couch he looked very restless. I asked him if he was all right. He said he was fine. I heard someone on the stairs and I turned around to look; it was Sister Linda carrying her crochet project. She went out the back door to the patio. I followed her. She looked at the cement patio and decided to scrub it before putting her project on it to dry after soaking it in sugar water. Wilson came to the back door and asked us what we were doing. I told him Linda was cleaning the patio so she could dry her school project after soaking it in sugar water. He said why don't she use the cloth line? I said she soak it in sugar water and shape it into whatever design she like and then let it dry. The sugar water makes it stiff. He said you are going to have a lot of ants crawling in the apartment. I said they would not bother it once it is dry that's why we are drying it outside. He went back to the living room and sat down and I followed him and sat on the opposite end of the couch. He said come here and sat beside me so I can comb your hair. I said I could do it. He said yes I know you can, but I want you to sit beside me, so I moved over close to him on the couch. As soon as I got close enough he started kissing me all over my neck. I said don't start doing that because we can't make love now. He said why not? We have our own room. He took the comb out of my hand and started combing my hair. Linda came in and asked me if I wanted her to cook some rice for lunch. I said yes and go outside and wait for someone to come by selling fresh fish and vegetable so we can have some for lunch. I asked Wilson if he wanted me to get him something from the restaurant for his lunch. He said just cook me some corn beef if you have some and I will eat it with rice…if you are going to the store buy me a couple of beers. I said o.k. And went out the door; I saw Sister Linda trying to bargain with the old lady that was selling fish and vegetables. When I passed her I told her to get whatever we needed and I was going to the store to get Wilson some beer. I bought beer and decided to buy coke and ice too. When I returned I gave Wilson one of his beer and took the other one in the kitchen with the ice and coke and put everything in the sink. Linda came over and rinsed the ice off and chopped it up and put some in the water pitcher. Then she started cleaning the fish and vegetable. I told her I was going to cook the corn beef first before she started cooking the fish and vegetables.

When I finished stir frying the corn beef I served it with rice to Wilson. He asked me if I were going to eat and I told him I was waiting for Linda to finish cooking the fish and vegetables. He asked me to sit beside him while he ate his food. I told him I was very hot and wanted to sit on the stair where a cool breeze was coming from upstairs. I also reminded him that we still need an electric fan to cool down our apartment. Finally Sister Linda finished cooking and we sat down and ate our meal. When we finished she washed the dishes and cleaned the kitchen. I noticed her going out the back door, so I went to see what she was doing. She was checking on her crochet design to see if it was dry and in the shape she had formed. It had dried and was very pretty. I decided I would make one like that when I finished the one I was working on. Wilson got curious and came to the door and asked what we were doing. I told him we were checking on Linda project. He said o.k. When you finish I have something to talk to you about. I left Linda outside and went back inside to see what he wanted. He said let your sister take care of her project and you come and spend some time with me. I said I was trying to see how she got her project to stand up so I would know what to do when I finish my design. He said you have plenty of time to do that later when I am not at home. I thought to myself...he is jealous of my crochet. He said would you get me a couple of beers from the store? I told him we had plenty of coke. He said he didn't want to drink coke he wanted to drink beer. I went to the store and got him two beers; on my way back I thought to myself...if we only had a refrigerator I could buy him a whole case of beer and I wouldn't have to keep making these trip to the store, plus I would save money too. When I returned to the apartment I put one beer in the sink and gave the other one to King Wilson. He motioned for me to sit down beside him. I sat down and he kissed me. The smell of cigarette and beer on his breath was almost unbearable and being pregnant didn't help at all. It made me dizzy at times but I would take it to make him happy. I really don't think he is aware of how bad the smell of cigarettes and beer can affect someone else.

Most of the time when he not drunk he will brush his teeth before we start making out. I never complain about the smell of his cigarette and beer breath; I just turn my head in the opposite direction and take a deep breath. Sometime while making love the smell takes the fire right out of my body and I end up having to fake an organism. When he is drinking a lot he never realize I am faking anyway. Wilson got up and went to the bathroom; I guess he is going to brush his teeth. When he came back he said let's go upstairs for a while. I agreed and followed him upstairs. It was real pleasant in the room because the window was down and a nice breeze was coming in the room. We went straight to the bed because there was any doubt as to why we came to our bedroom. We jumped in the bed and had one of our daily doses of lovemaking. Lying in his arms completely relaxed; I thought to myself...this is the way I want to die...happy and completely relaxed. We lay there speechless and finally drifted off to sleep. The sound of thunder woke me up and I noticed it was lighting too; I got up and got dressed and went down stairs. Sister Linda was there so I asked her was it supposes to rain in December. She said yes, where have you been; of course it rains in December. I said here it is only ten more days before Christmas and its raining; you better bring in your crochet before it gets wet. She said I have brought it in already and put it in my room...the crochet is dry, I can take it to school and get my grade for it...next week our two weeks Christmas holiday begins. I said that's right! What are you going to do for two weeks... are you and Mother going to visit Sister Melda? She said I don't think so...Sister Rose and Gina are suppose to spend Christmas in Calapacuan at Mother's house...are you coming too. I said I don't know what Wilson's plans are for the holidays; we have a lot going on right now...you go and enjoy your Christmas. I will spend Christmas with Wilson maybe he will decide to come to Calapacuan, but if not, you know I will be with him where ever he goes. Suddenly the rain started pouring down real hard; I went back upstairs to close the windows. I went into our bedroom and started closing the windows. Wilson said where have you been...don't close the windows all the way down, so we can still get a bit of fresh air in here...come here and sit on the bed with me. When I sat down he lay back on the bed and pulled me down with him. We lay there listening to the rain on the tin roof and finally drifted off to sleep again.

We slept for quite a while then Wilson woke up and started moving around and woke me. I asked him what the time was. He said its four thirty and got up and started dressing. When he finished dressing he left going down stairs. I got up got dressed and made the bed before following him downstairs. When I got downstairs he was still in the bathroom; Sister Linda was in the kitchen cooking rice. I sit down in the living room to wait for him to come out of the bathroom. Finally he came out of the bathroom and I asked him what he wanted to eat for dinner. He said don't cook anything for me I am going on the base to see a friend it shouldn't take very long, but I will eat there. I asked him if he wanted me to go with him. He said no! I have something I need to check with him about and I will be right back. Sitting there on the couch my mind started wondering again...what is he going to do that he can't take me with him...is he going to the club instead of the base...is he happy being alone with me? I really don't know what to think it look like every time we start to get real close he find reason to leave and do something stupid. I often wonder if he think I am stupid and believe all the lies he tell me to explain the thing he do. Here it is Sunday afternoon and he want to go back to the base to see a friend. Why can't he wait till Monday to see this friend? Wilson went back upstairs and changed his shirt and came back downstairs and kissed me and said I will see you later. When he kissed me I could smell the fresh cologne he had put on; I knew then where he was going; I would have to share him again with the Club Hostesses. I sat there on the couch watching him through the window until he disappeared through the gate leading to our apartment. I started to feel sorry for myself because I didn't know anything else I could do to make him satisfied with me. I felt something pulling on my shoulder and I turned and saw it was Sister Linda; I turned and asked her what she wanted. She said what you are thinking about...I wanted to tell you what I was cooking. I said go ahead and cook whatever you want to cook. I continued to sit there on the couch next to the window hoping that he would change his mind and come back. I really do believe Wilson love me, but he has strong issues that I don't understand...smoking, drinking and chasing other girl even though he has one at home.

I pray to God that I will be strong enough to stay with him until he realizes that he doesn't need another woman. I want to show him that I really love him no matter what he does I will be around. I felt that same tugging on my shoulder and someone calling out my name; I looked around and saw Linda. She said let's eat...what are you looking at out the window? I didn't answer I just went to the bathroom and washed my hands and came back to the table. Linda and I sat down at the table. She said you can have the fish head this time; I just smiled at her because we normally argue about who would get the fish head. As we ate our dinner she broke the silence and said what are you going to do the two weeks I am not here...are you going to sit and stare out the window all of the time...are you going to be all right? I said don't worry enjoy your vacation Wilson will take care of me. My mind started to wondering again...yes he is going to take care of me all right...worrying me to death...getting drunk running around with the girls in the club...coming home with liquor on his breath and cheap perfume on his clothes...of course, I will get mad and would probably flip out if I wasn't thinking about the baby I am carrying...the only thing he seem to be interested in is running the streets and partying. Vicky! Vicky! Linda said you had better finish eating your food is getting cold. I said o.k. And hurried to finish my food because I didn't know how much longer I could hold back the tears. When I finished eating I went straight upstairs and got into the bed and put my pillow over my head and let it out. I cried myself to sleep. Sometime later Sister Linda started banging on my bedroom door and woke me up. She said Brother Wilson is downstairs on the couch drunk. I said what time is it? She said it is almost ten o, clock. I got up and went downstairs with her and we helped him to get upstairs to bed. She said what is wrong with Brother Wilson... he always gets drunk. I said when he go to a party he get drunk... don't worry about it just lock the door downstairs and go to bed. She closed the bedroom door and went back downstairs.

I pulled off Wilson shoes as he sat on the side of the bed. He tried to pull me down beside him; I said stop it...do you think I want to get close to you the way you smell of cheap perfume. He managed to get undress and lie down; I pushed him to the far side of the bed and covered him. I lay down and started thinking again...why is this happening to me...I thought he was going to make me happy, because I love him very much and he said that he love me...all he seem to do is hurt my feeling...I don't know how much longer I can take this treatment...sometimes it seems like I want to die. I started crying again, so I put my pillow over my head again and cried myself to sleep. The next morning the alarm clock started ringing and Wilson shut it off and slowly got out of the bed. I knew he had a hangover again; I didn't say a word I just laid there with my back to him. He got dressed and asked me where the aspirin were. I told him the aspirin was inside one of the cabinets in the kitchen. I really didn't want to say anything to him not even goodbye. He came back to the bed and leaned over and kissed me on the cheek and said he love me. He knew I was really upset with him, so he tried to hug me. I pushed him away and said please go to work and leave me alone. He said please don't get mad at me I have a bad headache. I said it's not my fault you are the one that went out and got drunk partying with your girlfriends...look at your shirt there is lipstick all over it. He said I don't know how it got there. I said if you don't know I don't know either...you even smell like cheap perfume. He said I have to go to work and left. I guess he took some aspirin when he got downstairs. I looked out of the bedroom window and saw him walking toward Rizal Avenue. I got back into bed and hugged my pillow as my mind started to wonder again...he went to work with a bad headache...I feel sorry that I acted so mad at him before he left...I love him so much sometimes I can't think straight...I guess I shouldn't worry too much about him because I am second in his life and partying with his girlfriends is first. Sometimes I wonder how he finds his way back to the apartment when he is so drunk. I would ask him how he manages to get so drunk and he would say he didn't know he only had three or four beers.

Then he would start telling me how much he loves me. I would just give up and start crying and turn my back to him and go to sleep. Crying is the only way I can keep my sanity in this relationship. Suddenly I hear Sister Linda footsteps going downstairs; I decided to get up and see what she plans to cook for breakfast. When I got downstairs she was coming out of the bathroom; I asked her if she was going back to bed. She said no I am fully awake now. I said are you ready to start breakfast now? She said yes, but I need to go to the store and buy some bread rolls. When I come back I will fry some eggs and Spam. I said o.k. You get the bread rolls and I will boil some water for the coffee or oval tine. When Linda came back from the store she cooked breakfast and we sat down at the table and ate while talking girl talk. After breakfast Sister Linda and I went to the furniture store to make a payment on my bedroom set, after that we went shopping for food. We returned home around ten that morning and I told her to start cooking lunch; I decided to take a shower and lay down for a while before lunch. After my shower I went upstairs and towel dried my hair. When I finished with my hair I laid across my bed and my mind started to wondering...if I marry Wilson will he leave me at home when he visit his friends...I guess I will be left at home with our baby...that's o.k. We will just go watch movies together...maybe he will run around more once we get married then I will be home alone all of the time...I am too young to be stuck at home alone with a baby...I guess I will find out very soon because

I am pregnant and we are getting married real soon...what am I going to do...after we get married and move to the United States will he continue to get drunk maybe the baby will get sick while he is drunk...I can't speak good English...what will I do...what if he decided to leave us once we arrive in the States...oh! My poor baby what will we do; I am scared for us, but don't worry baby no matter what happens I will take care of you ...I promise to never leave you alone like I am now...we will be together no matter where your Father take us. A knock on the bedroom door broke my chain of thought; it was Linda she said it was time to eat. I got up and went to the mirror and wiped the tears and smudge from my face and went down stairs to join her for lunch.

She was in the kitchen cooking the food. She asked me to taste it to make sure there was enough seasoning. I tasted the food and told her it was good. She said do the food I cook taste as good as the food you and Mother cook? I said your food taste as good as or better than mines, but never as good as Mother...let's eat I am hungry. Linda fixed my plate with the head section of the fish in it; I was very surprised. I told her she could have the head section of the fish this time. She said no I want you to have it I am use to eating the tail section of the fish now...even when I am at Mother's house she like the head section of the fish so I end up eating the tail section...it doesn't matter to me what section of the fish I eat now. I said I guess we have grown out of those foolish things we use to say and do. She said yes, just thinking about it is embarrassing now. We ate our lunch in silent and when we finished I told her I would wash the dishes and clean the kitchen. She said o.k. And went upstairs and got her crochet project and came back down stairs and started crocheting. When I finished with the kitchen I went upstairs and got my crochet and came back and started crocheting with her. She said when her teacher give her a grade on her project she would put it on the coffee table in our apartment and I told her I would put my crochet on the end table when I finish it. She said my last day of school before Christmas vacation is Wednesday, I will be on vacation for two weeks...I will leave for Calapacuan Thursday will you be all right? I said I would be all right, because I don't have the morning sickness anymore, so go and enjoy your vacation...two weeks will not last very long. We crochet for a while then she decided to take a shower I kept crocheting. When she came out of the shower and went upstairs I had just finished a flower design. All of a sudden the apartment door came open and Wilson came in, I didn't hear him trying to open the door. He came and sat beside me on the couch and tried to hug and kiss me, but I didn't pay attention to him I kept crocheting. He started kissing my neck and I told him to stop. He said are you still mad at me? I turned toward him and said what do you think...if I came home smelling like men cologne and drunk wouldn't you be mad? Just as he went to answer Linda came down the stairs and said hi Brother and went over to the dining room table and started crocheting. Wilson said let's go upstairs I want to talk to you. I told him I didn't want to go upstairs and if he had something he wanted to tell me he could tell me where I was sitting.

He said please Sweetheart I really need to talk to you upstairs. I really didn't want Sister Linda to know I was mad and upset with him, so I got up and started upstairs. He followed me upstairs to our bedroom and closed the door and sat down beside me on the bed. He started hugging and kissing me and I pushed him away and asked him what he wanted to talk about. He stopped and gathered his composure and said with all seriousness, you know I love and care for you, and even if I get drunk you are on my mind...the girls in the club don't mean anything to me. I said if they don't why do you keep partying with them and getting cheap perfume and lipstick all over you? He said I don't know maybe it was your lipstick. Now he wanted to blame me for the red lipstick that I never use or have on his shirt. I couldn't control my tears any longer, so I laid back and pulled my pillow over my head and let it out. I really couldn't believe that he was saying that the red lipstick belong to me...I must be going crazy...maybe I have a split personality. I got up and started looking for the red lipstick I am suppose to have in my makeup kit...I looked in my closet for clothes that I didn't recognize. He asked me what I was doing. I said nothing I was just checking for something. I didn't find any red lipstick or clothes in the closet that I didn't recognize...I am not going crazy...I am eighteen years old and in love with an American Sailor... we suppose to be married very soon and I am pregnant. I went back to the bed and lay down; I asked Wilson if I was dreaming and he said no and started kissing me. I turned away from him and he said are you all right? He started to kiss me again. I told him I needed to use the bathroom, so I got up and went downstairs to the bathroom. When I left the bathroom I went into the living room and sat down on the couch next to the window. I sat there for quite a while before Wilson came down and sat in the chair across from me. He said why you didn't come back upstairs. I said because I wanted to sit down here and try to figure out just what I mean to you. Sister Linda got up from the dining table and said she had to leave for school. I said good luck with your project. She said goodbye Brother Wilson. He said goodbye to her and got up and told me he was going to the store for beer. I continued to sit there next to the window and enjoying the view. When he returned from the store he took the beer, coke and ice to the kitchen. He chopped up the ice and put some in a glass and poured some coke over it.

He brought the glass of coke to me and sat down in his chair with his beer. He started drinking his beer and watching me; finally he asked me if I was going to drink my coke. I said yes and took a sip of it. I drunk the rest of the coke and realized that I was very thirsty, so I went in the kitchen for more. When I came back Wilson asked me to sit beside him on the couch. We sat there silently for a few brief minutes as we drunk our drinks. He said please don't get mad at me because I can't take it. I said if you can't take it why do you always run around partying with the girl in the club and you know it makes me mad? He said I was only having fun with some friends. That's the problem, the friends you party with are the girl in the clubs...that what I am mad about. He said what you want me to do...get down on my knees and ask for forgiveness...o.k. I will do it even if I don't know what I have done that so bad. He got down on his knees. I told him to get up I didn't want him to do that I just wanted him to stop lying to me. I guess I have to forgive him, so I said o.k. I forgive you until you get drunk again...maybe today or the next day. He kissed me and asked me if I still love him. I said yes I still love you if I didn't I would not keep forgiving you for the thing you keep doing. He said you know I love you too. Then the kissing and hugging began and I said let's go upstairs it should be cooler there. We got up and hurried upstairs and opened the bedroom windows. It was fairly cool in the room with the cool breeze coming through the windows. We got into bed and things started heating up again. I said we had better hurry up and buy an electric fan. He said this want take long we will be out of here before you know it. He was right it didn't take long. I wanted to lie there and relax but the cool breeze had stop coming through the window. I said I have to get me something to drink or you will have to carry me downstairs. My body was completely drained. He said let's go downstairs. Downstairs we drunk the cold water we had in our water pitcher. He said I really do need to get you an electric fan. He opened all the windows in the living room and the room did cool down a little.

The next week Wilson would go to work and come straight home every day. Sister Linda got a B on her crochet project. She went home to Calapacuan for her Christmas vacation. Wilson and I only went to the movies and back to our apartment. We made love in the morning and at night, we tried not to do it in the middle of the day because it was so hot, but sometimes we couldn't help ourselves.

Two days before Christmas I went shopping for Wilson's present, I got him a seven-day handkerchief set and wrapped it and hid it in Linda closet. That's all I could afford to get him it left me with ten pesos for emergencies. On Christmas Eve I was waiting for Wilson to come home at one that afternoon, but he finally came around three. I almost panic I said to myself here we go again...I could have went to Calapacuan with Sister Linda if I had known he was going to do this. Here I am again waiting for him. Why does he always break his promises especially on Christmas Eve? I sat on the couch next to the window listening to Larry and Pat playing Christmas Carols. We didn't have a radio or anything to listen to music on. I could hear the music real clear coming from next door it sounded real good. I begin to feel lonely sitting there by myself. Around four o, clock Wilson came home, he had being drinking, but he was not drunk yet. Two or three drinks more I am sure he will be drunk and won't remember a thing tomorrow. I said where have you been? He said we have been invited to a Christmas Eve Party on base. I said I don't feel like going anywhere on Christmas Eve... You go! I don't know any of those people. He said CB and Jean will be there and I know you know them...please get ready. I went upstairs and put a nice dress and my makeup on; then I looked in the mirror at myself and said not bad. I went downstairs to join Wilson and he said let's go back upstairs. I said you don't like what I am wearing. He said you look so good I could have you for my dinner...I like what you are wearing. We hurried out the door and walked down to Rizal Avenue and caught a jeepney to the Navy Base. After getting a visitor pass for me at the gate we caught a taxi to the Kalayaan Housing area. We found the house and knocked on the door; a man opened the door and introduced himself as our host and introduced us to his wife and the rest of the guest that had arrived. CB and Jean were there and CB was drinking already. Jean was in the kitchen with the host wife while she was cooking something. I stayed in the kitchen with them.

The lady asked me if I speak English and I said yes a little bit, she said would you like something to drink. I told her I would like some water. She said we have plenty of beer and liquor you can have some if you like. I didn't know what to do or say. Jean said Vicky don't drink alcohol. She said who brought her here and where did he find someone that only drink water. She thought I was one of the girl picked up from one of the club in town. They didn't think I understood what she was saying. Jean got up and asked to speak to the lady privately, so they went out on the balcony for a couple of minutes. When they returned the lady asked me to come over to the table to see all of the food she had prepared. I said that's a lot of food...I am trying to learn to cook American food. We went into the living room and she asked her husband who came in with me. He introduced Wilson to her. She said that's you! I guess she had met Wilson before. Jean said Vicky is Wilson's Fiancé. The lady said oh lord; she is only a kid, she look smaller than my Daughter...she looks just like a baby. I said to myself...first she think I drink liquor and was picked up from one of the clubs out in town; now she says I am a little girl. Jean said Vicky is Filipino size...if she was like our size she would be taller. I said to myself...now she is saying I am a kid size...how about her size...she is taller than her husband she has to bind down to kiss him...she look like she is from the land of the giants...I am the right size for Wilson he doesn't have to get on his toes to kiss me...she should take a second look in her mirror before she start talking about someone else. I looked at Wilson he didn't say a thing when the lady was talking about me. He is drinking liquor now and he hasn't eaten any food, he will get drunk if he doesn't eat something. The lady husband asked if the food was ready and she said yes, I am slicing the ham now...everyone should start fixing theirs plates. The lady husband got in front of the line. I told Wilson to come on and get something to eat. He got up and came over to the line and Jean and I followed him. I tried to put some of everything on my plate so I could taste all of the American food. I stayed close to Jean so I could ask her the name of the food I had on my plate. I asked her what was the name of the white potato mixed she said that's potato salad and it is very easy to make.

She told me the name of all the food on my plate and how to cook it. She said if you can cook Filipino food then you can cook American food or Soul food as we call it. Jean said the main thing you have to do when cooking Soul food is read and follow the direction of the ingredients label and before you know it you will be cooking Wilson Soul food. I said I have learn something tonight thank you for explaining to me about the food. Jean smiled and said Merry Christmas Vicky and I said Merry Christmas to her and thanks again for your help. Jean is a very nice person and real pleasant to talk to. My English is not very good, but Jean unlike the other American listen and try to understand what I say. I went across the room to where Wilson was setting and took a seat beside him. I asked him what time was we going home...don't we need to call a taxi now? He acted as if he didn't hear what I said. Jean came over and said don't worry Vicky let him sleep for a while...look at CB he is drunk too... we are going to take you and Wilson back to your apartment. Finally everyone started to leave going home. The lady of the house came over to me and said I hope you enjoyed the party. I said I really did enjoy the party and thanks for inviting us. She said you are always welcome to my house. As I walked away I could hear her say to jean, she is not like the other local I have met she is a real nice kid. Jean said yes, and she has the same problem as I have, we have men that like to drink and can't control it. She said I think CB and Wilson was here earlier today, I was real busy and really wasn't paying attention as to who was coming and going. She started putting up the leftover food and I heard Jean said I guess we will be going now, I forgot that

I have my two kids riding with us. She said don't worry my husband is not drunk he can drive Vicky and Wilson home. The lady husband woke Wilson up and told him he had to take his lady home. Wilson said could I get you to call me a taxi? I just sat there looking around thinking…here we go again…he take me out and he get drunk and forget about me. Jean got CB up and they got their kids and left. The lady's husband asked Wilson if he was all right. Wilson said yes man I am all right. He said o.k. Let's go to my car I am going to take you and your lady home. I said goodbye and thank you to the lady of the house. She told her husband to be very careful driving outside of the Base. When he drove off the Base he asked Wilson where we lived and he kept talking to Wilson to keep him awake. When we arrive at our apartment he asked Wilson if he could walk to the door. Wilson said I am all right man. I said thank you for the ride. He said you are welcome; take care of your man. I said o.k. Good night. He drove away. Wilson walked inside of the apartment and went straight to the bathroom. When he came out I asked him if he could climb the stairs to our bedroom. I took his arm to make sure he didn't fall as he climbed the stairs. When we got in our bedroom he sat on the side of the bed and started to remove his shoes. I started to undress and asked him to unzip my dress in the back. He stood up and unzips my dress and started kissing my neck and shoulder. I said wait I have something for you; I went to Linda room and got his present out of her closet and gave it to him. I said merry Christmas to him. He looked at me and I said yes, you can open it. He took it and said I am really surprised that you got me a gift. He opened the present and was surprised. I said do you like your present? He said yes I love it. I said I thought you would like the seven-day set so you could have a clean handkerchief every day. He said I really love it, but I didn't get you a Christmas present. I said don't worry about it I just wanted you to have the seven-day set so you could have a clean handkerchief every day. Wilson kissed me and said thank you. He pulled out his wallet and gave me forty pesos. He said merry Christmas Sweetheart, I want you to get something for yourself…I am sorry I didn't get you something. I said thank you. I put my nightgown on and Wilson was still looking at the handkerchiefs. I said are you going to sleep or do you want to set up for a while? He stood up and finished undressing and got into bed beside me. I turned and asked him if he was all right. He said I am very happy that I met you...you just don't know how much I love you. Then he started kissing me as if he was completely sober. I thought to myself...it's a miracle he is awake and not drunk...was he faking being drunk at the party...he looked like he couldn't keep his eyes open there...but that's o.k. Thank God he is not drunk anymore. He said you love me too, right. I said right, I love you too. Then he drew me real close to him and started kissing me. I gave myself to him and he did likewise. Holding me in his arm he said thank you Sweetheart for loving me and he kissed me and said goodnight. I said I love you and goodnight. I closed my eyes and fell asleep.

Then next morning was Christmas day and Wilson didn't have to go to work so he slept in. I went down stairs to take a shower, the water pressure was real good and I really enjoyed the shower. When I finished my shower I felt a little dizzy, so I hurriedly towel myself off and sat down in the living room. After a few minutes I felt as if I wanted to vomit. I thought to myself...I feel as if I am having morning sickness all over again...I had better get something to eat and take my medicine...did I take my medicine yesterday? I heard Wilson coming down stairs; he said Sweetheart why did you get up so early? I said I just felt like I wanted to take a long shower. He went to the bathroom too. When he came out I asked him if he wanted me to cook breakfast. He said today is Christmas day do you think the restaurant are open so I can take you to breakfast? I said I don't think so, in the Philippines on Christmas day we stay home and sleep all day, because we stay awake on Christmas Eve eating and opening our presents. Wilson said in the States we open our present and eat on Christmas day. I said we celebrate Christmas the opposite way, but we still celebrate and that's what matters. I am going to the store and get some hot bread rolls and walked out the door. I went to two Sari Sari Stores and they both were closed. On my way back to the apartment I thought to myself...I guess we will eat the sandwich bread. When I walked in the door Wilson was going to the shower, so I told him the stores are closed too. I went into the kitchen and washed up and started cooking breakfast. When I finish cooking Wilson was coming out of the shower. I said its time to eat the food is cooked.

He got dressed and came to the table and started eating. I set down and I felt as if the room was moving. Wilson asked me if I was all right. I said I am dizzy. He said have you taken you medicine? I said not yet, after I eat I would take it...I will be all right the Doctor said some people don't get sick doing their pregnancy and some be sick the whole nine months...so don't worry I will be all right. When I finish eating I will lay down on the couch for a while. When we finished eating Wilson collected the dirty dishes and put them in the sink. I said don't worry about the dishes I will wash them when I feel better. He said maybe you should go back and see the Doctor again. I said I will be all right I feel this way once in a while. He sat down on the couch and I laid my head in his lap. Wilson asked me when Linda would be back. I said she would be back when school start again after New Years. After relaxing for a few minutes on the couch the dizziness passed and I felt like getting up. I said to myself...maybe I did forget to take my medicine...I feel all right now. I started to get up and Wilson said you should lie down. I said I am all right now, I told you I would be all right. He said that's good! I could tell he was happy to see that I was feeling better. I got up and went into the kitchen and washed the dishes. After my dizzy spell we didn't do anything except sat around and eat, Wilson drunk his beer. When we went to bed that night Wilson held me close and kissed me goodnight. I think he was afraid that I would get sick again.

The next morning the day after Christmas Wilson had to go back to work, as usually the alarm clock started to ring around four thirty that morning. When he got dress he left for work. I watch him from our bedroom window as he walked to Rizal Avenue to catch a jeepney to the Base Main gate. Sometimes there is no jeepney passing by around four thirty in the morning, so often times he had to walk to the base. I really don't like for him to have to walk the streets this early in the morning, because sometimes American is robbed when they are out early in the morning. I watched him all of the way to Rizal Avenue and saw a jeepney come by and stop to pickup him. I was happy now, so I went back to bed and hugged his pillow and went back to sleep. I woke up around eight thirty and felt hungry; I decided to go to the market and have breakfast there, so I hurried and fixed my bed and went down stairs and took my shower. I came back upstairs and got dressed. When I left for the market I made sure I took my medicine with me so I won't repeat what happened yesterday. I had forty extra pesos half of my monthly wages when I worked at the Money Exchange. I decided to eat first, so I went to a small restaurant and ordered chicken soup. When I finished eating I started looking around and saw a stand with electric fans; there was small, medium and large fans and I looked at the prices and decided to buy the medium size fan. Then I went over into the clothing section to look for me a dress. I found one that I really liked, so I tried it on and it fitted perfectly. I counted my money and with the ten pesos I already had I had enough to buy the fan and a dress. I saw another dress that I liked better, but I really didn't want to spend all of my money I wanted to keep at least three pesos for emergency.

Wilson is going to be surprised when he sees the electric fan; he told me to buy what I wanted to buy. I looked at the electric fan again and said to myself...this is big enough to help cool down our bedroom. I went to the jeepney stop and caught a jeepney going down Rizal Avenue. I stopped at Second Street and walked to our apartment. On my way to the apartment the electric fan seem to get heavier every step I made. When I got inside of our apartment I got a drink of water and sat down and relaxed for a while. Finally I decided to take the fan upstairs and try it out. I put the fan on the dresser across from our bed and turned it on. I lie on the bed and felt the cool breeze from the fan; it felt good   blowing on my body. I know Wilson will be surprised to see what I bought with the money he gave me for a Christmas present. I decided to take a quick shower before Wilson came, so I got everything together and went down to the shower. I showered quickly and came out to the living room and sat by the window as I toweled dry my hair. I was anxious for Wilson to come home and see the electric fan. I kept looking for him out of the window until around eleven o, clock, because he said he would be home early. I thought to myself...I guess I had better get me something to eat for lunch...I need ice for my coke and the water pitcher. When I got outside on my way to the store I met the couple living four apartments down from us. They introduced themselves and we chitchat for a while. I told her we would talk more later I had to go to the store. The lady was very nice to talk to. I thought to myself...I have met everyone except the Mother and Daughter living in the third apartment...I am not going to worry about that now, I need ice from the store. When I came back to the apartment I felt very lonely. I thought...where could he be...he always say he will be home early and never show up...I thought he was a little worry about my condition when he left for work...I guess he was just pretending. I sat down at the table and ate my lunch. When I finished eating I cleaned up the kitchen and took my coke in the living room and sat down beside the window so I could watch for Wilson. When I finished drinking my coke I decided to go upstairs and watch for him out of the bedroom window. I went upstairs and turned the electric fan on and sat close to the window. I got tired looking for him so I lay down and closed my eyes and said to myself...why did I fall in love with an American that lie to you...if he wouldn't drink so much he would be here with me...he said he would be home early...I tried to surprised him and got surprised myself. I reached over and got his pillow and hugged it, but I kept feeling very, very lonely. I said to myself...I should have went home...maybe I wouldn't be this lonely...what did I do to be treated like this...if you love someone you don't treat them as second best. I cried myself to sleep again. I woke up around two that afternoon and I was feeling very chilly because I had the electric fan on. I combed my hair and straightened up my face and went down stairs, feeling a little hungry I decide to start cooking me something to eat. When I got my food on the stove cooking I went outside for a while hoping to see Wilson coming home. I wonder where he was at...maybe with one of his girlfriend because we didn't make love last night. I decide to go back inside and check on my food that was cooking. I checked my food and went into the living room and sat by the window so I could watch for him when he comes through the gate of the apartment. I looked at the brick fence of the apartment compound and started counting the layer of bricks. I thought to myself...I look like a fool setting here waiting for him to come home, so I got up again went into the kitchen and checked on my food. My food was finally ready so I fixed my plate and took it into the living room and set down close to the window to eat. When I finished eating Wilson still had not come home. I washed the dishes and cleaned the kitchen. After I finished in the kitchen I tried to think of something to do while waiting for him...my crochet, I would work on my design, so I got my crochet and sat at the dining room table and started crocheting. I worked on my crochet until around five that afternoon and Wilson still had not come home. I said to myself...I am going to change my clothes and walk to Rizal Avenue and get me some barbecue for dinner...After I changed my clothes I locked up the apartment and walked to Rizal Avenue where the barbecue stands was located. There were barbecue hot dogs, chicken, pork and even barbecue squid and all of it smelled good; I decided to get the barbecue pork and squid.

There was American Sailors in uniform all up and down Rizal Avenue. I thought to myself...there must be two or three big Navy ships in port. When I got my barbecue I walked back to the apartment hoping to see Wilson there. Wilson wasn't there, so I went into the kitchen and put me some left over rice on a plate and sat down at the dining room table and ate it with my barbecue. My mind started wondering again...what happened to him...is he partying in one of the club...I guess whatever he is doing is more important than being with me...I never thought for one minute that I would be alone the day after Christmas...I could went home and spent time with my family, but I stayed here to be with him...he tells me that I am always on his mind, because he really and truly love me...where is he at now. I looked at the time it was eight o, clock now and he still haven't showed up. I often wonder whether he love me from his heart or his mouth. What can I do to change his way of thinking, because I really love him and will always forgive him when he comes home? I guess I have to be satisfied with being second in his life until he finally realize that everything he is looking for out in the street is at home waiting for him. I hope he hurry up and realize that he already have what he is searching for, I don't know how long I can hold on and wait, because what he is doing is a drain on my love for him. I said to myself...I had better get up and clean this table before I fall asleep... why does love hurt sometimes...love is good when two people share the same feeling. I have often daydream about seeing what on the other side of the world and when I fell in love with Wilson I could see that happening to me, but things are looking very dim now. Wilson asked me to marry him I really love and want to marry him, but I am not sure now that it is the right thing for me to do. Right now all

I see is misery and disappointment. Maybe I will still get to see the other side of the world, but not with Wilson. Wilson is a loving and caring person when he is not drinking, but when he start drinking he change and I see a bad side of him. I know his good side love me and everything is all right until he start drinking and his bad side come out. When he is not drinking it is like heaven between us, but if he start drinking everything turn to hell. I guess I might as well go upstairs maybe he will come home when he spend all of his money on liquor and the girls. I undressed and put on my nightgown and sat in front of the dresser and started looking at myself.

I thought to myself...I don't look bad at all...why does Wilson put me second in his life...I look and feel real sexy too...everyone like me when I worked in the Money Exchange booth...that's why Wilson don't want me to work, because all of the young guys like me...this pretty face catch a lot of eyes...but Wilson caught my heart and my heart belong to him now...cupid arrow pierced my heart the first time I saw him...the first time we met I knew then that I wanted to spend my whole life with him if he wanted me. I lay down on the bed and hugged my pillow and pretended it was him as I kissed it and closed my eyes and went to sleep. The front door opened and closed downstairs woke me up and I could hear Wilson coming up the stairs it sounded like he stumbled a couple of times; it is good the stair has a balancer to hold on too. I looked at the time it was eleven o, clock. When he came in the bedroom I pretended to be sleep. I could smell the liquor and smoke on him. I felt the bed move when he sat down to remove his shoes. He kissed me on the cheek I didn't move I kept pretending to be sleep. I wanted to set up and tell him what I thought about him, but I knew he was very drunk and wouldn't remember a thing the next day, so I didn't say a word. He lay down without removing his clothes. I kept my back to him until I heard him snoring. I opened my eyes and saw that he left the light on too, I got up and went downstairs to the bathroom and when I came back I cut off the light and went back to bed. I turned my back to him as I hugged my pillow and finally went back to sleep.

The next morning when I woke up he was still asleep so I checked the calendar to make sure of the date, all the worrying I had done about him caused me to forget what day of the week it were. I checked the calendar and saw that today was Saturday, so I decided to let him sleep and get mad at him later today when he wake up. I got up and got dressed and went to the store to buy bread rolls. When I came back Wilson was still sleeping, I decided to let him sleep while I cooked breakfast. When I finished cooking I went upstairs to check on him, he was still sleeping, so I went back down stairs and ate breakfast alone as always. I decided to go outside for a while. When I got outside I walked the length of the compound several times and didn't see any of the neighbors, but I could hear them talking and could smell the food they were cooking.

The aroma made me feel hungry again. Finally I went back inside and I heard Wilson in the bathroom, so I sat down in the living room and started crocheting. When he came out of the bathroom he was surprised to see me sitting in the living room and crocheting. I guess he thought I had left and went to Calapacuan. He said hi Sweetheart... where did you go? I didn't say a word I just continued to crochet. He came and sat down beside me and kissed me. I stopped crocheting and rolled my eyes at him without saying a word. He asked again where did I go. I said where do you think I went...I am always here where you left me all day...you told me you would be home early, but I didn't see you until eleven o, clock last night when you came home drunk...where did you go? He started thinking how the best way to answer my question. I said why do you bother coming home if you rather party with your girlfriends, you don't need or love me. Why do you do this all of the time? If you don't want to be with me just say so and I will pack my bag and leave. I am tired of what you are doing, I told you once before you would have to choose your girlfriends or me. I can deal with your drinking, but I won't share you with your girlfriends...you always tell me you are coming home early, but you come home late and drunk...I can't take this anymore. I started crying because when I get real upset and mad that the only way I can relieve the stress. He hugged and kissed me trying to calm me down, he still didn't tell me where he had been, but I knew where he had been...in the hotel with one of his girlfriend. I really don't understand him the hotel has plenty of water he should at least take a shower before he come home and wash the cheap perfume off him, so I can't smell it on him. It really hurt to know for sure what he has been doing. He said please don't cry. I said I was trying to surprise you and I end up being surprised when you didn't come home. He said what is the surprise? I said follow me and I took him upstairs to our bedroom and showed him the electric fan. He had been in the room half of the night and almost a half-day and had not seen the fan. When we got in the room he still didn't see it until I pointed to it. When he saw it he were surprised and seem happy. I told him that I bought it with the money he gave me for Christmas. He said I gave that to you so you could buy yourself something. I said I did buy something for me; then I showed him the dress I even tried it on. He looked at it and said that is nice and it fit perfectly. I told him to go downstairs and eat his breakfast because it is getting cold. He said the food will warm up when it get into my stomach. We went down stairs and Wilson got his food and sat at the dining table and asked me to sit down beside him. When he finished eating I washed the dishes and cleaned the kitchen. Wilson said he wanted to talk to me about the wedding. I sat down beside him in the living room. He said how long do you think it will take the Dressmaker to make your wedding gown? I said one to two weeks if it's a simple gown, but if it an expensive gown maybe a month. I know we don't have money for an expensive gown so don't worry about trying to get me one I prefer a simple gown anyway just something to wear to the wedding. He said I want you to check with the Dress Shops and find out how much it would cost for your gown and when we get the gown we will get your ring. I said I would start looking after the Holidays things will be cheaper then. I said to myself...here we go again every time I get mad and asked him where he been he always comes up with something to distract me from staying upset with him. Wilson looked at me real serious and said I want you to remember that I will always love you; I know I get drunk and like partying, but I will always come home to you... you are the one I want to spend the rest of my life with...I know that I get drunk sometimes and can't remember what I did, but I will try to change...it take time to do it...I am sorry that I make you mad I really don't mean to...sometimes when I am out with my friends I forget the time and end up getting drunk, but I come home to you. I said to myself...yea! You come home all right after you spend all of your money in the club and on the girls...you come home with the smell of cheap perfume…I guess the only way you can get that smell on you is dancing real close or in the hotel…either way I am tired of smelling it. I got up and went outside for a while, because I could feel myself getting upset again. When I got up he asked where I was going. I told him I was going outside, so I walked around outside for a while trying to calm down. I tried to understand my situation…am I always going to be second in his life…I know I am second to his drinking. Drinking seems to be the most important thing in his life now and when he start drinking he like to go nightclubbing. I know I can't stop him from drinking and I know drinking is what causes him to act like he does. When he gets drunk he says that he doesn't know what he does, but he always remember the way home.

I had better let this go for now because I am only making myself upset again. I went back inside the house and Wilson wave for me to come and sit by him. He asked me if I was feeling all right. I said yes even though I was feeling worse. He started kissing me and I couldn't help from responding. I forgot that I was mad and the next thing I knew we were rushing upstairs to our bedroom. Nature took it course as we lay completely spent in each other arms enjoying our little electric fan. That weekend went very fast the only thing we did was go to the movies and lay around the apartment enjoying each other company. For the next few days before New Year Eve Wilson went to work and came straight home without stopping and getting drunk. New Year Eve he came home from work around four o, clock and had being drinking, but he was not drunk. He asked me to go with him to a New Year Eve party on the Naval Base. I asked him to stay at home with me because I really didn't want go…every time I go to someone house on the Base they think I am a Hostess from one of the Club in town. The Club Hostess have a reputation of taking married men away from their wives and most of the married women living on base don't like to see them around. They think that all Filipino girls that marry American Sailors work in the Club at one time, but not all of the girls work in the clubs just like me. The girls working in the club are not all bad the majority of them is just trying to make a living, because job opportunities in the Philippines is very scarce for uneducated girls. Wilson kept begging me to go with him, so I gave in and went upstairs to get ready. Wilson followed me upstairs and helped me with the zipper in my new dress. He started kissing my neck and I said you had better stop that or we going to be late for the party. He sat and watched me as I put my make up on. He said you are a very cute woman and I love you. I asked him if he knew the people having the party. He said yes the guy works on a Tug Boat like me. I thought to myself…I am glad he is not drunk yet because I don't know anything about these people. When I finished dressing we left for the party. When we arrive at the party CB and Jean and a few other couples were already there. I was introduced to Wilson friend wife in the kitchen so I stayed in the kitchen with her and Jean. Jean asked me if I like Chit ling. I said what is that? She said come over here and I will show you what it looks like. I looked in the pot as she stirred up the chit ling. I said yes we eat those, but we don't boil it we fry it. Jean said that one of the Soul Food dishes the lady is cooking. I asked the lady how do you cook the Chit ling. She said can you smell them cooking. I said no and she said that because I boil them first with celery to take away the smell…then I separate the water and celery and add new water, salt and black pepper and boil it until it done. Jean said now I have learn to cook my Chit ling without them smelling up everything…just like Vicky I have learn something too. The lady husband came and asks her if she needed something from the Mini Mart, He was going to the Package Store for more beer and liquor. Wilson came over and told me he was going with the guys and kissed me. The lady looked at us and said how nice, then she turned to her husband and said how about me. He said oh you! He turned and left with all of the guys. I took a seat in the living room and started watching television. Jean and the lady were still in the kitchen talking. I heard Jean said I am going next door to check on my kids. Then the lady said come on Vicky we're going too. She lowered the fire under the pots on the stove and we went out the back door to see her friend next door. We knocked on the door and Jean friend opened the door. Jean introduced me to her friend. Her friend said who are you with…I hope it not a married man. The lady I came with said my husband invited Wilson to our party and this is Wilson Fiancé. She said I know Wilson, so this is his girlfriend. I sat down and listen to their conversation. The lady I came with asked her if she coming to the party. She said if my husband is there I am not coming...we're not talking...I am mad at him for what he did; so I try to avoid him...I don't want to kill him... you know, I want go out in town with my husband any more, the last time we were out in a club one of the Hostess came and sat in his lap...I almost got up and knocked the hell out of her, so I stay home before I kill someone. Then everyone started looking at me as if I had did something wrong. Jean quickly came to my rescue and said Vicky is not like that she is a very nice girl and is getting married to Wilson very soon...she is Wilson Fiancé. Jean friend looked at my hand and said if she is his Fiancé where is the ring? I could tell Jean was getting upset with her friend when she said I know Vicky and Wilson is planning to get married very soon maybe he doesn't have the money for the ring yet...everyone doesn't have the money right away to plan a wedding.

CB and I are living from payday to payday and he is a first class petty officer...everyone doesn't have the luxury to plan a wedding right away Wilson is a second class petty officer and your husband is a chief he doesn't have the kind of money your husband have. Then the lady having the party said we're going back to my house you should try and come. I didn't say anything I just followed her and the lady as we left. When we left Jean was still somewhat upset at the way her friend was acting. She said what was wrong with her? The lady said about her being so frustrated with her husband...what he did was real bad that why she is still mad at the world. Jean said what did her husband do that was so bad? When she had a Maid, she went shopping one day and on her way she forgot something she needed, so she came back home and found her husband in bed with the Maid... that why she doesn't have a Maid right now. Jean said I am sorry that happened to her, but she shouldn't blame all girls for what one did... her husband is as much to blame as the Maid. The lady said that's why I don't have a maid...what time is it? Jean said it is almost nine o, clock. The lady said that what I am talking about, when it come to drinking our husbands forget to come home on time...my husband know we're having a party...I bet they are in town again in the club. I said to myself...they have problems to with their husbands drinking and lying just like I do with Wilson...the American Sailors all act the same they like partying, girls, liquor and beer...they lie a lot too.

The lady said if you are hungry you might as well get yourself a plate and eat because I don't know when our men will be back. Jean and I sat down in the living room to wait for the guys to come back. The lady went to her bedroom to check on her kids and see if they were hungry. She came back and said the kids had been eating snacks while we were next door and was not hungry. I was hungry, but I sat quietly on the couch waiting for everyone else to eat. Then we heard someone knock on the door it was the lady from next door, she asked if the guys was back. The lady told her we were still waiting for them to return so we could eat. Jean stood up and said let go in the kitchen and gets a drink while we're waiting. I followed her to the kitchen and the lady gave me a piece of ham and asked how it taste. I said it taste good and it have a pineapple taste. She said thank you I am glad you Like it. Jean got a piece too and told me the pineapple was used to dress up your ham when you cook it. I said to myself...I wish they would come back now so we can eat...I hope Wilson is not too drunk, but they have been going for almost four hours...I know everyone of them will be drunk when they return. The lady started to get real upset because her husband had not return. The guests were still coming in and everyone was hungry. Finally she said it is time to eat, so everyone got a plate and got in line. I tried to get some of all of the food especially the one I have never eaten. When Jean and I fixed our plates and sit down to eat the guys came in. The lady husband was drunk already and CB was almost drunk and the other guys didn't seem to be drunk. Wilson was the last to come in and sat down beside me and kissed me, thank God he wasn't drunk. He said are you all right? I said yes, get yourself something to eat. Wilson got up and went into the dining room and fixed his plate. The lady of the house told her husband they needed to talk in the bedroom. When they returned they acted as if nothing had happened. He came over and sat by Wilson and me and asked me how I liked the food. I said the food is very good. Then his wife came and gave him his plate and told him to stop bothering me so I could enjoy eating my food. While everyone was eating the lady from next-door came over even though her husband was there, but they did managed to stay away from each other. Wilson said I am sorry I didn't know that they wanted to go barhopping, if I had known I would have stayed here with you. I said don't worry about it I am getting use to being left alone whether it's at home or out somewhere you always leave me alone. Next time you take me somewhere you better not leave me because if you do I want be there when you return...you know some people are nice and some are not. Wilson said I am so sorry. Then CB came over and asked me if I drink Champaign. Jean said CB leave Vicky alone; you know she doesn't drink alcohol. CB said she could take a sip. I took the glass and held it out like everyone else and when the clock were straight up midnight I said happy New Year and pretended to take a sip. Wilson said give the Champaign to me and I will drink it. He said happy New Year to me and kissed me like he had never kissed me before and everyone was looking at us. I started to blush. The lady said leave the young couple alone let them enjoy their kisses we have had our long kisses.

Jean said look at Vicky she is blushing. The lady from next door said you had better enjoy your boyfriend and keep a chastity belt on him when he go to the club in town so he can't use his gun. Everyone started laughing, I didn't really understand what she was talking about and really didn't care. Wilson didn't get it either or just ignored what she said. He was still holding my hand and had that bedroom look in his eyes. After the toasting to the New Year it was time to go home, so everyone started leaving. Wilson asked his friend to call us a Base taxi. Our taxi arrived around one thirty in the morning; we took it to the Base main gate and caught a jeepney to our apartment. When we arrived the owner of the apartment complex was locking the gate. We had forgotten that he told us he lock the gate around two in the morning for Security reasons. We rushed into our apartment and went upstairs and I put on my nightgown and we went to bed. We were real tired so we kissed each other goodnight and went to sleep. We slept to around ten in the morning New Years day January 1, 1969. We stayed in bed until I heard my stomach growling. Wilson said we had better get up and get something to eat before his stomach start growling too. I got up and went down stairs to the bathroom and cleaned up and started breakfast. Wilson followed me downstairs. When I came out of the bathroom he was sitting in the living room waiting for me to finish. He asked me what I was going to cook for breakfast. I told him I was going to cook me some dried fish and rice and cook him fried eggs and Spam. When I finished frying the Spam and egg I went to the store and bought bread because Wilson like to eat bread for breakfast. Wilson was sitting at the dining table when I returned; so I fixed our plates and sat down to eat. I looked at the time and said we are eating breakfast and lunch together it is eleven fifteen. We finished eating our food and Wilson took a seat in the living room and I washed the dishes and cleaned the kitchen. When I finished in the kitchen I went and sat down with Wilson in the living room. I said I still feel sleepy. He said lie down on the couch and put your head on my lap. I put my head on his lap and closed my eyes; he started rubbing my head and playing with my hair and I went to sleep.

I slept for around half an hour and started moving around. Wilson said are you awake now? I said yes and sat up. He said I think I will go to the store and get some beer and ice. I said I will go for you how many beers do you want. He said two beers and gave me the money. I got up and started to the store; when I got outside I saw the American couple washing their car. I said to myself...I guess they are going somewhere later on. When I passed by them they said Happy New Year to me and I said the same to them. On my way back to the apartment I noticed the gate to the compound was open and I didn't see their car. I thought to myself...it must be nice to have your own car and be able to go whenever you want to and didn't have to be bumped around with other passengers in a jeepney...you will be away from all the different smells of perfume and plain unwashed body odor. I walked in the door of our apartment and went straight to the kitchen and chopped up the ice and put it in our water pitcher and took Wilson one of his beers. He said who were you talking to outside. I said it was the American couple that lives next door. I sat down on the couch close to the window and Wilson said why are you sitting over there...come sit by me. I said I want to sit by the window because it hot and a cool breeze come in this window sometimes. He said are you hot? I will go upstairs and get the electric fan, so he went upstairs and came back with the fan. He plugged the fan and we sat down together as he drunk his beer and kissed me every now and then. He seem to be relaxed and happy being home with me. He broke the silence and said six more days before my birthday. I said what do you plan to do on your birthday...have you planned something? He said I have no plans maybe we will go to the movies or just stay home. We didn't do anything that afternoon but lay around and went back upstairs because he had his strength back and took our little fan with us. We relaxed and fell asleep. The noise from opening the front door down stairs woke me up. I got up and put my clothes on and went to see if it was Sister Linda coming back from her vacation. I closed our bedroom door because Wilson was still sleeping. I went to Linda room and to my surprise it was her, I was real glad to see her back. I asked how was her vacation. She said it was good and tiring. I said what did you do to make yourself tired?

She said everybody was home for Christmas...Brother Celino and his wife, Sister Rose and Gina they all spent Xmas and New Years there. So Brother Etong and me had to clean up all of their mess...Sister Rose and Brother Celino wife are pregnant and they sat around and don't help do anything. I said Brother Celino have a house next door. She said I know but they always come and eat at Mother House...Brother Celino is still looking for a job...Mother end up having to feed them until he get a job. Brother Etong and I had to wash clothes and do everything to try and help Mother. My vacation was a working vacation...oh! I almost forgot, Sister Melda came before Xmas and gave Mother some money for Xmas and went back to Cavite City. I said she didn't come to see us. Sister Linda said she only stayed one day, but she did manage to go and see Mama Ligaya at White Rock Beach. When Mother and I were going to the Market in Subic she said she was going to see Mama Ligaya. I said what different food did you have for New Years Eve? She said Mother made sweet rice wrap on banana leaves, cooked neck bones with plenty of vegetables, Sister Maria cooked rice noodles with pork and vegetables and Sister Rose bought the bread rolls...we had a lot of food for New Years too. She asked me what I cooked. I said nothing, we were invited to a New Years Eve Party in Base Housing...they had a lot of different kind of foods. She said it is good you had different kind of food to eat...Mother was a little worry about you, but she knew you were with Wilson. We went downstairs to start cooking dinner. Sister Linda started cooking some rice and vegetable for her and me, but we were trying to figure out what we could cook that

Wilson would like. I thought of the corn beef we had in the cabinet, so I chopped up some onions and Irish potatoes and stir-fried it with the corn beef. I fixed his plate with rice and corn beef on top and took it to the table to him. We all sat down and ate our dinner. When we finished Sister Linda washed the dishes and cleaned the kitchen. I asked her if her school uniforms were ready for the next day. She said yes all of my uniforms are clean and ironed. I gave her some money for jeepney fare when she returns to school tomorrow. She took her crochet upstairs to her room and Wilson and I were left sitting on the couch. He said he wanted beer so I went to the store and bought three beers for him. When I returned we sat on the couch and made small talk while he drunk his beer. Finally we started to get sleepy so we went upstairs to bed. The light in Linda room was off so I guess she was sleep.

In our room we turned the electric fan on and got ready for bed. Wilson sat on the bed until he finished his last beer, then he started kissing me and one thing led to another. Before long we were laying in each other arms totally relaxed and minutes later we were asleep. Four thirty came and the alarm clock went off, Wilson shut it off and got up to get dress for work. I said to myself …it that time again as I looked at the clock hoping it had made a mistake. He said Sweetheart I have to go to work go back to sleep and he kissed me goodbye. I got up after he went downstairs to watch him from our bedroom until he catch a jeepney at the stop…I saw him catch a jeepney right away, so I went back to bed. When Linda and I finally woke up that morning we got dressed and went to the market to buy food for the next two weeks. We came back home around lunchtime so we had lunch. I told Linda when I finish lunch I was going to some of the Dress shop to see how much a wedding dress and a bride Maid dress would cost to be made and while I am at the Market area I would check on the price of a wedding ring. After lunch I went to two dress shop one told me they could make the wedding dress and the bride maid dress for eighty five pesos each and the other shop said they would do it for one hundred and thirty five pesos each. I told the cheaper dress shop I would be back in one month to have the two dresses made. I left there and went to a jewelry store and saw a wedding ring that I really like and it fitted perfectly on my finger. The ring cost one hundred sixty pesos. After pricing the gown and ring I went back home, because I was feeling hungry even thou I had recently ate breakfast. I guess all of the walking and shopping had made me hungry. When I got back to the apartment Linda ask if I were all right. She said I looked very tired. I said just bring me a cold drink because I feel as if I am going to pass out. Linda hurried and brought me a cold drink and went upstairs for the electric fan. She said you should not be doing all of this walking around, because you are pregnant. I said I only wanted to price the gowns and rings so Wilson would have and ideal as to how much they were going to cost him. Linda said how many people in the wedding party would have a gown? I said only you and me would have a gown. I will have one bride maid and Wilson will have only one best man. I need to find a Godmother...I know I can't count on Sister Melda, because she didn't visit me when she was here a few days ago.

I am only counting on you and Mother to be at the wedding, but if anyone else wants to come I will be happy to have him or her. I want Wilson to call and tell Brother Smitty the date of our wedding as soon as possible so they will know; if they come it will be nice, but my real concern is getting married before my baby is born. I decided to take a shower to help me cool down. I got in the shower and stayed under the water for quite a while and it really did help me to cool down and relax. I finished my shower and towel dried my hair and went into the kitchen to get me something to eat. Sister Linda said you got hungry too...the food is on the stove. It was around one thirty in the afternoon when I finished eating. As I got up from the table Wilson was coming in the front gate of the apartment complex. I hurried to the bathroom to brush my teeth. When he came in the apartment he said hi Sweetheart and hi Linda. Linda said hi and picked up her crochet and started upstairs. Wilson said Linda you don't have to leave just because I am here. She said I have to get ready for school. Wilson and I sat down in the living room and I started telling him about the wedding gowns and the ring. He said I am sorry you have to buy your own ring, but you know that if I walk in the jewelry store the price of your ring will double...I will give you the money for the ring the end of January and February the fifteen you can have the dress shop to start making Linda and your gowns. I asked him what we would eat at the wedding reception. He said leave that to me I will take care of it and let you know. I said I am going to need a God Mother and someone to give me away, because I don't have a Father. He said I would take care of that too. Why don't you ask Ligaya to be your God Mother...you worked for her plus she is Melda's adoptive Mother? I said o.k. I will ask her...now that's settled what do we do for money? He said we will take care of one thing at a time when I get paid...I will also go to Colomban Catholic Church and see what I will have to do to get married in the Catholic Church. I said what Church do you belongs to. He said I am a Baptist...do we have a coke in the house? I said I don't know I will go and see. I went into the kitchen and found coke in a liter bottle. I said this is good, so I took some ice from the water pitcher for his glass and poured coke over it. I gave the coke to him and he drunk almost all of it at one time. I told him I was going to the store to get more coke. He said since you are going would you bring back me a couple of beers. I took the empty bottles with me so I would not have to pay a deposit for more bottles. I bought coke, beer and some more ice.

I came home and chopped some ice for my coke and the water pitcher and gave Wilson his beer. He was very happy because the beer was real cold. When Sister Linda came downstairs on her way to school, I told her she should drink some cold coke before leaving because it was very hot outside. Wilson said Linda if you need money for your school or transportation let me know. She said thank you Brother, Vicky gave me some money already. She drunk her coke and left for school. We were left sitting on the couch Wilson drinking beer and I was drinking coke. We hugged and kissed and talked more about the wedding. He told me that in America the woman parents paid for the wedding. I said what! I was really surprised to hear that. I said that's wrong, in the Philippines especially in the Province area the man had to work for the girl parent for a while and give the parent a Water Buffalo, a Cow or whatever money he had. The man still had to pay for the wedding. Don't worry that only in the Province not in the city...my Mother don't want anything from you other than wanting you to make me happy...she know you work hard and is going to marry me, right! He said right! He said I love you and want to marry you now, but you want to get married in the Church...we could also get married by the Justice of the Peace...I will be patience and do that for you, but soon you will be Mrs. Wilson. I said Mrs. Wilson! What going to happen to my last name? He said when we get married you will be Mrs. Rosario Wilson and he kissed me and said do you think you will like being called Mrs. Wilson? I said I always call you Wilson. He said you need to call me Honey, Sweetheart or JC like I call you Sweetheart, but if you want to you can still call me Wilson it's up to you...do you like being called Sweetheart? I said yes I like it and I like being called Mrs. Wilson too. That afternoon we talked more about our wedding and our families. I asked him if his family would like him marrying a Filipino. He said don't worry about it, I am the one you are marrying not my family, but I am sure they will like you...my Mother is just like your Mother she is very nice and kind to everyone...I have three Sisters and a Brother. He showed me the picture of his baby Sister she looked skinny and pretty like me. He said her name was Bobbie. When he pulled her picture out of his wallet I saw another girl picture and asked to see it. I asked him why was he still keeping another girl picture in his wallet...I thought you got rid of all of her pictures a long time ago? I said you are still in love with her...I thought you was trying to forget about her...how can you forget her if you're still carrying her picture around?

I got up from the couch and went outside and stood at the entrance gate to the Apartment complex watching the people walking by. Wilson followed me outside and said please let go inside so I can talk to you. I followed him back inside and he showed me where he had burned the picture in the ashtray. He said I am sorry I didn't know that picture was still in my wallet behind Bobbie picture I thought I got rid of that picture a long time before I met you. I said to myself... what other surprises I am going to have...He know what to say or do when he get caught in a lie...I know it hard for him to forget someone he love even if she with another man back in the United States...its o.k. I got to see what she looked like before he burned the picture. He said I am sorry that picture made you upset, as you can see I have burned it so you want get upset again. He hugged and kissed me and said he love me very much. I said what else are you hiding in your wallet? He took his wallet out and gave it to me. I knew there was no other picture in his wallet but I looked anyway. I took his sister picture out and looked behind it again…his wallet was real old, so I know what I will get him for his birthday. I was happy now that I knew what to get him for his birthday. He said please don't get mad anymore. To show him I wasn't mad I turn around and kissed him and he kissed me back. He kept kissing me and I knew he wanted to go upstairs, but I told him I had to cook dinner. He said he wasn't hungry because he ate a big lunch, but he would like a beer. I said o.k. I will go to the store and get you some beer…how many do you want me to get? He said three should be enough. I left and went to the store right down the street, but their beer was not cold so I went to the store behind the apartment and got the beer. When I came back Wilson was standing in the door waiting for me, he wanted to know what took so long. I told him I had to go to the store behind the apartment to get cold beer. He said next time the store down the street doesn't have cold beer just forget it and come back home, because he don't want me walking around on the back streets when it almost dark. I said don't worry I will be all right. I went into the kitchen and put the beer in the sink and Wilson opened one and sat down in the kitchen to watch me cook. I boiled some eggplant when it was done I took it and chopped it up with some tomatoes and put salt and pepper on it. I got me one of the fried milkfish we had for lunch and rice. I sat down to the table and started eating.

Wilson said why don't you buy some beef or chicken sometimes? I said this is what we can afford to eat now…don't worry when we get some extra money I will buy some beef and chicken and cook it for you. He said don't worry about me I eat well on my Tug Boat, I want you to eat good like I do. I said what I am eating is good some people only eat boil rice and salt…I am happy I have vegetables, fish and of course rice. He said well if you are happy and enjoy what you are eating I am happy too. He got up and went in the living room and I finished eating and washed the dishes. When I joined him in the living room we talked some more about his family. The more I heard the more I wanted to see and meet them. Wilson finished his beer around nine thirty and I was getting sleepy to, so we decided to go to bed. We went upstairs and I started to undress and Wilson remembered we left the fan downstairs, so he went down stairs and got it. We got in the bed and Wilson wanted to finish what we started earlier and we did. We said goodnight and went to sleep. I woke up around two in the morning and turned off the electric fan, it and the open windows put out too much cool air. I covered Wilson up with the sheet and went back to sleep. Four thirty came quick that morning and Wilson got up and got dressed for work he said he would stop by Colomban Catholic Church on his way back home this afternoon and find out what need to be done in order for us to be married in the Catholic Church. I said o.k. And he said I love you Sweetheart and kissed me goodbye. I said I love you to Tiger Dear and He said I think I like that goodbye Sweetheart and left on his way to work. As always I watched him from our bedroom window until he got to the jeepney stop and caught a ride or he had to keep walking because there was no jeepney at the stop. I was always worrying about him having to walk to the Base Gate sometimes when there was no jeepney at the stop. He told me there is a lot of American walking with him to the base when they can't catch a jeepney, so I don't have to worry as much. When he caught a ride I went back to bed and tried to go to sleep, but I couldn't go back to sleep. I just stayed in bed thinking about everything until I heard Sister Linda going downstairs. I quickly got up and made the bed and went downstairs to see what she was doing. She was boiling hot water for coffee. I told her to go to the store and get bread rolls for breakfast.

When she left I went into the bathroom and washed up and brushed my teeth. When she came back she said what do you want to eat with the rolls I said open a can of Ligo Sardines, I feel like eating Sardines. She said I guess when you are pregnant you will eat anything at anytime of the day. When we sat at the table eating our breakfast I asked her to accompany me to the market to buy Wilson a wallet for his Birthday. She said when is Brother Wilson's Birthday. I said in three days January 7, 1969. When we finished our breakfast I took a quick shower before we left for the market. I showed her the dress Shop that making our gowns as we passed by in the jeepney. I told her we would price some white shoes to wear with our gown. She said why do we have to wear white shoes I have some black shoes? I said I like white for my gown better. She said o.k. It's your wedding you can spend more money if you like. When we got to the market we walked around for a while and finally saw a brown wallet and a black one, I bought the black one because he always wears a black shirt. We looked at some Philippine made shirts. I saw a yellow gold that worn on the outside of a man pants it called a Barong-Tagalong shirt. It cost fifteen pesos, I told her that was too much for a readymade shirt. She said if you buy the material and get someone to sew it, it will cost as much as that shirt, maybe a little less…you will have to wait one to two weeks for them to make it…you had better buy it now, because if you change your mind and come back for it tomorrow it probably want be here. I bought the shirt and told Linda I wanted her to hide it in her bedroom until Wilson birthday. We looked at some white shoes and tried a couple of them on, the salesgirl said they fit perfectly you should take them today, but I told her we would be back. Linda said I don't like the shoe with the real high heel I like the one with about an inch high so I want fall down when I wear it. We caught a jeepney and went back to the apartment. It was time to start cooking something for lunch. Sister Linda started cooking the rice and asked what else I wanted her to cook. I said why don't you go to the Shangri-La Restaurant and order some big noodles with plenty of vegetables. I have a taste for big noodles. She said you always have a taste for something. I will be back in a few minutes with the noodles. I turned the gas down under the rice and followed her out the door; I went to the store and bought coke and ice. When I returned I decided to take another shower and try to cool down my body.

Since I have been pregnant I have experienced a lot of different sickness…morning sickness, dizziness, and wanting to eat all kinds of food. I finished my shower and came out of the bathroom and started towel dried my hair while waiting for Sister Linda to come back. She came back with the food and I got my plate with rice on it and was putting the noodle on top of my rice when I remembered what Mother said about eating with someone when you're pregnant… the person that with you are not suppose to eat what you are eating or eat after you. If they do they will be sick or sleepy all the time, so I gave Sister Linda my plate and waited until she started eating before I fixed another plate for me so she wouldn't get sick or sleepy. When I finished eating my noodles I was very happy and strong, I guess that because I wanted to eat noodles very bad. I asked Sister Linda what she thought Sister Rose and Brother Celino wife will do if they want to eat something real bad but don't have the money to buy it. She said I don't know, I hope they don't lose their baby because they can't eat what they want...you know Sister Rose always go to Mother house and get her to cook what she want to eat...Brother Celino wife do the same whenever she smell something cooking at mother house she come right over and sit in the kitchen waiting for it to get done. I said then that's good. Sister Linda said that good for them, but bad for Mother because she works very hard trying to take care of Brother Etong and herself, now she has more mouths to feed...Brother Celino is still trying to find a job...it really bad for Mother, I know you and Sister Melda give her money sometimes; it would be nice for just her and Brother Etong, but a few more mouths to feed is very bad for her. I said I try and help Mother as much as I can, but I have my problems too...Wilson doesn't have very much money either, we live from payday to payday you should know that. I give you money for your school every two weeks and we buy food and whatever left I try and give her some...we are trying to pay for our furniture and the wedding is coming up it is stretching his paycheck real thin. I sat down in the living room next to the window towel drying my hair. Sister Linda went and got her crochet and started crocheting. When I finished drying my hair I got my crochet and started working on my design. She said you are really doing good with your design it going to look good on the end table. I was real happy I was almost finished, so I could start a new design. I finally finished the flower arrangement and put it on top of the table and Linda and I sat admiring it. Sister Linda said it is three o, clock I have to get ready for school and she went upstairs. Then I heard the front door open it was Wilson. He kissed me and sat down in front of the electric fan. I went and got him a glass of cold water. He said thanks very much for the cold water. I said what happened...why are you so hot and tired? He said in a very low voice, forget getting married in the Catholic Church...they want me to go to school for one month and become a Catholic before I can marry you in the Catholic Church...I can't do it because I work and stand duty sometimes at night. I said what are we going to do? He said don't worry about it I have found a church that will be glad to marry us...it is a Methodist Church. I said I guess it is o.k. It is a church. He said I would show it to you tomorrow when we go see

Ligaya about being your Godmother...the church is very close to the Swan Club where Ligaya lives. Sister Linda came by on her way out and said goodbye I am off to school. I turned and started following her out. Wilson said where are you going? I said where else, I am going to buy beer for you. Outside Linda asked me when we were going to buy a refrigerator so I want having to go to the store every day. I said as soon as we get ahead. She walked with me across the street and we said goodbye. I bought Wilson beer and hurried back to the apartment. He had not drunk anything because he had to talk to the Priest in the church, so he was really ready for a cold beer. He said planning a wedding takes a lot out of you. I said money is our problem, if we had money we would be married a long time ago. He said sorry Sweetheart, but you are not marrying a rich man I am only a Sailor making blue-collar wages. I said don't be sorry I know it take time for everything, but if you let me work I can help out a little bit. He said no way a girlfriend or wife of mines going to work; I am the man of the house and I put food on the table...my wife is suppose to stay home and take care of the house, baby and of course me...o.k. Sweetheart. I said o.k. Have it your way. He said I don't want you to talk about getting a job again, remove that thought from your pretty little head...no job for you except here in the house. I said o.k. Tiger Dear. He said I like you calling me dear, but what with the Tiger? I said you always attack me when you want to make love so I call you my Tiger Dear. He said o.k. O.k.! And he pulled me down on the couch and started kissing me. I said hold on Tiger take it easy. He laughed and said is that the way a Tiger does it? I said yes, but we had better go upstairs and finish what you have started. I pick up his beer and he followed with the electric fan. Upstairs I said I thought you were very tired walking around today. He said I am never too tired to make love. He plugged up the electric fan and we jumped in the bed and it was on. A few minutes later we lay in each other arms totally spent and it didn't take long before we were sound asleep. Sometime later I felt the bed moving and woke up. Wilson was sitting on the side of the bed smoking a cigarette. I asked him what was wrong. He said nothing I just wanted to smoke a cigarette. I sat down beside him and looked at the time it was six o, clock. I said what do you want to eat? He said let go downstairs and see what you have. We went downstairs to the kitchen and looked in the cabinet. We found some sausage in the can and Wilson said he would eat the sausage with crackers. I said we don't have crackers but we have bread. I said I would go to the store and get some crackers. He said if you get crackers you might as well get me some beer. I went to the store and got crackers and beer. I opened a can of sardines and chopped up some onion and garlic and stir-fried it together. Wilson said that smell good. I said you should try some maybe you will like it. He said I would try a little bit. I put some rice on his plate and some of the stir-fry on top of it. I was so surprised, Wilson loved it, and He ate that and asked for more. He said that stir-fry is very good I like it. I said you should eat some more of the food that I cook you may like it too...you will never no unless you try it. After we finished eating I washed the dishes and cleaned the kitchen. We sat in the living room for a while and talked about our wedding. Finally it was time to go to bed, so we went upstairs and went to bed.

The next morning I didn't hear the alarm clock sound. I didn't know Wilson had kissed me goodbye and left for work. I thought to myself...what wrong with me? I got up and made up the bed and went downstairs. Sister Linda was boiling the water for the coffee. I told her that I really need some coffee to wake me up; I don't know what wrong with me.

She said you are pregnant...come on and get your coffee I am cooking fried garlic rice and fried dried fish. I said put a lot of garlic in the fried rice. After we ate breakfast I laid down on the couch in the living room and went to sleep. I was sleeping real well until someone tap me on the shoulder. I opened my eyes and Wilson was standing by the couch looking down at me. He asked me if I was all right. I said you are home early. He said I finished work early so I decided to come home early so we can go see mama Ligaya about being your Godmother. I said I forgot about going to see mama Ligaya today; I will go and take a shower and get ready. When I took my shower and started upstairs to get dressed Wilson was worried about me so he followed me upstairs and watched me dress. Finally I was ready so we went downstairs on our way out. I told Sister Linda we was leaving and to cook vegetables for lunch. On our way to mama Ligaya place Wilson showed me the Church where we would be married. I said that dress shop beside the church is the shop that making my wedding gown. He said that really nice we have the entire place concerning our wedding on the same side of the street even mama Ligaya live just a few steps away. When we arrived at mama Ligaya house her housekeeper told us she had just left for White Rock Beach. We hurried and caught a jeepney to White Rock Beach and when we got there we was told that she was in the office by the swimming pool. We quickly went to the office and asked to see her. We were brought into her office and we asked her if she would be my Godmother at our wedding. She said first of all I like to congratulate you on your wedding and yes I will be happy to be Vicky's Godmother at the wedding...Vicky is just like a Daughter to me anyway. Wilson said we haven't set the date yet, but we will let you know as soon as we do. She asked us where we were going to have the reception. Wilson told her we were going to have it at his friend house. She said you could have it here at White Rock Beach resort. Wilson said thank you very much for the offer, but we have decided to have it at my friend place. We knew she was very busy so we said goodbye and went walking around the beach area for a while. Finally we decide to go back to Olongapo City, so we caught a jeepney. On our way back we decided to go and watch a movie at the Grand Theater. When we arrived at the theater, we found out the movie we wanted to see would start in about a hour later. We went to the Grand Restaurant to get a sandwich while waiting for the movie to start. We ordered a tuna fish sandwiches and coke for our lunch. When we finished we went back to the Movie to watch the Western movie that I like.

Wilson likes Chinese movies and I like the Western movies. We went straight home after the movie and sat around talking about the movie we saw and our wedding until it was time to go to bed. The next day when I woke up Wilson was still sleeping, so I got up and went down stairs to say goodbye to Sister Linda because she was going home for the weekend. I told her to say hello to everybody for me and to tell Mother I would be coming to see her next week. She said tell Brother Wilson I said happy birthday to him and don't forget his present is in my closet. I said o.k. My goodness his birthday is today I almost forgot it. She said I would see you Sunday afternoon...I have all of the dirty clothes to be washed. I gave her twenty pesos to give Mother. I went to the bathroom and washed up and brushed my teeth. Just before I finished in the bathroom Wilson came downstairs and said I thought you left because I heard the front door open and close. I said happy birthday Tiger. He said it is my birthday today…I forgot it. I said when you finish in the bathroom come back upstairs. I went upstairs and fixed the bed and went into Linda closet and got his birthday present. I put one peso in the wallet for luck. When he came into our bedroom I gave the present to him. He opened the box and said a new wallet it is just what I need. I said I want you to try on this shirt. He was very surprised to see the shirt. He put the shirt on and tried to put it in his pants. I said this shirt is a Philippines Barong shirt and is suppose to be worn outside of your pant. He said thank you for the gifts; I love you very much. Then he started taking everything out of his old wallet and put it in the new one…he saw the one peso bill in the wallet and said it have money in it too. I said that to make the wallet lucky and never be empty. He said thanks again Sweetheart. After we had breakfast we sat around the house and talked about the wedding and our relatives. When we finished lunch that after noon we decided to go to the movies. After the movies we came back home and sat around for a while and Wilson asked me to go with him to see CB and Jean. I said o.k. And we went to their place. We knock on the door and CB answered it and said come on in and sits down. We came in and sat on the couch together. CB told Wilson to fix himself a drink. Jean came out of the bedroom and said why you didn't call me and let me know we had company. CB said you always like to stay in the bedroom with the kids, so I don't bother you with my company visiting me.

Jean laughs at CB and said you could have called me I was just playing with the kids. CB asked Jean when she was going to start cooking dinner. She said in a little while and sat down to watch television with us. Wilson asked CB if he would give me away at our wedding. CB said what wrong with her Father? Wilson said Vicky doesn't have a Father to give her away that why I am asking you… you and Jean are our close friend and is the only one I can count on to be a part of our wedding. Jean said you are planning your wedding already. CB said yes, don't you remember we talk about the reception being here in our house? Jean with a big happy smile said I didn't think you was serious about having the reception here. CB said if I am the Father figure that giving Vicky away, of course I am serious o.k. He looked at me and said Vicky you have my permission to marry this boy. Jean laughed at CB and said it too late for him to be asking your permission to marry her; they are getting married very soon and having little Wilson. Jean asked Wilson when were the wedding date. He said maybe in two months probably March. She said that want take long. She excused herself and went into the kitchen and started cooking dinner. They asked us to have dinner with them and we accepted. Wilson and CB had started drinking liquor, but they stopped long enough to eat their dinner. I told Jean today was Wilson birthday. She asked him how old he was today. He said I am twenty-three years old. She said you are still very young, I bet Vicky need to get her parents' permission to get married. Wilson said yes and we have taken care of that already, because that the law in the Philippines. We talked about the wedding and everything else we thought of that evening. We left their place around ten-thirty and went home. Wilson was not drunk he was walking very straight when we left their place. When we got back to our apartment we went up to bedroom and got ready for bed. We lay around and talked about our wedding. Wilson said Sweetheart I know I told you to buy your own wedding ring that because we don't have very much money and you need a ring for the wedding, but I promise you after we get married and settle I will buy you a real nice wedding ring myself and put it on your finger. I said I am not worry about the ring I just want to get married in the church. He said Sweetheart we are still getting married in a church it just not a Catholic Church. I said as long as it a church; we are doing all right all we have to do is stick to our plan and everything will be all right. Wilson kissed me goodnight and I kissed him back and we went to sleep.

The month of January came and went very fast. We didn't go out because we were trying to save our money. Around the end of January Sister Linda and I went in for our measurement for our gowns. I gave Mother some money so she could get her a dress made for the wedding. She bought the material and found a cheaper dressmaker in Calapacuan. She told me my dressmaker charge too much. I couldn't argue with Mother because she did found a cheaper dressmaker. The material that I saw and wanted were gone and the dressmaker would have to order it from Manila and that would take almost three months before she can finish with my dress. I wish I had the money the first time I saw the material and I would have it now. That's okay. They know where to get the material and I am happy about that. I will just put a deposit on it so when it comes in they will hold it for me. We will wait until next payday to get the shoes and my ring. Wilson and I was tired and completely drain from running around planning our wedding it look as though things was closing in on us. The closer the wedding got the more it took out of us. Wilson would come home from work and we would be out running around doing something for the wedding. We lost a lot of sleep and didn't make lover as often. I am not complaining I just want the wedding planning to be over.

During the month of February we didn't do or go anywhere even on Valentine Day we just stayed home. One day when we were out and about we stopped by the Dress shop and the Seamstress said the material was in and they wanted Sister Linda and me to come in the next week for our fitting. The next week we went to the Dress shop and tried on our gowns. The gowns fitted perfectly all they had left to do was the sequences. I stopped by the jewelry store and picked up my ring and it was very nice. I liked it very much even though I had to select it myself. When I got home I hid the ring in one of the dresser draws in our bedroom; I will give it to Wilson the day before the wedding. Sister Linda and I picked up our gowns and shoes the end of February I hid the gown in her closet so Wilson wouldn't see it before the wedding. We have three weeks left before March 22, 1969 the day of the wedding. We have everything we need for the wedding all we have to do now is wait. I don't know what come over Wilson he has started coming home late and drunk. We seem to be getting mad at each other all of the time; it looks like the closer we get to the wedding date the more we get on each nerves. One day Mother and Brother Celino came by to see if we needed someone to help cook for the reception. I told her that we were having the reception at one of his friend's house and the cook on Wilson Boat was doing the cooking for the reception. Before I could finish explaining what was going on Wilson and his friend CB came in and Wilson was very drunk.

He saw Brother Celino sitting on the couch and said he was my boyfriend. He was so drunk that he didn't recognize Brother Celino and my Mother sitting on the couch. He accused me of having my boyfriend in the house and when I tried to explain to him that he didn't know what he was talking about he slap me in the face. My Brother was so upset that he walked outside of the house and Mother followed him. CB said JC that Vicky Mother what are you doing man? Mother came back and said I never hurt you when you was growing up...now you have someone that I know love you, but I know that he is hurting you...I see with my own eyes he is a drunk and a girlfriend beater. I am sorry that I signed your paperwork for you to get married...if I knew he was hurting you I would never have signed it. Vicky you need to come home you don't need this kind of life...we can make it even if we have to scrub some floor for a living it is better than being beaten up. I said don't get mad at him he is drunk and don't know what he is saying. Mother said it up to you if you want to marry him...you are grown now, so

you have to decide if this is the kind of life you want. Mother and Brother Celino left and went home they were very mad at Wilson. I said to myself...why did he have to come home drunk when my family is visiting...he even called me a bitch and slap me in front of them...he really made a bad impression on my Mother. I need to get out of here for a while so I can think. I stayed outside of the apartment trying desperately to figure out what to do next. We really need a break from each other. Wilson act like he losing his mind thinking that Brother Celino was my boyfriend. If he is that jealous I don't know if I can live with him in the States or anywhere else...I can't imagine him slapping my pretty face all of the time. His friend came to the door and told me Wilson wanted to talk to me. I told him I didn't want to talk to him I have had enough of his drinking. When CB went back inside of the house I could hear him and Wilson talking. Wilson said where is the bitch? CB said she is outside and don't want to come in and talk to you...Mama son left already and was very upset. Wilson said they can leave if they want to this is my house. Finally I had to use the bathroom so I went inside and I saw CB sitting in the chair across from Wilson and Wilson laying on the couch sleep. CB stood up and said Vicky I am sorry the boy got drunk and acted up like that I will see you around.

I went on into the bathroom and when I came back I decided to let Wilson stay on the couch. I thought to myself...I don't care about the wedding anymore, I have tried my best to make him happy but his drinking is destroying everything we have...only three weeks left before the wedding and he is doing these crazy things. I went upstairs and got the alarm clock and put it beside the couch so he would hear it the next day and wouldn't be late for work. I went back upstairs and went to bed; after tossing and turning for one or two hours I went to sleep. The next day when I woke up I went into Sister Linda room and woke her and told her we was going to Calapacuan and stay at Mother's house for a while. I told her to take her schoolbooks and things so she could go to school from Calapacuan. We closed the apartment up and left for Calapacuan; on our way we stopped and bought bread rolls and some can food to take with us. When we arrive at Mother's house everyone was glad to see us. Sister Rose and Gina had spent the night and were there. Mother asked me if I was all right. I said I am all right Wilson doesn't know what he doing when he is drunk. She looked closely at my face for a mark of some kind. She said it is good that he didn't slap you very hard...I wanted to get a stick and knock him out maybe when he wake up he will stop drinking so much. Sister Rose said in English...Wilson got drunk. I didn't try to explain anything else to them. Mother couldn't speak English and she didn't need to know what Wilson said to me after she left. I looked at Mother and said in Tagalog, Wilson has a lot on his mind and he didn't mean to slap me. Brother Celino came in the house and tried to find out if I was all right. He said if Wilson wasn't drunk he would have beaten him up for slapping me. Mother got up and went into the kitchen and started making coffee. Sister Rose asked Mother what she was cooking for breakfast. Mother said I am cooking eggs, Spam and dried fish your Sister Vicky brought bread rolls. Mother told Brother Etong to bring more wood for the fire in the stove. Brother Celino told Brother Etong to get water he would get the wood. Gina was still lying on her mat so I lay down beside her on the mat. Brother Celino wife came in the house. When Mother finished cooking breakfast the pregnant women let everyone else get their food first so they wouldn't get sick or sleepy. The pregnant women compared their stomach to see who had the biggest stomach.

Sister Rose stomach was the biggest; my stomach wasn't showing yet I guess it is because I am skinny. You couldn't tell by just looking at me if I was pregnant. We didn't have any ideal as to who would have their baby first. Sister Linda said I hope you are not having the baby the same Month, because Mother will be too busy trying to take care of three grandchildren. I said I want Mother to be with me when I have my baby because I don't know what to do...Sister Rose have had two babies already and she know what to do, But Brother Celino wife and me haven't had a baby before. I said Wilson said he want our baby to drink bottle milk. Brother Celino wife said this is my first baby and she will drink my milk. When everyone finished breakfast Sister Linda and Brother Etong washed the dishes and cleaned the kitchen Mother said I am going to the market in Subic to buy rice and a few more grocery. I asked Mother to buy neck bones because I wanted to eat it with vegetables. Sister Rose said bring some star apples and Brother Celino wife said I want to eat sweet rice. Mother said I would buy what you want if you give me the money. Everybody looked at me. Sister Linda said Vicky they want you to give Mother money so she can buy the stuff they want. I gave Mother the money I was going to give her anyway. Mother and Brother Etong went to the market. Brother Celino and his wife went home. I asked Sister Rose to walk with me next door to Sister Maria's house. When we got there she was sitting on her porch that she calls a balcony. I said hello how are you doing? She said I am doing fine...I haven't seen you for a long time; I see Rose here all of the time, but I never see her husband. Sister Rose said my husband works at night and he have a part-time job at day time and when he is not working he try and get some sleep...we're trying to save a little money to have when the baby comes. We talked for a while until I started to feel sleepy, so I told her I have to go and lay down for a while. Sister Rose said I would go with you. We went back to Mother's house. Before I could lie down Sister Rose said look out the window Vicky...that looks like Wilson. I said yes that's Wilson. I went ahead and lay down on the mat in the corner. Sister Rose said Mother and Brother Etong are coming too. I said I guess Wilson is helping them carry the food to the house. I heard Mother calling me saying; Vicky, Vicky Wilson is here. Sister Rose got up from the mat. I didn't get up; everyone was so excited to see him if they knew what he called me before he slap me they wouldn't be so excited to see him. I am not glad to see him after he called me a bitch and slap me; I didn't do anything bad to deserve being slap. When they came inside Mother said in English...don't be a foolish dog Wilson and everyone laughed. She was trying to say don't be a bad man Wilson when you are drunk. Wilson said what is everybody laughing about? Sister Rose tried to explain to Mother what she had said. Wilson asked me what everybody was talking about? I said Mother said to you don't be a foolish dog that what they are laughing about...she was trying to say don't be a foolish man when you are drunk and slap my Daughter. He said it o.k. Your Mother trying to speak English...tell your Mother I am very sorry I hurt you and it will never happen again. I told Mother what he said. Mother said no more foolish dog o.k. Wilson. Everyone started laughing again and Mother said get serious and stop laughing at what I say. Mother got up and went into the kitchen and started washing the neck bones in the sink; then she started talking with her back to us. She said when you were kids I never spanked you because I don't believe in spanking...you are suppose to protect and show your love for your kids not spank and hurting them...Rose I know you are always spank Gina because I can see the marks on her legs...I don't know why you do it...I never spanked you when you were little. Now that you are grown you become the devil to your kids. Everybody in the room became very quiet you couldn't hear a sound. Wilson said what is going on? I said don't talk Mother is talking to Sister Rose. Mother said I haven't said anything to you yet because you are pregnant, but if you are hurting her because of your pregnancy just leave her here so you want have to beat her all of the time...she is only five years old... still a baby...I can't understand what you could be thinking about... beating a baby. When Mother finished talking to Sister Rose; Sister Linda went into the kitchen to help Mother with the cooking. Brother Etong went to the store for coke and ice. Mother called Gina and gave her some candy and the star apples to give to her Mother. Gina came smiling over to where Sister Rose and I was setting and gave her the star apples.

Sister Rose gave me one of her star apples and I got up and went into the kitchen and washed it and started eating it right away. Sister Rose followed me into the kitchen and washed her star apple and start eating it; she asked Wilson if he wanted one. He said no thank you and looked at me and asked what is it? I said it is a fruit and it is called a star apple. Sister Linda went next door and took the sweet rice to Brother Celino wife. Everyone have what they asked for to eat but me mines is still cooking in the pot. Brother Etong returned from the store with coke and ice. He gave it to Mother and she chopped some of the ice and put it in a glass and poured coke over it. She gave it to Brother Etong to give to Wilson. He said thank you. Watching him drinking the cold coke made me want some too; so I went in the kitchen and got me a glass of coke. I came back and sat by Wilson on my favorite wood box. I could tell that he was waiting for the right time to ask me to come back with him to Olongapo, so I told him I was going to stay in Calapacuan for a while. He was very surprised when I said that. He said if you stay I am going to stay. I said do whatever you want to do. He said I am sorry I slap you; I was very drunk you know that I wouldn't have slapped you if I were sober. I said that why I am scared to go home with you; if you will slap me in front of my Mother I know you could slap or hurt me when no one is looking. He said I would never hurt you because I love you; I was drunk and had too much on my mind…it just happened I don't really know what happened. I said I really don't need this kind of treatment; you had the nerve to slap me for nothing your drinking is getting bad, very bad I am afraid that the next time you get drunk and get mad at me I will end up in the hospital. He said if it gets to the point that I start beating you up I would leave you first. I said you could leave me now before it get worse. He said no, no! I will quit drinking before I leave you; I promise you and your Mother that I will never put my hands on you again. He tried to kiss me but I turned away. He tried to see if there was a mark or soreness on my face. I said please leave my face alone; I don't want you touching my face right now. He said very sadly, I guess I really hurt your feeling…I can't touch your face…I just want to see it. I am so sorry that I did it; I never ever in my wildest dream wanted to hurt you, I love you.

I heard Mother say let's eat the food is ready…Vicky fix Wilson plate first before you fix yours. Wilson said what did she say about me? I said she want me to fix your plate. He said I am not hungry. I said you had better eat even a little bit so she want start preaching to you or me. He said o.k. Just fix me a little bit. I went into the kitchen to fix his plate. I put neck bones, cabbage, potatoes and carrot on top of his rice and gave it to him. He said that look good; I went back to the kitchen to fix my plate. Sister Rose, Gina, Brother Etong and Mother were setting at the table. Mother took Sister Maria some food and came right back. Someone called Brother Celino and he came over to get his food. He said his wife was not going to eat lunch because she ate all of the sweet rice. I said more for me. I got boil banana, cabbage, potato and carrot to eat with my neck bones; I didn't get any rice. When I came back to sit on the box with him, he asked what was the brown food in my plate? I told him it was boil ripe banana mother cooked with the neck bones. Would you like some? He said no thank you I was just wondering what it was. I enjoyed eating my neck bones; I ate so much I could hardly get up. Wilson said tell your Mother the food was real delicious and I really enjoyed it. When I told Mother what Wilson said I thought I saw a smile for a brief moment? When everyone finished eating we just lounged around for a while; then finally everyone started drifting away. Wilson said where did everyone go? I said maybe next door. He said what are you going to do? I said I told you before I want to stay here for a while and try and sort things out. He said I guess I will stay here with you then. I said no! You need to go back to Olongapo so you can go to work tomorrow. He said today is Friday and I don't have to go to work tomorrow...that why I am out early today and I feel real bad because you didn't want to talk to me this morning. I said what do you think I felt when you came home drunk and say my Brother was my boyfriend and if that wasn't enough you slap me...you really scared me that time, so tell me how do I know that you want do it again when we are married...maybe we shouldn't get married right now and give you some time to get all of your running around and getting drunk done.

Go find someone you can slap around in front of your friend to show them that you are a man...your drinking is causing you to lose me and your baby...I have tried very hard to please you, but all you do is come home drunk and take out your frustration on me. If you want out of this relationship you don't have to hurt me just stop coming home and I will understand that you don't want to marry a Filipino.

The baby and I will be all right…I am still young and can work for a living…there are plenty job waiting for me or maybe I will work in the club like all of the other girls do that have baby by American… maybe that what I will do, you think I am having an affair anyway; maybe this time I will have a lot of American boyfriends. Wilson said please stop talking like that I know I made a terrible mistake; please forgive me I am only human…I will stop drinking before I let it cause me to lose you…you know I was drunk when I did that and I have apologized to you and your Mother and I want to say I am sorry to you again and I realize the big mistake I made…you said you love me and if you really do then give me one more chance and I promise you it will never happen again. He kissed me gently on the cheek and tried for my lips but I turned away. I calmed my anger down a little bit because I really love him very much. It hurt me to see him begging for forgiveness even though I knew his drinking was destroying the goodness in him. He said how about we spend the night here tonight. I said you don't have to stay because I want to stay. He said I want to stay and be with you. I didn't say anything I just got me a mat for the floor and put a blanket on it and got my pillow and lay down on it. Wilson just sits there on the wood box looking at me. Sister Linda came over and asked me if we were going home. I said I am not going home because I am at home already. She said I am talking about the apartment in Olongapo. I said no, you could go home and go to school. Linda said I don't have to go to school today; I will just wait to Monday. I said you don't have to be absent Brother Etong can wait for you over at the jeepney stop when you come back tonight. She said I can be absent for one day; I have never been absent since I started school. I said you are going to mess up your perfect attendance record. She said it is o.k. It is just one day I will tell them we had an emergency in the family. I said Linda I will talk to you later I am very tired, I am going to sleep.

Wilson said what is going on? I said Sister Linda don't want to go to school because I am not going home to Olongapo. Wilson said why can't we go back to Olongapo so she can go to school? I said no, if you want to go then go…if Linda doesn't want to go to school it is her decision she is old enough to make that decision. I have to many problems myself to worry about somebody else problems…I have to think about myself before I get sick. I closed my eyes as I hug my pillow and went to sleep. I don't know how long I slept, but when I woke up Wilson was lying beside me. I got up and got me some water. Wilson asked me if I was all right and got up and sat on the wood box. Mother came back from next door and started frying sweet potatoes and bananas for our snack. I went in the kitchen to the sink and washed my face one side felt a little sore. Mother was watching me; she asked me if I was all right. I said I am all right I feel better after I took a nap. I asked Mother if Linda went to school? She said no, she is next door talking with your Sister Rose and your Sister-in-Law. Everybody came back to eat fried sweet potatoes and bananas. Gina was sleeping across the room, but all of the talking woke her up. I gave Wilson some of the fried sweet potatoes so he could taste it. Mother gave Wilson the last of the coke. I told her we would be spending the night. She said o.k. I will prepare the bedroom for you. Sister Linda and Brother Etong help Mother to prepare the bedroom for us. Around four that afternoon Mother told Brother Etong to go out in the yard and catch a chicken for her to cook. She said she was going to fry half of the chicken for Wilson and cook the other half with papaya and make a soup. I said Mother will you please add some additional vegetable in the soup; She said o.k. I will be right back. Sister Linda came into the kitchen and I asked her to go to the store for ice, coke and three beers for Wilson and take Brother Etong with you. When I gave her the money Sister Rose told her she would walk with her. Gina said I want to go too. We were left in the house alone again. Wilson asked me where could he go to use the rest room. Mother didn't have indoor plumbing in her house; so I showed him the Doe and Jane bucket. He said he wanted to do number two. I looked for some paper towels, but I couldn't find where Mother had put them. I found a magazine and wet some of the pages and gave them to him to use. I took him outside and showed him where to go. When he finished we walked back to Mother's House holding hands. When Mother saw us she said what are you trying to do, lose your baby? I said we're being very careful. Mother said if you slide down that hill you will be sorry and it will be too late. Mother started cooking dinner; she cooked chicken and French fried potatoes for Wilson and the papaya chicken soup for everyone else.

We ate dinner around six o, clock: I fixed Wilson plate and gave it to him along with a cold beer. He was very surprised to see the beer. He said where did you get the beer? I said that what everyone went to the store for. Wilson was ashamed to drink the beer in front of Mother. She knew that he was hesitating to drink his beer when she asked him in Tagalog how did he like the chicken. I told him what she said and he said tell her it is very good. He saw her smiling and nodding her head in agreement. He knew then that she didn't mind him drinking his beer as long as he didn't get drunk and was willing to forgive him for what he did to me. I could see that he was happy to know that Mother was not holding one bad thing against him. My Mother is not an evil woman she only want her kids to have a nice life. She knows that Wilson is a good man, he just need to control his drinking. I could see that she wasn't mad at him anymore and I wasn't mad at him either. Every time I touched the side of my face the soreness was still there; I am glad that it didn't turn red or blue. At bedtime Mother gave me an extra blanket for Wilson and me. I put it on the mat so it would make the mat a little softer. When Wilson finished his beer we laid down on our mat and he held me tight and kissed me. He said I love you Sweetheart and I said I love you too. We went to sleep.

Saturday morning Mother got up early and started cooking breakfast. Wilson said why does everybody wake up so early? I said because they are use to getting up early; go back to sleep I will get up and see what Mother is doing. Mother was in the kitchen; I asked her what was she getting ready to do? She said I couldn't sleep any longer so I decided to get up and fix some coffee. I got a wash pan and asked for some of the hot water to wash my face and brush my teeth. Mother said how is Wilson doing sleeping on the floor? I said he is all right I fixed the mat nice and soft. When I went back to the bedroom Wilson had went back to sleep. I turned around and left him to continue sleeping and went back to the kitchen.

I told Mother Wilson was still sleeping. I sat down in the kitchen and drunk hot oval tine while she cooked breakfast. Mother said would you like some hot chocolate? Melda left some here the last time she were here; I drink it once in a while so it will last longer. I said no I would just drink the oval tine. She said what is the date of your wedding? It will be in about three weeks; I will send Linda to tell you the exact date. Try to come to my apartment about five days before the wedding. I told Sister Melda, but I don't know if she is coming. Mother said I think Rose is going to Pangasinan to visit her Husband relative next week before she gets too far along in her pregnancy. That why her and Gina is staying here; I think she will leave Gina here with me, but don't worry I will be at your wedding. Your sister-in-law will be here and Etong will be here too...I don't know Celino plans he still trying to find a job. Your Brother Etong will have to stay here because if everyone leaves when we come back everything will be gone. Finally everyone started waking up and moving around. Wilson got up and asked me if there were some mouthwash available. I said no, but he could put some salt on his finger and scrub his teeth. He did that and goggled with water. Mother gave him a towel to use when he washed his face. Brother Etong got a small branch from the Guava tree and cut it into small pieces and showed Wilson how to use it for a toothbrush. Wilson tried it and said it works and thanked Brother Etong. When we finished breakfast Wilson said Sweetheart I need to take a bath and change clothes. I said go home and take your shower and change clothes. He said I won't go without you; I can stay as long as you stay. I knew that we should go home so he could take his shower plus everyone was looking as if they wanted me to go even Mother I think she had been praying that Wilson and I could resolve our difference and get married. So to make everybody happy I said Wilson and I are going home so he can shower and change his clothes. Everyone was so happy I thought they were going to start clapping their hands. Wilson said what's going on? I said I told them we are going home. Wilson was about to boil over with excitement; he asked me if I was serious about going home. I said yes, let get ready to go. Brother Etong was very excited he indicated to me that he wanted us to love each other. Sister Rose said I would see you when I come back from Pangasinan. Mother told Wilson no more foolish dog and everyone said no more foolish man. She said o.k. No more foolish man.

She told Wilson that he speaks English, why didn't he say something instead of laughing at her? I told him what she said. He said what do you call your Mother in Tagalog? I said Inay. He turned to her and said I promise to tell you next time Inay. She was very happy to hear him call her Inay. He was glad to say it too, because he just kept repeating it to himself. Everybody except Brother Celino and his wife came out to see us off. I looked at the time it was eight o, clock in the morning; I guess Brother Celino and his wife is still sleep. We walked across the field to the jeepney stop. Wilson held on to my hand as if he thought I was going to run away. We caught a jeepney to Olongapo and Wilson kissed me on my neck in the jeepney. I said in a real low voice stop it. When we got to our apartment Wilson hugged me so tight I couldn't hardly breath. He said thank you for coming home Sweetheart. I quickly went to the couch and sat down. He asked me if I was all right. I said I feel a little dizzy from smelling the gasoline from the jeepney. I said would you go to the store and get coke and ice. He said yes and went right away. When he returned he fixes me a glass of coke with ice. I drunk the coke and a few minutes later I felt much better. Wilson sat beside me on the couch worried even though I told him I felt much better. I told him to go and take his shower and I will follow him. He went upstairs and got everything he needed and came back and took his shower. When he came out I went in and took a long shower to make sure I got the smell of gasoline from my body. When I came out I felt like a new person. I sat down beside him on the couch as I towel dried my hair. Wilson said let me do that, so I gave him the towel and comb and he started rubbing my hair with the towel and finally started combing it. It felt so good I almost fell asleep. I felt just like I feel when my Mother comb my hair. Wilson said would you like to go out for lunch with me? I said let stay home and eat here. He said o.k. I didn't want you to have to cook. He said how about me ordering some food from Shangri la Restaurant? I said o.k. That would be nice. He said what do you want to eat? I said I want to eat big noodle and plenty of vegetables. He kissed me and left for the restaurant. When he left I decided to go to the store and get some more ice, coke and beer. When I returned I put two beers in a bucket and put some chopped ice on it and covered it with a towel to keep it cool longer. When Wilson returned he had my noodles and fried chicken. We sat at the dining table to eat our food. Wilson said I am going to the store right quick and get you a Coke.I said I went to the store already. I gave him his beer and chopped some ice for my coke. He gave me some of his fried chicken and I gave him some of my noodles. We were happy we decide to order take out instead of going out to eat. When we finished eating I put the leftover away and cleaned the dining table. Wilson said maybe we should go and tell mama Ligaya about the wedding date tonight. I said that would be good so she want plan anything on our wedding date. That night we went to the Swan Club and asked for her. We were told that she haven't arrive from the White Rock Beach so we wait for her almost a half-hour in the Swan Club. Finally she came home so we went out to meet her before she went inside of her house behind the club. We caught up with her and said hello; we like to talk to you. She smiled and said hello come on upstairs I have something for you. She said have a seat. We sat down and Wilson said our wedding date is March 22 at one o, clock in the afternoon. She said what church are we getting married in? Wilson said the Methodist Church that's about one block from here...the church on the corner of the street next to the movie theater. She said oh yes, I know where it is I have been to a wedding there before. She said I will be there March 22 at one o, clock. Then she wrote it down on her calendar. She got up and went to her closet and came back with something in her hand. She said I didn't know what to get for both of you, so I got this Philippine made material so you Vicky can get you a dress made and Wilson can get him a shirt made with the material. She said where are you having the reception? Wilson gave her the address and said we are just having a few friends and my In-laws...just a small gathering to celebrate our wedding. She said the important thing is you are getting married. We said thank for the gift and we will be going so you can relax after a day in the office. When we left mama Ligaya house I was real happy and I know Wilson was happy too because we had taken care of everything we need to do before the wedding. All we have to do now is wait and don't fall apart. Wilson said I hope you don't change your mind about marrying me. I said just don't slap the other side of my face. A jeepney came by with horn blasting and Wilson said what did you say? I said nothing, I didn't want to take away the joy he was feeling now. We caught a jeepney and went home. When we got home in our apartment Wilson held me real tight and kissed me.

We sat down on the couch to relax for a while. I asked him what food was his friend preparing for our reception. He said just snacks and drinks...don't worry I have that taken care of...just relax show up at the wedding. When we went to bed that night we had enough energy to make a fire and we tried to use it all up. The electric fan came in handy again to cool us down so we could go to sleep. Around two o, clock in the morning we were awaken by loud voices and the sound of bottles and bricks hitting the roof and the outside of our apartment. I got up and tried to look out of the window. Wilson said close the window and don't stand near it because they may start shooting. Wilson said maybe someone got drunk and started a fight. I said I think it is a Gang that came in the wrong territory and they are fighting that why there are so many people involved. He said yeah! Maybe so, but you don't want to be a witness to someone getting hurt or killed. Then we heard a siren from an Ambulance or a police car that was running real fast down the street by our apartment going somewhere in the back of our apartment. Wilson and I got up and stood to the side and looked out our window, but we couldn't see anything it was too dark. We figured someone got arrested or hurt. Wilson went downstairs to use the bathroom and I followed him. We could hear people talking outside of our apartment. I got close to the window in the living room and I could hear what they was saying. The Owner of the Apartment complex and the American couple was outside checking their cars for damage. I heard one of them say yes, bottles and bricks hit both cars. When I hear them go in and close their doors I went upstairs. Wilson said what's going on down there? I said I heard the neighbor talking and they said broken bottles and bricks hit both cars in the driveway. He said that's ashamed...you never know what can happen while you are lying in bed trying to sleep. That why I don't won't you standing close to the window, because if they decide to shoot a stray bullet may hit you. He said lets go back to sleep. He pulled me close to him and kissed me goodnight. The next morning I got up and got dressed and went to the store to get bread rolls. I saw Mr. Blanco out sweeping up glass in front of our apartment. I didn't stop I kept going. When I came back he was still outside sweeping; I asked him if he needed some help and he said no. I said do you know what happened last night? He said the people that live behind our apartment complex had a party and got drunk and notice that some people from another Gang was there and they started fighting. I said I thought someone got mad at you and started throwing stuff at your apartments. He said no, it was a Gang fight they do that every once in a while when they find someone in their territory from another Gang. When I got back inside of our apartment Wilson was sitting downstairs in the living room. I said I thought you was still asleep. I went into the kitchen and washed my hands and started cooking breakfast. We ate our breakfast almost in silence. When we finished I washed the dishes and cleaned the kitchen. We went outside to see some of the damages that was done last night. We looked at the two cars and the only damage was the paint chipped in several place. I asked Wilson if he knew how to drive a car; he said yes, then I asked if he had a car. He said I don't have a car but when we get to the States I will get one for us and teach you how to drive it. I said is it very hard to learn to drive a car? He said it is not hard at all…we have two more weeks before the wedding. I said I don't want to think about it; I am scare that something will change your mind about marrying me. He said I am the one that worried sometimes I can't sleep at night thinking you may change your mind or disappear when the time comes. I said I will not change my mind in a million years I am worried about you…maybe while you are drinking your friend will talk you out of marrying a Filipino…you always listen to your friends. He said don't worry or be scared I love you and want to marry you and I promised I will take care of you and our baby…you are the most important thing in my life. We hugged and kissed and before we knew it we were upstairs in bed. After we made love we lounged around in bed until lunchtime. I told Wilson I was going to get up take a shower and cook lunch. He said I am going to take a shower with you. We got in the shower but Wilson was interested in doing everything except showering, we ended up going back upstairs and finishing up what we started in the shower. Now we're real hungry now after exerting all of that energy. Finally I was on my way downstairs to cook lunch. I was so hungry I couldn't think of anything to cook. I looked in the kitchen cabinets and saw Spam and Sardine so I decided to run to the store and get some bread to make Spam sandwiches for lunch. I bought bread, ice, coke and beer. When I returned I saw Wilson going into the bathroom to finish taking his shower.

I hurried and fried the Spam and made Spam sandwiches. When he came out of the shower I said lunch is ready we're having sandwiches for lunch. He came over and kissed me on the neck and said you are a lifesaver. We sat in the living room and ate our sandwiches. When we finished I said I am going to take my shower now. He said do you want some company, and he started smiling. I knew what he was thinking about; I said no. After my shower I came into the living room to towel dry my hair. Wilson sat watching me towel drying and comb my hair. He said your hair is almost to your waistline. I said to myself…it is good Wilson can't tell that I got an inch trimmed off a few days ago. I said I want to cut my hair to shoulder length. He said don't cut your hair I want it to hang down past your waistline. I said it would be too long to manage. He said just don't cut it Sweetheart and kissed me so I couldn't say anything else about my hair. We sat there talking for a while then we heard Sister Linda coming in the front door. She had a bag of clothes. She said hi and went up to her room. I got up and told Wilson I would be right back; I followed her into her room. She was hanging up her uniform in her closet. I separated my nicely ironed clothes and put them in my closet. I asked her how did everything go after we left Mother's house this morning. She said Brother Celino went with another guy somewhere looking for a job and had not returned when she left…Sister Rose left Gina at Mother's house because they are going to Pangasinan. She said oh! Before I forget it do you think when you get some extra money you can give it to me so I can get Mother some nice Sandal to wear to your wedding…I know Mother wouldn't ask you. I said I plan to do that anyway. When you go home Saturday, I will give you some money so you can buy Mother some new sandal when you go to the market. I said are you tired now? She said I am not tired. I said would you go to the market and buy fish and vegetables? She said yes; let me finish hanging the clothes here. I gave her the money for the food and went back downstairs. Wilson as always wanted to know what I was doing upstairs and I told him I was talking to Linda. When Sister Linda came downstairs on her way to the market; I told her to get one-half of chicken and one-fourth pound of potatoes. I went into the kitchen to start cooking the rice. Wilson asked me what I was doing? I said I am cooking rice. He said this early; it is only three in the afternoon. I want to have the rice done when Linda come back from the market so all we will have left to cook is the chicken, vegetable and potatoes.

Finally the rice were done so I turned it down so it would simmer and went into the living room and sat down with him. He said I missed you. I said I was only in the kitchen. I kissed him to shut him up...when he is home he wants all of my attention...sometimes I get hungry staying by his side because he don't want me to leave him. He can't understand that I am pregnant and want to eat very often...I am trying to feed two. When Sister Linda came back from the market; I went in the kitchen and helped her get started cooking the food. Then I came back and sat in the living room with Wilson. He was sitting patiently on the couch and I told him I was going to the store for beer his eyes lit up. I went to the store and bought ice and beer. When I returned the rest of the food was done so I fixed Wilson plate and gave him a beer and he was happy. I told Sister Linda I was going to set in the living room with him. I asked him how was the fried chicken? I told him I know it doesn't taste as good as his cook on his Boat, but that was the best I could do. He said don't worry about it I like the way you cook it. When we went to bed that night we went to sleep right away for a change; we had a very exciting day so we needed the rest. Around three-thirty in the morning Wilson started kissing me and woke me up. I thought to myself...what is wrong with this man...I guess he want to get what he missed when we went to bed earlier...I gave in and started responding. When it was over the alarm went off; I looked at the clock it was four in the morning. I said it four o, clock not four thirty. He said I have to go in a little early today. He got up and got ready for work and kissed me goodbye and left. I watched him from the bedroom window until he caught a jeepney to the Base. I went back to bed and hugged his pillow pretending it was him until I fell asleep. I woke up around nine that morning and I could smell fried dried fish. I got up and hurriedly fixed the bed and went downstairs. Sister Linda had finished eating and was sitting by the window crocheting. She looked up and said I cooked garlic fried rice and fried dried fish the water for the coffee is probably cold now. I

Chapter 6
The Wedding

Said the food would be good with hot coffee so I turned the fire up on the water kettle to heat it up again. Linda said when you finish your breakfast I will wash the dishes. When the coffee was ready I sat down and ate so much I could hardly get up from the table. She said what wrong with you? I said I think I have had too much to eat. She laughed and said I guess that one of the foods you crave to eat. I went outside to try and walk my food down; I saw the neighbor living in number five standing outside waiting for the moving van; they had a lot of boxes outside in the driveway. I guess number five will be empty for a while. I decided to go back inside and take a shower, so I went in and got everything I needed and went to the bathroom and showered. After I showered I came out and sat on the couch as I towel dried my hair. Sister Linda said is there going to be a lot of people at the wedding? I said why? She said I am scared that I may fall down in the church aisle. I said there is no need to be scared only a few people will be there...just pretend you are walking down the hall of your school...there are more people there than will be at my wedding. She said are you sure the church want be filled up? I said the only people that will be there is mama Ligaya who you know already and a few friends of Wilson...just walk and I will follow you. She stood up and said how do I walk fast or slow? I said I think slow would be better, so we practice walking until she felt comfortable with it. She said I am not nervous I am afraid I will fall down. I said get the heel you will be wearing at the wedding; She put them on and we practiced until she said I am ready now. I said thank God! We sat down and talked about the wedding...her getting a haircut and how I am going to get my hair fixed. Linda said Vicky the wedding is next Saturday. I said I know and I try not to think about it because sometimes I have a nightmare. The time passed real fast; three days before the wedding we went to visit CB and Jean. We talked about everything that was going to happen during the ceremony. CB said tomorrow night the guys are going to take Wilson out for a stag party. Jean said if you guys have Wilson a party somewhere we are going to have Vicky a party here. I didn't say anything because I didn't know anything about a stag party. When we got back to the apartment I asked Wilson what CB was talking about? He said it is a party the guys give you the last night you are a single man. I said oh! Do you mean getting drunk and being with girls? He said I don't know who will be there the guys are the one that set it up. We went up to our bedroom and Wilson asked me for my wedding ring so he could give it to the best man.

That night when we went to bed we were thinking about everything and couldn't really concentrate on anything. We kissed and said goodnight. The next morning Wilson woke me up with a kiss and told me he love me very much. He said meet me at CB house this afternoon and remember I will be spending the night there and you will be here...leave the apartment tomorrow at least by eleven and go to CB house so you will have plenty of time to dress for the wedding...Sanders and I will be here in the apartment changing for the wedding. He said I don't really know what going to happen tonight at the stag party, but please show up for the wedding and remember I love you very much. He said Sweetheart CB is going to have someone to pick you up at his house and drive you to the church. I said o.k. I will still see you tonight, right. He said yes, but you will have to go home alone because I will be spending the night there. I said why? He said the Groom is not to see the Bride before the wedding that a tradition...do you love me? I said I love you very much and I am scare because I don't know what going to happen tonight. He held me close and kissed me and kissed me some more and before we knew it we were experiencing our best when we're together…it happened very fast I guess it was because Wilson had to go to work. He got up and managed to get dress and kissed me and said he love me over and over. The last thing he said as he was going downstairs was I would see you tonight at CB's house. Again I watched him from the bedroom window until he caught a jeepney to the Base. I went back to bed but I couldn't go to sleep. I thought about everything he told me about tonight and tomorrow. Sometimes I wished we had went to the Justice of The Peace…I really don't know what to think, but that's o.k. Tomorrow is the big day; I can make it through tonight no matter what happens. I promised him that I would show up at the wedding; why is he worried that I want show up for our wedding. I am the one that should be worried because I am carrying his baby…suppose he change his mind about getting married, what happens then? The knock on the door brought me out of my deep thought. It was Sister Linda she asked if I was coming downstairs. I got up and opened the bedroom door. She came in and said Vicky tomorrow is your wedding day; Mother said she was going straight to the church. I said that o.k. Because she knows what time everything will get started.

I said tomorrow after I get my hair fix I will come back here then we will go to Wilson friend house to dress for the wedding. We will get dressed there and his friend will pick us up and drive us to the church. Linda said why couldn't we change here? I said because Wilson and his Best Man will be changing here…things are a little mixed up so we will do what we are supposed to do. She said I will just follow you wherever you go…it is your day tomorrow. We went downstairs and Linda started cooking breakfast and I decided to take a shower before I forget to. When I went into the shower Sister Linda said she was going to the store for bread rolls. I finished my shower and went upstairs to my bedroom and set down in front of the dresser; I tried to imagine what I would look like with my hair up and then I put it down. I decided to wear it up in the front and down in the back tomorrow. Sister Linda came to the door and said let eat. That afternoon when she left for school I just sat around in the apartment hoping Wilson would come home even though he told me to meet him at CB's house. Around four I decided to get ready to go. Then I fixed me a sardine sandwich I didn't feel like eating a big meal. I thought to myself...I better brush my teeth. When I finished brushing my teeth I started thinking that I didn't want go to CB's house; then I said to myself...they are nice people they are having our wedding reception at their house, so I got ready and left. When I got to their house Wilson was already there and very drunk. I said Jean what happened did they have the stag party already? It is only six thirty. She said I don't know why Wilson got drunk. CB and Wilson started to whisper to each other; then CB said go-ahead man. Wilson stood up and went into one of their bedroom. Then I heard him calling my name; CB said Wilson is calling you. I didn't really want to go, but they said that the room he will stay in tonight. I got up and went in the room to see what he wanted. He said sat down beside me. I said what do you want. He started unzipping my dress in the back. I said what are you doing? Stop we are not in our apartment. He said it is o.k. They said I can use this bedroom; so don't worry about anything. He pushed me over and started removing my clothing. I pushed him back and said don't treat me like your girlfriend in the club. If you love me, don't do this there isn't any lock on the door. Please don't do this here if you want to make love we can go to our apartment.

Wilson had made up his mind, so he tried to pin me down and I started screaming no, no real loud. CB and Jean opened the door. I was half naked and very embarrassed, but Wilson did stop trying to rape me. I got up crying and got dressed; Wilson stayed there on the bed and didn't say he was sorry to them or me. I told Jean I was going home. She said sit down for a minute and she went and got me a drink and tried to calm me down. I told her I was sorry that it happened in their house. She said I know you are sorry and hurt about what Wilson done, but remember he is drunk and tomorrow is your wedding day...I am sorry he is drunk and I am sorry we had to open the door but I didn't want him to force himself on you and hurt you because you are pregnant. I said I am going back to our apartment. She said think about your wedding tomorrow...we will just let Wilson sleep for a while I don't think he will go anywhere because he is drunk already. We will lock him down for tonight... don't worry everything will be all right...remember your wedding is tomorrow...you and Wilson been waiting for this day to come, don't think about what happened tonight just think about the good things you and Wilson have...put that in your mind and you will be all right. CB asked if I wanted him to drive me home; I told him no thanks and went out and caught a jeepney. I was in the jeepney feeling real down and missed my stop, so I got out of the jeepney and started walking back to Second Street. I heard someone calling my name so I stop and looked it was one of the girls I met when I worked in the Money Exchange. She said I heard you got married; where is your husband? I said he have duty tonight. She said where are you going? I said I came out to get some barbecue chicken from one of the stands. She said o.k. I will talk to you some other time my boyfriend and I are in a hurry; nice seeing you again. I guess they were in a hurry to go in that club. I was in a hurry to walk back to Second Street and get home. When I got in our apartment I started crying; I never felt so bad in my life. I guess Wilson drinking has taken over his way of thinking. CB and Jean saw me naked that is really embarrassing and humiliating. Did he really want to do that or did someone put him up to it? I know he was drunk but he almost hurt the baby and me... even though it was embarrassing I am really glad they came in the room. I went to my bedroom and cried some more. I know Wilson love me he just got some bad advice from a friend and his drinking clouded his thinking. I cried myself to sleep.

The morning of my wedding day I woke up early I looked in the mirror at my eyes to see if they was swollen from crying half the night. They were swollen a little; I went down stairs to take a shower and try to feel jolly, because today is my wedding day. After my shower I came back to my room and sat down in front of the dresser and draped a wet towel over my eyes. Sitting there I thought to myself...I Am going to my wedding with or without Wilson... nothing can destroy my love for him not even his friends or his drinking...I am going to be married today. I heard Sister Linda come in and I took my towel off of my eyes; she said I am going to start cooking breakfast. I said o.k. I am leaving at nine to get my hair fix; do you want to get yours fix? She said I will just comb my short hair; you are the one that need to get your hair fix and you are the one that getting married. I said we had better go and eat because we have to leave here around eleven o, clock. After we ate breakfast I left going to get my hair fixed. It took them an hour to fix my hair; when I looked in the mirror I thought I was looking at someone else. I were very happy about the way my hair looked. When I got home I told Sister Linda to fix us some sandwiches to eat before we went to CB's house. She kept looking at me and finally said if I didn't hear your voice I would think you were someone else...you look real different. When we finished eating our sandwiches we got a taxi to go to CB's house. When we arrive at CB's house Jean ask me if I wanted her to help me with my gown. I said would you please? She said you are a very pretty Bride. I said thank you very much. She said the guy that going to drive you to the Church is on his way; then she left with CB and her kids. The guy finally arrived about twelve fifteen. I was getting worried when he showed up; I could smell liquor on his breath. When we left the driver went past the church down Rizal Avenue close to my apartment; I didn't know what he was thinking about, so I told his wife if she didn't mind please tell her husband to drop us off at the church...I don't want to ride all over Olongapo in the dangerous streets. She told him what I said and he yelled at her saying I am looking for a shop to get my car fixed. I said if he want to get his car fix just take us to the church and drop us off. Then the driver stop in the street talking to some of the guys he knew. I looked at the time it was one fifteen. I was getting upset so I said to him if you have something else to do just let me out I will get a taxi. His wife said let go right now it is getting late. He said as if he was mad, why is she in a hurry to get married? I said is he drunk already? She said he has been drinking but he is not drunk...he is trying to find a shop so he can get his car fix. I said he can do that later. Finally he started driving toward the church. When we got there everyone were happy even me. They told me Wilson was very nervous and worried. CB said it is good you made it everyone were worried, what happened? I didn't answer I just asked if they were ready for us to come in. CB said as soon as Linda get started down the aisle you and I will follow her...are you ready to go? He took my hand and put it on his arm and we walked slowly down the aisle. I thought I was going to faint; I told Linda not to be scared and I am the one shaking and tears running down my face. I guess I was so happy to see Wilson waiting at the altar for me. He was standing beside his Best Man and Linda was standing across from them they all was watching me come down the aisle to the altar. When we got to the altar CB gave my hand to Wilson. Wilson was so glad to see me he said I thought you had changed your mind. I almost tried to tell him what happened, but the Preacher asked who was giving me away...I heard CB say I do. I remembered the Preacher asking me do you take this man to be your lawful wedded husband and I said I do...I couldn't keep from crying, so the Best Man gave me his handkerchief and said don't cry you are almost married now. Then Wilson put the ring on my finger and I put his ring on too and the Preacher said I pronounce you man and wife...you may kiss the Bride. Wilson kissed me like he would never let me go. The Preacher had us to sign our marriage certificate. After signing our marriage certificate we went outside to take some more pictures. I wanted to take a picture with Mother and Linda, but they ran out of film. Everyone left to go to CB's house for the reception. Wilson asked CB to drive us to the Photo Studio so we could take some pictures in our wedding gown. When we finished we went to the reception. We had a wedding cake and snacks. Mama Ligaya said if I knew you were only having snacks I would have given you a big reception. Mama Ligaya son surprised me because I didn't know he was at the wedding; he came and congratulated me. Mama Ligaya and him ate and left. I asked Sister Linda to go to the dress shop and get my dress; I forgot to pickup and Mother said she would go and get it for me. It was the dress I had planned to wear after I took off my wedding gown. I received hugs and congratulation from all of our guests. I had problem talking to them because Wilson was always telling me how beautiful I was and how much he loved me. I started to worry about Mother because it had been quite a while since she left to pick up my dress at the dress shop. Finally Mother came in the house; she was looking real tired. I asked her what was wrong. She said she forgot the address of CB' house and if she had not seen him outside she would still be walking around looking for this apartment. I said I am sorry Mother you got loss. I said Linda will you please get Mother something to eat and drink while I change out of my wedding dress? When I changed my clothes and came out of the bedroom; I told Linda to bring my dress to the apartment because Wilson and I were leaving. She said o.k. Mother and I are going to Calapacuan. I said o.k. I will see you Sunday. Jean came over and said you and Wilson should go now. Wilson and I said goodbye and left for our apartment. When we went out the door one of Wilson friend came out behind us and asked if he could walk with us. Wilson said yes man come on we are walking down to the Magsaysay Drive and catch a jeepney home. He said I had better go with you to your apartment. Wilson said o.k. Come on! When we arrived at our apartment Wilson friend asked if he could get a kiss from the Bride. So I kissed him on the cheek and said thank you for everything. He said that's not a kiss you are supposed to kiss me on the lips. I said no! Your wife or girlfriend should do that not me. I kissed Wilson on the lips and said he is my Husband now. Wilson said that's right man. His friend looked very disappointed and said I have to go man; I will see you when you come back to work, congratulation again. Wilson walked him to the door and said thank you very much for your help. When he came back inside he grab me and kissed me like I was going away for a year. He said we are finally married and you're Mrs. Wilson. Looking at him he seemed to be glowing from being so happy. I was happy too; it felt like a real heavy weight was lifted off of my back. We went upstairs to our bedroom and took off our street clothes and got into the bed. He kissed and held me real tight and said the wait is over…Monday we will pick up our Marriage Contract from the church and take it on the base and get your Military Dependent ID card.

When we get your ID card we will go to the Naval Hospital and get you a complete physical to make sure you and the baby is all right. I will check in with the Base Housing office so they can have someone come out and inspect the apartment, so we can get our housing allowance. I said are you going to be here when they come? He said yes, I am letting you know just in case they get here before I can get off from work; I don't want them to surprise you…just keep the place spotless like you and Linda do all of the time and everything will be all right…check the patio in back and make sure all of the garbage is picked up. I said o.k. Sweetheart. He said I am very happy now I can relax the wedding planning was real nerve racking…I don't think we could have taken another week of that agony…now that you are mine, oh! Completely mines. I was very happy too because I was scare that we would end up breaking up. Wilson did the majority of the planning; I guess that why he drunk so much, it helped him sleep.

I almost gave up several times because things were piling up on me and Wilson was no help. I guess the real reason we stayed together is because we really do love each other and that love is very strong. I don't think I could make it without Wilson in my life...thank God our love was stronger enough to survive all of our problems. Wilson asked me what was I thinking; I said nothing, I was just thinking how happy I am because we have each other. He said I am happy too Sweetheart...I thought you had changed your mind when you were late getting to the church. I said your friend that picked us up drove us all over Olongapo; he said he was looking for a shop to get his car fixed. He said that's what happened? That's why you were late? I said don't worry we're married now...he was one of our problems, thank God the wedding is over. Wilson said I am sorry Sweetheart not very many guys have a car around here; he wanted to help so he volunteered to pick up the Bride. Finally the talking was over and Wilson kissed me and I kissed him back; we made love for the first time as Husband and Wife. Afterward just like always we expressed our love for each other and Wilson held me real tight in his arms and we went to sleep. I always like for Wilson to put his arms around me, because it makes me feel safe when I sleep...there are two things that make me very happy before I go to sleep is knowing that I am healthy and in the arms of the man I love. Sunday Morning the day after the wedding I woke up and Wilson was just laying there looking at me. He said good morning Sweetheart. I said good morning; what time is it?

He said it is almost ten o, clock. I said you mean I have slept that long and don't feel hungry? He said don't worry just go and take a shower we're going out for lunch. I said o.k. And got up got my things and went down stairs to take my shower. When I came back upstairs I saw Wilson up and fixing the bed. I said don't worry about fixing the bed that's my job. He said o.k. I will let you do it next time; I am going to take my shower now. I sat in front of the dresser and just looked at myself in the mirror. I looked different my face had a glow to it. I guess it is because I am a married woman and is very happy. I thought to myself...I better hurry and towel dry my hair; I turned the electric fan on to help dry my hair. Wilson came back upstairs and looked at me and said great! You haven't dress yet. He tried to pull me back on the bed as he kissed me all over. I said Sweetheart, are you not hungry yet? I said I am very hungry and your baby is hungry too. He said o.k. I will let you go ahead and get ready. I quickly got dressed. He said the last one downstairs pay for lunch. I moved like I was rushing to the stairs and he beat me downstairs and said I guess you lost, but I will pay the bill. We laughed and held hands as we walked out of the apartment and started down the street to Rizal Avenue to catch a jeepney. He said we would go first to the Base and check what time the ID card office is opened Monday so we can get your ID card. We arrive at the Gate and Wilson got me a gate pass and we decided to go to the Bowling alley because they had a restaurant inside. When we got to the Bowling alley it was closed. Wilson said oh yes, today is Sunday and the ID card office will be closed too, so we went back off Base to the Grand Restaurant. I said what are we going to eat today? He said whatever you want to eat remember you are my wife. I thought to myself...that sound good, his wife and he is my husband, but we don't have to spend over our budget...I will have big noodles. He said there is plenty other food on the menu... just order what you want to eat. I said Sweetheart just order me big noodles. He called the waiter and ordered me big noodles and beef fried rice and two cokes. I was very surprised when he didn't order a beer for himself. I said you didn't order your beer. He said I don't need one. He said I think the ID card section in the Personnel Office opens the same time as the rest of the office 9 to 5, we want have a problem getting you your ID card after I come home from work Monday. When our food came I ate all of my food; I was real hungry because we missed breakfast.

Wilson said when we finish lunch let go see CB and Jean. I said o.k. After we ate our lunch we was walking down the street on our way to CB's house pass the Del Rosario Theater and Wilson looked at the movie billboard and said this is a good movie showing here we can go to CB's house some other time. I said o.k. It starts in about ten minutes. We got our tickets and went in the theater and found two chairs with our name on them way off in a corner. It was a Chinese movie Wilson said it wasn't as good as he expected it to be. After it was over we went home walking holding hands like teenagers. When we got home Wilson said when is Linda coming back? I said she is supposed to come today. He said I would like to have a cold drink. I said I would go to the store and get coke and ice. When I came back with coke, ice and beer he was very surprised to see the beer. I took the beer ice and coke in the kitchen I chopped some ice for my coke and put the rest in our water pitcher and opened one of the beers for him. I went back into the living room and gave Wilson his beer and we sat drinking our drinks. He stood up and started looking around in the living room, dining room and kitchen. I said what's wrong? He said I am trying to locate the electrical outlet so when the inspectors come I will know where they are. I said o.k. Then he came back and sat down. We can't set very long beside each other before we start kissing; we did and before long we were on our way upstairs to bed. We did our best to satisfy each other and we were very successful; our little electric fan was running full speed trying to cool us off, but wasn't having much luck because it seems as if we were moving faster than it was. We lay completely drain in each other arms and drifted off to sleep.

I don't know how long I slept before I woke and had to go to the bathroom. When I opened our bedroom door I smelled the aroma of food being cook. I closed the bedroom door and went downstairs. I saw Sister Linda in the kitchen cooking vegetables. Walking over to her I said when did you come home I didn't hear you come in? She said when I came upstairs I saw your bedroom door closed, so I came back downstairs and started cooking because I figured you were sleeping...how does it feel to be married and called Mrs. Wilson? I said it feel good...this is the first and last wedding I am going to have; Wilson and I are going to grow old together...I don't want to plan anything again except maybe my Daughter wedding.

She said the wedding was real nice; I even liked walking down the aisle in my gown and high heel shoes...I didn't like that guy that drove us around this bad neighborhood...do you know him? No that was my first time seeing him too. Wilson said he volunteered to drive us to the church in his car. Don't worry that is probably the last times we will see that old guy...I rather walk than ride in his car? Then I remembered I left Wilson upstairs so I decided to go and check on him. He was sitting on the side of the bed. He said hi Sweetheart is you cooking now? I said no but Linda is cooking vegetables.

I sat beside him and asked him what did he want to eat. He said don't worry about cooking something for me I will eat sausage and crackers later...do we have some more coke? I am thirsty. I said let go downstairs and I will get you a cold drink. Some coke was left in the kitchen, but there was no ice left, so I sent Linda to the store to get ice. She brought the ice back and I put some in the coke glass and gave it to him. He sat drinking his coke while Sister Linda and I ate dinner. When I finished eating dinner I joined him on the couch he was looking a little loss. So I said what wrong Sweetheart? He said I was waiting for you to finish eating so I could ask you to get me some beer. I said don't hesitate to ask us to get you some beer we know you drink; it is no problem for us to get it for you. I said Linda would you walk outside with me I am going to the store and it is getting dark. When we got outside Linda said just stay at the gate and watch me I will go to the store. There are drug users and dealers and gangs that walk up and down Second Street so we always watch each other when it get dark. Wilson should ask for his beer earlier before it got dark. He could go to the store for his own beer but the store will charge him more because he is an American. When Sister Linda got back to the gate I told her she was walking fast like she was in a walkathon contest. She said that is what I do when I am on my way back from school at night, but no one bother me because they know that I live here. I said good, because I don't want you to have problems from the drug dealers across the street. I remember when we first moved here on Second Street the drug dealers try to get me to buy drugs, but since they found out that I live here they don't bother me anymore. Even though they don't bother me I still don't trust them. She gave me the three beers and I took them inside of the apartment. I put two inside a big pot and put the left over ice we had on top of them and took the other one to Wilson. I really want him to enjoy being at home so I did everything I could to make him happy. Sister Linda told me she was going to bed if I didn't need her for something else. I asked her to check the cabinet in the kitchen and see if we still have crackers. She said Vicky we have six packages of crackers and a loaf of bread in case you want to make sandwiches for Brother Wilson. Wilson said what is Linda talking about, I heard her call my name? I said she was telling me about the bread in the cabinet if I wanted to make sandwiches for you…do you want a sandwich? He said no I am not hungry yet. Then he changed his mind. He said maybe I had better eat some sausage and cracker, so I want get hungry before we go to bed. When he finished eating he started smiling and said thank you Sweetheart, now that I have my strength back I am ready for another round. I said what are you talking about…do you want another beer? He said no, when we go to bed I will explain. Around ten o, clock Wilson took the last sip of his beer and said let go to bed. He went to the kitchen and got the last beer to take upstairs. We passed by Sister Linda's room and could see that her light was out; I guess she got tired of crocheting and went to sleep. When we went into our room I started to undress for bed; he said let me help you and he unzipped my dress and helped me take it off. He kissed me as he guided me down to the bed. He started smiling and said are you ready for another round? I thought to myself…that's what he was talking about downstairs. I said yes I am ready for another round, let the fight begin and it did. It didn't last too long both of us was knocked out in the end. About ten minutes later I said teasingly, do you want to go for another round? He said no, no that it for tonight he sat up and drunk the rest of his beer. I said do you have your strength back? He said no, no go to sleep. As always he held me in his arm and we drifted off to sleep. We was awaken by loud gun- fire coming from outside. Wilson said don't go to the window, because the shooter may fire into the window if he see a person in it. I heard Linda making noise so I crawled on the floor to her room to try and comfort her. She said it sounded like a bullet hit the other side of our apartment. I said just stay away from the windows and stay down. We sat on the floor until the gunfire stopped; then I went back to my bedroom to Wilson. He said is Linda all right I said she was just scared because she thought she heard a bullet hit the other side of our apartment. He said that why I don't want you to look out of the window when you hear Gangs fighting. I looked at the clock, it was two o, clock in the morning. I said what are they doing don't they ever sleep? He said they fight late while all the clubs are closed and everyone is off the streets. There is no one to witness what they are doing…you better go back to sleep. We heard two more gunfire; Wilson said it sounded like it came from the next street over from us. I said we better try and go to sleep in a few more hours and you have to go to work. At four thirty that morning I didn't hear the alarm clock ring; all I remembered was Wilson kissing me and saying I see you later Sweetheart. I was so sleepy I didn't get up and watch him until he got to the jeepney stop to catch a jeepney. I was mad at myself for not getting up and mad at the Gangs for waking us up at two in the morning. I got up and went to Sister Linda room she wasn't there so I went downstairs to the bathroom and the door was closed. I sat and waited for her to come out. Finally she did and I asked her if she heard Wilson when he left this morning? She said no, I didn't hear him; I was sleeping real good trying to make up for the interrupting we had last night, but I had to use the bathroom. I went into the bathroom and washed my face and brushed my teeth. When I came out she was sitting waiting for me. She said now that we are up we might as well eat breakfast, what do you want to eat? I said pancakes. She said I don't know how to cook pancakes. I said o.k. I will show you. Do you remember how the pancakes look that they cook in the market restaurant? Linda said yes they put margarine on the pancakes and sprinkled it with sugar. We had all of the ingredients except margarine so Sister Linda went to the store and got margarine. We cooked the pancakes and they were very good. Linda said she really like them with fried Spam. She said Vicky you are learning to cook American food real fast. I said yes, I keep trying and if I don't know I would ask somebody, because I really want to please Wilson and keep him from having to go to the restaurant to eat American food. When we finished eating our breakfast she cleaned the kitchen and washed the dishes.

I told her when we finish taking our showers I wanted her to go with me to the church where we had our wedding and pick up my Marriage License. When Linda and I finished showering and getting dressed we left for the church. When we arrive and talked to the church administrator they said that our License was not ready and we would have to come back the next day. I felt real down all the way back home. When we got back to the apartment I lay down on the couch and closed my eyes. Sister Linda got her crochet and started to crocheting. I drifted off to sleep. All of a sudden I could hear someone talking; I ignored the sound and kept trying to sleep until Sister Linda started tugging on my shoulder and saying Vicky, Vicky

Brother Wilson is here. I opened my eyes and said hi Sweetheart you are early today. He said yes I got off work early today...did you get the license? I said Linda and I went to the church but they said it was not ready today and come back tomorrow. He said did you go to the office in the back? I said yes at the back of the church. He said yes that is the place...we can't do anything but wait till tomorrow...I was really hoping you would have it so we could get your ID card. I said if we could wait a long time for our wedding; we can wait one more day for the license. I asked Sister Linda to go to the store for coke, ice and beer. When she came back she said a lady was outside selling fresh fish to the Owner of the apartment. I told Wilson I would be right back; Sister Linda and I went back outside to catch the lady selling fish. I bought fresh fish and vegetables from the lady. When I came back in the apartment Wilson asked me what did I buy? I showed him the fish and asked him if he would like fresh fish for lunch. He said I ate lunch before I left my Boat. Sister Linda and I got busy cooking lunch I told her to cook the eggplant and rice while I cleaned the fish. When I finished cleaning the fish I went into the bathroom and washed my hands. I came out and sat beside Wilson, as always he can't keep his hands off of me. He kissed my hand and said your hands smell like fish. I washed my hands again, but the smell still remained, so I went upstairs and rubbed them with Johnson Baby Powder. I came back downstairs and sat beside him. He said now you smell like a baby. I said which smell do you prefer fish or Baby Powder. He started smiling and said fish and kept laughing. I started to get up and he pulled me back down and said I was just kidding around and he kissed me.

He kept kissing me and I pulled away, because I was hungry; I went in the kitchen to check on Sister Linda and the food. She said the food is almost ready, so I put the rice in our plates so it would cool down a little before we start eating. I asked Wilson if he wanted anything else before we start eating; he said you could bring me another beer. When we finished eating Linda cleaned the kitchen and washed the dishes. Wilson and I sat in the living room and talked about what we wanted to do the next day. The number one thing was to pick up the marriage license, because we need that to accomplish just about everything else. The evening went by quickly and before we knew it we were on our way to bed. The alarm went off at four thirty. Wilson got up and got dress and was off to work. Finally I got up and got cleaned up and had breakfast; then I was off to the church to pick up our marriage license. When I got back home Wilson arrived about five minutes later, so we went to the base to get my ID card. When I got my ID card we went to the Base Housing office and signed up for them to come out and inspect our house; after we left the Housing Office we stopped by the Navy Exchange Store and the Commissary where you buy the food. I said food cost more here than it does in Olongapo. He said yes, and you can come here and do your shopping anytime. We decided to go by the Naval Hospital and make an appointment for me to get a complete physical. They set up an appointment for me to come back in two weeks. I was very happy that I was getting a complete physical to see if anything besides being pregnant was wrong with me. We caught the bus going back to the Main Gate. I asked Wilson was he going with me when I get my physical; he said of course I am going, but if you have any other appointments after this one you have to go by yourself unless I am off work...remember this bus makes a complete circle it stops at the Navy Exchange, the Commissary and Cubi Point where the Naval Hospital is located...just allow yourself some extra time if you have an appointment or if you think you are running late get a taxi so you want be late for your appointment. When we arrived at the Main Gate Wilson said we're here. When we got off the bus he asked me if I was hungry. I said yes I am hungry. He is so nice and pleasant to talk to when he hasn't been drinking. I enjoyed the bus ride while he explained very clearly to me how to get around on the base.

This time I felt good and happy to be the wife of a Military Man. He said let go to the Base Club. We held hands as we walked down the streets on the base. He said we had better get something to eat first...there is a hamburger stand close to the gate...what do you want to eat? I said I guess hamburger and coke. I said to myself... they don't have noodles and rice at hamburger stands. Wilson went up to the window and ordered our food. I looked at the sign they serve hot dogs too. Wilson came back with our food. He said I got you some French fries too. I said thank you sweetheart. He said don't thank me all of the time I am the one that should be thanking you because you are my wife; you married me even though I get crazy and drunk sometimes which I promise to control...you have made me the happiest man in the world. We enjoyed ourselves sitting there on the bench out in the open; Wilson set beside me so he could kiss me. The people looked at us a little bit and we didn't kiss too much because we didn't want to be in the news...once we start kissing it hard for us to control ourselves. We finished eating and started walking to the club holding hands. When we got there we were disappointed when they said I couldn't come in because I had to be Nineteen years old. Wilson was real disappointed because he wanted me to see the club on base. I said don't worry I will be nineteen in four months... it is only a club...I have seen plenty of clubs in Olongapo...what is the different...all I have seen is people dancing and getting drunk... so what is the big deal? He said I am sorry Sweetheart that you are too young to go to the club on base. I said I thought if I have my Dependent ID card I could go anywhere on base. He said to them it doesn't matter you are only eighteen and not old enough to go to the club...lets go to the club in town they never check ID's. I said o.k. Let go. We walked back to the gate and caught a jeepney outside the gate to the Supreme Club. We went in and found a table and Wilson went up to the bar and got our drinks. Sanders saw us and came by and said hi to us. He asked Wilson how was married life treating him? I don't know what Wilson said but Sanders started laughing. Wilson asked me to dance and while we were dancing he said something, but the music was to loud for me to understand what he said; then he started blowing in my ear.

I said stop it because you don't want to start something we can't finish here. We finished the dance and went back to our table. He said he had to go to the rest room. On his way back he saw a Sailor ask me to dance; he rushed over and told the Sailor I was his woman. The Sailor said I am sorry I didn't know. Wilson sat down he said I only went to the bathroom and someone want to dance with you already. I said he didn't know I was with you; he just saw a girl sitting by herself and he wanted to dance so he came over and asked me to dance...do you remember when you were out here before you met me and saw a girl alone you would ask her to dance...this is a club and people come here to dance...forget about it. He said yea, you are my wife.

I said he didn't know that I was married…if you are worried about someone asking me to dance maybe we better go home. Sanders came back over to our table and Wilson told him what had happened. He even pointed out the Sailor. I said to myself…I hope they don't start a fight…they talked for a while I couldn't hear what they said. Sanders went to the other side of the room and started talking to the guy. A few minutes later the Sailor left. I said thank God he left. A few minutes later someone started a fight on the other side of the club and the Armed Forces Police broke it up. Sanders came by our table and said man I have to go now; I will see you tomorrow. Wilson said we are going home in a few minutes. When he finished his beer he said are you ready Sweetheart? He took my hand and we walked out of the club and to our apartment. We went upstairs to our bedroom and started getting ready for bed. Then Wilson said next time we go to the club and someone asks you to dance, show them your ring. I thought he had forgotten about what happened in the club. I said the Sailor asked me to dance and I said no and that was enough because he went away. You should know that there are plenty of Service Men in the club that alone and want to dance and have fun; they ask girls to dance, even me. They don't mean any harm they just want to dance. If you don't want someone to ask me to dance then we shouldn't go to the club. I didn't ask to go to the club anyway; you wanted to go to the club. He said I don't want anyone messing around with my wife. I said no one is going to mess with me if I stay away from the club… why make a big deal out of nothing. He said Sweetheart I love you then he started kissing my neck. I said Sweetheart could we go to sleep I don't feel good. We went to bed and went to sleep.

The next morning before the alarm went off I felt his kisses. I said are you all right? He said yes! I love you very much…do you love me? I said of course I love you, but you have to trust me to do and say the right thing. He said would you forgive your jealous husband? I said yes, and then he kissed me and started our morning exercise. When it was over I lay relaxed in the bed and he was scrambling to get ready for work. I went back to sleep. When I woke up I went downstairs took my shower and ate breakfast. ; Then I went back upstairs and changed my clothes. When I came downstairs I told Sister Linda I was going to the base. She said what do you want me to tell Brother

Wilson if he come home early. I said just tell him I went on the base. I left and went to the Naval Base Main gate. I stopped and pretended to be looking for something in my bag, but I was watching what the people were doing when they went through the gate. I took my ID card out and got in the line of people going pass the Gate Guard; when I got to him he looked at my ID card and wave me through the gate. I caught the bus going to the Navy Exchange and Commissary and paid my ten-cent and rode it to the Navy Exchange; I got off and caught the next bus going to the Main Gate. I said to myself…now I can go anywhere on base except the clubs…when I get money I will go to the Navy Exchange and shop. I was very proud of myself; I had accomplished something real important and that being on base as Mrs. Wilson. When I got back to the apartment, Sister Linda said its good you are back before Brother Wilson come home because I wouldn't know what else to tell him if he start asking questions…how is the base? I said it is still the same as it was when Brother Smitty use to take us on base. I just wanted to learn to ride the bus by myself, so when the time comes for me to go to my appointment I want get on the bus acting stupid. She said I remembered when we use to ride the bus with Brother Smitty to the Cubi Point Theater to watch movie. He would buy us lot of candy, popcorn, snacks and coke. When we finish our coke in the theater we would be shaking because we were cold, but we learn our lesson and started taking our sweater to the movies. I said yes he was really good about taking us to the movies. I said do you remember Brother Smitty taking us to see the Boxing in the Gym on the base? Brother Smitty was so into the fight that I thought he was going to get in the ring and start boxing those guys.

She said I ended up watching Brother Smitty more than the guys in the ring because he was actually punching the air like he was punching somebody. We started laughing thinking about Sister Melda; she thought Brother Smitty was going to have a heart attack, so she kept watching him and trying to calm him down. She said after the fight was over I remember Brother Smitty asking for Aspirin because he had a tension headache. Brother Smitty is a great guy he would always take us with him to different thing on the base. Linda said we better eat lunch now; I said that is a good idea; we quickly prepared our lunch and ate it. After we finished eating we saw Wilson with something in his arm and trying to open the door. He left the box outside and came in and said Sweetheart I have a surprise for you. He kissed me and got the box from outside of the door; it was a black and white thirteen-inch television. Linda saw the TV and was very surprised and happy. I was very happy Wilson was thinking of me; I didn't have to watch someone else TV through their window. He put it on the table and plugs it up to see what kind of reception we would get; it was snowy but you could see the peoples on the screen. Wilson said we need an antenna so he went outside to see if he could hook our TV to the apartment owner antenna. I went and got some aluminum foil and wrapped it around the rabbit ears and the picture cleared up a bit. He came back and said he would ask the owner of the apartment later on. He said what did you do to the antenna it cleared up a little bit. I told him I had wrapped some aluminum foil on the rabbit ears like the people in apartment number three. He kissed me and said now you have a TV to watch…it is not color but it is something to watch when I am not home. Sister Linda said let watch the game show. We changed the channel and found a game show; Sister Linda and I were real happy. Wilson said the Housing Inspector from the base is going to inspect our apartment in two days. Try and keep an eye on the bathroom and the patio in the back everything is spotless as usual. I said Sweetheart I think the apartment is spotless, but if you see something just let me know and we will take care of it. He said I am going to tell the apartment owner about the inspection he may be able to tell us about something we over looked about the inspection. I followed him to Mr. Blanco door and he knocked and asked for him. Mr. and Mrs. Blanco came outside of their apartment and Wilson explained to them what was going on. Mrs. Blanco said we did know you had gotten married. I said yes we're newlywed. She said congratulation. I said thank you.

Mr. Blanco said don't put anything over the fire escape because they always check it and you should be all right because our apartments never fail an inspection by the Base Housing Office. He walked in our apartment and looked around a little and said you are ready for the inspection the place is spotless. He looked at me and said you keep your place very clean…we like to rent our apartment to people like you…you will pass the inspection with flying colors. We said thanks again and went inside. Wilson said let move the dresser in our room from over the fire escape. We rearrange our bedroom and I came back down stair to watch some more Philippine drama on our TV. Sister Linda came by and said I have to go to school enjoy your new TV. When she left Wilson said he wanted something cold to drink. I asked him what did he want to drink? He said a cold beer if you don't mind going and getting it. I took my shopping bag and bought ice, a big liter bottle of coke and beer; I carried it back in my shopping bag. When Wilson saw me with the bag he quickly took it and carried it in the kitchen. He said you are not supposed to carry something that heavy. I said Linda is gone to school and if you go to the store they will charge you twice as much as they charge me so I have to go. He said next time I will ask before Linda go to school. After I finished in the kitchen chopping up the ice and icing down his last two beers, I came back in the living room and sat down to watch TV with him. He said is there any programs on TV in English? I said the Let make a Deal show is over. Pretty soon they will have an English show again. He said don't worry about it just watch your TV. He sat back and drunk his beer. He said when I get paid Friday we will go to the Navy Exchange and look for some baby clothes and furniture. I said I bought a few baby clothes from the market. He said we could look for a baby bed. He said we will have some extra money soon; the payment we make Friday on the furniture is the last one and the Navy will start giving us a housing allowance. We can start saving and get a living room set...pretty soon you will have wall to wall new furniture. He kissed me and asked me if I loved him. I said I love you, I love you and I kissed him back. We started kissing and I thought I was going to melt. I got up and started walking toward the stairs and said the last one upstairs have to fix dinner. I was the first to get in our bedroom. I quickly undressed and he noticed my stomach for the first time. He said your stomach is getting big will we hurt the baby.

I said the Doctor said it is all right and the baby would be all right... We did exactly what we do best together. We took a short nap after we finished. After our nap we took a shower and went to visit CB and Jean. The kids answered the door. We sat down on their couch and CB came in the room shirtless and said how is the married man doing? And Jean came out just like she just woke up. I said to myself...they was doing what we just got threw doing. Jean said I been waiting for you to come visit; I have something for you. She went into her bedroom and came back with a small picture album with pictures of our wedding. It was a very nice compact album; I showed it to Wilson and he like it very much. We thanked them for the album. We talked about the wedding and finally Jean asked me if I had told Wilson about what he did the night before our wedding. I told her I had not told him about it because he was drunk and wouldn't remember what happened anyway. Plus I really didn't want him to feel bad since things are going real good now...I am real sorry it happened at your house. Jean said it wasn't your fault don't worry about it; no one knows what happened but us. I said I don't blame Wilson I blame his drinking. Jean said Wilson is a very nice guy if he not drinking a lot. I said what happened is like a bad dream to me. She said CB is a nice guy too if he is not drinking; when he is drinking and talking I want to wash his mouth out with soap. She said I know he is going to drink, so I rather he do his drinking here in the house because his big mouth can get him in trouble out in the clubs. I said Wilson like to drink and party too. She said well we married Sailors and they like to drink and party; when they are single it is all right but when they get married and have kids it is time to change; I am hoping CB will slow down and stop drinking so much, but I haven't had any luck thus far. She said I have to feed the kids would you like something to eat? I said no we had dinner before we left our apartment. I went back in the living room and watched television. CB and Wilson were having a loud conversation. CB was using all kinds of nasty words. I thought to myself...why does he talk like that? Wilson is a Sailor too and he doesn't use nasty words like that. I started yawning and Wilson asked me if I was all right. He said we would go home when I finish my drink. CB and Jean kids came in and said goodnight to their parents and us. Wilson said we are going home now tomorrow is a workday.

We said thanks for the gift and went home. When we got to the apartment Sister Linda was watching TV. She asked me if I wanted to watch the movie with her. I told her I was tired and I showed her the picture album. She was surprised to see her picture in it. We went up to our bedroom and Wilson asked me if I still love him. I said yes I love you…are you glad that you married me? He said yes you have made me the happiest man in the world. We undressed and went to bed. Wilson held my stomach as if he was trying to feel movement. I said I haven't felt the baby move maybe soon. He said your appointment at the Naval Hospital is next week; I am glad so we can be sure there is nothing wrong with you and the baby. He held me tight in his arms and kissed me goodnight. I said to myself…why we can't have a good night like this all of the time…we visit a friend he drinks and don't get drunk…I really wish thing will be like this always. I held his hand and kissed it to say I love him and closed my eyes to try and go to sleep in the arms of my husband. Husband, Mrs. Wilson, and my Wife really sounds good to me. I pinched my arm and it hurt…I know I am not dreaming…he is my Husband and I am his Wife. Oh! I better go to sleep it is very late. When Wilson left the next morning I was so sleepy I didn't know he was leaving; I thought I was dreaming. I am sorry I didn't say goodbye to him; I promised myself that it want happen again. I got up and fixed the bed and went downstairs. Sister Linda was watching TV early in the morning. I asked her how was the movie she watched last night? She said I will never watch a scary movie by myself again I had a nightmare last night…it was a Vampire Tagalog movie. I said why did you watch it if it was scary. She said it started off like a love story then it got scary, but I wanted to see the end even though it was scary. When I went to bed I covered my head because I was scared the Vampire would get me…it was so hot under my sheet I could hardly breath and I was soaking wet with sweat. I laughed and said you almost drowned in your own sweat; don't watch Vampire movies at night so you want have a nightmare. We better cook breakfast I am getting hungry. She said let eat garlic-fried rice the Vampire is afraid of garlic and the cross. She said do we have a cross in the apartment. I said yes it is on the shelf over there. She said I would take that and some garlic in my room tonight to put in my window. I said don't forget to remove the garlic tomorrow morning because the Housing Inspector is coming.

She said don't worry I will hide it in my shoebox; I need it only at night. I said Linda we had better take our showers tonight so when the Inspector comes the shower want be too wet. She said if we take our showers around six in the morning I would dry the shower right away.

Finally breakfast was ready and we fixed our plates and sat at the dining table. I took a spoon full of food and said oh! My mouth is burning the garlic is melting my teeth.Sister Linda jumped up from the table and turned red and was really scared. I wanted to laugh at her but I realize she was really scared. She said you're crazy Vicky, I thought you had turn into a Vampire. We laugh when she settled down. I said let eat and enjoy our breakfast and no more joking. She said who is that standing behind you? I turned and looked because I thought it was Wilson coming home early. She said I got you and started laughing. I said let get serious, do you remember when we live in Canan, Pangasinan and Mother started choking on something she didn't know what it could be and Father cut a thread that was hanging from the roof, the Vampire's tongue, so Mother wouldn't get choke anymore. He even went outside to see if something was on the roof. He said a woman with a half body flew away. Mother asked him what was he talking about? He said it was a half woman and half bat; he thinks it was a girl that liked him and followed him home. He said there is family of Vampires living in some part of Visaya, Province. Do you remember Mother being very mad that night at Father? Mother said why are you messing around with other women anyway...causing them follow you back here...you know we have kids...what if they get hurt? Father said they won't get hurt, because the Vampire comes out only at night; I am going to get a lot of salt and garlic and sprinkle it on the roof and put some around the windows and doors of the house. Mother said why is this happening to us we haven't done anyone any harm...some of your girlfriend followed you here to kill the children and me. Father said she is not my girlfriend I just know her; I didn't know that she belong to a family of half Bats and half human called Vampires. I heard that one of her great, great Aunt fell in love with a rich guy that own a Banana Plantation and got married to him. They say every full moon the wife disappears. The Husband heard peoples in his Barrio telling stories about Vampire peoples he didn't know he was married to one; he wondered why every full moon she would leave. The Husband decided to follow her one night and she went to their Banana Plantation and left half of her body beside a Banana tree. He decided to put salt and garlic on the half of her body that was left by the Banana tree, because the guy love his wife so much he killed himself by his wife half body. When the people found his body they knew he killed himself because his wife was a Vampire; they also knew that his wife was the one killing people in their Barrio. Sister Linda said that why the movie I was watching last night on the TV was real scary, but I had to watch it. I said Linda don't forget to give me some garlic so I can put some in my window too; I don't want to take a chance, I rather be safe and protect my baby. The Vampire likes to kill pregnant women. She said what do you think happened to the Vampire that fell in love with Father? I said she is somewhere without a tongue; if you see a woman with her tongue removed that is the woman that almost killed my Mother. She said I had better put some garlic in my bag. I said that's a good ideal Linda. I better give you some more money to buy more garlic. She said what if Brother Wilson sees the garlic in the window? I said we would only put it in the windows at night so he want see it, but if he does I will explain to him that it's for our protection because there are a lot of things happening here in the Philippines that hard to explain. I said Linda don't go to the store yet I am going to take a shower. She said o.k. I will just watch TV while I wait for you. I hurried and took my shower and came out and towel dried my hair. Then I told her to go to the store. I walked around outside in the apartment complex. I met a new neighbor she was a Filipino married to a white American Sailor. When Sister Linda came back from the store I walked inside the apartment with her. She said are you doing your exercise or are you scared to stay inside? I said it is daytime now why should I be scared, but in the back of my head I wonder what really happened to that Vampire...did she follow us to Olongapo City? I thought...I am pregnant, Sister Rose is pregnant and Brother Celino wife is pregnant...I better tell Linda to remind Mother about the Vampire that almost killed her. I said Linda when you go home Saturday tell Mother about the Vampire. She said haven't you seen the bundle of garlic hanging from the door of Mother's house in Calapacuan? She haven't forgotten she doesn't want us to be scare anymore it been a long time, but she is still very careful.

I said that why I always smell garlic in Mother's house. Sister Linda said even Sister Rose and Brother Celino know about it. I said no one told me. She said they wanted to tell you, because you like to eat a lot of garlic in your food Mother said you would be all right. I said Yeah! I always brush my teeth and the smell is gone. She said don't worry you know it now; just do what we plan to do for protection. I said when you go upstairs put two pieces of garlic in my drawer on my side. She said I am going to take a shower. I said go ahead and take your shower I am just going to set here and watch TV. She said I was just letting you know so you want go outside. I said go ahead and take your shower I am not going outside. I said to myself…between this Vampire movie on TV and what happen to us a long time ago; it looks like something or someone is telling us to be careful. I said it is better to be safe than sorry. Then I heard Sister Linda singing in the shower; she never sing before I guess she is scared. When she came out of the shower I told her she had ran all of the bugs in the apartment away. She said that good we don't have to buy bug spray now. Someone came and knocked on the door and I opened it. It was the lady selling fish and vegetables. Sister Linda said just buy fish Vicky we have vegetables. I bought the fish and sweet potato leaves and the lady went next door. I told Sister Linda when she cook lunch make sure she use plenty of garlic and salt. She said Vicky would you cook lunch I forgot to do my homework last night after I watched the Vampire movie on TV. I said o.k. Go ahead and do your homework; always let me know if you have homework. She said I always do it before I go to sleep, but I was to scare to stay up by myself and do it. I started making preparation to cook. I saw the ants come in from the patio. I said to myself…here you come again… when I spray they multiply…if I leave them alone it doesn't seem to be as many…I really don't know what to do about them…I guess I will keep spraying even though they seem to be laughing at us…it look like when I spray they play dead and when I go away they get up and keep moving across the patio to our kitchen. The ants are very smart. I cooked lunch and covered it up. I called Sister Linda to see if she had finished with her homework. I told her we better eat before the food get cold. We fixed our plates and sat at the dining table and ate lunch. Sister Linda said the food was real good and it tasted like the food Mother cooked. She said if I keep cooking like this we would gain a lot of weight. I told her I wanted to gain some weight anyway. Since I have been pregnant the only place I gain weight is my stomach. I am pregnant and still skinny.

We finished our lunch and Linda cleaned the kitchen and washed the dishes. After lunch we decided to watch TV for a while. Someone knocked on the door and I opened it. Mr. Blanco kids wanted to watch TV with us. I didn't know they had kids because we never hear them or see them around. I invited the two boys and a girl to come in and watched a game show with us then they said thank you for letting us watch your TV then they left. We finally figured that they went to Columban High School just around the corner and they were home for lunch when they came over to watch TV. I said they are lucky to have a school just around the corner and they can come home for lunch. Sister Linda said I am lucky too even though I ride a jeepney to school. I said yes, you are very lucky that you still go to school. If Sister Melda hadn't stop helping me maybe I would have went to college, but you know what, I am very, very lucky because I met Wilson. I don't feel so bad now that I didn't finish High School. I will finish someday maybe when I go to America, if Wilson let me go. She said you could go to school here after you have your baby. I said I want to but we are leaving next year. She said do you mean to say that you are leaving the Philippine next year...you will be far away from us. I said we can visit, Wilson promised me that I will come home to visit even in America. She said that is too far away you will need a lot of money to ride a plane or ship. Which one are you going to ride? I said I don't know right now, but Wilson rode a ship coming over here maybe we will ride one going back to America. Wilson came home from work and said hello to us and kissed me. I told Linda before she change clothes go to the store and get beer and ice. Wilson said are you feeling all right? I said I feel fine. He said would you like to go and see a movie? I said yes, I would go upstairs and change. He said we're not going now we will go around five this afternoon and in the mean time you can sit beside your Husband and give him a big kiss. I sat down beside him and gave him a big kiss. A few minutes later Linda came back with the beer. She said they didn't have cold beer across the street; she had to go to the other store in the back. I said o.k. Just put the beer in the sink and I will take care of it. I went in the kitchen and chopped the ice and put it on top of the beer in a big pot. Then I gave Wilson one to drink. He said thank you Sweetheart; I really need this cold beer it is getting real hot outside.

I said in a few more days it will be April one of the hottest months in the Philippines, so you better get ready for it. He said I remembered in August when I met you it rained just about every day that month. Before I met you I tried carrying an umbrella, but I kept losing it, so I stop buying them; when I was in town nightclubbing I would run from club to club. I said I met the Blanco kids; I didn't think they had kids because I never see or hear them. He said I saw one, but I didn't know how many they had. I said they came over and asked to watch TV with me. He said now you have someone to keep you company while you watch TV. Wilson scooted over close to me on the couch and started kissing me. I said wait a minute I thought we were going to the movie. He said yes, but I missed you so much today I just want to kiss you and hold you. I said I missed you too. I heard Sister Linda say I have to go to school I will see you tonight. I said be careful and don't watch scary movie when you get home. I saw her smiling as she walked out the door. Wilson said do I have another beer left? I went into the kitchen and got a beer from the big pot and gave it to him. When I sat down beside him on the couch he turned the TV off; he wanted all of my attention. He asked me if I still love him. I knew then we were not going to make it to the movies, so I said I love you, I love you and started kissing him. We knew it was time to go upstairs; Wilson unplugged the electric fan and followed me upstairs. He was so charged up he forgot to plug in the electric fan. We realized that the fan wasn't plug in the outlet when we lay there soaked in sweat trying to cool off and relax at the same time. Wilson got up and plugs the fan in the outlet and got back in bed. Finally we cooled off and drifted off to sleep.

When the alarm went off the next morning Wilson got up and dressed for work; he was in a real good mood. I asked him what time was he coming home to meet the Inspector; he said just get everything ready…the Inspector suppose to be here at ten and I will be here too. This morning I watch him from my bedroom window as he boarded a jeepney for the Base. I didn't go back to bed I fixed the bed and got my things together to take a shower. I went downstairs to the bathroom and took my shower. When I came out Sister Linda was waiting to take her shower. I told her to scrub the shower before she takes a shower then we could wipe the walls down with towels to dry it after she shower.

After I towel dried my hair and Linda finished her shower we got busy cleaning, dusting, mopping, and buffering the place. We check and double-checked the apartment; we even sprayed a nice fragrance in the apartment so it would smell good. We didn't cook or fry anything for breakfast because we didn't want the place to smell like dried fish. Mr. Blanco took care of the outside area; he swept the front of the compound and sprinkled water on the street to keep the dust down. Finally we were finished and we sat down to rest before the Inspector arrives. Sister Linda said Vicky look, the floor is shinning you can see your reflection. I said well maybe they would give us a big A ok. She said they should give us an A+ because the apartment is spotless. I said the only thing I want is their approval, but I am not worried because the Owner of the apartment said these apartments never fail an inspection. I turned the TV on so we could watch it until the Inspector arrives. I was a little nervous about the inspection and Sister Linda was nervous too. She showed me her fingers crossed. I said yes maybe we should cross our toes too. She tried to cross her toes and she did on one foot but she couldn't on the other foot. We started laughing. I said maybe I better cross mine too. She said I didn't know I could cross my toes on one foot and not the other one. I said hold the other one with your hand. We started laughing again. I said don't worry Linda you are just nervous; if they don't approve our apartment I want you to beat them up o.k. She said then they would put me in prison. Then we heard Wilson outside talking to someone. I opened the door and they came in. Sister Linda and I sat on the couch and watch them. They looked everywhere and finally the inspector asked where the fire escape was. Mr. Blanco pointed to it. The inspector went upstairs and looked at it and came back down stairs and checked it on his list. The Inspector said something to Wilson and the Owner and shook hands; I did hear him say thank you when he turned to leave. Wilson and the Owner looked real happy. Wilson came back in the apartment and said we passed the inspection now we can relax. Sister Linda and I were very happy, I told her we could cook us some food now. Even the Lady that sell fish and vegetables arrive in the nick of time. I bought a fish and told Linda to clean it. Wilson said now we will have housing allowance…thank God it is over…you can even make a mess if you want too…they want be back. He said thank you Linda for helping your sister and me pass the inspection...I will drink a cold beer if we have one.

I said I would go to the store and get some. I left and went to the store, on my way back I said to myself...I hope the next thing he buy is a refrigerator to put his beer in because going back and forth to the store everyday is tiresome...I bet if I counted the miles I have walked to and from the store it would be the same amount from here to America. When I returned to the apartment I didn't see Wilson so I asked Linda if she knew where he went; she said he is in the bathroom. I took the beer and ice in the kitchen and put it away. When Wilson came out he said would you and Linda like to go out for dinner? I said o.k. Linda go get ready we're going out for lunch. She said what about the food I am cooking? I said we would have it for dinner. I gave him one of the beers and said we will be ready by the time you finish your beer. Sister Linda and I went upstairs to change our clothes. Sister Linda came into my room and asked for some lotion. I gave the bottle to her and told her to keep it. I would get some more today at the Navy Exchange; I would get Jergens lotion like Sister Melda always bought. She said you are going to the Base Exchange? I said yes Wilson and I are going to look at a baby bed and see how much it cost and compare it with the price of one out here in town. I said are you ready? We better go before he change his mind. We hurried downstairs. Wilson said take it easy I don't want you to fall and hurt yourself. We left and went to the Shangri La Restaurant and Linda asked me what I was going to order; I said I am going to order big noodles and vegetables. She said how about me ordering fried chicken? I said yes you can order it and we can share each other order. Wilson ordered a beer right away and the Waiter gave us a menu. When the Waiter came back with the beer Wilson ordered the fried chicken and noodles and beef fried rice for himself; he told the Waiter he want a refill on our cokes. They gave us large portion of food; we ate what we could and asked the Waiter to wrap up the rest and Linda took it home. Wilson and I went to the Navy base. We caught the bus to the Navy Exchange; Wilson started explaining to me about the bus ride; I reminded him that he had told me before and that I had been on base by myself. He said where did you go? I said to the Exchange and back to the Main gate and went home. Wilson gave me twenty more dollars in case I wanted to buy something in the Exchange. We looked around at baby furniture and saw a basinet. Wilson said he was going to get one for our baby when it is born. I said o.k. I want to look around some more because I want to buy some Jergens lotion and maybe some more things.

We looked around and found everything I wanted and we paid for it. Wilson said make sure you keep the receipt, because they have what they call Merchandise Control here on the base and they keep up with everything you buy. I put the receipt in my bag. When we got to the gate, sure enough they asked for the receipt and compared everything in our bags with it. I said to myself…even if you have an ID card they still think you would steal from the base. Wilson said are you all right? I said even if you are an American Sailor they still check what you take off the base. He said yes, they want to make sure you only take out what is on that receipt…they are trying to control the black market…people buying stuff on the base and taking it to town and selling it for a big profit. I said they don't have to worry about me because they have almost everything I want in town. When we got home Sister Linda had already left for school; there were only one beer left for Wilson and I went to the store and got more. While we were sitting in our living room we heard our next-door neighbor the white American couple arguing. She wanted to go out but her husband wanted to stay home because he thought she was to drunk. She came outside to their car and almost fell down; he got her back inside and we could hear them argue for a while. Finally it was quiet. I asked Wilson if he wanted something to eat. He said he was not hungry. I went in the kitchen and ate the fish Sister Linda had cooked before we went to lunch. When I finished I brushed my teeth; I know Wilson like to kiss and I didn't want him to smell fish on my breath. I came back to the living room and set beside Wilson on the couch; I asked him if he heard anymore from our neighbor apartment? He said no not yet. I said they are trying to make up. He said like this, and he started kissing me all over. I knew what was coming next; we would get the electric fan and go upstairs. Since the wedding Wilson seem more responsible now; he come straight home from work and maybe drink two beers and we have fun together in our bedroom or watching TV. If we go anywhere it is usually to a movie and back home.

Finally my Hospital appointment date came Wilson took the day off of work and went with me. They had a lot of paperwork for me to read and fill out. Wilson filled out the paper and I signed them. They took fluid samples and gave me an x ray. Finally the Doctor told me the baby was all right, but I needed iron in additional to my medicine.

He said eat liver and drink vegetable juice. The Doctor said I was anemic and he wanted to see me again in a month. He asked if my Husband was with me; I said yes he is in the waiting room, so the Nurse went and got Wilson. The Doctor told him the same thing about iron and me being anemic and to make sure I took my medicine. I was a little frightened at first when they called my name, but the Nurses and Doctor were so nice they made me feel real comfortable. I won't mind coming back to my appointment even if Wilson doesn't come with me. We went by the Commissary and bought some beef liver and vegetable juice. When we got home Wilson and I cooked the beef liver and I ate some and drunk vegetable juice. The liver was all right, but I didn't like the taste of the vegetable juice. Wilson said Sweetheart, you don't have to force yourself to drink the vegetable juice just eat plenty of beef liver. The day and week passed by very fast, but Wilson never forgot to remind me about taking my medicine. I went to my appointments at the Hospital alone. Wilson would ask me what the Doctor said about the baby and me. He seemed to be relieved when I tell him the Doctor said we were doing fine.

During my seventh month of pregnancy we made love one night and afterward the baby kick me. I said oh! Out loud and Wilson almost fainted. He asked me what was wrong. I told him the baby kicked me and I took his hand and put it on my stomach so he could feel the baby move. He asked me what the Doctor said about having sex while I was pregnant. I told him the Doctor at the Hospital told me we could have sex up to the ninth month just be careful...he also told me to start getting some exercise. He said I should get out and walk in the morning or late in the afternoon. I said maybe I walk with you to the Gate in the morning. Wilson said whatever you want to do Sweetheart. The baby moved again and I grab Wilson hand and place it on my stomach where the baby moved. He said baby don't hurt mommy go to sleep now. He kept rubbing my stomach. He is very thoughtful, caring and loving since we been married; he has cut back on the amount of beer he drinks and he continue to maintain control of himself. I am very happy about everything that happening I don't know how long it will last, but I hope it will last forever. He is making me very happy to be his wife and soon the Mother of his kid.

Then Wilson said go to sleep Sweetheart so you can get up and walk with me to the gate tomorrow morning. When the clock alarm went off the next morning I quickly got up got dressed and went downstairs to the bathroom. When I came out of the bathroom Wilson was standing in the living room waiting for me. He said are you ready? I said yes, and he took my hand and we were on our way to the Base main Gate. On our way I told Wilson that I could see him as he passed different places on his way to the gate. He said do you mean that you watch me as I walk to work. I said yes I watch you from the bedroom all the time if I am not too sleepy. He said it is all right because a lot of people walk to work in the morning. I said yes it is all right, but it is cool in the morning...are you cold? He said no this feel good...how about you Sweetheart...you have your sweater on are you cold? I said I am all right it feel good to walk early in the morning; there are not too many jeepney out in the street with the smell of gasoline that make me feel dizzy. When we got to the bridge next to the Military base Wilson kissed me goodbye and asked me if I would be all right walking to the apartment. I said I would be all right. He said I think you should ride a jeepney back, so I caught a jeepney and went back home. Wilson watched me until I got into a jeepney and the jeepney pulled off. When I got back to the apartment I decide to walk around the compound for a while. I walked until I started sweating then I went inside. Sister Linda saw me sweating and said Vicky where have you been? I said I have been exercising walking with Wilson all the way to the gate. She said that's too far for you to walk especially you being pregnant. I said the Doctor told me to walk everyday and get plenty of exercise. I sat down and the baby started moving; I called Linda so she could feel the baby moving. She said the baby kicked her hand. I said the baby have been moving like that since last night. When he move like that sometime I can hardly breathe. She said Sister Rose tie something around her waist above the baby so if it kick it want reach her heart. I said yes I saw her do that with her first baby. Maybe you better go upstairs and get me something I can make a band and put around my bust. She did and it felt better when the baby kicked. Then the baby started moving even more and Linda started laughing and said the baby must be exercising or hungry. We cooked our breakfast of fried eggs, bread rolls and onions. We sat down to eat and I had a taste for sardine so Linda opened a can of sardine and I ate sardine with my fried eggs and onion.

Sister Linda said I thought you passed that stage where you want to eat weird food. I said the sardine is good. The baby moved around in my stomach a lot while I was eating. The baby stopped moving when I finished eating. I sat in the living room to see if it was going to start moving again. When I turned the TV on the baby moved once and quit. I rubbed my stomach to reassure my baby that I was going to protect it from the new noise of the TV. I kept rubbing my stomach and I fell asleep. Sometime later someone knock on the door and Sister Linda opened it. It was the oldies son of the building owner coming to watch TV. I got up and went to the bathroom; when I came back I asked the boy if he went to school today. He said no I am not going to school for a while because there is something wrong with my stomach; we're going to America next month to see a Specialist to try to find out what wrong with my stomach. I said what wrong with the Doctors here? He said I have been to different Doctors here but they don't know what is wrong with my stomach. They are sending me to see a Specialist Doctor in America. He watched TV with us for about thirty minutes and he started holding his stomach. He said I have to go home now my stomach is hurting, thank you. When he left Linda said you could tell something is wrong with him because he is very skinny. I said yes, maybe he has ulcers or something. I asked Sister Linda had she taken a shower. She said yes I took a shower while you were sleeping on the couch. I said I guess I better take my shower before Wilson comes home. Then before I could go upstairs the lady selling fish knock on the door. I opened the door to see what she was selling today. She was selling pork, beef, fish and vegetables. I bought some pork, eggplant and tomatoes. And hurried to take my shower; it felt real good under the running water. When I came out Sister Linda said you stayed in there so long I thought you were going to use all of the water in the water tower. I went upstairs and towel dried my hair and came back down stairs. She said now that you are finish let eat. We ate our lunch and really enjoyed the pork adobo. I told Sister Linda if the lady come by selling pork tomorrow buy some more. She said it is cheaper in the market. I said o.k. You go to the market tomorrow and buy pork and whatever else we need; oh yes, we need to buy some can food for Wilson; tomorrow is Friday sometime he eat sausage and corn beef on the weekend. Sister Linda said I have one more Month to go before school is out for a three month summer vacation…you're going to have your baby pretty soon and I will be here to help you with it…Mother will be here too she said this is your first baby and she would be here to help you with it.

I said I need Mother help because I don't know what to do. She said don't worry everybody will be here to help you with your baby… just be careful Mother had you when she was seven month pregnant. I said do you think I am going to have the baby now because the baby moves a lot? She said I don't think so, I hope not, because if you do the baby will be premature. I said I was a premature baby, but look at me now…do I look all right…do I look complete…do I look pretty and sexy? And skinny, she said, but you look real good for a

premature baby. I said yes, but my problem is I need to gain some weight…I am too skinny. Sister Linda said if I was you I would be happy to be skinny and not have blobs of fat all over me. I said Wilson married me and I am skinny; I guess he like me the way I am. She said Brother Wilson is too protective and jealous of you; I know he love you very much even if you are skinny, so be happy you have everything now…I am going upstairs and finish my homework. I decided to go outside and walk around in the apartment compound and get a little more exercise. After walking around the compound several times I saw Wilson standing inside the gate watching me; I don't know how long he had been standing there before I saw him. He came over and kiss me and said Sweetheart what are you doing out here. I told him I was getting some more exercise. He said Sweetheart you got your exercise this morning. I told him when I walk with him to the gate the next morning I wanted to take Magsaysay Drive back to Rizal Avenue and down to Second Street where we live. He said Sweetheart that is the long way back home and I think it is too far for you to be walking plus there are more jeepney and gasoline smell on Magsaysay Drive. I said Sweetheart if I walk that way I promise if I get tired or feel dizzy I will catch a jeepney home. He said o.k. He held the door open for me to go in our apartment. Sister Linda heard us come inside and came down and asked if we need her to do something before she got ready for school. I said yes I want you to go to the store and get ice, coke and beer. When she came back from the store I took the ice and chopped it up and put some in our water pitcher and the rest in the pot on top of Wilson beers. I took him one to drink and sat down beside him on the couch. Linda started talking about how hot it was upstairs. I told her April and May was the hottest Month in the Year. Wilson said what Linda is talking about. I said she is talking about how hot the weather is now.

He said it is real hot now; just before I left my Boat I took a shower and before I could
walk to the bus stop I was sweating...the only thing that can cool you down is an air condition building, a good electric fan or a real cold beer like this one. I said yes, but if you drink a lot you will end up drunk and hot. He said if I were drunk I would fall asleep and won't feel hot anymore. I said just enjoy your beer. He said scoot closer to me. I said if I sat any closer to you I would really get hot...I know what you want to do. When Sister Linda finished her shower and got dressed for school. She came downstairs and said I feel much better after the shower. I said take your umbrella it will keep the sun off of you for a while. Wilson looked happy that she was leaving going to school. He became real aggressive in his caressing and kissing. He said do you think it is too hot for us upstairs; I said yes three o, clock in the afternoon it is very hot upstairs. He said we have an electric fan you will be all right. We went upstairs; he said there is a breeze coming in the windows and when I turn this fan on it will be nice up here. When he turned on the fan it wasn't bad at all in the bedroom, so we proceeded with caution because we knew we had a baby onboard to Christian our bed. When we finished and I was lying in the arms of the man I love, I started starring at the small electric fan on the dressed that was doing it best to cool us down. I thought

to myself...I would always try providing his sexual needs and any other needs he may have. Wilson drifted off to sleep. I watched him he looked so peaceful while he slept. I started thinking to myself again...Wilson like to make love two sometimes three times a day, what is he going to do when I have the baby and he have to wait for a few weeks...would he wait or go to the clubs...I know he ran around in the clubs before we got married...will I marriage change his way of thinking...I hope so...I will find out very soon because this baby is coming. Wilson opened his eyes and asked why I wasn't sleeping. I said I am not sleepy now. He said what are you thinking about? I said I am worried that if I can't make love for a few weeks after I have the baby will you change me. He said don't worry about that, I love you and can wait for you until you are ready...just trust me...I love you and always remember that. I know I have to believe that he would do the right thing just like he said, but thinking about the way things use to be makes it real hard.

In my eight month of pregnancy my Auntie from Pangasinan, Mother's youngest sister came to visit me. She stayed for a while to help out around the apartment while Sister Linda was in school. Sister Rose had her baby I thought I was going to have my baby before she had hers. That same month Mr. Blanco left to take his son to America for his Medical appointment. They always kept me informed as to how the boy was doing, because he spent a lot of time with me watching TV in my apartment. I really felt bad about the boy being sick like that and I couldn't do anything to help him. Wilson started to change too, he would come home late after drinking somewhere; he started looking at me as if something was wrong with me that he didn't like. When we made love he would turn off the light so he couldn't see me. Sometimes I cry to relieve the tension; I would cover my head with my pillow so my Aunt and Linda couldn't hear me. Mr. Blanco notice him coming home late one night drunk and told me he was surprised to see him that way because he thought Wilson was a very nice guy. I made excuses about him going to a party. Finally everyone at one time or another saw him come home drunk. One day I was outside and Mrs. Blanco told me her son had died and they were bringing his body home from America. She said the doctor in America said the cancer was too far along for them to be able to help her son. She said the cancer had spread throughout her son body. I told her how sorry I was about the boy's death and came back inside our apartment and sat on the couch. I told my Aunt and Linda about the boy passing. My Aunt said don't you go over there because you are pregnant. I said the body is not here yet maybe two days before it gets here. My Aunt said just listen to me, when someone dies young like that; they ask for someone to die too. Someone always die following the young. I asked Linda what Auntie was talking about. She said I don't know, but if I were you I would listen to her. Do you remember when our Great Grand Mother died; I almost died too and I still have the scar on my leg to prove it. I said oh yea! That right. When the body comes I will send Auntie over to help with the cooking and tell them I can't come because I am pregnant. After the funeral I saw Mrs. Blanco and I told her why I couldn't come. She said she understood; she said her son always talked about me and said I was nice and very pretty. She said thank you for being nice to my son.

Sister Linda, Auntie and I was watching TV when Wilson came home; he had been drinking but I didn't say anything to him. He kissed me and sat down beside me watching TV. When the program was over Linda and Auntie went upstairs. I asked Wilson why does he always stop somewhere and drink before he comes home. He said one of the guys on his Boat invited him to his house and they started drinking. I said I never see you very much now because you stay away more than you stay here? What wrong...are you ashamed of me because I have a big stomach? He didn't answer my question; he got up and went in the kitchen and got a can of Vienna sausage and started eating. I said to myself...what's going on...why is he treating me like this...I thought we were doing real good and we were very happy...he even started controlling his drinking, but now it is worse. When he finished eating he asked me if I was going to bed. I followed him upstairs and took off my clothes and put on my nightgown he looked at me as if I had leprosy. He turned off the light and got in the bed. He pulled me close and started caressing me; I wanted to tell him to stop, but I knew that he was determine so I responded to get it over with. Sometimes I feel that he have sex with me because he thinks that it is his duty as a husband. I really don't know what to do or think. He seems to be letting my pregnancy come between our relationships; he doesn't seem to understand that when you are eight months pregnant you will not look the same, because of the disfigurement of the body. I can tell that he is doing the same thing he did before the wedding; he is acting out of tension and his perception as to what things should be and when things are not like what he think they should be he start drinking. For whatever the reason he is acting out of context; I will wait until he start to see thing a little clearer and start acting like a good husband and the soon to be Father. On July the fourth I was setting in the living room waiting for Wilson to come home. I could hear the music coming from next door. I said to myself…our neighbors are having a party. A few minutes later Wilson came home he had been next door drinking with our neighbor. He said we are going next door to their party, so I went with him. Larry and Pat was a white American couple they both were drinking a lot, but Pat was drunk and wanted Wilson to dance with her.

Wilson wanted to do it anyway because he was almost drunk too. They was acting up on the floor trying to dance; Larry wanted his wife to set down and stop acting crazy, but she was drunk and didn't pay him any attention. I was upset with Wilson too and tried to get him to go home. Finally I left and went back to our apartment; I was upset with myself because I couldn't control the situation. I told Sister Linda and Auntie tomorrow we would go to Calapacuan. I would have gone tonight but it is too late. I went upstairs and went to bed and cried myself to sleep. I don't know what time he finally came home, but he did because when the alarm clock ringed he got up and went to work. I didn't say anything and he was silent too. I got up the next morning and got ready and we went to Calapacuan. Everyone was very surprised to see me. Mother was upset because I was riding in a jeepney. She said do you want to have your baby in a jeepney? Then she took a good look at me and realizes that I had a problem, so she just got busy cooking breakfast for the whole family. Everybody was there Sister Rose, her Daughter Gina, and her new baby Robert. Brother Celino and his wife were there too, and or course Brother Etong. My Auntie Daughter Enyang and her new baby were there. After I arrived Sister Maria came over to Mother's house. I saw Sister Rose new baby for the first time he was real fat and cute. Enyang baby was fat too. Both of them say they are breastfeeding their baby because they don't have the money to buy milk. They asked me if I was going to breastfeed my baby and I told them I wasn't sure yet. I went into the kitchen to see what Mother was cooking; Sister Maria was in the kitchen with her. Everyone followed me wanted to know why my stomach was so big and I am so little. They asked me if the baby was heavy to carry around. I said the baby is not heavy, but is moving a lot. Enyang baby started to cry and she started breastfeeding it. I asked her if it hurt when the baby is sucking her breast. She said no, he doesn't have teeth yet. Sister Rose said wait until he starts teething and biting, then it would hurt. I asked Mother if she was going to cook dried fish; I said don't worry about it if you don't have some. She said I could send your Brother Etong to the store and get some. She looked for Brother Etong, but he left going to get water. Brother Celino said I will go to the store what do you want? I said dried fish and a coke and ice. Then everyone said I want coke too. So I told him to get a case of coke and plenty of ice. When Brother Etong came back from getting water and firewood he came close to me and pointed at my stomach. I said yes, it is big and the baby will come very soon. He pointed at Sister Rose and Enyang. I said yes they have their baby already. He pointed to his finger like he was counting. I said yes you would have a lot of nieces and nephews pretty soon. He just smiled. When Brother Celino returned from the store the dried fish was fried and breakfast was ready. Everyone even Sister Rose's Husband made it in time for breakfast. Everyone was real happy laughing and talking, but me I almost had tears at one time thinking about the way Wilson is acting now, but I don't want them to know about my problem. I know Mother knew from the time she saw me when I came in the house this morning that I was having a problem, but I think

I have managed to hide it from everyone else. When I finished eating I sat on my favorite wood box in the corner looking out the window. I heard Mother ask Auntie if she would wash the clothes she took in from someone in Olongapo, because she had to go to the market to buy fish and vegetables. Auntie said could we split the money you get for washing the clothes because I am trying to save some money to visit my kids in Manila. Mother said who is in Manila? Auntie said three of my kids...your oldest nephew and the other two next to Enyang...they never write so I want to find out what going on...when I return I could go to Vicky's house and help her with the baby or Enyang and I could stay here and do your washing. Mother asked Auntie what happened to Enyang Husband. She said he is a drunk and like to hang around with drunker and one time he got in a fight with them and they stab him with a knife; they took him to the hospital and he stayed there for a week. His parents sold all of their land paying his hospital bill and he died anyway. After he died the parent wanted to take their Grandson, so Enyang and I left Pangasinan and came here to Subic. We had planned to go to Manila because I have kids there, but they know I have kids there, so we came here. Enyang said he was a no good Husband all he wanted to do is drink; he left me when I got pregnant that's why I don't feel bad that someone killed him. I said I guess she lost interest in him; like Wilson I will always love him, but if he keeps treating me like he is ashamed of me, I guess we can forget this marriage too. Lately we could never have a good conversation because he always comes home after he had been drinking. I am in my ninth month of pregnancy and he doesn't seem to know it or care. I can't wait to have this baby; even though I am married to him maybe I will run away somewhere with my baby and let him go back to America alone...he will never change his ways. Mother told me she was going to the market in Subic. I told her I was going to stay with her for a while and gave her some money to buy neck bones and vegetables. Mother asked Brother Etong to go with her to the market. He wanted to know if I was going to be at Mother's house when they returned from the market. I said yes I am going to eat lunch here. Auntie and I went outside right behind Mother and Brother Etong, I went to Sister Maria's house and Auntie went to get started washing the clothes for Mother. Sister Maria was setting on her porch although she likes to call it a balcony. When I got there she was happy to see me; I sat down beside her and we chitchat for a while. Finally I asked her about her Daughter, she said her Daughter was getting alone fine with her boyfriend, but as far as she knows they don't plan to get married. Sister Maria always have a real nice altitude about everything that's what I like about her. My Brother Celino brought his new wife right there in the neighborhood and built a house for them about a hundred yards away and it don't seem to faze her. Sister Linda came and said Vicky they have started drinking your coke. I said it is all right just bring Sister Maria and me a coke, get one for yourself too. When she came back she said Vicky there are too many people staying in Mother's house are we going back to Olongapo tonight? I said no we would sleep in Mother's bedroom. Sister Maria said I have plenty of room here your Auntie and Enyang can sleep here. I said see Linda we have a place to sleep tonight. She said what about Brother Wilson? I said he has duty tonight don't worry he will be all right. Sister Rose Husband walked by Sister Maria house and said goodbye to us on his way to work. Sister Maria said he always works day and night. I said that's good because they need the money. I asked whether Brother Celino had a job; Sister Linda said she think he has a part-time job making bricks. I said that great, because his wife is going to have a baby just like me any day. Sister Maria said you better stay home, because you don't want to have your baby in the rice field or a jeepney. I saw Mother and Brother Etong coming back from the market. Brother Etong was smiling just like always when he sees me; he gave me some fruit they bought from the market. I can't hide my feeling from Brother Etong either; he can tell if something going wrong with me.

I told Sister Maria I was going back to Mother's house; I followed Mother and Brother Etong to the house. When I came in the door Gina saw my fruit and asked if she could have some. Mother told her she can't have my fruit but she had something in her bag for her. Mother gave her a piece of a sweet rice cake that she bought for our dessert. Mother started cooking and Linda and I started helping to cut up all of the vegetables. Auntie and Enyang finished washing the clothes and came in the house. Auntie asked if she could have a cold coke. Mother yelled at her and said you know every time you drink coke you get a stomach ache, why do you want to drink it if you know it would hurt your stomach? Auntie said I want just a swallow or two just to kill my thirst; I haven't drunk a coke in a very long time. Mother said if your stomach starts hurting don't tell me about it. Auntie said I am not drinking it… are you happy now? Everyone start laughing at Mother and Auntie because they were real comical yelling back at each other. When the food was cook Mother said it is time to eat. Sister Linda and Brother Etong put the plates and dishes of food on the floor so everyone could get around it and eat. Everyone was eating and looking real happy but me, I missed Wilson even though he is not home very much. I started thinking the thing he had being doing the last few weeks. Mother said Vicky do you want some more vegetable? I said no I have enough. She said you haven't eaten very much are you all right...are you feeling bad? I said I am all right; the baby is moving a lot. She said that's why you need to eat because the baby needs to eat too. When you get back home and if you hurting or you see blood or water coming out; I want you to send Linda to get me day or night...when I get there I will stay until you have the baby and understand how to take care of it. So you need to eat more so you will be strong when you have your baby. Stop thinking so much, you don't want it to affect your baby...remember if you laugh the baby is happy too and if you cry the baby feel that too...you have to stay strong, because you are going to be a Mother very soon.

Auntie said Vicky is worried because Wilson is always drunk when he comes home. Mother said is Wilson still drinking a lot? I said when he is invited to a party. Auntie said sometimes he scare me when he go upstairs, because he look like he is going to fall, but he always find his way home. I said to myself...Auntie Talks too much I don't want everyone to know that Wilson drinks too much. Auntie said Vicky will tell you that he comes home drunk. In a very strong voice I said Auntie he gets drunk when his friend invites him to a party; you know yourself when people get invited to a party or festival they get drunk. She understood that I wanted her to stop talking about Wilson and she started talking about her late Son-in Law. I said to myself...thank God...I hope she never repeat that again. I know Auntie was telling the truth, because she set up watching TV at night when Wilson comes home. Well everybody have problems, but I don't want her to tell my Mother about mine while everyone is listening. Mother came in the room with a large pan with warm water in it. She was going to give Sister Rose baby a bath. I made sure I had a ringside seat so I could see everything that was happening. As Mother bathes the baby she explained what we should do and what we shouldn't do while bathing a baby. After bathing the baby she dressed him. I saw her put mittens on the baby hands. I said why are you putting mittens on the baby it is not cold.

Mother said the mittens keep him from scratching his face. Enyang said my baby is next. I said Sister Linda when you go to the market get some mitten for my baby and keep watching; maybe we will see something else we need. Sister Linda made a list of everything else we needed for my baby. I said o.k. Linda when we get home I want you to go to the market and get everything on that list. She said what time are we going home? I said no we're going to stay here tonight. Mother heard what we were talking about and said does Wilson know you are staying here tonight? I said he has to work tonight and if he comes home he will know I am here. She said I don't mind you staying here, but if your husband doesn't know where you are you better go home...if you have problem you need to talk them out you just don't leave your house without telling him where you are going. I said to myself...if you only knew what going on with my marriage you would be telling me to come home. I am the only one holding this marriage together; if I wasn't so in love with him I would have ran away a long time ago. I have chosen this man to spend the rest of my life with: I will follow him wherever he goes if he wants me. So I am prepared to wait until he finally realize his mistakes and start being the Husband I married him to be.

Mother said o.k. You can stay if he have to work tonight...you need to relax...don't think too much...if you are worried about having your baby, you will be all right; just look at your Sister Rose and your Cousin Enyang they are all right. They had their baby without a Doctor; I know Wilson is going to take you to the Hospital on Base and they have very good Doctors...don't worry everything is going to be all right...take care of yourself and don't think too much. Mother gave me a mat, a pillow and a blanket. After the bedroom was rearranged I put my mat down and tried to relax. Gina came to me and asked if she could comb my hair. I said yes, I would give her twenty centavos later to buy her some candy. She was very happy, so she combed my hair ever so gentle and before I realize it I was sleep. I don't know how long I slept before Enyang baby started crying because he was hungry. Enyang was sleep and didn't want to wake up long enough to feed the baby. The baby kept crying and finally Auntie told Enyang if she didn't wake up and feed the baby she would dump a bucket of water on her. Enyang started mumbling...I want to sleep too…this baby wants to eat every hour. Auntie said you was in a big hurry to marry your no good dead Husband…now you don't want to feed your baby…the baby didn't ask to be born…you were in a hurry to climb the tree to get the apple; now you have it and don't want to take care of it. Sister Linda said what is Auntie talking about? I said Enyang don't want to feed the baby. She said Enyang climbing the tree…what tree is that? I said it is the other kind of tree…oh! Forget it, you will know that when it's your time to be married like us. We just lied there listening to Auntie and Enyang talking back and forth. I thought to myself…everyone has a problem no matter what it maybe…my biggest problem is Wilson drinking too much, but I am not going to give up on him I will stay with him until he tell me he don't love me…I pray that one day he will wake up and pay attention to me without drinking a drop of liquor and start being the Husband he should be. He doesn't know that I really need his love and assurance that everything will be all right. Around bedtime everyone started trying to find a place to sleep. Auntie Took Enyang and went to stay in Brother Celino house so she could watch her and make sure she feed the baby. Mother said Enyang is too young to have a baby. I said how old Enyang is. Mother said she is only sixteen a few years younger than you. Sister Maria was sitting on her balcony in the cool and she saw Wilson coming across the field and it was almost dark. She started shouting; Vicky, Vicky Wilson is coming.

We were in Mother's house next door and we could hear her. Brother Etong went out and met him with a flashlight. Sister Linda said you are in trouble now; you told Mother Wilson had to work tonight. I said what I am I going to tell her… Wilson drinks too much. She said you should tell her the truth, Wilson does drink too much…I can hear your arguments and hear you crying at night. I said I don't want Mother to know my problem she has enough problems to deal with now. She said what happened to Brother Wilson…he wasn't drinking too much before. I said I don't know. Wilson came into the house he said hi Inay to Mother in Tagalog. Mother smiled and said hi to him. I didn't get up I just sat there on the floor in the bedroom. Sister Linda said I am going to sleep beside Mother, you and Brother Wilson need to talk. Brother Etong pointed to the bedroom where I was. Wilson came in and sat beside me on the floor. He asked me if I was all right. I said why you want to know; I thought you had forgotten me already. You love your drinking more than the baby and me, so I decided to come home and have my baby here. You don't care anymore why should I stay there and watch you come home every night drunk…you have lost interest in me…you never kiss me or make love to me anymore. I know you are going to say you were drunk and didn't know what you were doing; well I don't know what I am doing either, I am just pregnant and want to have my baby here. He said no! I don't want you to have our baby here without a Doctor; I am scare something may happen to you. I said you are scared something may happen to me? That's something new coming from you; you never care since my stomach got big like a Volcano. You think my stomach is going to blow. He said no Sweetheart I am scared that when you have our baby you will never come home. I said what do you mean? I didn't want to tell you this, but I had a sister that died having her baby, that why I am scared for us. I said I am sorry to hear that your sister died in childbirth, but don't think that will happen to me. If God want us there is nothing we can do; we just have to pray that the baby and I will be all right. He said I think about you a lot, I think you are too little to have a baby and I start drinking and end up drunk before I come home. I said don't use my pregnancy to get drunk…If I die during childbirth then it is God will, but you have to stop hurting me with your drinking and staying away from home. Wilson said I told you I am scare that I am going to lose you that is why I drink more.

I said o.k. Go ahead and kept drinking and think I am gone from your life…I will stay here and have our baby. I lay down on the mat and turned my back to him. I heard Mother say if Wilson hasn't eaten yet I could cook something for him. With my back to him I said have you eaten already? He said yes I ate before I left my Boat. I said you go to the club and drink some more I am staying here. Mother asked again if Wilson had eaten. I said yes. Wilson said what is Inay talking about? I said your Mother-in-law want to cook you something to eat if you have not eaten. He said you see, your Mother care about me. I said everybody care about you except you. You are destroying the one that love you no matter what. He said you still love me right? I said why I should say I love you and I am mad at you. Right now I don't have to prove to you that I love you, because I haven't did anything wrong to you. If you don't know by now that I love you; then you really have a problem and you should go I won't try and stop you. The only thing I want right now is to have my baby and find me a job. You could go back to Olongapo and do your running around without me. He said I told you I started drinking because I was afraid of losing you. I said please don't use that again as an excuse. I am here now just go and enjoy your life if that the way you want to live it. I am a Filipino I am use to a hard life my baby is going to be all right, because it will be surrounded by the love of my family. You said that you are scared, well the way you treat me makes me afraid. I thought being married would change your way of thinking, but it made it worse. I said you always use different excuses to keep me around; if you don't love me like you said you do, just forget we're married and we can go our separate ways…life doesn't treat you well sometimes, but I will always love you. He said Sweetheart I am sorry I hurt you, but you know I love you…I am stupid and drink too much…please forgive me…you are my wife and we have a baby coming very soon; I want you and the baby home. I promised I would change my way of drinking; I did it before and can do it again. I said just go home I will think about forgiving you. I want to stay here maybe a week. He said I will stay here too…I can catch a jeepney to work tomorrow. Mother came to the door and said I sent Etong to

Chapter 7

Our First Born

Borrow Maria big flashlight; you can use it when you leave to go home...just go home your Husband have to work tomorrow, you can talk when you get home. Wilson said is Inay Mad? I said no she just want me to go home. Wilson got up and said thank you Inay. And Linda told her what he said. Mother said o.k. Wilson no more foolish and no more beer. I got ready to leave because Mother wants us to go; I told Linda get ready we are leaving for Olongapo. We left walking cross the rice field; Brother Etong led the way with the big flashlight. Wilson held my hand real tight and we carefully walked toward the jeepney stop. When we got to the road we told Brother Etong thank and be careful on his way back home. He was glad to see us back together; he signaled by pointing at us. When we caught a jeepney he stood waving at us saying good bye. Wilson held me real close in the jeepney. Linda asked me about Auntie. I told her when we get a lot of dirty clothes she could tell Auntie to come over every two weeks and wash. Wilson said we forgot Auntie. I said she is not coming because her Daughter had a baby and don't want to feed him. I just want her to come over maybe once a week and do the washing. He said o.k. I could get you a Maid when you have the baby. I said not now! When we got to our apartment I sat down on the couch in the living room and Wilson sat by me. He kissed me and said thank you Sweetheart for coming home the apartment isn't lonely anymore. When I came home everyone was gone I thought the wall was caving in on me. I said oh! You felt that way too; I feel that way all of the time when I am alone and lonely…when you don't come home I go to bed and cry myself to sleep. He said you won't have to cry anymore because I will be here. I didn't say anything, because he has made promises before and broke them. I really didn't feel angry with him anymore, so I told him I was going to bed. He said if you are ready to go to bed let's go; I have to work tomorrow. We went upstairs and Wilson held my hand as we mounted the stairs. In our bedroom I took off my clothes and put my nightgown on. He asked me if the baby still moving. I said yes and took his hand and placed it on my stomach. He started smiling and said the baby kicked my hand. Then he kissed my stomach and said go to sleep baby. Then he gently kissed me on my lips; I almost cried, because I missed him so much. He said are you all right Sweetheart? I said yes. He started to caressing and kissing me. I said turn off the light. He said no! Leave the light on. I knew he wanted to make love and I did too. He said do you think you would be all right if we made love? I said the Doctor said it would be all right up to my ninth month, just don't overdo it. When we finished making love he said I really missed being with you like this. I said it been a while because you are always to drunk. He said Sweetheart don't get mad at me anymore; if you do I will tell your Inay. I said turn off the light so we can go to sleep. He said let me look at you for a while; I want to see the face I missed seeing. I said you are saying that now because we just finished making love; just wait until tomorrow you will forget that I am alive…lets go to sleep before I get upset. He said o.k. Sweetheart lets go to sleep. He kissed me and held me close like he always do and I went to sleep.

That month Wilson did what he promised; he came straight home from work and cut down on his drinking. One morning I woke up early because my lower back was hurting I went to the bathroom and saw blood on my underwear. Wilson said I want you to go see the Doctor today. I called Sister Linda and told her to go to Calapacuan as soon as she get dress and get Mother, because I want to make sure she is here when I have my baby. Wilson went to work and Sister Linda went to get Mother and around eight that morning I went to The Naval Hospital on Base. When I arrive I was feeling worse; finally I saw the Doctor and he examined me and measured my stomach. He told me to return home because it would be about two more weeks before I had my baby. The last thing he told me was to get plenty of exercise, so when I left the base I walked down Magsaysay Drive to Rizal Avenue and to Second Street; I took the long way home to make sure I did my exercise. When I got home Mother was there waiting for me. She examined me and told me the Doctor didn't know what he was talking about, because I was going to have my baby that day or that night. I kept going to the bathroom and Mother said if you don't stop using the bathroom so much you are going to drop your baby in the commode. I said I am hurting and I feel like I need to use the bathroom. She said you feel like that because you are going to have your baby. Wilson came home and asked me what the Doctor said and I told him the Doctor told me it would be another two weeks before I had my baby. My Mother said I am going to have the baby today or tonight. Wilson said maybe the Doctor messed up counting the days; if your Mother said you would have the baby today. He said what do you want to do? I said I don't know...I could tell Wilson was getting nervous.

Wilson opened one of his beers and started drinking it. I kept going back and forth to the bathroom and nothing happened. Finally my water broke and Mother said you are having the baby now. I was so scared I couldn't talk. Wilson ran next door with my bag and told our neighbor I was having the baby. He came back and picked me up and carried me to the car and dropped me in the seat. I said don't kill me I haven't had the baby yet. He said I am sorry I am very nervous. I said I am the one having the baby not you. He kept telling me he love me on the way to the Hospital. I told him I love him too. When I got to the Hospital they put me in a wheel chair and took me to the delivery room. Wilson was looking at me as he said goodbye; I could tell he was very worried about me. In the delivery room I just concentrated on having my baby. They put me to sleep; I don't know how long I was out; the only thing I remembered was hearing them spank my baby to make it cry. Someone said you have a baby girl. I could hear the baby cry it sounded good. When the Doctor came to check on me I told him I had pain when I urinate; he said you are not suppose to be feeling pain because I gave you medicine for it. I said well I still feel it. He said close your eyes and go to sleep. I closed my eyes and finally drifted off to sleep. I slept until I felt something dripping in my face. I opened my eyes and saw that my bed was in the hallway. I thought I could hear the sound of rain coming from outside. Wilson came to my bed and told me he had to leave because it was getting late and he wanted to make sure I was all right before he left the Hospital. A few minutes after he left I went back to sleep and slept the rest of the night. The next morning a Nurse came and asked me if I wanted to see my baby girl. I said yes, where is she? The Nurse brought the baby to me and gave me a small bottle of milk. I tried my best to keep awake while I was holding the baby, but I couldn't keep my eyes opened, so I fell asleep with my baby. The next thing I remembered was hearing the Nurse say Mrs. Wilson, Mrs. Wilson you almost laid on top of your baby. I said you better take the baby because I am too sleepy and can't watch her. That afternoon Wilson came he was looking very happy; he gave me a big kiss and asked if I was all right and what do I wanted to name the baby I said Rebecca. He said Rebecca that sounds good to me. I said have you seen the baby? He said not yet. I told him I had seen the baby but I felt asleep trying to hold her and she is very cute. He asked me if the baby was born complete. I said what do you mean? He said does she have all of her fingers and toes? I said she have everything a normal baby suppose to have and she is very cute...you better go and see her.

He said I will go see the baby after I give the name of the Baby to the Nurse so they can complete her birth certificate...do you feel better now? I showed him my stomach and said I feel much better. He kissed me and said thank God you both are all right...now I can relax; I can't wait to take you home. I said when are you taking me home? He said in four more days, because you have to stay in the Hospital five days when you have a baby. I said did you tell Mother and Linda that I had a baby girl. He said no but I will when I go to the apartment...after I tell them about the baby; I am going to stay on the Boat until you come home. I said to myself...we have an apartment why don't he stay at home...I am in the Hospital I can't argue or worry about why he don't want to stay at our apartment. When he left I tried to figure out why he wanted to stay on his Boat instead of the apartment..He came back to see me two days later. The excuse he gave me for waiting two day before he came to see me was he had to work at night now. I thought...he never work at night before, why now while I am in the Hospital. When he left I cried to try and clear my mind, because I felt he was doing something other than what he told me. On my discharge date Wilson arrived about one in the afternoon. I know he was drinking somewhere before he came to pick up me because I could smell it on him. On our way home he asked me if we could go see a movie later on. I said I guess so if we only going to watch a movie. When we got to the apartment Mother and Linda was real happy to see the baby and me. Linda was real crazy about the way the baby looked; she said this baby look so cute after just being born. When we settled down for a while I asked Mother if she could keep the baby while Wilson and I went to the movies. She said I don't mind keeping the baby, but you just came out of the Hospital you need to stay home, plus it is raining. I said I would be all right. We went anyway, but Mother was still upset when we left. In the movie Wilson started acting like we were on a date. He was holding me so tight and kissing me I couldn't see the movie. He kept telling me he loved me. I just listened to what he was saying and thought...if he really and truly loved me he wouldn't be worrying about watching a movie; he would listen to me when I tell him I still have some pain and when I told him the Doctor gave me seven stitches...maybe he would want to hold the baby, but the only thing he thought about was going to a movie. After the movie he asked me if I wanted to go to a club. I said no you go, just take me home I have to take my medicine and I am still having pain. He acted a little disappointed, but he didn't argue about it and we came home. When we got home Rebecca was sleeping very soundly and looking as cute as can be. Mother said she had just fed her and I need to lie down because I didn't look good. I told Wilson to get the special lamp I was supposed to use to dry my stitches.

I got in bed and set the lamp up so I could dry my stitches. Wilson asked me how I felt and I told him I still have some pain. Mother brought me some food. I asked Wilson if he wanted something to eat. He said he wasn't hungry. I turned off the lamp. Mother said where are you going? I said I want to go down stairs and check on my baby before I eat. Mother said the baby is all right don't worry I will take care of her...you should have stayed home instead of going to a movie; I hope you don't get sick. Wilson said lie down and relax...I shouldn't have taken you to the movie. I said it too late to think about that now. He didn't say anything more he just sat there on the side of the bed. A few minutes later he got up and went downstairs and came back and told me our baby was still sleeping. He said she is so cute and she doesn't cry. I said I guess she knows that she is safe here with her Mom and Dad, Grandmother and Auntie looking out for her. Wilson said Rebecca is a nice name. I said are you disappointed that she is a girl? He said I wanted a boy, but the girl is all right; maybe in two or three years we would have a boy. I said why don't we bring the baby in our room? He said let Linda and your Mother take care of the baby until you are all right...just relax for a week or two until you feel better. I said o.k. But I want to see my baby now. I got up and started to go downstairs. Wilson said o.k. I am going with you downstairs your Mother and Linda is watching TV. Rebecca was still sleeping in her Basinet when we got down stairs; Mother said she was taking Rebecca up to Linda's room when they finish watching TV. I said o.k. And leaned over the basinet and kissed the baby goodnight. I said Mother if she doesn't finish her milk just throw it away, because we don't have a refrigerator to keep it from spoiling. Mother said don't worry just go back to bed. Wilson and I went back upstairs to our bedroom. He hugged and kissed me; I didn't know what he was thinking, but I knew what I was thinking and I said no not now. He said I know I just want to hold you.

He held me in his arms as we slept. Around two o, clock in the morning I heard my baby crying; just when I was about to get up and see what was wrong with my baby I heard either Mother or Linda get up. A couple of minutes later the baby was quiet. Wilson said go back to sleep the baby is all right your Mother and Sister is taking care of her. I went back to sleep.

My pain came back I looked at the clock it was four-thirty in the morning, so I woke up Wilson so he could get ready for work. He said Sweetheart what do you need? I said the alarm clock didn't ring it is four-thirty. He said today is Saturday I don't work today. I said o.k. Would you go downstairs and get me a glass of water I need to take my pain medicine again. He got up and put on his pants and went downstairs and got me a glass of water. I took my medicine and Wilson said go back to sleep. I lay back down quietly and before long my pain was gone and I went to sleep. I slept to around nine o, clock that morning and when I opened my eyes Wilson was watching me sleep. He said you look beautiful and peaceful while you sleep. He asked if I was going to get up. I said yes I am going to check on the baby. He said would you make a list of the things you need from the base because Iam going to get the baby diapers and milk. I said I don't need anything right now. I am going to send Linda to the market. He said oh! I forgot to give you some money. He gave me money for food and my money. When we went down stairs Mother asked us if we were hungry. I said yes, but I wanted to see my baby first. She said I cooked fried eggs and Spam. I said where is the baby? Linda said I have the baby I am coming downstairs I just changed her diaper. I held my baby and kissed her; Wilson gave her a kiss too. Sister Linda brought the basinet and put it beside me and I put her in it and ate breakfast. When we finished breakfast Wilson left and went to the Navy Exchange to get our baby diapers and milk. I sat in the living room and told Mother about my seven stitches. She said I am going to Calapacuan and get some Guava leaves and boil them and let you set in the warm water. I gave her twenty pesos so she could buy whatever she needed to take to Calapacuan when she leaves the next day. I told Linda I wanted her to go to the market and buy grocery. Mother said Linda would stay and watch the baby and she would go to the market and she wanted me to go back to bed. I said could I lay here on the couch? She said o.k.

But you must lay down...get well first then go running around... you are sick now because you wouldn't listen to me. She said Linda go up stairs and get a pillow and blanket for Vicky. Before I could lie down Rebecca started crying. I picked her up and Linda said she just ate and I changed her diaper; she better not be hungry again. I said she just want her Mother to hold her. She stopped crying. Sister Linda said if she is not crying put her down so you can lay down before Mother come back and get mad at me...Mother was really mad when you went out yesterday after just coming from the Hospital. I said my head and stitches are hurting. She said I am sorry you are hurting, but you need to lie down before Mother comes back. We looked at Rebecca and started talking about who she looked like. I said she looks like me. Linda said now she does, but she is going to have a big nose like Brother Wilson; her face will look like yours. I said it is good she looks like both of us. Sister Linda said yes, half you and half Brother Wilson. I said Linda did Wilson come and tell you that I had a baby girl before he go and stay on his Boat? Linda said Vicky Brother Wilson came home every night you were in the Hospital. Most of the time he was drunk but he came home. Sometimes his friend came with him and Mother would tell them no more foolish dog, no beer, no good. His friend wouldn't come inside they would bring Wilson home and drop him off at the door. Mother and I had to help Wilson upstairs sometimes. I think he got drunk because he missed you a lot. I said thanks for telling me that about him; I guess he forgot to tell me he changed his mind about staying on his Boat. Linda said if he is out in town the apartment is closer than his Boat…I better clean the kitchen so when Mother get back from the market I can leave right away for Calapacuan to get the Guava Leaves. I said I better lay down before Wilson or Mother walk in and catch me setting up. Before I could get my pillow arranged Wilson walk in the door with a case of Similac milk and a box of diapers. He had a bag with a pacifier, a small baby toy and M and M candy for me. I said thank you Sweetheart for the candy. He kissed me and bended over the basinet looking at our baby. He said she is sleeping very well in her basinet. I said yes that why I want to lay here on the couch and watch her. He said o.k. As long as you are comfortable here; he sat down in a chair across from me and said the baby milk is very expensive if you by one can at a time it is cheaper to buy a whole case. I said do we have enough money to buy everything our baby need.

He said we have money don't worry about that, just worry about getting strong…I am real happy you and the baby is at home. Sister Linda came in the living room and said I am going to the store to buy ice and coke. Wilson said bring me some beer too; he got up and gave her money for the beer. When she came back from the store I asked her about Mother because she should have been back. She said you are right because she left right after Brother Wilson left to go to the base and he is back already. Wilson said is Inay gone? I said she left for the market right after you left and she is not back yet. I said what time is it? Wilson said it is almost eleven o, clock. Then the door open and Mother came in with two big bags of food. Mother said I got Guava leaves for your bath. I said you went to Calapacuan and the market too; that why it took so long for you to come back. Wilson said what is going on? I said Mother went to Calapacuan that is the reason it took her so long to come back. He said what is she going to do with Guava leaves? I said she would boil the leaves and I would set in the water and soak my stitches. Mother said I am going to cook Wilson some adobo chicken for lunch. Wilson said what Inay said about me. I said she told me she was cooking you some adobo chicken for lunch...if you hear your name when my family is speaking Tagalog it is always something good about you nothing bad, so don't worry yourself. He said I thought she was telling you about me coming home drunk. I said I know all about it don't worry I am not mad because I know you drink...stop being paranoid when you hear someone speaks your name. Mother said lets eat lunch... Linda fix Wilson plate. I said I would hold the baby while Linda fixes Wilson plate. Mother said why are you insisting on doing something? Linda and I will fix the plates and take care of the baby...you set up and eat...that is all you need to do. Linda put the baby in the basinet beside the couch and they brought Wilson and my plate so we could eat together. I asked Linda if she would bring me a glass of cold coke. Mother said you could have coke but no ice...we don't know whether you caught cold or not so it best to be careful. After lunch Wilson told Mother he really enjoyed the adobo. She said o.k. And got busy in the kitchen preparing the Guava leaves so I could soak my stitches. When Mother had everything ready I went into the bathroom to soak my stitches. Finally Mother said you have soaked long enough, so she helped me take a shower. When I finished I went upstairs to use the lamp to dry my stitches.

Wilson helped me to get the lamp set up. I asked him if he wanted to see my stitches. He looked and said he was sorry they had to cut me when I had the baby. He said it would be quite a while before we could have another baby, but I do want to have a boy so he can carry the Wilson name...I guess the way you are feeling now you don't want to talk about having another baby. I said it is o.k. Maybe when Rebecca starts walking and talking we could have another baby. Wilson said yes as he kissed me. We heard Rebecca start crying. I started to get up and go downstairs to check on her. Wilson said no! You stay in bed your Mother and Linda would take care of her. You need to take it east so my Sweetheart can get well soon...we need you...I want you to be strong for the baby and me. I said o.k. and I lay back down; I said Sweetheart I am going to take a nap for a while the medicine is making me sleepy. Around three that afternoon I started having pain and woke up. Wilson was sleeping beside me. I got up and went downstairs for water to take my medicine. Mother said where are you going? I said I came to get water so I could take my medicine. She said what happened to Wilson? I said he is sleep and I didn't want to wake him. I took my medicine and looked at Rebecca sleeping. I decided to set for a while in the living room with Mother. I said where is Linda. Mother said she is upstairs studying. I said that good she is studying while the baby is sleep, tomorrow when she go to school she won't have to rush to study before she leaves. Pretty soon I will be able to take care of the baby; I am just having pain once in a while now. Mother said you are lucky you have pain medicine to take when you are hurting; most of the women here in the Philippines can't afford anything but aspirin...just like me all my kids were delivered by a Midwife even premature birth like you...with God help you all made it in this world without a Doctor or medicine...just a few good neighbors to help me get well and you get strong...I even thought for a while maybe you wouldn't make it, but you were strong and wanted to drink milk every hour and sometimes less than an hour. When you wanted to eat all of the time I knew then you would make it. I said do you think Rebecca is all right she always sleeping. Mother said if she isn't hungry or wet she would be sleeping all of the time...remember the only time a baby cry is when it is wet, hungry and maybe her Angel make her cry or she is dreaming...after you feed her always make her burp. I said yes that was the first thing they told me to do in the Hospital. Mother said Rebecca is twice the size you was when you was a baby; that's why you were my miracle baby...everybody was waiting for you to die they didn't think you was going to make it, but God had a different ideal, he wanted you to grow up and have a baby to love just like me.

Wilson came downstairs looking for me. He said why are you downstairs? I said I had to get water to take my medicine. He said

Sweetheart you could have woke me up. I said you were sleeping so good I didn't want to wake you. Mother said I think I will lie down for a while if you are going to watch Rebecca until Linda come downstairs. I said go ahead Mother Wilson and I are here. When Wilson sat down beside me he said you look much better than you did yesterday. I said after I soaked my stitches and took a hot shower I feel much better. He said I am sorry I didn't know you were hurting and sick; I thought you was all right...I didn't know about the stitches either...I was only thinking about taking you out for a while because you had been in the Hospital cooped up. I said don't worry about it; I was trying to please you too that why I didn't say no, I have learned my lesson even though it was the hard way. Next time I will listen to Mother. Sister Linda came downstairs and said I am through with my homework you can go upstairs and lie down. I said I don't want to lie down right now I would set here on the couch and watch Rebecca while she sleep; would you go to the store and get your Brother some beer? She said yes and left for the store. Wilson said thank you Sweetheart I was just getting ready to ask her myself. Rebecca started to cry so I took her up and prepared to change her diaper. After I changed her diaper she kept crying. Wilson asked me what did I want him to do. I told him to go in the kitchen and get the baby milk. He went and got the milk and I started feeding her. Wilson was laughing at Rebecca, because she was sucking the bottle real fast as if she was very, very hungry. He said drink all of the milk you want and Daddy will get you some more. Sister Linda came back from the store and gave Wilson one of the beers and took the rest in the kitchen. She washed her hands and came over to me and asked me if I wanted her to feed the baby. I told her I would finish feeding her. When I finished feeding the baby I tried to make her burp. Wilson said let me do it. I gave him the baby and went to the bathroom; when I came back he said the baby burp already. I said o.k. Now put her back in the basinet. Right after he put her in the basinet she went to sleep. He told me to lie down on the couch and put my head in his lap. He seems to be very happy sipping his beer and playing with my hair; every once in a while he would look over in the basinet at Rebecca. I said to myself... this is just like heaven being here with my Husband and baby girl... if Wilson stayed sober we could be the happiest family in the world.

Wilson said what are you thinking about?   I said I am thinking of you and the baby; I have you both right here with me. He said I am the happiest man on earth to have you and the baby and your love. He said what is that red on the baby cheek. I said I don't know I will ask Mother when she wakes up. I was about to go to sleep when I heard Mother and Linda coming downstairs. I heard Mother leave to go to the store and buy an onion for the Mongo Beans. I set up and asked Mother to come see the red on the baby cheek. She looked at the baby and told me to tell Wilson to stop kissing the baby when he is unshaven because that is what irritating the baby skin causing it to turn red. I told Wilson what Mother said. He said I would stop kissing her cheek and kiss her hand. I said you still should shave, just in case you forget. He said I promise I will shave before I kiss our baby. Mother said no kissing, no kissing Wilson. I guess Linda told Mother what to say in English to Wilson; don't kiss the baby. After dinner Mother showed me how to give the baby a bath, because she was only staying until Friday. When I went upstairs to be with Wilson; he asked me what I was doing. I told him Mother was showing me how to give Rebecca a bath, because she have to go home Friday to catch up on the washing she have been taking in. He said are you ready to take care of her now? I said I am ready now, but Mother wants me to get stronger before she leaves me alone. Wilson said who is going to wash our clothes? I said Auntie is coming once a week. He said tell her I will pay her. He said Larry our next-door neighbor is moving pretty soon we can get their Maid. I said o.k. When they leave I will get Luz their Maid, but for now Auntie could do the washing for a while. He started caressing and kissing me. I said Sweetheart we have at least three more weeks before we can make love…do you remember the stitches I showed you? He said I am sorry Sweetheart sometimes I forget. He held me as we drifted off to sleep. Friday didn't take very long to come and Mother was getting ready to leave. She went over everything she could think to tell and show me about the baby. She showed me how to take care of the baby belly button too. I was feeling real strong I could do everything I normally do around the house. Mother told me Auntie was coming that Monday to wash and help out around the house. I gave Mother some money for her and Brother Etong. She said if you have any problem just send

Linda to get me. She said goodbye to her Grand Daughter. She told Linda and me to take care of her Grand Baby.

When she left I was a little frightened because even though she showed me how to take care of Rebecca I still felt a little unsure. The first time the baby cried after Mother left; I said I can do this, I checked her diaper to see if she was wet. She was wet so I changed it and put her back in the basinet; she kept crying so I told Linda to get me her milk. I gave her the milk and she started sucking the bottle real fast and Sister Linda started laughing at her sucking like that. She said don't forget to burp her. When she finished sucking I put her against my shoulder and burped her. Linda said you look like you have been doing this all of the time. I held her until she fell asleep; then I put her in her basinet. Linda started cooking lunch; she said now we have to cook I miss Mother good cooking already I even gained a few pounds. I said we have been spoiled for two weeks; we should be thankful that we have her. She needs to go home Brother Etong needs her too. When we finished eating we cleaned the kitchen and sterilized the baby bottle. Sister Linda said Vicky why don't you go and rest a while I will finish up here in the kitchen. I went into the living room and sat down on the couch and turned on the TV. I said if I go to sleep wake me if you hear the baby cry or before you leave to go to school. I got a little sleepy watching TV so I lay down and went to sleep. I slept for a while then I heard Rebecca cry so I got up and changed her diaper and gave her some milk. Sister Linda came downstairs on her way to school. She said I heard Rebecca cry and started downstairs to wake you but you were awake already. I said goodbye to Linda; I walked her out the door with Rebecca. Right after we got outside it started to rain and I took Rebecca back in the house. After I burp Rebecca I laid her in the basinet and she went to sleep. I ran upstairs to straighten up my face before Wilson comes home. As I brushed my hair I said to myself...my hair is too long I have problem trying to manage it...I really need to cut it...Wilson don't want me to cut it, but it is still very hard to manage; I am going to have to do something about it. I rushed back downstairs to set by Rebecca's basinet; she was moving around maybe she is dreaming or her Angel is trying to make her cry. I started thinking...Wilson use to be at home about this time, but they change his work hours while

I was in the Hospital, now he has to work until five o, clock. If I didn't have Rebecca I would be lonely, because Linda went to school and Mother went home. It is rainy season now and it is raining now. We will probably have a problem drying the baby clothes; I guess we will have to put up a cloth line in Linda's room so we can dry the baby clothes. I looked in Rebecca's basinet she was still sleeping and enjoying the cool breeze that the rain brought on. I would like to curl up with someone and enjoy this cool breeze too. I had better stop thinking about making love or doing anything for the next two weeks. Suddenly the front door opened and Wilson stood in it dripping wet. I went to the bathroom and got his towel to help him dry off. I told him to go upstairs and change his shirt. He kissed me and looked at Rebecca before he went upstairs. After he changed his clothing he hurried back downstairs. I asked him what happened to his umbrella. He said I forgot to carry it. I said you better start carrying it. He said I think I will go to the Navy Exchange tomorrow and look for a raincoat. I said remind me to give you a list of the things we need from the Exchange. He said did your Mother leave already? I said yes, after she showed me how to take care of the baby. He said you really need a Maid. I said it is o.k. I can take care of my baby; she sleeps all of the time anyway. He said you still need someone to help you when Linda goes to school. I said Sweetheart I need to get use to doing this without anyone help. Can we afford a Maid in America? He said no we cannot, but you can have one here. I said well Larry and Pat are leaving very soon and I have told their Maid I wanted her when they leave. He said o.k. That is good, because you need time for yourself and for me too. I said I will always have time for you. He said I almost forgot to tell you that I made First Class Petty Officer; I am just waiting for the promotion date. I said what does that mean? He said that means more money for us and I can buy furniture for our living room and more clothes for you and the baby. The month of August was over along with the rainy season. It rains a little in September but nothing like July and August. My first appointment with the Doctor after the baby was born finally came and Wilson went with us. The Doctor examined the baby and me; he said we were doing all right. I said does that mean I can start having sex? He said you mean you haven't yet? I said no! He said you can start now, but use some protection because the baby is not even a year old yet...tell your Husband to use condom. I said thank you Doctor. When we came out in the waiting room to meet Wilson he met me and took the baby. He said what the Doctor said. I said the Doctor said we can make love but we have to use protection. He said tell you to buy condom in the Exchange. I said what is this condom the Doctor is talking about...how do we use it so I won't get pregnant? He said I am the one that use it; I will show it to you tonight...we need to go to the Exchange before we go home. He looked around and found the condom and I bought diaper and some more stuff we needed. Wilson gave me Rebecca so he could carry all of our bags; that when I realized Rebecca was putting on some weight. When we got home I changed Rebecca diaper, clothes and fed her. I told Linda to watch her for a while so I could go upstairs with Wilson to see what he had to show me. Wilson and I went upstairs and he showed me the condom. I said so that what the Doctor was talking about. He said we would try it tonight when the baby goes to sleep. We went back downstairs and Wilson asked Linda to go to the store for beer. While she was gone Wilson started caressing and kissing me. I said you better stop Linda haven't left for school yet. When Linda returned she gave Wilson one of the beers and put the other one in the kitchen on ice. She came back and asked me what I wanted her to start cooking for lunch. I said how you would like to go to the Shangri La Restaurant and get two big orders of noodles. She said o.k. I said Sweetheart do you want to eat noodles too. Wilson said yes that would be fine. I gave her the money for the food and she left. Wilson said Sweetheart the baby is asleep and Linda is gone; could we go upstairs and try out my new condoms. Wilson grabs the baby basinet and took it and the baby upstairs and put it in Linda's room and came back to me in our room. We made love like it would be another month before we could do it again. I asked Wilson how did the condom work he said he didn't have a problem with it. We had our little electric fan working overtime to give us a cool down so we could go back downstairs before Sister Linda Returned. Wilson said thank you Sweetheart. I said why are you thinking me I liked it as much as you did. When we cooled down, we got up and got the baby and went back downstairs. We got comfortable on the couch in the living room.

Wilson said when do you think we should have our baby baptized? I said how about when she turns three months old. I said I want to barbecue a whole pig. He said I will give you the money and you can get what we need. I said o.k. When Sister Linda came back from the restaurant with the food she took it in the kitchen to fix our plates. I got up and went in and told her I would fix Wilson and my plate. She said two big orders is a lot of noodles. I said I would have leftover for my dinner and when she came back from school stop by a barbecue stand and get her something. She said I cooked rice earlier today; I will open a can of sardine to eat with it that will be my dinner. I said o.k. whatever you want. Rebecca started crying and Wilson said good timing baby; I guess it is your lunchtime too. I stood up to get the baby and Wilson said finish your lunch I will take care of the baby. He fed the baby and burped her too, but the baby kept crying. I said maybe she is wet. He said don't worry I can change the diaper; where are the diapers? I gave him a cloth diaper. He looked at it and said what happened to the diapers we bought? I said we use them at night; if we use them at daytime we would use a lot of pampers. Wilson said you are going to be washing all of the time. I said that no problem. He kept fumbling around with the diaper; I got up and showed him how to use the cloth diaper. He said it didn't take you long at all. I said Mother taught me how to do everything for our baby. He said now I know what to do if she cries; he held her for a while and the baby went to sleep. He said Sweetheart our baby is sleep again. Linda said Brother Wilson know how to put the baby to sleep. He put the baby back in her basinet. He looked so proud, happy and relaxed. I hope he stays this way. He sat down on the couch beside me and said pretty soon I will have to start work on the paperwork for you and the baby to go to the States with me; it takes about one to two months to process the paperwork.

October nineteen sixty-nine Larry and Pat move away and we got their Maid Luz. Luz would be a live-in Maid so she shared a bedroom with Sister Linda. I showed her what to do to take care of Rebecca because that was the main reason Wilson wanted a Maid. I taught her everything Mother taught me about babies. She was to take care of the baby most of the time when Wilson was at home especially at night. When Wilson went to work I would take care of my baby because I wanted to spend time with my baby so she would get use to being with me too. Everybody in the apartment complex fell in love with my baby they wanted to hold her. Luz would take her outside during the day and everyone was just crazy about her. Wilson didn't like the baby being away when he came home, so I told Luz to make sure she bring the baby back in the apartment before Wilson came home.

Finally we decided to have the baby baptized and CB and Jean would be her Godfather and Godmother. I told Mother and Brother Celino and Mother said just give us the money for the pig and charcoal and tell us the date and we will do the rest. I invited the neighbors and everyone wanted to bring something. One afternoon Rebecca started vomiting every time she drinks her milk she would vomit. I asked Luz who was the last person she let hold the baby. She told me it was the lady living in the apartment down from us. I told her to take the baby back to the lady apartment and have her to make a cross sign on the baby stomach. When she came back I told her don't take the baby there anymore, because sometimes people can hurt a baby and never know it. After that Rebecca stopped vomiting and went to sleep. That night around six o, clock Wilson came home in his uniform; I was a little surprised because he had been drinking already. I said why you are in uniform; I didn't notice that his stripes had changed. He said Sweetheart this is my surprise for you this is my promotion day to first class petty officer. I have been waiting for a whole month to wear my uniform. I said now you are a first class petty officer. I gave him a kiss. I just wanted to come and tell you first; I want to meet some friends that got promoted and celebrate. He kissed me and left. I said to myself…wait a minute I am his wife and he didn't ask me to go with him to celebrate…he is acting like he just arrived here on a ship wearing his uniform…what is he trying to do…impress some girl that he is a first class petty officer? I just sat there and watch TV and waited for him to come home. Then I heard Rebecca crying; I went upstairs to see what was wrong. Luz said I am changing her diaper, but she is still crying. I went and got her milk so Luz could feed her, when I got the milk I took her and fed her but she kept crying, I told Luz to warm some water I wanted to give the baby a sponge bath. I gave her a nice bath and she stopped crying and went to sleep. I told Luz not to put to many clothes on her because she was very hot; just put a baby shirt on her with her diaper. Luz said I am going to sleep so I want be too sleepy when it time to feed her again. I told Luz if you need me just knock on my bedroom door anytime. I went downstairs and I saw Sister Linda coming in the door. I said you are early tonight. She said they let us out early tonight the Teachers have a meeting tonight. I said this late at night they have meetings? She said yes the Teacher that teach night classes have to have meetings too…where is Luz and Rebecca?

I said upstairs sleeping. She said it is only eight-thirty. Linda started upstairs. I said try not to make noise Rebecca has been fussy tonight; I had a hard time putting her to sleep. I had to give her a sponge bath before she would go to sleep. I sat and watch TV while waiting for Wilson to come home. Linda came back downstairs to get her something to eat. She said Brother Wilson is not home yet. I said no he is out celebrating; he made First Class. She said is Brother Wilson a First Class already. I said yes. Well being a First Class Petty Officer didn't change Wilson way of thinking; he still drinks a lot. We went out once in a while to the movies, but he stopped taking me out to the clubs. I really don't know why. He started back stopping and drinking before he come home; sometimes I am in the bed when he get home and when he comes to bed I would act like I am sleep so he would let me alone.

One Sunday morning I was feeding the baby and she kept spitting up the milk. Wilson said I think she need to see the Doctor…take her to the Hospital tomorrow morning and let the Doctor see her. After Wilson left for work the next morning Luz and I got ready and took Rebecca to the Base Hospital. We waited for a while because we didn't have an appointment. Finally we saw the Doctor and he examined her for marks and bruises. Then after further examination he told me we would have to change her milk. He recommended changing to carnation milk mixed half and half with water. He said try that for a couple of days and if she continues to vomit bring her back, but if she stop don't bring her back until her regular appointment. Luz and I were very happy that was the only thing wrong with the baby. We went home and I told Linda to go to the market and get a case of carnation milk in small cans, because we don't have a refrigerator to keep it if we get a big can. Wilson came home early and wanted to know what the Doctor says about the baby. I told him the Doctor wanted us to change the baby milk; he wanted us to give her carnation milk. We have to mix it half milk and half water. It will take one can of milk every time we feed her because we don't have a refrigerator to keep the left over. What do you think we should do? He said we have to buy a refrigerator for the baby milk. I said we don't have that kind of money do we? He said don't worry, I plan to buy one anyway; I will get it now instead of later. Wilson bought a refrigerator the next day and had it delivered. He came home and turned it on. We were very happy to have a refrigerator because it helped us in more way than one.

Rebecca liked the carnation milk and with the refrigerator we could mix as much milk as we wanted. We set the date for Rebecca baptism and the Godparents bought the baby clothes for the ceremony. We went to the church that Sunday and when we got there I had to go to the bathroom and I told them to take the baby and go ahead to see the priest and I would catch up later, but by the time I came out of the bathroom they was finished with the ceremony. We went home and Mother and my Brother had all the food prepared and the neighbors brought their present and what they promised to cook. Everyone really enjoyed the food and drinks especially Wilson because he got drunk before everyone left. I let him sleep it off on the couch until bedtime. Linda and I helped him upstairs to the bedroom. He got undress and got into the bed. I put my nightgown on and got into bed too. He put his arm around me and went to sleep.

After the baby's christening we bought a new living room set and a bar; both of them was made from rattan wood. We returned Sister Melda's living room set to Mother house in Calapacuan. We started back going to the movies; every time a new movie came out we watched it.

One day Wilson wanted to eat Chittling and the only place in town that served them was Old Toby Club. We went to the club and Wilson took something to the Owner so we went back to his office. He introduced me to the Owner of the club and asked if the Chittling was cooked already He told Wilson that they would be ready in about thirty minutes. We sat in his office for a while, while they talked business. Then Wilson had to use the bathroom and he left me in the office of the club Owner. The club Owner closed the door to his office and asked me why I married Wilson knowing he drink too much and run around with the girls in the clubs? He said I was too young to be with a guy like that; he drinks too much. I didn't say a thing I just sat and listen to what he was saying. When Wilson came back he told Wilson he was telling his old lady that he wasn't any good. Wilson said you better stop telling my old lady that; you know I am a good man. Finally a guy came to the door and told the Owner the Chittling was done. We went to a table and ordered the food every girl passed by the table said hello to Wilson. I asked him who

Chapter 8
Planning Our Move to the USA

The first girl was. He said that is the Owner wife. The girls kept coming and I didn't ask again. I said to myself...that why he doesn't want to take me nightclubbing. When we finished eating and were on our way out of the club; the Owner said you better keep an eye on Wilson. Wilson said man stop telling my wife stuff like that. We walked home down Rizal Avenue where all of the clubs were located. Every club we passed and some of the hostess standing in the door would say hi to Wilson. I said to myself...Wilson must think I am stupid; these girls are his girlfriend if they was not they wouldn't be speaking to him like they are. When we got home Luz and the baby was sleep already and we went straight upstairs to our bedroom. Wilson started taking off his shoes and dropped one. I said be quiet you will wake the baby. Then we heard the door downstairs close I said that is Linda coming home from school. He said lets go to sleep. Around two in the morning I heard Rebecca crying very loud and I got up and went into Linda's room to see what was wrong with her. I said why is the baby crying like that. Luz said I guess she want her bottle; I am changing her diaper now. I took the baby and told Luz to go downstairs and get the baby's milk. When Luz came back with the bottle I took it and fed my baby and finally she went to sleep. When I went back to my bedroom Wilson was awake and he asked what was wrong with the baby. I said she just want to fuss a little. He said you better go back to sleep, Rebecca will be all right.

In February Sister Melda and Brother Smitty came to Calapacuan to visit Mother and before Sister Melda left to go back to Sangley Point she stopped by our apartment. Sister Melda and Sister Linda talked about something. When they stopped talking Sister Melda asked Wilson why he wasn't giving Linda money to go to school. I was upstairs changing the baby diaper. When I came downstairs and Wilson told me what was going on I was really surprised, because I knew Wilson and I were giving her money to go to school. Sister Linda went upstairs and pack her clothes and left with Sister Melda. Wilson was very upset and he said It was hard believe to Linda told Melda that I didn't give her money to go to school. I said I would find out one of these days the real reason Sister Linda was leaving. I think Sister Melda is jealous of me having a Husband that is a First Class Petty Officer the same as her Husband; I guess she think if she takes Linda from us it would somehow hurt me and cause trouble in my family. I know for a fact that Wilson on more than one occasion told Sister Linda whenever she need money for her schooling to come to him and he would be happy to give it to her; how she tricked Linda to say that is beyond anything I can think of. Wilson said I am sorry Sweetheart you Sister Linda told a story like that…I guess Melda got to her.

After Linda left we moved on because we had a Maid to help me with Rebecca and Auntie came and visited and help out. December came and Brother Celino Wife finally had a baby girl and they were very happy because she was their firstborn. When Wilson got promoted he was also transferred to another Boat and he ended up working longer hours; when he come home he would be tired and sometimes he would stop and drink before he got home. Our lovemaking slowed down a lot I think it is because he has to wear protection at least I hope that is the reason. Sometimes he looks at me as if something is wrong with me; I still try my best to make myself appealing to him. I still have my long hair, but I wish I could cut it to shoulder length, but he said don't cut it because that's his hair. I really don't know what to do right now to help or control him. One weekend after CB and Jean moved on base they invited us to their house. We went and took Rebecca; their kids really like her and wanted to hold her, but their Mother wouldn't let them. I was sitting on the other side of the room with Jean but I could hear CB and Wilson talking about a passport photo. Jean heard what they were saying and told Wilson he needs to get a separate photo for Rebecca and me. Wilson told me to go to the Navy Exchange Photo Shop and get some passport photo made of Rebecca and me. I said o.k. I would go tomorrow. Jean asked me to go in the kitchen with her because she had to check on the food she was cooking. Rebecca was sleeping so I told Wilson to keep an eye on her I was going in the kitchen. He said o.k. I will, but he started drinking with CB. When we got in the kitchen I asked Jean how did she like living on base. She said I love it, because everything is very close to us…the School, the Mini Mart and Swimming pool; the Commissary and Exchange is just down the hill two miles away. I said that good everything is very close to you. She said I really like it here the neighbor are quiet not like when we lived out in town with too much noise…the jeepney and neighbors. Rebecca started crying and Wilson called me he didn't try to check and see if she was wet he just kept drinking with CB. I came and got my baby and gave her the bottle of milk; she stops crying. I told Wilson we better go because it is getting dark, but what I really mint was before he got drunk. I don't know if he understood what I was trying to say or not, but he agreed to go home and that what I wanted. As we left to go to the bus stop CB kept trying to explain to Wilson how the buses run. Wilson kept telling him this wasn't the first time he rode the bus. When we got home Rebecca was still asleep. When we came in with Rebecca Luz asked me if I wanted her to take Rebecca upstairs; I said yes you carry the basinet and I will follow you. When we got to her room she put the basinet down and I put Rebecca in it. I came back downstairs to find out what Wilson and CB had been talking about at his house. I said what about the pictures I am suppose to take tomorrow. He said go to the Photo Shot and asks them to take some passport photo for you and the baby…take Luz with you.

The next morning before he left for work he said don't forget to get your passport photo made today. I said o.k. I would go to the shop right after I have my breakfast. After breakfast I dressed Rebecca and put a little hat on that match her outfit; Luz and I left for the photo shop. When we arrived the guy took the pictures and he didn't say anything about her hat. Luz and I left and went back home. When

Wilson came home from work I showed him the pictures and he said they were cute. He said lets go by CB house tonight…leave the baby with Luz. When we got there Wilson showed CB the passport pictures and CB asked me why I put a hat on the baby's head… was I ashamed to show her hair? Jean said she could dress her baby anyway she like. He said she is covering the baby head so you can't tell she is black. I said I am not ashamed of the way my baby looks, I love her. Wilson didn't say a word to try and defend me. CB kept rattling alone, but I ignored him. Around ten Wilson asked CB to call a taxi for us. When we got the taxi and was on our way home I asked Wilson what CB means when he says I am ashamed to have a black baby? He said don't worry about what CB said just get another photo of Rebecca made tomorrow. I said to myself…I don't know what going on with Wilson…if he let somebody talk to me like this…would he do the same in America…what am I going to do if he mistreat me in America? He said what are you thinking about? I said if I go to the States with you and you keep drinking too much; what is going to happen to Rebecca and me? He said don't worry I will take care of you even if I drink. I said that what you say; how about right now…you act like you don't have time for the baby and me. He said things are going to change pretty soon right now I am working a lot of hours.

He kissed me hoping to shut me up. I said if you are working too many hours how do you have time to drink before you come home?   He said sometimes I meet a few friends and they ask me to go and have a beer with them. I didn't respond because I knew this conversation was not going anywhere. We got out of the taxi and went through the main gate. I kept walking ahead of him and he said hey wait for me. He caught up and took my hand and we walked across the bridge to the jeepney stop. We caught a jeepney and a guy was riding with us; he said he was a (PC) Police Constabulary. He asked me which club I worked in; I said what do you mean? He said you are with an American, what club do you work at; I said I don't work in the club this is my Husband. Wilson said what is he talking about? Then the PC stopped the jeepney and got out and left. The jeepney driver said the PC is trying to make some money that why he asked you where you work. He knew you were young so he figured he could scare you and the American would pay him to let you go. When we got to our apartment I told Wilson what the PC asked me. Wilson said my police friend told me to make sure I kept my outer bound pass in my pocket when we were dating, because if they catch me with a girl that don't work in a club they would fine me two hundred pesos. I said I didn't know that; he said don't worry about it we're married now. We went upstairs to our bedroom I didn't see a light in Luz room so I knew her and the baby were asleep. When we got in our bedroom and started undressing for bed; Wilson said come here. I said what do you want? He started kissing me on my neck and the next thing I knew I was on the bed; we made love very quietly because we didn't want to wake the baby in the next room. Wilson started a period of coming straight home and if he wanted a cold beer he would get one from our refrigerator. We knew it wouldn't be long before we leave the Philippines and go to the United States. Wilson suggested to me about trying to get our family together especially the one that had a new baby that was born the same year as Rebecca to take a family portrait. I liked the ideal and contacted everyone; I told them we liked for them come to our apartment to take a family portrait and have lunch afterward. Everyone except Auntie and Brother Etong, Auntie had to finish the washing she had took in and Brother Etong had to stay and watch the house in Calapacuan. The list of participant was Brother Celino, His wife Rose, their new baby Gloria, Sister Rose, her new baby Robert, Gina, Sister Maria, Enyang and her new baby boy, Mother, Sister Linda, Luz the Maid, Wilson, Rebecca and Me. After the photo and lunch we all set around and talked for a while, because everyone knew I would be leaving very soon. Finally everyone started to go home because it was getting dark. I gave Mother some money to help her and Brother Etong. Wilson said the picture would be ready in a few days. After everyone left Wilson and I sat in the living room and talked about some of the things we had to do to get ready for our move to the States. Wilson said next month we would go to Manila and get Rebecca and my passport. I said o.k. It looks like we really going to leave. The next week Luz and I took Rebecca to the Hospital for her check up. When we got there I saw a long time friend setting on the steps leading into the Hospital with her Husband. She said you have a baby and stood up to see Rebecca;

she said your baby is real cute. I said thank you. I didn't think for a second about people making other people sick in the Philippines; I had really tried to erase that from my way of thinking. We went in and saw the Doctor and he said your baby is doing fine and have gained some weight; he said the carnation milk really helped her. When we were leaving the Hospital my friend was still setting on the steps with her Husband. Her Husband had inpatient clothing on so he must be sick and she is visiting him. When we came down the steps she stood up again to see and touch Rebecca. We left and went to the bus stop and caught a bus to the Main Gate. While we were on our way I noticed Rebecca not moving around at all; I shook her but she didn't respond. We got off of the bus at the next stop and caught a taxi back to the Hospital. The first thing that came to my mind... my friend had done something to hurt my baby and didn't know it...maybe she did it to her Husband and that the reason he is sick. When we got to the Hospital she was still sitting on the steps with her Husband. I went up to her and told her she had made my baby sick; Before I could tell her what to do, she put some spit on her finger and made a cross on my baby forehead and stomach. She said I know I make people sick sometimes. I said maybe you are the one making your Husband sick; you better take care of him when he gets back to his room. After she made the cross on Rebecca head and stomach Rebecca started moving as if nothing happened. Luz said could you do the same to me because I don't know where you live? She said yes and did it to Luz and me. After that we hurried over to the bus stop because we wanted to get away from her. When the bus came and we was on our way to the Main Gate; Luz said she has strong power to hurt peoples...why does she do it? I said I don't know but I thank God she was still outside when we got back to the Hospital, because I don't know where she live either...the first time I met her I was working in the Money Exchange Booth in front of the Jet Club and she worked there. When she got married I didn't see her anymore until today. Luz said why did she hurt your baby if she knows you? I said I don't know some people are evil you never know what they have on their minds. Luz said we had a lady like that in our Barrio and she did it to the wrong person and that person reversed it on her. I said yes it is hard to explain everything that happens around us, but

I am glad my baby is all right. I looked at her she was wide-awake and trying to pull my hair. I shook Rebecca again to make sure she was all right and she started crying real loud. I hurried to give her bottle to stop her from crying as Luz and I laughed. I told Luz I had to see Mother so she could make some type of protection for my baby, because you never know what can happen these days. Luz said I bet she is the one making her Husband sick. I said I agree with you, I feel sorry for the man she married, but I am sure God watch over him and protect him like my baby.

When we arrive home I told Luz not to take my baby next door until I got some protection for her. She said o.k. I will keep her inside of our apartment. When Wilson came home and asked how the baby's appointment go; I told him the appointment went well. Then I told him what happened to the baby when the girl touched her. He didn't believe me; he said maybe the baby was tired and sleepy. I didn't argue with him about it because he is from America…I don't know if they have witches and witch doctors there…I just left it alone…I didn't speak very good English and it was hard to explain. The next day when Auntie came to wash I told her to tell Mother what happened and so she could get some protection for my baby…she is too little to get sick and I don't know what makes her sick. Auntie said do you mean to say that they have people here in the city like that…I thought they were only in the Barrio. I said look like they have moved from the Barrio to the city. She said well I would tell your Mother I know she will be mad again…why someone would want to do something like that to a baby. Then she started washing the clothes. When Luz came back from the market the girl that made Rebecca sick stopped her to talk about something. Luz told me she asked why I stopped bringing the baby outside. I said did you tell her there were evil people outside that like to hurt little babies. She said no! I told her you don't want me to take Rebecca outside. I told Luz to start cooking and I was going to give Rebecca a bath. When I gave her the bath she liked to splash in the bath water; Rebecca was continuing to gain weight, you could tell because her little face got fat and round. When I finished bathing her; I gave her some milk and she went to sleep. Luz came over and tried to kiss Rebecca. I told her she better wash her hand. She said yes that's right I forgot I was cleaning fish. Auntie came inside and got some water; she told me she was almost through washing and asked me if I wanted her to cook the vegetables. I said yes. I knew Auntie cook real good vegetable like Mother does, so I couldn't wait to taste the vegetables when she finishes cooking. When I finished feeding and burping Rebecca; I lie on the couch and put her head on my chest and she went to sleep. When Auntie finished washing and came inside she said why don't you get a walker for Rebecca she has strong legs and they have some made small enough for her. I told her I would tell Rebecca's Father about it. After we finished lunch; Auntie asked me why Wilson dungaree pants were so hard to iron. I told her it wasn't that hard because I have ironed them before. I said did you put the dungaree in the boiling starch? She said yes! When I finish ironing them they will be stiff enough to stand by itself...why does Wilson like a lot of starch in his dungaree? I said he like to wear them more than one day and the starch keep them looking good after one or two days wearing. When the clothes dried Auntie started ironing; when she finished ironing one of Wilson dungaree pants she show it to me; I said you have to iron his dungaree on the wrong side and it want be as hard to iron. She said I forgot you told me that once before. When she finished ironing I gave her money for the jeepney and I pay her once a month for washing and ironing so she won't spend it because she is saving to go to Manila to visit her kids. When Wilson came home I asked him if they have a baby walker in the Navy Exchange. He said they should have some. I said could we go and buy one for Rebecca? He said yes we would go Saturday. I said Auntie said they have baby walker in the market too. He said o.k. We would check there too. After we finished dinner, Luz washed the dishes and cleaned the kitchen and was on her way into the living room to watch TV. Someone knocked on the door and Luz went to answer it. She talked to someone outside for a brief moment. Finally the person left and Luz came to me and told me the person that was at the door was her cousin. Her cousin came to get her, because her Mother was very sick. Luz wanted to get one-month advance pay before she went home. I told Wilson what she said. Wilson said he didn't have enough money on him to give her one-month pay, but if she waited until tomorrow he would go to the bank and get some more money and give it to her, but today he only have enough for two-week pay. She said she would take that because her cousin was waiting for her at the Victory Liner Bus terminal. We gave her two-week advance pay and she left. Wilson said now we can't go to the movie; I had planned to take you to the movie tonight...I guess we have to wait until she comes back. Rebecca started crying and I checked her diaper and it was wet; I told Wilson to go upstairs to Luz room and get a pamper diaper. I gave Rebecca a quick sponge bath and put her pamper on. Wilson took her on his lap. She kept playing with her rattler; shaking it in Wilson face. He said what time does Rebecca goes to sleep? I said she goes to sleep when she get ready...Luz plays with her until she goes to sleep. We played with her until she finally went to sleep. I told Wilson to bring her basinet into our room. He said no let her stay in Luz room we can keep the door open. I said I want to put her in our room. He said he couldn't make love with the baby in the room...she will be all right in Luz room. I looked in my drawer and got some garlic and put some in Luz bedroom window and some in Rebecca basinet; I wanted to be sure my baby would be all right. When I came back in our bedroom and took off my dress to put on my nightgown. Wilson said you want need that for a while. He was right; I wouldn't need it. He was back to his old self again and I was happy. When we settled down he went to sleep. I got up and rolled my baby's basinet in our room before I went to sleep. The next morning Wilson got up and got ready for work; he said he might be home early today. He kissed me and he kissed Rebecca on her hand. He said you brought Rebecca in our room anyway. I said I feel better if she is in here with us. When he left Rebecca woke up and started crying; I changed her diaper and went downstairs and got her some milk. I put her in her basinet and went down stairs to use the bathroom. When I came back she was sound asleep. I got back in bed and went to sleep too. That afternoon right after Wilson came home; Mother and Brother Etong came by our apartment. Mother wanted to take Rebecca home with her for the weekend. I asked Wilson if it would be all right if Mother and Brother Etong take Rebecca to Calapacuan for the weekend. He said sure, She is her Grandmother and Brother Etong is her uncle, why not? I packed Rebecca things in her baby bag. I told Mother to boil the water for her milk. Mother said I know what to do with the baby...you worry too much just relax. I gave Mother some money to buy milk and whatever she need. I kissed my baby goodbye and Wilson kissed her too. When he kissed her he said look no beard Inay; she just smiled and walked out the door with my baby. After they left we sat quietly on the couch looking at each other. Wilson broke the silence and said get ready we are going out to lunch and a movie. When we got to the Grand Restaurant I ordered fried chicken and Wilson ordered spaghetti; I thought to myself…both of us ordered something different than we usually order. When we finished our dinner we watched the movie, "My Name is Nobody" it was a Western comedy movie. When the movie was over people was still laughing at it outside of the theater. When we got home Wilson got him a beer from the refrigerator and we sat down on the couch. I asked Wilson if he thinks our baby was going to be all right. He said we could go tomorrow and get her if you are worried. I said I miss my baby… maybe she is crying wondering where we are at. Wilson said do you want to go tonight and get her? I said no, we would go tomorrow after we find a walker for her. Wilson said lets go upstairs so you can stop worrying about our baby. He got another beer from the refrigerator and I went upstairs. I sat on the bed thinking about Rebecca. Wilson came in and said our baby will be all right with your Mother… remember she raised six kid by herself; I know she can take care of Rebecca…you are mines tonight…you need to take care of me…I am the baby tonight. We got in the bed and I looked at the electric fan and said to myself…you got to do your thing tonight again. We made love and afterward Wilson said everything would be better if I didn't have to use this condom. I said you don't have to use it. He said we couldn't afford to have another baby right now…this is the only protection I know to use. I said when we go to America do you think they may have something else we could use? He said next time you go to the Naval Hospital ask the Doctor if there is something else we can use for protection. I said o.k. Sweetheart, next time I will ask the Doctor. He hugged me and said stop worrying about Rebecca she would be all right tonight and remember I love you. When I heard him say I love you, my heart came alive; It's been a while since I heard him say he love me in that tone. I guess it is because he has been working very hard and didn't really have time to settle down and hold me and tell me he love me like he is doing tonight. I said I love you too.

I woke up early the next morning thinking about my baby and worried that she maybe crying for me and I am not there to hold her. I went down stairs and took a shower and got dressed. Wilson was still sleep. I wanted him to get up so I could cook breakfast. Finally he did wake up and I told him to go and take his shower and I would start cooking breakfast. After breakfast Wilson said let go and find our baby a walker here in town she would only use it a few months only before we leave for the States. We looked around in the furniture stores and found one just her size; we bought it and took it to the apartment and left to go to Calapacuan to get our baby. When we arrive at Mother's house I saw Brother Etong watching Rebecca as she slept in a makeshift swing made out of a bed sheet with a string tired on each end. He was fanning the flies away with a piece of cardboard. Wilson said I told you Brother Etong and your Mother would take care of our baby. I went into the kitchen to see Mother; she said I fed her some rice soup you need to start feeding her some solid food a little at a time. I said o.k. And went into the room where Brother Etong had Rebecca. I told him he could stop fanning her and let her wake up. Mother said she just went to sleep a few minutes before you arrived. I said we would wait until she woke up. Mother said your Brother Etong really like Rebecca he haven't let her out of his sight since she been here. Rebecca is really playful and Etong likes that. I told Brother Etong thanks for taking care of Rebecca. He smiled and signaled to me "when I go to the United States write him about Rebecca and send him a picture" I said o.k. And I would tell her about her Uncle Etong. Mother told Brother Etong to get some wood for the stove. He signaled for me to start swinging Rebecca in the sheet when he left to go get wood. I said o.k. I would swing her, but Wilson came and started swinging her. Wilson said this is nice they have made a swing for her; I told you she would be all right. I asked Mother where were Auntie; she said your Auntie and Enyang went to wash someone clothes in Olongapo and Celino and his wife went to Barrio, Burretto. Celino is trying to find a job as a Carpenter. I said I thought he had a part-time job making bricks? She said yes, but he need more work. When Mother finished frying sweet potatoes she gave us some. Wilson said this is real good…tell Inay what I said. She smiled and asked him if he wanted some more. He said no I have enough. He said this makes me thirsty. Brother Etong had just come back from the store getting ice and coke. I went into the kitchen and got him a glass of ice and coke. I told him Brother Etong had just returned from the store. He said Brother Etong is a lifesaver; tell him thanks for the coke and tell Inay thanks for the snack.

Finally Rebecca woke up and I changed her diaper and Mother got her bottle and I fed her. After Rebecca burp I told Mother we was leaving and going back to Olongapo. Tell Auntie to come to my apartment Monday because I don't know when Luz would be back. Brother Etong and Mother kissed Rebecca goodbye. They seem a little sad that we were taking Rebecca away. We said our goodbyes and left. When we got to our apartment Rebecca was still asleep; I put her in her basinet. Wilson stood over the basinet looking at Rebecca; then he looked at me and said I love you Sweetheart. I said I love you too. He said we have to go to Manila next week to file for your Passport do you think Luz would be back by then? I said don't worry Auntie would be here to take care of Rebecca. I said if Auntie can't make it then we will take the baby with us. He said oh yes, Bailey's wife wants to go with us. I will let you know the date as soon as I check with Special Services and see what day they have a car available. I said just let me know as soon as possible. I am going to ask Auntie to stay with us for a while. He said do that even if Luz come back; I will pay her.

Later that afternoon Wilson said don't cook anything I will go to the restaurant and get us some food. I said are you sure you want to do that? He said yes. I will leave in a little while. When he left Rebecca woke up and I changed her diaper and shirt. When I was changing her shirt I saw a small red square bag made out of cloth pinned to the inside of her shirt sleeve. I said to myself…Mother made a protection bag for Rebecca and forgot to tell me about it. I looked at Rebecca and said your Grandmother is thinking about you. Now I can take you outside and get some fresh air. After I fed her I took her outside, but it was getting dark so I came back inside. I decide I would watch TV and let Rebecca try out her walker. I turned on the TV and tried to put her in the walker, but she was still a couple of inches too short. I told her that it wouldn't be long before she could use it. I took her and prop her up on one side of the couch and she looked like a little old lady sitting there with only a few teeth in the front. I kept watching the front door because I figured Wilson would be coming in any minute. Three hours later he still had not returned. I thought to myself... three hours just to go to the restaurant for takeout...I wonder what happened to him. I got hungry so I put Rebecca in her basinet and made me a sardine sandwich.

When I finished my sandwich I checked on Rebecca in her basinet. I thought...she is seven months old and getting very big pretty soon she will be too big for her basinet...I can't count on Wilson to go to a restaurant without him forgetting to come back. Finally I decided to give Rebecca her bath so she would feel good tonight when she goes to sleep. I started talking to Rebecca I said I hope your Daddy don't act like this when we get to America or I will be forced to get a job to take care of us...your Daddy always tell me he love me, but he keep doing thing like this. It was getting late so I put Rebecca down on the floor and took her basinet up to my bedroom. I went back downstairs and got Rebecca and her milk. I fed and burp her then she started closing her eyes to go to sleep. I held her for a while until I were sure she was sound asleep. Then I took her upstairs and put her in her basinet. A few minutes later I heard the front door close. I went downstairs to see who had come in; it was Wilson drunk and falling all over the place. I asked him where had he been, but all he said was "man it is your turn" then he said some woman name. I was really mad but I helped him upstairs to our bedroom. I thought to myself...I had to take care of our baby; now I have to take care of a grown drunk man. I helped him to get undress for bed. I checked the baby again and put on my nightgown and went to bed. I heard Wilson call a woman name in his sleep. I wonder why he does this to me...is this a marriage or what? If I ask him about what he said tomorrow; I know what he going to say, "I was drunk I don't know what you are talking about"...I was just dreaming. The next morning when I woke up he was still sleeping; I took Rebecca downstairs and fed her. I put a blanket on the floor so she could play. Finally Wilson came downstairs and tried to kiss me. I turned away and told him I don't want him to kiss me; he should kiss the girl he was calling in his sleep last night. I said where did you go last night...you were supposed to get some food what happened to it? He said I am sorry, I saw a friend that I know from my last ship and we started drinking and before I knew it I was waking up in our bedroom. I said I know your drinking comes before us; I don't think I want to go with you to America. Wilson said Sweetheart if you see a friend you have known for a long time you would talk to them too. I said yes, but I don't party with men and call their names in my sleep... you always hurt my feeling...what if I do that to you...you would get mad too. I thought when we got married and we had the baby you would change if only a little bit, but you are acting like you are still single running around in the clubs chasing girls. Then I started to cry, because I couldn't hold my tears back any longer. It really hurt to think that Wilson is with someone else. I thought I could take it, but it's getting harder each time, because I get jealous just thinking about him dancing with someone else. Wilson tried to consul me and gets me to stop crying. I told him to go brush his teeth and take a shower, because I hate the smell of liquor on his breath and I didn't like smelling the cheap perfume left on his body by his girlfriend. He said I told you I was out having a drink with a long time friend. I said then your friend must be a sissy that wears lipstick because he left some on your shirt. He didn't say another word he·just went upstairs and got clean underwear and came back downstairs and went into the bathroom. I took Rebecca outside to get some fresh air and I saw Sally one of our neighbors and we talked for a while. I asked her when she and her husband plan to have children. She said they have been trying but they haven't had any luck. I told her to talk to some of the older Filipino ladies and they would tell her what do to stay pregnant and stop having miscarriages. She said she would try it when she visits her realities on Visayan Island. She invited us in her apartment and I followed her in and sat down. As soon as I sat down I heard Wilson calling me as he walked down the corridor looking for me. I said goodbye to Sally and went outside to see what he wanted. I said what do you want? Wilson said I knew you were mad I wanted to make sure you hadn't left. I said I am planning to leave; I am tired of what you are doing to me. Wilson said you know I love you...you and the baby is the most important thing in my life.

I said next to your drinking and girls. Rebecca started to cry and I checked her diaper and told him to get me one. I changed her diaper and gave her a bottle. He started laughing and said look at our baby she is holding her bottle with her hands and feet. I said to myself... if you were here more often you would see her do more than that. He said I am going to cook breakfast. I said no I would do that when Rebecca goes to sleep. He decided to cook anyway. When he finished cooking he said breakfast is ready. We ate breakfast and he asked me how did I like the food. I said it is good...not bad at all. When we finished Rebecca was asleep so I washed the dishes and clean the kitchen. He said when you finish in the kitchen come in the living room I want to talk to you. When I finished I came in the living room he asked me to sit by him. He said traveling on Military Chartered Flights require you to wear pants; maybe you could get you a pantsuit made...I will buy you a coat upon arrival in America. I said I would do that after I get my passport.

Monday morning Wilson went back to work and Auntie came to stay with us. I don't know what happened with Luz; she haven't returned or sent anyone to tell us what going on. Auntie is here to help us with Rebecca and the washing. Wilson was finally able to schedule a Special Service car and driver for our trip to Manila. Wilson friend wife went with us because she wanted to find out what she would have to do when it was time for her to get her passport. We filled out my application and turned it in; we were told to come back in two hours. We went to Manila's famous Luneta Park and hung out until lunchtime then we went to lunch. After lunch we went back to the passport office and we were told because of the amount of people applying they didn't know how long we would have to wait. We decided to wait another hour. After waiting another hour Wilson checked again on my passport; the guy told him he didn't know how long it would take, but if we came back tomorrow he would guarantee it would be ready. Wilson was really upset because our driver had to have the car back before dark and we had to leave right away to make it before dark. Wilson told me I would have to ride the bus back tomorrow to get my passport because he had to work. Mrs. Bailey said she wanted to go back with me the next day so we decided to meet at the Victory Liner Bus station at seven the next morning. When we got back to Olongapo the driver dropped us at our apartment. Auntie was giving Rebecca her milk when we got there; she said I cooked some vegetable with fish. I said o.k. Thank you, I am very hungry. I said sweetheart what do you want to eat? He said whatever is easy to fix. I looked in the kitchen cabinet and saw a can of beef stew; I asked him how about some beef stew? He said it fine with me. I warmed up his beef stew and we sat at the table to eat; Wilson was still upset about the passport. He said I know that guy was trying to make some extra money for the passport, because I was told how much I was to pay at my personnel office on the base. I said I don't know why they make the American pay more than everyone else; they always do that to American they think American have a lot of money. They don't seem to realize that the American works hard for their money too. Wilson said here is the money for your passport asked if the passport ready; get it before you give them the money. I said o.k. I will. He said I am sorry I can't go with you tomorrow, but as you know I have to work. I said that's o.k. Mrs. Bailey is going with me. Wilson said if she changes her mind about going will you be all right? I said I would be all right. The next morning Wilson got up reminding me about when to give the money for the passport. I didn't go back to sleep I got up and took my shower and got dressed for my trip. Auntie said where are you going I said I have to go to Manila to pick up my passport. On my way out I gave Auntie money to buy fish and vegetables. I caught a jeepney and to the Victory Liner Station; Mrs. Bailey was at the station waiting for me. We bought our ticket and boarded the bus. We tried to get, as close to the front as possible so we wouldn't have to smell all of the different fragrances. I asked her when was she going to have her baby; she said in about four months. That's why I want to find out what I have to do to apply for my passport…my husband has almost completed his tour of duty here in the Philippines…thank you for allowing me to accompany you… now I will know what to do when I apply for mines. I said thank you too, for going with me today. When we arrive it was lunchtime so we went to a nearby restaurant and got some food. While we was having lunch we saw the guy from the passport office in the restaurant eating; I went and asked him if my passport was ready. He said yes, it was ready about thirty minutes after we left. He had my passport in his brief case as if he knew I would be coming back for it. He gave it to me and I gave him the money in the envelope Wilson gave me. I said thank you and went back to my table. When he finished eating he came over to our table and talked to us for a while about the traffic in Manila. Mrs. Bailey got his name so she could ask for him when she came back for her passport. She asked me how much money was in the envelope I told her it was twenty-five pesos.

She said twenty-five pesos not bad. I will give him the extra money so I can get the passport right away. She said money talks in the Philippines. I said yes especially if they know you are married to an American. Mrs. Bailey said if you want something done right away just put some money under the table. Before we arrived in Olongapo Mrs. Bailey said why don't you call me Rose, when you call me Mrs. Bailey it make me feel real old. I said I was only respecting my elder. She said I know, but just call me Rose it makes me feel better. When we arrived in Olongapo we parted with our goodbye and good luck. When I got to the apartment it was four in the afternoon and Auntie had started cooking dinner. I check on Rebecca and she was still sleep; I went upstairs and changed my clothes and freshen up before Wilson came home. When I finished I came down stairs and started watching TV. Auntie finished cooking dinner and came in the living room and said dinner is ready if you are hungry. I said yes I am hungry and I got up and fixed my plate. Auntie cooked adobo pork and boil cabbage; I ate too much so I went outside to try to walk it down. I saw the sister of the pregnant girl that lives in the last apartment to our left. She told me her sister had a baby boy. I said tell your sister I said congratulation. Then I heard the gate to the compound open and Wilson walked through it. We almost ran to meet each other. He said I am happy to see you are back safe and sound. We hugged and kissed in front of our front door. I led him inside of the apartment to show him my passport. He said now we can submit the paperwork for your Visa to go to the United States of America. When we get your visa we should have a couple of months left before we leave the Philippines. The following week Luz came back and we decided to keep Auntie on for a while longer. One afternoon Wilson boss, Jack came home with him. Jack is a white American. He appears to be a very nice guy, he told me I look like his Sister very little and cute. He and Wilson was setting in the living room drinking a beer and he was looking out of the window and saw Evelyn, the girl that lives with her mother a couple of doors down from us. He asked Wilson if she live here in the neighborhood or was she visiting? Wilson said he didn't know and asked me if I knew her. I said yes I know her she lives a couple of doors down from us with her very strict Mother. Jack said I know her she was my Secretary where I use to work. He asked me if I would tell her he would like to see her again and he would be at our apartment tomorrow afternoon around four.

I said o.k. I would tell her but I can't guarantee she would be there when he comes. Wilson walked to the compound gate with him. When he came back inside he said the apartment owner has invited us to a party at Baloy Long Beach. Wilson said I will let them know whether we are going or not tomorrow. I said we can go, it been a long time since we were at the beach.

The next day I went to Evelyn's apartment and before I could explain why I had come she told me everything; I guess she saw him when he came to our apartment and decided to walk by to let him see her. She was very surprised that Jack was a friend of our family. She said he was her boss before he transferred to another office and she like him very much. I said the reason I am here is he like you very much too and would like to see you at my apartment this afternoon. She said don't talk too loud my Mother is listening. I said o.k. When you see him come to my apartment, come on over. She said I really need an excuse to leave my apartment, because Mother always wants to know where I am going. Would you do me a favor and come get me when he comes; you can say you have something to show me in your apartment. Around four that afternoon Jack came with Wilson to our apartment again. I went to Evelyn apartment and asked for her; the Maid called her to the door. I could hear her Mother ask her where she was going. She said I am going to Vicky's apartment she have something to show me I will be right back. She was so anxious to get to my apartment she was leading the way. When we got inside of my apartment and her eyes met Jack; I could tell that they just wanted to grab each other and kiss, but they controlled themselves until they was in our patio in the back. We couldn't hear what they were saying, but between kisses they were mumbling something. I was really happy for them because I know how it feels to be in love. Finally they came back inside in our kitchen because they didn't want to be seen outside kissing in the patio. They talked in our kitchen until her Maid came calling for her. The maid said Evelyn's Mother wanted her to come back to their apartment. Wilson said our apartment owner is having a party at Baloy Long Beach tomorrow if you guys want to meet there I could check and see if he would let me bring a couple of friends. They agreed to go if we could take them. Wilson went to Mr. Blanco apartment and asks if he could bring a couple of friends and the owner said we have plenty of food the more the merrier. He asked Mr. Blanco if he wanted him to bring something. He said no just bring yourself and your friend. Saturday morning we got ready to go to the beach; Wilson rented a jeepney and waited to follow Mr. Blanco to the beach. Evelyn didn't have a problem getting away because her Mother knew the apartment owner real well. We took Rebecca and Luz with us. When we arrive at the beach and found our hut everybody went swimming except Evelyn and me. Evelyn was worried that Jack wouldn't come; I tried to reassure her that he would come by telling her he had promised. Finally we saw Jack coming and Evelyn was very happy; I was happy too, because she kept worrying me about him coming. They found them a place near the water and started enjoying themselves; if you didn't know better you would think they was performing a love scene for a movie. I told Luz to take care of Rebecca while Wilson and I went swimming in the Ocean. When I came out of the water Luz said I didn't know Evelyn had a boyfriend and the apartment owner said he didn't know she would kiss like that in public, because her Mother is very religious and old fashion. I said I guess when you are in love you don't waste time to pick a place to express it. He said I guess you are right; let's eat. They really had a lot of food and everybody enjoyed swimming and eating. After we ate we stayed for about two more hour and left. Jack left with us. When we got to our apartment Jack asked me to keep his camera, because he had been drinking and he didn't want someone to snatch it on his way back to the base; he kept thanking us for inviting him to the party. We went in and took our shower and tried to relax. Wilson said he had to go see someone; I said you have been drinking stay home, but he left anyway. I went to sleep for about two hours. Auntie told me I had better eat because they ate while I was asleep. I got up and ate a little bit. Around eight that night the power went off in Olongapo. Luz and Auntie lighted candle for the apartment. Then someone came knocking at the door looking for Wilson. He said where is Wilson, Olongapo is burning. I said he is not home yet. The guy left to help put out the fire. The apartment owner said the old market is burning it has reached all the way to Rizal Avenue. I started worrying about Wilson; the whole city of Olongapo was dark even the clubs. Wilson friend came back again asking for Wilson; I said I am sorry but he is not back yet. His friend seems upset and said the whole city of Olongapo is burning and no one is helping to put out the fire. I guess about nine o, clock Wilson came home; I asked him where he had been. He said he was at one of his friend house. He said the fire had burned the old market and was real close to the Swan club. I said there are no lights I am going to bed. We went upstairs we could still hear the siren they seem to be coming closer. We got into bed it was very hot without the electric fan. Rebecca started crying in Luz room and I got up and went in to see what was wrong. Auntie was setting holding Rebecca and Luz had went down for her milk. I stayed there until she quiet down then I went back to my bedroom.

The next day there was no power the city was at almost a stand still. The ice in our refrigerator had melted and we had to go buy some small can of milk for Rebecca, because we didn't want a lot of it to spoil. I was glad that I had not gone shopping for food because we would have lost a lot of frozen food. We were down to candles for light and we had a gas stove for cooking; I had been there before so it wasn't a big deal to me. We went without power for two days; I was surprised it didn't take longer, but the reason they got it up so quick is because the Naval Base Electrician came out and helped. We heard rumor about how the fire got started: faulty wiring, and arson, but regardless of the reason everybody loss. When the power finally came back on everyone was happy even Wilson so he could go back to the clubs. One day Evelyn nephew went to the market with me; he wanted to buy beefsteak and I went to buy fresh shrimp. When I returned around four that afternoon Luz told me Wilson had a broken leg and the Armed Forces Police took him to the Emergency room on the base. I quickly put everything in the refrigerator and went to Alice and Bob our neighbor house to get Bob to go with me to find out what was wrong with Wilson. Alice didn't want him to go, but he went with me anyway. We went to the Dispensary on base and no one knew anything about him being there or coming. Bob wanted to go to the Staff NCO club and ask around in there. When we got there I waited in the hallway for him about an hour; then I decided to go in and see what he was doing, I found him drinking with his friend. I told him I was going home; he said I am going with you. When we got back to the apartment Wilson was soaking his feet. I said what happened to you? Wilson said where did you go? I said I went to the Base Dispensary, but they didn't know anything about you being there...where did they take you? He said he didn't know. He was acting drunk, but I think he really knew where they took him. I think he was acting drunk so he wouldn't have to explain how he got hurt. Bob cursed and said he was going home. Bob like to curse just like CB every other word come out of his mouth is nasty. Wilson foot was hurting him real bad. I asked him if he would be all right. He said I am all right. I asked him again what happened; he said I got into a fight with a guy. I said what were you fighting about? I don't really know it just happened. I was upset with Wilson and didn't ask him again about what had happened to him; I guess maybe he was fighting over a girl and if so, I think he got what he deserve. When it was time for bed I helped him upstairs and helped him to undress and get in the bed. I got in the bed too. I was real upset as I lay there thinking...was he fighting in the club...why is he still getting drunk before he comes home...now he got himself hurt...what is next? Do I deserve this kind of marriage? I closed my eyes and tried to go to sleep, but I kept thinking...if he acting like this here, what is he going to do in the States? I know that once I get to the States the only person I can count on is him, but can I really count on him? I was laying with my back to him and he pulled me close to him and said don't worry I will be all right. I just closed my eyes and finally did go to sleep. The next day Wilson left for work on his crutches. I was really worried because I thought his feet were broken, but he had a spring his ankle. It good he didn't get hurt real bad, but if he were at home with his family he would be all right. I wonder why he got married if he had not planned to stop running around in the club; he should have stayed single and left the baby and me out of this mess. Next time he start acting up I am going to visit Sister Melda in Cavity City; I really need a break so I can clear my head, because I haven't really made up my mind to go to the States with him. Wilson came home before lunch and said the Doctor gave him five days to stay off his feet. He said he was to soak his foot in warm water with Epsom salt for the spring. He soaked his feet for the rest of the week; by the end of the week all of the soreness was gone. Bob and Alice finally decided to get married at the Justice of the Peace. We were asked to be witnesses. Wilson told them how easy it was to get our apartment approve, so they moved into one of the vacant apartment in our compound. Wilson started drinking even more once his friend moved in a few doors down from us.

Rebecca is tall enough now to use her walker; she is so cute walking around in the walker. The owner of the apartment Brother works in a furniture shop. Wilson hired him to refinish our dining table and chairs because of cigarette burns. It took him about three days to finish the job. Wilson was at Bob and Alice house drinking one day and she told Wilson she saw a Filipino guy coming out of our apartment. Wilson was half drunk and he rushed home to ask me about it. I said there hasn't been a Filipino guy coming out of our apartment, but the owner Brother when he was working on the furniture. I said you better tell Bob to tell Alice to stop worrying about what's going on in someone else house and mind her own business. Wilson said maybe you better tell the owner Brother if he is not finish to stop coming. I said you tell him yourself because you hired him. He knew I was upset so he didn't say anything else about it.

The next day I went to see Alice; I told her to stop watching my apartment and telling her Husband about who she see coming in and out. I said mind you own business and stop trying to mind mines. I left and went back to my apartment. Since then we never speak. Wilson goes there and drinks, but I don't go with him. I don't understand Wilson way of thinking; he is quick to believe anything someone tells him about me; he doesn't bother to ask me if it is true or not. He just assumes that I did whatever they said I did. I have never met a woman like Alice she likes to mind other people business and she is very, very jealous of anyone that talks to her Husband. She got mad at another neighbor because their Maid stop to talk with Bob and he was the one that stopped her. Bob is very friendly he always stopping and talking with everyone in the neighborhood. Mrs. Blanco said one day Bob stopped to talk to her and Alice saw him talking; she called him and told him to come home. All of the women in the apartment complex dislike her. Finally it was time to go to the American Embassy in Manila to get my visa. Wilson told me we would be sharing a Special Service car with Bob and Alice. I didn't say anything even though Alice and I weren't talking. When we got there and turn in my request we had to set and wait to be interviewed. Bob and Alice did the same. When I was called in for my interview the guy asked me a lot of questions and one I didn't understand. He told me to go out and ask my Husband; I did and Wilson explained it to me and I went back inside and told him I understand the question. The guy said have a seat outside and I will call you in a few minutes. When I came back to my seat Alice asked me how the interview went. I told her what they asked. Bob told her to tell him she understand everything he ask so we could go home. They called her and she went in and came back out to wait with us. While we were waiting I could tell Bob was real nervous; he told Wilson he need a drink. A few minutes later he called me to the window and told me I was ready to go to the United States. We waited a little while longer and Alice was called in for her interview. When she returned she said everything went all right. We sat and waited a few minute longer then they called her back and gave her visa. On our way back home we stopped at several stores and Wilson and Bob bought beer; when we got home they were almost too drunk to get out of the car. After that trip Wilson and Bob stop hanging around drinking together; I really don't know what happened, but I am not sorry. Wilson continued stopping and drinking before he came home. On March twenty-second our wedding anniversary Wilson said he was taking me out for dinner and a movie. He was out drinking with some friends and forgot. I didn't make a big deal about it; because I was use to him forgetting about what he tell me. One night I was at home waiting for him; it was around two in the morning. I went to my friend Sally apartment and asked her if she would come and help me find him. We went to three of his friend house and they said they haven't seen him; we thought about the hotels but we figured he would use another name so we just came back home. I thanked Sally for trying to help me find him. She said just ask anytime she didn't mind helping me. That night I couldn't take the pressure anymore so I packed some clothing for Rebecca and me. The next morning real early I went on the base to Wilson Boat I asked if Wilson were there they said he is not here yet. Then I saw him get off a bus and come toward his Boat. I was so upset I didn't know what to do, because I figured he had spent the night in a hotel in town. I started walking to the bus stop in a hurry to catch a bus or anything to get me back to the main gate. Wilson saw me and begged me to wait for a minute. I told him I was leaving him; he said please don't leave wait until I get home. I started crying and left and went on to the bus stop. When I got on the bus everyone was very concern as to my welfare I said I am all right. One of the passengers gave me a napkin so I could wipe my face. When I got back to the apartment I told Auntie to stay in the apartment until I came back I was going to Cavity City to visit Sister Melda. I took Rebecca and our bag and left for the bus station. I caught a bus to Cavity City. When I arrived I went to the house I thought she lived in, but she had moved. I decided to go toward the Base Gate because I remembered she said something about moving in the opposite direction from where she lived before. I had so much on my mind it was a little mixed up. When I was walking down the street a black Filipino boy asked me whom I was trying to find. I said I am trying to find my sister house she use to live on the other end of the street. He said is she married to a black guy name Smith? I said yes she is married to Arnold C. Smith. He said follow me I know just where they live. I was carrying Rebecca and our bags. The boy said let me help you with your bags. I gave him our bags and we walked about two blocks from the base gate to her house. He stayed there until Sister Melda came to the door; she was very surprised. She said we were just talking about you and Wilson. I gave the boy some money for helping me with direction and my bags. Sister Melda asked me where did I find the boy that helped me with my bags. I told her near the base gate. Then Mother came in the room and really surprised me. I said what are you doing here? She said your Sister Linda got hurt fishing and I came to help take care of her; I have been here over a month. Mother said why are you traveling by yourself with a baby? I said I came to visit Sister Melda. Sister Melda took Rebecca and started playing with her. I asked Sister Melda was Linda still in the Hospital? She said no Linda was well and back in school. We talked and Sister Melda played with Rebecca until Mother finished cooking lunch. After lunch Sister Melda showed me where I would sleep. Mother took Rebecca and started giving her milk. I lay down and took a nap. When Brother Smitty came home from work he was surprised to see Rebecca and me. He asked where was Wilson; I told him Wilson had duty so I came to visit. He talked for a couple of minutes then he went to his room. I lay back down. A few minutes later I could hear Sister Melda talking to Mother in Tagalog. She said I bet you Vicky and Wilson had a fight...I told Vicky he have kids in the States...I know he have a lot of girlfriends in the club. Mother said I know Wilson drinks when Vicky in the Hospital, but he always came home early even if he is drunk; I know he don't have time to be messing around with some girl because he likes to drink. Sister Melda said he could have a girl first then get drunk, so Vicky don't have time to get mad because he is drunk when he get home. Mother said I believe Wilson love your sister very much; if he didn't he wouldn't have came home every night when she was in the Hospital. Sister Melda said I know Wilson have kids in the States. I said to myself...I came here to visit and clear my head and she is adding more to it. I didn't say anything I just acted like I was sleep. When I went to the bathroom and came out; Mother called me in the kitchen. I saw Brother Smitty in the living room watching TV. Sister Melda was very upset because someone had stolen her clothes off her cloth line. Sister Melda said have Wilson finished getting my passport... you think Wilson is going to take you to the States and he have kids there? I didn't tell her anything about my passport and visa I just kept quiet and let her talk. She always tries to act like she has all of the answers for everything. Sister Linda said do you want me to give Rebecca a bath. Sister Melda said just go ahead and give her a bath so she will sleep tonight. Mother said Vicky are you all right? I said I am all right. I had to get away from them for a while because I was going to start crying so I said I want to lie down for a while I don't feel good. Mother said go ahead and lie down I will take care of Rebecca tonight. I got in bed and put my pillow over my head and let it out; I cried myself to sleep. The next morning I woke up and waited until Brother Smitty went to work before I got up and took a shower. After breakfast I told them I was going home. I asked Sister Melda if there were bus service to Olongapo from this area. She said yes, they have Victory Liner Bus Service here in Cavity City; you better hurry they have one leaving in about an hour. Everyone went to the bus station to see me off. When Rebecca and I boarded the bus I said to myself…whatever happens from now on I would have to take care of it without coming to Sister Melda's house…I came to visit maybe stay a week, but I just can't take anymore of her big mouth. I hugged my baby and put her on my lap and she slept all the way to Olongapo City.

When we got home Auntie said Wilson went to Cavity City to get you. A Filipino guy was with him. I said whatever! Auntie took Rebecca and put her on the floor on a blanket, because she always turn on her stomach so we don't put her in the basinet anymore. Around four that afternoon Wilson made it back from Cavity City. He was so happy to see me; he hugged and kissed me. I went to Cavity City to bring you home, but your Sister told me you had just left coming home. I said stop playing around; if you don't want me in your life please tell me. You know I love you but you always do crazy things like you don't have any responsibility at all. You have the baby and me, but you still want to run around in the clubs and get drunk every night…I don't want to go with you to America…just leave Rebecca and me here we will be all right…this marriage is not going to work…I thought when we got married you would slow down, but you have gotten worse. Which one of your girlfriend did you spend the night with when I met you at your Boat? You was surprised to see me there. Now you can't say you slept on your Boat so what other story you are going to tell me? I started crying and Wilson took me up to our bedroom and turned on the electric fan. It felt good even though I was crying. He said Sweetheart please don't cry anymore; I promise I won't get drunk anymore and I will come straight home after work. The only girls in my life are you and Rebecca and no one else. I said yes and the girl you slept with when you didn't come home. He said I slept at that Filipino couple house, you remember Mr. and Mrs. Burnell invited us to their baby christening. I said to myself...he have black friends living close by how did he get over there in another neighborhood when he is drunk...he have only been there once before...I just listen to his explanation. It is hard to believe him because he always tell me a lie. He tried to kiss me and I turned away. I said stop trying to kiss me you smell like liquor. He left and went downstairs and brushed his teeth and came back and tried to kiss me again. I said do you think just because you brush your teeth I want to kiss you? He said yes. I was sitting on the side of the bed. When he said yes I started to get up but he grab my arm and pushed me down on the bed and kissed me. I said is this the way you do your girlfriends? He let me go. I lay down in the bed and turned my back to him. He stood there and looked at me for a while, and then he lay down beside me and hugged me from the back. Finally we went to sleep. I guess he was as tired as I was from my trip. That week came and went pretty fast, Wilson kept his word he came straight home every day. Auntie finally figured she had enough money to go to Manila and visit her kids; she told me she had to say goodbye for a while because she wanted to see her kids, but when she come back she was going to stay in Calapacuan with Mother. I told her if I don't see her before we leave I really appreciate all she done to help me and make sure Wilson is always ready for work in a clean pressed uniform. I gave her the money I had been saving for her and Wilson gave her some extra money. When she left I felt that I had lost a very good family member and a friend. Auntie was always jolly and funny, even Wilson like her.

Two weeks after Auntie left Brother Etong came to our apartment and gave me a note telling me Mother was sick and need some money to buy some food and medicine. Wilson gave him twenty pesos and jeepney fare. I was a little worry about him going back alone and couldn't talk. Wilson said he would be all right, because he came here by himself, he would be all right going home by himself. He Played with Rebecca a little while before he left. When he left Luz said I didn't know your Brother can't talk; I was talking to him and he was giving me sign language. Wilson told me to tell Luz we want need her after April so she can start looking for another job. I said I would tell her later. He said what wrong? I said I am worry about Mother. Wilson said you have sent her money to buy food and medicine don't worry everything would be all right. Wilson said when your family come again tell them to take some of the things we are not going to pack especially the stove because it is dangerous to ship. I said o.k. I will when someone come to visit. Around the end of the week Sister Linda and Brother Etong stop by to get a cold drink. I asked Sister Linda what was she doing here I thought she were in school. She said forget that school, Sister Melda has become crazy again. Now I am helping Mother, our sister-in- law and Brother Etong sell vegetables in the market. They are over there behind where you use to live on Twenty-Fifth Street in the new market. I was surprised to hear what they was doing and about the new market. I thought about going to see what going on, but Wilson don't want me to go anywhere not even to Calapacuan. I told Wilson what was going on with the family especially Linda. He said Linda had a chance to go to school here, but she lied and said I wasn't giving her money to go to school, so she is on her own now I am out of the picture. The next day Sister Linda and Mother came back and tried to sell fish and vegetables to the Landlord wife. She said I didn't know she was your Mother I said yes. She said your Mother have been coming here for quite a while selling fish and vegetables. I said they never stop at my apartment. Mother said Vicky have her own family and problems and don't need mines…I am still strong and can take care of myself. The Lady said you are right please come inside for a while. Mother went inside for a while and when she came out. She came to my apartment. I told her when we leave Wilson want her to have our stove and electric fan. They left to go back to the little market where Brother Etong and my Sister-in-law was selling vegetables and fish. That night Wilson asked me to walk down Rizal Avenue with him before it get dark; I went with him and we saw a girl on the second floor of the club trying desperately to say something. I knew her when I worked in the Money Exchange booth she can't talk like Brother Etong. She was trying to tell me something using sign language, but Wilson said don't stop lets go home. When we got to our apartment I asked him why he didn't want to stop. He said he didn't want her telling me something that wasn't true. I said if you don't do or say anything to that girl she wouldn't have anything to say about you. I had problem going to sleep that night thinking about that girl wanting to tell me something. Wilson went to sleep right away; he was very relaxed and content. He told me he loved me very much before he went to sleep. The next morning when Wilson got up to go to work; when he got dressed he asked me if I would be home today when he came back. I said I am not going anywhere today. He kissed me goodbye and walked to the bedroom door; he turned around and said I love you very, very much. I said I love you too. He left with a smile on his face. When Wilson got outside I could hear Bob nasty mouth talking to him. Bob is a nice guy, but he has a real nasty mouth just like CB. Wilson is a Sailor but he doesn't talk like that. Maybe he talks like that somewhere else but not around me. Every other word that comes out of CB and Bob mouth is nasty. A few minutes later I heard Rebecca crying; I got up and went in Luz room to help her with Rebecca. I took Rebecca and changed her diaper while Luz went downstairs for her milk. When Luz came back with her milk I put her in the middle of my bed and gave her the bottle. She held it herself using her hand and feet. Luz started laughing at her because she uses her feet to help hold the bottle. While we sat on the bed watching Rebecca, Luz said she was talking to some of the other Maids in the apartment complex and they said a family that move in the complex need a made. I said make sure you tell them you will be available the end of the month. She said I am going to miss you, Rebecca and Brother Wilson. I said I am going to miss you too, because you are just like family. Luz asked if I wanted her to watch Rebecca as she slept. I said no she would be all right here. I put pillows around her as she slept. Luz left to clean her room and cook breakfast. I went down stairs and took my shower and came back to fight with my long hair trying to dry it. When I finally got it dried I went downstairs and told Luz to get a blanket and spread it on the living room floor; then I went upstairs to get Rebecca. I don't like leaving her on the bed because she likes to roll around a lot. I am glad Wilson bought the rug for the living room, now all we have to do is put a clean blanket down on it and Rebecca can sleep or play on it. Rebecca was still sleep when I brought her downstairs. I put her on the blanket and went to the table to eat breakfast. Luz asked me if I think they have dried fish in America. I said I don't know, but

Wilson told me they have plenty of fish. I can start drying fish there; I know how to dry fish in the sun.

Wilson came home around four that afternoon he hugged and kissed me; he had been drinking. He said in two weeks the movers would come and pack all of our furniture. I want you to separate the things we would need before the furniture get there. Things like... iron, ironing board, baby clothes and pot and pans. He said where are Rebecca and Luz? I said I guess they are still sleep upstairs. I heard someone knocking on the door. I went to answer it. It was the girl on the second floor of the club that couldn't talk. She started explaining to me about Wilson using her hands. I understood what she was saying because Brother Etong uses sign language. She told me enough for me to understand Wilson had made love to her. I pretended I didn't understand what she was telling me; finally she just left. When she left the door I asked Wilson why she told me that he made love to her. He said she was someone that was jealous of what I had and wanted to destroy it.   He just sat there with a look on his face that was completely flushed. My heart ached all the way to my stomach; I had promised myself a long time ago if one of his girlfriends came knocking at my door I wouldn't believe anything they say because I know they are jealous of me, but this time I know within my heart this girl was telling the truth. I walked outside to get some fresh air; I was so upset I didn't know what to do. I tried desperately to understand why this is happening to me...my Mother had a hard time with my Father he would go and come when he got ready and she would forgive him and take him back...now it is happening to me...I guess she loved him no matter what happened just like I love Wilson. I love him very, very much, but the hurt I feel I guess it will heal because my love is strong. Wilson came outside and asked to talk to me. I went inside the apartment and said I don't want to talk about anything I just want to forget that it happened. He didn't know what to say he just sat down on the couch with a blank face. Luz came downstairs with Rebecca and broke the silence. She gave Rebecca to me because she had to start cooking. Wilson said let me have her. He sat holding her on his lap then he said Sweetheart Rebecca has two small teeth coming out in front. I said they have been out for a long time you are late. You never have a chance to play with her because you always come home late. Luz said it is time to eat. I asked Wilson if he wanted to eat he said no I ate before I left my Boat. Luz and I ate our food. Luz is not a very good cook, but she takes very good care of Rebecca. When we finished our meal Luz washed the dishes and cleaned the kitchen. Then she came and got Rebecca to give her a bath. I sat on the couch with Wilson. He asked me if I had my pant suit already. I said yes it is in my closet I will let you see it when we go upstairs. He kissed me very gentle on my lips; it felt like lighting hit me and ran through my body. I guess when you love someone it always feel good to kiss. I will love him no matter what happens to us. I still want to spend my life with him right or wrong...good or bad. What happened here today show me that I can deal with anything because of my love for him? His drinking is a bad thing, but we can deal with that too...one day at a time. He is a good loving and caring man that always makes sure Rebecca and me have plenty to eat and a place to stay. When Luz finished giving Rebecca her bath she brought her back to me. Wilson wanted to hold her, but she started yawning and acting like she wanted to go to sleep. I told Luz to take her upstairs and give her milk so she can go to sleep. Wilson said our baby is getting heavy. I said since her last check up she has gain a lot of weight. He said when we get to the States we would start her on fresh milk. I said I guess we can do that. The days and weeks kept zipping right on by and before we realized the date the movers came by to check how much household effect we had so they would know how much manpower to bring the next day. The next day they came and packed all of our house effects. The apartment owner told Wilson don't worry about trying to clean the apartment because it is real clean all it need is a little dusting and he would do that. He said we could stay in his sister-in-law failed clinic next door to his apartment for free and he would furnish the bed. His Sister-in-Law had long since closed up her clinic. He said he just wanted to show the apartment right away. We weren't going to stay in the apartment any longer once they packed us out. Wilson accepted his offer because he didn't want to stay in a hotel or my Mother's house for three weeks. The owner fumigated the place and cleaned it up for us. The place had two rooms. We used one room for the bedroom and the other one for our kitchen. Wilson said this is not bad; we will stay in the same area until we leave and it will be easy for our Special Service driver to find us. Luz stayed with us a few more days and then went to stay with her new employer. She said if I need her to baby-sit at night just call her; she would be in the apartment in back of this apartment complex. She said she would visit once in a while before I leave. I said o.k. Thank you I will do that. The day after we moved in to the new place Mother and Sister Linda came by and knock on our apartment door. The owner wife told them we had pack up all of our furniture and moved out. She brought them to the little place we were staying. When I opened the door Mother looked as if she wanted to cry, because she thought we had left without saying goodbye. She said I thought you were gone already. I said the owner said we could stay her until we leave for free, so we don't have to stay in the hotel. I said you need to come here early on the nineteenth of this month and get the electric fan, the stove, food and the rest of the stuff we would be leaving behind. Please come early so we will have time to say goodbye. Mother held Rebecca and played with her. She said it would be a long time before she saw her grandchild again. I said don't worry we will be all right. Wilson promised we would visit when we save enough money for the airline ticket. She said yes, but that is too far away.

I said I would write and let her know how we are doing. Mother said I am worried that Wilson will mistreat you and no one can help you...I know he love you, because he takes very good care of you and the baby, but I don't know how he is going to treat you when you get to America. I said Mother he is going to treat me just like he does here; I don't think he will change just like that. Rebecca started smiling at her Grandmother. Sister Linda laughed at Rebecca, she say Rebecca look like an old lady without teeth. Mother said take care of yourself and the baby over there; don't worry about us here we will be all right. My Mother always say she would be all right because she don't want to tell me her problems, because she know I have problems too. I said let eat some breakfast; Mother said let me cook it. I said we have Spam, coffee and eggs; Linda would you go to the store and buy bread rolls. When breakfast was ready we put a blanket over the bed and we sat on it and ate our breakfast. Rebecca grabs one of the bread roll and tried to eat it. Mother said maybe her gums itch. Then she got a piece of the roll in her mouth and liked to choke. Mother quickly retrieved it from her mouth. Rebecca started crying for more bread. Mother said don't give her bread give her a cracker. We gave her a cracker and she made a mess with cracker crumbs all over the blanket. We cleaned it up and gave her some milk. She was holding her bottle by herself with her hands and feet. Linda said she really have grown and can hold her bottle by herself. Finally Rebecca went to sleep. We talked for quite a while about me leaving. Mother said you are going to the other side of the world and the only way we can communicate is to write, so please write and send me pictures of your family. I said make sure Linda writes me too, because I want to know how everyone is doing. I said Linda write me right away when you receive my letters. Linda said don't worry I will write you right away. I said Mother would you stay until sometimes this afternoon. She said we would stay until four o, clock. I said o.k. That would be good. I said Linda check out front and see if anyone is selling fish and vegetables. Mother said how about I go to the market and get a kilo of pork and we cook adobo pork for lunch? I said that would be even better. When Mother left Linda and I started talking about what she was going to do now that she is not going to school. She said she was going to find a job so she could help Mother. I said why not go to Ligaya and ask for a job in the Money Exchange. She said so I can get fired by Sister Melda again...no way...I have had enough of Sister Melda...don't worry I can read and write, I can find a job somewhere else.

Remember what Mother said take care of yourself and Rebecca and write us a few lines and let us know how you are doing. I said tell Brother Etong to take care of himself; I have a picture of Rebecca I want you to give it to him because he really like her. Tell him even if he can't come to see me off I love him and I will send him some more pictures when I get to America. When Mother returned from the market she started cooking; she said you have a lot of ants coming in here. I said Linda would you spray the wall outside for me. I followed her outside and the owner saw what we were doing and said you still have ants coming inside? I said yes. He said I will be right back; I am going to buy something to get rid of those ants. When he came back he mixed something up and sprayed all over the wall outside and surrounding area. I told him thanks for spraying. He said now I know they want be back for a while. Mother said that spray has a very strong smell it is making me dizzy turn the electric fan this way. I went over by Mother I said yes it is very strong; Linda would you please close the window before we end up in the Hospital. We set the fan on high so it could blow the fumes out so it wouldn't bother Rebecca. I sprayed a little of Wilson cologne in the air so the smell wouldn't be too bad. Mother said what kind of spray he uses? I said I don't know he mixed up something. She said it almost made me sick. Don't spray that here anymore. I said the owner said it would take a while before the ants came back. She said the food is ready let eat. I said the smell of the adobo have made me hungry. Rebecca woke up too; I don't know if the smell of the adobo woke her up or not. When we started eating Mother fed Rebecca some pork fat; she said it is good for babies that saliva a lot. When Mother stops feeding Rebecca the pork fat Rebecca started crying, she wanted more and I gave her the bottle of milk. Mother said if she doesn't stop salivating give her some more pork fat. I said if she keeps salivating I would give her some. Sister Linda washed the dishes and clean the kitchen area. I said take the leftovers home. I gave Mother twenty pesos and some more stuff left from packing. Mother put everything in her shopping bag and played with Rebecca a few minutes before they left going home. I said come back anytime you get a chance, but remember we're leaving May nineteenth please come early so we can say goodbye. When they left for a brief moment I felt alone; then Luz knocked on the door. She wanted to know if I wanted her to baby-sit Rebecca. I said she is sleep now; maybe you could baby-sit for us at night when we go out. She said I don't work at night I can watch Rebecca for a while…just let me know you know where I work. When I closed the door I lay down beside Rebecca and went to sleep. When Wilson came home Rebecca and I were still asleep. He came in and woke me up with a kiss. I said I didn't hear you come in the door. I got up and washed my face and brushed my teeth. He said do you think we could get a baby-sitter tonight to watch Rebecca while we go out with Jones and his girlfriend. I said yes I can get Luz. I went to the apartment where she worked and asked for her. I said would you watch Rebecca tonight for us. She asked her employer and they said you can if you want to. She said I will be over in a few minute. I came back to our place and told Wilson she was going to baby-sit. I got ready to go. When Luz came in I told her where everything was at and we left to meet Jones and his friend in the Supreme Club. Wilson and Jones had a couple of drinks and decided to go to a movie. We went outside and caught a jeepney to go to the Grand Theater. On our way Jones girlfriend started talking about how fat Jones was in our dialect, Tagalog. She said Jones was fat like a pig "Matabang Baboy". I said maybe he is big and fat, but he is not a pig "Baboy". Jones understood a little Tagalog; He said fat yes, but not a pig "Baboy". Wilson thought I was the one saying it and he got mad at me. I told him it was Jones girlfriend saying it. She started laughing. I didn't understand her talking about how Jones look like a pig; she should look at her nose it look like a pig nose. I said to myself...I really feel sorry for Jones he always find a no good girl; the first one was a Gang Member and used drugs and this one tries to humiliate him...she just want Jones money. When we got in the movie I didn't set by Wilson because I was mad at him for accusing me of calling Jones a pig. Then suddenly the theater started shaking; Wilson grabs me by the arm and said let go Sweetheart it is an earthquake. He protected me from the people running out of the movie. It stopped as suddenly as it started. Wilson started kissing me he said I am sorry about the misunderstanding about who called Jones a pig. Sweetheart I grab your arm because I thought you might get hurt when everyone was panicking because of the earthquake. I said I am sorry too. I said to myself...I didn't do anything wrong; I just tried to stop Jones girlfriend from calling him a pig. Wilson just assumed that I said it and took the girl side. I don't know why he never take my side every time there is an incident Wilson believe someone else before he would believe me. When the movie was over we went back to the Supreme Club. I said lets go home. Wilson said just a couple of drinks and we would go. I sat there watching him and Jones drink. Jones was drinking beer and liquor. I told Wilson we have to go, because I told Luz we would be gone maybe two or three hours. I don't want to take advantage of her because we may need her again before we leave. Wilson said Jones we have to go home man. Jones said o.k. We will walk

Chapter 9

Realizing a Dream

Outside with you. When we got outside we said goodnight. Jones was really drunk and his girlfriend was still talking about him. She said if he falls on her she would be mashed flat as a piece of paper. They caught a jeepney going somewhere; we walked home because it was only one block. I said Sweetheart do you think Jones would be all right he is very drunk? Wilson said he will be all right he always drinks a lot...don't worry about him worry about me your Husband. I said I always worry about you. When we got back to the house Luz and Rebecca was asleep. I tried to wake her and ask if she wanted to stay tonight and go home early tomorrow; she said tomorrow is Saturday I will stay here tonight if you don't mind. I said o.k. Wilson and I went into the other room and went to bed. Saturday morning I got up early so Luz could go to her place. When she left Rebecca got fussy. I changed her and gave her some milk; then she started crying. Wilson said bring her here so she want wake up Luz. I said Luz left early this morning. I put her on the bed beside Wilson and she started pulling on his nose and ears. Wilson said not my nose, I know my nose is big, but you are hurting Daddy's big nose. Wilson started tickling her stomach and she was just giggling and trying to hold on to his nose. I gave her the bottle again; she took it and tried to hold on to Daddy's nose. I held her hand and told her don't do that to Daddy. Wilson said that o.k. Let her have some fun. I said I am going to cook breakfast. He said just fry some Spam for me I will eat bread and Spam. I said are you sure that all you want to eat? He said yes. I fried the Spam and I gave him Spam and two slices of bread and a glass of water. We put pillows around Rebecca so she wouldn't roll off the bed. Wilson went to the bathroom and washed his face and brushed his teeth. When he came back we ate a Spam sandwich for breakfast. After breakfast I took my shower. Wilson watched Rebecca until I finished my shower and dried my hair. Then he took his shower while Rebecca and I played on the bed. When he came out of the bathroom Rebecca and I was laughing and having fun. He said you guys are having fun. I said I am going to the market and I am taking Rebecca with me, so I can buy her a small pantsuit and I will look for some shoes to match my suit. He said o.k. I will be here when you come back. Rebecca and I left for the market. When we were going out the door Wilson said hurry back home I miss you already. When we got to the market Rebecca was getting heavy. We went to the shoe place first I decided to get me a pair of black shoes, a pair of Sandals and a red striped dress and a pair of red shoes for Rebecca. I put everything in a big bag and tried to carry Rebecca on one side and the bag on the other side. I said to myself…this is a bad ideal trying to carry Rebecca on my hip and the bag on the other side. I caught a jeepney right away and went home. When we got back to the house I didn't see Wilson anywhere. I said where do you think your Daddy went? I put everything inside and went back outside with Rebecca. I saw Mrs. Blanco outside she said Wilson went with this girl that said her boyfriend died. I said do you know her name? She said no, but I do remember her nose; this is embarrassing to me because I don't like to talk about how someone looks, but her nose look like a pig nose. I said that is Jones girlfriend; she said yes, I think I heard her say Jones, but I am not sure. I said thank you. I was a little worried about who died. I went inside to put Rebecca to sleep so I could cook me some rice. After Rebecca went to sleep I cooked my lunch and ate it while waiting for Wilson to come home. I guess it was about twelve-thirty when Wilson came back; he looked real puzzled. I said who died… Mrs. Blanco said one of your friend died. He hugged me and said Jones. I said Jones! I was very surprised. I said we went out with them last night…what happened? Wilson said his girlfriend woke up and found him dead beside her; she didn't know what to do so she came and got me. I called the Armed Forces Police and they came and took his body on the base. They said he took drugs and strangled on his saliva. I guess he tried to wake up but was to overcome by the drugs. I said to myself…someone put drugs in his drink…I know he was drunk but he always get drunk…someone did it to him. Wilson still couldn't believe Jones had passed. I had problems believing it too. After Jones death Wilson started thinking about how short life can be, I think he started thinking twice before he get drunk. We stayed in the house most of the time. We spent our time together with our baby. Wilson went and pick up my X-ray and our Medical records the day before we left May eighteenth.

The morning of May nineteenth Mother and Linda came to say goodbye to us. They came very early so we could spend a few hours together before we left. They played with Rebecca for a while. Wilson gave Mother all of his leftover Philippine money. Mother said no foolish Wilson, no drinking. Wilson told my Mother he promise to take care of me. Linda told her what he said in Tagalog. Mother said very good, very good Wilson no foolish. She tried to say in English, "take care of my Daughter and don't drink too much you have a baby already". Wilson repeated that he promise to take good care of the baby and me. I asked Mother where was Brother Etong? She said he had to stay and watch the house because no one was there. He wanted to come but your Sister-in-Law had to go and wash clothes at someone house. He told me to give you and Rebecca a big hug and a kiss for him. Mother hugs and kissed Rebecca and me. When the Special Service car arrive to pick us up everyone came out to say goodbye… Mr. and Mrs. Blanco, Bob and Alice, Luz and of course, Mother and Linda. Bob said I see you in the States in two months. Luz was holding Rebecca and saying goodbye. I felt real down when I looked at Mother and saw the tears in her eyes and still trying to smile at me. She said take care of yourself and tried to wipe her face. Linda said goodbye and take care. When we left I kept waving to Mother and Linda as long as I could see them. Wilson hugged me and told me everything would be all right. I was hugging Rebecca and Wilson was hugging me. I knew then it would be a long time before I see my family again. Wilson was my family and I would put myself in his hand, because he is the one I will spend the rest of my life with on the other side of the mountain in the United States of America. When we arrive at Clark Air Base we got accommodation for that night at the Base Guest House. The next morning we got up early and had our breakfast and went to the Air Terminal to board our Military Chartered flight to Travis Air Force Base in California. When we boarded the plane and took our seats I started to get scared; I felt like getting off the plane. Wilson sensed how I felt and hugged me and told me everything would be all right. When the plane started moving I knew then that it would be a long time before I return to my country and see my family again. When the plane was airborne I said to myself…goodbye Philippines I will come back and see you one of these days…I thought of the dream I had as a little girl sitting in my window looking out at the Sea and mountains…I dreamed of someday going on the other side of the mountains…I also thought of the old lady fortune teller telling me I would leave the Philippines and go far away…my dream is my Destiny. Wilson said are you all right? I said yes I am all right now. He said I know you have mixed feeling about leaving your Family and Country, but I want you to remember that you are with me; I love you and Rebecca more than anything in this world and I am going to take care of you.